THE ACADIENSIS READER: VOLUME ONE

Atlantic Canada
Before Confederation

THE ACADIENSIS READER: VOLUME ONE
THIRD EDITION

EDITORS:

P.A. BUCKNER
GAIL G. CAMPBELL
DAVID FRANK

ACADIENSIS PRESS
FREDERICTON
1998

© ACADIENSIS PRESS 1998

Canadian Cataloguing in Publication Data

Main entry under title:
Atlantic Canada before Confederation

3rd ed.

Includes bibliographical references.
ISBN 0-919107-44-3

1. Maritime Provinces — History — To 1867.* 2. Newfoundland — History. I. Buckner, Phillip
A. (Phillip Alfred), 1942-   II. Frank, David, 1949-   III. Campbell, Gail Grace, 1945-
IV. Title: The Acadiensis Reader, volume one.

FC2011.A86 1998   971.502   C98-950128-0
F1032.A86   1998

Acadiensis Press is an affiliate of CANCOPY, the Canadian Reprography Collective. Permission
for photocopying or other reprographic copying may be obtained from CANCOPY, 214 King
Street West, Suite 312, Toronto, Ontario M5H 3S6.

Acadiensis Press
Campus House
University of New Brunswick
Fredericton, N.B.
E3B 5A3

Telephone: (506) 453-4978
E-mail: acadnsis@unb.ca

QUEBECOR PRINTING ATLANTIC

CONTENTS

Preface (with Note to the Third Edition)... 7

RALPH PASTORE
The Collapse of the Beothuk World 11

JOHN G. REID
An International Region of the Northeast:
Rise and Decline, 1635-1762.. 31

KENNETH DONOVAN
Slaves and Their Owners in Ile Royale, 1713-1760................................. 47

STEPHEN E. PATTERSON
Indian-White Relations in Nova Scotia, 1749-1761:
A Study in Political Interaction 77

NAOMI GRIFFITHS
Acadians in Exile:
The Experiences of the Acadians in the British Seaports........................ 114

J.M. BUMSTED
The Origins of the Land Question on Prince Edward Island,
1767-1805 132

BARRY CAHILL
The Treason of the Merchants: Dissent and Repression
in Halifax in the Era of the American Revolution.................................... 146

NEIL MACKINNON
The Changing Attitudes of the Nova Scotia Loyalists
towards the United States, 1783-1791 165

SHANNON RYAN
Fishery to Colony: A Newfoundland Watershed, 1793-1815.................... 177

WILLIAM SPRAY
The Settlement of the Black Refugees in New Brunswick,
1815-1836 196

T.W. ACHESON
The Great Merchant and Economic Development in Saint John,
1820-1850 212

JUDITH FINGARD
The Relief of the Unemployed Poor in Saint John,
Halifax and St. John's, 1815-1860... 237

RUSTY BITTERMANN
The Hierarchy of the Soil: Land and Labour
in a 19th Century Cape Breton Community 259

GAIL G. CAMPBELL
Disfranchised but not Quiescent:
Women Petitioners in New Brunswick in the mid-19th Century............. 282

JANET GUILDFORD
    Separate Spheres: The Feminization of Public School Teaching
    in Nova Scotia, 1838-1880 315

IAN ROSS ROBERTSON
    Political Realignment in Pre-Confederation
    Prince Edward Island, 1863-1870.. 336

PHILLIP A. BUCKNER
    The Maritimes and Confederation: A Reassessment................................ 360

PREFACE

During the 1960s and 1970s a revolution began to take place in Canadian historiography. The traditional focus on "national" themes was abandoned by a growing number of historians who turned to a wide range of more limited topics. Regionalism was one of those topics and was eagerly embraced by scholars in the hinterlands of Canada who felt that the older emphasis on nation-building relegated their regions to a secondary and largely reactive position in Canada history.[1] These developments were viewed with approval -- and even encouraged -- by such leading figures in the Canadian historical profession as Ramsay Cook and Maurice Careless. In 1967 Cook had suggested that "Perhaps instead of constantly deploring our lack of identity we should attempt to understand and explain the regional, ethnic and class identities that we do have. It might just be that it is in these limited identities that 'Canadianism' is found". In a widely quoted article published in 1969 Careless popularized the term "limited identities", which became the most important new concept employed by Canadian historians in the 1970s.[2]

It was against this background that *Acadiensis* was launched in 1971.[3] The pressure to found *Acadiensis* came from many directions but a key role was played by the late Ken Windsor who insisted on the need for a journal which would -- in his words -- "recover the past" of the Atlantic Region. The timing was fortuitous. University history departments in the region were still in the process of expansion and a substantial number of graduate students were in the process of completing theses on regional topics. George Rawlyk, whose graduate seminar at Queen's University produced many of these students, predicted in 1969 that a new "Golden Age of Maritime Historiography" was about to begin.[4] During the 1970s his prophecy seemed on the verge of fulfillment. Particularly through the pages of *Acadiensis*, a new generation of scholars began to reshape the contours of our regional and national historiography.[5] There was also a refreshing amount of interdisciplinary con-

1 For a brilliant critique of the traditional historiography, see E.R. Forbes, "In Search of a Post-Confederation Maritime Historiography, 1900-1967", *Acadiensis*, VIII, 1 (Autumn 1978), pp. 3-21.

2 Ramsay Cook, "Canadian Centennial Cerebrations", *International Journal*, XXXI (Autumn 1967), p. 663; J.M.S. Careless, " 'Limited Identities' in Canada", *Canadian Historical Review*, L (March 1969), pp. 1-10.

3 For comments on the origins of the journal and its antecedents, see P.A. Buckner, "Acadiensis II", *Acadiensis*, I, 1 (Autumn 1971), pp. 3-9, and "Acadiensis: The First Decade", *Acadiensis*, X, 2 (Spring 1981), pp. 3-4.

4 George Rawlyk, "A New Golden Age of Maritime Historiography?", *Queen's Quarterly*, 76 (Spring 1969), pp. 55-65.

5 See W.G. Godfrey, " 'A New Golden Age': Recent Historical Writing on the Maritimes", *Queen's Quarterly*, 91 (Summer 1984), pp. 35-82.

tact in the journal, which was most notable in the contributions of historical geographers. In 1977 an historian from outside Canada, commissioned to prepare a survey of "Canadian History in the 1970s", declared: "I am conscious in reading *Acadiensis* that work on Maritime history is cumulative in a sense in which work published in the *Canadian Historical Review* is not and perhaps cannot be because the range of topics covered is so wide".[6]

Ironically just as the new Golden Age seemed to have arrived, some historians began to predict its demise. In 1977 Ramsay Cook, while praising the results of the new historiography, cautiously warned regional historians not to ignore "the 'national' experience".[7] In 1978 Lovell Clark delivered an attack on those Canadian historians who "add to the focus of disunity by jumping on the bandwagon of regionalism", and in 1980 Donald Swainson emphasized that Canadian historians had "allowed the pendulum to swing too far" in the direction of regionalism.[8] Maurice Careless -- once described by Ramsay Cook as "the patron saint of the new approaches to our history" -- announced that the search for "limited identities" had gone too far: "limited identities threaten to take over, and settle the matter of a Canadian national identity, by ending it outright, leaving perhaps a loose league of survivor states essentially existing on American outdoor relief".[9] Even those who remained sympathetic to the more general historiographical revolution that had taken place wondered whether the "increasing emphasis on 'region' as the crucial variable which explains sundry problems of Canadian development" was not "misplaced".[10]

The flight from regional studies was due to several factors. As Ramsay Cook pointed out, the historians "at least partly reflected the direction in which the society itself was moving".[11] The growing fear of Quebec separatism in the late 1960s and early 1970s had inspired the desire to find an explanatory concept which all Canadians -- including Québécois -- could accept. Limited identities seemed to provide that concept. But after the Quebec referendum separatism no longer seemed a threat and Canadian historians -- in tune with the national mood -- began to re-emphasize their commitment to the search for

6 H.J. Hanham, "Canadian History in the 1970s", *Canadian Historical Review,* LVIII (March 1977), p. 10.

7 Ramsay Cook, "The Golden Age of Canadian Historical Writing", *Historical Reflections,* 14 (Summer 1977), p. 148.

8 Lovell Clark, "Regionalism? or Irrationalism?", *Journal of Canadian Studies,* 13/2 (Summer 1978), p. 119; D. Swainson, "Regionalism and the Social Scientists", *Acadiensis,* X, 1 (Autumn 1980), p. 144.

9 Cook, "The Golden Age", p. 139; J.M.S. Careless, "Limited Identities -- ten years later", *Manitoba History,* I (1980), p. 3.

10 Greg Kealey, "Labour and Working-Class History in Canada: Prospects in the 1980s", *Labour/Le Travailleur,* 8 (Spring, 1981), p. 74. Compare Bryan Palmer's 1972 assessment in "Most Uncommon Common Men: Craft and Culture in Historical Perspective", *Labour/Le Travailleur,* 1 (1976), p. 21.

11 Cook, "The Golden Age", p. 139.

a "national" identity. Too few were prepared to heed David Alexander's pleas for a stronger Canadianism which might learn something of value from the regional experience and incorporate some of the virtues of the other identities in which Canadians have participated.[12] There was also a feeling -- particularly among the older generation of historians -- that the profession and the discipline had been fragmented by the variety of new approaches which had developed in the 1970s. Some historians legitimately criticized the imprecision with which the terms "region" and "regionalism" were -- and are -- used.[13] There was nothing "peculiarly Canadian" about these developments. American historiography, which so greatly influences Canadian, followed a similar pattern in the 1980s.[14]

One might have some sympathy with these attitudes if an historiographical revolution really had taken place in Canada. Yet, as Chad Gaffield has written, the new approaches of the 1970s have become "institutionalized" in new journals in the "periphery" while "mainstream" historical attention focuses on traditional topics.[15] While work in new fields such as social history, women's history and working-class history is frequently welcomed, few historians have been prepared to accept the need to re-think some of the traditional categories and periodization of Canadian history.[16] Even a cursory examination of the recent literature reveals the limited impact of the new scholarship. Most books on "national" subjects pay lip-service to the need to convey the variety of the regional experience in Canada but too frequently contain only token materials or passing reference to the Atlantic Region. And most textbooks in Canadian history retain their traditional Central Canadian and to a lesser degree Western Canadian focus.[17] Until our national historiography really does incorporate the insights contained in journals like *Acadiensis* the flight from regional concerns in the 1980s seems, at best, premature.

It is to make these insights more widely accessible that we have decided to issue two volumes of essays drawn from *Acadiensis*. Since our primary concern was to choose articles which were most likely to be of use in undergraduate survey courses, a large number of scholars were asked to par-

12 David Alexander, *Atlantic Canada and Confederation: Essays in Canadian Political Economy* (Toronto 1983).

13 See Ramsay Cook, "Regionalism Unmasked", *Acadiensis*, XIII, 1 (Autumn 1983), pp. 137-42.

14 For example, see Carl N. Degler, "Remaking American History", *The Journal of American History,* 67 (1980), pp. 7-25 and Thomas Bender, "The New History -- Then and Now", *Reviews in American History*, 12 (December 1984), pp. 612-22.

15 See his review of *Hopeful Travellers* in the *Urban History Review*, XI (February 1983), p. 81.

16 For efforts to do so, see Michael S. Cross and Gregory S. Kealey, eds., *Readings in Canadian Social History*, 5 vols. (1983-1984), and Marie Lavigne, Jennifer Stoddart, Micheline Dumont et Michèle Jean, *L'histoire des femmes au Québec depuis quatre siècles* (Montréal 1982).

17 See Bill Godfrey, "Canadian History Textbooks and the Maritimes", *Acadiensis*, X, 1 (Autumn 1980), pp. 131-5.

ticipate in the process of selection. The end product is not comprehensive and many fine articles had to be omitted. In order to publish the volumes as inexpensively as possible, the articles also had to be reprinted precisely as they originally appeared in the journal and they are presented without comment by the editors. Nonetheless, we hope that these volumes will introduce students, both within and without the Atlantic Region, to some of the important literature that has appeared in *Acadiensis* and whet their appetite for more. If they do serve that function, they will help not only to fulfill Ken Windsor's dream of recovering the past of this region but also to re-integrate this history into the mainstream.

NOTE TO THE THIRD EDITION

The debate over the place of the regional approach to Canadian history continues. In a recent book entitled *Who Killed Canadian History?*, Jack Granatstein worried that the rise of new approaches based on themes such as class, gender, ethnicity and region had destroyed the narrative unity of Canadian history. A more subtle critique was presented by Michael Bliss, who shared some of the same concerns but also argued for the integration of this new work into the main body of Canadian history.[1] Meanwhile, regional history has continued to follow its own path of evolution. Perhaps the most notable achievement was the publication of a new general history of Atlantic Canada in the form of a two-volume work that incorporated much of the research published in the pages of *Acadiensis* since the 1970s.[2] For specialists there was also a retrospective index to the contents of the journal.[3] The success of *Acadiensis*, and the continuing demand for the earlier editions of *The Acadiensis Reader*, have helped sustain the case for the relevance of regional history. Moreover, recent general histories of Canada have made some measurable efforts to address the significance of the regional experience.[4] The present edition of this anthology was prepared after consulting the needs of those involved in teaching Atlantic Provinces history at the university level. This edition reproduces much of the contents of the previous two editions and also includes several more recent articles. The addition of a third name to the editorial team for this edition recognizes the contributions of Gail Campbell, who has served as the most recent editor of the journal.

DF
1998

1. J.L. Granatstein, *Who Killed Canadian History?* (Toronto, 1998); Michael Bliss, "Privatizing the Mind: The Sundering of Canadian History, the Sundering of Canada", *Journal of Canadian Studies*, Vol. 26, No. 4 (Winter 1991-92), pp. 5-19, and the responses in the same journal, Vol. 27, No. 2 (Summer 1992).

2. Phillip A. Buckner and John G. Reid, eds., *The Atlantic Region to Confederation: A History* (Fredericton/Toronto, 1994); E.R. Forbes and D.A. Muise, eds., *The Atlantic Provinces in Confederation* (Fredericton/Toronto, 1993).

3. Eric Swanick and David Frank, eds., *The Acadiensis Index, 1971-1991* (Fredericton, 1992).

4. Janet Guildford and Michael Earle, "On Choosing a Textbook: Recent Canadian History Surveys and Readers", *Acadiensis*, XXVII, 1 (Autumn 1997).

RALPH PASTORE

Reprinted from Vol. XIX, No. 1
(Autumn 1989)

The Collapse of the Beothuk World*

UNTIL RECENTLY, THE BEOTHUKS, NEWFOUNDLAND'S ABORIGINAL people who became extinct in 1829, were a shadowy people whose origins, culture, and demise were little understood. In the past 15 years, however, archaeological, historical, and linguistic investigation has produced answers to a number of significant questions about them. It is now clear that the Beothuks were a hunting and gathering people of Algonkian stock,[1] whose ancestors in Newfoundland produced tools typologically similar to the late prehistoric Indian inhabitants of coastal Labrador and the Quebec North Shore.[2] It is also clear that, prior to the coming of Europeans, the Beothuk occupied, or at least used, all of the island of Newfoundland with the possible exception of the Avalon peninsula east of Trinity Bay. This island, despite its enormous size, has a simplified ecosystem characterized by a disproportionately small number of prey species relative to the large number of predators. Those predators included wolves, bears, lynx, marten, mink, weasels, otter, fox, and human beings. The major native interior prey species were caribou, beaver, and arctic hare (although the bones of the latter have never been identified from an archaeological site on the island). In essence, then, the island is a rather impoverished piece of the boreal forest in the mouth of the St. Lawrence. Of course, the surrounding waters are much richer in available food. Most important of the marine mammals to native hunters were harbour, harp, grey, and hooded seals, and walruses, all of which were once found in abundance off the coasts. Other marine resources available to the Beothuks included cod, salmon, flounder, smelt, capelin, mussels, soft-shelled clams, and lobsters. A number of avian species also contributed to the aboriginal diet including the now extinct great auk as well as murres and a wide variety of ducks and geese.[3]

---

*An earlier version of this works was presented at the Seventh Atlantic Canada Studies Conference, Edinburgh, May 4-7, 1988. I am indebted to Laurel Doucette, Charles Martijn, Douglas Robbins and Jim Tuck for their comments.

1   John Hewson, *Beothuk Vocabularies: A Comparative Study* (St. John's, 1978), pp. 135-46. Hewson also noted that the Beothuk language "appears to show" a "feature...normally considered diagnostic" of Central rather than Eastern Algonkian (p. 146). The present-day Naskapi-Montagnais of Labrador are also classfied as part of the Central Algonkian subgroup.

2   Ralph T. Pastore,"Excavations at Boyd's Cove — 1984: a Preliminary Report", in J.S. Thomson and C. Thomson, eds., *Archaeology in Newfoundland and Labrador, 1984* (St. John's, 1985), pp. 322-37 and R.T. Pastore, "Investigations at Boyd's Cove: The 1985 Field Season, a Preliminary Report", in J.S. and C. Thomson, eds. *Archaeology in Newfoundland and Labrador, 1985* (St. John's, 1986), pp. 218-32.

3   A.T. Bergerud, "Prey Switching in a Simple Ecosystem", *Scientific American*, 249 (December

The majority of prehistoric Beothuk sites are found along stretches of coastline that allowed them to exploit the resources of both the near shore and the interior of the island. This site distribution leaves the impression of a people who were not specialized in their hunting and fishing strategies,[4] an hypothesis strengthened by the few samples of prehistoric Beothuk food remains that have been recovered from archaeological sites.[5] A generalized subsistence pattern was probably necessary for the island's peoples because, despite the rich resources of the sea, prehistoric human populations in Newfoundland have always been vulnerable to changes in the availability of animal stocks. One of the most significant marine resources would have been the harp seal which is usually present, even today, in herds numbering more than a million. Yet there have been times in the historic period when, due to strong offshore winds, the unsuitability of the ice, or factors not yet understood, these seals unaccountably failed to arrive off the island's coast.[6] There is no reason to believe that prehistoric harp seal stocks would have been any more reliable. The most important land resource, caribou, may have been equally unreliable. A successful caribou hunt involved intercepting the animals primarily upon their fall migration.[7] Caribou movements are notoriously unpredictable and may be affected by factors as diverse as insects and ice storms. As illustrated in Figure 1, Newfoundland's native peoples, like most hunting and gathering bands, had to time their own seasonal movements to coincide with the availability of their prey. If that prey was not there, hunters would have to fall back on less important substitutes. Unfortunately, the island of Newfoundland lacked many of "fall-back" species — the moose, deer, and porcupine — found on the mainland. Even less important prey species such as beaver and freshwater fish are much less abundant than on the mainland. Newfoundland native groups, therefore, had little margin for survival if one of their major food resources, caribou or harp seal, failed. A few years of such

1983), pp. 130-41; J.A. Tuck and R.T. Pastore, "A Nice Place to Visit, but...Prehistoric Human Extinctions on the Island of Newfoundland", *Canadian Journal of Archaeology*, 9 (1985), pp. 69-80.

4   R.T. Pastore, "The Spatial Distribution of Late Palaeo-Eskimo Sites on the Island of Newfoundland", in *Palaeo-Eskimo Cultures in Newfoundland, Labrador and Ungava* (St. John's, 1986), pp. 125-34.

5   David Simpson, "Prehistoric Archaeology of the Port au Port Peninsula", M.A. thesis, Memorial University of Newfoundland, 1986. Fieldwork under my direction in the summer of 1987 at a Beothuk site on an island in Notre Dame Bay revealed a prehistoric Beothuk midden made up of bones from a broad range of food species.

6   L. Chafe, *Chafe's Sealing Book: A History of the Newfoundland Sealfishery from the Earliest Available Records Down to and Including the Voyage of 1923* (3rd ed., St. John's, 1924), p. 19.

7   Arthur E. Speiss, *Reindeer and Caribou Hunters: An Archaeological Study* (New York, 1979), p. 124.

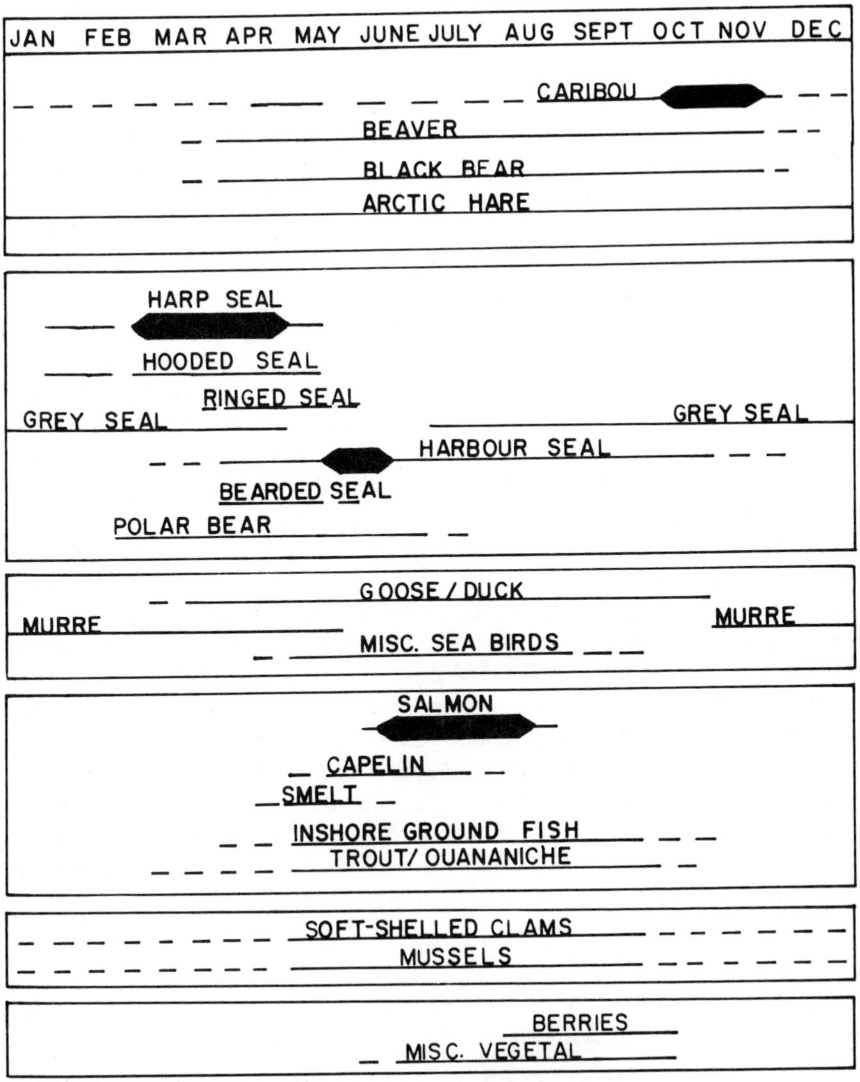

JAN	FEB	MAR	APR	MAY	JUNE	JULY	AUG	SEPT	OCT	NOV	DEC

CARIBOU

BEAVER

BLACK BEAR

ARCTIC HARE

HARP SEAL

HOODED SEAL

RINGED SEAL

GREY SEAL   GREY SEAL

HARBOUR SEAL

BEARDED SEAL

POLAR BEAR

GOOSE / DUCK

MURRE   MURRE

MISC. SEA BIRDS

SALMON

CAPELIN

SMELT

INSHORE GROUND FISH

TROUT/ OUANANICHE

SOFT-SHELLED CLAMS

MUSSELS

BERRIES

MISC. VEGETAL

Figure I. SEASONAL AVAILABILITY OF
NEWFOUNDLAND FOOD RESOURCES

From Tuck and Pastore, "Extinctions".

failures might well cause the sort of extinctions that appear to be characteristic of Newfoundland's prehistory. Indeed, archaeological research has demonstrated that in least three instances before the arrival of Europeans, prehistoric native populations have become extinct — very likely because of changes in the availability of vital food resources.[8]

Although archaeology has provided at least the outlines of the prehistoric Beothuk subsistence pattern, it is not possible to determine the size of the Beothuk population at the time of European contact. Such a determination would require a systematic survey of the entire coast and much of the interior of the island as well as a programme of excavation designed to reveal site size and population and, given the expense involved, such an undertaking is unlikely. Even the fortuituous discovery of archaeological sites is less likely in Newfoundland. Elsewhere, many archaeological sites are discovered because of modern building and road construction, but the island's poverty, sparse population, and rugged terrain make extensive activity of this sort highly improbable. In the absence of such a programme of reconnaissance and excavation, estimates of Beothuk population can only be informed guesses. Perhaps the first recorded estimate was by Joseph Banks who noted in 1766 that Beothuks were "thought to be very few as I have been told not Exceeding 500 in number but why that should be imagind I cannot tell as we Know nothing at all of the Interior Parts of the Island nor Ever had the Least Connextion with them tho the french we are told had".[9] Although Banks believed that by the 1760s the Beothuks had retreated into the interior, there is evidence that they were still visiting the coast to hunt and fish, even if their permanent residence had shifted to the interior.[10] He was, however, correct in regarding that population estimate with some scepticism, for there really was no sound basis for estimating their numbers.[11]

Ignorance about the size of the Beothuk population at a time when the numbers of other native peoples of the northeast were quite well known to whites is not surprising. Some time after about the second decade of the 17th century, the Beothuks followed a pattern of withdrawal from contact with Europeans which culminated in their extinction early in the 19th century. The

---

8   Tuck and Pastore, "Extinctions".

9   A.M. Lysaght, ed., *Joseph Banks in Newfoundland and Labrador, 1766: His Diary, Manuscripts and Collections* (Berkeley, 1971), p. 132.

10 For example, see "The narrative of Lt. John Cartwright's journey up the Exploits River, 1768", in J.P. Howley, *The Beothucks or Red Indians* (Cambridge, 1915), p. 33.

11 For a discussion of the debate on Beothuk population size see Ingeborg Marshall, "An Unpublished Map Made By John Cartwright Between 1768 and 1773 Showing Beothuck Indian Settlements and Artifacts And Allowing a New Population Estimate", *Ethnohistory*, 24 (Summer 1977), pp. 223-49.

tragedy of that extinction, unique in Canadian history, has attracted a great deal of attention from both scholarly and popular writers. The Newfoundland geologist, James P. Howley, whose remarkable collection of documents pertaining to the Beothuks was published in 1915, concluded that the Beothuks had been hunted and harrassed to extinction. Although Howley discounted many of the more lurid oral accounts of Beothuk persecution, his documentary collection was eagerly used by a number of popular writers, most notably Harold Horwood and Pierre Berton, to spin out a sensational tale of "the people who were murdered for fun".[12]

Given the fact that researchers limited to the documentary record were faced with a number of accounts, some trustworthy, others not, of Europeans killing Beothuks, it is perhaps not surprising that a monocausal explanation of the Beothuk demise was accepted. That would change after the results of James Tuck's archaeological investigations of a number of Newfoundland sites were published. He found that for thousands of years prior to the coming of Europeans, Newfoundland's inhabitants had depended upon the resources of the sea for most of their food. He also noted that when Europeans began to settle the island, of necessity they were drawn to the same resource-rich areas of the coastline that the Beothuks inhabited. As Tuck put it: "An unknown number of natives were actually killed outright by Europeans. But more important to the survival or extinction of the race, the remaining Beothuks were denied access to the coast and forced to try and survive on the resources of the interior".[13] In an important article published in 1977 Leslie Upton argued that "despite these tales of slaughter, common to all North American frontiers, the decrease in Beothuck population over a period of three hundred years was unspectacular". Positing a population of about 2,000 at the time of European contact, Upton found nothing unusual about a rate of decline due to epidemic disease and loss of hunting territory that was, in fact, less than what other researchers had found for New England. In a suggestive comparsion between the Micmac and the Beothuk experience Upton speculated that "the Beothuks died because they did not have enough contacts with the whites". He noted that the course of Beothuk-white relations had been remarkably different from that of other Indian peples in North America. Upton stated that "the Beothuk strategy of withdrawal has no parallel elsewhere in the region, and its cause cannot be known: epidemic disease may have been the catalyst that prompted the decision".[14] The problem with this explanation is that

---

12 Harold Horwood, "The People Who Were Murdered for Fun", *MacLean's Magazine*, 10 October 1959; Pierre Berton, *My Country: The Remarkable Past* (Toronto, 1976).

13 James A. Tuck, *Newfoundland and Labrador Prehistory* (Ottawa, 1976), p. 75.

14 Leslie Upton, "The Extermination of the Beothucks of Newfoundland", *The Canadian Historical Review,* 58 (June 1977), pp. 133-53.

every other native people in North America also suffered the ravages of epidemic disease; none, however, withdrew so determinedly from European contact.

Throughout North America, the lure that drew native peoples to European contact was trade. The knives, axes, kettles, blankets and guns of the newcomers were immensely desired by Indians. Elsewhere in North America Indians endured disease, violence, alcoholism, and an assault on their most deeply held beliefs in order to trade furs for European goods. The fact that the Beothuks did not do so is remarkable, perhaps unique. Since Upton's work, archaeologists working on Beothuk sites have done much to suggest a possible reason for the Beothuk failure to participate in a fur trade.[15] In brief, it is argued that because of the unusual nature of the early Newfoundland economy, the Beothuks did not *need* to enter into a fur trade to obtain European goods — especially metal objects. Once European fishermen began to dry fish on shore, they left behind, each winter, flakes, wharves, stages and a variety of debris associated with an onshore fishery. For the Beothuks, these seasonally-abandoned fishing premises were treasure troves of metal objects, particularly nails. Archaeological work at two Beothuk sites in Notre Dame Bay, in fact, has resulted in the recovery of hundreds of nails (many of them modified into projectile points), as well as scraps of iron and brass kettles, fish hooks, awls, and numerous other metal pieces. Although a marginal trade between European fishermen and Beothuks may have existed in the 16th and early 17th centuries,[16] by the latter date the Beothuks had been drawn into a pattern of pilfering European goods from seasonally-abandoned fishing premises. As a result, the first European settlers on the island had to trap their own furs. The Newfoundland "furrier", as he was called, dates to at least 1612-1613.[17] Although more research is needed, the practise of whites trapping furs in the 17th century appears to have little parallel in the rest of North America.[18] When whites were forced to trap their own furs,

---

15 The following argument is a brief summary of the material presented in R.T. Pastore, "Fishermen, Furriers, and Beothuks: The Economy of Extinction", *Man in the Northeast*, 33 (Spring 1987), pp. 47-62.

16 For example, in 1612 when the would-be colonizer, John Guy, encountered Beothuks in Trinity Bay, the Beothuks attempted to trade with the English by leaving behind poles with furs on them, but the English were not equipped with trade goods. As Cell noted, the Beothuks, unlike this particular group of Englishmen, appear to have engaged in a fur trade before. John Guy's Journal of a Voyage to Trinity Bay, 7 October 1612 to 25 November 1612, in Gillian Cell, ed., *Newfoundland Discovered: English Attempts at Colonization, 1610-1630* (London, 1982), p. 76.

17 "Occurrents in Newfoundland", 1 September 1612-1 April 1613, in David B. Quinn, ed., *New American World* (New York, 1979), IV, pp. 166, 169, 170, 172-5.

18 Although the Hudson's Bay Company did allow its men to trap privately at least by the 18th century (see for example Instructions of Joseph Isbister, Chief Trader at Albany Fort to John Yarrow, Master at Eastmain House, 15 September 1753, HBCA B.59/a/22, fo 4, extract provided by Toby Morantz), Morantz believes that such trapping by whites was "was on a very small scale".

there was, of course, even less possibility that a systematic fur trade would emerge on the island between settlers and Beothuks.

The absence of fur traders in Newfoundland was paralleled by an absence of missionaries. Elsewhere in North America, one of the more important ways in which native peoples were drawn into interaction with Europeans was through the activities of missionaries. Newfoundland's seasonal fishery and tiny year-round British population (estimated at about 1200 in the last quarter of the 17th century),[19] however, could not support a missionary effort to the Beothuks. Nor is there any evidence that the colony of Placentia, occupied by the French during the period, 1662-1713, sent misionaries to the Beothuks.[20] The other usual medium for peaceful contact between Indians and whites in the European colonies was the official assigned by the metropolitan powers to deal with native groups. Such officials generally had two functions: to secure the assistance or the neutrality of Indians, and to negotiate the sale of Indian land. But the British Crown did not make the commanders of the Newfoundland convoy governors nor did it provide for the creation of magistrates who would spend the winter on the island until 1724.[21] By then there was certainly no need for Indian agents since the Beothuk pattern of withdrawal was well established. Nor was there any need to secure the assistance of the Beothuks in the wars between Britain and France. As a people who lacked firearms, they would have counted for very little and, in any case, the contest for supremacy in Newfoundland would be won by the power which had naval, not land, supremacy.

Without these Indian agents, fur traders, and missionaries, there was no one to stand between the Beothuks and the white settlers, their competitors for the resources of the coast.[22] Because the vast majority of those European occupiers left no written records, the historian of the Beothuk experience is forced to rely much more than usual upon archaeological data even for information as basic as the plotting of the Beothuk retreat from encroaching white settlement. In an attempt to delineate the shrinking world of the Beothuks, evidence from published and unpublished archaeological reports, site record forms on file in the Newfoundland Museum in St. John's, and a few scattered documentary references, have been used to note the location of both prehistoric and historic Beothuk sites in Newfoundland and related sites in Labrador and Quebec.[23]

---

19 Grant Head, *Eighteenth Century Newfoundland* (Toronto, 1976), p. 82.

20 See Ministère de la France d'Outre-Mer, Archives des Colonies, Serie C11C, Amérique du Nord, vols. 1-7, Terre-Neuve (Plaisance), Microfilm in the PAC.

21 Keith Matthews, *Lectures on the History of Newfoundland, 1500-1830* (St. John's, 1973), pp. 141-50.

22 Upton, "The Extermination of the Beothuks", p. 153.

23 Earlier results of this research were published in Graeme Wynn, Ralph Pastore, and Bernard Hoffman, "The Atlantic Realm" in R. Cole Harris, ed., *Historical Atlas of Canada*, I (Toronto,

The question of what constitutes prehistoric Beothuk needs some explanation. It now is clear that the immediate prehistoric predecessors of the Beothuk on the island of Newfoundland were the possessors of the Little Passage complex. At two important sites in Notre Dame Bay, for example, there was no evidence of another occupation intervening between that of the Little Passage people and the Beothuks.[24] In addition, the strong resemblance between the stone tools used by both groups suggested a continuity over time. That hypothesis has been strengthened by a detailed attribute analysis of Beothuk and Little Passage stone projectile points which identified a number of trends in attributes extending from the prehistoric period to perhaps the beginning of the 18th century.[25]

On the other side of the Strait of Belle Isle, William Fitzhugh first identified a late prehistoric/early historic Indian presence extending along the coast of Labrador from Saglek Bay to the Quebec Lower North Shore, which he named the Point Revenge complex. "The geographic extent of Point Revenge occupation and its persistence into the historic period", he argued, "make it the most likely progenitor of the modern Indians of Labrador". He also noted that "sites related to Point Revenge in Newfoundland are thought to be ancestral to Beothuck culture, and on the Quebec north shore, prehistoric continuity into historic Montagnais is also suggested".[26] The posited relationship between Little Passage and Point Revenge is based both on a similarity of projectile point styles and an apparent preference in both cases for locating sites in similar areas. Little Passage and Point Revenge sites are often found in an inner coastal zone which suggests a subsistence pattern described by Fitzhugh as "Modified-Interior", *i.e.*, a "generalized" rather than "specialized" dependency on coastal and interior resources.[27]

Although more research on both Little Passage and Point Revenge is needed, current evidence does suggest a relationship. Figure 2 is predicated on this premise and indicates 16 Point Revenge sites on the central Labrador coast, two

1987). Results of archaeological research undertaken since the preparation of that volume have been incorporated in this work.

24 Ralph Pastore, "Excavations at Boyd's Cove, Notre Dame Bay — 1983", in J.S. Thomson and C. Thomson, eds., *Archaeology in Newfoundland and Labrador, 1983* (St. John's, 1984), pp. 98-125; Ralph Pastore, "Excavations at Inspector Island, 1987: A Preliminary Report", in *Archaeology in Newfoundland and Labrador, 1987* (in press).

25 Fred Schwarz, "The Little Passage Complex in Newfoundland: A Comparative Study of Assemblages", Honours thesis, Memorial University of Newfoundland, 1984.

26 William W. Fitzhugh, "Indian and Eskimo/Inuit Settlement History in Labrador: An Archaeological View", in Carol Brice-Bennett, ed., *Our Footprints are Everywhere: Inuit Land Use and Occupancy in Labrador* (Nain, Newfoundland, 1977), p. 14.

27 Schwarz, "The Little Passage Complex", pp. 43-7.

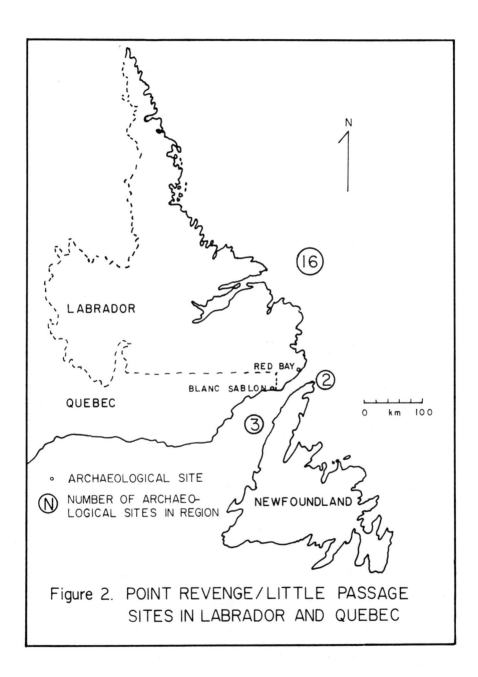

Figure 2. POINT REVENGE/LITTLE PASSAGE
SITES IN LABRADOR AND QUEBEC

Little Passage sites in the Strait of Belle Isle, and three Little Passage or Point Revenge sites on Quebec Lower North Shore.[28] At present, James Tuck, the excavator of the Red Bay site, believes that the diagnostic artifacts of the two sites in the Strait of Belle Isle would fit generally within the assemblages recovered from prehistoric Beothuk (Little Passage) sites on the island. This should not be surprising. The much earlier Maritime Archaic and Palaeo-Eskimo traditions have been reported from both Quebec-Labrador and the island,[29] and it would be unusual if the Beothuks and neighboring Quebec-Labrador groups were an exception to the general rule that related subarctic hunter-gatherer cultures tend to be scattered over quite wide distances. Still, there are locations within these huge areas which were quite crucial for hunter-gatherers, and the Strait of Belle Isle would have been exactly such a place. It has quite rightly been referred to as a "resource funnel" for a variety of marine resources including many species of whales and seals.[30]

On the island itself, as Figure 3 reveals, six prehistoric sites have been discovered in Bonavista Bay, five in Notre Dame Bay, five on the south coast, two each in the interior and Trinity Bay, and one each in Placentia Bay and on the west. One explanation for the preponderance of sites in the island's northeast is illustrated by Figure 4 which shows the migration of harp seals and their breeding areas.[31] Clearly, Notre Dame Bay would have been very appealing to prehistoric Beothuk seal hunters. The attraction of the south coast is more difficult to explain, but since this coast tends to be ice-free all year long,[32] its coves and bays

28 At present there is some confusion in the usage of the terms "Point Revenge" and "Little Passage". While Fitzhugh designates Indian occupations on the coast of central Labrador from about A.D. 1000 to A.D. 1650, as Point Revenge, the excavators of the Quebec sites perceive Point Revenge as antecedent to Little Passage. Until the results of recent research on both sides of the Quebec Labrador border appear, I have chosen not to attempt to reconcile the terminology, but simply to present the data as reported. William W. Fitzhugh, "Winter Cove 4 and the Point Revenge Occupation of the Central Labrador Coast", *Arctic Anthropology*, XV, 2 (1978), pp. 146-74; Hélène Taillon and Georges Barré, eds., *Datations au ¹⁴C des sites archéologiques du Québec* (Quebec City, 1987), pp. 480-1.

29 James A. Tuck, "Prehistoric Archaeology in Atlantic Canada since 1975", *Canadian Journal of Archaeology*, 6 (1982), p. 203.

30 F.A. Aldrich, "The Resource funnel of the Strait of Belle Isle", paper delivered to the International Symposium on Early European Settlement and Exploitation in Atlantic Canada, St. John's, October 1979.

31 Based on A.W. Mansfield, *Seals of Arctic and Eastern Canada* (Ottawa, 1964), p.12, and D.E. Segeant, "Migrations of harp Seals *Pagophilus groenlandicus* (Erxleben) in the Northwest Atlantic", *Journal of the Fisheries Research Board of Canada*, 22 (1965), pp. 433-64.

32 Chesley Sanger, "The Evolution of Sealing and the Spread of Permanent Settlement in Northeastern Newfoundland", in J.J. Mannion, ed., *The Peopling of Newfoundland* (St. John's, 1977), p.139.

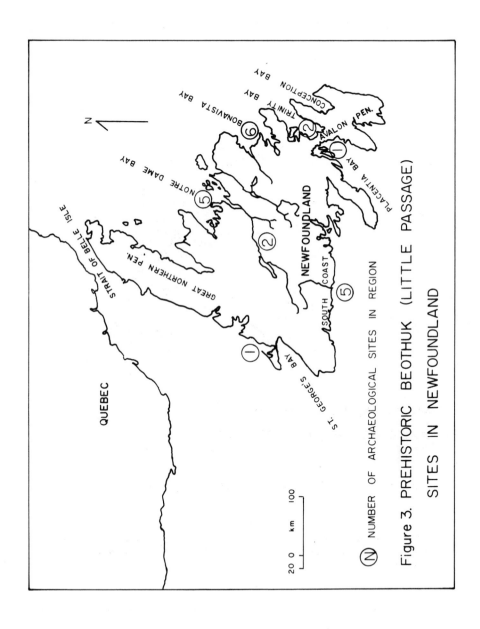

Figure 3. PREHISTORIC BEOTHUK (LITTLE PASSAGE)
SITES IN NEWFOUNDLAND

Ⓝ NUMBER OF ARCHAEOLOGICAL SITES IN REGION

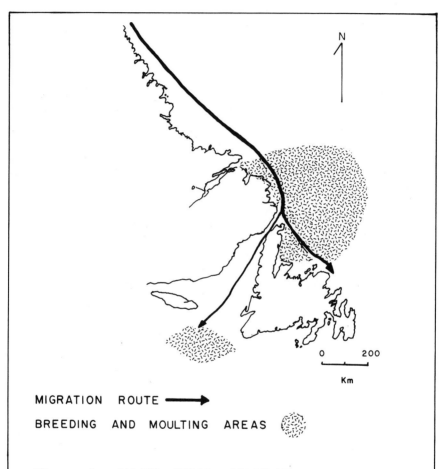

MIGRATION ROUTE ➡

BREEDING AND MOULTING AREAS

Figure 4. HARP SEAL MIGRATIONS

AFTER A.W. MANSFIELD, SEALS OF ARCTIC AND EASTERN CANADA,
BULLETIN No. 137. FISHERIES RESEARCH BOARD OF CANADA
(OTTAWA, 1964), p. 12.

once had harbour and grey seals in abundance.[33] In addition, prehistoric hunters may well have been drawn to the south coast to hunt caribou in the winter since the largest winter concentrations of caribou on the island are to be found along the south coast and its interior.[34]

Figure 5 reveals a somewhat different pattern in the distribution of historic sites.[35] That pattern would be much clearer if it were possible to establish an age for each site, but in many instances the surviving material is simply not datable. The sites at both extremes of Figure 5 may be among the oldest. In the far southeast, the Ferryland site is also the location of Lord Baltimore's colony, founded in 1621, and evidence of an Indian presence here lies beneath a stone wall attributed to Baltimore and is found with European artifacts which date to the late 16th century. In the far northwest, material from Blanc Sablon in the Strait of Belle Isle is still undergoing analysis, but according to its most recent excavator, aboriginally produced stone tools have been found at the same level with European artifacts.[36] Preliminary work from the nearby site of Red Bay, a Basque whaling station occupied from ca. 1540 to ca. 1610, indicates an association of 16th century Basque features with an Indian occupation. The stone projectile points produced by those Indians, both at Blanc Sablon and Red Bay, may in fact be a variant of those produced by historic Beothuks on the island. The island itself is clearly visible from the Labrador side of the narrow (20 km) Strait of Belle Isle, and it is inconceivable that native groups on either side would have been prevented from traversing it throughout the year. Indeed, for much of the year travel by canoe across the Strait would be far easier than an inland journey of 20 km by foot. The Strait of Belle Isle, in fact, should be viewed as a highway, not a barrier.[37]

Whatever the nature of the relationship between the historic Indians of Quebec-Labrador and those of the island, it is clear that both groups had access

33 Even now there are major concentrations of harbour seals found from Placentia Bay to the southwest corner of the island. J. Boulva and I.A. McLaren, "Biology of the Harbor Seal, *Phoca vitulina*, in Eastern Canada", Department of Fisheries and Oceans Bulletin, No. 200 (Ottawa, 1979), p. 2.

34 During the period 1957 to 1967, the largest concentration of caribou was found along the south coast and its interior. A.T. Bergerud, "The Population Dynamics of the Newfoundland Caribou", Wildlife Society, Wildlife Monograph No. 25 (Washington, D.C., 1971). Whether this was true in the prehistoric period is not known.

35 These sites include: archaeological sites, both living and burial; burials reported by non-professionals; and living sites, burials, and storehouses reported by contemporary observers. Documentary and other references for these sites are to be found in the appendices at the end of the paper.

36 Jean-Yves Pintal, personal communication.

37 I am indebted to Marguerite MacKenzie, Memorial University Department of Linguistics, for this observation.

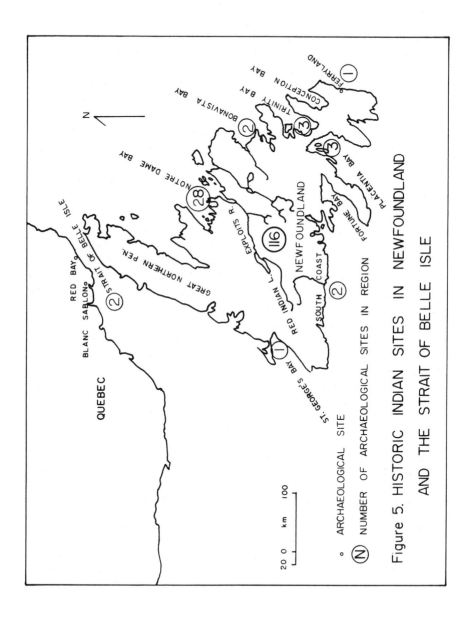

Figure 5. HISTORIC INDIAN SITES IN NEWFOUNDLAND
AND THE STRAIT OF BELLE ISLE

to European goods in a similar manner. That access is clearly indicated by the presence of native hearths found at both Red Bay and Ferryland which are located in and among European structures. This has led the director of excavations at those sites to suggest that the Indians in question had been visiting the two locations to scavenge European iron from seasonally-abandoned shore stations. The one site from the southwest corner of the island, in St. George's Bay, was reported in 1594 by the master of the *Grace* of Bristol who found a Beothuk camp in that bay, along with the wrecks of two Basque ships. The other sites along the South Coast and Placentia Bay are either burials or archaeological sites, none of which can be dated with any confidence. The three sites from Trinity Bay are drawn from the account of John Guy who met a Beothuk group camped there in 1612, and from a work by an early Newfoundland entrepreneur who reported an encounter between Beothuks and European mariners around the turn of the 17th century. Only two sites are listed for Bonavista Bay, perhaps because of a lack of archaeological surveys in the area. Of these two, one is a burial, the other a living site. Unfortunately, neither has been dated with any precision.

The 28 sites in Notre Dame Bay and all but one of the 116 sites from the interior represent the Beothuk response to increased European utilization of Newfoundland. Most of these living sites date to the late 18th-early 19th centuries when the Beothuk presence in the bay was restricted to furtive fishing and hunting forays carried out under the guns of white settlers. Two of these sites, Boyd's Cove and Inspector Island, however, have been dated to ca. 1650-1730, and merit special attention.[38] They are situated in eastern Notre Dame Bay and were occupied at a time when English permanent settlement ended in Bonavista Bay, and a French migratory fishery was carried on in the western portion of the bay. These two living sites were positioned in an area safely between the two zones of European exploitation from which it was possible to visit the seasonally abandoned French fishery to the west for European iron, and occasionally to steal from the English settlements and fisheries to the southeast.[39] These sites may well have been occupied at a time when Beothuk culture entered a period of florescence — when it was still possible to hunt and fish in safety, and still possible to acquire the iron from which to fashion the tremendously useful metal cutting and piercing tools that made their lives so much easier. Faunal analysis of the animal remains from the Boyd's Cove site bears this out. The wide range of species taken prompted the

---

38 Pastore, "Fishermen, Furriers, and Beothuks" and "Excavations at Inspector Island, 1987". The Beothuk component at Inspector Island appears to date to ca. 1720-1730, although future analysis may result in modification of this conclusion.

39 Pastore, "Fishermen, Furriers, and Beothuks".

analyst, Stephen Cumbaa, to note: "At Boyd's Cove we have a glimpse of a people at ease in their environment and obviously exercising a fair degree of control over use of its resources. The contrasting picture we have a century later of a beleaguered and dwindling population eking out a living on the run from a dominant culture is all the sadder for the comparison".[40] The other sites in Notre Dame Bay represent archaeological sites, both living and burial, and bone ornament caches. None has been dated with any more accuracy other than to the historic period.

The sites clustered along the Red Indian Lake-Exploits River system represent the last refuges of the Beothuk. Many of these sites have been excavated, and they have produced a large quantity of knives, scissors, trap parts, and other European objects.[41] The abundance of European objects, coupled with the relative lack of stone tools, as well as the dates assigned to a number of artifacts from the Wigwam Brook site, support the evidence from the documentary record that this region was intensively occupied during the late 18th and early 19th centuries.[42] This was a period when the Beothuks were hindered by white settlement from access to the resources of the coast and were forced to try to subsist on the meagre resources of Newfoundland's interior. The nature of those last days is graphically revealed in the archaeological evidence. Animal bones from one late 18th/early 19th century site on the Exploits River, for example, revealed that not only were the Beothuks subsisting almost entirely upon caribou, but they were attempting to do so all year round.[43] One leading authority on caribou hunting has noted that in an area such as Newfoundland, where caribou migrate over short distances, it would have been possible for aboriginal groups to prey on caribou year-round, but "humans usually found easier resources to harvest for part of the year, mostly anadromaous fish, beaver, or moose".[44] Moose, of course, were not introduced to the island until the late

---

40 Stephen Cumbaa, " 'Diverse Furres and Deeres Flesh' — Animal Use by a 17th Century Beothuk Population at Boyd's Cove, Notre Dame Bay, Newfoundland" (unpublished report, Zooarchaeological Identification Centre, National Museum of Natural Sciences, National Museums, Canada, 1984).

41 Don Locke, *Beothuck Artifacts* (Grand Falls, Newfoundland., n.d.); Helen Devereaux, "The Pope's Point Site", unpublished report, Newfoundland Museum, 1965; Helen Devereaux, "A Preliminary Report on the Indian Point Site, A Stratified Beothuk Site", unpublished report, Newfoundland Museum, 1970; Raymond LeBlanc, "The Wigwam Brook Site and the Historic Beothuk Indians", M.A. thesis, Memorial University of Newfoundland, 1973.

42 Ingeborg Marshall, "An Unpublished Map", pp. 223-49; Maps of the Red Indian Lake-Exploits River region drawn by Shanawdithit in 1829, in Howley, *The Beothucks*, pp. 238-45.

43 Frances L. Stewart, "Faunal Analysis of the Wigwam Brook Site, Newfoundland", Appendix 1, in LeBlanc, "The Wigwam Brook Site".

44 Speiss, *Reindeer and Caribou Hunters*, p. 138.

19th century, and the island's fish and beaver populations are both much smaller than those on the mainland.[45] Conventional anthropological thinking has it that caribou "can theoretically supply all of the requirements of a human population, but the chances of this occurring are in fact extremely small".[46] In fact, Newfoundland's stark interior supported only 14 indigenous mammalian species, and there is no evidence in the archaeological record that any aboriginal culture lived there for 12 months of the year. When the Beothuks were forced to do so, the results were tragic. Detailed analysis of a child's garments from a contemporaneous burial provides a graphic picture of Beothuk life during those last days. The shroud of one child (now in the Newfoundland Museum) was found to be a woman's legging, made from five pieces of skin, most of which had been patched and repaired. The child's moccasins exhibited similar careful patching and repairing; most surprising was the use of spruce root rather than the usual caribou sinew to repair the moccasins. All of this suggests a people on the ragged edge of desperation who did not even have enough animal skins to clothe a child properly.[47]

This pattern of gradual Beothuk withdrawal from a territory which once encompassed almost all of Newfoundland and perhaps the Strait of Belle Isle to the banks of the Exploits River has been constructed largely on the basis of archaeological evidence. However, the same pattern is evident in the documentary record. For example, as late as 1612 John Guy noted the presence of Beothuks on the Avalon peninsula. Ten years later, the experienced sea captain Richard Whitbourne stated that although Beothuks from Bonavista Bay stole into Trinity Bay to pilfer "Hatchets, Hookes, Kniues, and such like" he implied that they no longer lived in Trinity Bay.[48]

The Beothuks who had once lived in Trinity Bay appear to have travelled back and forth across the narrow isthmus of the Avalon peninsula to gain access to the considerable resources of Placentia Bay, especially the harbour seals.[49] The

45 W.B. Scott, and E.J. Crossman, *Fishes Occurring in the Fresh Waters of Insular Newfoundland* (Ottawa, 1964); Thomas Northcott, "An Investigation of the Factors Affecting Carrying Capacity of Selected Areas in Newfoundland for the Beaver (*Castor canadensis caector* Bangs 1913)", M.Sc. thesis, Memorial University of Newfoundland, 1964, p. 117.

46 Ernest S. Burch, "The Caribou-Wild Reindeer as a human resource", *American Antiquity*, 37 (1972), p. 363, quoted in Speiss, *Reindeer and Caribou Hunters*, p. 139.

47 Ruth Holmes Whitehead, "I Have Lived Here Since the World Began: Atlantic Coast Traditions" in Julia D. Harrison, ed., *The Spirit Sings: Artistic Traditions of Canada's First Peoples* (Toronto, 1987), p. 40.

48 Richard Whitbourne, *A Discourse and Discovery in New Found-land* (London, 1622), in Gillian Cell, ed., *Newfoundland Discovered* (London, 1982), p. 118.

49 Guy, "Journal", p.72. Boulva and McLaren "Biology of the Harbour Seal", p.2, found the largest concentration of harbour seals on the island in Placentia Bay.

Beothuks may have also occupied that narrow neck of land in order to intercept caribou herds passing from the main part of the island to the isthmus.[50] The importance of that isthmus to the Beothuks is underscored by the presence of two large prehistoric Beothuk sites there. Thus, the year-round occupation of Trinity Bay by the English by 1675 and the French occupation of Placentia Bay by at least 1662 had the effect of denying these two important food sources to the Beothuk.[51] By 1694, de Brouillan, the commandant of the French garrison of Placentia, could write about "la decouverte des sauvages qui habitent au sud de l'isle", clearly indicating that the French at Placentia had not been in contact with the Beothuks, if indeed they ever had, for some time.[52] De Brouillan's information was given to him by a band of Micmacs who had come to Newfoundland from Cape Breton. Their arrival in Newfoundland meant yet another competitor for the island's resources. While it is possible that there were Micmacs in Newfoundland in the 16th century,[53] given the report by de Brouillan, it does not appear as if their presence on the south coast was intensive enough to disrupt Beothuk use of that portion of the island. However, it is clear that by the middle of the 18th century, Micmac use of the southern portion of the island from St. George's Bay to Placentia Bay had denied yet another area of the island — and its caribou and seals — to its aboriginal inhabitants.[54]

50 The narrow necks of peninsulas are ideal for intercepting caribou migrations. M.A.P. Renouf, "Prehistoric Coastal Economy in Varangerfjord, North Norway", Ph.D. thesis, Cambridge University, 1981.

51 Gordon Hancock, "English Migration to Newfoundland", in Mannion, ed., *The Peopling of Newfoundland*, pp. 16-7; Jean Pierre Proulx, *The Military History of Placentia* (Ottawa, 1979), pp. 9-12.

52 Jacques-François de Mombeton de Brouillan to the Minister of Marine, 25 October 1694, Archives des Colonies, C11C, II, 20.

53 The evidence for this is summarized in Charles A. Martijn, "Voyages des Micmacs dans la vallée du Saint-Laurent, sur la Cote-Nord et à Terre-Neuve", in Charles Martijn, ed., *Les Micmacs et la Mer* (Quebec, 1986), pp. 215-21.

54 Ralph T. Pastore, *The Newfoundland Micmacs*, Newfoundland Historical Society Pamphlet No. 5 (St. John's, 1978), pp. 9-19. While the present article was undergoing editorial review, Ingeborg Marshall's "Beothuk and Micmac: Re-examining Relationships", *Acadiensis*, XVII, 1 (Autumn 1988), pp. 52-82, appeared. While I would agree with Ms Marshall that the Micmacs played a greater role in the extinction of the Beothuks than has been previously recognized, I have argued that this was because of Micmac displacement of the Beothuks from an area necessary to their subsistence. Until some direct evidence is produced, I remain unconvinced that the French paid a bounty to the Micmacs for Beothuk heads. I find even more dubious Marshall's uncritical use of an oral account of an alleged "critical turning point" when a group of Beothuks discovered a number of Micmacs with the heads of Beothuks for which they expected a reward from the French. The Beothuks supposedly then invited the offending Micmacs to a feast and slaughtered the erstwhile murderers. This is in fact a variant of a European folk motif, Motif K811.1 "Enemies invited to a feast and killed", in Stith Thompson, ed., *Motif Index of Folk Literature*

By the middle of the 18th century, then, the Beothuk range had shrunk considerably. The contraction of the Beothuk world would have meant more than just reduced access to food resources. Given the presence in a number of prehistoric Beohtuk sites on the island of Ramah chert, a translucent silicate found only in Ramah Bay in northern Labrador, it can be assumed that a trade across the Strait of Belle Isle existed in prehistoric times. Since trade between band level societies also implies the exchange of marriage partners, it is possible that at the point in Beothuk history when contact with Indian peoples in Labrador was either lost or reduced, the subsequent reduced gene pool would have further imperiled the survival of the island's natives.

It is difficult to determine when contact with Labrador may have been interrupted. There is some evidence that the Basques who carried on a whale hunt in the Strait of Belle Isle, during the period ca. 1540 to ca. 1610, employed native people at the shore stations.[55] Although there is some controversy — and no direct evidence — relating to the incidence of European epidemic disease among the native peoples of the Northeast in the 16th century,[56] there are two factors about this Basque-native contact which might have made the trans- mission of epidemic disease more likely. First, the distance from Europe to the Strait of Belle Isle was shorter than that to New England or the Maritimes, thus increasing the likelihood that a disease carried by a crew member would not yet have run its course prior to landing. Second, if the Basques employed Indians in shore-based activities throughout the season, the prolonged close contact implied would have been more conducive to the spread of pathogens than would be the case in a fur trade where contacts between the two groups would have been of much shorter duration.

Assuming that the Indians of the Strait of Belle Isle survived the Basque whale fishery of the 16th century, they would have had to face an invasion of the Strait by Inuit in the 17th century. There is evidence that by the last half of the 17th century there was an Inuit population living in the region throughout the year,[57]

(rev. ed., Bloomington, 1955), IV, p. 340. I also find puzzling the use of a term such as "nations" to describe the Micmac and the Beothuk, and a sentence such as: "The Beothuks were evidently not in a position to enforce their claim on this territory and may have relinquished the land voluntarily in order to remain on good terms with their Micmac neighbors". Such terminology is inappropriate when dealing with hunting bands.

55 Selma Barkham, "A note on the Strait of Belle Isle during the period of Basque contact with Indians and Inuit", *Etudes/ Inuit/ Studies*, 4, 1-2 (1980), pp. 51-8.

56 Dean Snow and Kim Lanphear, "European Contact and Indian Depopulation in the Northeast: The Timing of the first Epidemics", *Ethnohistory*, 35 (Winter 1988), pp. 15-33; Bruce Trigger, *Natives and Newcomers* (Montreal, 1985), pp. 237-9.

57 Charles Martijn, "La présence inuit sur la Cote-Nord du Golfe St-Laurent à l'époque historique", *Etudes/Inuit/Studies*, 4, 1-2 (1980), pp. 105-25.

and it is quite likely that Indian use of the Strait was either severely curtailed or ended. In 1705 Augustin LeGardeur de Courtemanche established a trading post at Brador, near Blanc Sablon, and it is significant that he had to bring a group of Montagnais families with him to hunt fur bearers and to prosecute a (salmon ?) fishery.[58] The well-documented hostility between the Inuit and French traders and fishermen in the Strait of Belle Isle casts further doubt on the likelihood that normal communication between the Indian populations of the Island and Labrador could have persisted in the last half of the 17th and first half of the 18th century.[59]   Those French posts were established to trade with the Montagnais whose persistence today underscores the hypothesis that it was the Beothuk decision to withdraw from the fur trade which was the most important factor in their demise. The effects of that decision, however, were reinforced by the growing exploitation of Newfoundland's resources by other ethnic groups. Although the spread of permanent English settlement on the island may have been the most important factor denying the Beothuks access to vitally needed coastal resources, to that equation must now be added the Basque and Inuit presence in the Strait of Belle Isle, the Micmac use of the southern third of the island, and the French base at Placentia. A complete understanding of all of the effects of these arrivals upon the Beothuks may not yet be attainable, but the pattern revealed by the distribution of Beothuk sites over time is clear enough. As contact with Labrador was lost, and as the various regions of the island were denied to the Beothuks, they were forced to withdraw to the island's impoverished interior where there could be but one outcome for them.

58 "Anonymous Memoir, 1715, Concerning Labrador", No. 1419, in Privy Council, *In the Matter of the Boundary Dispute Between the Dominion of Canada and the Colony of Newfoundland in the Labrador Peninsual* (Ottawa, 1927), VII, p. 3694.

59 François Trudel, "Les relations entre les Français et les Inuit au Labrador méridional, 1660-1760", *Etudes/Inuit/Studies*, 4, 1-2 (1980), pp. 135-46.

JOHN G. REID

Reprinted from *The Northeastern Borderlands*
(Acadiensis Press, 1989)

An International Region
of the Northeast:
Rise and Decline, 1635-1762

IN ONE SENSE, THE EXISTENCE OF an international region of the northeast in the seventeenth and early eighteenth centuries is easy enough to establish. The absence of generally agreed land frontiers made it inevitable that the spheres of influence of European and native peoples would shift and overlap. As early as the 1620s, the territory which today comprises the State of Maine and the Maritime provinces had been claimed partly or wholly by four European nations: France, England, Scotland, and the Netherlands. The established native populations were also diverse — Micmac, Maliseet-Passamaquoddy, and Abenaki — and they retained considerable cultural integrity and military power despite the disastrous effects of epidemic disease. Clearly, the scene was set for international conflict, as European invaders contended with Indian peoples and with each other. Borderland interaction there would be, interaction in all likelihood marked by violence and bloodshed.

Violent conflict, between European and native and between European nationalities, duly emerged, and has been treated as a major theme in the history of this northeastern region in the colonial era. Not for nothing did J.B. Brebner begin his classic 1927 study of *New England's Outpost: Acadia Before the Conquest of Canada* with the sombre observation that "ever since the coming of European settlers, Nova Scotia has had a peculiarly troubled history."[1] This comment could be applied to the whole of the French colony of Acadia, which in the seventeenth century covered not only today's Maritime provinces but extended southwest as far as the Penobscot river, and also to the English province of Maine, between the Kennebec and Piscataqua rivers. The territory between the Penobscot and the Kennebec was intermittently the subject of active dispute between French, English, and native inhabitants.[2]

Warfare was a recurring element of the experience of all those who lived in the region from early colonial times until the mid-eighteenth century. In Acadia, there were frequent conflicts between French and English, and, after the conquest of 1710, between British and Micmac. Southwest of the

---

1 John Bartlet Brebner, *New England's Outpost: Acadia Before the Conquest of Canada* (New York: Columbia University Press, 1927), p. 15.

2 For more detailed discussion of the development of spheres of influence in the region, see John G. Reid, *Acadia, Maine, and New Scotland: Marginal Colonies in the Seventeenth Century* (Toronto: University of Toronto Press, 1981), *passim*.

Penobscot, in the disputed territory and in Maine, the English and Abenaki fought a series of bitter wars, complicated at times by the intervention of the French and other native peoples. Although it is not necessary here to review in detail the complex and often repetitive patterns of these conflicts, a few examples will serve to illustrate their persistence. As early as 1613, the principal Acadian centre of Port Royal was burned by an expedition from Virginia, which also destroyed a short-lived French settlement near Mount Desert Island. Between 1629 and 1632, a small Scottish colony was established at Port Royal, at a time when the few French inhabitants were living elsewhere in the colony. The Scots departed as a result of European treaty negotiations, but not before they had fought one significant battle in capturing a French fort at the mouth of the St. John river. In 1654, by which time the colonization of Acadia by French family groups had begun, the chief Acadian settlements were again raided by English forces, and the Acadians lived under English occupation for 16 years. In 1675, following many years of intermittent tensions, the first major English-Abenaki war began, and it lasted three years. The general series of wars between 1689 and 1713 further confirmed the patterns of British-native and British-French conflict. Even after the Treaty of Utrecht in 1713, the sequences continued. New England aggression put the Abenaki on the defensive in a new war from 1722 to 1727, and the remnants of native military power — in Acadia as well as in Maine — were effectively undermined by British victory in the general North American conflict from 1754 to 1763. That great war also resulted in the expulsion of the majority of the Acadians from their land in Nova Scotia, following their ultimately unsuccessful attempt to establish a position of neutrality between French and British forces.

Apparently, therefore, the history of this region in the colonial period is characterized by violent disputes: by conflicts which, though often obscure and complicated in the details of their development, essentially conform to patterns that have become well-established in North American colonial historiography. They confirm the hostility between English and French, and between European and native, and thus bear out the conclusions of such recent scholars of the general phenomenon of European colonization as Kenneth Andrews and Donald Meinig. Andrews has subtly documented the sharpening of international rivalries in the late sixteenth century, and the resulting delineation of North American spheres of influence:

The invasion of North America was a European movement. Throughout the sixteenth century Portuguese, Spanish, French and English explorers and fishermen reconnoitred the coasts from Florida to Baffin Island. For a long time among these early pioneers collaboration between men of different nationality was not uncommon — indeed it was normal in the Newfoundland fishery. Towards the end of the century, however, national rivalry intensified for economic as well as political reasons.[3]

Meinig, meanwhile, has analysed the interaction of Europeans and indigenous peoples into three general patterns:

1. expulsion of the native population from the colonized area and the creation of a firm frontier of separation between the two peoples, as in Virginia;
2. benign articulation of the two peoples at a point of exchange, each group operating largely within a separate territory but bound together in an encompassing economic system, as in Canada; and
3. stratification within a single complex society, exhibiting varying degrees of racial and cultural mixture and fusion, as in Mexico.[4]

In all of these cases, Meinig emphasizes, "an imperial relationship was...assumed" on the European side, and ultimately "resistance, conflict, and dislocations were sure to follow."[5]

This paper will argue, however, that in the international region of the northeast — notwithstanding the apparently overwhelming evidence of conflict-dominated relationships — there were also important elements of peaceful interaction and attempts at mutual adaptation among peoples who, if their experience had conformed to the more general North American norms, ought to have been in conflict. To adopt the terms used by Andrews and Meinig, a case will be made for the extension in time and scope of the phenomena of "collaboration" and "benign articulation." Beginning with a review of recent literature on the region itself, the paper will sketch an interpretation of the rise and decline of what was, for a time, an unconventional society in colonial North America: one where the necessities of survival led to conscious efforts to restrain violent conflict. Finally, some questions will be identified that must be considered en route to a firm reinterpretation of the balance between conflict and coexistence, and of the resulting significance of the northeastern region in the wider

3 Kenneth R. Andrews, *Trade, Plunder and Settlement: Maritime Enterprise and the Genesis of the British Empire, 1480-1630* (Cambridge: Cambridge University Press, 1984), p. 304.

4 D.W. Meinig, *The Shaping of America: A Geographical Perspective on 500 Years of History, Volume 1, Atlantic America, 1492-1800* (New Haven and London: Yale University Press, 1986), pp. 70-72.

5 *Ibid.*, p. 70.

historiography of colonial North America.

As so often in the colonial history of the northeast, the seeds of reinterpretation can be found in the work of Brebner, and notably in his well-known dictum that "there were, in effect, two Acadies, each important in its own way. The one was the Acadie of the international conflict, the other the land settled and developed by the Acadians."[6] Brebner's preoccupation, however, was to trace the steps that led to what he considered to be an inevitable tragedy: the way in which international tensions and "the expanding energies of New England" led to the expulsion of "Evangeline's people...from the land which they called Acadie and which, unfortunately for them, they had conquered as husbandmen but lost as Frenchmen."[7] Thus, although Brebner rightly distinguished between the warlike impulses that proceeded from imperial rivalry, and on the other hand the peaceful aspirations of the Acadians, he offered only a simplistic paradigm to explain their interaction. For him, "the simple Acadians" were overwhelmed by forces they could not even begin to understand, because "high politics were beyond them."[8]

Only in the last fifteen years have the questions that Brebner raised been reconsidered by a new generation of historians who have sought to evaluate more thoroughly the experience of those who lived in this region.[9] None of these authors has sought to minimize the conflicts that took place. All, however, have also brought to light evidence of efforts to achieve inter-national reconciliation. George A. Rawlyk, writing in 1973, posed an explicit challenge to Brebner's emphasis on New England expansionism. The Massachusetts interest in Acadia, Rawlyk argued, was sporadic and was influenced by certain identifiable interest groups. By the middle of the seventeenth century, a *modus vivendi* had been established, by which the

6   Brebner, *New England's Outpost*, p. 45.

7   *Ibid.*, pp. 15, 233.

8   *Ibid.*, pp. 8, 204.

9   In identifying these recent studies, I have included only those which focus on international themes — the relationship between European nationalities and between Europeans and native people — and so have not dealt with such other works on early Acadia and Maine as Edwin A. Churchill, "Too Great the Challenge: The Birth and Death of Falmouth, Maine, 1624-1676" (Ph.D. thesis, University of Maine, 1979); Andrew Hill Clark, *Acadia: The Geography of Early Nova Scotia to 1760* (Madison: University of Wisconsin Press, 1968); Charles E. Clark, *The Eastern Frontier: The Settlement of Northern New England, 1610-1763* (New York: Alfred A. Knopf, 1970); Gordon E. Kerhsaw, "*Gentlemen of Large Property and Judicious Men": The Kennebeck Proprietors, 1749-1755* (Somersworth, N.H., and Portland, Me.: New Hampshire Publishing Company and Maine Historical Society, 1975); Calvin Martin, *Keepers of the Game: Indian-Animal Relationships and the Fur Trade* (Berkeley: University of California Press, 1978); and John G. Reid, *Maine, Charles II, and Massachusetts: Governmental Relationships in Early Northern New England* (Portland: Maine Historical Society, 1977).

Penobscot river was unofficially recognized as the French-English boundary, and it was tacitly understood that Massachusetts fishermen and traders would have access to Acadian natural resources and that northeastern Indian peoples would not be encouraged by the French to make war on the English settlements. Increasingly, towards and beyond the turn of the century, these understandings were weakened and military conflicts resulted, but there was never a single consistent pattern of aggression by either side.[10]

Writing in the same year, and in a 1979 introductory essay to Volume IV of the *Dictionary of Canadian Biography*, Naomi Griffiths emphasized the pragmatism of the Acadian people, and their conscious search for a "policy" which would allow them to survive in the dangerous region they inhabited. The Acadians were, for Griffiths, "as much a people of the frontier as the inhabitants of Monmouthshire, Cumberland, Alsace-Lorraine, or the Basque country."[11] Central to the Acadian strategy was the forging of "contacts with other people [which] were considerably wider than has usually been accounted:" with New England traders, and with native people. As regards European imperial powers, Griffiths argued, the Acadian stance was one of neutrality, but this was not just the haphazard reaction of an ignorant people. It was, rather, "[a] policy of their own making."[12]

In 1975, in a University of Maine doctoral thesis significantly entitled "Nos amis les ennemis," Jean Daigle analysed the commercial interactions between New England and Acadia in the late seventeenth and early eighteenth centuries. Daigle, like Griffiths, stressed the self-conscious efforts of Acadians to reach a practical relationship with the powerful Massachusetts colony. Acadian merchants were no mere tools of English exploiters, but were, in reality, "dynamiques et clairvoyants."[13] They pursued their own interests, and those of the Acadian people, with skill and vigour. "La poursuite d'une politique de neutralité de non-alignement," Daigle argued, "laisse sous-entendre que les commerçants acadiens comprirent le rapport de forces en présence en Amérique; l'accommoda-

10 George A. Rawlyk, *Nova Scotia's Massachusetts: A Study of Massachusetts - Nova Scotia Relations, 1630 to 1784* (Montreal: McGill-Queen's University Press, 1973), pp. 17-19 and *passim*.

11 N.E.S. Griffiths, "The Acadians," in *Dictionary of Canadian Biography* (hereafter *DCB*), ed. George W. Brown *et al.* (10 vols. to date; Toronto: University of Toronto Press, 1966-), IV, pp.xvii, xxi; also Naomi Griffiths, *The Acadians: Creation of a People* (Toronto: McGraw-Hill Ryerson, 1973).

12 Griffiths, "The Acadians," pp.xvii, xxi.

13 Jean Daigle, "Nos amis les ennemis: relations commerciales de l'Acadie avec le Massachusetts, 1690-1711" (Ph.D. thesis, University of Maine, 1975), p. 200.

tion avec leurs amis les ennemis du Massachusetts fut pour eux la seule alternative valable."[14]

Four years after Daigle had written, another scholar turned to international relationships in the colonial era of the northeastern region, though of a different kind. The late Leslie Upton's study of *Micmacs and Colonists* presented a more conventional, conflict-centered, interpretation. Given that he began at 1713, and focused on the troubled relations between the Micmac and the British colony of Nova Scotia which they had never recognized as legitimate, the emphasis on tension and hostility was justifiable. Upton too, however, commented on the Acadian-Micmac bond: "there was such a close connection between the early Acadians and the Micmacs that beleaguered British officials often complained they they could not tell the two apart. But the peoples concerned knew who they were and, despite the ties of blood and friendship, pursued their separate courses."[15] Upton was also at pains to portray the strategic sophistication with which the Micmac regulated their military affairs. Unwilling to be lured into a major war which they could not win, the Micmac were content to resist the British presence through an intermittent raiding warfare, punctuated by negotiations that led, as in the case of the treaty ratified at Annapolis Royal in 1726, to short periods of peace.[16]

John G. Reid's 1981 comparative study of the "marginal colonies" of Acadia, Maine, and New Scotland in the seventeenth century also dealt with matters of war and peace. Persistent efforts by competing imperial authorities to assert control over the northeastern colonies led to the development of "a basic pragmatism" among the colonial populations.[17] Expressed in a willingness to adapt to changing regimes — as, for example, in the case of the Acadian adaptation to English rule between 1654 and 1670 — while also developing effective forms of local self-government through leaders generated by the communities themselves, this approach offered a means of survival and even prosperity despite the armed conflicts that swirled around the areas of settlement. By the later years of the century, international tensions had reached the point where the outbreak of war in 1689 unleashed violence on a scale that could only be destructive for all those who lived in the region. Pragmatism could offer only limited protection, but at times during the seventeenth century it had served the colonists well.

The colonists were not the only populations in the northeastern region

14 *Ibid.*, p. 9.
15 L.F.S. Upton, *Micmacs and Colonists: Indian-White Relations in the Maritimes, 1713-1867* (Vancouver: University of British Columbia Press, 1979), p. xv.
16 *Ibid.*, pp. 43-45.
17 Reid, *Acadia, Maine, and New Scotland*, p. 188.

who had to respond to the threat of violent disruption. Kenneth M. Morrison's *The Embattled Northeast*, published in 1984, provided a subtle reinterpretation of the struggle of the Abenaki to adapt to the changed circumstances created by European colonization. Morrison emphasized that the military alliance of French and Abenaki was slow to evolve. Although the various branches of the Abenaki — which continued well into the eighteenth century to act independently of each other — were willing when necessary to defend themselves against English aggression, their consistent preference was "to forestall hostilities, repeatedly seeking to communicate and negotiate their differences." Ultimately, by the 1720s, the Abenaki recognized the need for a close internal unity and a firm alliance with the French. Their longstanding efforts to deal diplomatically with English ethnocentrism, however, illustrated for Morrison that "Abenaki responses to Euramericans depart considerably from the general character of colonial Indian-white relations."[18]

Most recently, the archaeological work of Alaric Faulkner and Gretchen Fearon Faulkner has offered new insights into the nature of international interaction in the colonial northeast. In their 1987 study of *The French at Pentagöet, 1635-1674*, the Faulkners provided a detailed account of the important French fort and trading outpost on Penobscot Bay. While showing clearly, from the range of artifacts found on the site, that Fort Pentagöet was not in a position of dependence on Massachusetts traders, but rather was able to maintain trade relationships with French merchants, the evidence also demonstrated that a cordial relationship with neighbouring English settlers in the Penobscot-Kennebec territory was fostered actively by French governor Hector d'Andigné de Grandfontaine during the early 1670s. The Faulkners also found that regular trade with Massachusetts did take place as one part of Pentagöet's pattern of commercial relationships. "Commerce with one's potential enemies," they commented, "seems to have been a way of life on a frontier where opportunity took precedence over political allegiance."[19]

Thus, we are left with an apparent historiographical paradox. General interpretations of the effects of European imperialism in North America have emphasized violent conflict as a theme of seventeenth and early eighteenth century interactions, whether between European nations or

18 Kenneth M. Morrison, *The Embattled Northeast: The Elusive Ideal of Alliance in Abenaki-Euramerican Relations* (Berkeley: University of California Press, 1984), p. 193.

19 Alaric Faulkner and Gretchen Fearon Faulkner, *The French at Pentagöet, 1635-1674: An Archaeological Portrait of the Acadian Frontier* (Augusta, Me., and Saint John, N.B.: The Maine Historic Preservation Commission and the New Brunswick Museum, 1987), pp. 28, 168.

between European and Indian. In the early northeast, war between French and English is not hard to exemplify, from the Argall raid of 1613 to the final conflict that brought about the expulsion of the Acadians and culminated with the virtual elimination of France from North America in the early 1760s. Likewise, from the outbreak of the first major war in 1675 to the involvement of the Penobscot in the same great conflict of the late 1750s and early 1760s, English and Abenaki fought no fewer than five wars. It is on the basis of such evidence that we have been told in general histories that in the northeast "the English and French were usually at war," or that in New England as in other parts of Anglo-America "the sporadic warfare of the seventeenth-century frontier...generally resulted in the defeat and degradation of the Indians who set themselves in opposition to the white advance."[20] Yet every scholar who has systematically examined international relationships in the northeastern colonies, in studies written over the past fifteen years, has cast doubt on such generalizations and has called attention to hitherto unexplored areas of peaceful interaction. Taken together, these studies suggest the need for a reinterpretation of questions of war and peace in the region.

In offering a possible framework for reinterpretation, this paper will proceed from certain basic premises. First, the paper will deal with Acadia and with the disputed territory bounded to the southwest by the Kennebec river. The English province of Maine will not be included, as from the mid-seventeenth century onwards its experience was more directly influenced by southern New England than was true further to the northeast. Secondly, the paper will treat this northeastern region as an area of European colonization which was unsuccessful from an imperial standpoint. No European power was able to establish a substantial colonial population, or to draw clear economic benefits from this territory. No European power, at any time prior to the British ascendency that was established by the Seven Years' War, succeeded in making the area militarily secure. This was, in short, a debatable territory, a borderland. From that characteristic came the series of conflicts which took place. But from that same characteristic came the realization by both colonial and native populations that war could all too easily destroy them and therefore must be avoided whenever possible.

The result of this recognition was the development of a series of unusual international relationships, which can be examined in three distinct time periods. The relationships were essentially four in number: between

20 J.L. Finlay and D.N. Sprague, *The Structure of Canadian History* (Scarborough, Ont.: Prentice-Hall, 2nd ed. 1984), p. 39; Douglas Edward Leach, *Arms for Empire: A Military History of the British Colonies in North America, 1607-1763* (New York: Macmillan, 1973), p. 68.

French in Acadia and native people; between English in northern New England and native people; between French in Acadia and southern New Englanders; between English in northern New England and visiting French envoys and traders. The time periods were those from 1635 to 1689, the period of establishment of the respective relationships; the pivotal period of war from 1689 to 1713; and the period of decline from 1713 to 1762, during which vestiges of the old international region remained, but were steadily eroded by the growth of imperial conflict between France and Great Britain.

Between 1635 and 1689 there existed a genuinely international region of the northeast. The date 1635 is important because it marked important changes that would influence subsequent international contacts. The death of the Acadian-based governor of New France, Isaac de Razilly, in that year led to his effective succession by his lieutenant Charles de Menou d'Aulnay Charnisay. D'Aulnay, at Razilly's behest, had just completed the conquest for France of the Plymouth colony's trading post at Pentagöet, at the mouth of the Penobscot river. Among d'Aulnay's first acts after succeeding Razilly was to move the headquarters of the colony of Acadia, and the few colonists, to Port Royal from La Hève. D'Aulnay had a rival, however, in the person of Charles de Saint-Etienne de la Tour, who had been in Acadia since 1610 — much longer than either Razilly or d'Aulnay — and claimed to rule the colony as governor by virtue of a commission issued by the French crown in 1631. La Tour, like d'Aulnay, had fur-trading interests on the coasts of the modern New Brunswick and northeastern Maine, and in early 1635 he issued a warning to all New Englanders that "if they traded to the east of Pemaquid, he would make prize of them."[21]

This interconnected series of events in 1635 had profound consequences. The removal of the chief Acadian settlement to Port Royal, where the first family groups of settlers would shortly arrive, influenced the course of the colony's economic development. Marshland agriculture, combined with fishing and fur trading, would increasingly form the economic basis of Acadian communities. Reclaimed marshes had no economic or other significance for the Micmac, so that competition for land would not here be an issue between natives and settlers. At the same time, the continuing fur trade provided an economic basis for cooperation between the two peoples, and the intermittent presence of French religious missionaries led to further peaceful contacts. Eventually formal kinship ties developed through intermarriage. The most famous example was the marriage of the French military officer Jean-Vincent d'Abbadie de Saint-Castin in the 1670s to his Penobscot wife Pidianske, known to the French as

21 John Winthrop, *Winthrop's Journal*, ed. James Kendall Hosmer (2 vols.; New York: Charles Scribner's Sons, 1908), I, p.146.

Marie-Mathilde, but there were other instances in all of the major Acadian communities, such as the case of the marriage of Claude Petitpas at Port Royal in or about 1686 to his Micmac wife known as Marie-Thérèse.[22] These family connections were important elements of the successful coexistence of the Acadian colonial population with Indian peoples.

Acadians also forged a successful relationship with their New England neighbours: one which, until century's end, endured in spite of occasional interruptions by war. Again, the events of 1635 were important in delineating the effective boundaries of French and English spheres of influence. D'Aulnay and La Tour had separately made clear the French determination to maintain control of Pentagöet and all lands further northeast. The existence of English settlements at Pemaquid, Sheepscott, and other places between the Penobscot and Kennebec rivers was tacitly recognized by them as legitimate, and although later French claims would be advanced to that border territory between the two rivers there was, until 1689, no serious doubt that southwest of the Kennebec was an area of exclusively English colonization. With those distinctions established, Acadian-New England relationships could begin to assume their interactive pattern. The d'Aulnay-La Tour dispute of the 1640s, which ended with the defeat of La Tour in 1645, was instrumental in advancing the trading relationship between French and English, when Massachusetts merchants traded with La Tour in 1641 at his request, although the dispute also brought the two nationalities to the brink of war two years later. In 1643, La Tour used New England mercenary troops in an unsuccessful assault on d'Aulnay at Port Royal. D'Aulnay's understandable outrage led to his threatening to make war on Massachusetts. Ultimately, however, New England promises of "love and peace" led d'Aulnay to undertake in October 1644 "that whatever troubles may fall out between the two Crownes of France and England...to keep inviolably with you...that peace and intelligence which is requisite in these beginnings...."[23] A treaty to that effect was signed in Boston in the same month, albeit without the knowledge of the European parent country of either colony.

The treaty of 1644 did not stand. Six years later d'Aulnay died in an accident at sea, and political control of Acadia again fell into dispute. The resulting internal conflicts were barely resolved when the 1654 English occupation of the Acadian settlements took place. Yet the results of that

---

22 Georges Cerbelaud Salagnac, "Jean Vincent d'Abbadie de Saint-Castin," *DCB*, II, pp. 5-6; Clarence J. d'Entremont, "Claude Petitpas," *ibid.*, p. 524; Griffiths, "The Acadians," pp. xvii-xviii.

23 Governor and Council of Massachusetts to d'Aulnay [1644], Massachusetts Archives, vol. 2, ff. 482-83; d'Aulnay to Magistrates of Massachusetts, 21 October 1644, *ibid.*, ff. 478-81.

16-year conquest showed that the principle of Acadian-New England accommodation was not lost. Scanty evidence suggests that the Acadians at Port Royal adapted readily to the English presence, and even took advantage of it to free themselves from the sway of their previous French seigneurial landlords.[24] Trading contacts with Massachusetts continued to flourish long after the English departure in 1670, with some New England merchants establishing warehouses and residences in Port Royal itself. The Acadians also began to generate their own community-based structures for local government, which fostered their increasing reluctance to accept without question the orders issued by colonial administrators. Not for nothing did a puzzled Governor Frontenac of New France write in 1679 of the Acadians' "Inclination Anglaise et Parlementaire, que leur inspire la frequentation et le commerce qu'ils ont avec ceux de Baston...."[25]

At the same time, a similar pragmatism was developing among English settlers in the Penobscot-Kennebec territory. Two French official reports in 1671 suggested that the inhabitants of these communities would willingly adapt to French rule if the territory's status was resolved in favour of France. Jean Talon, Intendant of New France, reported on the "joye sensible" with which these English had welcomed a French emissary.[26] Although, as Talon was well aware, the settlers' joyfulness may have been exaggerated for the occasion, it was entirely consistent with the courteous reception given to other French visitors such as the Jesuit missionary Gabriel Druillettes in 1647, and to the merchant Henri Brunet on a series of trading visits beginning in 1673. Pemaquid merchants such as Abraham Shurt in the 1640s, and Thomas Gardner and Silvanus Davis in the 1670s, were active in commerce with the French, just as the Acadians of Port Royal dealt with merchants of New England.[27] Significantly, Shurt and Gardner also sought to preserve the peace between English and Abenaki. Shurt traded for many years with both Kennebec and Penobscot Abenaki, while Gardner in 1675 — with King Philip's War already in progress in southern New England — reported to the governor of Massachusetts that "I do not find by Any thing I Can discerne that the Indianes East of us are in the least our Ennimies," and squarely blamed the aggressiveness of his English neighbours for any hostility that existed.[28] In this most northeas-

24 See Reid, *Acadia, Maine, and New Scotland*, pp. 140-41.

25 Frontenac to Louis XIV, 6 November 1679, France, Archives des Colonies (hereafter AC), C11A, vol. 5, f. 16.

26 Talon to Jean-Baptiste Colbert, 11 November 1671, AC, C11A, vol. 3, ff. 187-88.

27 See John G. Reid, "French Aspirations in the Kennebec-Penobscot Region, 1671," *Maine Historical Society Quarterly*, 23 (1983-4), pp. 85-92.

28 Thomas Gardner to Governor John Leverett, 22 September 1675, *Documentary History of the State of Maine*, Maine Historical Society Collections, series 2 (24 vols.; Portland,

terly part of New England, no clear parallel with the Acadian-Micmac relationship would emerge: the news from southern New England created too strong and fearful a reaction from many of the English colonists. Nevertheless, there were others of the colonists who consistently sought, like the Abenaki themselves, to resolve disputes through diplomatic rather than violent means. War between English and Abenaki took place between 1675 and 1678, but in the northeast it was intermittent, thanks to the efforts of Gardner and of such native leaders as the Kennebec and Penobscot chiefs Mogg and Madockawando.[29]

More destructive for all inhabitants of the northeastern region was the complex series of wars waged between 1689 and 1713. Although these conflicts did not end the efforts of diverse peoples to coexist in the region, they created the circumstances that would ultimately make it impossible for them to do so. None of the wars originated in the region itself. A dispute between the English of Maine — that is, southwest of the Kennebec — and the western Abenaki broke out at Saco, Maine, in 1688. By the following year it had spread northeastwards, and in August 1689 Pemaquid fell to Penobscot Abenaki forces, soon to be followed by all other English settlements to the southwest as far as the outskirts of Wells. New England observers suspected collusion between French and Abenaki, and in response a New England fleet under the command of William Phips successfully attacked Port Royal in May 1690. Although the captors stayed only long enough to plunder the settlement, before returning to Massachusetts, this was only the first of a series of destructive raids which culminated in the final conquest of 1710. Early in the war, the English fears of an outright French-Abenaki alliance had proved self-fulfilling, and from 1690 until the short-lived peace treaty of Ryswick in 1697, the French commander Joseph Robinau de Villebon co-ordinated an effective guerrilla war on New England by French and Indian war parties from his base at Fort Naxouat, on the St. John river.

Even during this chaotic period, however, certain elements of the old international co-existence persisted. The relationship between Acadians and native people was not compromised. Neither, more surprisingly, was the trading contact between Acadia and New England: "Every year," wrote a French official in 1697 of the major Acadian settlements, "the English bring to these places trade-goods, brandy, sugar cane from Barbadoes, molasses and the utensils which are needed, taking in exchange pelts and grain, which has been a great boon during the recent years of famine in

Me., and Cambridge, Mass.: Maine Historical Society, 1869-1916), vol. VI, *The Baxter Manuscripts*, pp. 91-93.

29 See Morrison, *The Embattled Northeast*, pp. 108-11.

Boston."[30] Even Villebon recognized the necessity of the Acadian-New England trade, although he could not officially condone it, and was not above absenting himself from an Acadian settlement where English vessels were expected, "[so] that I might not be a witness to their trading...."[31] In the extreme northeast of New England, meanwhile, English settlement had been eliminated for the time being, and with it the old patterns of English-French and English-Indian interaction. The predilection of the eastern Abenaki for peaceful diplomacy had not disappeared, however. Mutual mistrust between English and Abenaki persisted throughout the period following the outbreak of war, and yet the Abenaki had quickly become disillusioned with the long-term military entanglements that their alliance with the French seemed to demand. As early as 1693, Madocka-wando signed a treaty with Phips, now governor of Massachusetts. Madockawando had acted without first going through normal processes of discussion with his Penobscot advisers, and community pressure forced him to repudiate the agreement shortly afterwards. Yet renewed negotiations led to a more acceptable treaty in 1699, and further conflicts during the later phases of the British-French war were brought to an end by the English-Abenaki treaty signed at Portsmouth, New Hampshire in 1713. As Kenneth Morrison has observed, the eastern Abenaki had sought, albeit without complete success, "to reach a middle ground between contending English and French colonies."[32]

The year 1713 was also the year of the Treaty of Utrecht, by which all of peninsular Acadia was ceded by France to Great Britain, to become known as the colony of Nova Scotia. Cape Breton Island — now known as Ile Royale — and the Ile St-Jean (later named Prince Edward Island) were retained by France, and the territory later known as New Brunswick remained a matter of French-English dispute, but all the main Acadian settlements on the peninsula and the isthmus were now brought under British rule. This cession of territory would obviously change radically the pattern of political and military power in the northeastern region. Furthermore, the ambiguities in the treaty — relating not only to the boundaries of Nova Scotia but also to such other important matters as the extent of English control of the land adjoining Hudson Bay, and the status of the Iroquois — ensured that further tensions would arise between

---

30 Memoir of M. Tibierge, 30 June-1 October 1697, in John Clarence Webster (ed.), *Acadia at the End of the Seventeenth Century: Letters, Journals and Memoirs of Joseph Robineau de Villebon, Commandant in Acadia, 1690-1700, and Other Contemporary Documents* (Saint John: New Brunswick Museum, 1934), p. 155.

31 Villebon's Journal, 17 April 1693, *ibid.*, p. 46.

32 Morrison, *The Embattled Northeast*, p. 163, and pp. 133-64 *passim*.

France and Britain in North America. Given the strategic importance of Nova Scotia/Acadia as an area where the two nationalities were now in close proximity, the increasing militarization of the region during the ensuing four decades was hardly surprising.

Among the results of this process was the steady destruction of the old international relationships. Although kinship ties persisted between Acadians and Micmac, even this long-established relationship came under strain. Among the reasons consistently cited by Acadians for their refusal to sign an unconditional oath of allegiance to Great Britain was the fear of Micmac reprisals. "Si nous ne pouvons pas être a couvert de cette Nation [the Micmac]," wrote one Acadian group to the British authorities in 1717, "nous ne Scaurions prester le Serment qu'on nous demande Sans nous Exposer a estre Esgorge dans nos Maisons...."[33] British officials were inclined to see this argument as a mere excuse for recalcitrance, and yet the Acadian claim was later given substance when a Micmac force burned the Acadian settlement of Beaubassin for strategic reasons in 1750. Although evidence regarding the episode is sparse, it is likely that the French missionary accompanying the Micmac, Jean-Louis Le Loutre, forced the Beaubassin Acadians to leave their village by threats of outright violence.[34]

As for the British relationship with the Indian peoples of the northeast after 1713, it too was increasingly troubled. War broke out again between the Abenaki and Massachusetts in 1722. By the end of the fighting five years later, it had become clear to the Abenaki that all they could now hope to achieve was to contain English expansion as best they could, with assistance from New France when needed. Led by the Penobscot, they pursued a cautious policy involving the creation of a defensive intertribal confederacy. When the final conflict between French and British began in the 1750s, the Penobscot attempted to maintain neutrality, but were soon drawn in on the French side. Their position was decisively undermined by the fall of New France, and their treaty with the victors in 1762 has been described by one scholar as "essentially a capitulation to the English."[35] The Micmac, meanwhile, faced a similar loss of military effectiveness following the capture of Ile Royale and Ile St-Jean by the British in 1758. The Micmac had rejected the terms of the Treaty of Utrecht from the beginning, although they had proved willing to use diplomacy as well as

---

33 [T. B. Akins, (ed.)], *Nova Scotia Archives II: A Calendar of Two Letter-Books and one Commission-Book in the Possession of the Government of Nova Scotia, 1713-1741* (Halifax: Government of Nova Scotia, 1900), pp. 52-53.

34 See Gérard Finn, "Jean-Louis Le Loutre," *DCB*, IV, p. 455.

35 Dean R. Snow, "Eastern Abenaki," in Bruce G. Trigger, (ed.), *Handbook of North American Indians: Volume 1, Northeast* (Washington, D.C.: Smithsonian Institution, 1978), p. 144; Morrison, *The Embattled Northeast*, pp. 185-93.

war to attempt to safeguard their lands. Now they fought intermittently on, but the balance of power had turned permanently against them.[36]

The capture of the two French islands in 1758 was also one major phase in the expulsion of the Acadians from Nova Scotia which took place between 1755 and 1762. Acadian efforts between 1713 and 1755 to maintain, through diplomacy, a neutral position in the gathering conflict between the British and French had ultimately made the Acadian communities vulnerable to both sides. The burning of Beaubassin in 1750 had been followed by the issuing of an order by the Governor of New France that "all Acadians who (within eight days of the publication of this) have not taken the oath of fidelity [to France] and are not incorporated within the Militia companies which we have created, will be declared rebels to the orders of the King and as such expelled from the lands which they hold."[37] Although the French lacked the power to enforce such an order, the British did not. As a result of a decision taken in Halifax — albeit on questionable grounds — by the governor and council of Nova Scotia in the summer of 1755, most Acadians were expelled as untrustworthy subjects in time of war.[38] By 1762, therefore, few vestiges remained of the old international region of the northeast. The very populations whose interactions had created the unique pattern of peaceful inter-relationships during the seventeenth century were either gone altogether, as in the case of the original English of the Kennebec-Penobscot territory, or crucially weakened, as were the Acadians and the Indian peoples. The sequence of events that had begun with the destructive wars between 1689 and 1713 had culminated in the decisive clash of European imperialisms in the mid-eighteenth century. Violence and forced submission, it would seem, had ultimately triumphed over adaptation and coexistence. So it had. And yet the manner in which it had done so, and the long persistence of efforts within the region to resolve conflicts peacefully, give rise to certain historiographical reflections that deserve to be tested by further research.

First and most obviously, it is clear that the history of the northeast in the colonial era cannot be understood unless traditional compartmentalization is abandoned. The region must be interpreted not only by cross-border study but also through cross-cultural approaches. This relatively small territory in North America was inhabited by peoples, native and

36 Upton, *Micmacs and Colonists*, pp. 48-60.

37 Ordinance of the Marquis de La Jonquière, 12 April 1751, printed in N.E. S. Griffiths (ed.), *The Acadian Deportation: Deliberate Perfidy or Cruel Necessity?* (Toronto: Copp Clark, 1969), p. 83.

38 For a recent summary of the events surrounding the expulsion, see John G. Reid, *Six Crucial Decades: Times of Change in the History of the Maritimes* (Halifax: Nimbus Publishing, 1987), pp. 29-48.

European, who differed radically by culture and ethnicity but who never-theless attempted over a long period of time to resolve or minimize their potential conflicts. The full subtlety of those efforts can only be captured through equally subtle historical methods.

Secondly, the question arises of the exceptional character of the north-eastern region in colonial North America. From the European imperial standpoint, this was an area of failure in the seventeenth century, and only gradually was it later brought closer to the mainstream of the development of Euro-America. In the early years, relatively small populations — Indian, Acadian, and English — coexisted, and there was room for all, provided only that violent tendencies were restrained. The restraint was no easy task, given the frequent intervention, even in the seventeenth century, of rivalries that originated in Europe or in southern New England. Yet the extent to which violence could be, and was avoided suggests that in this region the general notions advanced by Andrews and Meinig — of "col-laboration between men of different nationality" and of "benign articula-tion between...two peoples" — can be given much stronger emphasis than those scholars, or others, have felt able to accord in the more general North American context.

Thirdly, the northeastern experience may suggest some change in conventional approaches to the entire question of violence and non-violence in colonial North America. Many scholars have contrasted the frontier violence of the early colonial era with the later development of more peaceful and ordered societies. In his recent Curti lectures at the University of Wisconsin, Bernard Bailyn went some way towards modify-ing this picture. Early America, for him, was "a borderland world" on the periphery of Europe, where "savagery and the breakdown of ordered life lay everywhere;" there was also, he argued, a "growing civility," but it was one that could incorporate institutionalized violence in the form of slavery.[39] In the northeastern region, however, peace and civility were the goals and, for a time, the accomplishments of early native and colonial communities. Only later did an official culture of violence intrude. Bailyn rightly pointed to the "complex mixture" of violence and civil order in North America.[40] The unconventional but revealing history of the north-eastern borderlands may suggest that the complexity was greater than even he was prepared to allow.

---

39 Bernard Bailyn, *The Peopling of British North America: An Introduction* (New York: Alfred A. Knopf, 1986), pp. 112-18.

40 *Ibid.*, p. 114.

KENNETH DONOVAN

Reprinted from Vol. XXV, No. 1
(Autumn 1995)

Slaves and Their Owners in Ile Royale, 1713-1760*

IN 1733, CHARLES, AN 18-YEAR OLD black slave, produced much of the food consumed in his owner's household. Charles was the property of Pierre Benoist, an ensign in the garrison at Louisbourg, who lived with his family in block 2 of the town. By 1733, Pierre and his wife, Anne Levron, residents of the town since 1722, had two daughters, 15-year-old Anne and eight-year-old Marie Anne. Maintaining the Benoist household was a full-time job for Charles. The courtyard of the property had a garden measuring 34 by 45 feet and three animal sheds housing two goats, a sow, 30 hens and roosters, eight ducks and six turkeys. In addition, Benoist had a half share of an ox and a heifer. Besides their backyard garden, the Benoists had another 90 square-foot garden in nearby block 22 of the town. When not planting, weeding, harvesting the vegetables or feeding the livestock, Charles would have been busy cutting kindling and keeping the stoves and fireplaces supplied with wood. By December 1733 the Benoists had 10 cords of wood in their backyard. A prized member of the household, Charles was valued at 512 *livres* in 1733.[1]

At least 216 individuals such as Charles were enslaved in Ile Royale, most in Louisbourg.[2] As the capital and commercial centre of the colony, Louisbourg had an economy which depended on the fishery, the military and trade.[3] Its stratified

---

* Earlier versions of this paper were presented at the Atlantic Canada Workshop, Carleton University, Ottawa, Ontario, 14-17 August 1991; The Southeastern American Society for 18th Century Studies, University of Alabama, Birmingham, Alabama, 4-6 March 1993; the Planter's Studies Conference, Acadia University, Wolfville, Nova Scotia, 30 September-3 October 1993; and the French Colonial Historical Society, Sydney, Nova Scotia, 31 May-3 June 1995. I would like to thank Sandy Balcom, Philip Boucher, Pierre Boulle, Carolyn Fick, Robert Forster, Cornelius Jaenen, John Johnston, Martin A. Klein, Bill O'Shea, Sue Peabody, Graham Reynolds, Hilary Russell, David Schmidt, David States, and the four anonymous *Acadiensis* readers for their comments on this paper.

1 Inventory after death of Anne Levron at the request of Pierre Benoist, her husband, 19 December 1733, G 2, vol. 182, fols. 986-1009, Aix-en-Provence, France, Archives Nationales, Section d'Outre-Mer [A.N., Outre-mer]. See also Brenda Dunn, "The Private Properties of Block 2", unpublished manuscript, Fortress of Louisbourg, 1978 [revised], pp. 78-85.

2 The colony of Ile Royale included the islands of Ile Royale (Cape Breton) and Ile St. Jean (Prince Edward Island). The French used the names Ile Royale and "Cap Breton" interchangeably. I have compiled a nominal list of the 216 slaves found in the Ile Royale documentation. See Kenneth Donovan, "A Nominal List of Slaves and Their Owners in Ile Royale, 1713-1760", *Nova Scotia Historical Review*, 16, 1 (June 1996), pp. 151-62. The list includes the name, age and origin of the slaves, if available, together with the date of their arrival in the colony. The names and occupations of the owners are also part of the data.

3 Louisbourg's permanent civilian population was 633 in 1720; 813 in 1724; 1463 in 1737; and 2690 in 1752. These figures do not include totals for the garrison, fishermen or other transients who were

society was dominated by senior colonial officials, military officers and successful merchants — categories that were not mutually exclusive. Down the social scale, petty merchants, innkeepers and artisans served garrison, port and fishery. Each summer French and Basque migrant fishermen swelled the population throughout Ile Royale. In Louisbourg's newly formed society, people tended to change occupations more readily than in France but, because almost all manufactures were imported, their occupational choice was narrow. As in small French towns of the day, people of different status lived side by side.[4] Slaves were part of the local society.

Most of the slaves in Ile Royale were involved in some sort of domestic service. The women among them performed a wide range of duties, from looking after children to cleaning clothes, scrubbing floors, preparing meals and washing dishes. The men, like Charles, performed many outdoor functions. They tended gardens, fed animals, cleaned stables, carried water and cut firewood. Thus, for those who could afford it, purchasing a slave brought higher status and improved living conditions. Since they could not write, slaves in 18th-century Cape Breton left few records of the kind that are usually used by scholars. Yet the Louisbourg archives contain evidence that relates to the African presence on the island. Few in numbers, the slaves in Ile Royale would have known each other, and there is evidence they gathered together on occasions such as slave baptisms and weddings. Of the slaves whose birthplaces are known, 28 individuals were born in Louisbourg, 21 were from the French West Indies and another 12 were natives of French West Africa. Most of these people, with different backgrounds, but a common experience as slaves, would have spoken French, and had a variety of occupations. On Ile Royale they became servants, gardeners, bakers, tavern keepers, stone masons, musicians, laundry workers, soldiers, sailors, fishermen, hospital workers, ferry men, executioners and nursemaids. Most important, the enslaved people of this society became mothers and fathers; they were part of an evolving African-French colonial culture.

Slave holding in Ile Royale was part of a broader phenomenon that began in the 16th century, when the first slaves were brought from Africa to America. By 1750, 3,800,000 African slaves had been sent across the Atlantic. More than half were sent to Brazil and Spanish America; the rest (1,700,000) were transported to the British, French, Dutch and Danish colonies. A small proportion of this latter number, 120,000, had been shipped directly to the North American mainland north

in the colony on a seasonal basis. By the late 1750s Ile Royale's population, including soldiers, approached 10,000 people. See A.J.B. Johnston, "The Population of Eighteenth-Century Louisbourg", *Nova Scotia Historical Review*, 11, 2 (December, 1991), pp. 75-86.

4   Kenneth Donovan, "Ile Royale, 18th Century", in Cole Harris, ed., *Historical Atlas of Canada: From the Beginning to 1800*, Vol. 1 (Toronto, 1987), plate 24; Kenneth Donovan, "Tattered Clothes and Powdered Wigs: Case Studies of the Poor and Well-to-Do in Eighteenth-Century Louisbourg", in Kenneth Donovan, ed., *Cape Breton at 200: Historical Essays in Honour of the Island's Bicentennial* (Sydney, 1985), pp. 2-3. See also Peter N. Moogk, "Rank in New France: Reconstructing a Society from Notarial Documents", *Histoire Sociale/Social History*, VIII, 15 (May, 1975), pp. 34-53; and his "'Thieving Buggars' and 'Stupid Sluts': Insults and Popular Culture in New France", *William and Mary Quarterly*, XXXVI (October, 1979), pp. 524-47; W. J. Eccles, "The Social, Economic, and Political Signigicance of the Military Establishment in New France", *Canadian Historical Review*, LII, 1 (March, 1971), pp. 1-22.

of Florida and Texas.5 Of the 120,000 slaves sent to North America by 1750, only a small proportion, 1400 people, came to New France, an area which encompassed the territory from the Gaspé peninsula up to and including Detroit and Michilimackinac. From 1681 to 1818 there were approximately 4100 slaves in French Canada, representing less than one per cent of the population. Within the boundaries of present-day Quebec, there were 2,092 slaves from 1681 to 1759. During the period under study here, Ile Royale, which had a smaller population than the communities along the St. Lawrence, included some 216 slaves: 136 males, 70 females and ten whose gender could not be determined. In Canada, the majority of the slaves, almost 2700, or 65 per cent, were Panis Indians.6 In Ile Royale, by contrast, over 90 per cent of the slaves were Blacks, reflecting the colony's close trade links with the French West Indies.

For the French, as for the Spanish and the Portuguese, slavery was a social as well as an economic system in so far as it enabled slave owners to attain higher status within various French colonies. Official French policy towards slavery was established in 1685 with the adoption of the Black Code for the West Indies. Reissued, with minor revisions, in 1724, the Black Code offered some protection to slaves in the West Indies. Composed of 60 articles, the Black Code "insisted on the basic humanity of the slave: each was to be instructed, baptized, and ministered unto as a Christian, families were to be recognized, and freed slaves were to receive the rights of common citizens — in theory the African could aspire to become a Frenchman".7 There was a wide gap, however, between theory and practice. And in Canada and Ile Royale the Black Code was not even registered, although it was observed to the extent that slaves were to be baptized and adults were not to work on Sundays and holy days of obligation.8 In effect, the Black Code was ignored in most French colonies.

Yet some scholars maintain that French racial attitudes were more subtle and not as harsh as those of the British and Dutch. The more subtle French racial attitude, so the argument goes, was reflected in miscegenation, acculturation and manumission. Writing in 1986, historical geographer Donald Meinig argued that a flourishing Afro-Catholicism, with its elaborate rituals, together with numerous mulattoes and the wide acceptance of different degrees of colour, to say nothing of free black plantation owners with their own black slaves, reflected the open,

---

5 Phillip Curtin, *The Atlantic Slave Trade: A Census* (Madison, WI., 1969); D.W. Meinig, *The Shaping of America. Atlantic America, 1492-1800* (New Haven/London, 1986), p. 226.

6 Marcel Trudel, *Dictionnaire des esclaves et de leurs propriétaires au Canada français* (Québec, 1990), pp. xiii-xxviii. See also Marcel Trudel, *L'esclavage au Canada français: Histoire et conditions de l'esclavage* (Québec, 1960), pp. 20-1.

7 Meinig, *The Shaping of America*, p. 171. For a contemporary description of the Black Code, see Le Romain, "Negroes", in *Encyclopedia Selections Diderot, D'Alembert and A Society of Men of Letters,* trans. with an Introduction by Nelly S. Hoyt and Thomas Cassirer (Indianapolis, 1965), pp. 258-73. The Black Code has been printed in Mederic Louis Elie Moreau de Saint-Méry, ed., *Loix et constitutions des colonies françoises* (Paris, 1784-1790). A complete version is available in *Le Code Noir, au Recueil des Reglemens* (Basse Terre, 1980), p. 446.

8 Cornelius J. Jaenen, *The Role of the Church in New France* (Toronto, 1976), p. 152.

intimate and vibrant nature of creole society.[9] Such a view must be questioned within the context of creole society in the French West Indies and cannot be extended to include France's possessions in the northern part of North America. In Canada and Ile Royale there is little evidence that slave society was less repressive than in New England and the Middle Colonies of British North America.[10]

Throughout the northern colonies of British America, living conditions mitigated the harshest aspects of slavery. Employed on farms throughout the countryside, and working as house servants in the towns, slaves lived in close proximity to whites. Owning only one or two slaves, most slave holders remained confident of their hegemony, and hence slaves were allowed a certain degree of autonomy.[11] Similar slave-holding patterns emerged in Ile Royale. As in New England, few slaves (six out of a total of 216) were freed in Ile Royale.

In most Roman Catholic colonies the church's response to slavery was driven not so much by a humanitarian concern about the plight of slaves in colonial society as by a religious conviction that slaves had souls to save and therefore represented potential converts. Accordingly, the church maintained that the moral and spiritual nature of the slave was more significant than the slave's temporary servile status.[12] The Catholic Church did not make the temporal or spiritual lives of

9   Meinig, *The Shaping of America*, p. 171. For other scholars who maintain that French racial attitudes were more subtle, see Robin W. Winks, *The Blacks in Canada, A History* (New Haven, 1971), pp. 12, 21; Michael Zuckerman, "Identity in British America: Unease in Eden", in Nicholas Canny and Anthony Pagden, eds., *Colonial Identity in the Atlantic World, 1500-1800* (Princeton, 1987), p. 150, n. 101; Carl J. Ekberg, *Colonial Ste. Genevieve: An Adventure on the Mississippi Frontier* (Gerald, Missouri, 1985), pp. 197-239. For a contrary interpretation, see William Cohen, *The French Encounter with Africans: White Response to Blacks, 1530-1880* (Bloomington, 1980); Philip Boucher, *Les Nouvelles Frances. France in America, 1500-1815: An Imperial Perspective* (Providence, 1989), pp. 49-52.

10 In a recent work, Gwendolyn Midlo Hall maintains that the French in Louisiana showed little contempt for blacks and that French officials did not consider the Africans uncivilized. See *Africans in Colonial Louisiana: The Development of Afro-Creole Culture in the Eighteenth Century* (Baton Rouge, 1992), p. 150. For a less sympathetic interpretation, see Daniel H. Usner, *Indians, Settlers, and Slaves in a Frontier Exchange Economy: The Lower Mississippi Valley Before 1783* (Chapel Hill, 1992), pp. 36, 40.

11 Ira Berlin, "Time, Space, and the Evolution of Afro-American Society on British Mainland North America", *American Historical Review*, 85, 1 (February, 1980), pp. 44-78. During the 18th century slaves comprised a small proportion of the population of New England and the Middle Colonies (e.g. eight per cent of the population of New Jersey and less than four per cent in Connecticut and Massachusetts). See also Gary Nash, *Forging Freedom: The Formation of Philadephia's Black Community, 1720-1840* (Cambridge, Mass., 1988); William Pierson, *Black Yankees: The Development of an Afro-American Subculture in Eighteenth-Century New England* (Amherst, Mass., 1988); Shane White, *Somewhat More Independent: The End of Slavery in New York City, 1770-1810* (Athens, Georgia, 1991); Joyce D. Goodfriend, *Before the Melting Pot: Society and Culture in Colonial New York City, 1664-1730* (Princeton, 1992).

12 Jaenen, *The Role of the Church*, pp. 151-52; Winks, *The Blacks in Canada*, p. 12. See also Marcel Trudel, "L'attitude de l'église Catholique vis à vis l'esclavage au Canada français", Canadian Historical Association *Report* (1961) and the "The Attitude of the Roman Catholic Church toward the Negro during Slavery", in W.D. Weatherford, *American Churches and the Negro* (Boston, 1957); Mary Veronica Miceli, "The Influence of the Roman Catholic Church on Slavery in Colonial Louisiana under French Domination, 1718-1763", Ph.D. dissertation, Tulane University, 1979.

slaves any easier in Ile Royale. Admittedly, slaves in Cape Breton were baptized and acquired Christian names from the master's family. Ninety-seven black and Amerindian slaves appear in the Louisbourg parish records; 57 of those were records of baptism. Even though many of the 57 had come from the French West Indies, where, according to the stipulations of the Black Code, slaves "were to be baptized" and "masters were to instruct their slaves in the Catholic religion, on pain of a discretionary fine", they had not been baptized before their arrival in Louisbourg.13 Slaves were baptized more readily in Cape Breton, and throughout New France, because there were no powerful interests — primarily slave owners and plantation managers — who opposed religious instruction of the slaves.14 But in some cases such baptisms occurred only on their death beds, after years of service in their masters' households. Moreover, the baptismal ceremony often became a demeaning experience for slaves. Young children of the slave's owners served as godparents at most baptisms. Chattel slaves did not usually merit the appearance of adults as godparents or witnesses. The baptismal ceremony only became more elaborate to suit the whims and social aspirations of powerful slave owners.

The founding of Ile Royale in 1713 coincided with the rapid expansion of the French slave trade. Throughout the 17th and 18th centuries, French merchants purchased more than a million men, women and children of African origin to be sent to the New World as slaves. It was the establishment of the French empire in the West Indies, specifically the colonies of Saint Domingue (Haiti), Martinique and Guadeloupe in the second quarter of the 17th century, that provided the impetus for the French slave trade. Tropical commodities, such as tobacco and indigo in the 17th century, and sugar and coffee in the 18th century, required a large labour force. Amerindians and black slaves provided the least expensive source of labour for the plantation economies. These non-white people were thought to be more suited to the tropical climate of the Antilles. The dark skin of the Amerindians and the Africans also helped the French to overcome any moral doubts about slavery.15

More recent scholarship has challenged the role of all Christian churches, citing an "African spiritual holocaust" in which the psychological balm of Christianity helped to control slaves. See Jon F. Sensbach, "Charting a Course in Early African-American History", *William and Mary Quarterly*, L, 2 (April 1993), p. 401; Norrece T. Jones, *Born a Child of Freedom, Yet A Slave: Mechanisms of Slave Control and Strategies of Resistance in Antebellum South Carolina* (New London, Conn., 1990); Peter Kolchin, *Unfree Labour: American Slavery and Russian Serfdom* (Cambridge, 1987); and Jon Butler, *Awash in a Sea of Faith: Christianizing the American People* (Cambridge, 1990).

13 Le Romain, "Negroes", p. 270. See also E.V. Goveia, *The West Indian Slave Laws of the 18th Century* (Barbados, 1970) p. 39.

14 Many plantation managers opposed religious instruction of the slaves in the West Indies. The French Catholic Church in the sugar islands during the 18th century was also a pale imitation of the church in France. See Robert Forster, "Slavery in Virginia and Saint-Domingue in the Late Eighteenth- Century", in Philip Boucher, ed., *Proceedings of the Thirteenth and Fourteenth Meetings of the French Colonial Historical Society* (Lanham, Maryland, 1990), p. 9; Eugene D. Genovese, *Roll, Jordan, Roll: The World the Slaves Made* (New York, 1972), p. 174; C.L.R. James, *The Black Jacobins* (London, 1980); Alfred Metraux, *Voodoo in Haiti*, translated by H. Charteris, (New York, 1972); A. Gisler, *L'esclavage aux Antilles françaises, XVIIIe et XIXe siècles* (Paris, 1981).

15 Robert Louis Stein, *The French Slave Trade in the Eighteenth Century: An Old Regime Business* (Madison, WI., 1979), p. XIV. See also, Jean Mettas, *Repertoire de la traite negrière française au XVIII siècle*, Serge Daget, ed., 2 vols (Paris, 1978, 1984); Robert Louis Stein, *The French Sugar*

By 1718, Ile Royale had become a thriving French colony, producing and exporting 150,000 quintals of dried codfish. Throughout the 1720s and 1730s production of cod ranged between 120,000 and 160,000 quintals annually. Cape Breton cod production in the first half of the 18th century accounted for one-third of all the cod caught by the French in North American waters. Much of Ile Royale's fish was marketed in Europe and the Caribbean. As the slave population of the French West Indies expanded, the French Caribbean demand for dried cod increased dramatically and Ile Royale provided a portion of this trade. By the 1740s, Ile Royale was selling up to 40,000 quintals of cod per year in the West Indies, particularly in Saint Domingue. The colony also became a market for Caribbean products. Shiploads of sugar, molasses and rum were brought to Ile Royale and immediately re-exported, primarily to the British American Colonies. So extensive was the trade in rum and molasses that, by the 1750s, the value of Ile Royale sugar products rivalled the value of the colony's codfish production.[16]

Import records for the colony have not generally survived, yet the few records that remain can provide some indication of the extent to which the 18th-century slave trade touched Cape Breton. Three slaves brought to the island in 1737 were valued at a total of 1800 *livres*. In 1752, two vessels, out of a total of 57 coming from the West Indies, carried slaves for sale in Cape Breton: a female arrived in April on *L'Hirondelle*, and, two months later, a male debarked from *Le Bien*. Ship captains from the West Indies occasionally came to Cape Breton and sold their slaves to prospective buyers or used them as barter for the purchase of trade items. On 10 November 1734, for example, 12-year-old Cesard found himself with a new master on an unfamiliar shore when his owner, Captain Charles Le Roy, struck a bargain with a merchant, Louis Lachaume. According to the sale agreement, Lachaume "inspected and was content" with Cesard for the price of 350 *livres*.[17] Cesard was only one of tens of slaves sold in Cape Breton by captains of merchant vessels. In 1742, Arny, a Guadeloupe mulatto, likewise became a resident of the island, when Captain Pierre Cosset sold him to Julien Bannier for 800 *livres*.[18] Some captains brought more than one slave. Captain du Houe, commander of a Malouin merchant vessel, arrived in 1755 with two slaves, one for sale and one for his personal use. Since most ships departed soon after discharging their cargoes, some captains hired commission agents to sell their slaves. Thus, in 1757, Captain Sieur Villard asked Louisbourg councillor Guillaume Delort to sell his slave,

---

Business in the Eighteenth Century (Baton Rouge/London, 1988).

16 Christopher Moore, "Cape Breton and the North Atlantic World in the Eighteenth Century", in Kenneth Donovan, ed., *The Island: New Perspectives on Cape Breton History 1713-1990* (Fredericton/Sydney, 1990), pp. 40-1.

17 Contract of transfer of a negro named Cesard from Charles LeRoy to Louis LaChaume, 10 November 1734, G 3, 2039-1, pièce 57, A.N., Outre-Mer; Recapitulation of cargo brought from the French West Indies to Cape Breton, 1737, C11C, vol. 9, fol. 94, Archives Nationales, Archives des Colonies, Paris, France [A.N., Colonies]; Table of commerce, list of vessels coming from the French West Indies to Louisbourg and the merchandise which they are transporting, 1752, C11C, F 2, B, vol. 2, A.N., Colonies.

18 The sale of a mulatto named Arny from Guadeloupe, 1742, B, 275, fols. 47-47v., Archives départementales, Charente-Maritimes, La Rochelle, France [A.C.M.]. See also Louisbourg merchant Josse Bette who bought 11-year-old Jean from Captain James Spellen of New York on 27 April 1753 for 420 *livres*, G 3, 2047-2, no. 74, A.N., Outre-Mer.

Jacques, to the financial commissary of the troops for 800 *livres*.[19]

For tens of slaves, perhaps hundreds, who came to Cape Breton during the 18th century, the island was merely a port of call. These men and boys served as crew members on merchant ships or as personal slaves of officers on the King's vessels.[20] Louisbourg vessels also had slaves among their crews. In July 1724 Michel Daccarette sent one of his ships to Bordeaux loaded with codfish. The vessel departed Bordeaux at the end of September for the return voyage, only to be wrecked with all hands lost on Sable Island. Included among the dead was "a small negro". Thirty years later, another Louisbourg vessel foundered in a storm off Portsmouth, New Hampshire. Of the 12 men aboard the ship, 10 drowned, including the captain and four slaves.[21] New England and Halifax merchant ships also had slaves among their crews. On 22 November 1752 the brigantine *Portsmouth* left Piscataqua, New Hampshire, bound for Louisbourg with a crew of nine, including Longford, a black man.[22] Some slaves, apparently, even experienced a measure of independence on board ship. Halifax merchant Joshua Mauger, who traded with Louisbourg throughout the 1750s, "owned three vessels, manned by his own slaves, captains and crews all Black".[23]

19 Sale of Jacques to Pierre De La Croix, 11 October 1757, G 3, vol. 2045, no. 49, A.N., Outre-Mer. For the two slaves of Captain du Houe, see Thomas Pichon to A. Hinchelwood, 9 October 1755 in J.C. Webster, *Thomas Pichon the Spy of Beausejour, An Account of his Career in Europe and America* (Sackville, 1937), p. 115.

20 The French and British navies had black seamen, slave and free, among their crews. See N.A.M. Rodger, *The Wooden World: The Manning of the Georgian Navy* (Annapolis, 1986), pp. 159-60; W. Jeffrey Bolster, "'To Feel Like a Man': Black Seamen in the Northern States, 1800-1860", *The Journal of American History*, 76, 4 (March, 1990), pp. 1173-99. For officers on the King's vessels who had slaves at Louisbourg, see 1 July 1755, G 1, vol. 409, register 1, fol. 62, A.N., Colonies. Numerous slaves arrived in Cape Breton in 1757 as part of Admiral De la Motte's fleet. Guy Fregault, *Canada: The War of the Conquest* (Toronto, 1969), p.149; James Lind, *An Essay on the Most Effectual Means of Preserving The Health of Seamen in the Royal Navy and a Dissertation on Fevers and Infection* (London, 1779), in Christopher Lloyd, ed., *The Health of Seamen: Selections from the Works of Dr. James Lind, Sir Gilbert Blane and Dr. Thomas Trotter* (London, 1965), pp. 96-7; Boyce Richardson, "1757, Year of Failure and Tragedy", *The Beaver*, 66, 2 (April-May, 1986), p. 38.

21 *The Boston Weekly Newsletter*, 7 November 1754. For the slave aboard Daccarette's ship, see Officers of the Admiralty to the Minister, 17 December 1725, C11B, fols. 396-99, A.N., Colonies. For the career of Michel Daccarette, see T.J.A. Le Goff, "Michel Daccarette", in *Dictionary of Canadian Biography*, [DCB] III (Toronto, 1974), pp. 156-7; Christian Pouyez et Gilles Proulx, "L'Ile Du Quai De Louisbourg", *Travail Inédit Numéro 149* (Ottawa, 1972), pp. 35-8.

22 *The Halifax Gazette*, 21 July 1753.

23 James S. MacDonald, "Life and Administration of Governor Charles Lawrence 1749-1760", *Collections of the Nova Scotia Historical Society, XII* (Halifax, 1905), p. 23. For other slaves arriving in Louisbourg as crew members on merchant ships, see "Roles d' equipage", for the *King George*, 1735, Series 9 B, vol. 643, Archives départementales D'Ille et Vilaine, Rennes. I want to thank Olaf Janzen for this reference. See also, Statement of payment by Nicolas Botte of Louisbourg for various services, including slaves, for the outfitting of the *St. Michel*, 5 November 1741, B, 275, fols. 37v-39, A.C.M. For the slave aboard the brigantine *L'Aigle*, see 6 February 1740, G 2, vol. 186, fol. 208, A.N., Outre-Mer. There are also numerous references in the Louisbourg parish records to ship captains of merchant vessels having their slaves baptized shortly before the death of the slave.

Although Louisbourg was home to the colony's largest slave community, not all slaves purchased there remained in the bustling port town. In 1734, Jean Pierre Roma, director of a company founded to set up a large fishing operation and concession on Prince Edward Island, wanted slaves to work for his company. Beginning in 1732, Roma established the headquarters for his settlement, Trois Rivières, at Brudenelle Point on the eastern tip of the island.[24] Agreeing to bring 80 people the first year and 30 each year thereafter, Roma ensured that slaves were an integral part of the settlement. Coming to Louisbourg in 1732, he sold a ship, valued at 3,000 *livres*, for four slaves, "2 negroes prime slaves and 2 negresses prime slaves, of the aradan nation". The Aradas were Africans from the coast of Ouidah in Benin.[25] During the years 1732 to 1749 Roma owned 12 slaves, making him the largest slave owner in the colony. Drawing upon his experience in Saint Domingue where he had been a landowner, Roma wanted the slaves to help develop Trois Rivières by rearing their own children there.

Twenty-two slaves in Ile Royale were born in the French West Indies, but those of African origin — 12 people in total — were often described as a "native of Grada in Guinée" or a "native of Gorée". The African-born slaves in Ile Royale came primarily from four West African points of departure: the Congo, Benin, Guinea and Senegal. During the 18th century, the French in the West Indies, like Roma, developed a fine sense of distinguishing among African peoples. Although some of the supposed distinctions were based on myths among the planters, they did represent a recognition of different ethnic groups and different cultures among Africans. Jean Baptiste Labat, a French missionary in the West Indies during the latter part of the 17th century, discussed such distinctions in travel accounts of his journeys throughout West Africa. Slaves of Guinea were thought to be most suitable for heavy work, whereas those of Senegal were judged to be good domestic servants and craftsmen. As for the Aradas, Labat judged them to be the finest slaves: "Enslavement disturbs them little because they are born as slaves".[26] Jean Pierre Roma agreed with Labat: Aradan slaves were superior to those from the Congo. Since the Aradas were prime slaves, Roma paid a premium price, some 4,000 *livres* for four slaves, *"pièce d'inde"*. (A *"pièce d'Inde"* or prime slave was the theoretical value of a healthy, young, adult male slave.)[27] Roma's payment was the most costly transaction for slaves in Ile Royale. But he apparently believed the investment had been worthwhile since he returned to Louisbourg five years later seeking another four Blacks, two males and two females between 15 and 20 years old and of "good quality". He arranged to pay for the slaves, who were to be

24 D.C. Harvey, *The French Regime in Prince Edward Island* ([1926] New York, 1970), pp. 73-93; Margaret Coleman, "Jean-Pierre Roma", *DCB*, III, pp. 566-7; J.M. Bumsted, *Land, Settlement and Politics on Eighteenth-Century Prince Edward Island* (Kingston/Montreal, 1987), pp. 6-7.

25 Sale of the vessel *St. Jean*, Jean-Pierre Roma to Jean Baptiste Morel, 3 September 1734, B, 276, fols. 24v-27, A.C.M. On the Aradas, see Karl Polanyi, *Dahomey and the Slave Trade, An Analysis of an Archaic Economy* (Seattle/London, 1966), pp. 105-9, and Le Romain "Negroes", p. 263.

26 Father Labat's observations are cited in Cohen, *The French Encounter*, p. 27.

27 All slaves that were sold were valued in terms of the "pièce d'Inde". For the value of a prime slave, see Stein, *The French Slave Trade*, p. 85.

delivered in July of the following year.[28]

Such transactions indicated a growing wealth among most members of Louisbourg's familial and economic elite, who could now afford to purchase slaves. Slaves not only performed valuable services, they also reflected the social aspirations and affluence of the owner's household. Most of Ile Royale's governors and *commissaires-ordonnateur* had slaves. Since the governor and the *commissaire* were the two most powerful men in the colony, their actions set the tone for social behaviour in Ile Royale. The first governor of the colony, Pasteur de Costebelle, purchased a slave, Georges, in 1713, four years after slavery had been officially recognized in New France. Costebelle's successor, St. Ovide de Brouillan, bought two slaves: 10-year-old Jean-Baptiste in 1728 and 10-year-old Charles Joseph, the following year. St. Ovide was succeeded, in 1739, by Governor Issac Louis de Forant. Departing France on 30 July 1739, De Forant brought a domestic staff of four men and two women. Although this large staff was undoubtedly fully adequate to meet the day to day needs of his household, nevertheless, de Forant purchased a young male slave within a few months of his arrival.[29]

Ile Royale's *commissaires-ordonnateur*, prominent members of the governing elite of the colony, were, with few exceptions, also prominent slave-holders. Jacques Prévost, who became *commissaire-ordonnateur* in 1749, was typical. Prévost had first come to Louisbourg in 1735. The following year he served as godfather at the baptism of 17-year-old Jacques, the slave of merchant Louis Jouet. Prévost's wife, Marie Thérèse Carrerot, had long been accustomed to having slaves in her household; she was only nine when her parents purchased 14-year-old Rosalie to help raise their family of five children.[30] In 1749 the Prévosts had a household staff of 10 people, including a slave, Angelique, and her infant son. Four years later Prévost bought two more slaves, Jean Narcisse and Pierre, both of whom were baptized on 13 April 1754. The baptism of the newly acquired slaves was a social occasion; the witnesses at the ceremony included the Prévosts, the godparents and four other townspeople.[31]

Since most of Ile Royale's *commissaires-ordonnateur* and governors acquired

28 Sale of the vessel *St. Jean du Port* by Jean Pierre Roma to Jean François Morel and Pierre Maurice, 2 July 1739 for the four slaves, G 3, 2046-1, no. 175, A.N., Colonies. See also Louisbourg, 22 October 1740, B, 269, fols. 25v-26, A.C.M.

29 See Accounts of Monsieurs Lasson and Laccarette with Governor Costebelle, 1713, G 2, vol. 178, fols. 18-23, A.N., Outre-mer; Baptism of Jean Baptiste, 12 August 1728, G 1, vol. 406, register 4; Baptism of Charles Joseph, 5 April 1729, G 1, vol. 406, register 4. See also "Issac-Louis de Forant", in *DCB*, II (Toronto, 1969), pp. 224-6. For official approval of the "long-standing" practice of owning slaves in New France, see Dale Miquelon, *New France: A Supplement to Europe* (Toronto, 1987), p. 239; Daniel G. Hill, *The Freedom Seekers: Blacks in Early Canada* (Agincourt, 1981), p. 4; Winks, *The Blacks in Canada*, p. 3.

30 Sale of the slave Rosalie, 19 June 1736, G 3, 2039-1, no.168, A.N., Outre-Mer. For Prévost as godfather to the slave Jacques, see 23 May 1736, G 1, vol. 406, register 4, fol. 61v.

31 Baptism of Jean Narcisse and Pierre, 13 April 1754, G 1, vol. 409, register 1, fol. 9v, A.N., Outre-Mer; Census of families returning to Ile Royale, 1749, G 1, vol. 462. For a biographical description of Prévost, see T.A. Crowley, "Jacques Prévost De La Croix", *DCB*, IV, (Toronto, 1979), pp. 643-6.

By 1754 four slaves, Jean Narcisse, Pierre, Angelique and her five-year-old son, lived and worked in this building, the residence of the Commissaire-Ordonnateur. Aix-en-Province, France, Archives Nationales, Dépôt des Fortifications des Colonies, Amérique Septentrionale, no. d'ordre 199, 1743.

Pompée, a 12-year-old slave, died in this Louisbourg house during the smallpox epidemic in March 1732. The burial entry noted that Pompée "had been baptised during his sickness". Paris, Archives Nationales, Archives des Colonies, Dossiers Personnels, Series E, no. 258, 1753.

slaves, it became fashionable for other members of the bureaucracy, including representatives of the Superior Council and officers of the garrison, to do so as well. At least nine of the 14 members of the Superior Council purchased slaves.[32] Few heeded the advice of Louisbourg *ordonnateur* De Mezy, who noted, in 1724, that he preferred white indentured servants to slaves because they were less expensive.[33] Evidence in the Louisbourg archives supports De Mezy's contention. Slaves in Louisbourg cost anywhere from 10 to 20 times more than a typical servant. Throughout the first half of the 18th century, the services of a full-time servant could be purchased for approximately 50 livres per year.[34] During the 1740s an indentured servant could be hired for a three-year contract at 110 livres.[35] There were also hundreds of fishermen who hired their services to families during the fall and winter in return for room and board.[36] Of course, the governor and others who purchased 10-year-old boys could not have been seeking servants capable of heavy work.

Perhaps those who purchased young children believed they were making a long-term investment. If so, at least some were doomed to disappointment. Councillor Joseph Lartigue, born in Newfoundland, had come to Cape Breton as a fishing proprietor and eventually diversified, becoming involved in the mercantile trade. Lartigue's 12-year-old slave, Pompée, died in March 1732; the burial entry noted that Pompée "had been baptised during his sickness."[37] One fellow member of the Superior Council, Pierre Martissans, followed much the same route to commercial success and high status in the town as Lartigue. Martissans and his wife Jeanne had seven children by the time their slave Jeanneton died in April

32 The nine members of the Superior Council who purchased slaves included: Joseph Lartigue, Guillaume Delort, Louis Delort, Nicolas Larcher, Pierre Martissans, Alexandre-Rene Beaudeduit, Philippe Leneuf de Beaubassin, Guillaume Delort junior and André Carrerot.

33 De Mezy to the Minister of the Marine, 1724, C11B, vol. 7, fols. 68-74, A.N., Colonies.

34 There are numerous contracts for the services of domestic servants in the Louisbourg archives. In 1728, 11-year-old Marie Doucet was hired out to Anne Guyon Depres at the rate of 40 *livres* in the first year of the contract, 50 *livres* in the second and 60 in the third, 30 June 1728, G 3, 2037, no. 20, A.N., Outre-Mer. The cost of slaves in Ile Royale, in comparison to the cost of a servant, was roughly the same as in Philadelphia throughout the 18th century. "At an average price of £45, an adult slave would have to serve for 11 years to match the £4 per year cost of an indentured servant." See Susan E. Klepp, "Seasoning and Society: Racial Differences in Mortality in Eighteenth-Century Philadelphia", *William and Mary Quarterly*, LI, 3 (July 1994), p. 474, n. 3.

35 See, for example, indenture of Jean Chartier to Sieur Philipot of Scatary, 11 October 1741, B, 6113, dossier 24, p. 5, A.C.M.

36 For two examples of fishermen working for their room and board, see François Bernard, 6 October 1755, G 2, vol. 203, dossier 373, A.N., Outre-Mer, and Jean Eu, April 1752, "Tour of Inspection made by the Sieur De La Roque", *Report Concerning Canadian Archives for the Year 1905*, 11 (Ottawa, 1906), p. 61.

37 Burial of Pompée, 13 March 1732, G 1, vol. 406, register 4, vol. 406, fol. 34v, A.N., Outre-mer. For background on Lartigue, see Kenneth Donovan, "Communities and Families: Family Life and Living Conditions in Eighteenth-Century Louisbourg", in Eric Krause, Carol Corbin, William O'Shea, eds., *Aspects of Louisbourg: Essays on the History of an Eighteenth-Century French Community in North America* (Sydney, 1995), p. 131.

1739. Described as a "creole of St. Domingue", Jeanneton was only 14 years old.[38]

Slaves such as Jeanneton and Pompée were more expensive as well as much riskier investments than ordinary servants, yet merchants, officers of the garrison and members of the bureaucracy were willing to spend money to enhance their stature in the community. The merchant Louis Jouet owned 11 slaves during his residence in Ile Royale from 1724 to 1758.[39] One of Jouet's associates, Jean Laborde, owned five slaves in Louisbourg during the 1750s. By the time he left for France, in 1758, his property and holdings were valued at a quarter of a million *livres*.[40]

Even people who could not afford a slave desired one. Thomas Pichon, secretary to Ile Royale Governor Comte de Raymond during the 1750s, regretted that he could not afford a slave. Writing in 1755, Pichon wistfully noted: "I have no servant. My resources are, at present, too limited. M. Desages..., a Malouin merchant captain, has 2 negroes, one of whom he wishes to sell, but the price is much too high".[41] Pichon was one of the few government officials unable or unwilling to become indebted to purchase a slave. Since he was a bachelor, Pichon was not preoccupied with the status of his family in Louisbourg's tight social circles.

As status symbols, slaves could expect to be well provided for, if not necessarily well treated. In France, employers, notably women, hired handsome servants, including tall and robust young men, to serve as lackeys and pages. Waiting at doors and antechambers, these young men were an extravagant display of the owner's wealth. Among the most highly prized servants and pages, largely because of their distinctive appearance, were black slaves from Africa. One caption on a 17th-century fashion plate extolled the value of a Moorish page for those women who wanted to highlight a pale complexion.[42] At least 14 women in Louisbourg owned slaves. Some, like Marie Anne Joseph Cheron, the widow of André Carrerot, who co-inherited a St. Domingue plantation from her brother Étienne in 1752, were women of considerable wealth. The plantation, including slaves, was sold for a net value of 75,000 *livres*. Marie Anne also inherited a slave named Françoise, presumably her brother's personal slave, who was estimated to be worth 1,000 *livres*. There are a few examples in the Louisbourg documentation of such women slave owners visiting boutiques to purchase clothing for their slaves. The widow Madame Desmarest bought shoes for her slave at a cost of four *livres* per pair on at

---

38 Burial of Jeanneton, 13 April 1739, G 1, vol. 407, register 1, fol. 25v, A.N., Outre-Mer.

39 Terraance D. Maclean, "H History of Block 4: 1713-1758", *Manuscript Report* 176 (Ottawa, 1975), pp. 30-5.

40 T.A.Crowley, "Government and Interests: French Colonial Administration at Louisbourg 1713-1758", Ph.D. thesis, Duke University, 1975, p. 298; J.F. Bosher, "Jean Laborde", *DCB*, IV, p. 421.

41 Thomas Pichon to A. Hinchelwood, 9 October 1755, in J.C. Webster, *Thomas Pichon,* p. 115. For a biographical description of Pichon, see T.A. Crowley, "Thomas Pichon", *DCB*, IV, pp. 630-32.

42 Sarah C. Maza, *Servants and Masters in Eighteenth-Century France* (Princeton, 1983), pp. 206-9. See also Shelby T. McCloy, *The Negro in France* (Lexington, 1961), pp. 30-1; Olando Patterson, *Slavery and Social Death, A Comparative Study* (Cambridge, 1982), p. 178.

least three occasions from 1739 to 1741.[43] Yet the slaves of even the wealthiest residents of the colony were not merely status symbols; they were expected to perform a range of domestic duties.

The more typical experience of slaves in the colony was that represented by 18-year-old Charles, kept so busy in the Benoist household, and the other slaves who, like him, lived in block 2 of the town. The slaves in block 2 undoubtedly knew each other, although their work would have left them little time for developing close friendships. In a few cases, however, some may have found a degree of friendship and companionship within their own households. Purchased in 1738 by Julien Grandchamp, Asar, a young black slave, may well have welcomed the addition to the household of Louis, a Panis, three years later. Grandchamp and his wife Thérèse had operated a modest inn in block 2 of the town since 1724. By the late 1730s Grandchamp was approaching his late 60s and the duties of managing an inn were becoming onerous. Besides a garden, the Grandchamps had sheep, chickens, turkeys and ducks. They purchased Asar to help with the chores, and he must have proved satisfactory since they bought another slave, Louis, in 1741.[44]

Houses along the Louisbourg waterfront. By 1741, the two houses in the centre, which comprised the Grandchamp inn, were the home for Asar, a black slave, and Louis Joseph, a Panis slave. Vincennes, France, Archives du ministère des Armées, Archives du Génie, article 14, Louisbourg tablette 22, 1731.

43 Buying of shoes, 1739-1741, G 2, dossier 475, fol. 63, A.N., Outre-Mer; Cheron inheriting Françoise, 29 April, 15 July 1752, G 3, vol. 2047-2, nos. 50 and 51.

44 Inventory after death of the estate of the late Julien Auger dit Grandchamp, 19 April 1741, G 2, vol. 197-2, dossier 142, no. 5, A.N., Outre-Mer; Sale of the estate of the late Thérèse Petit, widow of Julien Auger dit Grandchamp, 20 September 1753, G 2, vol. 202, dossier 286. See also Dunn, "The Private Properties in Block 2", pp. 46-61.

Pierre Josselin scarcely had time either to make acquaintances among his fellow blacks or to prove his worth to the Acadian family who had purchased him. Joseph and Marguerite Dugas lived across the yard from the Grandchamps. Natives of Minas Basin, the couple had married in 1711 and, by 1722, had moved to Louisbourg. A carpenter, Joseph Dugas supplied wood and foodstuffs to the garrison as well as participating in the coasting trade. Although they had nine children and lived in a small house, the Dugas family purchased Pierre Josselin in the 1730s. Perhaps they felt some social pressure, since six of the 10 households within their block had slaves. On 20 January 1733, however, 25-year-old Josselin died of smallpox, a victim of an epidemic that recognized no colour bar and also took the lives of Charles' mistress, Anne Benoist, and her 15-year-old daughter.[45]

In a world where life was so precarious, slaves were particularly vulnerable. Those who did not predecease their owners were left with no recourse and virtually no protection under the law. At such times, even slaves who had provided long years of service were treated as commodities, their future to be decided in a sale agreement or at an auction. There is no way to determine how long Anne Despres' female slave had served her mistress by the time she faced auction in March 1745. A widow for 25 years, Anne Despres had maintained her independence by operating her husband's merchandising business and teaching sewing to young girls. Madame Despres had become a modestly successful business woman whose estate sold for 1,453 *livres* after her death in August 1744. Her slave had continued to live with her son Pierre Bellair and his family until the day of the auction, in March 1745.[46] At 2 o'clock on the afternoon of 22 March the judge of the Superior Council, accompanied by the King's proctor, the court clerk and the usher, proceeded "in front of the door of the house of the said Mr. Bellair to conduct the sale of a negress belonging to the estate of Madame Anne Guyon Despres". After the drummer had notified the public of the auction, and several people had appeared, the woman "was exhibited in public". In this case, perhaps partly out of a sense of filial obligation, Pierre Bellair did bid for the woman but only obtained her after the sixth bid.[47] Since she sold for the small amount of 350 *livres*, the slave was likely a young girl or an elderly woman.

Held against their will, some slaves attempted to flee from their owners. According to Mi'kmaq oral tradition, the Mi'kmaq helped some slaves to escape during the French regime. Moreover, there was at least one marriage between a

---

45 Burial of Pierre Josselin, 20 January 1733, G 1, vol. 406, register 4, A.N., Outre-Mer; Inventory of the Dugas estate, 19 September 1733, G 2, vol. 182, pp. 641-58.

46 For Anne Despre's mercantile success, see Pouyez et Proulx, "L'Ile du Quai de Louisbourg", pp. 23-6 and Criminal proceeding against Charles Durand accused of theft from the home of the widow Chevalier, 19 August 1724, G 2, vol. 178, fol. 447, A.N., Outre-Mer. Two other auctions of slaves have survived in the Ile Royale documentation. In 1757 Madame Poincu purchased a 12-year-old slave from the estate of Captain Pierre Montalambert for 1300 *livres* . Four years earlier, Louisbourg merchant Milly Daccarette successfully bid 450 *livres* for a slave recently arrived from Martinique. Inventory and sale of the estate of Pierre Montalambert de Cert, 1757, G 2, vol. 209, dossier 513; 28 December 1753, G 2, vol. 202, no. 298.

47 Inventory and sale of the estate of Anne Guyon Despres, auction of the negress, 22 March 1745, G 2, vol. 199, pièce 187, A.N., Outre-Mer.

Mi'kmaq male and a freed black slave woman at Louisbourg.[48] This marriage underscores a degree of interracial acceptance beween Mi'kmaq and black slaves in 18th-century Cape Breton. Without Mi'kmaq assistance, an inhospitable wilderness offered little consolation to any slave seeking freedom. The only alternative appeared to be as a stowaway on vessels departing Ile Royale. In the spring of 1750, Jean Baptiste Estienne, a slave of the Brothers of Charity, attempted to leave Louisbourg on board the vessel *Iphigenie*. Twenty-eight-years old, Jean Baptiste had worked at the King's Hospital since 1742. A refugee in Rochefort following the siege of Louisbourg, he had returned to Ile Royale with Brother Gregoire Chomey in 1749. Desiring freedom, Jean Baptiste wanted to return to France, but he was discovered aboard the *Iphigenie* and returned to Louisbourg.[49]

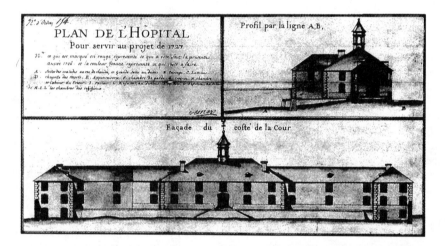

At least four slaves, Jean Baptiste Estienne, Madelaine, Hector and Jean La Vielle worked in the Louisbourg hospital, seen here in 1726. Aix-en Provence, France, Archives Nationales, Dépôt des Fortifications des Colonies, Carton no. 3, no. 154, 1726.

48 For the marriage of a Mi'kmaq male and a freed slave woman, see below. For oral evidence of Mi'kmaq helping slaves to escape, based on personal communication with anthropologist David Schmidt, University College of Cape Breton. See also the black slave, Isaac, in Canada, who could speak Mi'kmaq, French and English and the Panis slave Jacques, who married a Mi'kmaq woman in Acadia, Trudel, *Dictionnaire des esclaves*, pps. 18, 122.

49 Prévost to the Minister of the Marine, 19 May 1750, B, vol. 91, A.N., Colonies. For the four slaves in the service of the Brothers of Charity, see Terry Crowley, "Religion in New France: Church and State at Louisbourg", in Philip B. Boucher, ed., *Proceedings of the Tenth Meeting of the French Colonial Historical Society* (Lanham, Md., 1985), pp. 139-60. Jean Baptiste had been a slave for the Brothers since 1742. Baptism of Jean Baptiste, 24 March 1742, vol. 407, register 1, A.N., Outre-Mer. For Jean Baptiste's stay in Rochefort, see 23 July 1749, Series 1 E, vol. 146, fol. 493, Archives du port de Rochefort.

Jean Baptiste was one of four slaves who returned to Cape Breton with the Brothers of Charity in 1749. The remaining three included Magdeline, Hector and Jean La Vielle. In total, 28 slaves came back to Louisbourg after Cape Breton was returned to the French. The returning settlers numbered just under 2000 men, women and children as well as a garrison of more than 1000 men. Deported from Cape Breton in 1745, the French had to surrender their property and, more critical, their means of earning a living. Since they were refugees, many of the former residents of Ile Royale had to petition the government for assistance. Only the wealthiest merchants, men such as Louis Jouet and Louis Delort, together with military and government personnel on fixed incomes, could afford to keep their slaves. Besides the Brothers of Charity, 17 individuals and their families owned 24 slaves.[50] The legal status of the slave in France remained confused throughout much of the 18th century. No French citizen could be enslaved, yet slavery had official recognition in the colonies. Slaves in France were technically free since, by custom, all slaves who set foot on French soil were free. Royal decrees of 1716 and 1738, however, suspended the custom by permitting colonial masters to retain their slaves in France so long as they fulfilled certain formalities. Some slaves won their freedom in French courts on the basis of custom but the outcome of these cases was not always assured.[51] Rather than challenging their masters' ownership, it appears that many slaves who served the wealthiest owners of Ile Royale opted to return with them to the colony as slaves in 1749. Thus the slaves deported from Cape Breton to the metropole in 1745 remained slaves in France.

Like the Brothers of Charity, the Government also occasionally found it expedient to purchase slaves. At least one occupation in New France, that of torturer and executioner, was reserved primarily for social outcasts, such as convicted criminals and slaves, because it was considered to be such a degrading and shameful position. Of the seven executioners and torturers at Louisbourg, two had been convicted for theft, one had been sent to Ile Royale as a salt smuggler, and another, a slave, had been convicted of murder. In seeking a slave as executioner after 1740, Ile Royale officials adopted the precedent established in Quebec, where Mathieu Leveille, a slave from Martinique, had been an executioner since 1733.[52]

50 Census of settlers returning to Ile Royale in 1749-1750, G 1, vol. 466, pièce 76, A.N., Outre-Mer. There were 1966 men, women and children enumerated on the Louisbourg census for 1749. Another 21 people were described as inhabitants of Ile Royale living at Rochefort, 17 August 1749. See Series IR, vol. 47, Archives Maritimes, Port de Rochefort. Seven of the 24 slaves who returned to Ile Royale were located in Series F 5B, A.N. For the names of the 24 slaves returning to Cape Breton in 1749-50, see the longer version of this paper in the Fortress of Louisbourg library.

51 Sue Peabody, "'There Are No Slaves in France': Law, Culture, and Society in Early Modern France, 1685-1789", Ph.D. thesis, University of Iowa, 1993, pp. 98-111; Cohen, *The French Encounter*, pp. 45-6; Lucien Peytraud, *L'esclavage aux antilles françaises* (Paris, 1897), pp. 374-5; McCloy, *The Negro in France*, pp. 21-2.

52 Andre Lachance, "Mathieu Leveille", in *DCB*, III, pp. 398-9. For a list of the executioners and torturers at Ile Royale, see Gilles Proulx, "Tribunaux et Lois de Louisbourg", *Manuscript Report*, 303 (Ottawa, 1975), p. 26. Proulx lists only six executioners and torturers. For the seventh, Jean Baptiste, see Bordereaux, 1757, C11C, vol. 14, fol. 91v, A.N., Colonies. For background on

Louisbourg *commissaire-ordonnateur* Francis Bigot wrote the minister of the marine in 1740 asking that a slave from the West Indies be sent to Ile Royale to act as executioner. Acting on the Minister's request, the Superior Council of Martinique selected François, a slave who had been convicted of the unpremeditated murder of a small black boy. The court in Martinique offered François the choice of either being executed for the murder or taking the position of hangman at Louisbourg. François thanked the councillors and "voluntarily accepted the said charge".[53] Accordingly, the Intendant of Martinique, Monsieur de la Croix, purchased François for 1,800 *livres* and permitted him "to practise the skills of torture and execution at Fort Royal" before going to Louisbourg. De la Croix wrote to Bigot advising him to watch François carefully because "The negroes are for the most part of a difficult conception and very maladroit".[54] To ensure that François remained obedient, the Louisbourg authorities provided him with rations from the King's storehouse, paid him 300 *livres* per year, and, in 1743, purchased "an English slave" from Simone Millou, a Louisbourg widow, for 154 *livres,* to become his wife. Clearly, François and his bride, although still slaves, were granted a measure of independence.[55]

Black people were the most numerous slaves in Louisbourg, but there were at least 18 Amerindians enslaved in the town as well. In the Louisbourg parish records, Amerindian slaves were usually referred to as "sauvage" or "Panis".[56] Among the Panis slaves baptized in Louisbourg were Louis Joseph, described as a 14 or 15-year-old "who does not have any father or mother", and 17-year-old Marie Joseph. Sold to people in Montreal and raised in the Catholic religion from the age of four, Marie, nevertheless, had not been formally baptized. Most Panis slaves in Ile Royale, like Marie, came to the island by way of Canada. At least one Panis, however, was sent to Louisbourg via France. On 16 March 1743 the *Cire* departed LaRochelle for Louisbourg, but the "little Indian named Cola who was for M. Delort died during the voyage".[57]

At least three Panis slaves bore children in Louisbourg. Françoise was already a member of the household of a prominent Louisbourg merchant, Michel Dumoncel,

attitudes toward executioners, see Pieter Spierenburg, *The Spectacle of Suffering. Executions and the Evolution of Repression from a Preindustrial Metropolis to the European Experience* (Cambridge, 1984), pp. 13-42.

53 Extract from the registers of the Superior Council of Martinique, 9 September 1741, G 2, vol. 186, fols. 437-38, A.N., Outre-mer. See also letter to de la Croix, 26 July 1742, B, vol. 74, fol. 89, A.N., Colonies; Bigot to the Minister of the Marine, 23 December 1740, C11B, vol. 22, fol. 223, ; de la Croix to Maurepas, 30 April 1742, F 3, vol. 80, fol. 249.

54 De la Croix to Bigot, 30 April 1742, C8A, vol. 54, fol. 273, A.N., Colonies.

55 Expenses and receipts for the colony, purchase of a wife for the excutiner, 1743, C11C, vol. 12, fol. 107 v, A.N., Colonies; Rations for the executioner, 1742, C11B, vol. 26, fol. 149.

56 The term "Panis" derived from the enslaved Pawnee tribe, located in the region that would eventually become the state of Nebraska. The French name Panis had become a generic term for Amerindian slave by the mid-18th century. See Cornelius J. Jaenen, *Friend and Foe. Aspects of French-Amerindian Cultural Contact in the Sixteenth and Seventeenth Centuries* (Toronto, 1976), p. 139; Miquelon, *New France 1701-1744*, pp. 238-9; James Cleland Hamilton, "The Panis — An Historical Outline of Canadian Indian Slavery in the Eighteenth Century", *Proceedings of the Canadian Institute* (February 1897), pp. 19-27; Trudel, *L'esclavage au Canada*, pp. 60-4.

57 Louisbourg, 2 May 1743, B, vol. 272, fol. 137, A.C.M.; Baptism of Marie Joseph, 28 October 1749, and Louis Joseph, 7 July 1739, G 1, vol. 407, register 1, fols, 63, 29v-30, A.N., Outre-Mer.

when she became pregnant. A resident of the town since 1733, Dumoncel and his wife Genevieve Clermont had six children when they bought Françoise in 1754. Within three years of her arrival, Françoise gave birth to a daughter, Marie Jeanne. As was customary when a slave had a child, the name of the father was not mentioned in the baptismal records. Like Dumoncel, another prominent Louisbourg merchant, Louis LaGroix, and his wife Magdelaine Morin purchased a Panis slave named Marie Anne in the 1750s. Marie Anne helped to look after the three young LaGroix children and had her own child, Jeanne Josephe, out of wedlock in 1758. Again, the father's name was not listed in the records.[58]

Female slaves in Louisbourg, like other women in service, were vulnerable to sexual exploitation by their owners, or those in authority over them. Louisbourg's illegitimacy rate of 4.5 per cent represented 101 children out of a total of 2233 baptisms in the parish records. Twelve slave women gave birth to 20 per cent (20 of 101) of the town's illegitimate babies. In five instances, the women voluntarily identifed fathers who were not their owners, but in the remaining 15 cases the fathers were listed as unknown.[59]

The clearest case of sexual exploitation in the Louisbourg records is that of the Panis slave, Louise, who arrived from Quebec during the summer of 1727. Louisbourg innkeeper Jean Seigneur purchased 25-year-old Louise from captain Pierre Dauteuil in order to use her as a servant in his inn. Seigneur gave Dauteuil two barrels of red wine for Louise; he agreed to complete the transaction the following year with two more barrels of wine. By February 1728, however, Seigneur realized that Louise was eight or nine months pregnant and therefore unsuitable as a servant in his establishment. In Louisbourg, as in France, it was customary to discharge servant girls as soon as they became pregnant in order to avoid public scandal.[60] Seigneur now refused to keep Louise, on the grounds that she "gave a poor example to his family, especially his young daughters, and because he could not call on her services which he needed in his inn".[61] He took Dauteil to court, claiming that he had purchased Louise under false pretenses. A priest, Michel Leduff, was summoned for a private discussion with Louise and learned that, on the voyage from Quebec during the summer of 1727, when "the crew were quiet", Louise had slept in Dauteil's cabin and was now expecting his child. Even though Louise was pregnant, Dauteuil had sold her to Seigneur, warning her to say nothing, but promising to return for her prior to the birth of the

58 Baptism of Jeanne Josephe, 14 March 1758, G 1, vol. 409, register 2; baptism of Françoise, 4 June 1754, G 1, vol. 409, register 1, fol. 17; baptism of Marie Jeanne, 14 March 1758, G 1, register 2, A.N., Outre-Mer.

59 See A.J.B. Johnston, "Women as Victims in 18th-Century Cape Breton: Violence at Home and in the Street", paper presented at the French Colonial Historical Society Conference, Montreal, McGill University, 21-23 May 1992.

60 Donovan, "Tattered Clothes and Powdered Wigs", p. 10; Jean Louis Flandrin, *Families in Former Times, Kinship, Household, and Sexuality* (Cambridge, 1979), p. 94.

61 Sale of an Indian to LaRiviere by Delamolottiere, 20 August 1727, G 3, 2058, no. 15, A.N., Outre-Mer; Process concerning Louise, Panis Indian, 19 February to 2 March 1728, G 2, vol. 190, no. 3, fol. 74-76v.

baby. Since she was a slave, Louise had little choice but to obey Dauteil and no recourse should he fail to keep his promise. Louise delivered baby Louis on 3 April, and he was baptized, with Seigneur's daughter Angelique acting as godmother. Four months after the birth, Dauteuil and Seigneur appeared before a Louisbourg notary and agreed that Louise and her baby should be sold in Martinique in favour of another slave. One year later, Louise had been sold in Martinique for 600 *livres* and replaced by 14-year-old Etienne, who cost 650 *livres*.62 Upon his arrival in Louisbourg, Etienne was baptized and put to work in Seigneur's inn.

Slavery depended on racial differences: it served as a model for social subordination since it could only be applied to black and Panis slaves. The status of the slave became the model of what whites could not be.63 In his work on *The French Encounter With Africans*, Willian Cohen has examined racial attitudes prevalent in France from medieval times to the end of the Enlightenment. Cohen has argued that the African's blackness was unpleasing to the French: black skin was a sign of some "inner depravity".64 Other European nations reacted in a similar fashion: "the colour bar stood between black and white". Africans were thought to be inferior.65

Racism — based upon the theory of the innate differences and permanent inferiority of certain human groups — was more subtle throughout New France because it was displayed in people's attitudes and actions rather than in formal expressions of opinion. In contrast, throughout the British American Colonies, where there was a well established press by the mid-18th century, published references to slavery, including metaphorical references, were common.66 One corresponent from Cologne, writing in the *Boston Post Boy* in 1748, compared negotiations over the possible return of Cape Breton to France to taming a "rusty negro" without a whip.67 Although there was no press in New France, Cape Breton's French-regime documentation reveals similar white racist attitudes. Such attitudes were expressed most clearly in written negotiations for the purchase of slaves. Boston merchant Peter Faneuil, who sent slaves to Cape Breton in exchange for French goods, instructed ship captain Peter Buckley, in 1738, to buy him a slave in Antigua that was "a straight negro lad, 12 or 15 years old, having

---

62 Agreement between Delamolottiere and Seigneur, 28 August 1729, G 3, 2037, no. 58, A.N., Outre-Mer. For the baptism of Louis, see 3 April 1728, G 1, vol. 406, fol. 36v.

63 Winthrop D. Jordan, *White Over Black: American Attitudes Toward the Negro, 1550-1812* ([1968] New York, 1977), p. 134.

64 Cohen, *The French Encounter*, p. 14.

65 James A. Rawley, *The Transatlantic Slave Trade A History* (New York, 1981), p. 13.

66 See, for example, a poem entitled "On the Clemency shown the French at Louisbourg", *The Boston News Letter*, 4 January 1759. See also a note "concerning the imperious and haughty terms in which the French speak," *ibid*., 21 August 1760. For background on the press in the British American Colonies, see Ian K. Steele, *The English Atlantic 1675-1740: An Exploration of Communication and Community* (New York, 1986), pp. 132-67; Charles E. Clark, *The Public Prints: The Newspaper in Anglo-American Culture, 1665-1740* (New York, 1994); William D. Sloan and Julie H. Williams, *The Early American Press, 1690-1783* (Westport, Conn., 1994).

67 *The Boston Weekly Post Boy*, 7 March 1748. The letter from Cologne was dated 1 November 1747.

had the smallpox if possible". Since the slave was for his own household, Faneuil wanted a negro with as "tractable a disposition" as possible.[68]

Slaves without tractable dispositions were usually punished or sold to new owners. Some were sent out of the colonies because owners feared that their independent behaviour would unduly influence fellow slaves. Witness the case of the slave Toussaint, a baker known for his obstinate behaviour in St. Pierre, Martinique. On 20 September 1753, Monsieur Dauberminy, a Martinique merchant, wrote to the Louisbourg merchant firm of Beaubassin and Silvain asking them to sell Toussaint:

> I have put aboard the Ste Rose a Negro by the name of Toussaint, to ask you to get rid of him for me at any price. He belongs to one of my friends who wants to get [him] out of these islands because of the excessively strong habits he has here. Please do me the pleasure of rendering him the service of having him remain in Louisbourg, and of selling him to someone who will never bring him back here. He is a baker by trade. As for the price of the sale, you can use it for whatever you think best, whether cod or something else.[69]

Beaubassin and Silvain sold Toussaint at an auction in December 1753. Slaves such as Toussaint had to temper their "strong habits" or face the consequences.

Psychological abuse and physical cruelty were inherent features of chattel slavery in Ile Royale. One example of such abuse comes from the trial record of Jean Landry, a soldier, arrested in 1734 for theft at the home of merchant Michel Daccarette. Two years earlier, Daccarette had purchased two slaves, 15-year-old Blaise Simon and 11-year-old Jean, as household servants. During Landry's trial, Blaise Simon, a native of Grada in Guinée, was called upon to testify. Simon's deposition revealed that slaves were subject to corporal punishment at the slightest provocation. Daccarette returned home at four o'clock on a Saturday morning. Upon discovering his slave asleep in the kitchen, Daccarette gave him "several cracks with his cane" and told him to go out and investigate a noise in the yard. Blaise Simon stated that "his master had not returned for supper" that evening. After a late night, Daccarette's slave bore the brunt of his master's ill temper.[70]

Slaves had to be at the service of their masters even as they slept. Pierre Prévost,

68 William B. Weeden, *Economic and Social History of New England 1620-1789*, II (New York, 1963), p. 627. For Peter Faneuil sending slaves to Louisbourg, see Peter Faneuil to Thomas Kilby, Boston, 20 June 1737, Faneuil Letter Book, Baker Library, Harvard University, Boston. For background information on Faneuil's trade with Cape Breton, see Donald F. Chard, "The Price and Profits of Accommodation: Massachusetts-Louisbourg Trade, 1713-1744", *Seafaring in Colonial Massachusetts* (Boston, 1980), pp. 131-51.

69 Dauberminy to Beaubassin, Silvain and Company, 20 September 1753, G 2, vol. 202, No. 298, A.N., Colonies. For the sale of Toussaint by auction, see 28 December 1753, G 2.

70 Criminal procedure against Jean Manier dit Landry, 1734, G2, vol. 183, fols. 78-91. See 6 July 1732, G 1, vol. 406, register 4, fol. 37, for the baptism of Blaise Simon and Jean, slaves in the household of Michel Daccarette.

a soldier on guard duty, stole 40 silver coins from the home of Lieutenant Jean de Pensens one morning in September 1740. Since he had previously worked as a servant in the house, Prévost knew that the coins were kept in a desk drawer. Marie Charlotte, de Pensens' wife, testified that she had been alerted by her female slave who slept "near her bed".[71]

Slave owners wanted slaves willing to accept their subordinate status without questioning authority. And a few slaves were rewarded for such faithful service with the promise of freedom upon the death of the master. Louisbourg merchant Pierre Augruax freed his slave Moll after his death.[72] Boston merchant Thomas Hancock wrote in his will that he would free his slave Cato "if he behaved well till the age of thirty".[73] No stranger to Louisbourg, Hancock supplied provisions to the New England forces during their occupation of the town from 1745 to 1749 and to the British garrison in the 1760s.

During the 1745 and 1758 sieges of Louisbourg, 32 slaves, as well as one free black man, served in the New England and British forces there. One Louisbourg diarist noted on 24 November 1745: "this day were Burid Capt Glovers negro, Peter, and Newport Cofew, a free Negro, of Capt Mountfords company".[74] Since the beginning of the 18th Century, slaves in New England had been required to take militia training, and to serve in the military with whites, even though they were legally excluded from the militia. Theodore Atkinson, a member of the governing council of New Hampshire, sent his slave, John Gloster, to Louisbourg as a private in the New Hampshire forces. Slave recruits such as Gloster were usually forced to give back at least half of any monies received for military service to their owners.[75] Even slaves who worked on the fortifications as labourers or tradesmen would have to give up part of their wages to their owners. During the summer and autumn of 1747, a black labourer, Quash, received the same pay as 43 white co-workers. Two black tradesmen, "Negro Tom" and "Negro Will", were also paid at the same rate as their fellow white masons and bricklayers.[76] It is unlikely, however, that the

71 Criminal Procedure against Pierre Prévost de La Fleur, 23 September 1740, G 2, vol. 197, no. 135, fol. 9, A.N., Outre-Mer.

72 Pierre Augruax frees his slave, 21 August 1751, G 3, 2041-1, pièce 29, A.N., Outre-Mer.

73 W.T. Baxter, *The House of Hancock Business in Boston 1724-1775* (New York, 1965), p. 46; *Dictionary of American Biography*, IV (New York, 1960), pp. 220-1.

74 Louis Effingham de Forest, ed., *Louisbourg Journals 1745* (New York, 1932), p. 163.

75 Bernard C. Nalty, *Strength for the Fight: A History of Black Americans in the Military* (New York, 1986), pp. 7-8; Harold E. Selesky, *War and Society in Colonial Connecticut* (New Haven/London, 1990), p.63; *Roll of New Hampshire Men at Louisbourg, Cape Breton, 1745* (Concord, 1896), pps. 6, 35. The original muster roles for the New England forces in the 1745 expedition have not survived. Three slaves are recorded in Massachusetts regiments. See the *Collections of the Massachusetts Historical Society*, 6th series, X, (Boston, 1899), Pepperrell papers: Ruben, Negro, served under Daniel Bacon at Louisbourg, 24 May 1745, pp. 515-16; Gambo, Negro, served under Colonel Samuel Moore at Louisbourg, 20 November 1745 p. 553; Cuffey, Negro, served under Captain Samuel Lumbert, 20 November 1745, p. 554. See also "Nathan Whiting's List of Soldiers", *Collections of the Connecticut Historical Society*, XIII (Hartford, 1911), pp. 68-82.

76 "List of New England Artificers, Labourers and others who have been employed in the month of August last on the several works and repairs in this garrison, 1 September 1747", British Colonies,

black men were permitted to keep all of their wages.

Slaves were in demand at Louisbourg during the New England occupation from 1745 to 1749. Many of the military leaders of the New England expedition against Louisbourg owned slaves and participated in the slave trade. William Pepperell usually kept 10 or 12 slaves and "maintained a splendid barge with a black crew dressed in uniform".[77] One of those slaves, Catto, accompanied Pepperell to Louisbourg and remained in the town throughout the fall and winter of 1745-46.[78] Brigadier General Samuel Waldo invested heavily in the slave trade and sold slaves from his business quarters in Boston.[79] Peter Warren was one of the largest slave owners in New York when the province had "the largest slave force in any English colony north of Maryland". One of Warren's slaves, a musician, came to Louisbourg and played for public celebrations in the occupied town. Writing in July 1745, a Louisbourg diarist noted that "for the space of 2 hours the Commodore's Negro played upon the trumpit Elevatingly".[80] When Major Israel Newton of Connecticut died at Louisbourg in 1745, his estate included three slaves. Another New England officer, Captain David Donahew, had almost lost his life at the hands of Africans after his ship was wrecked on the River Gambia during a slaving expedition in 1742.[81] Donahew and his fellow New England officers, like their French counterparts, had a slave-owning mentality. Thus, it is not surprising that the government agent, Thomas Hancock, received a number of requests for slaves from Louisbourg officers. Writing to David Rogers, Captain of the Royal Artillery at Louisbourg, Hancock noted, in a 1747 letter from Boston, that "I shall speak for a negro Boy and advise you, they are very scarce here". Slaves were scarce in Boston because, as Hancock wrote, they "are good for anything".[82]

Scarce or not, slaves were recruited not only by the New Englanders, but also by the British to meet the operational requirements of their army in North America. Unskilled slaves were mostly involved in manual labour such as digging latrines, opening trenches, constructing batteries and repairing lines in support of the regular

Military Affairs at Louisbourg 1747, Washington, Library of Congress.

77 Joseph Williamson, "Slavery in Maine", *Maine Historical Society Collections*, 7, Series 1, 1876, pp. 213-14; Byron Fairchild, "William Pepperrell", *DCB*, III, pp. 505-8; Chard, "The Price and Profits of Accommodation", pp. 144-6; Byron Fairchild, *Messrs. William Pepperrell: Merchants at Piscataqua* (Ithaca, 1954), p. 118.

78 William Pepperrell to his wife, Louisbourg, 11 September 1745, in *The New England Historical and Genealogical Register*, 19 (1865), p. 229; Thomas Waldron to Richard Waldron, Canso, 22 April 1745, Louisbourg, 1745 Siege Papers, William L. Clements Library, University of Michigan, Ann Arbor.

79 Donald F. Chard, "The Impact of Ile Royale on New England 1713-1763", Ph.D. thesis, University of Ottawa, 1976, p. 88; Dumas Malone, ed., *Dictionary of American Biography*, X (New York, 1964), p. 333.

80 "Journal of private George Mygate of Springfield, Massachusetts", in de Forest, ed., *Louisbourg Journals 1745*, p. 103; Julian Gwyn, *The Enterprising Admiral. The Personal Fortune of Sir Peter Warren* (Montreal/London, 1974), pp. 72-3; Chard, "The Price and Profits of Accommodation", p. 148.

81 See de Forest, ed., *Louisbourg Journals, 1745*, p. 33; Howard M. Chapin, "New England Vessels in the Expedition Against Louisbourg, 1745" (Boston, 1923), p. 24; Selesky, *War and Society in Colonial Connecticut*, p. 87.

82 Thomas Hancock to J.H. Bastide, 24 September 1745, and Hancock to Captain David Rogers 23 July and 13 August 1747, Hancock Papers, Harvard University.

troops. By the end of the Seven Years' War (1756-1763), thousands of blacks were serving in the British military in North America.[83] At Louisbourg, slaves in the British Army and the New England militia were paid one quarter of the money due them for their labour. On 13 September 1759 Gibson Clough, a stonemason from Salem, Massachusetts, and a member of Colonel Jonathan Bagley's Essex Regiment, noted:

> The Capt or Commanding offrs of Companys that have any Negroes in their Companys who are not allowed to do Duty in the Ranks are hearby Directed to Receive all mony that is or Shall be Due for their Works and when Received to Give one Quorter part of Such money to ye Negroe or negroes Who Wrought and the other three parts to mr Commessary Sheaff director of ye Horsptal takeing his Receite for ye Same and By him to be Converted to ye use of ye Sick in the horsptal and are allso Directed to take care that the Negroes are keept to work for ye use above menchend.[84]

Fourteen days later, Jonathan Proctor, another member of Bagley's Regiment, wrote: "Died Last Night a Negrow felow Belonging to Capt Parkers Compt". The owners of slaves who died in the service of Massachusetts and the other New England Colonies were usually compensated for their loss of property. Slaves in the New England militia had no say in how or where they would serve; their masters usually sent them off to war while they stayed at home. Other slaves accompanied their masters to Cape Breton. Edward Sheaffe, commissary in Bagley's Regiment, brought his slave Catto to Louisbourg in 1760. Slaves such as Catto Sheaffe, a private in the same regiment as his master, had little incentive to fight since Massachusetts' slaves were not offered freedom for battlefield heroism.[85]

At least one Louisbourg slave, however, was freed for meritorious service. Louisbourg port captain Pierre Morpain had his seven-year-old slave Georges Sauzy baptized on 17 June 1732. When he left for France in October of the following year, Morpain left his young slave with Hyppolite Lespaines, superior of the Recollet priests at Louisbourg. Father Lespaines was instructed to keep Sauzy for "Morpain until he returns from France or sends orders to sell him". Morpain eventually returned and reclaimed young Sauzy, who remained a slave in his household for the next 12 years. As port captain, Morpain was one of the key

83 Roger Norman Buckley, *Slaves in Red Coats: The British West India Regiments, 1795-1815* (New Haven/London, 1979), pp. 1-3; Sylvia R. Frey, *The British Soldier in America: A Social History of Military Life in the Revolutionary Period* (Austin, 1981), pp. 17-20; Sylvia R. Frey, *Water from the Rock: Black Resistance in a Revolutionary Age* (Princeton, 1991).

84 "A Journal of Mr. Gibson Clough until he arrived at Louisbourg and what happened there from the First of June until the End of the Year", unpublished diary, 1759-1761, 13 September 1759, in Fortress of Louisbourg National Historic Site library.

85 Nalty, *Strength For the Fight*, pp. 6-9. For Edward Sheaffe's slave Catto, see vol. 98, pps. 482, 494, Massachusetts State Archives, Boston; Captain Newhall's Company, Treasury -1, 398, p. 33, Public Record Office, London. For the death of the slave belonging to Captain Parker's Company, see "Diary Kept at Louisbourg, 1759-1760 by Jonathan Proctor", *The Essex Institute Historical Collections* (Salem, 1934) p. 49.

defenders of Louisbourg during the siege of 1745, leading a detachment of 80 men to Gabarus Bay to prevent a landing by the New Englanders. Faced with overwhelming odds, Morpain ordered his men to continue the assault. Only after his recruits were threatened with certain defeat, did he order them to retreat. Although wounded during the fray, Morpain was saved by his slave. According to Antoine de la Boularderie, co-leader of the expedition, "His negro carried him, dragged him, hid him under some leaves and saved him. In recognition of his services, he gave him his liberty and they only returned to the town three days later, under great personal risk".[86]

Morpain's emancipation of his slave was in keeping with French colonial policy, since the Council of the Marine had proposed as early as 1722 that "freedom be granted only to those slaves who, by acts of devotion, had saved the lives of their masters, mistresses, or the children of their owners". Moreover, war often increased the number of freedmen since local authorities recruited slaves with the promise of freedom for those who distinguished themselves in military action.[87] Judging by the diary of a New England officer in the 1745 capture of Cape Breton, other slaves besides Georges Sauzy participated in the defence of Louisbourg. "Our men took one french man and one negro man", wrote Benjamin Stearns on 5 May 1745.[88] Georges Sauzy, however, was the only slave known to be freed because of his heroic efforts during the siege. After the French reoccupation of Cape Breton in 1749, Sauzy, only 24-years old, returned to Louisbourg and settled on the Mira River, a free man.

Of all the slaves in Cape Breton during the first occupation (1713-1745), Georges Sauzy was the only person recorded as being emancipated. As the 18th century progressed, it had become increasingly difficult, especially in the French West Indies, for slaves to gain their freedom legally by manumission. Judging by the experiences of slaves in Ile Royale and Canada, New France was little different. By 1721 an ordinance in the West Indies restricted the right of slave owners to free their slaves, and eventually imposed high fees for the right to free a slave.[89] An ordinance restricting the right of slave owners to free their slaves was also issued for Ile Royale in 1721. The new law stipulated that minors could not sell slaves from their inherited estates until they reached the age of 25.[90] The intent of the edict

86   Gaston Du Boscq De Beaumont, ed., *Les derniers jours de l'Acadie (1748-1758): Correspondances et mémoires; extraits du portefeuille de M. le Courteois de Surlaville* (Paris, 1899), p. 290. For the baptism of Sauzy, see 17 June 1732, G 1, vol. 406, register 4, fol. 36v., A.N., Outre-mer. For Morpain leaving his slave with Lespaines, see Acknowledgement by Hyppolite Lespaines that he is keeping a negro for Pierre Morpain until he returns from France, 21 October 1733, B, 274, A.C.M.

87   Leo Elizabeth, "The French Antilles", in David W. Cohen and Jack P. Greene, *Neither Slave Nor Free: The Freedmen of African Descent in the Slave Societies of the New World* (Baltimore/London, 1972), pp. 136, 140-1.

88   "Benjamin Stearn's Diary, Journal -1745", *Massachusetts Historical Society Proceedings* (1909), p. 139. See also de Forest, ed., *Louisbourg Journals, 1745*, p. 12.

89   Cohen, *The French Encounter*, pp. 55-6, 101; Gabriel Debien, *Les Esclaves aux antilles françaises, XVII - XVIII siècles* (Basse Terre, Guadeloupe, 1974), p. 374.

90   Declaration of the King concerning the manner of appointing tutors and guardians, 14 December 1721, G 2, vol. 178, fols. 256-62, A.N., Outre-Mer.

was to restrict the manumission of slaves. In Ile Royale there were few manumissions: of the 35 illegitimate children born to slave mothers in Louisbourg, none was freed.

There were, however, a few free blacks in Ile Royale. George, "the Black", a fisherman, was one of only two black men, slave or free, who worked in the Ile Royale fishery.[91] The only other black man known to work in the fishery was 25-year-old François Xavier, a free black, born and raised in France. Recruited to come to Louisbourg in 1751, François was to serve as an indentured servant in the fishery for three years.[92] There were also a few blacks employed in other endeavours. In 1752, Vincent Vinette, a free black, became an apprentice baker to master baker Gerome Larrieux. Vinette was to be paid 72 *livres* per year during the first two years of his five-year apprenticeship and 144 *livres* per year during the last three years of his contract. Larrieux also agreed to provide room and board as well as laundry services.[93]

Georges, "the Black", a free man, worked for fishing proprietor Marie Anne Peré in 1735. Georges would have lived in one of the fisherman's sheds, seen on the right, in this 1730 view of the Peré property. Paris, Archives du Génie, article 14, Louisbourg tablette, no. 9, 1730.

91 1735, G 2, vol. 194, dossier 80, A.N., Outre-Mer. George worked for Marie Peré, a widow of fishing proprietor Antoine Peré. Included among the debts owed to Madame Peré was a list of her fishermen who owed for supplies. Georges, "the Black", owed 70 *livres*.

92 M. Gaucher, M. Delafosse, G. Debien, "Les Engagés Pour Le Canada au XVIII Siècle", *Revue d'Histoire de l'Amérique Française*, XIV, 3 (December 1960), p. 439.

93 Apprenticeship of Vincent Vinette, 5 December 1752, G 3, 2047-suite, pièce 29, A.N., Outre-Mer.

At least three enslaved black women were eventually freed and married in Louisbourg. One of the freed women, Marie Marguerite Rose, was a native of Guinée and a slave of Louisbourg officer Jean Chrysostome Loppinot. Purchased in 1736, Marguerite was baptized on 27 September and was described as being "around 19 years old". Two years later, she gave birth to a son, Jean François, who automatically became a slave, the father being listed as "unknown".[94] In 1745, Marguerite Rose, then 28, lived with ensign Loppinot, his wife Magadeline and their eight young children. She was kept busy looking after the Loppinot household, but she had some assistance from a domestic, her son Jean. After the capture of Louisbourg in 1745, Marguerite Rose and her son went to Rochefort with the Loppinots, returning with the family to Ile Royale in 1749.[95] Two years after their return to Cape Breton, Marguerite's son, Jean François, described as a slave "in the service of Mr. Loppinot", died, just 11 days after his 13th birthday. After having devoted her adult life (19 years) to helping to raise the 12 Loppinot children, Marguerite obtained her freedom sometime before her wedding in 1755. On 27 November 1755, Marguerite Rose was married to Jean Baptiste Laurent, who was described as an "Indian" on his marriage certificate.[96]

In the spring of 1756 the newly married couple rented part of the house next door to Marguerite's former owners, the Loppinots. The rental agreement stated: "We the undersigned J. Bte Indian and Marguerite negress, husband and wife, both free, have rented a house located on St. Louis street from Bernard Paris to commence the 10 April of the present year and finish the last of September of the following" at 50 *livres* per month. Located on Block 16, the half-timbered house had been divided into two apartments. Jean Baptiste and Marguerite's apartment had two rooms downstairs, one with a brick fireplace and four windows. There was also an area upstairs which could be used as bedrooms or storage. The couple had access to the yard, which had a well and a garden. With her new freedom, Marguerite had improved her living conditions. She and Jean Baptiste established a tavern in their Block 16 house and appear to have been equal partners in the business. Whether purchasing liquor or foodstuffs for the business, or taking in sailors for room and board, "Madame Rose negress" appeared on many of the receipts. Marguerite also had a significant account, amounting to 226 *livres* with her former owner, Jean Loppinot, who supplied the tavern with meat and rum.[97] Although a slave for most

94 Baptism of Jean François, 7 October 1738, G 1, vol 407, register 1, fol. 14, A.N. Outre-Mer.

95 Baptism of Marguerite Rose, 27 September 1736, G 1, vol. 406, register 4, fol. 63, A.N., Outre-Mer; Census of 1749-1750, pièce 76, G 1, vol. 466. For Loppinot at Rochefort, see 17 September 1747, B, vol. 86-1, p. 184, and 13 May 1748, B, vol. 88-2, p. 301, A.N., Colonies.

96 Act of marriage between Jean Baptiste Laurent, Indian, and Marguerite Rose of Guinée, 27 November 1755, G 1, vol. 409, register 1, fol 77v., A.N., Outre-Mer. For the death of Marguerite's son, Jean, see 18 October 1751, G 1, vol. 408, register 1, fol. 160v. Marguerite's husband was likely a Mi'kmaq since there are still Mi'kmaqs living in Nova Scotia with the surname Laurent. See, for example, Micheline Johnson "Paul Laurent", in *DCB*, III, pp. 358-9.

97 For information on Marguerite's business, see 10 November 1755, G 2, vol. 212, dossier 552, pièce 9, A.N., Outre-Mer; 17 September 1755, pièce 5; 19 May 1756; 1755-1756, pièces 1 to 4. For the rental agreement, see pièce 22.

of her life, Marguerite had acquired considerable business and management skills.

The marital bliss of Marguerite and Jean Baptiste was to be short lived, since Marguerite died in 1757, less than two years after her marriage.[98] Forty years old, Marguerite had lived nearly all of her life in bondage, yet she accumulated possessions in her few years of freedom. On the day of her death, Louisbourg authorities conducted an inventory of Marguerite's estate. The tavern was simply furnished, with a buffet, a dresser, a long wooden table with two benches and various earthen ware and faience dishes. The inventory also listed Marguerite's clothes, most of which were described as being worn or used. The value of the estate amounted to 274 *livres* when sold to the highest bidders at the estate sale.

Marguerite's ability to open a business, establish credit, and gain acceptance in the community suggests a certain degree of "limited opportunity" in Louisbourg society. This "limited opportunity" reflected current mores in the French West Indies since "tavernkeeping was one of the most important occupations of the free-coloured people" as early as 1713. There, a number of enterprising free-coloured women had established taverns, one of the few avenues to commercial success.[99] Thus, when newly freed Marguerite opened a tavern in Louisbourg, she was following a precedent that had long been established in the French-plantation colonies.

There is no evidence about how or why Marguerite Rose was freed from slavery. She may have purchased her own freedom, but it is more likely that Jean Baptiste Laurent bought her, in order to marry her. Such was the case with Jean Baptiste Cupidon, a former slave of Louis Delort, who bought a slave named Catherine from Blaisse Cassaignoles for 500 *livres* and married her in 1753. A long-time Louisbourg merchant, Blaisse Cassaignoles was active in the cod fishery, shipping and supply trade and had been a slave owner in Louisbourg over a 20-year-period. Following his marriage in 1735, Cassaignoles and his wife Marie Jeanne Seaux had four children, and his slave, Catherine Françoise, had doubtless helped to raise the family.[100]

Cupidon, a native of Dakar, Senegal, had planned for his marriage by buying a small house near the Royal Battery, in November 1752, for 200 *livres*, which he agreed to pay over the following year. On 1 March 1753, Cupidon and Cassaignoles signed a contract for the purchase of Catherine; Cupidon agreed to pay Cassaignoles 120 *livres* immediately and 80 *livres* in September. The remaining 300 *livres* was to be paid in 100 *livres* installments over the next three years. As security for payment of the balance owing, Cupidon and Catherine agreed to present, as mortgage, themselves as well as all of their present and future estate, including moveable and immoveable goods. For his part, Cassaignoles agreed to

---

98 Act of Burial of Marguerite Rose, 28 August 1757, G 1, vol. 409, register 2, fol. 25v., A.N., Outre-Mer. For a description of the house and its interior, see Morgan, "A History of Block 16", pp. 18-23.

99 Elizabeth, "The French Antilles", pp. 160-1.

100 For information on Cassaignoles, see MacLean,"A History of Block 4", pp. 45-50. For the purchase of Catherine by Jean Baptiste Cupidon, see 1 March 1753, G 3, 2041-1, A.N., Outre-Mer.

"give liberty and emancipate by this agreement the forementioned Catherine negress his slave and this day and for always without any restrictions, the said Catherine to be independent and free of his will and servitude as if she had never been in slavery".[101] An experienced merchant, 63-year old Cassaignolles was protecting his investment by insisting on a mortgage. Catherine Françoise was his property, a piece of chattel to be bought and sold. For Jean Baptiste Cupidon, Catherine Françoise was his bride to be, and buying her freedom was the equivalent of a significant dowry. Purchasing a wife was not necessarily an alien experience for Africans such as Cupidon, since they were familar with the custom of making bridewealth payments as part of the commitment to marriage.[102]

The third enslaved woman to be freed and married was Marie Louise, who had been a slave of merchant Louis Jouet for 18 years by the time of her marriage. Marie Louise married 25-year-old Louis Coustard on 21 January 1754. Recruited in La Rochelle in 1751, Coustard was an indentured servant who was described as having no profession. He was the only white man to marry a black slave in Ile Royale. Since her arrival in Louisbourg in 1736, Marie Louise had given birth to seven illegitimate children, all of whom became slaves. Pregnant at the time of her marriage, she delivered a son, Michael, on 25 May. Within three years, she gave birth to a daughter, Thérèse, born 6 January 1757.[103] Since Marie Louise had been freed upon her marriage to a caucasian, her two children by Louis Coustard were born free.

Athough slaves such as Marie Louise lived in the homes of their owners, there is little evidence of emotional attachment between master and slave. Marie Louise, for example, did not receive any compensation, nor was she protected from further sexual exploitation after she identified the white fathers of two of her illegitimate children. And two of the three women freed in Louisbourg during the 1750s were only freed near the end of their lives, thereby absolving the owners from the responsibility of caring for the women in their old age. The owner of the third freed woman was fully compensated for the freedom of his slave.

On at least one occasion, in January 1758, a young enslaved couple, Joseph *dit* Hector and Victoire, were permitted to marry. The wedding appears to have been a social gathering for some members of the Louisbourg slave community; four of the six participants at the ceremony were slaves. The owners of the married couple, Jean Baptiste Morin and Marie Charlotte Saint Martin, were well-to-do. An aspiring member of the bureaucracy, Morin was a royal notary and clerk of the Superior Council. With the naval blockade of Louisbourg and the impending siege of the town, the Morins' willingness to allow their slaves to marry could be

101 Sale of Catharine to Cupidon, 1 March 1753, G 3, 2041-1, A.N., Outre-Mer; Purchase of house from Jean Marcadet by Cupidon, 2 November, 1752, G 3, vol. 2041-1, no. 161.

102 Pierson, *Black Yankees*, p. 93.

103 Baptism of Thérèse Coustard, 8 January 1757, G 1, vol. 409, 2nd register, fol. 13, A.N., Colonies; Baptism of Michael Coustard, 25 May 1754, G 1, vol. 409, register 1; Marriage of Louis Coustard and Marie Louise, 21 January 1754, G 1, vol. 408, register 2, fol. 62v.; Recruitement of Louis Coustard, see M. Gaucher, M. Delafosse, et G. Debien, "Les engagés pour le Canada au XVIII siècle", *Revue D'Histoire De L'Amérique Française*, XIV, 4 (mars 1961), p. 584.

interpreted as a magnanimous gesture, especially since Joseph and Victoire were the only enslaved couple permitted to marry in Louisbourg. The marriage did not last long though; 17-year-old Victoire died on 15 February, just five weeks after her wedding.[104]

A few other occasions in the records hint at some semblance of slave social life in Louisbourg. In December 1734, the slave, Magdelaine Acheury, delivered a boy. Six months later the child was baptized and given the name Philippe in a ceremony that included the mother, the father, Jacques, as well as two slave godparents, Philippe and Marie Jeanne. This was one of just two, out of a total of 58 slave baptisms in the Ile Royale records, in which five slaves were permitted to gather together at a baptismal ceremony. The only other baptism with slaves as godparents occurred seven years later, in March 1742, when 20-year-old Jean Baptiste Estienne was baptized, with two slaves, Estienne and Marie, serving as godparents. Jean Baptiste belonged to the Brothers of Charity.[105]

Such social occasions suggest that at least some slaves were accorded a measure of independence. The month before Jean Baptiste's baptism, Jean La Vielle, another slave owned by the Brothers of Charity, was present at the auction of the estate of the deceased Philibert Genier. La Vielle had considerable responsibility, since he bid six *livres* five *sols* for two pairs of mittens, two pairs of wool pants, and four caps.[106] The only other references to slaves in Louisbourg acting independently occurred in the 1750s. On 26 March 1750 a mulatto named Antoine departed Louisbourg on a schooner bound for France. Antoine was listed as a "voluntary passenger". Similarily, in the summer of 1752, the slave, Louis, left Louisbourg on the ship the *St. Augustin de Cherbourg*, arriving in France on 20 October.[107]

The relatively independent actions by Louis, Antoine and Jean La Vielle were rare in Cape Breton because slavery perpetuated a culture of oppression. Owners might be cruel or kind, but whatever the treatment accorded them, the shared experience of slaves was usually oppressive and humilitating. Nonetheless, an analysis of the individual experiences of slaves at Louisbourg suggests that the nature of that experience defies easy generalization. Some, like Charles, Asar, Marie Marguerite Rose and Catharine Françoise, helped to maintain households, growing the food and raising the children. A rare few, like Marie Marguerite Rose, managed to achieve a modest level of literacy, a rare accomplishment for someone of her sex at this time. Others, like Tom and Will, were skilled tradesmen, helping

104 Death of Victoire, 15 February 1758, G 1, vol. 409, register 2, fol. 37v, A.N., Outre-Mer; Marriage of Joseph dit Hector and Victoire, 7 January 1758, G 1, vol. 409, register 2, fol. 34. For biographical information on Jean Baptiste Morin and Marie Charlotte, see H. Paul Thibault, "L'Ilot 17 de Louisbourg 1713-1768", *Travail Inédit Numéro 99* (Ottawa, 1972), pp. 137-41.

105 Baptism of Jean Baptiste Éstienne, 24 March 1742, G 1, vol. 407, register 1, fol. 82, A.N., Outre-Mer. For the baptism of Philippe, see 2 June 1735, G 1, vol. 406, register 4, fol. 57.

106 Papers concerning the estate of Philibert Genier, 8 February 1742, G 2, vol. 198, dossier 158, A. N., Outre-mer.

107 Arrival of the "negre Louis" on the *St. Augustin de Cherbourg*, 20 October 1752, Series F 5B, fol. 102, A.N.; Departure of the mulatto Antoine from Louisbourg, 26 March 1750, F 5B.

to build and repair Louisbourg's fortifications. The experience of Blaise Simon, who was subject to regular beatings at the hands of his master, was surely far different from that of George Sauzy, who developed a bond of loyalty so strong he was prepared to risk his own life to save his master. Some, like Jean Baptiste, refused to accept their fate, while others, like Jean la Vielle, were prepared to make compromises in order to gain a measure of independence and responsibility. Yet, no matter what their particular situation, slaves in Ile Royale were forced to adapt to a life they did not choose and could rarely control. Nevertheless, in spite of the indignities they suffered, the spirit of people such as George Sauzy, Louise, Touissant, Blaise Simon, Marie Marguerite Rose, Jean Baptiste Cupidon, Catharine François and Marie Louise remained undaunted. Ile Royale, like most of the Western Hemisphere, was a multiracial society. And although the remaining records can provide only a glimpse of the world of the slaves in 18th-century Louisbourg, they do demonstrate that black and Panis slaves were neither invisible nor peripheral to Ile Royale society.

STEPHEN E. PATTERSON

Reprinted from Vol. XXIII, No. 1
(Autumn 1993)

Indian-White Relations in Nova Scotia, 1749-61: A Study in Political Interaction

THERE IS A POPULAR VIEW TODAY that native people were simply the victims of history, implying that they passively fell before a European juggernaut. This viewpoint not only distorts history but also inadvertently disparages the historic role of native people themselves. In Nova Scotia the Micmac, Maliseet and Passamaquoddy behaved as autonomous peoples throughout the contact period, exercising choices which represented their best efforts to accommodate the European intruders and adjust to the challenges and opportunities they posed. If we think of contact, as the ethnohistorians encourage us to do, as a process rather than as a point in time, we can see that in Nova Scotia it lasted for centuries, perhaps reaching a decisive phase in the mid-18th century. Yet what had begun, at least arguably, as a conflict of cultures — now well-documented in studies by anthropologists and ethnohistorians[1] — had by the 18th century become a conflict for space, for control, for power — or in a word, politics. By this stage in their dealings with each other, natives and non-natives alike faced choices which were essentially political, although the options had diminished in number, and the option of avoiding a decision was frequently no longer possible. In part, this politics was a politics of war, illustrative of Clausewitz's famous dictum that war is "politics by other means". This was a conflict of diverse peoples in a frontier setting where authority was far from omnipresent. While French and British civil and military authorities sought to implement their respective official policies, New England fishermen and merchants largely did what they wanted, French

---

1   The seminal statement is Alfred Goldsworthy Bailey, *The Conflict of European and Eastern Algonkian Cultures, 1504-1700: A Study in Canadian Civilization* ([1937] Toronto, 1969). More recent studies include Bernard G. Hoffman, "Historical Ethnography of the Micmac in the Sixteenth and Seventeenth Centuries", Ph.D. thesis, University of California, Berkeley, 1955; Wilson D. Wallis and Ruth Sawtell Wallis, *The Micmac Indians of Eastern Canada* (Minneapolis, 1955); Harold Franklin McGee, Jr., ed., *The Native Peoples of Atlantic Canada: A History of Ethnic Interaction* (Toronto, 1974); Philip K. Bock, "Micmac" and Vincent Erickson, "Maliseet-Passamaquoddy", in Bruce G. Trigger, ed., *Handbook of North American Indians, v. 15: The Northeast* (Washington, 1978), pp. 109-36; Virginia P. Miller, "Social and Political Complexity on the East Coast: the Micmac Case", in R.J. Nash, ed., *The Evolution of Maritime Cultures on the Northeast and the Northwest Coasts of America* (Burnaby, 1983), pp. 41-55; Ronald J. Nash and Virginia P. Miller, "Model Building and the Case of the Micmac Economy", *Man in the Northeast*, no. 34 (1987), pp. 43-56; Ronald J. Nash, "An Alternative History: Uninterrupted Views of Micmac Society", in D.C. Tkaczuk and B.C. Vivian, eds., *Cultures in Conflict: Current Archaelogical Perspectives* (Calgary, 1989), pp. 187-94; Frances L. Stewart, "Seasonal Movements of Indians in Acadia as Evidenced by Historical Documents and Vertebrate Faunal Remains from Archaeological Sites", *Man in the Northeast*, no. 38 (1989), pp. 55-77.

missionaries dabbled in politics and diplomacy, and Acadians did their best to avoid either British or French control. Interests were fragmented and behaviours frequently individualistic. What applied to the newcomers applied equally to the natives, who did not behave as a uniform bloc, but rather sometimes disagreed with one another, occasionally had to deal with renegade individuals and often subordinated their broad common interests to the immediate imperatives of time and place.

A political framework, understood broadly, makes a good deal of sense when applied to the Nova Scotia of the mid-18th century, certainly more sense than the old imperial model which placed Nova Scotia within the essentially French-British struggle for control of North America, or that variation on the frontier thesis which described Nova Scotia's early history as one aspect of the New England frontier experience. The interaction of indigenous and colonial peoples is best understood from the inside. Both natives and non-natives viewed the options open to them in any given situation and acted accordingly, and local conditions and immediate necessity frequently took priority over external pressures, distant alliances or broader visions.

The tools of political analysis can help sort out this complexity. Politics, of course, is in important ways an expression of culture. Broadly defined, politics is a conflict of values. To understand the conflict, we have to know about the sources of the values. Political historians have become used to describing the "political culture" within which organized or semi-organized groups make political choices.[2] They have long taken for granted that political choices reflect underlying interests and that the politically motivated will make conscious decisions based on self-interest. They have not been surprised when communities split apart along lines of interest when values collide, nor when groups with common interests coalesce to achieve a common purpose. Such modes of analysis can usefully be employed in interpreting the complex of war, quasi-war and alliance, the attempts at treaty-making and the population movements which characterized Nova Scotia's history in the mid-18th century. What they show is that Indian-White relations were driven by conscious political choices rooted in people's often imperfect understanding of their own self-interest.

For a period of 150 years the principal contact of Nova Scotia's Indians was with the French, who came as missionaries, fishermen, civil and military officials and Acadian farmers. The process of cultural transfer was still very much in train

2   Political culture may be defined as the framework of ideas, beliefs and assumptions within which individuals and groups make political choices. Since the early 1970s historians have found this concept, along with an expanded definition of politics, useful in transcending the biases inherent in the narrow examination of the politics of white, male power elites. Examples include Stephen E. Patterson, "The Roots of Massachusetts Federalism: Conservative Politics and Political Culture before 1787", in Ronald Hoffman and Peter J. Albert, eds., *Sovereign States in an Age of Uncertainty* (Charlottesville, 1981), pp. 31-61, and Ronald P. Formisano, *The Transformation of Political Culture: Massachusetts Parties, 1790s-1840s* (New York, 1983). The need to redefine politics in a more inclusive fashion is suggested by Paula Baker, "The Domestication of Politics: Women and American Political Society, 1780-1920", *American Historical Review*, LXXXIX (1984), pp. 620-47.

in the 18th century, yet by the time the Indians had to deal with British intruders in Nova Scotia, whose numbers dramatically increased with the founding of Halifax in 1749, they had already been conditioned to dealing with Europeans by the practices and values of the French. Of approximately 3,000 Indians in Nova Scotia, the Micmac were most numerous, 1,500 to 2,000 spread throughout present Nova Scotia and eastern New Brunswick as far as the Gaspé; the Maliseet of the St. John River valley numbered fewer than 1,000; and the closely related Passamaquoddy, whose territory spread from the St. Croix valley to Mount Desert Island, may have numbered no more than 100.[3] The French influence was substantial. Maliseets in the 1740s referred to the king of France as "our king" and were to continue to call themselves "French Indians" even years after French power in North America had ended. By mid-century, many Indian leaders could speak or at least understand some French, and the adoption of French names was spreading rapidly, at first in combination with an Indian name, and then altogether in French with a man's first name becoming the family name of his children. The process reflected both the spread of Christianity, widely disseminated throughout the region by French Roman Catholic priests, and the practice of interracial marriage, most commonly of Acadian men with native women. The blend of French and native cultures expressed itself in such things as the annual summer pilgrimage of Micmacs to Chapel Island on Cape Breton, which began around 1750 when Father Pierre Maillard turned his Holy Family Mission into a sort of cultural shrine.

The cultural interaction of Indians and French represented the natives' first accommodation with Europeans, and cultural ties were a significant factor in the natives' decision to support the French in time of war. The official French position, however, was that the alliance with natives was the direct result of French policy. Beginning in the late 17th century, officials in New France had formally drawn together the Indian tribes within the territories they claimed and by the 1720s thought of their alliances as a system.[4] With the help of Jesuit missionaries and by pursuing a policy of encouragement to tribes alarmed by the more rapidly growing English colonies to the south, the French became friends and allies with the Abenaki of northern New England, the Montagnais, Nipissing and Algonquin of the St. Lawrence waterway, and the Potawatomi, Ottawa, Puan (or Winnebago), Sauk, Illinois and Huron from the region of the Great Lakes. Their friendship with the French drew the Micmac, Maliseet and Passamaquoddy of old

---

3   Among the best treatments of the Indians in the region during the 18th century are L.F.S. Upton, *Micmacs and Colonists: Indian-White Relations in the Maritimes, 1713-1867* (Vancouver, 1979); Andrew Hill Clark, *Acadia: The Geography of Early Nova Scotia to 1760* (Madison, 1968), esp. pp. 56-70; Olive Patricia Dickason, *Louisbourg and the Indians: A Study in Imperial Relations, 1713-1760* (Ottawa, 1976); Dickason, "Amerindians between French and English in Nova Scotia, 1713-1763", *American Indian Culture and Research Journal*, vol. 10, no. 4 (1986), pp. 31-56.

4   Yves F. Zoltvany, "The Frontier Policy of Philippe de Rigaud de Vaudreuil, 1713-1725", *Canadian Historical Review* [*CHR*], XLVIII (1967), pp. 227-50; "Philippe de Rigaud de Vaudreuil", *Dictionary of Canadian Biography*, [*DCB*], II (Toronto, 1969), pp. 565-74; W.J. Eccles, "Sovereignty-Association, 1500-1783", *CHR*, LXV (1984), pp. 475-510; Richard White, *The Middle Ground: Indians, empires, and republics in the Great Lakes region, 1650-1815* (Cambridge, 1991), pp. 142-85.

Acadia into this network. Even after Acadia was formally ceded by France to Britain in the Treaty of Utrecht (1713), the natives of Nova Scotia retained their alliance with France and with France's other Indian allies.[5] From 1722 to 1725 they openly participated with the eastern Abenaki, Penobscot and other northern New England tribes in war against the British. New Englanders called it Dummer's War (after the Massachusetts governor), but Micmacs in Nova Scotia carried on hostilities against British fishermen and fishing stations quite independently of the actions of other tribes, including the Maliseet and Passamaquoddy, who were chiefly interested in the steady advance of Massachusetts settlers into their lands on the Maine frontier.

All of Nova Scotia's Indians, however, agreed in 1725 to follow their New England allies in accepting peace terms from the British, which were negotiated in Boston that year by four Penobscot delegates and commissioners from Massachusetts, New Hampshire and Nova Scotia. In 1726 representatives of the three Nova Scotia tribes gathered at Annapolis where they ratified one of the several treaties drafted at Boston, acknowledging British sovereignty in Nova Scotia and pledging future peace. In exchange, Lieutenant Governor John Doucett made several promises to the Indian signatories in a separate written document. It pledged that the Indians "Shall not be molested in their persons, hunting, fishing and their planting on their planting ground, nor in any other their lawful occasions".[6] Several dozen Indians signed the 1726 treaty, but there was nothing in their experience with the French to prepare them for a legal accommodation with Europeans. What they were used to were the powerful ties of culture and in some cases consanguinity reinforced by regular presents and trading opportunities. Moreover, they were encouraged by the French to believe that paper promises meant nothing. For all of these reasons, when war broke out in 1744 between France and Britain — the War of the Austrian Succession, concluded in 1748 by the Treaty of Aix-la-Chapelle — all three tribes set their treaties aside and actively supported France.[7] The vigorous military role of Indians in the region convinced British officials that Indians were no more than puppets in the hands of the French.

But were they? Despite the powerful French influence, the facts indicate that natives retained considerable independence of judgement and action. When, for example, in the 1710s the French urged Micmacs to resettle Cape Breton to contribute to its defence, Micmac bands divided in their response. Some were

5   Dickason, *Canada's First Nations; A History of Founding Peoples from Earliest Times* (Toronto, 1992), pp. 108-12, 159-62; Dean R. Snow, "Eastern Abenaki", *Handbook of North American Indians, vol. 15*, pp. 137-47.

6   Several copies of the Treaty of Submission and Agreement dated 4 June 1726 appear in C.O. 217/38 and C.O. 217/4, Colonial Office Records, Public Record Office (PRO), Great Britain [microfilm copies in Harriet Irving Library, University of New Brunswick]. For printed copies of the treaties, see W.E. Daugherty, *Maritime Indian Treaties in Historical Perspective* (Ottawa, 1983), pp. 75-8.

7   Messrs. de Beauharnois and Hocquart to Count de Maurepas, Quebec, 12 September 1745, "Military and other Operations in Canada during the years 1745-1746", and "Journal of Occurrences in Canada; 1746, 1747", in E.B. O'Callaghan, ed., *Documents Relative to the Colonial History of New-York, X* (Albany, 1858), pp. 3-19, 38-88, 89-132.

willing to move to Cape Breton and to accept a greater dependence on the French
for foodstuffs, while others realized that to do so ran contrary to their traditional
subsistence patterns. A hunting people understood the need to distribute themselves
across the range of moose and other animals and to continue their pursuit of fish
and game as the seasons dictated. On the other hand, the need to guard against the
growing power of the British also seemed compelling. As with Indians elsewhere,
Micmacs weighed the relative strength of the European intruders, made strategic
decisions about alliances in relation to their need to survive and did not all make
the same decision. Some went to Cape Breton; others did not. Similarly, the peace
treaty of 1726 divided Micmacs. Bands closest to Annapolis as well as along the
present east coast of New Brunswick supported it, while bands on the North Shore
and on Cape Breton Island did not. French officials at Louisbourg made clear their
own opposition to the treaty and succeeded in keeping some Micmacs from signing
it, but many others simply ignored the French pressures.[8] Europeans had their own
ways of interpreting native decisions, of course, but the evidence does not suggest
that Nova Scotia natives, any more than natives elsewhere, were simply the pawns
or puppets of European imperialists.

The divided response of Micmac bands can be explained in part by the nature of
their political structure and traditions. Where the Maliseet and Passamaquoddy
were small, fairly homogeneous tribes, the Micmac, in contrast, had always been a
decentralized people: organized in bands or districts which were largely family
groupings, they had spread out over their territory in order to keep population and
food resources in balance. Each band had its own chief or sagamo (sagamore) who
was chosen from within and whose principal duty was to allot hunting grounds to
the families within the band. Traditionally, life revolved around hunting, and the
seasonal movements of the band within its district corresponded with the natural
shifts in the availability of fish, fowl and mammals. By the mid-18th century,
there were still 14 or 15 such bands, each identified with the island, bay or river
system which marked their district. Occasionally, the leading men in some or all of
the bands would meet in council, but even as late as 1750 there was no permanent
or regular centralized structure and no overall authority. Sagamos met together as
equals, and their efforts could as often end in general disagreement as in
agreement.[9] The concepts of grand chief and grand council were to come later,
following the collapse of French power in America and perhaps as a direct
consequence. Until then, decision-making among Micmacs could be fragmented as
bands or districts assessed their interests in their own way. Europeans could deal

---

8   Dickason, *Louisbourg and the Indians*, pp. 68-72, 78-9; Dickason, *Canada's First Nations*, p.
     118; L. Armstrong to Secretary of State, Annapolis Royal, 9 July 1728, C.O. 217/38. See also the
     interesting discussion by Bill Wicken, "Living Within the Imperial Vice: The Mi'kmaq and
     Acadians of La Have, 1690-1726", paper presented to the Canadian Historical Association,
     Kingston, June 1991, pp. 28-9.

9   Reuben Gold Thwaites, ed., *The Jesuit Relations and Allied Documents: Travels and Explorations
     of the Jesuit Missionaries in New France, 1610-1791*, 73 vols. (Cleveland, 1896-1901), III (1897),
     pp. 87-97; Chrestien Le Clercq, *New Relations of Gaspesia* ([1691] Toronto, 1908), pp. 234-7;
     Sieur de Dièreville, *Relation of the Voyage to Port Royal in Acadia or New France* (Toronto,
     1933), p. 157.

with no single leader or body and thus had no reliable assurance that all Micmacs would follow a given course.

Yet at the same time, the French understood this better than the British and had already influenced native political culture with French ideas of power and religion, even if such ideas coexisted in uneasy tension with native tradition. According to Sieur de Dièreville, who visited Port Royal in the 1690s, the rhetoric of chiefs assembled at a war council lavishly praised the French monarch and called upon Micmacs to fight for their king. In the 18th century, both the alliance and the network of Catholic missions had a centralizing and unifying effect. Moreover, by then the range of choice still open to natives had been severely limited by some of the choices of the past. Contact with Europeans had radically altered the native economy and established a degree of dependence which was difficult to escape. For example, natives eagerly adopted the use of firearms for hunting and thus became dependent on the French not only to supply them with powder and shot but also on French gunsmiths for periodic repairs to their weapons. The adoption of firearms also changed hunting practices, as many hunters gave up hunting small animals altogether and reserved their precious supply of powder and shot for large game animals, principally moose.[10]

Hunting practices were even more radically altered in times of war, for hunting required dispersion while fighting required the concentration of forces. The French offered two solutions: they regularly dispensed supplies and provisions from Louisbourg or elsewhere, or they paid Acadians to provide foodstuffs directly. Despite their claims to neutrality, the Acadians became regular providers to the natives. Even Penobscot Indians from Maine travelled to Minas in the 1720s to receive supplies, and the British periodically complained that Acadian food made it possible for Micmacs to pursue hostilities.[11] The cost of provisioning their Indian allies was a burden to French officials, but as they saw it, it was unavoidable. "It is highly important to preserve these Indians attached as they have always been to France; the English have been deterred from forming any settlement in Acadia solely by the dread of these Indians", wrote authorities at Quebec City. "All this consumption greatly increases the expenses, but it is impossible to avoid them, without abandoning the Indians of Acadia and the Micmacs, who, of all the nations, are the most faithful to us".[12] War in fact

---

10   Nicolas Denys, *The Description and Natural History of the Coasts of North America (Acadia)* [1672], translated and edited by William F. Ganong (Toronto, 1908), p. 187; Dièreville, *Relation* , pp. 139-41; Armstrong to Duke of Newcastle, Canso, 5 September 1725, C.O. 217/38, pp. 50-3.

11   Dièreville, *Relation*, p. 156; Dummer to Armstrong, c. October 1725, *Collections of the Maine Historical Society*, 2d series, X (Portland, Me., 1907), p. 351; "The State and Condition of His Majesty's Province of Nova Scotia truely Represented", 8 May 1728, C.O. 217/5, pp. 17-18; Armstrong to Newcastle, Canso, 5 September 1725; E.J. Philipps to Armstrong, C.O. 217/38, pp. 50-3, 143-5; "Remarks Concerning the Settlement of Nova Scotia, by Judge [Charles] Morris, 1753", *Documents Inédits sur le Canada et l'Amérique Publiés par le Canada-Français*, 3 vols. (Quebec, 1888-90), II, pp. 97-101.

12   O'Callaghan, ed., *Documents*, X, p. 126. For a discussion of the cost of providing presents to natives, see Catherine M. Desbarats, "Amerindians and Colonial Government Finances in New France, 1700-1750", paper presented to the Canadian Historical Association, Kingston, June 1991.

reinforced the changes already taking place in the native economy; the shift was away from dispersion and self-reliance towards concentration and dependence. The end of war in 1748 might have permitted a return to more traditional ways, but the choice for natives was complicated by the sudden arrival of large numbers of British settlers.

When the French and British ended their war in 1748, the British returned Louisbourg, captured by New Englanders and the British navy in 1745, to France. The Maritimes as we know them were divided between the two powers: Île Royale and Île St. Jean (Cape Breton and Prince Edward Islands) in French hands, peninsular Nova Scotia in British, with present-day New Brunswick claimed by both. While agreeing to the restoration of France's power-base at Louisbourg, the British immediately decided to erect a new heavily fortified town beside the excellent harbor at Chebucto "as a counterweight [to Louisbourg] and as a protection for New England and her trade" and to bring in new English and foreign Protestant settlers.[13] In June 1749 Governor Edward Cornwallis and 2,500 settlers arrived to establish Halifax. Native people reacted, but not all in the same way. Even before Cornwallis and his settlers were settled on shore, three natives arrived in Chebucto Bay to treat with the governor and his council. Two of the three were Maliseets from the St. John River — Francois Aurodowish and Jean Battiste, claiming to represent the chief of the Passamaquoddy and Maliseet chiefs from Octpagh (Aucpec, above Fredericton) and Meductic. The third was a Micmac, Jean Pedousaghtigh of the Chignecto band. Claiming that they had seen the treaty signed by France with Britain "and are glad of it", they declared that "We reckon ourselves included in the peace made by the Kings of Great Britain and France", curiously implying not only that the Maliseet acknowledged their close alliance with France but also that they expected France to exercise sovereign rights on their behalf. Cornwallis, however, demanded to know if they were "empowered from your Chiefs to make a particular treaty with me", and they replied that they were, whereupon the treaty of 1726 was read to them and they agreed to renew it. All of these discussions were in French, and they were translated for the Indians by their own interpreter named Martin and an Acadian named André from Minas.[14] Once signed, the treaty was taken by Captain Edward Howe to the mouth of the St. John River for ratification by the Indians there.

Howe's purpose was to gain through their direct participation the widest possible acceptance of the treaty by the Indians. On 4 September 1749 he was at the mouth of the St. John River where several "chiefs and captains of the River St. Johns and places adjacent", including Chief Pierre Paul Neptune of the neighboring Passamaquoddy, ratified the treaty. Even though this was a renewal of an earlier treaty, the new treaty was most specific in repeating verbatim the obligations of the Indians. Beyond the general and implied offers of amity, peace and protection offered by the British, however, there were no specific British obligations. In fact, none of the recorded discussions with the Indians either at Halifax or at the mouth

---

13 As quoted by J. Murray Beck, "Edward Cornwallis", *DCB*, IV (Toronto, 1979), pp. 168-71.

14 Council Minutes, 13-14 August 1749, vol. 186, RG1, Public Archives of Nova Scotia, Halifax [PANS].

of the St. John refer to any of the specific promises made by Lieutenant Governor John Doucett to those Indians who signed the 1726 treaty. By its silence on such matters, the 1749 treaty was no more than a simple peace treaty, and as it turned out, it failed to bring about the general peace that the British hoped for.

Indeed, British hopes were dashed within days when Cornwallis received a letter from the Micmac of Cape Breton and Antigonish. The letter was in French and it was dated "au Port Toulouse, 5 jours avant le St.-Michel", indicating that it was the work of Micmacs gathered on Chapel Island near the Cape Breton community also known as St. Peter's on 24 September. Father Maillard's mission there was already becoming a favourite resort of Micmac people in the summer months. Maillard had enormous influence with them, not only because he had become accepted as their spiritual leader but also because he had succeeded in learning the Micmac language, for which he had developed an orthography in the European style. While hieroglyphs may have been used by the Micmac people earlier, Maillard, drawing on the work of an earlier priest, Chrestien Le Clercq, developed and taught his orthography to aid his religious instruction, confining his translation to the catechism, the Lord's Prayer and other parts of the liturgy. However, he declined to teach the Micmacs how to read or write French, which he claimed they would abuse by learning what was evil rather than what was good.[15] Instead, he offered to write for them, and thus it was that he wrote the letter which Cornwallis received in September and from which the British learned how some Micmac people felt about British peace overtures to the Indians of Nova Scotia.

The letter was direct: "Mon Roi et ton Roi font entre eux la distribution des terres", it said, acknowledging as the Maliseet had done that Micmacs saw themselves as allies of France, "c'est ce qui fait que présentement ils sont en paix, mais pour moi, je ne puis faire alliance ni paix avec toi".[16] Did this then mean that the Micmacs would remain at war with the British? Taken with reports that British officials were receiving from elsewhere, the letter appeared to them to have this meaning. Only shortly before, they had received two letters reporting that Micmacs at Chignecto — with whom presumably Cornwallis had just signed a treaty — had attacked two vessels and that three Englishmen and seven Indians had been killed in the attack. When the council discussed the matter, they concluded that this treachery was the work of another French priest, the Abbé Jean-Louis Le Loutre, who was then with the Indians at Chignecto, "and it is highly probable that he is there on purpose to excite them to war".[17] Whatever the source of their information, the British had reason to be suspicious of Le Loutre. Only

---

15   Micheline D. Johnson, "Pierre Maillard", *DCB*, III (Toronto, 1974), pp. 415-19; "Lettre de M. L'Abbé Maillard sur les Missions de l'Acadie et particulièrement sur les Missions Micmaques", *Les Soirées Canadiennes: Recueil de Littérature Nationale*, III (Quebec, 1863), p. 358.

16   Micmacs to Cornwallis, [22 September] 1749, C.O. 217/9, p. 116. Author's translation: "My king and your king together distribute these lands; it is because of that they they are now at peace, but for me I can make neither alliance or peace with you". Maillard sent a copy of the letter written in Micmac and a French translation to his superior in Paris which has since been printed in *Collections de Documents Inédits Publiés par le Canada-Français*, I, pp. 17-19. This printed version of the letter is similar to, but not precisely identical with, the version received in Halifax.

17   Council Minutes, 18 September 1749, vol. 186, RG1, PANS.

shortly before, Le Loutre had written to the Minister of Marine in France: "As we cannot openly oppose the English ventures, I think that we cannot do better than to incite the Indians to continue warring on the English; my plan is to persuade the Indians to send word to the English that they will not permit new settlements to be made in Acadia...I shall do my best to make it look to the English as if this plan comes from the Indians and that I have no part in it".[18] He obviously failed in covering up his own role and it appears likely that both the incidents at Chignecto and Maillard's letter were the products of Le Loutre's plan. In addition, the British soon had information about Micmac seizures of a number of other sailing vessels and the taking of 20 English prisoners at the fishing village of Canso. When on 30 September a Micmac raiding party killed four unarmed men and carried away another as they worked at a saw mill near Halifax harbour, British officials angrily took action. Refusing to declare war on the Micmac because to do so "would be a manner to own them a free and Independent people", governor and council issued a proclamation ordering British subjects to "annoy, destroy, take or destroy the savage commonly called Micmacks wherever they are found" and offering a reward for every Indian taken alive or killed "to be paid upon producing such savage taken or his scalp (as is the custom of America)".[19]

Intelligence reports and the facts at hand told the British that they were at war, which they called simply "the Indian war" but which historians have since referred to as the Micmac War or the Anglo-Micmac War.[20] In effect it continued the war begun in 1744, and it eventually blended into the next major conflict between Britain and France, the Seven Years' War (usually called in the British colonies the French and Indian War) which broke out in 1754. The Indian war ended in 1760 when Micmacs finally agreed to treaty terms, after several earlier failed attempts.[21] During the war, the British remained hopeful that their treaty with the Maliseet would work, and they therefore exempted both the Maliseet and the Passamaquoddy from the Proclamation of 1749. Only the Micmac were to be destroyed. But it soon became apparent that the Maliseet were actively engaged, and again French missionaries appeared to be the culprits. While it was easy for the British to exaggerate the ability of the French to manipulate the Indians as they wished, documents now available from the French side, including a lengthy autobiography by Le Loutre himself, show conclusively that French intentions were as the British feared.[22] British officials were bound by treaty to consider the French friendly, but what followed in Nova Scotia was at best a half-peace; the

18   29 July 1749, as quoted by Gérard Finn, "Jean-Louis Le Loutre", *DCB*, IV, p. 455.
19   Council Minutes, 1-2 October 1749, C.O. 217/9, pp. 117-18.
20   See, for example, Micheline D. Johnson, "Jean-Baptiste Cope", *DCB*, III, pp. 136-7; Olive Patricia Dickason, "La 'guerre navale' contre les Britanniques, 1713-1763", in Charles A. Martijn, ed., *Les Micmacs et la mer* (Quebec, 1986), pp. 233-48; Dickason, *Canada's First Nations*, pp. 159-62.
21   The limited literature on treaties includes the old and sketchy article by R.O. MacFarlane, "British Indian Policy in Nova Scotia to 1760", *CHR*, XIX (1938), pp. 154-67.
22   John Clarence Webster, *The Career of the Abbé Le Loutre in Nova Scotia with a Translation of his Autobiography* (Shediac, 1933).

diplomatic and military niceties were observed and polite letters were exchanged, but Halifax did demand that the governor at Louisbourg remove Le Loutre from Nova Scotia, which he did not do. In fact, French civil and military officials both in Quebec and at Louisbourg directed the missionaries, and the missionaries directed "their Indians", in what was in reality a war.

Yet because the Micmac and Maliseet fought for their own purposes, not as subordinates to the French in any strategic sense, it was a war which the French could not contain. The Micmac, and especially some bands among them, were independent-minded and were willing when it seemed in their interest to strike a course that neither French officials nor missionaries would approve. While British officials never fully understood this, they nevertheless retained a flexible attitude, looking for opportunities to separate the Indians from their French allies, or in a phrase, to divide and conquer. Nova Scotia's governors from 1749 to 1760 — Cornwallis, Peregrine Thomas Hopson and Charles Lawrence, all of whom were military men — looked constantly for opportunities to bring the Indians to the peace table, but in the meantime, as one might expect of military men, they maintained a defensive posture and took the steps necessary to protect what tiny, scattered British settlements there were.

There were other tensions between Britain and France that complicated the Micmac War, among them a disagreement over the precise boundaries of Nova Scotia. In 1713 the French had surrendered Acadia "according to its ancient boundaries" with the exception of Île Royale and Île St. Jean. The British believed that they had won all of the territory of present Nova Scotia, New Brunswick and eastern Maine, although the boundaries with Massachusetts' Maine and with Quebec remained vague. Yet French soldiers continued to travel through parts of the old Acadia without challenge until the British arrived in numbers in 1749. At this stage the French asserted their claim to the present New Brunswick by building a small earthenworks fort at Beauséjour on the Isthmus of Chignecto. To avoid war over the issue, both sides agreed to establish a boundaries commission, which met in Paris for several years without success.[23] War would eventually decide the issue, but before it did the French decided to make Beauséjour much more than a frontier outpost; they saw in it the opportunity to build a new Acadia by attracting to the lands they claimed the approximately 8,000 Acadians who lived in coastal settlements around Minas Basin, near the mouth of the Annapolis River or in various other places within Nova Scotia. If Acadians could be persuaded to move north of the Bay of Fundy or to Île St. Jean, they could build a self-sufficient society and strengthen French claims. Le Loutre took credit for the idea, and it was he, with full official sanction, who attempted to implement it.

Le Loutre has always been an enigmatic and fascinating historical figure. Arriving in Cape Breton in 1737 from the Paris-based Séminaire des Missions Etrangères, he was sent into Nova Scotia to minister to the Micmacs.[24] He "fixed on Chigabenakady [i.e. Shubenacadie] as his headquarters and there he erected a

---

23   John Clarence Webster, *The Forts of Chignecto* (Shediac, 1930); Max Savelle, *The Origins of American Diplomacy* (New York, 1967), pp. 386-419.

24   Finn, "Le Loutre", *DCB*, IV, pp. 456, 453.

church and presbytery", travelling widely from this centre to visit Micmacs who, as he explained, "lived in scattered communities widely separated from each other". At first, the British had no objections to his activity, believing that Christian Indians would remain peaceable. But in 1744, after war broke out between Britain and France, Commandant Jean-Baptiste-Louis Le Prévost Du Quesnel at Louisbourg sent orders to Le Loutre "that the Indians were to declare war against the English and that he must accompany them as chaplain in all their expeditions", and they were particularly to block food supplies to the British from Acadian farmlands.[25]

After the war, Louisbourg officials, alarmed by the news that the Maliseet had signed a treaty and taken British presents, ordered Le Loutre to remove his headquarters from Shubenacadie to Beauséjour and to take with him "the Indians from Chigabenakady and the other tribes dependent on it as far away as Cape Sable, as they were too near Halifax". Yet again the Micmac divided, some following Le Loutre and others declining. The group who went with him to Beauséjour he called "my Indians"; once there, they held a council in which they "decided to oppose the unjust invasions of the English", sent necklaces to the Maliseet "to induce them to break the treaty which they had made with the English" and fought off two English vessels which had arrived in Beaubassin to look things over. Le Loutre wrote in his autobiography that this is why immediately afterwards the British "declared war on the Indians", adding that "on receipt of this news all the Indians went on the warpath, and, everywhere they rose in arms and resumed acts of hostility". But this attempt to blame the British for the resumption of hostilities flies in the face of Le Loutre's private letters which clearly show that his initial object was to encourage British-Indian conflict. In his autobiography he claimed only the role of spiritual advisor who urged the Micmacs to treat their prisoners with humanity, but he also advised them "to uphold their rights and their claims to their lands, their hunting areas and their fishing of which the English wished to gain control". These in themselves were powerful enough incentives to resist British intrusion; whether the Micmacs also needed Le Loutre's prodding is difficult to know. Whatever the mix of motives, these Micmacs chose to fight and in doing so they accepted Le Loutre's political as well as his spiritual guidance. Moreover, they were soon joined by Maliseets who apparently also accepted Le Loutre's direction, for when winter approached "the Missionary [as Le Loutre called himself] dismissed the Malecites until spring time and retained only his own Indians".[26]

The plan to resettle Acadians north of the Missaguash soon became apparent to the British. Cornwallis' excellent intelligence network reported that Le Loutre went to Cobequid (now Truro) to get Acadians to move to the Beauséjour area and that he was even threatening them with Indian massacre if they did not obey him. From a reconnaissance party sent to Chignecto under Major Charles Lawrence, he

25   Le Loutre, *Autobiography*, pp. 33, 35-8.

26   Le Loutre, *Autobiography*, pp. 39-42. Whether French missionaries were principally interested in religion or politics is explored in Micheline Dumont-Johnson, *Apôtres ou Agitateurs: La France missionnaire en Acadie* (Trois-Rivières, 1970).

learned that a French company of regular troops had already located there and that as many as 1,000 Acadians were dispersed in the Memramcook-Petitcodiac-Shepody area, all of them claiming that this was the territory of the King of France. Cornwallis countered by planning his own fort and a small settlement for the isthmus, yet he warned his London superiors that "those parts will be so infested with Indians that without guards, it will be dangerous to go into the woods for materials or firewood".[27]

Cornwallis implemented his counterstroke in the summer and fall of 1750, with landings at Chignecto and a supporting mission at the mouth of the St. John River. In both places his forces came up against stiff opposition from French soldiers with strong Indian reinforcements. At Baie Verte on the northern side of the Isthmus of Chignecto, a British naval vessel seized a French sloop which had just unloaded arms and ammunition from Quebec destined for "Loutre and his Indians". In the same catch were several damning letters, including orders from the Quebec intendant to the master of the French vessel "to follow Loutre or LaCorne's orders", thus showing clearly that Le Loutre was acting under direction from the very top.[28] Both sides suffered losses in the Chignecto landing, but the British came ashore and erected their fort on the high ground east of the Missaguash, naming it Fort Lawrence after their commander. During a lull in the fighting, Captain Edward Howe, by now experienced in dealing with the natives, asked for and received permission to meet with French officers by the riverside under a flag of truce to effect a prisoner exchange. As the meeting concluded, however, shots rang out — purportedly from Indians who were concealed behind a dyke — and Howe was mortally wounded. The facts of the killing were never settled with any certainty, although the British talked about it for years as an example of French and Indian treachery; there were also those from the French side who saw it as a dishonourable violation of the rules of war and who blamed it all on Le Loutre and his Indians.[29] The uneasy standoff between British and French at Chignecto continued for almost five years while Micmac raids and skirmishes around the British settlement became so common as to attract scant mention.

Meanwhile, the Micmac War, openly supported by the French, manifested itself in other parts of the province. Off Cape Sable, the navy seized a French vessel headed from Quebec to the St. John River carrying "Arms, Ammunition, and Provisions for the Indians, who are at open War with His Brittanick Majesty's

27   Cornwallis to [Lt.] Gov. [Spencer] Phips [of Massachusetts], 3 May 1750; Cornwallis to Board of Trade, 10 July 1750, C.O. 217/10; Charles Lawrence, "A Journal of the Proceedings of the Detachment under my Command after entering the Basin of Chignecto [April, 1750]", in John Clarence Webster, ed., *The Journal of Joshua Winslow* (Saint John, 1936), pp. 32-4.

28   Cornwallis to Board of Trade, 19 August 1750, C.O. 217/10. The letter is immediately followed by "Extract[s] of some letters found in the sloop London taken in Baie Verte by Captain LeCras". See also Cornwallis to Duke of Bedford, 19 August 1750, in Webster, ed., *Journal of Joshua Winslow*, pp. 35-6.

29   John Rous to Cornwallis, 6 September 1750; Cornwallis to Bedford, Halifax, 20 September 1750; Cornwallis to Board of Trade, 22 September and 27 November 1750, in Webster, ed., *Journal of Joshua Winslow*, pp. 36-40; Beamish Murdoch, *History of Nova Scotia*, (Halifax, 1866), II, pp. 192-3.

Subjects". Cornwallis found such activities "so bold and daring, in direct Violation of express Treatys, that I own it astonishes me". In May 1751, a well-organized body of about 60 Indians swooped down on the tiny British settlement at Dartmouth, across the harbour from Halifax, catching the small garrison and most of the inhabitants in their beds. Accounts varied in their descriptions of the event, but they agreed that eight settlers were killed, six soldiers and several settlers were taken prisoner and the village was ransacked. The Indians, too, suffered casualties, including three killed, although they again carefully removed their dead and wounded. A furious Cornwallis immediately ordered a court-martial to discover how a British garrison numbering as many as 60 could have allowed this massacre, as they now called it, to occur. But intelligence information helped answer the question: the French had sent Indians in from Quebec "to join the St. John's and Mickmacks and to do what mischief they could in this Province", and, as a further incentive, "the Governor of Canada gave them a reward for every prisoner and scalp they bring of the English". Cornwallis also learned directly from some Acadians that they had been warned "not to go as courriers or assist the English in anything upon pain of death". He counteracted this French interference by sending British regulars amongst the large Acadian settlements at Minas and Pisiquid (Grand Pré and Windsor). But news from Louisbourg that the French navy was operating eight men-of-war in the region, two of which were known to be headed for the mouth of the St. John River, considerably altered the equation. With inadequate men and material resources on the one hand and the vigorous French and Indian activity on the other, Cornwallis knew that it would be dangerous and foolhardy to attempt new settlements away from the immediate vicinity of Halifax until the threat to their security could be removed. "War is not a time to settle inhabitants", he wrote despairingly, "and that it is so here no person that sees it and hears the transactions here can doubt".[30]

By the late summer of 1751, however, Cornwallis saw promising signs of peace. The governments of New England regularly held conferences with the Algonkian Indians of the Maine district, and Nova Scotia continued to be represented there by Paul Mascarene, who had negotiated the 1725 treaty. In August commissioners met some of these Indians at Fort George on Casco Bay, and among them were eight Maliseets, or St. John's Indians as the British called them. Mascarene informed Cornwallis that they had with them a chief named Monsarrett, who "promised to go to Halifax with some deputies from his tribe to treat a peace with Your Excellency and to bring the Micquemacques in, and in the meantime to cease all acts of hostility". As summer gave way to fall, British optimism increased: Cornwallis could report that the Indians "have commenced no hostilities" since Mascarene's meeting, although he still had seen none of them at Halifax; he also found that the Acadians seemed more contented having just harvested a bumper crop. Moreover, while several British troops at Chignecto had fallen into the hands of Indians there, they had been ransomed through the efforts of Le Loutre and had been released unharmed. By February 1752 the pattern

---

30 Murdoch, *History of Nova Scotia*, II, pp. 200-1; Cornwallis to Board of Trade, Halifax, 27 November 1750; 24 June and 24 July 1751, C.O. 217/11, 217/12 and 217/13.

seemed even more assuring: "nothing extraordinary has happened. The Indians have not come to make peace, but have not committed any acts of hostilities". When another summer rolled around and there were still no signs of conflict, Cornwallis decided that it was time to remove the old injunction against the Micmac. On 18 July he issued a proclamation forbidding hostilities against the Indians, which had the effect of cancelling the proclamation he had issued in 1749.[31] Cornwallis did this on the eve of another conference in Maine, perhaps to indicate that he anticipated a formal renewal of peace with the Indians of Nova Scotia, but he did not act soon enough to prevent a most embarrassing incident. Three young Micmacs had boarded a New England schooner near Cape Sable only recently, apparently with some assurance that the crew was friendly, and they had been seized and killed. Cornwallis' proclamation condemned the act and made clear the government's policy of pursuing peace with the Indians, but this in fact was a policy that had not been publicly articulated before this time. Cornwallis now left Nova Scotia, and his place was taken by another British colonel who had served in Nova Scotia since the founding of Halifax, Peregrine Thomas Hopson.

Hopson was not quite sure why the Indians were quiet, but he was distrustful enough of the French to believe that whatever happened was their doing, and their purposes seemed best served at present by a period of peace. Whatever their motives, however, he believed that British interests demanded a formal treaty with the Micmac and he decided to pursue one with vigour. If the Micmac were not going to come to him, he would go to them and invite them to come in to sign a treaty, promising them whatever gifts and other assurances for the future it might take. The best chances for contact were in Cape Breton, where New England and Nova Scotia merchants carried on trade with the French at Louisbourg despite the risks, since some of the trade was illegal and getting caught could mean the loss of ship and cargo. There were risks from the Micmac too. These Indians had always been skilled canoeists and, after the first contact, had acquired European shallops and the skill to sail them;[32] by the mid-18th century they were capable of overtaking slow-moving or becalmed sailing vessels off the coast, and once aboard and in control, they navigated the vessels into French fishing ports such as St. Peter's where they ransomed them back to their British owners. It was precisely an episode of this sort which gave Hopson his opportunity to seek out a Micmac chief

31   Paul Mascarene to Cornwallis, 27 August 1751, Cornwallis to Board of Trade, 4 September and 3 November 1751, 16 February 1752, C.O. 217/13, Council Minutes, 17 July 1752, vol. 186, RG1, PANS.

32   The transference of European sailing technology and skill to Micmacs was noted by several early observers. Marc Lescarbot reported Micmacs and fishermen from St. Malo sailing identical small vessels off Cape Breton in 1606: *The History of New France*, II (Toronto, 1911), pp. 308-9. LeClerqc wrote of Gaspé Micmacs in the late 17th century: "ils s'embarquent dans des chaloupes, & traversent aux Isles de Maingan, païs des petits Eskimaux": *New Relations of Gaspesia*, pp. 418, 269n. Denys explained how the Micmac acquired shallops from the French (as translated by William F. Ganong): "These they sometimes buy from the Captains who are about to leave after having completed the fishery; but the greater part they take from the places in which the Captains have had them hidden on the coasts or in the ponds, in order to make use of them on another voyage": *Description and Natural History*, pp. 196, 230, 422. The maritime experience of the Micmac is examined by several authors in Martijn, ed., *Les Micmacs et la mer*.

who might sign a treaty.

Early in August two British fishing schooners (one from Nova Scotia and the other from New England) were seized by Micmacs while fishing off Canso and both ships and their 15 crew members were taken into St. Peter's. Hopson negotiated their release through the Comte de Raymond, governor at Louisbourg, who volunteered the information that a third vessel, "appartenant au nommé Picquet d'Halifax" (probably William Piggott, who was a Halifax shipowner) had also been seized at Petit-de-Grat. Raymond promised that the latter would be returned without ransom since it was taken in French territory, but the best he could offer on the others was that the prisoners would be released unharmed and their English owners could come and pay the ransom for their vessels. The affair was handled with great politeness on both sides; but behind the careful diplomacy there appears to have been a secret mission. For while in Petit-de-Grat, Piggott sought out a Micmac chief who lived on the east coast of Nova Scotia named Jean-Baptiste Cope, offered him presents and told him that there would be more awaiting him if he would come into Halifax and sign a peace treaty on behalf of his band.[33] He was probably also given a letter or pass from the governor to ensure that he would encounter no difficulty in coming to Halifax. This approach worked and on 14 September 1752 Jean-Baptiste Cope appeared before the governor and council.

We know a fair amount about Cope. He appears frequently in the records during these years, particularly in French documents, and we know that he spent time at Beauséjour, Louisbourg and elsewhere on Cape Breton, and on the eastern shore of Nova Scotia, which he considered his home. His name, obviously, was thoroughly French and it appears that he spoke French. He went by the title "Major", which may have been given him by the French military in recognition of his service to them or may indicate that his father was a French soldier. Leslie Upton claims that the title "Captain" was commonly taken by métis men and that they frequently were given the task of dealing with Europeans by fellow Micmacs. Cope was well-known to French officials, who believed that he was completely untrustworthy and duplicitous. One French account identifies him as the murderer of Captain Howe, although it was probably his reputation rather than first-hand evidence that led to this conclusion. Both the French and Cope himself suggested that many Micmacs had no use for him and that he was considered something of a renegade. Le Loutre knew him and despised him, and while he never explained why, the circumstantial evidence is suggestive. Cope was a Shubenacadie Micmac. Shubenacadie was also Le Loutre's headquarters until he moved with "his Indians" to Beauséjour in the period around 1750. It is likely that at some point this band split in two and that those who did not want to follow Le Loutre and serve the French interest withdrew to lands on the eastern shore near Musquodoboit which had traditionally been

33   T.A. Crowley, "Jean-Louis de Raymond", *DCB*, IV, pp. 655-7; Hopson to the comte de Raymond, 10 August 1752; Raymond to Hopson, 30 August 1752, Hopson to Board of Trade, 16 October 1752, C.O. 217/13; Prévost to [?], 10 September 1752, MG1, Archives des Colonies, Série C11B Correspondance generale, Île Royale, vol. 33, pp. 163-6, Archives Nationales, Paris [AC] [microfilm in le Centre d'études acadiennes, Université de Moncton].

within the territory of the Shubenacadie band (the Shubenacadie River and a series of lakes and streams traverse the province from Minas Basin to Musquodoboit, and this waterway had traditionally carried the seasonal migrations of the band which on some occasions was called the Shubenacadie-Musquodoboit "tribe"). These Micmacs along the eastern shore considered Cope their chief; they numbered 90 persons, including men, women and children.[34]

Cope represented only a very small part of the Micmac people and he never pretended otherwise. In his first meeting with governor and council in Halifax, they asked him if he were a Micmac chief and he replied "that he was chief of that part of the nation that lived in these parts of the province and had about 40 men under him". Asked what proposals he had for them, Cope replied "that the Indians should be paid for the land the English had settled upon in this country". Could he bring "the other tribes of the Micmac nation to a conference here"? "He would return to his own people and inform them what he had done here and then would go to the other chiefs and propose to them to come in and renew the peace". This he thought he could accomplish in about a month, and if he could not, he would return with their answer. On this basis, the council decided to draw up their own written proposal, which they presented to Cope the next day. He agreed to what they read him, a kind of preliminary peace treaty, and the council ordered that it be written up on parchment "in French and English to be ratified and exchanged on the morrow".[35]

The proposed peace treaty owed much to the thinking of a British regular officer named George Scott, who only the previous month had sketched out a plan for the governor based on his experience in attempting to pacify the Micmac over several years. The French held the allegiance of the Indians through trade and bribery, he believed; the Indians expected presents and they received them regularly. The British, he proposed, must do likewise and the Shubenacadie River was the place to do it. The route taken by Micmac raiders into Dartmouth led straight from the Shubenacadie, and even when at peace this is where the Indians came and went. The British should locate a fort here and attached to it should be a trading post where Indians could get high quality European merchandise at good prices in exchange for their furs and feathers. An advantageous trade would cement the friendship of the Indians, he believed, and even if the British operated at a loss, it would be well worth it if it succeeded in bringing about the desired pacification.[36]

The proposal to Cope built on these ideas. "If you shall think fit to settle your wives and children upon the River Shubenacadie no person shall hinder it nor shall meddle with the lands where you are", it declared. "And the Governor will put up a

34   Johnson, "Jean-Baptiste Cope", *DCB*, III, pp. 136-7; Upton, *Micmacs and Colonists*, pp. 26-7; "From a ms. by a person who served at Louisbourg from 1750 to 1758", in Murdoch, *History of Nova Scotia*, II, p. 193; "Anthony Casteel's Journal", *Le Canada-Français*, XX (Quebec, 1889), p. 125; Hopson to Board of Trade, 6 December 1752, C.O. 217/13, pp. 384-8; Prévost to Minister [of Marine], 12 May 1753, MG1, C¹¹B, vol. 33, pp. 159 ff., AC.

35   Council Minutes, 14 September 1752, vol. 186, RG1; Treaty proposal, 16 September 1752, C.O. 217/13, pp. 306-7.

36   George Scott to Hopson, 17 August 1752, C.O. 217/13, p. 292.

Truckhouse of merchandize there where you may have everything you stand in need of at a reasonable price and where shall be given unto you the full value for the peltries, feathers, or other things which you shall have to sell". The British also promised that "we will not suffer that you be hindered from hunting or fishing in this Country as you have been used to do", that the disputes of the past would be "buried in oblivion", and that the Indians could expect annual presents "while you behave yourselves as good and faithful children to our great King". In return for this, the British expected that in addition to "the Burying of the Hatchet" the Micmac would acknowledge the British king as their "great chief and Father". Cope agreed to this and promised also that he would bring his own people in within a month to ratify a treaty based on these terms and that he would use his "utmost endeavors to bring here the other Tribes of Mickmacks to make peace".[37]

The British in Nova Scotia were novices at Indian treaty-making. They had relied in the past on New Englanders to negotiate treaties through distant intermediaries, and even when they met the Maliseet in 1749, it was an old treaty which they renewed rather than negotiate a new one. But this treaty of 1752 now in process was in fact the first to be negotiated entirely in Nova Scotia, and the British were feeling their way. Prior to this the most extensive British experience with North American Indians had been with the Iroquois, and there clearly was in their discussions with Cope more than a little of the diplomatic language and style which the British had developed in their dealing with the Iroquois. At one point the British wrote that "we hope to brighten the chain in our hearts and to continue our Friendship every year", language reminiscent of the Covenant Chain alliance system that the British had with the Iroquois, even though the Micmac were no part of this alliance system. The father-child metaphor was also one from the Anglo-Iroquois past, although by the mid-18th century, the British had actually progressed beyond this: they were both children of the same father-King and therefore they addressed the Iroquois as "brethren".[38] Another significant point was that the British understood Micmac organization well enough by now to know that they did not have a highly centralized political structure, that they were organized in bands with many chiefs rather than with one and that the British were going to have to bring them in one band at a time before they could effectively establish peace with the whole Micmac people. Unfortunately, the British used the term "tribe" loosely when they meant "band", and they therefore wrote that Cope was chief of the Shubenacadie tribe, in fact that he was the "chief sachem", a term that was used in New England but which apparently was not in usage among the Micmac. Despite such loose terminology, the British understood what they were doing. The negotiation with Cope was seen and fully understood as a beginning, and it was with a band of Micmacs rather than the whole tribe.

---

37 Treaty proposal, 16 September 1752, C.O. 217/13, pp. 306-7.

38 See, for example, *An Account of the Treaty between His Excellency Benjamin Fletcher...and the Indians of the Five Nations* (New York, 1694) [Early American Imprints, no. 702]. For a discussion of the Covenant Chain, see Francis Jennings, *The Invasion of America: Indians, Colonialism, and the Cant of Conquest* (New York, 1976), pp. 322-4; Stephen Saunders Webb, *1676: the End of American Independence* (New York, 1984).

Cope went away loaded down with presents, and a little more than a month later, two Micmacs of Cope's band arrived in Halifax, apparently as his emissaries. Hopson therefore commissioned William Piggott to take a ship eastward, guided by the two Indians, to a place called Beaver Harbour where he understood that Cope and his people were living; the ship was to carry three weeks' provisions for "near fifty persons" — obviously for the wives and children, since Hopson expected that Cope's men would return with Piggott "to confirm and ratify the peace according to Treaty already made with Major Cope". Upon signing, each family would receive six months' provisions, a blanket and other articles. Since it was now late October, Piggott was urged to make haste so that the Indians might be back with their families before winter weather set in. They came. At least the principal men of Cope's band came with him prepared to sign a treaty even though Cope had had no success to this date in bringing in the chiefs of other bands. Hopson proceeded to settle for what he could, which was a full-scale treaty with Cope and his band, drawn up in both English and French and signed by both sides on 22 November 1752.[39]

It was called a "treaty or Articles of Peace and Friendship" between the British and "Major Jean Baptiste Cope, Chief Sachem of the X X X Tribe of MickMack Indians Inhabiting the Eastern Coast of the said Province and Andrew Hadley Martin, Gabriel Martin and Francis Jeremiah members and Delegates of the said Tribe for themselves and their said Tribe their heirs and the heirs of their heirs forever". The name of the band was not given, although it was identified as the "Chibenacadie" in the proclamation that followed. Instead, the clerk seems to have left a space which was filled with three Xs either then or later. Unfortunately, some 20th-century transcriptions have omitted this, making it appear that Cope was "Chief Sachem of the Tribe of MickMack Indians", and thus leading readers to a most erroneous conclusion about who was actually covered by the Treaty of 1752. It was never meant to apply to all of the Micmac people, as the wording of the treaty itself and all of the other evidence surrounding it, including the proclamation that immediately followed and the governor's subsequent report to his superiors in Britain, prove categorically. This was a treaty with one band which Halifax officials hoped would serve as a model for dealing with all of the Micmac people.[40]

The treaty began by recalling the treaty negotiated in Boston in 1725 and ratified in Annapolis in 1726 and renewed by some Indians in 1749; the terms of this treaty were now renewed by the signatories. Secondly, it acknowledged in several ways that the British and the Indians had been in conflict, but that now "all Transactions during the late War shall on both sides be buried in Oblivion with the Hatchet" and the Indians should enjoy British "favour, Friendship and

---

39   William Cotterell to William Piggot, 25 October 1752, vol. 163, RG1, pp. 25-6; Treaty of 1752, 22 November 1752, C.O. 217/40, p. 229.

40   The Treaty of 1752 is in C.O. 217/40, p. 229. This, as noted by the secretary on the document itself, is a copy taken from the Council Minutes of 22 November 1752 which appear, along with the Proclamation of 24 November 1752 and a printed broadside of the proclamation, in vol. 186, RG1, PANS.

Protection". Indicating the limited scope of this treaty, another clause had the Indians promise to "use their utmost endeavours to bring in the other Indians to Renew and Ratify this peace" and to inform the British of any Indians "or any enemy whatever" (presumably meaning the French) who had designs against the British. If the signatories, because of their friendship with the British, found themselves attacked by other Indians, the British promised to come to their aid. The treaty also promised that the Shubenacadie band "shall not be hindered from, but have free liberty of Hunting and Fishing as usual" and, "if they shall think a Truckhouse needfull", it would be built on the Shubenacadie or any other place the Indians frequented. This left George Scott's plan conditional and open-ended, and as it turned out, no truckhouse was built in accordance with this provision. The treaty also provided for an immediate presentation of gifts, a promise of similar presents "to the other Tribes that shall hereafter Agree to renew and Ratify the Peace" and more gifts to the treaty-Indians half-yearly "for the time to come" and then every October first "so long as they shall Continue in Friendship". The Indians promised that they would help save the lives and goods of people shipwrecked on the coasts, and perhaps most importantly from the British perspective, that they would settle all future disputes with His Majesty's subjects "in His Majesty's Court of Civil Judicature, where the Indians shall have the same benefit, advantage and Priviledges as any others of His Majesty's Subjects".[41]

While Hopson was happy to have his treaty, he was also realistically cautious about what it meant. As he wrote to the Board of Trade in London, he had a treaty "with one tribe of the Mickmack Indians; tho it is but a small tribe I hope it may have the good effect to bring over the Rest but this is more to be hoped for than trusted to". More specifically, he added: "I have given provisions for Six months to this Tribe; which amounts (their familys included) to ninety persons". The proclamation issued a few days earlier was equally clear. It informed the people of Nova Scotia (on beautifully printed broadsides bearing the royal coat of arms and in both English and French) that the treaty was between the government and "Major Jean Baptiste Cope, Chief Sachem of the Chibenaccadie Tribe of Mick Mack Indians, Inhabiting the Eastern Coast of this Province", and it warned all of His Majesty's subjects that they should "forbear all Acts of Hostilities against the aforesaid Major Jean Baptiste Cope or His Tribe of Chibenaccadie Mick Mack Indians". Within days, these broadsides appeared in forts, settlements and public places all over the province, and French officials in far off Louisbourg were soon worrying about the impact it was having on the 2,000 or so other Micmacs who had not signed this treaty.[42]

French officials, in fact, followed all of these proceedings with great interest, having in their possession key pieces of the puzzle with which the British were wrestling. Authorities at Louisbourg had good contacts with the Micmac and understood what the Indians were doing and why. The commissary at Louisbourg,

---

41 C.O. 217/40, p. 229.

42 Hopson to Board of Trade, 6 December 1752, C.O. 217/13, pp. 384-8; Council Minutes, 24 November 1752, vol. 186, RG1, PANS; Prévost to Minister [of Marine], 12 May 1753, MG1, C11B, vol. 33, pp. 159 ff., AC.

Jacques Prévost, learned about William Piggott's visit with Jean-Baptiste Cope on Cape Breton and about Cope's subsequent visit to Halifax to sign a treaty. He dismissed it as a treaty with "quatre vingt dix à cent Sauvages tous mauvais sujets et tant hommes, femmes qu'enfants." "Les Anglais", he said, "ont voulu se servir de ce traité pour attirer tous les autres Sauvages" but as he heard the story, it had split the Micmac people, most of whom were angry at Cope and had no intention of following his lead. He pointed out to his superiors in France that Cope had a reputation for being perfidious with both the English and the French, and the story was about that Cope and the chief of the Cape Sable Indians had together planned to sign a treaty with the British in order to get their presents, but that they had no intention of honoring it. Prévost's accounts have the quality of hearsay, but in a number of respects, the information appeared accurate. If Cope's treaty had angered other Micmacs — and there are other indications that it did — it may have made sense for Cope to disavow it by spreading the story that he had never meant it to be a serious undertaking. All he had to do now was to prove this, and in fact he very shortly did so.[43]

The other point missing from British knowledge had to do with the activities of Le Loutre, whose power over the Micmacs seemed curiously lacking through the period of the treaty and its aftermath. Le Loutre, as he explains in his autobiography, had in the summer of 1752 reached a critical point in the development of his Acadian settlement north and west of the Missaguash. There were more than 2,000 settlers, an enormous shortage of provisions, and the great marshlands near Beauséjour needed draining and dyking if the Acadians were to practise their special type of agriculture and thus become self-sufficient. As a result, Le Loutre had left Beauséjour in August 1752 and had gone first to Quebec to get approval of a mammoth land reclamation project, back to Beauséjour briefly to put a fellow priest named Manach in charge, then to Louisbourg to get needed foodstuffs sent back to Beauséjour, and thence to France where he went to the highest authorities for 50,000 livres to pay for the massive draining and dyking project he had in mind. Le Loutre succeeded in all of this, but it was June of 1753 before he was back at Louisbourg; when he learned about the Treaty of 1752, he was enraged. He claimed that Cope was not the head of the Shubenacadie but the "tail". If the British wanted to deal with these Indians, he fumed in what may have been a moment of supreme candour, they should have done so through him.[44] Le Loutre's absence may explain a lot; his return coincided with a dramatic turn for the worse in Anglo-Micmac relations.

Hopson lacked detailed knowledge of what the French were doing, but was prepared to speculate in a letter to the Board of Trade: "I conclude this Letter with a conjecture of my own which the behaviour of the French at this Juncture helps to confirm me in", he wrote in the winter following the treaty, "it is, that their ceasing

---

43   Le Loutre, *Autobiography*, pp. 44-8; "Anthony Casteel's Journal", *Le Canada-Français*, XX, pp. 125-6.

44   Prévost to Minister, 12 May 1753, MG1, C¹¹B, vol. 33, pp. 159 ff., AC. Author's translation: "ninety to one hundred Indians, all evil subjects, men, women and children"; "The English wanted to use this treaty to attract all the other Indians".

to urge the Indians to annoy us is only with a view of Employing themselves and the expence they were at in that Service to Strengthen their own colony and thereby enable themselves to give a Surer and more decisive blow". Hopson could have been reading Le Loutre's mind; the realist in him said that he must use the brief hiatus afforded by the treaty to plant settlements and strengthen the position of the English in Nova Scotia, while the optimist clung to his original hope that Cope would keep his promise and bring in more Micmac bands to sign treaties. By March 1753 he had word of the killing and scalping of two British soldiers at Chignecto, but that Micmacs in the vicinity had disavowed the act. Meanwhile, he said, "the Indians on this side remain quiet", meaning presumably the Indians nearer to Halifax. In fact, by April he was reporting with great confidence that he had letters and other information to confirm that "the remainder of the Mickmack Indians will very soon be here to make peace". And on 12 April Glaude Gisigash, "an Indian who stiles himself Governor of LaHave", arrived before the council in Halifax to agree to terms like those settled with Cope and to promise to return with his own interpreter and several members of his band to ratify a treaty. Hopson was not sure how much longer his luck would last, but for the moment at least he claimed that "our design seems to be much favoured by the Indians remaining quiet".[45] Without his knowing it, however, the period of peace had already ended.

On 16 April 1753 two English settlers, John Conner and James Grace, paddled into Halifax harbour in an Indian canoe with six Indian scalps and a frightening story. They were part of a party of four, they reported to council, which had left Halifax by schooner in February and proceeded along the eastern shore to Jeddore and then points beyond. They were between Country Harbour and Torbay around 21 February when a canoe with four Indians came out, fired at them and pursued them as the wind drove them toward shore. Other Indians joined in and finally boarded the schooner, forcing them to submit and run their vessel into an inlet. Conner and Grace were sent into the woods to collect firewood and as they returned they saw Indians strike their companions, Michael Hagarthy and John Poor, in the head with axes "and killed and scalped them". From there, they claimed, they were taken "about 10 miles into the country where they continued prisoners until the 8th day of this month". At that point, they were left in the care of six Indians, including a woman and a boy, while the others went off. Seizing an opportunity when the men were separated from the woman and boy, Conner and Grace claimed that they killed the latter, secured arms and ammunition and then killed the four men on their return, permitting their escape. They had the scalps to prove it.[46]

It was a harrowing story, and Conner and Grace were immediately required to sign sworn depositions attesting to its validty. In fact, the Treaty of 1752, if followed to the letter, might bring in Cope's followers demanding satisfaction in the King's courts. Moreover, if the account were true, it would mean either that

45 Hopson to Board of Trade, 6 December 1752, C.O. 217/13, pp. 384-8; 28 March and 14 April 1753, C.O. 217/14, pp. 30-9, Council Minutes, 12 April 1753, vol. 186, RG1, PANS.

46 Council Minutes, 16 April 1753, vol. 186, RG1, PANS; Hopson to Board of Trade, 16 April 1753; "An Examination...of James Grace and John Conner taken April 16th 1753", C.O. 217/14, pp. 151-5.

Cope was failing in his bid to bring other Indians into the peace or, worse, that Cope himself had gone back on his word. Hopson did not particularly want to believe either of these things and decided to await further developments. He was in this quandary when Cope's own son arrived in Halifax with a story that seemed to make sense of what was going on. The son claimed that Cope and Glaude Gisigash had been to Chignecto to urge the band there to come into the peace, "but they could not succeed therein and the Chignecto and Cape Breton Indians would continue the war". Cope and Gisigash had decided that they "would bring their families and settle at Halifax and behave as good subjects to His Majesty". Would the governor send a ship to Cope's home along the eastern shore, take on board the provisions he had there, since "evil minded persons had stole several casks", and bring them back to the safety of the British settlement? Hopson and his council agreed.[47]

Hopson had a lot on his mind in May 1753 when he commissioned a local shipowner, Samuel Cleaveland, to take his sloop and a small crew, along with Joseph Cope and his two Indian companions, to rescue Cope's provisions somewhere near Jeddore on the eastern shore. His preoccupation was with settling German Protestants who had been assembling in Halifax for almost three years awaiting a time when they could safely plant a new community. Early plans had been to settle them at Musquodoboit, and surveys had actually been carried out there in 1752. But in the end, apprehension about Indians had led Hopson to fix on a site on the other side of Halifax, on the south shore at a place the Micmac and French called Mirligueche, but which the British now renamed Lunenburg. The German Protestants were part of a long-planned scheme to counterbalance the large Acadian population of Nova Scotia at a time when English migrants, it seemed, preferred to go to the better-established English colonies to the south. The arrival of the Germans and the necessity of feeding and housing them until they could be settled had contributed to the pressure on Nova Scotia governors to arrange a peace treaty with the Micmac. Hopson was now determined to get on with it, even though warning signs were up. In late May he received "an Express from the Officer commanding at Pisiquid [Windsor] advising me, that he is credibly informed that there are three bodys of Indians disposed of in those parts, amounting to about three hundred who lye there in readiness, as they give out, to oppose the Settlement of Merlegash and intend to begin the March there as soon as they have information when the Settlers are to Sail". The news was alarming but Hopson claimed that he was not as worried about the Indians at this point as he was about the French: another Nova Scotia schooner, he learned, had been taken by Indians while it was in a French harbour in Cape Breton; a considerable number of New England vessels trading into Louisbourg "have been detained there a long while by an Embargo"; and the small sloop he had sent with Cope's Indians had been gone so long that he was beginning to fear it had been "certainly stopped".[48]

His fears would undoubtedly have been greater still if he had been able to read

47   Council Minutes, 16 May 1753, vol. 186, RG1, PANS.
48   Hopson to Board of Trade, 29 May 1753, C.O. 217/14, pp. 177-8.

the correspondence of Jacques Prévost, the civilian administrator of Louisbourg, who explained that at this point there were few Indians in Cape Breton "parce que les principeaux guerriers suivis de la jeunesse courent la côte de l'est à l'Acadie", the name the French still used when referring to Nova Scotia. They were there "de venger la mort de leurs frères", according to Prévost, meaning those who had been killed by Grace and Conner. Commissary Prévost's sources of information among the Micmac were good, and he usually was able to sort out what they were doing and why. He wrote long, detailed letters to his superiors in the Ministry of Marine in France. He knew, for example, about the Grace and Conner incident and that the Indians claimed that their schooner had run aground and sank, drowning some of her crew. This much Prévost was not inclined to believe because, as he reasoned, the four men captured by the Indians were sufficient to man a small craft of this size. The Indians admitted that they had captured four men, and some of them claimed that two had died of illness while others said that they had killed them. Which was correct Prévost was unable to determine. But he did know that the two who survived had surprised their captors while they slept and had killed them and escaped.[49] What Prévost wrote certainly confirmed much of what Conner and Grace had sworn.

Prévost also quickly learned what had befallen Jean-Baptiste Cope. The Indians who set out to avenge the death of the Micmacs scalped by Conner and Grace came eventually upon the bodies of two Cape Sable Indians whom they knew to be a man named Joseph and his wife, both of whom they believed had been treacherously killed by the English. The source of the trouble, they concluded, was the treaty that Cope had signed with the British, for which they determined they must punish him. They therefore visited the Shubenacadie-Musquodoboit band, found Cope, took him to the Micmac village at Ramsheg (now Wallace on the north shore of Nova Scotia) and decided at first that he should be sent with several English prisoners to Quebec. At that point, however, their plan seems to have changed; instead, they devised a scheme whereby one of the adherents of Cope's treaty would be sent into Halifax with a request that the British send a vessel to the eastern shore to carry provisions and there it would be destroyed. Prévost's information was that this had happened, that the vessel had carried ten men and that of them the English crew had been killed while only an Acadian pilot had been spared. Afterwards, the Indians who carried out the attack "se sont ensuite retirés et dispersés de différents côtes dans l'Acadie pour continuer disent-ils à frapper dur leurs ennemis".[50] If Prévost was right, Joseph Cope's visit to Halifax had been part of a rather elaborate hoax and the Micmac war was on again with a vengeance.

---

49 T.A. Crowley, "Jacques Prévost de la Croix", *DCB*, IV, pp. 643-7; Prévost to Minister [of Marine], Louisbourg, 17 June 1753, MG1, C11B, vol. 33, pp. 181-3, AC. Author's translation: "because the main warriors followed by the young are travelling on the east coast of Acadia" and "to avenge the death of their brothers".

50 Prévost to Minister, 17 June 1753, MG1, C11B, vol. 33, pp. 181-3, AC. Author's translation: "withdrew and spread out into different parts of Acadia in order, according to them, to continue to strike their enemies with force".

For weeks Hopson had nothing but his own suspicions that things had gone awry. But by 23 July, as he wrote to the Board of Trade, he knew that peace had not been secured: "the almost continual war we have with the Indians prevents our mixing any English Settlers with these Inhabitants or instituting any sort of civil jurisdiction among them". He firmly believed that the French were at the root of the problem. The Indians, he claimed, "have been hitherto left open to the insinuations and evil practices of French Priests & other Emissaries that are sent amongst them from Canada and the French Fort at Beauséjour, who have at all times been endeavouring to prejudice them against an English Government, and to persuade them that the Country they live in will very shortly fall into the hands of the French either by negotiations or by force of Arms". The problem, as he analyzed it, was precisely the problem that had existed before the Treaty of 1752: "In fact what we call an Indian War here is no other than a pretense for the French to commit hostilities upon his Majesty's subjects".[51]

Hopson had the hard facts of missing or delayed ships and reports of Indians massed to oppose his settlements to convince him that he was at war; by 30 July he also had the story of Anthony Casteel, an Acadian in the British employ who now arrived in Halifax alone several weeks after having left on Cleaveland's schooner. Casteel was a French-English interpreter and messenger for the Nova Scotia council, a valued servant of the British given the fact that the largest part of the Nova Scotia population was French-speaking Acadian and that Micmacs and Maliseets could deal with Europeans only in French. Casteel knew Jean-Baptiste Cope, and it seems likely that it was he who translated for Cope and the council when Cope had originally negotiated his treaty. It therefore made sense for Casteel to be sent on this mission. Now Casteel returned, the sole survivor. The schooner, he reported, had gone along to Jeddore without incident, and there they were met by Major Cope who greeted him like a long-lost friend. Cope acknowledged that he was in deep trouble with the other Micmacs because of the treaty he had signed. But then things turned violent. Cope's Indians seized the Europeans and killed and scalped them all except Casteel — whom they spared after much deliberation because he was French.[52]

Casteel's adventure had just begun. Cope, he reported, seemed delighted that this ruse had worked; it proved that he was a "good soldier". Yet apparently there was more to prove. Casteel was taken by the Shubenacadie route across the province to Cobequid (Truro) where they stopped at an Acadian house to obtain provisions. Casteel claimed that his captors produced a written order from a French officer calling on Acadians to furnish ammunition and provisions to this "detachment" since it was "upon the Kings duty going to Chebucto". Here Casteel was shown Cope's copy of the Treaty of 1752 which he scarcely began to read when an Indian snatched it from him and threw it into the fire, "telling him `that was the way they made Peace with the English'". From there Casteel was taken to Tatamagouche and then to Ramsheg, and before he was taken finally to

---

51   Hopson to Board of Trade, from Letter Book, P.A.C./N.S./A:54, printed in N.E.S. Griffiths, ed., *The Acadian Deportation: Deliberate Perfidy or Cruel Necessity?* (Toronto, 1969), pp. 84-5.

52   "Deposition of Anthony Casteel", 30 July 1753, C.O. 217/14, p. 199.

Louisbourg, he visited Baie Verte, where a large council of Indians set a ransom of 300 livres upon his head, which he claimed was paid for him by a local Acadian. Once at Louisbourg, Casteel was thoroughly questioned by French officials about the military preparedness of the British in Halifax. Now in a totally different situation, Casteel, doubtless aware of the cartel by which the French and English had agreed the previous year to exchange military prisoners, insisted that he was British and was in the employ of the Nova Scotia government. After a final interview with Le Loutre, just returned from France — the occasion when the priest denounced Major Cope, his treaty and the British for toying in this fashion with the "souls" of the Micmacs — the French allowed Casteel to return to Halifax. What he had to tell Hopson would clearly be in the French interest since, however he phrased it, it would demonstrate that the Treaty of 1752 was dead and that attempting to lure the Micmac away from the French would not work. Le Loutre also had a special message for the governor; it was, according to Casteel, that "the English might build as many Forts as they pleased but he wou'd take care that they shou'd not come out of them, for he was resolved to torment them with his Indians and desired that the Governor might declare War Accordingly".[53]

Hopson understood the message clearly; he had failed in his bid to pacify the Micmac. To an official query about the volume of British trade with the Indians, he replied that it was negligible "and indeed the shortness of the time they were peaceable makes it impossible to form any right judgement of this matter". By mid-summer he had reports from Chignecto of Le Loutre's return and that he had 300 Micmac families there with him. His conclusion was that "very little progress can be made in the service I have the honor to be employed in, until the French flag is removed out of this province by some means or other; when that happens I have hopes that the Indians when their allies are withdrawn will no more be able to disturb us and that they will then make proper submissions to His Majesty's government and live under it in peace and quietness".[54]

Hopson was right in suggesting that the French had made use of their Indian allies to keep Nova Scotia unstable; specifically, the French sought to retard British settlement and buy time for France to implement its Acadian resettlement scheme. French accounts not only confirm the generality of Hopson's charge, but show that in this summer of 1753 Le Loutre paid out "1800 argent de L'Acadie" to Indians at Beauséjour in payment for "dix huit chevalures qu'ils ont levés aux anglois dans les differents courses qu'ils ont faites sur leurs etablissements pendant le mois dernier". But at this point, French Indian policy took a new turn. France's larger interests dictated that full-scale war with Britain be delayed, and the French were growing worried lest their Indian allies precipitate one before the French were

---

53 Casteel's deposition presents an abbreviated version of his story which appears in its complete form in "Anthony Casteel's Journal", *Le Canada-Français*, XX, pp.111-26. A handwritten transcript of this document by Dr. Andrew Brown was taken from the original at the British Museum and is located in the Public Archives of Nova Scotia in the Andrew Brown Manuscripts. Brown's marginally inserted opinions unfortunately influenced Leslie Upton in his interpretation of the Grace and Conner incident: see *Micmacs and Colonists*, p. 55.

54 Hopson to Board of Trade, two letters of 23 July 1753, C.O. 217/14, pp. 185-96; Letter Book, P.A.C./N.S./A:54, in Griffiths, ed., *Acadian Deportation*, pp. 84-5.

ready. Marquis Duquesne, governor general of New France, accordingly wrote his military commander at Beauséjour in July 1753 that he was giving orders "pour empêcher que l'ont tuat les Anglois", and "si les sauvages de votre contrée venoient vous demander pareille permission vous leur dirés que je leur ai deffendu de la leur donner". Duquesne knew that the French did not have, nor could they have, absolute control over what the Indians did. "Comme ce Mikmaks ont levé la hache contre les Anglois", he acknowledged, "vous ne pouver guerre les empêcher d'aller frapper au loin si c'est part esprit de vengeance, mais pour frapper à Beaubassin il ne conviendroit pas de le souffrir sans être exposé au risque detre insulté dans votre poste". Duquesne's order is useful evidence of the nature of French-Indian relations: the French knew what they wanted, but they also knew that the Micmacs had minds of their own. The Indians did become quiet around Beauséjour, however, and this benefited both the French and the English. With Le Loutre once again in charge, Acadians, French soldiers and their Indian allies worked diligently through the summer of 1754 building dykes, aboiteaux and roads at Chignecto, while his emissaries pressed Acadians at Minas and elsewhere to relocate there. This Duquesne approved: "Je ne puis qu'aprouver le mouvement que se donne Monsieur l'abbé Le Loutre pour faire occuper les terres qui restent en friche. Nul n'est pas capable que lui de faire cette repartition et d'engager l'habitant à un établissement solide".[55] Simultaneously the new British governor at Halifax, Charles Lawrence, continued work on his Lunenburg settlement, sent out a party of soldiers to explore the upper reaches of the Shubenacadie River and began planning a community at Musquodoboit to provide protection to Dartmouth from Indian attacks.[56]

British policy in Nova Scotia continued to steer between fear of Indians and hope for peaceful accommodation. Despite the collapse of peace on the eastern shore, the British did not formally renounce the Treaty of 1752 until 1756. Meanwhile, they had two encounters with the Micmac which demonstrated to them that some of the Indians were clearly under French control and others were not, suggesting the need for greater flexibility in their approach. In November 1753 representatives of the Cape Sable Indians arrived in Halifax with a peace message. The Cape Sables were a small band of about 60 Micmacs who lived on the South

55   Prévost to Roué, 16 August 1753, MG1, C11B, vol. 33, AC. Author's translation: "18 scalps which they took from the English in different incursions that they have made on their settlements during the last month". Duquesne to de la Martinière, 27 July and 10 September 1753, copy in Webster Collection, New Brunswick Museum, Saint John [NBM]. Author's translation: "prohibiting the killing of the English" and "if therefore, the Indians in your district ask for permission to do so, tell them that I have forbidden you to do so"; "As the Micmac have gone on the warpath against the English, you can scarcely prevent their striking at distant places in the spirit of vengeance, but it could not be tolerated at Beaubassin without exposing your post [i.e. Beauséjour] to the danger of attack"; "I cannot do otherwise than approve the efforts of the Abbé Le Loutre to have the uncultivated land occupied. No one is more capable than he is [to oversee this project] and to encourage the inhabitants to undertake a permanent settlement". Le Loutre, *Autobiography*; pp. 46-7; "Journal of Louis de Courville, 1755", in John Clarence Webster, ed., *Journals of Beauséjour* (Halifax, 1937), p. 45.

56   Abbé Daudin to Abbé de l'Isle Dieu, 26 September 1754, Copy in Webster Collection, NBM; Le Loutre, *Autobiography*, p. 47; Lawrence to Board of Trade, 1 March and 1 June 1754, C.O. 217/15, pp. 25-9, 32.

Shore. Their spokesmen included Baptiste Thomas, one of two chiefs of the band, who explained to the governor and council that they had "never joined with the other Indians in molesting the English" and because, to the contrary, they had occasionally helped Englishmen whose vessels had become storm-wrecked along their coast, they had "never received any assistance from the French". They were now nervous about going into British settlements, they explained, because "the other Indians have renewed hostilities" and they feared British retaliation against the Cape Sables even though they were innocent. The clarity of their message, and perhaps also their courage in coming in to give it, deeply impressed the council, who correctly deduced that some bands were under French influence and others were not, and that therefore their policy towards the Indians should be adjusted: "tho' it was highly proper as much as possible to annoy and destroy <u>such</u> of the Indians as continued to make war upon us", their minutes record, "yet on the other hand it might be of great advantage to support and encourage such of them as should come in and be willing to remain friends with us, and that by acts of friendship and kindness the whole of them might at length be convinced that it would be more for their interest to be our friends than enemies". In consequence, the council voted winter provisions for 60 people and the secretary even made an account of the bread, pork, blankets, powder, shot, tobacco, pipes and other items that made up the gift.[57]

The second encounter, however, raised skeptical eyebrows because Le Loutre attempted to serve as an intermediary. Through a British officer at Fort Lawrence, Le Loutre sent the message that the Indians wished to make proposals "towards establishing a General and lasting Peace". In a detailed letter, Le Loutre explained that Baptiste Cope had recently arrived at Chignecto with news that British soldiers had penetrated into Micmac hunting grounds on the Shubenacadie, and in their traditional fashion, Micmacs at Chignecto had called a council to settle on a course of action. According to Le Loutre, the Indians proposed that a large portion of Nova Scotia should be recognized by the British as Micmac territory. It would run from the Isthmus to Minas, then to Cobequid and Shubenacadie (including Le Loutre's old mission), across to Musquodoboit, then along the eastern shore to Canso and finally through the strait (or Fronsac), along the north shore and back to Baie Verte. For a people who lived by hunting and fishing, argued Le Loutre, this was a reasonable demand. What he did not say, of course, was that the land proposal would have the effect of creating an Indian buffer state between a rather truncated British Nova Scotia and his new French Acadia, limiting the British in fact to the small area which France now claimed it had surrendered to Britain in 1713. While the council in Halifax agreed that the Indians "or anybody on their behalf might come here with great security to make their proposals and that nothing should be wanting on our part to establish a general peace", they privately expressed their misgivings. The council's secretary wrote that he did not trust Le Loutre, whom he blamed for the treacherous murder of Captain Howe, and more than this, Le Loutre "cannot be ignorant that we are by no means the aggressors or

---

57   Council Minutes, 16 November 1753, vol. 187, RG1, PANS.

in any way desirous to begin or continue a war with the Indians if they would demean themselves as they ought to do towards his Majesty's subjects". The British had shown their good will in their treaty with Major Cope, he added, yet the treaty "has indeed since been broke through on their part, of which Transaction Mr. Le Loutre can probably give a better account than we". Suspicious of Le Loutre, whose ulterior motives seemed all too transparent and whose letter was "too insolent and absurd to be answered through the Author", the Nova Scotia council addressed a general letter to all Nova Scotia's Indians. If the Indians were at all serious about making peace, they could come into Halifax "where they will be treated with reasonable conditions".[58]

In February 1755 the Chignecto Micmacs by-passed Le Loutre and repeated their demand for the same area of land through a Micmac spokesman, Paul Laurent, who had for a time lived in captivity in Boston and could speak English.[59] Laurent's message to the governor and council was that a peace treaty depended on a land grant, and while he was not able to negotiate this, he asked for a reply in writing "and that the Council would specify therein the Quantity of Land, that they would allow them, if they thought what was required was too much". The council replied that the demand was "unreasonable" and that the Indians' peace overtures were "very general and the demands you make, in our opinion, are extremely exorbitant". But they hastened to add that they were quite willing to set aside a tract of land "for your hunting, fishing, etc. as shall be abundantly sufficient for you and what we make no doubt you, yourselves, will like and approve". To arrange this, they asked that the chiefs of the Micmac tribe come to Halifax to work out the details, insisting that the piecemeal approach of the past had not worked. With obvious reference to the treaties of 1749 and 1752, they wrote: "You are sensible that certain Captains of your Tribes, (at least Persons styling themselves such) have appeared here and made peace under promises of bringing in the other tribes, that instead of bringing those tribes, the treaties have been immediately and perfidiously broken; and that when these things had happened and we have complained of them, the tribes in general have disclaimed such proceedings from whence it is apparent we could have no certain dependence on overtures made by one or a few individuals". As skeptical as they were, the British made clear that they were ready to negotiate and that the concept of setting aside Indian lands was acceptable, but it must be within the framework of a general peace treaty and it must have the sanction of all of the Micmac chiefs together.[60] Unfortunately, that was to be the end of peace negotiations for the time being.

"In Acadia, during the winter of 1755, we lived in profound peace", a French soldier wrote in his journal. But in fact war had already broken out between English and French forces at the forks of the Ohio River. In no time, Acadia became the scene of some of the bitterest fighting that took place in the Seven

---

58   Council Minutes, 29 July, 9 September 1754, vol. 187, RG1, PANS; William Cotterell to Captain Hamilton, 3 June 1754, in Thomas Beamish Akins, ed., *Selections from the Public Documents of Nova Scotia* (Halifax, 1869), p. 210.

59   Micheline D. Johnson, "Paul Laurent", *DCB*, III, pp. 358-59.

60   Council Minutes, 12 and 13 February 1755, vol. 187, RG1, PANS.

Years' War. In June a force of 2,000 British regulars and colonial troops completely surprised the commander at Beauséjour, who tried briefly to muster his inadequate complement of French regulars, Acadian workers and Indian allies and then surrendered when all looked hopeless.[61] Le Loutre disappeared from Beauséjour before the British entered, and while his dream of a new Acadian homeland under the flag of France was now dashed forever, he and other French priests were still able to provide direction to Micmac and Maliseet warriors who had not conceded defeat. To deal with both the Indians and the French, whose stronghold at Louisbourg remained, the British at this point decided to destroy their logistical support; since they firmly believed that both were dependent on food provisions from the Acadians, they took the drastic decision to expel the entire Acadian population. Over the summer and fall of 1755, Acadian families were rounded up at Minas and Annapolis and deported. Hundreds more met a similar fate as the war progressed, while many others escaped to French territories — Quebec, Île Royale, or Île St. Jean — or to the relative security of the northern bays and forests of present-day New Brunswick which were beyond the effective limits of British administration. While the reasons for the expulsion were complicated, a significant factor in British thinking was their experience, since their arrival at Halifax in 1749, of war with Micmac and Maliseet Indians, a continuous war which British officials believed had been engineered by France. Moreover, the British also acted on the belief that the Acadians had become willing pawns in this contest. Lawrence claimed to have solid evidence that Acadians had provided both the French and the Indians with "intelligence, Quarters, provisions, and assistance in annoying the Government" during the Indian war.[62]

The British were wrong in thinking that Micmac and Maliseet warriors served only French interests. They had their own interests and they understood them. While they had been divided in accepting the guidance of French priests in the past, they now generally chose to fight in alliance with France and to accept their tactical direction. This decision turned out to be a serious miscalculation on their part, not so much because they chose the side that would eventually lose, but because their choice profoundly altered the very basis of their subsistence. The lives of hundreds of self-sufficient Indians were completely disrupted by their service to the French cause as they came to rely on regular supplies of food and ammunition from the French government. This in turn required food shipments from Acadian farmlands to supplement the inadequate supplies reaching Louisbourg and other French outposts from Quebec and from France itself. It was this fragile chain of

---

61 "Journal of Louis de Courville", in Webster, ed., *Journals of Beauséjour*, pp. 45-50; "Pichon's Journal of the Siege of Beauséjour", in John Clarence Webster, *Thomas Pichon, "The Spy of Beauséjour"* (Halifax, 1937), pp. 100-7; John Clarence Webster, ed., "Journal of Abijah Willard", *New Brunswick Historical Society Collections*, XIII (1930), p. 25; Lawrence to Board of Trade, 18 July 1755, C.O. 217/15.

62 Lawrence to Board of Trade, 11 August 1755, C.O. 217/15. The variety of interpretations of the expulsion is explored by Griffiths, ed., *The Acadian Deportation*. See also Jean Daigle, "Acadia, 1604-1763: An Historical Synthesis", in Jean Daigle, ed., *The Acadians of the Maritimes: Thematic Studies* (Moncton, 1982), pp. 17-46 and Naomi Griffiths, *The Acadians: Creation of a People* (Toronto, 1973), pp. 48-85.

supply which the British destroyèd by expelling the Acadians. The accuracy of their analysis immediately became apparent as the dependence of the Indians on the Acadians and on Beauséjour shifted to Louisbourg: "Nous nous appercevons déjà de la misère que les Sauvages éprouvent sur les frontières de l'Acadie par les visites qu'ils se font ici", wrote Louisbourg's highest officials. "Ils paraissent zélés et prêt à servir le roi, mais on saurait les employer sans les nourrir, et nous vous prions de nous procurer assez de vivres pour le pouvoir faire". What they asked was only the beginning. The supply problem plagued the French for the rest of the war and they never resolved it. More than any other single factor — including the massive assault that eventually forced the surrender of Louisbourg — the supply problem spelled doom to French power in the region. From Halifax Lawrence had clearly understood the relationship between supply and the ability to fight, and he believed that the expulsion not only reduced French power in region, but also that it "renders it difficult for the Indians, who cannot as formerly be supply'd with provisions and Intelligence, to make incursions upon our Settlers".[63]

While the expulsion seriously undermined the French position, it did not lessen their determination or the willingness of their Indian allies to wage war against the British using every means at their disposal. By the spring of 1756 Lawrence was receiving reports from all parts of the province describing the hit-and-run strikes of Micmac and Maliseet warriors. Schooners seized, British regulars killed and scalped at Fort Moncton, houses destroyed and settlers killed in Mahone Bay — this was the information laid before the provincial council on 14 May, when the council agreed to a new proclamation repealing that which had accompanied the signing of the Treaty of 1752. Notwithstanding this treaty, read the proclamation, "the Indians have of late, in a cruel and treacherous manner killed and carried away divers of his Majesty's subjects in different parts of the Province". The officers and subjects of the British crown in Nova Scotia were therefore commanded "to annoy, distress, take and destroy the Indians inhabiting different parts of this province, wherever they are found". A reward was offered for prisoners or scalps. Thereafter, reports of Indian attacks became so commonplace that Lawrence became offhand in his treatment of them. "Nothing extraordinary has happened since my last", he wrote the Board of Trade, "except that the Indians in Conjunction with some of the French inhabitants that were left behind, have scalped and carried off some People in different parts of the province".[64]

Effectively, the proclamation of 1756 ended British treaty-making attempts for the time being on the grounds that the Micmac themselves had violated earlier treaties. While the Micmac would have differed in their interpretation of events, they accepted that they were at war. As French correspondence from Louisbourg

63 Vaudreuil to the Minister [of Marine], 19 April 1757; Drucourt and Prévost to the Ministry [of Marine], 6 April 1756 and 12 May 1757, copies in Webster Collection, NBM [Author's translation of letter of 6 April 1756: "We already see the hardship that the Indians suffer on the frontiers of Acadia because of the visits they made here. They seem zealous and ready to serve the king, but we cannot employ them without feeding them, and we beg you to procure enough foodstuffs to be able to do it"]; Lawrence to Board of Trade, 18 October 1755, C.O. 217/15.

64 A Proclamation, C.O. 217/16; Council Minutes, 14 May 1756, vol. 187, RG1, PANS; Lawrence to Board of Trade, 25 May 1756, C.O. 217/16.

shows, the Micmac in general were most active in scouting and raiding, and even the Cape Sables, who had made such a point in 1753 of remaining peaceable, were now as involved as any other Micmac band. Indian warriors now regularly reported to Port Toulouse to receive French presents and military directions: some were employed in guarding the passages between Nova Scotia and Île Royale, some were sent to Chignecto to serve under the French officer Charles Deschamps de Boishébert and others were ordered directly to the Halifax area to spy and to conduct guerrilla-style attacks. Acadians and Indians at times worked together and were especially effective in capturing small British vessels that ventured near or through the Cabot Strait, from which escapades the Indians brought back scalps to collect French reward money. Lawrence reported that it had become common practice for Acadians and Indians to ambush British settlers and soldiers, killing and scalping them as they passed on the province's few usable roads, and that settlers in new towns such as Lunenburg and Lawrence Town had to observe the greatest precautions in venturing into the woods to gather firewood or clear land. Lawrence warned his superiors that he could not induce new settlers to come to Nova Scotia, since they were "liable to have their throats Cutt every moment by the most inveterate Enemies, well acquainted with every Creek and Corner of the Country by which they can make their Escape". Boishébert's force of Indians near the old Fort Beauséjour killed and scalped unwary soldiers, burned their wood supply and so frightened them that they ventured out only to get to their boats. As Marquis de Vaudreuil, governor general of New France, heard it, "Il a été envoyé de temps en temps d'autres partis sauvages qui ont toujours eu quelque succès".[65]

Such reports illustrated how completely the role of Indians had been integrated into French military operations. At Louisbourg, the commissary's account books showed increasing amounts set aside for Indian presents and provisions, which by late 1756 consisted of one and a half pounds of bread and a half- pound of meat for every warrior employed in guarding the coast. From 1756 to the fall of Louisbourg in 1758 the accounts show regular payments of scalp money — including notably one payment to Baptiste Cope — and they specify that supplies were regularly dispensed to 700 Indians. Micmac and Maliseet warriors had become indispensable defenders of Île Royale while also providing the French with their most effective raiding and intelligence capacity. Yet when the British assault on Louisbourg finally came in 1758, it was such a massive blow, delivered by a force so vastly outnumbering the defenders, that the French quickly capitulated, leaving their fleeing Indian allies to fend for themselves.[66]

---

65   Drucourt and Prévost to the Minister [of Marine], 6 April 1756, Prévost to Minister [of Marine], 27 September and 2 October 1756, Vaudreuil to Minister [of Marine], 19 April 1757, copies in Webster Collection, NBM [Author's translation: "From time to time other parties of Indians have been sent out, and they have always had some success"]; Prévost to unknown, 12 May 1756, MG1, C11B, vol. 33, pp. 105-6, AC; Lawrence to Board of Trade, Halifax, 3 November 1756, C.O. 217/16.

66   Accounts, 29 November, 20 December 1756, 30 September 1757, MG1, C11B, vol. 37, pp. 209 ff., vol. 36, pp. 221 ff., vol. 37, pp. 128 ff., AC. The most complete account of the military career of Louisbourg is J.S. McLennan, *Louisbourg from its Foundation to its Fall, 1713-1758* (Sydney, 1957). For numbers of men and details of the initial attack in 1758, see especially pages 247-60.

For a time, Micmac and Maliseet warriors tried to continue without French support, returning to the guerrilla tactics which they had employed so effectively at the high tide of the Micmac War in the early 1750s. Strike groups attacked fishermen along the eastern shore, taking them prisoner or killing and scalping them, while skilful sea raiders seized increasing numbers of British vessels. It was bad enough to lose civilians just outside the capital, lamented Lawrence, but "what is still more extraordinary they have now commenced a War upon us by Sea, and in one Month have taken ten Coasters between this Place [meaning Halifax] and Louisbourg in spite of every measure Mr. Whitmore and I could concert for the Protection of the Coast".[67] While Lawrence advertised in New England newspapers in 1758 that Nova Scotia was now open for settlement, incursions by Micmacs and Acadians in the Minas and Pisiquid areas effectively prevented it until 1760. But by then, native warriors were feeling the full impact of their loss of French logistical support; without the French to supply them with arms and ammunition and the Acadians or Louisbourg to feed them, they suddenly found themselves in the same desperate misery as the scattered groups of Acadians, convincing proof if ever it was needed of how completely they had lost their pre-war self-sufficiency. The Micmac and Maliseet, after 16 years of almost constant warfare, had become a dependent people. Only the belief that France would be able to reassert its power in the region kept them going; when news arrived that Quebec itself had fallen, the will to fight rapidly evaporated. Dire need forced them to capitulate wherever they could find British troops. Maliseets first presented themselves at Fort Frederick at the mouth of the St. John River in November 1759, and Micmacs appeared during 1760 at Louisbourg, Chignecto or Halifax. All were told to send representatives to Halifax to sign formal treaties with the governor and council.[68]

Ballomy Glode and Michel Neptune, respectively of the Maliseet and Passamaquoddy tribes, arrived in Halifax in February 1760, and the terms negotiated with them became a model for the several treaties which followed with the Micmac, although there was also an essential difference. The Maliseet and the Passamaquoddy had a treaty relationship with the British in Nova Scotia going back to the Treaty of 1725, which had been renewed in 1749. Even though Glode and Neptune were now willing to admit that they had broken the treaty, the British agreed to bury all former hostilities in oblivion, to incorporate these earlier agreements into the new treaty (in effect renewing them) and to propose an additional new arrangement for maintaining the peace through the establishment of a regulated trading system. There were no reciprocal obligations: no British

67   Lawrence to General Amherst, 17 September 1759, W.O. 34/11, War Office Records, PRO [microfilm in the Harriet Irving Library, University of New Brunswick]. The prowess of the Micmac at sea is explored by Dickason, "La 'guerre navale' contre les Britanniques, 1713-1763", in Martijn, ed., *Les Micmacs et la mer,* pp. 233-48.

68   Council Minutes, 30 November 1759. Several bands of Micmacs were represented by Roger Morris and four others who came directly into Halifax on 9 January 1760, and were given formal permission to come and go until a treaty could be negotiated: Council Minutes, vol. 188, RG1, PANS. For the capitulation of Cape Breton Micmacs, see the various letters of Whitmore to Amherst during 1760 in W.O. 34/17, pp. 87-183.

promises about fishing, hunting, land or anything other than the implied protection of Nova Scotia law. Subsequent treaties with the Micmac repeated the substance of these terms yet without reference to any earlier treaties, an approach that the records do not explain, but which clearly reflects the long history of British disillusionment with previous Micmac treaty arrangements, including the notoriously unsuccessful Treaty of 1752. Where the Maliseet and Passamaquoddy "hereby renew and Confirm the aforesaid Articles of Submission and Agreement, and every part thereof and do solemnly promise and engage that the same shall for ever hereafter be strictly observed and performed", the Micmac treaties began *de novo*. As "treaties of peace and friendship", they required the Micmac signatories to "acknowledge the jurisdiction and Dominion of His Majesty George the Second over the Territories of Nova Scotia or Accadia and [to] make submission to His majesty in the most perfect, ample, and solemn manner". Also, because there were so many bands of the Micmac and the assembling of them all could not be achieved without great difficulty, the council decided to treat with each band separately, a process which took more than 18 months.[69]

The novelty in all of the treaties was the establishment of government truckhouses in six different locations throughout Nova Scotia at which all trade between whites and Indians would be conducted. Every tribe or band was required to keep two or three "hostages" at one of these truckhouses "for the more effectual security of the due performance of this Treaty", and the trade was to be conducted according to a negotiated price list which a number of unidentified Indian chiefs worked out with the governor and council in Halifax at the time of the first treaties. Borrowed from New England and reflective of George Scott's arguments back in 1752, the truckhouse concept had admirable theoretical underpinnings in the liberal thought of the 18th century. Commerce, according to both Montesquieu and Hume, was the way to prevent war. Experience taught the British that commerce with the Indians, if it were to achieve the desired effect, must be regulated to prevent the abuses which governors in almost all colonies had reported in the past. By 1764 the Board of Trade itself proposed a massive plan to confine the Indian trade throughout North America to certain frontier posts and to license white traders to ensure their adherence to strict rules of fairness. The Nova Scotia experiment anticipated this imperial policy by four full years, although in its actual implementation, it was far too extended and costly for a small province to manage. Moreover, the first Indian commissary, Halifax merchant Benjamin

---

69 Council Minutes, 21, 22 and 29 February, 10 March, vol. 210, RG1, PANS, pp. 114, 115-16, 117-18. The Maliseet and Passamaquoddy Treaty was drafted and negotiated in French and the draft appears in vol. 258, MG1, PANS, pp. 66-83. Final drafts appear under date of 23 February 1760, in C.O. 217/18. The first Micmac treaties were signed on 10 March with the La Have and Richibucto bands, copies of which are in the PANS, the La Have Treaty in the Andrew Brown Manuscripts, #19071, p. 174. No copy of the treaty with the Shubenacadie-Musquodoboit band remains, although the council minutes report that one was signed on 10 March, and Lawrence reported to the Board of Trade that he had "made a peace on the same terms with the Tribes of Richibuctou, Musquadoboit and La Have, who sent their Chiefs here for that purpose": Council Minutes, 10 March 1760, vol. 210, RG1, PANS; Lawrence to Board of Trade, 11 May 1760, C.O. 217/17, p. 59.

Gerrish, managed the system so that it was the government which lost money while he profited usuriously.[70] By 1762 Gerrish was removed and the number of truckhouses was reduced to three. By 1764 the system itself was replaced by the imperial licensing of private traders, although the Indians themselves, if the Maliseet were representative in this respect, actually preferred the fixed prices of the truckhouses as opposed to the free market arrangement which followed. The Nova Scotia government lost heavily in the truckhouse system; they may also have bought a modicum of good will with the Indians.[71]

Despite an early plan to bring all of the Micmac bands together eventually for a grand reaffirmation of the treaties signed in 1760 and 1761, the Nova Scotia government never managed to do this. But on 25 June 1761 representatives of the Miramichi, Shediac, Pokemouche and Cape Breton bands — the largest gathering of Micmac chiefs to assemble to sign a treaty — gathered in Halifax. Council president Jonathan Belcher, who succeeded Lawrence as the king's representative when he died in 1760, marked the occasion with as impressive a ceremony as he could muster. They gathered in the open air at Belcher's farm on the edge of town, and there were speeches in Micmac and in English. Father Maillard, now devoting the last years of his life to bringing about a peaceful accommodation between the Micmac and the British, served as interpreter. Belcher spoke first and he was awkward; that is, not knowing how to approach the Micmac, he relied on the conventions established over the years between the British and the Iroquois; the rhetoric was Covenant Chain rhetoric even though the Micmac had never been part of the Iroquois alliance: "Protection and Allegiance are fastened together by Links", said Belcher, "if a Link is broken the Chain will be loose. You must preserve this Chain entire on your part by fidelity and Obedience to the Great King George the Third". But through all of the rhetoric, Belcher's explanation of the treaties they signed was also clear: the Micmac were to live now according to the laws of Nova Scotia: "The Laws will be like a great Hedge about your Rights and properties" and "your cause of War and Peace may be the same as ours under one mighty Chief and King, under the same Laws and for the same Rights and Liberties".[72]

When Belcher had finished, the treaties were signed and hatchets were ceremoniously buried. The chief of the Cape Breton band spoke (with Maillard translating from the Micmac). What he said represents the longest single recorded statement by any Indian in the region for the period. How much Maillard may have altered it in translation we can never know, although there were things in it that must have embarrassed Maillard mightily: "My Lord and Father", he addressed Belcher in a most abject way. "We come here . . . to yield ourselves up

70   Council Minutes, 13, 14 and 16 February 1760; Minutes of the House of Assembly, 18 and 19 February 1760, C.O. 217/20; "Plan for the Future Management of Indian Affairs, 1764", C.O. 324/17; Stephen E. Patterson, "Benjamin Gerrish", *DCB*, IV, pp. 290-1.

71   Representations of the Maliseet Indians, Council Minutes, 18 July 1768, vol. 189, RG1, p. 119, PANS; "Remarks on the Indian Commerce carried on by the Government of Nova Scotia in the Year 1760, 1761 and part of 1762", 15 April 1763, C.O. 217/20, pp. 160-5.

72   "Ceremonials at Concluding a Peace", 25 June 1761, C.O. 217/18, pp. 276-84.

to you without requiring any Terms on our part". They were motivated to do this, he said, because of "your Charitable, mercifull and bountifull behaviour to the poor French wandering up and down the Sea Coasts and Woods without any of the necessaries of Life; Certain it is that they, as well as we, must have wretchedly perished unless relieved by your humanity". The British, he went on, were now the masters here, "such has been the will of God, He has given you the Dominion of these vast Countries", and since the British were willing to forget the hostilities "committed by us against you and yours", he was willing to swear on behalf of all his people "that I sincerely comply with all and each of the Articles that you have proposed to be kept inviolably on both Sides". It was a promise without limits, he declared: "As long as the Sun and Moon shall endure, as long as the Earth on which I dwell shall exist in the same State you this day see it, so long will I be your friend and Ally, submitting myself to the Laws of your Government, faithful and obedient to the Crown". What he wanted most for his people, he said, was "your indulging me in the free Exercise of the Religion in which I have been instructed from my Cradle". He had never understood, he said, that the British were also Christians, and he was sorry they had fought, for Christians should not shed the blood of other Christians. But he now buried his hatchet "as a Dead Body that is only fit to become rotten, looking upon it as unlawful and impossible for me to make use of this Instrument of my Hostilities against you".[73] And so he ended. For the Cape Breton and other Micmacs of present-day Nova Scotia, this was their final treaty with the British, the basis upon which they must build their future relationship with the European intruder.

For the Miramichi and Shediac bands who were present, however, and for the Maliseet who had signed earlier, there were to be other treaties in 1778 and 1779, restoring their allegiance after a short-lived lapse during the American War of Independence.[74] But by 1761 the die had been cast: the numbers of British colonists now rapidly increased as New England planters responded to Nova Scotia's call for settlers, and within 20 years, the Loyalist influx would further reduce the native room for manoeuvre. The Maliseet, at least in the short run, proved to be more adept than the Micmac in pursuing their grievances and rights

73 "Ceremonials at Concluding a Peace", C.O. 217/18, pp. 276-84. This account includes the treaty signed with Claude Atonash, chief of the Shediac band, while indicating that treaties of the same "Tenor and Contents" were signed by the chiefs of Miramichi, Pokemouche and Cape Breton. The Miramichi treaty can be found in vol. 165, RG1, PANS, pp. 162-65. Maillard's role was instrumental in bringing the Micmac to accept terms of accommodation, according to a member of the Nova Scotia council: "they had Assurances given to them of the free Exercise of their Religion, without which it is certain they would not have come to any terms": Michael Franklin to Board of Trade, 3 September 1766, C.O. 217/21, pp. 342-7. The account of the ceremonials does not identify the chief of Cape Breton by name, but it was probably Jeannot who was identified as chief in Whitmore to Amherst, 1 December 1759, W.O. 34/17, pp. 46-7. See the discussion of Jeannot in Dennis A. Bartels and Olaf Uwe Janzen, "Micmac Migration to Western Newfoundland", *The Canadian Journal of Native Studies*, X, 1 (1990), pp. 71-96, n. 19.

74 See Alice R. Stewart, "John Allen", *DCB*, V (Toronto, 1983), pp. 15-17; "Déclaration addressée au nom du roi", Webster Collection, NBM; Richard Hughes to Lord George Germain, 12 October 1778 and 16 January 1779, C.O. 217/54; the Treaty with Miramichi, Restigouche, Richibucto and Shediac bands of 26 September 1779, is in C.O. 217/54, pp. 252-7.

through a process of negotiation, but by the time New Brunswick was separated from Nova Scotia in 1784, there was little to choose between them in their concern for native people and in neither an adequate foundation upon which natives might stand to exercise the political power they had enjoyed in the 1750s.

Native power in the 1750s derived from circumstances: relatively speaking their numbers were still meaningful in the conflicts between British and French, and they were able to operate between the two with a measure of independence. In resolving the political questions they faced — to fight or to treat for peace, to rely on customary hunting practices or to integrate into a French and Acadian economy, to remain on traditional territory or to remove to positions of greater security — natives made reasoned choices based on their best efforts to understand their own interests, although they did not all make the same choices. Most decisions involved risks which were largely unavoidable. Moreover, by the 1750s the range of choice had considerably narrowed. The ties of dependency determined that natives would cast their lot, for better or worse, with the fortunes of France. While reliance on French and Acadian arms and provisions seriously compromised native economic self-sufficiency, the arrangement worked for a time and might well have continued to work had the British not found its inherent weakness. On the other hand, the French association posed almost as many problems for natives as the British did. French policy was designed to serve French interests; far from benign in its treatment of natives, France wanted native military help in pursuing its Acadian resettlement scheme and defending French posts. Moreover, their longtime association with the French did not prepare natives for the challenges they met from the British in the 1750s. Natives had reached a cultural accommodation with the French, but this had done nothing to prepare them for the British official preoccupation with signed agreements and with questions of sovereignty, dominion and exclusive ownership.

Despite this handicap, natives met British officials at various times after the founding of Halifax, and their negotiations represented important examples of political interaction. The treaty terms the British offered the Indians over the space of a decade are measures both of early native political clout and the gradual power shift to the British that occurred during the 1750s. In 1749, without experience in drafting treaty arrangements, Halifax officials were happy to stick to terms that had been agreed on years before in Boston. In 1752, now desperate for a way of reaching the Micmac, they were prepared to offer trade opportunities and guarantees respecting hunting and fishing. In 1754 and 1755, while they balked at the specific land claim of some Micmacs, they made clear that the land question was negotiable if it could be done within the framework of a general treaty. Yet by 1760, when the cards were clearly in British hands, it appears that all that was left to negotiation was the price list for goods to be exchanged at truckhouses. After years of war or similar hostilities in which the native people had allied themselves with the losing side, natives had lost their political leverage, and questions of land, hunting and fishing rights and other questions relating to native autonomy, simply were not dealt with. The treaties of 1760 and 1761 were those of a conquering power; they said what the British wanted them to say. Moreover, since the British succeeded in establishing their laws, courts and legal practices in Nova

Scotia, the treaties have ever since been legally interpreted within the imperatives of that tradition.

As in most political interactions, numbers tend to triumph. There are always options open to minorities, however, and native people in Nova Scotia made the best of the ones they had. This is what is remarkable about these decisive years of political interaction. Despite the intensity of the cultural and political pressures they were under by the mid-18th century, native people still retained their independence of thought and action. Their flexibility and adaptability were already clearly in evidence under the French regime, and their responses to the British arrival demonstrated a continuing ability to weigh the options and pursue reasonable strategies in their struggle to survive.

NAOMI GRIFFITHS

Reprinted from Vol. IV, No. 1
(Autumn 1974)

Acadians in Exile: the Experiences of the Acadians in the British Seaports.

The story of how a number of Acadians, held in English sea-ports during the Seven Years' war, were shipped to France in 1763 reveals a great deal about the characteristics of Acadian society and about European perceptions of these characteristics. This particular crossing from England to France was the continuation of a voyage into exile which had begun eight years earlier. Although it involved only part of the total number of Acadians deported in 1755, this episode illustrates clearly many of the ways in which Acadians were more than just a fragment of French society.

At the time of the events which resulted in their dispersal, there were more than nine thousand Acadians within the boundaries of the then British colony of Nova Scotia.[1] Their ancestors had been the first settlers of the lands which today form New Brunswick, Nova Scotia, Prince Edward Island and part of the state of Maine. Their economy was based on a mixture of farming, fishing, hunting and smuggling and flourished sufficiently to support a population expansion that saw the numbers of the Acadians quadruple between 1710 and 1748.[2] By the mid-eighteenth century the Acadians were very definitely a separate people. They were accustomed to living on their lands according to traditions of political action which they had developed during the seventeenth century, when English influence upon their society had been as important as French authority. In 1755 there was once more open warfare between English and French in North America and the Acadian lands were part of the border, claimed by England and coveted by France.

To both sides the Acadians appeared as a possible military force. The French were convinced that Acadians would support their efforts and the English were dubious about Acadian promises of neutrality. The lieutenant

1 Estimates vary. This is based upon a comparison of the numbers reported as exiled and the numbers discovered within the colony in 1764 when they were once more allowed to own land in Nova Scotia. N. Griffiths, *The Acadians: Creation of a People* (Toronto, 1973), p. 66.
2 A.H. Clark, *Acadia: The Geography of Early Nova Scotia to 1760* (Madison, Wisconsin, 1968), p. 201.

governor of Nova Scotia, Colonel Charles Lawrence, and his advisers, decided to nullify this force by expelling it from the battle zone. On the 11th of August, 1755, Charles Lawrence wrote to his fellow governors on the continent to explain that this expulsion entailed the division of the Acadians "among the Colonies where they may be of some use, as most of them are healthy strong people; and as they cannot easily collect themselves together again it will be out of their power to do any mischief and they may become profitable and it is possible, in time, faithful subjects".[3] As summer gave way to fall, the transports left the shores of Nova Scotia and with them went the Acadian people bound for one or other of the thirteen colonies. The stated object of this exercise, the fragmentation of Acadian strength, was abundantly achieved. Eight years later the Acadians were to be found, a divided people, scattered from the shores of the Saint Lawrence to the Gulf of Mexico, and in the ports of England and France. Barely a thousand remained within Nova Scotia by the end of 1763.

The particular exiles who were in England in that same year had arrived there in 1756 by way of Virginia. In his plans for the redistribution of the Acadians Lawrence worked on the principle of act first, explain later; as a result there had been no prior consultation with his fellow colonial administrators. The circular, which contained Lawrence's justification of his action on grounds of military necessity, was sent to the governors on the same ships that carried the Acadians into exile. As the Acadians were landed, from Massachusetts to Georgia, each colony coped as best it might. Whether the exiles were in Massachusetts or further south, the problems they posed for the colonial authorities were fundamentally the same and foreshadowed those with which the metropolitan authorities were to be confronted. How were the immediate physical needs of the Acadians to be met? Were they to be treated as prisoners of war? How was their claim to be considered as British subjects to be met?

Varying answers were given by the colonial administrations. Massachusetts, for example, on the 16th of November, 1755, passed an act to cope with "divers of the Inhabitants and Familys in [sic] Nova Scotia". It placed the Acadians in the hands of the Justices of the Peace and Overseers of the Poor "to deal with them as by Law they would have been empowered to do were they inhabitants of the Province".[4] The lead given by the Commonwealth was followed, to a greater or lesser degree, by Pennsylvania, Connecticut and Maryland. But Virginia adopted a more complex method of dealing with these unexpected arrivals. On the 15th of November, 1755, Robert Dinwiddie, governor of that colony, wrote to the Board of Trade to report that more

3 Circular from Lawrence to the Governors on the Continent, Halifax, 11 August 1755, printed in the *Report of the Public Archives of Canada*, 1905, II, App. B, pp. 15-16.
4 Printed in *Acts and Resolves Public and Private of the Province of Massachusetts Bay*, Vol. III (Boston 1878), p. 951.

than a thousand of the French Neutrals from Nova Scotia had arrived and that as they "have refus'd to swear Allegiance to His Majesty, so we can have but a very poor Prospect of their being either good Subjects or useful People".[5] Two days later, he wrote to Sir Thomas Robinson, the Secretary of the Board, that "it is very disagreeable to the People to have imported to rest among us a No. of French People, w'n many of y't Nat'n joined with Ind's are now muder'g and scalp'g our Frontier Settlers".[6] The Acadians were French, they were Catholics, and Dinwiddie considered them "intestine Enemies":[7] Nevertheless, he was quickly brought to admit that he was confronted with something more than a number of enemy captives. This becomes clear in letters written by him on November 24th, 1755. After complaining that the Council were much against the Acadians and that a "great Drought" meant that he was short of Troops, Dinwiddie summarized a conversation he had had with the Acadians. His inquiries as to whether they would settle down as peaceable subjects according to the laws of the colony had brought the Acadian reply that they had already sworn allegiance to his Majesty and would not swear it again; that they had forfeited their rights through the faults of others; and that they desired the free exercise of their religion.[8] In his second letter Dinwiddie declared that the Acadians were "to be maintain'd till next Spring, w'n they shall have lands assigned to settle on".[9] In fact, next spring the Acadians were not assigned lands but put on board ships, and, at the cost of £5,000, sent to Britain.[10] If Lawrence could solve the problem of Acadian loyalty in Nova Scotia by re-locating the Acadians, Virginia, in a similar situation, could do likewise.

Colonel Lawrence had not seen fit to warn Virginia of his plans, and the British were likewise not notified in advance of this new deportation. News of Dinwiddie's action first came to the attention of British authorities via a firm of Bristol merchants, Messrs. Lidderdale Harmer and Farrell, who were advised by one of their ships returning from Virginia that they could expect the imminent arrival of another of their ships with a large number of "Neutral French on board".[11] On the 14th of June, 1756, these merchants wrote to the Secretary of State, Charles James Fox, "praying his orders for the disposal" of these people and were directed on the 18th of June to apply

5 Printed in R. Brooks, ed., *Dinwiddie Papers* (Richmond, Virginia Historical Collections, 1899), II, pp. 269-72.
6 17 November 1755, *ibid.*, p. 268.
7 Dinwiddie to Shirley, 28 April 1756, *ibid.*, pp. 394.
8 24 November 1755, *ibid.*, p. 284.
9 *Ibid.*, p. 281.
10 Dinwiddie to Dobbs, 11 June 1756, *ibid.*, pp. 442-443.
11 L.G. and H.T. to Hon. John Cleveland, 24 November 1756, Medical Board Out-Letters, Admiralty 98/5, Public Record Office, London. This letter is a summary of the events that occurred when the Acadians arrived in England made by clerks in the Medical Board, which at this time was part of the Sick and Hurt Board of the Admiralty.

to the Medical Department of the Sick and Hurt Board of the Admiralty, the authority generally responsible for prisoners of war in England, who, it was stated, would have received in the interim orders "to take care of the said Neutrals".[12] On the 22nd of June there was a meeting of this body with the Lords Commissioners of the Admiralty, and one of its members, Mr. Guiguer, set out that same night for Bristol. His instructions were "to make Provision for, and to cause them [the Neutral French] to be paid sixpence per day for their Subsistence, and to give to each what may be reasonable for Lodging or to provide the same as shall appear most for the service".[13] By the time Mr. Guiguer reached Bristol, the *Virginia Packet* with 289 Acadians aboard was already there.[14] As a result of his actions, they were landed on the 24th of June and housed in "Warehouses".[15] By the end of the month Falmouth had reported the arrival of 220 French Neutrals,[16] and Liverpool, 242.[17] Finally, in the first week of July, there was a report from Southampton of the arrival of 293 French neutrals.[18] Thus as summer opened families of Leblancs and Landrys, Boudraults and Melansons, born and bred in Nova Scotia, whose ancestors had first settled there in the seventeenth century, set about surviving internment in eighteenth-century England.

The Acadians were to remain in England for nearly seven years, but the most severe test of their capacity for survival was to come that first summer. An epidemic of small-pox attacked all four groups in the month of July, 1756. By the 9th of August the Medical Department computed that upwards of two hundred were ill.[19] So great was the death toll, removing approximately a quarter of their number,[20] that the Medical Department was called upon to defend its treatment of the Acadians. Rumour of the disaster had reached France and Louis XV's government protested to Fox that the Acadians had been inadequately housed and inhumanely neglected.[21] The Medical Department rebutted the charges vigorously, calling them "False, Indecent and Absurd".[22] They contended that the mortality suffered by the Neutrals, "great as it has been, really had not exceeded the common Computation at large

---

12 *Ibid.*
13 J.M. and J.B. to John Cleveland, 28 June 1756, *ibid.*
14 Minutes of the Medical Board, 21 June 1756, Admiralty 19/30.
15 J.M. and J.B. to John Cleveland, 28 June 1756, Admiralty 98/5.
16 J.M. and J.B. to John Cleveland, 23 June 1756, *ibid.*
17 Minutes of the Medical Board, 29 June 1956, Admiralty, 99/30.
18 *Ibid.*, July 1756.
19 J.M. and J.B. to John Cleveland, 9 August 1956, Admiralty 98/5.
20 The numbers reported as landed in 1756 were: Southampton 293; Bristol 289; Liverpool 242; Falmouth 250; total 1054. Numbers for these same towns in 1762 were: Southampton 220; Bristol 152; Liverpool 215; Falmouth 153; total 741. Of these last 149 were less than seven years old. L.G. and J.B. to John Cleveland, 23 November 1762, Admiralty 93/9.
21 J.B. and J.J. to John Cleveland, 17 September 1956, Admiralty 98/5.
22 J.B. and J.H. to John Cleveland, 30 September 1756, *ibid.*

so much as might reasonably have been expected". The root cause of the severity of the epidemic lay in the "Circumstances . . . of the People, their long Voyage, their Change of Climate, their Habits of Body, their other disorders and their irregularity and Obstinacy". They went on to affirm that "not only the Laws of nations and the principles of Justice have been Strictly Observed but that even the most imperfect right of Humanity have been scrupulously complyed with", and that "such Representations and Complaints" as had been made by the French were "very Dishonourable to the Nation and if causelessly made, matter ought to be set in a just light to Foreign States, to remove as much as possible the prejudices conceived upon the spreading such Complaints".[23]

Once past the small-pox disaster, the Acadians made the best of their situation. As a community they were extraordinarily well equipped to survive in exile. By 1755 there had been more than a hundred and fifty years of separate Acadian existence. Their history provided them with a traditional pattern of life to remember, something that could be recalled during their wanderings as a reality to be fought for and recovered. During the seventeenth century their political fate, to be ruled at times by France and at times by England, had encouraged Acadian settlers to have a strong sense of identification with their own communities. Their sense of loyalty to any particular European power was a matter of enthusiasms tempered by common sense. At no time did the majority of the Acadian community rise in support of either France or England, and, although the official control of their lands changed hands, the lands remained Acadian. By the middle of the eighteenth century Acadia was their natural homeland, a country created along the shores of the Bay of Fundy, spreading farms and settlements not only north and west but along the Atlantic coast northeast of the Chignecto isthmus. Comparatively isolated from the main stream of European settlement in North America, the Acadians had developed their own patterns of political action and government. Their expulsion did not expunge this country from their minds, but by depriving them of it made the Acadians remember it with desperate longing. Indeed, it was the remembrance of things past that was to enable the Acadians to resist the spiritual fragmentation which is frequently the lot of deported communities.

To the force of such a vision the Acadians added another strength: a powerful family structure. Large families connected to each other by intermarriage formed the basis of Acadian demography. Not only was each village a group of related families, but kinship lines linked the various settlements with one another[24] When sent into exile each group of Acadians was more than an assembly of individuals or of nuclear families concerned for a very

23 J.B. and J.H. to John Cleveland, 17 September 1756, *ibid.*
24 Griffiths, *The Acadians*, p. 18; G. Massignon, *Les Parlers français d'Acadie* (Paris, 1955), I, pp. 42-75.

small circle of people; it was an assembly of relatives. The traditions of the Acadian community had formed a social structure which automatically looked after weaker brethren. A lively interest on the part of every individual in the affairs of everyone else was an Acadian norm. Their emotions embraced the generations. Exile both tore at the heart of Acadian families and revealed the tenacity of Acadian emotions. Daniel Leblanc died in Philadelphia in 1756, protesting to the end his loyalty to the British and weeping because there were only sixteen of his descendants at his bedside instead of the gathering of sixteen children and a hundred and two grand-children to whom he wished to say good-bye.[25] Later records of Acadian experiences during the twenty-five years they remained in France, show both an extraordinary knowledge of where sisters, parents and other relatives were and a continuing concern for their welfare.[26] Although divided into widely separated groups, the Acadians confronted their exile as a community.

Further, this community had traditions of political action which were well suited to battle for Acadian interests in exile. The great American historian, J.B. Brebner, pointed the way to understanding Acadian history when he wrote that "There were in effect, two Acadies, each important in its own way. The one was the Acadie of the international conflict, the other the land settled and developed by the Acadians".[27] The Acadians not only managed the affairs of their villages with far less reference to outside authorities than might be imagined, but also learned to confront outside officialdom with a semblance of unity. These traditions originated in the seventeenth century when garrison and officials, the transient signs of European metropolitan government, were often located a considerable distance from the settlements. During British rule of the Acadians between 1710 and 1755 a number of Acadians acted as representatives of their villages, travelling to another locality to present the views of their communities about political matters. The Acadians took with them into exile habits of political organization which made them capable of reacting to what was happening to them instead of merely being a number of passive victims. They were accustomed to organizing their communities to present a particular point and to argue this viewpoint with officials representing more powerful authorities.

If the Acadians had strengths within their community which would help them to survive in exile, occasionally the very terms of that exile contributed to their needs. The Acadian claim to be British, to be "subjects of the King",[28]

25 Petition to the King of Great Britain, c. 1760, printed in P.H. Smith, *Acadia: A Lost Chapter in American History* (Boston, 1884), p. 236.
26 Commentary in miscellaneous papers, dated 1765, IF 2158, Archives Départementales [hereafter AD], Ille et Vilaine. None of the Acadian material in France has been catalogued. This particular collection is made up of eighteenth-century notes, brought together by the commissioners of the marine who were responsible for the Acadians.
27 J.B. Brebner, *New England's Outpost* (New York, 1927), p. 45.
28 J.M. and J.B. to John Cleveland, 28 June 1756, Admiralty 98/5.

was accepted by the authorities. As a result, they were provided with quarters that militated against social fragmentation, and with a reasonable standard of living. Whether established in Liverpool, Bristol, Southampton, or Penryn, the Acadians were kept together. In Liverpool a section of the town was set aside for them.[29] In Bristol warehouses were transformed for their use.[30] Whatever the pattern, the Acadians were grouped in communities of between 150 and 250 persons, large enough to give the individual some point of reference in an alien land. The separation of these communities from the surrounding population was further marked by regulations governing the Acadians' right to work and by the government pensions provided for them. The Admiralty generally ruled that "all the Neutrals were restrained from working to prevent the Clamor of the labouring People in the towns where they resided".[31] This embargo was by no means rigidly enforced, especially in Penryn and Southampton,[32] but it was sufficient to mark out the Acadians as a group from the working world that surrounded them.

Even more than this regulation, the Admiralty pension set them apart from the working people in the neighbourhood. The allowance which was given to them was sixpence per day per adult and threepence a day for those under seven years of age, for a total of £ 9.2.6 per annum per adult and £ 4.4.3. per annum per child.[33] A family of six, a size that was median for these communities in 1763,[34] received £ 36.10.0 per annum, considerably more than the average British labourer earned.[35] Further, this allowance was for subsistance; shelter, some clothing and other necessities were also provided.[36] While the standard of living was well below that experienced by the exiles before 1755, it did not affect seriously the Acadian birth-rate.[37] Infant mortality controlled the growth of the community until the end of 1757, but after that year the children born lived. An Admiralty survey made of the communities in November 1762 revealed a population with a quarter of its number

29 Nivernois à Prasline, Londres 17 fevrier, 1763, Archives des Affaires Etrangères [hereafter AAE], correspondence d'Angleterre, 449, f. 345, Archives Nationales.

30 J.M. and J.B. to John Cleveland, 28 June 1756, Admiralty 98/5.

31 J.M., J.B. and H.G. to John Cleveland, 21 May 1761, Admiralty 98/8.

32 L.G., J.B. and H.G. to John Cleveland, 19 July 1758, Admiralty 98/7.

33 J.M. and J.B. to John Cleveland, 28 June 1756, Admiralty 98/5; Minutes of the Medical Board, 6 and 7 July 1756, Admiralty 99/30.

34 Shipping lists of Acadian embarked for France, 1763, printed in M.P. and N.G. Reider, *The Acadians in France* (Louisiana, 1972), pp. 86-121.

35 Asa Briggs, *How they lived* (Oxford, 1969), III, p. 143. In the north of England in Cumberland, a housekeeper cook earned £5 per year; the Acadian allowance was £ 9. 7s 6d. See E. Hughes, *North Country Life in the Eighteenth Century* (London, 1865), II, p. 116.

36 L.G., J.M., J.B. and H.T. to John Cleveland, 8 February 1757, Admiralty 98/6.

37 For the effect of nutrition on fertility, see P. Goubert, *Cent Mille Provinciaux au XVII*e *siècle: Beauvais et Beauvais de 1600 à 1700* (Paris, 1968), pp. 49-106.

aged less than seven.[38] While such figures hint at the appalling impact of the small-pox epidemic of 1756, they also indicate the vitality of the Acadian communities.

This vitality showed itself unmistakably when in 1763 an enquiry was made of the Acadians as to "what manner they would chuse to be disposed of" when hostilities ceased. The summary of the replies from the Neutral French at Bristol made by the Admiralty reads as follows:

1 . . . . We hope We shall be sent into Our own Countries and that our Effects etc., which We have been dispossessed of (not withstanding the faithful neutrality which We have always observed) will be restored to Us.
2 . . . . If the first Article is allowed Us, it draws with it the free exercise of our Religion, which We shall not think we enjoy if the Priests that may be permitted to instruct Us are not sent by way of France.
3 We humbly beg His Majesty will grant Us all our Ancient Rights and Privileges which We enjoyed before, obediently consenting to pay the customary duties of the Country, and as proof of our integrity we will bind ourselves by an Oath of fidelity and neutrality, not to bear Arms against any warlike Nation whatsoever.
4 After His Majesty may have been pleased to indemnify us for our losses. We hope from his Goodness that he will please to provide Us with the necessary Provisions.
5 We earnestly desire that in case any fault would be laid to our Charge or that the Commander should complain of Us to the Court, that we may be permitted to chuse among us some persons whom We may depute to justify Us before those who are to judge.
6 If we could be exempted from having any fort among our habitations We should look upon that as an essential Point of happiness.
7 If another War should happen, We desire, in case we should be forced to declare Ourselves, that we may be permitted to retire where we may think proper.

The Admiralty noted that "the Neutrals at Southampton had at Liverpool desire to be on the same footing as those at Bristol", but that those at Penyrn asked for time to form their address.[39] This summary concludes with the remark that "A letter from Liverpool from some of the Neutral French, but which is not signed, desires that they may be under the French Government again, and that they may have what has been taken from them returned again if possible". After eight years in exile the majority of the Acadian communities asserted their right to be considered a neutral people. They demanded compensation for the troubles they had endured and asked that the provision

38 L.G. and J.B. to John Cleveland, 23 November 1762, Admiralty 98/9.
39 L.G. and J.B. to John Cleveland, 4 January 1763, *ibid.*

for their future should be a restoration of their past, changed only to ensure that no new deportation could trouble their lives.

Their actual fate, however, was to be closer to the desires expressed in the unsigned letter from Liverpool than to the vision outlined with such care by the Acadians of Bristol. This letter was sent by some Liverpool Acadians in September 1762 to one of the chief negotiators of the Peace of Paris, Louis Jules Barbon Mancini Mazarini, duc de Nivernois, Grandee of Spain, Knight of the King, Peer of France, who had recently arrived in London.[40] Nivernois was something very close to a "career diplomat", previously posted in Rome and Berlin, and was well known at Court, where he had played in Voltaire's *Enfant Prodigue* with Madame de Pompadour.[41] It is difficult to determine exactly what he knew about the Acadians when he received this letter. Nivernois' instructions had emphasized "the importance of hastening the signature of the preliminaries in order to ensure the cessation of hostilities and the conclusion of peace".[42] Since such preliminaries included Anglo-French disputes over most of the globe, it was obviously a task which would relegate the Acadians to a side-line. Nonetheless, Nivernois would be aware of Nova Scotia as a result of the negotiations of Aix-la-Chapelle in 1748, when the precise boundaries of the colony had raised much debate.[43] Further, over the last four years Acadians had landed in France itself, at Boulogne, Brest, Cherbourg and St. Malo in 1758; at Boulogne, Dunkerque and St. Malo in 1759; Cherbourg in 1760; and at Rochefort in 1761.[44]

Whatever Nivernois' knowledge of Acadian matters prior to September 1762, his reaction to the letter he received from Liverpool was a memoir to his superiors, in which he pointed out how valuable such subjects would be, if re-established in the French colonies.[45] Nivernois viewed the Acadian people at this time as unquestioningly loyal to France. Nor did he come to consider the Acadian people in any very different light during the months ahead. Indeed, the attitude of most of the French officials who dealt with the Acadians before the mid-1760's was based far more on French vision than on Acadian realities. It was a vision born from a marriage of political aim and philosophical belief. The surrender of "Acadie or Nova Scotia" by the terms of the Treaty of Utrecht, 1713, was never considered by the French

40 The report is published in the Report of the Public Archives of Canada, 1905, II, App. G, p. 150 *et seq.*
41 Jean Orieux, *Voltaire ou la Royauté de l'Esprit* (Paris, 1966), p. 325.
42 Z.E. Rashed, *The Peace of Paris*, 1763 (London, 1951), p. 165.
43 There had been a number of publications since then on the subject, among them M.F. Pidanzet de Mairobert's *Lettres sur les Véritables limites des possessions Anglaises et Françaises en Amérique* (Paris, 1755) and J.N. Moreau's *Mémoire contenant le précis des Faits, avec leurs Pièces Justicatives sur les limites d'Acadie* (Paris, 1756).
44 See the surveys of Acadians landing in France collected in IF. 2169, AD, Ille et Vilaine.
45 Nivernois à Etienne Francois, Duc de Choiseul, October 1762, cited in O.W. Winzerling, *Acadian Odyssey* (Louisiana, 1955), p. 26.

government officials as the final and immutable political settlement of these lands and the Acadians were looked upon by the French authorities as a people who, very probably, would one day again be ruled by France. The transmutation of Acadian loyalties was never considered, for the French saw in the existence of a common language and a common religion the foundation of nationality.[46] Though not the unique property of eighteenth-century French government officials, this belief was one which those who ruled France in the wake of Louis XIV held almost unquestioned. The unification of Breton peasant and Marseill es fisherman, Bordeaux trader and Champagne vinter, into subjects of France had led the administrators of the country to consider mere affection for land a very poor motivating force when placed besides the claims of tongue and faith. One French official, who had had some experience of the Acadians in the 1760's, asserted that their misfortunes arose from their "attachment à leur anciennes terres".[47] It was his view that such an attachment should be sacrificed to the wider claims of loyalty owed to the very embodiment of the French language and the Catholic religion, the French state. Thus, Nivernois was merely following the path taken by earlier French officials in their dealings with Acadians when he considered these newly discovered exiles solely as loyal Frenchmen, whom it was the duty of the King of France to rescue.

Such a path allowed a great deal about the Acadian people to go unperceived. Overemphasis of the fact that the first settlers to be established as Acadians were French, obscured the equally important evidence that the community, once established, had continuing and important contact with New England. The dominance of settlers of French descent hid the important evidence that the community, once established, had continuing and important contact with New England. The dominance of settlers of French descent hid the important influence of English, Irish and Scots families in the community.[48] The unbroken maintenance of French claims to "Acadie or Nova Scotia" blocked any clear view of the impact on the colony of English rule from 1654 to 1670. The overwhelming evidence that English administrators placed little or no reliance upon Acadian loyalty between 1710 and 1755 covered up the equally over-whelming evidence that the Acadian people, as a whole, never fought for France during this period. Nor was there any consideration of the possibility that any mark would have been made on the Acadian community by more than forty years of British rule. Yet this was an

46 Later when French officials had had direct experience of dealing with the Acadians, they modified their views. The records on the Acadian sojourn in France are voluminous. The most important collections are in the provincial archives of Morbihan (Vannes), Ille et Vilaine (Rennes), Loire Atlantique (Nantes), Charente-Maritime (LaRochelle), Vienne (Poitiers), and the Municipal Archives in Bordeaux.
47 La Galissonière au Evêque, Paris, 19 mai 1752, G.111.106, Archives de l'Archevêque de Québec.
48 Griffiths, *The Acadians*, chs. I and II, *passim.*

interval sufficient to ensure that the vast majority of the Acadians could have had little, if any, personal experience of French suzerainty.

Thus there was no French tradition of considering the Acadians as being a distinct entity or of having any kind of community identity separate from that of France and it is not surprising that in all his actions concerning them Nivernois always considered Acadians as basically and essentially French. His subsequent reports to the French government on Acadian matters contain the same opinions about Acadian political and religious loyalties that he expressed in his original memoir written in October 1762. He followed up this memoir by despatching his Secretary, de la Rochette, to Liverpool to make a first-hand report on the Acadian situation. Rochette not only went to Liverpool, on December 26th, 1762, but in the following weeks visited Southampton, Falmouth (Penryn) and Bristol.[49] On the 17th of February, 1763, Nivernois sent an account of his Secretary's work to France in the form of a lengthy report on the Acadian situation. The report presents Acadian history as the simple annals of the heroic peasant. After the Treaty of Utrecht, it is stated, the Acadians kept not only "leur eglises et leurs pretres" but also "l'attachement le plus profond et le plus tenace pour la France".[50] They practised their religion with a profound and unshakeable devotion. When faced with a demand by the English for an oath which "attaquoit leur religion", rather than betray their beliefs, the Acadians accepted exile.

From the general considerations the Report moves to discuss the realities of the Acadian position in England in 1763. The situation in Liverpool is first analysed. Until the question of peace had arisen the Acadians had been living unmolested, "peu inquites",[51] in a section of the town assigned to them, with Liverpool itself the limits of their prison. But the immediate effect for the Acadians of the news of the probably ending of the hostilities was an attempt by the British commissioner, Langton, whose charge they were, to persuade them to return to Nova Scotia as loyal British subjects. This man had stooped so low as to employ a Scots priest to further his designs, promising this unhappy creature his own parishes in Acadie in exchange for "des sermons scandaleux" in favour of Langton's designs.[52] The report comments that "54, parmi lesquels sont presque tous 'les vieillards' " accepted this offer, but they refused to commit the decision to paper and had since all written to Nivernois begging for his protection. The remainder, "170 personnes, faisant 38 famillies", were in despair and might also have succumbed, had not an alternative plan been proposed by a Frenchman, a pilot born at Le Havre and awaiting ransom at Liverpool, who suggested that a letter be

49 Nivernois à Praslin, Londres, 17 février 1763, AAE, Correspondance d'Angleterre, 449, f.345.
50 *Ibid.*, f.343.
51 *Ibid.*, f.346.
52 *Ibid.*, f.346 *verso*.

written to Nivernois. An Irishman, married to an Acadian, asking for his recompense to be allowed to remain with the Acadians, wherever Fortune
should lead them, took the letter to London.[53] The report denies the importance of the Acadian longing for their former lands and implies that Acadians could only be brought to return to their homeland by British trickery.
To emphasize this, the statistical comparison of the number in the group
who briefly wavered in their allegiance to France with the number that remained unswerving in their loyalty is enumerated differently; those who fell
victim to British traps are counted as individuals, but those who did not are
counted as men whose actions would also commit their families. No comment
is made on the fact that those who worked so determinedly for the interests
of French in Liverpool were not themselves of Acadian birth but two people
who had never seen Nova Scotia.

Rochette's experience in Southampton are recounted with the same emphasis. The lack of warmth with which he was welcomed is attributed to
Acadian suspicion that he might be an English spy, sent to trick them. Therefore, their very love for France was "l'unique motif de leur defiance".[54] It
is also suggested that Southampton was close enough to London to expose
the Acadians to a positive barrage of blandishments: "Le général Mordaunt
et même en ce dernier lieu le duc d'York n'avoient pas cru au dessous d'eux
de les solliciter de renoncer à la France".[55] The Acadians of Falmouth (Penryn) proved a little more difficult to tailor into the required pattern. Although
there had been some hitch in the payment of their allowance from the government and some of the Acadians were much in debt in this town, this group
had made more progress than their brethren elsewhere towards integration
with the people who surrounded them.[56] They had the freedom of the neighbourhood and were not confined to any special part of the town for their
living quarters, while the young people were apprenticed to English work-
men and had from this "contracte des inclinations peu francoises".[57] The
report admits that the good-will of these Acadians could not really be trusted
but makes no attempt to assess the possible importance of this evidence.
Instead, this section of the document concludes with a very cursory survey
of the situation in Bristol, where 180 Acadians "s'abandonnent entièrement
à la protection du Roy". The whole problem of the French preconceptions
of Acadian characteristics is highlighted by this summary treatment of the
Acadians in Bristol, for these were the same people who had recently an-

53 *Ibid.,* f.347.
54 *Ibid.*
55 *Ibid.,* f.347 *verso.*
56 A local diarist considered that "During their abode here by their industry and civil deport-
ment they have gained the esteem of all". See Felix Farley's Bristol Journal, cited in D. Vintner,
"The Acadian Exiles in England 1756-1763", *Dalhousie Review,* 36 (1967), p. 352.
57 Nivernois à Praslin, 17 fevrier 1763, AAE, Correspondance d'Angleterre, 449, f.348 *verso.*

swered the British Admiralty most trenchantly when questioned about their wishes for their future.

The Report contains an even greater volume of evidence of French misunderstanding of the Acadian identity. It notes that "il y a une defiance generale qui prevaut plus ou moins chez tous les Acadiens", but explanations are quickly offered for this attitude. The Acadians resident in England were aware that inadequate treatment had been accorded their kin who had already arrived in France and they had heard rumours that France intended to send them to her territories in the Caribbean, an idea which repelled them. Due basically, it is suggested, to the influence among the Acadians of priests, men who "sont Anglais ou Ecossais et que l'on a flatté de l'esperance de devenir leurs curés en Acadie", the Acadians were constantly thinking of their former lands: "Ils se flattent toujours de retourner en Acadie et d'y jouir du libre exercice de leur religion sous la protection du Roy. Ceux même qui sont en France, en Boulogne, St. Malo et Rochefort persistent dans cette opinion et l'ont même écrit aux Acadiens en Angleterre". Moreover, "ils craignent que le Roy n'abandonne leurs frères dispersés dans les colonies angloises du continent septentrional de l'Amerique".[58]

At no stage does the Report consider this evidence in detail. There is no comment made on the quite extraordinary level of communication which the widely scattered Acadians had maintained between themselves since their dispersal. Nothing is inferred from the evidence that a group of supposedly destitute refugees could be well-informed about policies, born in another country, affecting their future. Nor is there any discussion of the probable future behaviour of subjects who are prepared, while supposedly existing in deplorable circumstances, to query the plans of well-wishers. The statement of Acadian wishes, explicit though it is, is introduced with a verb that indicates self-deception: such wishes were in the eyes of French officials, unrealistic and therefore not worthy of serious consideration.

Instead of indulging in a commentary on the possible import of this evidence of Acadian complexity, the Report turns to a discussion of the problems of the Acadian people as a whole, the "plus de 10,000 [gens] qui meurent de faim".[59] Their characteristics are multiplied but the result is still a stereotype. French, Catholic, to these attributes are added the virtues of a pastoral people, and the Acadians become a simple people, who had led an existence far removed from the vanities and corruptions of Europe. Hard workers, "tous laboureurs ou percheurs", accustomed to the rigors of "un climat très rude" and "connoissent très peu de maladies",[60] the Acadian community is made up of individuals who are industrious, "malheureux et respect-

58 *Ibid.*
59 *Ibid.*, f.349.
60 *Ibid.*, f.349 *verso*.

able".[61] It was obviously both politic and just to encourage such paragons.

The report concludes by calling for the gathering up of the majority of Acadians, from wherever they were to be discovered, and their establishment within the dominion of the King of France, preferably in Brittany, preferably on the estates of Nivernois, and definitely with the aid of a considerable amount of government money. It is interesting to note that it proposes that the resettlement should imitate "la pratique constamment suivie des Anglois loursqu'il établissent des colonies", the settlement of the Acadians in villages of a hundred families, with lands distributed to them in lots, a pattern of settlement which the Acadians had never known. The support for each family should encompass "des vivres pour la première année et de la semence pour la second, des instruments de labourage et des instruments et matériaux à bâtir". Animals were also to be distributed and families to have their choice of a cow, or a mare, or two sows, or five sheep, with a stallion and a bull the common property of each village. Finally, these establishments should be "exempte de toutes impositions pendant 50 ans". Such proposals might seem an expensive solution to the problem of the Acadians but, the Report argues, it would pay considerable dividends in future years, for the Acadians, so treated, would develop into ideal French citizens.[62]

The immediate reaction of the French government to this scheme was favourable. Choiseul agreed to the settlement of at least some of the Acadians on the island owned by Nivernois off the coast of Brittany.[63] Even the revelation of the Acadian debts, approximately 14,000 livres, did not dampen this first enthusiasm, partly due to the fact that Nivernois claimed that just under half the sum could be paid by the Acadians themselves, taxing the group as a whole for the benefit of the indigent.[64] On the 6th of April 1763, Nivernois was informed that the King would advance the monies to clear this hurdle and that funds were immediately available to transport the Acadians to France. He was urged to spare no effort in the work of removing the Acadians.[65]

This task of moving the Acadians to France was placed in the hands of Nivernois' secretary, Rochette. He was informed that plans had been made by Choiseul for ships to go to Falmouth, Liverpool and Southampton and to return with the Acadians to St. Malo and Morlaix.[66] Writing from Bristol in the middle of May, 1763, Rochette posed a problem which, although he found the solution swiftly enough for himself, was to bedevil French

---

61 *Ibid.*, f.352.

62 *Ibid.*,

63 Duc de Praslin au duc le Nivernois, Versailles, 1 mars 1762, AAE, Correspondance d'Angleterre, 450, F.7 *verso*.

64 Nivernois à Praslin, 14 mars 1762, *ibid.*, f.83.

65 Choiseul à Nivernois, 6 avril 1763, *ibid.*, f.205 *verso*.

66 *Ibid.*

authorities considerably in the near future. It was the problem of who should be considered an Acadian, and in particular whether those whose North American homes had been Ile St. Jean were included in the term. Rochette decided affirmatively, adding forty more passengers to his lists, because, as he explained, "ils ont tous été réclaimés par les Acadiens euxmêmes".[67] As France attempted to assimilate her new citizens, the distinction between Acadian and Canadian was to prove a matter of importance, not merely in the distribution of pensions but also in the amount of liberty of action granted to the newcomers. On the whole, it was more advantageous to be considered Acadian than Canadian, for it meant that one would be the recipient of considerable government concern, and concerted efforts for resettlement. In 1763 it was even better to be an Acadian exile than a French officer, prisoner of war in England. On arrival at Southampton, Rochette wrote that he embarked a number of the latter on the ship provided for the Acadians, for their condition stirred his compassion.[68]

Rochette made considerable efforts to see that the sea passage would be as comfortable as possible. His major problem was the large number of women and children, who needed mattresses and shelter on board, and "plus de bagages à eux seuls que quatre régiments de dragons". He provisioned the ship with "pain blanc, de veau, d'oeufs, de beurre, et de lait pour l'usage de ces malades et des enfans", but left the distribution of these provisions in the hands of two of the older Acadians. He could not restrain himself from one final comment. "Si ces bonnes gens", he wrote, "n'avoient pas une quantité prodigieuse de *butin* (c'est le mot dont ils se servent à l'imitation des sauvages leurs anciens viosins et amis pour désigner leurs effets en général) ils auroient été plus à leur aise, mais ce butin remplit presque toute la calle et une grande partie de l'entrepont".[69] The next Acadians to be transported were those of Penryn, the group that Rochette had already noted as being more adapted to English ways than he considered fit. His first problem was that the town itself was in the midst of celebrating Whit Sunday with "une exactitude singulière". "Toute l'honorable corporation de Penryn", he wrote, "n'a pas cessé durant trois jours d'être yvre de cidre et d'eau-de-vie de Nantes". Business was impossible for a full day because men and women alike were engaged in watching the "combat du taureau". When he did manage to begin assembling the Acadians for their journey to Falmouth, Rochette found his work exasperating. He commented:

> Ils sone les plus opulens de les plus civilés de toute la bande, ils sont aussi les plus entêtée et les moins candides et ils m'ont donné plus de mal que je ne croyais. Cependant avec quilques grosses paroles, j'en suis venu à

67 Rochette à d'Eon, Bristol 14 mai 1762, AAE, Correspondance d'Angleterre, supp. 13, f.60.
68 Rochette à d'Eon, Southampton, 18 mai 1763, AAE, Correspondance d'Angleterre, supp. 13, f.72.
69 *Ibid.*

bout. Il y en a une leur gousset, ceux-là auroient traité volontiers d'argents dans compagnon Mr. le commissaire parce qu'il n'a point de montre. Ils n'en pourtant rien fait, grâces au ton despotique que j'ai pris. Au demarrant tout est bien, et ils sont regrettés genéralement . . . .[70]

So the Acadians from Penryn set out on further travels. Behind them they left those who had fallen to small-pox; more than sixty are named in the church register of Saint Gluvias for 1756.[71] Rochette, having parted with the Acadians from Penryn, concluded his work by supervising the Liverpool Acadians on board 'L'Esturgeon' on the 7th June.[72] Some five or six of the young men jumped ship at the last moment, but by the end of the second week in June the French embassy in London could report that the transportation of the Acadians from the British sea-ports to destinations on the French Atlantic coast had been completed.[73]

Writing to Choiseul on June 13th, 1763, another member of Nivernoi s' staff, d'Eon drew yet one more picture of the Acadian character:

Plusiers de nos prisonniers françois se sont laissés,éblouir par les promesses des Anglois et one marqué en ce point beaucoup moins de fidelité à la France et de désir de vengeance que les malheureaux Acadiens qui viennent de s'embarquer pour la France après avoir étonné toute l'Angleterre par leur probité, leurs moeurs et leur attachment inviolable à la misere effrainte qu'ils ont supportée jusqu'à la fin avec une courage heroique que tous les devraient avoir encore, s'ils eussent conse vé leurs moeurs et pas connu le luxe.[74]

But events were to show that a common language and a common religion did not by themselves render the Acadians French, nor did French generosity and Acadian gratitude dissolve the distinctiveness of this tiny people, and cause them to melt imperceptibly into the great mass of French people. In part this was due to the haphazard and dilatory way in which the French plans for Acadian re-settlement were actually put into practise. No major attempt to carry out their establishment in villages, on the lines proposed originally, took place before 1766-1767, when a concerted effort was made by a number

70 Rochette à d'Eon, Penryn, 26 mai 1753, AAE, Correspondance d'Angleterre, supp. 13, f.76.
71 R.S. Brun, "Le Séjour des Acadiens en Angleterre et leurs trous dans les Archives Brittaniques, 1750-1763", *La Société Historique Acadienne*, 32ème Cahier, Vol. IV (1971), pp. 65-66; M. Daligaut, "Les Acadiens prisonniers en Angleterre", *ibid.*, 34ème Cahier, Vol. IV (1972), p. 160.
72 Rochette à d'Eon, Liverpool, 6-8 juin 1763, AAE, Correspondance d'Angleterre, supp. 13, f.80.
73 D'Eon au duc de Choiseul, Londres, 13 juin 1763, AAE, Correspondance d'Angleterre, 450, f.405. D'Eon was born on 5th October 1728 and died in London 21 May 1810. Another career diplomat he was despatched from Russia to England in 1762 to serve as second-in-command to Nivernois.
74 *Ibid.*

of French officials to organize the Acadians into four villages on the island of Belle Isle, off the south coast of Brittany.[75] It failed. In 1773, the Acadians were to be found scattered throughout the Atlantic ports.[76] Another attempt was made to bring together in one place all the Acadians exiled in France, this time the area near Poitiers,[77] but this experiment also failed. Finally, through the work of Acadians who had reached Louisiana via Santo Domingo,[78] seven ship loads of Acadians left France for New Orleans and Spanish rule in the summer of 1785.[79] This represented just over two thirds of the Acadians then in France.[80] Those who remained behind were mostly the old, the ill, or the orphaned young.[81]

In sum, the attempt to establish the Acadians within the dominions of the King of France failed. In the spring of 1763, the French hoped that in acquiring the Acadians they were acquiring a number of particularly desirable French citizens. It was a hope destined to be frustrated, due in part to the nature of the Acadians and partly to the fallacious perception of that nature by the French. The plans of the latter were based upon an idealisation of the Acadian, upon the vision of the Acadian as a peasantry whose most important characteristics were their language and their religion. Little account was taken of any other element making up the Acadian communities. French bureaucracy was baffled by the Acadian sense of family. Any attempt to prevent them roaming the French Atlantic coast to discover or re-visit relatives, always failed. Those from England had barely landed when a harried French official wrote in August 1763, that it was impossible to confine them to St.

---

75 The records for this are scattered. The legal business, land grants, etc., are to be found in Assiegements, Série C, 5176, 5177, 5179, 5180, 5182, 5185, 5188, 1763-1770, AD, Ille et Vilaine. The day-to-day problems are recorded in Collection Lanco, AD, La Vendée. An overview of the project is in the Extrait des Rolles de familles, Le Moyne mss, Archives Municipales [hereafter AM], Bordeaux.

76 The Acadians were distributed as follows: in Bretagne, at St. Malo 1723, at Morlaix 179, at Lorient et Quimper 22, at Belle Isle 81, at Nantes 81, at Brest 3; in Rouen, at Le Havre 159; in Caen, at Cherbourg 214; in La Rochelle, at Rochefort 74, at La Rochelle 45; in Amiens, at Boulogne 2; in Bordeaux 10; total for France 2510. "Recueil de pièces relatif aux Acadiens", f. 312, AM, Bordeaux.

77 The papers relating to this are uncatalogued correspondence, 1763-1770, in the AD, Poitiers Vienne. A number of articles about this stage of Acadian experiences have been published in the *Bulletin de la Société des Antiquaires de l'ouest et des Musées de Poitiers*. In particular see Général A. Papuchon, "La colonie Acadienne en Poitou", Troisième Série, Tome I (1908), pp. 311-363.

78 Noticia de los accaimientos de la Luisiana en el ano de 1769, Miscelaneo, Tomo XIII, ff. 10-77, Palacio Real, Madrid.

79 Ships rolls, Marine 458, AD, Loire Attantigue, Nantes.

80 Winzerling, *Acadian Odyssey*, p. 154.

81 Their fates were various. Their lives can be traced as a separate thread through the welfare and pension activities of the various governments of the Revolution, of Napoleon and of Louis XVIII.

Malo and Morlaix.[82] Moreover, so vigorously did the Acadians comment on the actions of the French officials, that the latter were driven to respond in kind. One Bordeaux official wrote to his superiors that the Acadian attitude showed evidence almost of a revolt and was of a kind "à faire suspecter des intelligences criminelles".[83]

There was another factor which blocked the assimilation of the Acadians by eighteenth-century France — their inheritance from eighteenth-century Nova Scotia. A shrewd Breton lawyer remarked that the Acadians were used to a bountiful land, where the earth was not difficult to till, that they were accustomed to bread, milk and butter and meat, and looked down upon fish, cider and vegetables.[84] When the settlement of Belle Isle was founded, the Acadians had little idea of how to work in stone and demanded wood and even their methods of carpentry were much different from those practised by the French.[85] Above all, the Acadians were not used to the limitations which hedged the life of the average eighteenth-century Frenchman: the corvée, the restriction on travel within the country, the dominance of traditional concepts of occupations. The records of the Breton courts contain a considerable number of cases in which Acadians were on trial because they had tried to combine more than one career, farming and fishing, seaman and carpenter.[86] Acadian society in Nova Scotia had been a society in which individuals were accustomed to confront a number of tasks; eighteenth-century French society was one in which most people took up only one type of occupation. Once more the Acadians demonstrated a complexity beyond the experience of those who had to cope with them.

There had always been more to the Acadian community than a collection of expatriated French traits. In 1763, as in 1755, the Acadian identity was defined solely in terms of their language and religion. The Acadians of the British seaport found their longing for the land of their birth subordinated to an emphasis by French diplomats on their common speech and faith. During the next twenty years the French were to find that the Acadians looked upon their sea-ports as much a place of exile as had been Bristol or Liverpool. Acadian character would stand out against French society no less strongly than it had against British.

---

82 Unsigned report in letter book, 2 août 1763, C. 3819, f. 771, AD, Ille et Vilaine.
83 Torrey à Le noyne, 1773, Le Moyne Mss., AM, Bordeaux.
84 Lettre addressé à Guillot, Commissaire de la Marine à St. Malo, 10 mai 1759, IF 2159, AD, Ille et Vilaine.
85 *Ibid.*
86 E.G. LeLoutre à Warren 26 October 1768, Fonds Warren, Série E, AD, Morbihan.

J.M. BUMSTED

Reprinted from Vol. XI, No. 1
(Autumn 1981)

The Origins of
the Land Question on
Prince Edward Island, 1767-1805

The early history of the Island of St. John (or Prince Edward Island as it was called after 1798) retains a certain potential fascination for students of British North America, not least because the land-holding and administrative arrangements on the Island represented an experiment on the part of the mother country never replicated in other British colonies founded after 1750. As is well known, the land of the Island of St. John was totally granted — by lottery — to private proprietors in 1767, in return for their assumption of responsibility for its settlement and development, as well as the cost of its administration through the payment of substantial quitrents to the British Crown.[1] Divided into 67 lots of roughly 20,000 acres each by surveyor Samuel Holland in 1764-5 (lot 66 of 6,000 acres was reserved to the Crown), the Island's land was completely alienated in advance of the establishment of any formal government, a relatively uncommon practice in British colonial policy. In marked contrast to Nova Scotia, which had cost the Crown over £600,000 to establish, the Island was intended to be completely self-financing from the outset. The private proprietors were required to meet two conditions in order to maintain their grants: they were to improve and populate their lots with substantial numbers of foreign-born Protestants or settlers already resident in North America — one person for every 200 acres — and they were to pay a sizeable annual quitrent, ranging from six shillings per hundred acres for good lots to two shillings per hundred acres for poor ones.[2] The obvious expectation was that the profits of settlement would provide the proprietors with revenue to pay the quitrents, and while it was not specified in the grants, the general concept was that the money would come from rental of lands to tenants/settlers. Originally attached administratively to Nova Scotia, the Island was permitted a separate government in 1769 on the understanding that the costs of administration would be born entirely by the proprietors, most of whom had signed a pledge to meet this obligation.[3]

These intentions, commitments, and promises were never fulfilled. The proprietors did not produce the required number of settlers and many lots remained almost totally uninhabited. Quitrents to the Crown soon fell badly

1 The proceedings surrounding the lottery may be followed in documents reprinted in *Public Archives of Canada Sessional Paper Number 18* (Ottawa, 1906), pp. 3-22.

2 *Ibid.*, pp. 7-9.

3 "Court of St. James, 28 June 1769", Colonial Office [CO] 226/1, pp. 1-11, Public Record Office, London.

into arrears and the cost of governing the Island had to be assumed by the Crown during the War of the American Revolution. From the beginning of actual settlement, criticism of the proprietors was endemic, particularly on the Island itself, and the issue of escheat (the revocation of the original grants by the Crown for non-fulfillment of terms) ultimately became a central component of intense Island political and social conflict. By the mid-nineteenth century, conflict on the Island between the large proprietors and the tenants had become bitter and occasionally violent. Each side in this dispute had its own version of the early history of the Island, and subsequent historical accounts of the early days have invariably been strongly coloured by the partisan debates of the nineteenth century, which tended to assume that the land question on Prince Edward Island had remained virtually unaltered from the first granting of the Island in 1767.[4] This assumption was particularly powerful among the proponents of land reform who tended to view the previous history of the Island as a consistent one with clear-cut issues, and certainly clear-cut villains and heroes. The "bad guys" were obviously the proprietors, most of whom had remained inactive absentees since the 1767 lottery, and the British government which had consistently supported the property rights of the initial grantees and their heirs despite valiant efforts by the "good guys" — a series of Island administrations beginning with that of Walter Patterson, actively supported by the popularly-elected House of Assembly — to reform the landholding system.

The concern of this paper is not to deal with the issues of the land question as they ultimately emerged, but to raise the entire question of historical continuity and the prevailing assumption that the land question was the same from the outset of British settlement. The thesis is relatively simple and straightforward. During the first two gubernatorial administrations on the Island, that of Walter

---

4   For contemporary arguments, see Sir C.P. Lucas, ed., *Lord Durham's Report on the Affairs of British North America* (Oxford, 1912), II, pp. 198 ff.; George Young, *A Statement of the "Escheat Question", in the Island of Prince Edward; Together with the Causes of the Late Agitation, and the Remedies Proposed* (London, 1838); *Remarks upon that Portion of the Earl of Durham's Report Relating to Prince Edward Island, by a Proprietor* (London, 1839); "Report of the Commissioners", 1861, in *Prince Edward Island Assembly Journals*, 1862, Appendix O. The major historical works about the Island include Duncan Campbell, *History of Prince Edward Island* (Charlottetown, 1875); A.B. Warburton, *A History of Prince Edward Island* (St. John, N.B. 1923); Frank MacKinnon, *The Government of Prince Edward Island* (Toronto, 1951), especially pp. 105-19; Andrew Hill Clark, *Three Centuries and the Island: A Historical Geography of Settlement and Agriculture in Prince Edward Island, Canada* (Toronto, 1959); F.W.P. Bolger, ed., *Canada's Smallest Province: A History of P.E.I.* (Charlottetown, 1973), especially pp. 37-134. The best published study of the popular escheat movement is I.R. Robertson, "Highlanders, Irishmen, and the Land Question in Nineteenth-Century Prince Edward Island" in L.M. Cullen and T.C.Smout, eds., *Comparative Aspects of Scottish and Irish Economic and Social History 1600-1900* (Edinburgh, n.d., but 1977), pp. 227-40. I am indebted for discussions over the years with Robertson, Harry Holman, and Harry Baglole for much of the analysis which follows, especially to the last for letting me examine an unpublished paper with a title very similar to that of this paper.

Patterson from 1770 to 1787 and of Edmund Fanning from 1787 to 1805, the land question was not really a popular issue at all, but one created by contending factions of elites (chiefly officials and would-be officials) for their own political, economic, and social advantage. Their ambition was, as Captain John MacDonald put it to the Earl of Selkirk in 1810, one of taking down "the actual Proprietors and of placing themselves in their stead".[5] The land question during these administrations did not revolve around the form of tenure so much as over who were to be the Island's large land-holders. Although the rallying cry changed from "distraint" to "escheat", the principal confrontation was between the absentee proprietors (generally supported by the British government) and resident proprietors, most of whom were leading officials of the Island government.

The major question of who were to be the holders of those 66 20,000 acres lots was based upon three closely-related ambitions shared by nearly all leading Island figures during the period 1770-1805: the desire for at least effective control and preferably ownership of the Island's land and natural resources; the demand for remunerative public employment; and the hope for an enhanced social status. A truism of the development of new settlement colonies is that those who people them seek to better themselves economically and socially. Like most wilderness settlements, early Prince Edward Island attracted men on the make, many of them prepared to devote much energy to improving their position in life. The Island inevitably drew its fair share of individuals whose previous careers had been marked mainly by an absence of success — scape-grace younger sons of gentry families in England, Ireland and Scotland; lower-level military officers whose careers had become arrested for one reason or another; professional men often forced to leave their previous employment under a cloud; bankrupt or near-bankrupt merchants — who saw the Island as a chance to start afresh. But in several critical respects the Island was markedly different from other settlement colonies in British North America.

The assumptions with which the Island's development had been set under way were far more overtly class-conscious than in most other places on the American continent. Although Lord Egmont's proposals for replicating a feudal society on the Island had been ostensibly rejected by the British government, much of the personnel of the Island's first government and many of the implicit principles upon which the Island was being organized were closely connected to Egmont's scheme.[6] Both the British government and the proprietors assumed that the Island would have a landed interest of "gentlemen", dominating a population composed principally of tenant farmers, and the Island's geographical isolation

5 John MacDonald to Selkirk, 23 April 1810, Selkirk Papers, vol. 56, pp. 14981-15005, Public Archives of Canada [PAC].

6 See my "British Colonial Policy and the Island of St. John, 1763-1767", *Acadiensis*, IX (Autumn 1979), pp. 1-18.

encouraged a self-deceiving and exalted view of one's own importance, while failing to provide an economic base upon which such pretensions could be truly founded. The Island in its early years was desperately short of both cash and credit, and in order to maintain the lifestyle of a gentleman — the model for the Island's elite — it was absolutely essential to acquire some sort of dependable income. As Governor Patterson put it in 1773 when complaining about the failure of the payment of official salaries, the officers of the Island were deprived by their status of the "advantages of peasants" and were "obliged to support the Appearances of Gentlemen without the means".[7] Father James MacDonald wrote a few years later that "it is impossible for any man to live in this part of the world without some employment or other; unless a man should have a yearly income".[8] And, he added, only three gentlemen on the Island enjoyed one.

Virtually the only place one could turn for a regular income in an isolated wilderness settlement was to the government, and thus the press for places among those with social pretensions was intense, exacerbated naturally by the relatively small number of decent appointments and the relatively large number of aspiring candidates. Even if one acquired a place with a salary, there was the problem of actually receiving that salary in spendable form, for salaries (particularly in the first years) had to come from revenue, and the only major source of revenue before 1777 was the quitrents. The failure of the proprietors to provide the necessary funds for the payment of official salaries inevitably led to resentment on the part of the Island's officers, as well as to pressure exerted upon the proprietors either to fulfill their commitments or to turn the lands over to others.

To the official resentment over the inadequacy of the quitrent collection to finance the Island's officers was added yet another distinctive feature of the Island's early development: the fact that all the land had been allocated in advance of settlement. In most colonies, ambitious first-owners could expect to acquire large quantities of underdeveloped land at minimal cost, and land, it must be remembered, was both the most promising form of potential wealth and the visible mark of status in all colonial societies. In theory a divergence between first-comers and landholders ought not to have arisen on the Island, for the intention of the British government in allocating the land in 1767 had been that most of the original grantees would move to the Island in order to develop their holdings. As residents they would administer the government. Indeed, most of the first official appointments were made to proprietors. Had the original proprietors become residents and political leaders, most of the subsequent conflict over landholding during the first decades of settlement would never have occurred. What did occur was the extraordinarily rapid emergence of an

7   Walter Patterson to the Earl of Dartmouth, 17 February 1773, CO 226/5, pp. 103-10.
8   James MacDonald to George Hay, 4 November 1776, Blairs Letters, Scottish Catholic Archives, Edinburgh.

officeholding group on the Island who were not proprietors, who resented the proprietors for their failure to provide financially for the Island's political establishment, and who understandably thought that as Island residents *they* should be its principal landholders.

The quest for land, place, and social status under.peculiar conditions thus set the stage for the intense political conflicts of the Island's early years. From the outset the Island had more place seekers than places, a distinct shortage of alternate routes to success than through public involvement lending to public emolument, and most important of all, the curious situation of an absence of wilderness land to be aggrandized by the ambitious in a country totally unsettled and underdeveloped. When one adds the hothouse environment of a tiny elite community centred in Charlottetown, where the leading inhabitants soon intermarried and everyone knew everybody else's business, political conflict and factionalization was bound to be not only inevitable but fierce. Moreover, it was bound to turn, in the last analysis, around the issue of land. The peculiar conditions of the Island produced a circular effect upon its development. The Island's officials and leading citizens bitterly resented the proprietors for their failure to fulfill the terms of their grants, at the same time that their own economic and social needs led to a rapacious devouring of any capital invested by a proprietor seeking to comply with the conditions.[9] By the beginning of the nineteenth century, the experiences of a number of proprietors who had attempted to be active on the Island had graphically demonstrated the perils of involvement and investment. The wisest Island proprietor was he who did nothing and hoped his holdings would appreciate in value.

At the same time that the proprietors were being attacked by the officeholders, the documentable rapacity of the Island's officials vis-a-vis the proprietors was one of the principal factors behind the refusal of the British government to penalize the proprietors for their failures. Much was and still is made of the connections into government enjoyed by the absentees, but one of the main values of those connections was to assure that the authorities in London bothered to find out what was going on in the Gulf of St. Lawrence. The British government was not likely to attack private property, but the proprietors did not have to invent arguments to defend it; the behaviour of the Island's office-holders spoke for itself. The amount of time the Colonial Office and the Privy Council spent upon investigations into the events on the Island of St. John/Prince Edward Island between 1770 and 1805 bore absolutely no relationship to the size or importance of the colony, and invariably what the succession of lengthy hearings held in London demonstrated was the bad conduct of the Island's officials. Whenever distraint or escheat was mentioned or discussed in Britain, the proprietors were able to point to what had happened whenever one

9 See my "Sir James Montgomery and Prince Edward Island, 1767-1803", *Acadiensis*, VIII (Spring 1978), pp. 76-102.

of their number had actually attempted to honour his commitments. In this limited sense there is a true continuity between the early disputes over land and the land question of the nineteenth century. The proprietorial system survived well beyond any legitimate claim it could make to existence largely because its first enemies and critics had been so obviously self-seeking and rapacious (not to mention clumsy) in their attacks upon it. Had the disputes of the first years genuinely been matters of principle or genuinely revolved around the later issues of the form of tenure, the landholding system of Prince Edward Island might have been reformed far earlier and much more justly.

The land question on the Island from 1767 to 1805 did not emerge full-blown at the outset, and only gradually developed along lines which have any relationship with the later period. The first phase, from the initial allocation of the lots until 1780, was one of experimentation, rapid changes in the administrative arrangements for the Island, and substantial dislocation brought about by the warfare of the American rebellion. Uncertainty was the key in this initial period. Although the officers on the Island attempted to put pressure upon the proprietors to fulfill their obligations, their major concern was with their own salaries, which before 1777 could be paid only from the quitrent collections. The second phase, beginning in 1780 and lasting until the mid-1790s, was a period of blatant local land grabbing. In terms of the proprietorial grants the catchword was "distraint", the legal procedure so clumsily employed by the officers in 1781 to bring about a major transfer of land from absentee proprietors to resident ones (i.e., themselves). This action led to Walter Patterson's audacious attempts to defy both the proprietors and the British authorities over the transfers, a policy which brought Island development to a halt in a decade of peace when more could have been expected. Patterson's actions were the critical turning point in the early history of the land question (and arguably of the Island itself), because they effectively prevented any resumption of normal Island progress within the existing landholding arrangements without proposing any constructive alternative.

Not until the mid-1790s did the Island begin to recover from the Patterson ruckus, for his successor Edmund Fanning was forced to defend his behaviour (and that of his leading colleagues) against charges brought before the Privy Council in 1792 by proprietorial supporters of Patterson. The final period, from 1796 to 1805, saw the gradual consolidation of the land question and its many ramifications into the critical Island political issue — especially at election time — and the emergence of escheat as a preferable slogan to distraint. Yet one need not be overly cynical to recognize that there was more rhetoric than substance behind the early escheat movement, and that its leaders had merely found less public and obvious ways of advancing their landholding ambitions on the Island. Significantly enough, the land reformers under Fanning became the pro-proprietorial party under DesBarres, fending off a new thrust by a faction of recent arrivals and resident outsiders who were organized into the so-called

"Loyal Electors". But while the land question underwent many permutations in the first forty years of Island development under the British, it was in 1805 — and beyond — one debated by the Island's elite for their own purposes rather than a genuinely grass-roots issue.

In the first phase emphasis must be placed upon experimentation and rapid shifts in administrative arrangements. It is clear that the proprietors pressed for a separate government in 1769 to keep the rapacious Nova Scotians out, and that many of them expected to be able gradually to ease the new colony onto the British civil list. Solemn promises to finance the Island's establishment solely from the quitrents and never to seek government assistance were not to be taken entirely seriously, as the proposed budget which the proprietors advanced in 1769 plainly demonstrates, since it included no provisions for any public improvements whatsoever.[10] Some proprietors may genuinely have expected that the vast economic potential of the Island as reported by Samuel Holland would make rapid settlement possible, leading to self-financing with an Island assembly voting the necessary funds for local improvements. At best, one suspects, the proprietors hoped for settlement and self-financing simultaneously. A flourishing Island providing its own funds would encourage the British to take over most of the proprietorial obligations. In 1777, of course, the British government did place the Island's political establishment on the civil list, and this action ought to have contributed to a British re-evaluation of the role of proprietors at the end of the American War. That it did not was the result of the impetuosity, impatience, and stubborness of the Island factions.

Because the quitrents had to supply official salaries before 1777, and could do so only if regularly paid and efficiently collected, it is not surprising that the governor and his council (who were the very officials looking for the money) became very concerned over quitrent arrears from a very early stage. In 1771 the first quitrent legislation was adopted on the Island by the governor and council, providing a model which served as the basis for subsequent legislation well into the 1780s. Under this ordinance the lots in arrears of quitrent could be distrained by Island judicial procedure and sold on the Island.[11] The British government, however, refused to regard ordinances passed only by governor and council as having any legal force, and given the relatively inconsequential nature of other early ordinances, it would hardly be far-fetched to see the immediate Island response — to embody an assembly as quickly as possible — as mainly connected to the quitrent problem. In any event, an assembly was called in 1773, although Patterson himself acknowledged that he was hard-pressed to find enough "respectable" citizens to sit in it.[12] One of the assembly's first actions

10 "Court of St. James, 28 June 1769". CO 226/1, pp. 1-11.
11 "An Ordinance and Act of Council for the effectual recovery of certain of His Majesty's Quit Rents in the Island of Saint John", CO 225/4, pp. 161-5.
12 Patterson to Dartmouth, 17 February 1773, CO 226/5, pp. 87-9.

was to readopt the 1771 quitrent ordinance, and with some minor revisions in 1774, it was given the royal assent two years later. The Board of Trade, which vetted colonial legislation at this time, curiously failed to recognize the many disadvantages to those not resident upon the Island in the procedures for distraint and sale.[13]

Whatever the real intentions of the proprietors toward settlement and quitrents, the coming of the American Revolution disrupted any orderly progress on either front. Obviously settlement by rebellious Americans could not be encouraged, and the quasi-legal immigration of Scots and Irish which had been the main source of population was halted for the duration. Proprietors in Britain quickly put the Island out of their minds, rousing themselves only for a successful petition to place the Island's establishment upon the civil list.[14] This accomplished, they sat back to await the resolution of Britain's American problems. Meanwhile, those who remained in residence on the Island, struggled to survive. The local breakthrough came when Phillips Callbeck, acting governor from 1775 to 1779 while Patterson was in England, discovered the ease with which both the government and the proprietors could be exploited, thanks to the isolation of the Island and the confusion of the war.[15] This lesson would not be lost upon Walter Patterson when he returned to the Island in 1780.

Patterson's return in June of 1780 can be taken as the beginning of the second phase of the land question, in which land grabbing was naked and clumsy. Curiously enough, the first serious efforts in this direction were opposed by Patterson, when Lieutenant Governor Thomas Desbrisay and his fellow councillors took advantage of Patterson's absence in Halifax to strip the royalty of Charlottetown clean of desirable town and pasture lots, chiefly by granting them to themselves and garrison soldiers from whom the land was quickly purchased. Patterson was angered by this effort, although Desbrisay expostulated to the Colonial Secretary, "for Gods Sake what business is it of Mr. Paterson's if I procure honestly other people's Grants of Land to make a livelihood for my dear Children!"[16] Only a few days after Patterson exposed the culprits, the council decided to implement a treasury minute of 1776 authorizing legal action against delinquent proprietors based on the 1774 legislation, although that minute had obviously been prepared before anyone knew that the war with the Americans would last so long.[17] It is difficult to acquit Patterson of some forward planning in this action, since he had two months earlier (and before the Charlottetown lots business) appointed his brother-in-law as

---

13 "Report of Richard Jackson, 23 March 1774", CO 226/1 pp. 175-81.

14 Petition of Proprietors of St. John's Island to the King in Council, CO 226/1, pp. 207-14.

15 For Callbeck, see the sketch by Harry Holman in *Dictionary of Canadian Biography*, IV (Toronto, 1979), pp. 128-9.

16 Thomas Desbrisay to Lord George Germain, 23 November 1780, CO 226/7, pp. 219-23.

17 Executive Council Minutes, 26 November 1780, CO 229/1, p. 185.

Receiver of Quitrents and his private secretary as Deputy Receiver. Although it can never be proved, Patterson and Callbeck had probably made a deal shortly after the governor's return to the Island, in which Patterson promised not to examine too closely into Callbeck's wartime financial dealings with the British government and the Attorney General agreed to show Patterson how policy could be managed to the governor's advantage. In any event, it is difficult to isolate the critical point in the long fiasco which ensued, for everything seemed to follow cumulatively from the decision to auction (quite illegally) a number of proprietorial lots in November of 1781, a sale in which Patterson was virtually the only purchaser. The council had failed to allow time to notify the proprietors, and in the end had distrained most of the Island's land in the local Supreme Court without bothering to observe the terms of the legislation.[18] The auction was attended only by a small cadre of Island officials, for it was publicized only on the Island if at all, and of the 220,000 acres sold, Patterson (who was pointedly not present) ended up with 170,000 acres, bought by his private secretary in his own name and those of Irish friends.[19] Naturally the proprietors complained, and without realizing the extent of improper procedure or gubernatorial self-interest, the British government in 1783 attempted to reverse the sales as impolitic. Lord North sent a revised quitrent act to Patterson with instructions to place it before his assembly and an implicit order to see it passed.[20]

The refusal of Patterson to place the 1783 draft bill before the assembly — he suppressed it for nearly a year — was probably the critical step in the second phase. Indeed, it could well be argued that this action was the real turning point in the Island's history, for the bill was a good one. It would have brought quitrent arrears up-to-date as of 1783, giving the proprietors a fresh start in a time of peace, while providing legislation fully sanctioned by the British government for distraining lots of delinquent proprietors for local purchase. Moreover, it would have preserved most of the lots auctioned in 1781 in the hands of their resident buyers, since any proprietor who wished his land restored had to repurchase the lot and pay for any improvements, a trouble most proprietors probably would not have taken.[21] Why Patterson refused to accept this solution is not at all clear, although he undoubtedly recognized full well that the sales had been

---

18 *Ibid.*, 19 February 1781, CO 229/1, p. 190; Copy of Memorial from Chief Justice Peter Stewart, St. John's Island, 30 May 1789, Public Archives of Prince Edward Island, [PAPEI], 2652/4.

19 "Account of Sales of Sundry Townships and half Townships sold by Public Auction at the Suit of His Majesty for non payment of Quit Rents due to the 1st of May 1781", Selkirk Papers, vol. 56, pp. 15049-50.

20 Lord North to Patterson, 24 July 1783, CO 226/8, p. 60.

21 "An Act for Repealing an Act...and for the enforcing in future a due and regular payment of the Quit Rents", CO 226/3, pp. 62-71.

far less proper than the ministry realised, and was afraid of exposure. As well, one can imagine Phillips Callbeck at hand, advising against making needless concessions. Finally, Patterson's judgment may well have been clouded by the open eruption of a smouldering feud with Peter Stewart, caused partly by the governor's successful seduction of the Chief Justice's wife, Sarah.[22] Whatever his motivation, Patterson's decision to sit on the legislation rather firmly arrested any proprietorial investment in the Island. During the 1780s and early 1790s, the proprietors were far more concerned with their titles than with the development of their estates.

Patterson desperately tried to cover up and obstruct the attempts of the British government to resolve the quitrent disputes to everyone's satisfaction.[23] The settlement of Loyalists, whom both Patterson and the proprietors had been for several years attempting to lure to the Island, became part of the governor's strategy of obfuscation and preservation of the 1781 sales, rather than a constructive effort to re-establish some forward momentum to settlement. Instead of placing the Loyalists on uncontested property, those who arrived were given their land grants on Patterson's own purchases, with predictable results. The question of Loyalist titles remained a contentious one well into the nineteenth century, constituting yet another legacy of Patterson's policy.[24] Moreover, the Loyalist claims were only a small part of the larger issue of titles — both for proprietor and ordinary settler — created by the sales of 1781 and the subsequent moves of Patterson and a rump council. Finally, the factionalization of the later Patterson years prevented any serious housecleaning of the shady figures and incompetents who had opposed him for their own purposes. The Stewart/Desbrisay family alliance was scarcely composed of men whose probity was beyond dispute. But inevitably Patterson's successor Fanning was forced to turn to the alliance for political allies in order to establish his own position. The attempt in 1792 by a small group of Patterson die-hards among the proprietors to charge Fanning and the Stewart crowd with malfeasance failed dismally because it was too obviously politically inspired — and by a very dubious group.[25] Nevertheless, it seems likely that many of the charges, particularly

22 Peter Stewart to James Montgomery, 27 April 1783, GD 293/2/79, p. 46, Scottish Record Office [SRO], Edinburgh. David Lawson to James Montgomery, 31 May 1784, GD 293/2/78, p. 61, SRO.

23 They may be followed in Bolger, *Canada's Smallest Province*, pp. 57-65, a narrative sympathetic to Patterson, or in Harry Baglole, "Walter Patterson", *DCB*, IV, pp. 605-11.

24 The only detailed study of the early Loyalist question — getting nearly everything wrong — is Wilbur H. Sieburt and Florence E. Gilliam, "The Loyalists in Prince Edward Island", Royal Society of Canada *Transactions*, 3rd ser., IV, Sec. II (1910), pp. 109-17. This subject is much in need of further analysis.

25 *Report of the Right Honourable the Lords of the Committee of His Majesty's Most Honourable Privy Council on Certain Complaints against Lieutenant Governor Fanning, and other Officers of His Majesty's Government in the Island of St. John* (n.p., n.d., but London, 1792.)

those brought against Chief Justice Peter Stewart and his son-in-law William Townshend, represented legitimate grievances which were too readily dismissed by the British government.[26] Independent evidence does suggest that Stewart operated the Island's Supreme Court as a virtual family fiefdom, and that justice, especially for small landholders and tenants, was not readily obtainable there.[27]

Although it took Fanning and his associates some years to get established — the confusion caused by Patterson's refusal to be replaced was succeeded by the proceedings against the officers of 1792 — the new Lieutenant Governor and his allies were just as rapacious as Patterson and his supporters. The difference was that they were smoother ("audacious open tyranny" had been replaced by "deep far fetched despicable Yankey cunning" was the way John MacDonald trenchantly put it) and they were able to operate behind the scenes in the administrative, political, and legal chaos which Patterson had left in his wake.[28] Fanning himself purchased 60,000 acres of Patterson's land for less than £100, chiefly because his cronies privately fixed the bidding on the lots to prevent the price being raised.[29] The Lieutenant Governor and his colleagues found it more profitable to become the agents of the absentee proprietors than to take on the quitrent obligations themselves, and a good deal of asset-stripping went on, particularly after timbering became profitable at the beginning of the nineteenth century.[30] Supporters of Patterson and opponents of the government found themselves at considerable legal disadvantage on the Island.[31] The enemies of "Hellfire Jack" Stewart maintained that Stewart had become Receiver of the Island quitrents by buying off a rival candidate with an annual annuity of £80. When asked how he could afford to make such an offer, Stewart allegedly replied that "the Treasury never called the Receivers of American Quit Rents to Account and he would pocket what he received". Stewart added that Patterson's fault was "having forfeited the lots in an illegal manner; but he [Stewart] would go legally to work".[32]

---

26 Townshend's weak defence, dated 1791, is in PAC, MG23 E6. See also my forthcoming biographical sketches of Fanning, Stewart, and Attorney General Joseph Aplin (three of the officers involved) in the *DCB.*

27 "Sir James Montgomery and PEI", pp. 90 ff.

28 John MacDonald to Helen MacDonald, 7 July 1790, Acc. 2664, PAPEI.

29 James Douglas to James Montgomery, 15 September 1800, GD 293/2/19, p. 10, SRO.

30 Fanning, for example, was agent for James Montgomery, Viscount Townshend, and Robert Shuttleworth. Along with his own holdings, he was in charge of over 200,000 acres of Island property. See W.S. MacNutt, "Fanning's Regime on Prince Edward Island", *Acadiensis,* I (Autumn 1971), pp. 37-53.

31 See, for example, James Douglas to James Montgomery, 26 November 1797, GD 293/2/19, p. 9, SRO.

32 "John Stewart" in biographical appendix of Island officers attached to John Hill's 1801 "A Detail of Various Transactions at Prince Edward Island", CO 226/18, p. 433; see also John MacDonald to Helen MacDonaald, 7 July 1790, Acc. 2664, PAPEI.

Regardless of whether it is entirely fair to attribute to self-interest the 1795 Act to make seven years possession of land under a deed an indefragible title to the land, one chief beneficiary of the legislation was Edmund Fanning.[33]

Beginning in 1796, with the publication of Colonel Joseph Robinson's "To the Farmers in the Island of St. John, in the Gulf of St. Lawrence", the rallying cry of the government and the "reformers" was the establishment of a separate Court of Escheat on the Island.[34] Robinson's pamphlet is an extremely rare one, known usually only through hostile comments about it in the papers of the Colonial Office. Both his tone and argument are really far less radical than the criticisms of the pamphlet would suggest. Although he called for an end to the proprietorial system, Robinson was opposed neither to quitrents nor tenancy. What he advocated was a return of the land to the Crown, which would then act directly as the landlord of the small holder on the Island. Although many of the anguished screams and charges of proprietors and their allies ought not to be taken seriously, several of the points which the opponents of escheat made in the 1790s were valid. Several local observers detected behind Robinson's pamphlet and the subsequent political campaigning based upon it the fine hand of Edmund Fanning and the Stewarts, who as the local administration would in effect become the landlord if Robinson's recommendations were implemented.[35] Walter Patterson had sought to transfer some of the lots from one set of proprietors to another, but Edmund Fanning was far more subtle. In effect the Island's officials would collectively become THE PROPRIETOR. Moreover, there was the very real question of who would staff the proposed Court of Escheat and whether justice would be any more obtainable there than in the existing courts of the Island. At the same time that the agitation for an Escheat Court reached its height, between 1796 and 1803, the administration of justice on the Island reached a new low. The two trends were not entirely unconnected. The Chief Justice employed his office to prevent legal action being taken against him and his relatives by a number of creditors and small tenants, and there occurred a rapid turnover of Attorneys General, several of whom left the Island vowing never to return. Scotland's former Lord Advocate James Montgomery threatened to bring his own litigations against Stewart to London, where, he wrote to Fanning, "They will exhibit a Picture, if the same System is continued, that never before Appeared in any English judicature". Stewart's actions, added Montgomery in a nice piece of pawky Scots understatement, were "not a good Idea in a Chief Justice".[36]

When Attorney General John Wentworth, appointed by London to replace

33 35 George III, c.2, "An Act for Confirming Titles and Quieting Possessions".

34 A copy of this pamphlet has recently been acquired by the PAPEI.

35 These charges were advanced by James Douglas, John MacDonald, and Joseph Aplin on numerous occasions.

36 James Montgomery to Edmund Fanning, 18 September 1801, GD 293/2/17, p. 12, SRO.

Joseph Aplin (who in turn had been dismissed by Fanning for open criticism of the government), proved slow to take up his place, Fanning wrote to the Colonial Secretary seeking permission to appoint his own local candidate, Peter Magowan. Wentworth finally appeared on the Island in May 1800, and as the only alternative practising attorney to Magowan, immediately acquired all of the cases involving the Stewart family, a total of over 60 actions.[37] Many of these cases were defenses of the possessions of small property holders (a number of them Acadians), who were being evicted from their lands by Captain John Stewart and his brother-in-law William Townshend.[38] Not surprisingly, when Fanning received a warrant to appoint Magowan, granted on the assumption that something had happened to Wentworth, he immediately accused Wentworth of malpractice (a similar technique had been employed several times in the past against vocal Island lawyers), and replaced him.[39] Wentworth went home, wrote James Douglas to William Montgomery, "with such an Account of the Misconduct here that would quite surprize you", leaving but one lawyer on the Island.[40] Given the legal administration of the colony, it is difficult to conceive that the establishment of a local Court of Escheat would act to the benefit of the average small tenant.

In short, the famous legislative report of 1797 on the state of settlement on the Island, accompanied by a petition for a Court of Escheat, was designed less to achieve an equitable settlement of the land question (even in terms of the local population) than for other and deeper reasons, probably principally to enable John Stewart to renegotiate terms with the proprietors and extinguish as many old claims as possible, which Stewart did in London in 1802 and 1803. Satisfied with this settlement, the Fanning/Stewart party became pro-proprietorial, continuing to accumulate land and agencies for absentee proprietors throughout the first decades of the nineteenth century. Whether the appointment of Frederick DesBarres as Lieutenant Governor and the subsequent establishment of the Loyal Electors represented a genuine new hope for Island residents is doubtful, but as of the retirement of Edmund Fanning, the land question had become so hopelessly entangled with Island politics and official self-interest that a very new broom would be required to sweep the decks of nearly forty years of official obfuscation, maladministration, and chicanery. Proprietor John Hill was quite accurate in 1801 when he wrote, "No Man in his senses will trust his property in

37 James Douglas to James Montgomery, 15 September 1800, GD 293/2/19, p. 10, SRO. According to Douglas, Wentworth was attorney in over 200 actions.
38 *Ibid.* Some substantiation of these charges is provided by the incomplete Supreme Court Docket Book, 1801-1804, RG 6, PAPEI, which for Hilary Term 1801 lists over ten actions involving Stewarts in which Wentworth was plaintiff's attorney, and a number of actions for ejectment by Stewart.
39 See my forthcoming sketches of Magowan and Wentworth for the *DCB*.
40 James Douglas to William Montgomery, 26 November 1800, GD 293/2/19, p. 1, SRO.

a place that either does not afford the institutions necessary for protection, or where those institutions are used as the means of destruction".[41] Yet Hill did not take the next logical step: if proprietorial property was useless, why hold onto it? But even if he and his fellow proprietors had returned their lots to the Crown, there exists precious little evidence to suggest that the ordinary Island inhabitant would, in 1805 at least, have been appreciably better off.

41 John Hill, "A Detail of Various Transactions", CO 226/18, p. 282.

BARRY CAHILL

Reprinted from Vol. XXVI, No. 1
(Autumn 1996)

The Treason of the Merchants:
Dissent and Repression in Halifax in
the Era of the American Revolution

"The various events of the American revolution — the attempt on fort Cumberland — the design against Halifax, only set aside by the fear of the epidemic small pox [July 1775], and many other obvious causes, created a reign of terror in this province which continued to the close of the war in 1783."

— Beamish Murdoch, 1866

"There is an impression that in Nova Scotia only New Englanders were suspected of disloyalty and sympathy with the Revolutionists."

—Walter C. Murray, 1903

"'My son, a great rebel hunt is in progress. Every man of New England birth is suspect, and when he happens to be a merchant with many in his debt, there are sure to be certain ones eager to denounce him, truly or falsely, to bring about his ruin. Halifax is ringing with accusations and denunciations'."

— Thomas H. Raddall, His Majesty's Yankees, 1942

IN APRIL 1754 MALACHY SALTER, a 38-year-old *émigré* Boston merchant, sat on the grand jury which discharged a 'foreign Protestant' immigrant lying under an indictment of high treason. This was the first attempted prosecution for treason in what is now Canada.[1] Twenty-four years to the month later, Malachy Salter, ex-justice of the peace, himself stood indicted for sedition. It was the second occasion on which the Halifax grand jury — their heads turned by rebellion and civil war in America and insurrection in the Chignecto hinterland — had returned 'true bill' on an indictment against Salter for ancillary crime against the state. "During the American Revolt..." wrote Thomas Beamish Akins in 1895, "Mr. Salter, with several other gentlemen of the town, became suspected of treasonable correspondence. He was twice under prosecution, but on a full investigation nothing appeared to have been said or written by him of sufficient moment to warrant the charges".[2] Writing almost three decades earlier, the lawyer-chronicler Beamish Murdoch — a paternal great-grandson of Salter — adopted a somewhat different

---

1   *R. v. Hoffman* (N.S. Gen. Ct., 1754). See Barry Cahill, "The 'Hoffman Rebellion' (1753) and 'Hoffman's Trial' (1754): Constructive High Treason and Seditious Conspiracy in Nova Scotia under the Stratocracy", in F. Murray Greenwood and Barry Wright, eds., *Canadian State Trials [Volume One]: Law, Politics and Security Measures, 1608-1837* (Toronto, 1996), pp. 72-97.
    The author is grateful to Jim Phillips, Barry Wright and the three anonymous reviewers at *Acadiensis* for their critiques of earlier drafts of this article.

2   T.B. Akins, "History of Halifax City", *Collections* of the Nova Scotia Historical Society, 8 (1895), p. 235.

perspective: the Council, in November 1777, had ordered the arrest, detention and prosecution of his ancestor for corresponding with the enemy. Murdoch went on to assert, however inaccurately, that Salter was tried and acquitted at the next supreme court.[3] In fact, the accused, who had already been tried and convicted earlier the same year for uttering seditious words, was neither tried for nor acquitted of the more serious misdemeanour of treasonable correspondence. Trial was indefinitely postponed and the lingering threat of prosecution was removed only by Salter's death three years later. Murdoch's brief account bears contrasting with the slightly later and more expansive one provided by Salter's great-great-granddaughter, Susan Stairs:

> On October 10th, 1777, was passed an order-in-council for the arrest of Malachy Salter on a charge of corresponding with parties in Boston of a dangerous tendency, and a prosecution was ordered. The original indictment of the grand jury was found a few years ago in the court house, and is now in the possession of the [Nova Scotia] Historical Society. In this paper is stated that Malachy Salter is reported to have said, 'He did not think the rebels were so far wrong'; but upon this the grand jury indicted him for high treason, but Mr. Salter was allowed to give security himself in £500, and two others each £250 for his good behaviour. He was tried in the supreme court and acquitted....
>
> I have seen the indictment and am sorry that I did not copy the names of the grand jury.[4]

Taking the *Salter* case as its point of departure, this article provides an account of the sedition proceedings arising from the inability or unwillingness of the old New England mercantile elite of Halifax to navigate between the shoals of neutrality and disloyalty, and thus respond successfully to the challenge posed by the government's reaction to the emergency in the New England colonies. The Nova Scotia government attempted to suppress sedition in Halifax and elsewhere in the colony through a variety of measures, executive and judicial, which involved both

---

3   Beamish Murdoch, *A History of Nova-Scotia, or Acadie* (Halifax, 1866), vol. 2, pp. 587-8. Murdoch failed to mention that Salter had been tried and convicted of uttering seditious words in February 1777. The bias of the historiography — and it persists — is to paint Salter as a 'good' American; a loyal Yankee rather than a disloyal, or even 'neutral' one. See, for example, C. Bruce Fergusson, comp., *A Directory of the Members of the Legislative Assembly of Nova Scotia 1758-1958* (Halifax, 1958), p. 307; and Arthur Wentworth Hamilton Eaton, "Chapters in the History of Halifax, Nova Scotia, No. X: Halifax and the American Revolution", *Americana* 12, 2 (April 1918), p. 200.

4   [Anon., comp.], *Family History: Stairs Morrow: Including Letters, Diaries, Essays, Poems, Etc.* (Halifax, 1906), pp. 252-3. Susannah Duffus Morrow [Mrs William James Stairs], 1822-1906, began to compose "The Morrow Family" history in 1879. The court document to which she refers is no longer to be found in the Royal Nova Scotia Historical Society fonds, now held at the Public Archives of Nova Scotia [PANS], nor are other records extant of the Halifax grand jury of the time. It is nevertheless clear from Mrs Stairs' description of the proceeding that her ancestor Salter was charged not with high treason (rebellion) but with sedition (incitement to rebellion).

prosecution and persecution, legal repression and legal harassment. The use of the formal law in sedition trials was an essential aspect of the official response to the American Revolution. For a variety of reasons repression and not leniency marked the legal process. Official repression through the criminal justice system was distinguished by various methods of harassing suspected rebel sympathizers: arrest, imprisonment or detention without trial, oppressive recognizances, delay of trial through repeated continuances, pseudo-treason indictments disguised as high misdemeanour (serious sedition), and vexatious or malicious reindictment.

The causes and nature of the official response to sedition in Nova Scotia in the era of the American Revolution must be evaluated in the context of the aftermath of the patriot siege of Fort Cumberland in 1776.[5] In responding to the insurrection, the government, soon also facing legal constraints which prohibited trials for high treason, turned to the lesser charge of sedition as a means of suppressing dissent. Any account of rebellion and repression in the Revolutionary era would be incomplete, therefore, if trials for sedition such as Salter's were not placed in the broader context of the official reaction to political protest and dissent on the part of Nova Scotia's New Englanders. The government's reaction to Salter's articulation of his pro-patriot political views was characterized more by repression than by leniency, and, in particular, the heavy hand of the law of sedition was imposed. Yet Salter was one of only two patriot sympathizers actually tried for sedition, and, while both were found guilty, neither received a harsh sentence.[6]

Except for two of the patriot besiegers of Fort Cumberland, no one in Nova Scotia was tried for high treason during the period which encompassed the American Revolution.[7] This article attempts to show why Malachy Salter, an 'economic republican' who, nevertheless, did not favour American independence and who was not himself a rebel, was subjected to such an extreme degree of harassment and continuing legal repression. It also suggests that the only reason why Salter was not charged with high treason was that the imperial *Habeas Corpus Suspension Act* of 1777 effectively prevented treason trials. This is the reason why only two of the 40-odd insurrectionists indicted for high treason following the siege of Fort Cumberland were actually tried, and why no treason

---

5 See generally Ernest Clarke, *The Siege of Fort Cumberland, 1776* (Kingston & Montreal, 1995).

6 This and the paragraph following depends upon the introduction to Ernest A. Clarke and Jim Phillips, "Rebellion and Repression in Nova Scotia in the Era of the American Revolution", in Greenwood and Wright, eds., *Law, Politics, and Security Measures*, pp. 172-3.

7 The only other comparable proceedings were *R. v. Patten* (Hilary Term 1779) "For Treasonable Practices" and "for Encouraging Desertion from his Majesty's Troops". The Halifax grand jury initially declined to consider the former for want of crown witnesses, while returning true bill on the latter: N.S. Supreme Court, Pleas of the Crown, Easter Term 1765 to Michaelmas 1783: RG 39, series J (HX), vol. 1, pp. 333-4, 338, PANS. Patten was never tried, and all proceedings against him were finally ordered terminated by the lieutenant-governor in May 1780: Secretary [Bulkeley] to Attorney-General [Brenton], 9 May 1780, Secretary's letter-book, p. 279, RG 1, vol. 136, PANS. Joseph Patten JP (1710-1787), a New England Planter from Massachusetts, was the senior patriot leader in Granville Township, Annapolis County — a 'Yankee' by no means 'neutral'; see generally A.W. Savary, *Supplement* to [W.A. Calnek] *History of the County of Annapolis* (Toronto, 1913), pp. 35-6.

indictments were preferred after local proclamation of the act in August 1777.[8] The language of the second indictment preferred against Salter in April 1778[9] makes clear that the government thought they had good grounds for charging him with high treason and that they fully intended doing so should the inconvenient statutory bar be removed. Though the *Habeas Corpus Suspension Act* did not forbid charging a suspect with high treason — arrest, detention and indictment were allowed, while recognizance, bail and trial were prohibited — there was no point in doing so while the act was in force. Better, then, to confine formal charges to triable indictments than for the government to prefer a charge which could not proceed to trial without special permission from Whitehall.

The loyalty of the members of the pre-Planter New England mercantile elite[10] of Halifax, according to Lewis Fischer, was secured by their anticipation of sustained economic growth based on sharply rising pre-war levels of trade and commerce — in other words, the prospect of wresting control of the lucrative West Indies trade from their New England competitors.[11] It is ironic that Salter, who exemplified the entrepreneurial stratum within Halifax's New England mercantile elite,[12] ultimately became the victim of his own determination to compete with and remain independent of the old Anglo-European mercantile elite, personified by Joshua Mauger. Salter's biographer makes the telling point that he "was the only leading Haligonian prosecuted during the American revolution who was not defended by Mauger's associates"[13] — the reason being that Salter was indebted to Mauger's

8   These insights derive from Clarke and Phillips, "Rebellion and Repression".
    An Act to impower his Majesty to secure and detain Persons charged with, or suspected of, the Crime of High Treason, committed in any of his Majesty's Colonies or Plantations in America..., (1777) 17 Geo. 3, c. 9. The emergency measures *Habeas Corpus Suspension Act* was subject to annual renewal, and was renewed five times before being allowed to expire in January 1783. It is arguable that the proliferation of prosecutions for 'high misdemeanor' or 'treasonable practices', rather than high treason *per se,* can be attributed to the authorities' desire to circumvent the *Habeas Corpus Suspension Act,* which prevented them from either bailing or trying an accused for treason, and effectively suspended the legal right "to be tried within a reasonable time".

9   Depositions and Other Papers Connected with Crown Prosecutions between 1749 and 1780, RG 1, vol. 342, doc. 80, PANS.

10 It is necessary to distinguish between New England Planters of the period 1759-1764 and New England settlers of the decade preceding the Planter immigration. Pre-1759 emigrants from urban New England, such as Salter, were not 'Planters' in the same sense as post-1759 New England and Ulster immigrant farmers and fishermen who both colonized the vacant Acadian lands and founded new townships on the south and southwestern shores of Nova Scotia.

11 Lewis R. Fischer, "Revolution without Independence: The Canadian Colonies, 1749-1775", in Ronald Hoffman et al., eds., *The Economy of Early America: The Revolutionary Period, 1763-1790* (Charlottesville VA, 1988), pp. 94-5ff.

12 Lewis R. Fischer, "'Revolution without Independence': The Halifax Merchants and The American Revolution, 1749-1775", paper presented to the Annual Meeting of the Canadian Historical Association, June 1978, p. 12 [ms.]. Elsewhere, Fischer points out that "after 1764 New Englanders never comprised less than 85 per cent of all [Halifax] merchants": "Canadian Colonies", p. 107.

13 S. Buggey, "Salter, Malachy (Malachi)", in *Dictionary of Canadian Biography,* vol. IV, p. 696. The reason for Salter's isolation and vulnerability was that John Butler, Mauger's principal agent and the army paymaster, was not only Salter's most pressing creditor but also a member of Council. Some merchants being more equal than others, Butler was exonerated of the charge of

associates, who were not about to leap to the defence of a hard-pressed competitor, much less incriminate themselves by opposing government action against an exemplary seditionist. "Although Salter", writes Fischer,

> like so many successful merchants, managed to gain his share of place holdings, his principal interests were always in trade and commerce. His connections, both mercantile and familial, were chiefly with New England, but his network of commercial correspondents stretched at least as far down the coast as Philadelphia. To serve his expanding trading interests, Salter invested heavily in shipping, becoming the most important shipowner in the town [of Halifax] following Mauger's departure [in 1760].[14]

Salter, writes Brebner, "was notable in that he chose to maintain his commercial contacts with New England, which had been his home".[15] He was even more remarkable in that he chose to persevere following the outbreak of rebellion and civil war in New England, refusing to sacrifice his investment despite the trade embargo. Yet there also were pressing financial reasons for Salter's determination to take advantage of the new economic opportunities presented by what soon became a revolutionary war. Importuned by creditors, he had taken over as master of his newest and largest trading vessel, the brigantine *Rising Sun*. As early as 1774, his creditors, pursuing him down the south shore from Halifax to Liverpool, attempted, unsuccessfully, to have the vessel impounded.[16]

Though the ordeal of Malachy Salter was atypical of the experience of the old New England mercantile elite of Halifax, his very failure to capitalize on the war shows why Fischer's "revolution without independence" model, which draws heavily upon the evidence of Salter's career, forms the basis for a new economic interpretation of the failure of the American Revolution in Nova Scotia. Other scholars have also recognized the importance of mercantile issues and have identified Salter as one of those merchants who had "waxed fat from war contracts" during the previous war.[17] Fischer himself, however, neglects to consider the impact

corresponding with the enemy in February 1776; he was too powerful to be subjected to the indignity of a sedition indictment: Minutes of Council, 8 February 1776, RG 1, vol. 189, PANS.

14 Fischer, "Revolution without Independence", p. 103.

15 John Bartlet Brebner, *The Neutral Yankees of Nova Scotia: A Marginal Colony during the Revolutionary Years* ([1937] New York, 1970), p. 21.

16 Harold A. Innis, ed., *The Diary of Simeon Perkins, 1766-1780* (Toronto, 1948), pp. 72-3 (April-May 1774), 79 (Aug 1774), 157 (July 1777).

17 Wilfred Brenton Kerr, *The Maritime Provinces of British North America and the American Revolution* (Sackville NB, [1942]), p. 12; cf. Brebner, *Neutral Yankees*, pp. 19-20. The original proponent of the theory of an homogeneous merchant-loyalism was Viola F. Barnes, "Francis Legge, Governor of Loyalist Nova Scotia, 1773-1776", *New England Quarterly*, 4 (July 1931), pp. 425ff. In his article, "The Merchants of Nova Scotia and the American Revolution", *Canadian Historical Review*, 13, 1 (March 1932), pp. 20-36, W.B. Kerr offered a critique of the Barnes thesis "that the influential Halifax merchants were directly responsible for keeping Nova Scotia loyal to the Crown"; see George A. Rawlyk's important historiographical essay, "The American Revolution and Nova Scotia Reconsidered", *Dalhousie Review*, 43, 3 (Autumn 1963), pp. 379-80 and 391 n. 5. See also Reginald C. Stuart, *United States Expansionism and British North America, 1775-1871* (Chapel Hill NC & London, 1988), p. 18, and "A Revolution Repeatedly Rejected, 1774-1871", in

which Salter's indebtedness, not to mention his years-long persecution as a suspected state criminal, had on his commercial activities. Also left out of consideration are the kinship ties which bound the old New England mercantile elite, of which Salter was the most prominent and prestigious member, to the old New England official elite.[18]

The death of Chief Justice Jonathan Belcher, at the end of March 1776, seems to have removed the last restraint on legal repression of "the more radical New England element at Halifax" and elsewhere. Belcher was not replaced for two years and, during the hiatus, the government evinced no reluctance to suppress political dissent on the part of "the extreme New England republican wing of the local opposition".[19] As early as July 1776 Attorney-General William Nesbitt illegally laid an *ex officio* criminal information for high treason against one Thomas Falconer [Faulkner], a New England Planter of Londonderry Township.[20] Though prosecutions by way of information for anything other than high misdemeanours were *ultra vires* under the criminal procedure of England as in force in Nova Scotia, the offence was non-bailable and the accused was detained without trial until the next term, when the indictment (for "treasonable practices") which had afterwards been preferred against him was quashed by the grand jury.[21] It is inconceivable that Chief Justice Belcher would have tolerated this flagrant abuse of process — unless

John Herd Thompson and Stephen J. Randall, *Canada and the United States: Ambivalent Allies* (Montreal & Kingston, 1994), pp. 9-14. Yet neither Kerr's critique of Barnes nor Rawlyk's critique of Kerr really undermines the basis of the Barnes thesis, of which Fischer's economic reinterpretation is both a recapitulation and a revision. On the other hand, an inherent weakness of this whole approach may be that it confines the scope of the economic interpretation to the leverage exercised by the metropolitan mercantile elite.

18 Salter himself had been briefly an ally of Nova Scotia's Bostonian first chief justice, Jonathan Belcher. His son and namesake, Dr Malachy Salter Jr, would later marry a daughter of Justice Charles Morris of the Supreme Court of Nova Scotia. Councillor Morris, originally from Massachusetts, served as acting chief justice of the province from March 1776 to April 1778 and in that capacity presided not only at the treason trials of the patriot besiegers of Fort Cumberland, but also at Salter's trial, in February 1777, for uttering seditious words.

19 The phrase is Winthrop Bell's, used in reference to the administration of Charles Lawrence, 1754-60: W.P. Bell, *The "Foreign Protestants" and the Settlement of Nova Scotia: The History of a Piece of Arrested British Colonial Policy in the Eighteenth Century* ([1961] Fredericton and Sackville NB, 1990), p. 465.

20 Pleas of the Crown, 15 July and 11 October 1776, RG 39, series J (HX), vol. 1, pp. 257, 262; petition of Thomas Faulkner, 10 February 1777 (endorsement), RG 1, vol. 342 doc. 59, PANS. The original charge against Faulkner was changed from statutory high treason to the high misdemeanour of 'treasonable practices' because no grand jury could be persuaded to return true bill on an indictment for high treason unless the accused were shown to have taken up arms against the king. Faulkner, who afterwards led a contingent from the Cobequid townships at the siege of Fort Cumberland, was to be one of only two men indicted rebels tried for high treason in April 1777.

21 The high prerogative expedient of *ex officio* criminal informations was available only for prosecuting misdemeanours; ergo, the Faulkner prosecution was illegal and unconstitutional.
   The "quasi-independent township of Londonderry", as Brebner (*Neutral Yankees*, p. 39) calls it, though colonized 14 years earlier, was not formally erected until March 1775 — scarcely a month before the outbreak of rebellion in New England. Londonderry subsequently showed itself to be the least rebellious of the three Cobequid Bay townships, having been settled mainly by Ulstermen rather than by New England Planters. See generally Mary Ellen Wright, "'...of a Licentious and Rebellious disposition' — the Cobequid Townships and the American Revolution", *Collections* of the Royal Nova Scotia Historical Society, 42 (1986), pp. 27-40.

as an unavoidable side effect of the government's proclamation of martial law on 5 December 1775, in which the moribund chief justice, as *ex officio* president of the Council, had no choice but to acquiesce. Attorney-General Nesbitt probably took advantage of the fact that neither of the assistant judges of the Supreme Court — the senior of whom (Isaac Deschamps) replaced Belcher as acting chief justice — was a lawyer. Whether their ignorance of criminal procedure (not to mention the 1695/6 *Treason Trials Regulation Act*) excused the judges' failure to counter the abuse of process by the chief crown attorney begs the question of judicial complicity in official repression. The *Habeas Corpus Suspension Act,* which permitted arrest and detention without bail or trial — on mere suspicion, not to mention accusation or misprison of treason — cannot be pleaded in extenuation of the judges' action, because it was not passed and did not become law until 1777.

The late chief justice, concerning whom "the tradition is emphatic that he was distinctly in sympathy with the Revolution",[22] had had close links with Halifax's Protestant Dissenters' Meeting-House [Mather's Congregational], and with its interim supply, Parson Seccombe of Chester, afterwards accused of seditious preaching. Thanks to the proliferation of independently-minded New England merchants such as Salter among its lay leaders, Mather's Church came to be viewed by government as the seed-bed of whig-patriotism in the capital. "So much concern did the political sympathies of this congregation give the Governor", writes the church historian, "that extraordinary means were taken to thwart them".[23] In broader ideological terms, moreover, the significance of the ordeal of Malachy Salter was not lost on those of his New England compatriots whose Congregationalism accommodated both religious and political dissent. If "the Revolution made Congregationalism...unpleasantly synonymous with rebellious sympathies", then Salter was "naturally suspected" not only "because of his New England connections", but also because of "his leading position at Mather's".[24] Salter was thus trapped in a vicious circle: the fact that they had selected him as moderator drew suspicion upon the congregation, while the congregation's uncompromising New Englishness cast the veil of suspicion over its paramount leader. The government's continuing prosecution-cum-persecution of Malachy Salter cries out for detailed analysis as a case study of ambiguous or divided loyalty, combining elements of politics, trade and religion. As a conscientious patriot, as a seagoing merchant suspected of trading with the enemy and as a pillar of the New England Congregational 'mother church', Salter made altogether too conspicuous a

---

22 Eaton, "Halifax and the American Revolution", p. 198.

23 Walter C. Murray, "History of St. Matthew's Church, Halifax, N.S.", *Collections* of the Nova Scotia Historical Society, 16 (1912), p. 164. One of the foundational myths of Mather's church is that the 65-acre glebe was 'confiscated' as a result of the 'treason trials' of Parson Seccombe of Chester and Salter: ibid., p. 152; Ian F. MacKinnon, *Settlements and Churches in Nova Scotia 1749-1776* [Montreal, 1930], pp. 72 n. 3, 97 n. 4; [R.M. Hattie], *Looking Backward over Two Centuries: A Short History of St. Matthew's United Church...* (Halifax, 1949), p. 12. Of course, no such trials ever took place, and escheat and forfeiture could only follow a conviction for high treason or judgment of outlawry against the accused.

24 Brebner, *Neutral Yankees*, pp. 192, 340.

target.

The "ardent republican", who studied the biography of the regicide and observed the anniversary of King Charles I's execution as a private holiday,[25] was not about to renege on his political principles because those of like mind had taken up arms against King George in defence of the very principles to which Salter himself adhered. His reputation appears even to have preceded him to England, whither he had gone on a trading voyage, for, in July 1776, the secretary at the Treasury wrote to the permanent under-secretary at the American Department informing him that a vessel lying in the Thames, the owner-master of which was Malachy Salter, was suspected of being bound for Massachusetts — in direct violation of the *Boston Port Act.* The secretary of state himself was concerned enough to write on the same subject a few days later to the new lieutenant-governor of Nova Scotia, advising him that a vessel owned and commanded by Salter was believed to be carrying goods from London to Nova Scotia in transit to Boston, and instructing him to prevent all contraband trade with the colonies in rebellion.[26] Commodore Marriot Arbuthnot RN, commissioner of the naval dockyard, who had taken over the government in May, replied that he would do his "utmost to prevent any intercourse or Correspondence between the Colonies in Rebellion, and any Persons in this Province".[27] This blanket prohibition against written communication, which derived from Governor Legge's proclamation of 5 July 1775 forbidding aid to the rebels,[28] laid the groundwork for the government's four-year-long vendetta against Malachy Salter.

Salter returned from England in the autumn of 1776. His ordeal, which began in earnest in the aftermath of the raising of the patriot siege of Fort Cumberland, coincided with a period of accelerated legal repression. The government's

---

25 "My great-great-grandfather," wrote Susannah Duffus Morrow, "was an ardent republican; beside him in his portrait is painted the 'Life of Cromwell', the name distinctly marked on the back of the book; while on the anniversary of the death of King Charles, Mr. Salter always had a sheep's head for dinner. I do not just see the connection, unless he meant to imply a resemblance between the two heads": [Anon.], *Family History*, p. 252. The unsigned and undated painting to which Mrs Stairs referred (probably an early Copley) now hangs in the Legislative Library at Province House in Halifax.

26 J. Robinson to W. Knox, 12 July 1776, Colonial Office Series [CO] 5 (America and the West Indies — Original Correspondence, etc.)/ vol. 147/ folios 320-1, Public Record Office [PRO]; G. Germain to M. Arbuthnot, 20 July 1776, CO 217 (Nova Scotia — Original Correspondence)/ vol. 52/ folio 162 (draft), PRO (mfm at PANS). See Judith Norton, comp., *New England Planters in the Maritime Provinces of Canada, 1759-1800: Bibliography of Primary Sources* (Toronto, 1993), p. 21, §156.

27 Arbuthnot to Germain, 3 October 1776, CO 217/52/226r, PRO.

28 "Proclamation forbidding persons to Aid or Correspond with any persons in Rebellion", 5 July 1775, CO 217/51/282r-283v, PRO. Murdoch states, "the governor issued a proclamation, forbidding all persons in this province from corresponding with or assisting the 'rebels' in New England, and directed the justices of the peace to publish it, and cause it to be read several times in all places of public worship": *Nova-Scotia,* p. 548. Eaton ("Halifax and the American Revolution", p. 201) considers this to be an economic warfare measure in response to the Nonexportation Resolution of Congress (17 May 1775), which placed an embargo on trade with the other American colonies not yet in rebellion.

post-insurrection strategy aimed particularly at suppressing sedition through comprehensive use of the criminal law.[29] Indeed the two sedition trials — of Houghton first, then Salter — were held expeditiously in the winter of 1777, while the two treason trials were deferred until the spring. Salter was tried and convicted of uttering seditious words in February 1777. Indicted again, scarcely a year later, for corresponding with the enemy, he saw the indictment quashed on a technicality. His reindictment on a more substantive and serious charge,[30] was not proceeded with because it appeared to charge high treason in the guise of high misdemeanour. Treason trials were banned by the imperial *Habeas Corpus Suspension Act,* which was passed the very month of Salter's trial, and came into force six months later. Salter nevertheless lay under the third indictment for nearly three years, until his death in January 1781. The prosecutorial compromise struck between the law officers was indefinite continuance, only aggravating the tension which must have been felt by the victim of the prosecution. Like the New England Planter magistrate Timothy Houghton of Chester — tried and convicted for high misdemeanour a mere two days earlier than Salter[31] — the latter, whose "misfortunes seem to have broken him",[32] did not live to see the end of the war.

The proliferation of indictments for "treasonable practices" (constructive treason) rather than high treason *tout court,* as well as the tendency for indictments to be indefinitely continued and never to come to trial, can both be attributed to the overarching impact of the five-year-long *Habeas Corpus Suspension Act* on the government's tactical planning for the prosecution of crimes against the state. The misdemeanour classification was therefore little more than a convenient legal fiction. Salter eventually fled to England because he feared that all that stood between him and a treason trial was the renewal of the temporary *Habeas Corpus Suspension Act.* If it were not renewed, then the way was clear for him to be indicted and tried for high treason. Though Salter could have been indicted for outlawry (high treason *in absentia*), he could not have been tried while the *Habeas Corpus Suspension Act* was in force. Had the act not been renewed, however, there would have been more indictees on high treason than those three dozen arising from the patriot siege of Fort Cumberland, and Malachy Salter would surely have been one of them.

After his first return from England in October 1776, Salter had begun to interest himself in the welfare of American prisoners of war incarcerated at Halifax. His charitable ministrations to the sick or wounded Americans subsisting on board a

29 In contrast, Clarke and Phillips, "Rebellion and Repression", p. 200, argue that the 1777-80 *Salter* prosecution exemplified "a reluctance" on the part of government "to invoke the heavy hand of the law".

30 "Treason imputed to a person by law from his conduct or course of actions, though his deeds taken severally do not amount to actual [high] treason": *Black's Law Dictionary,* 6th ed. (St Paul MN, 1990), p. 1501.

31 See Barry Cahill, "The Sedition Trial of Timothy Houghton: Repression in a Marginal New England Planter Township during the Revolutionary Years", *Acadiensis,* XXIV, 1 (Autumn 1994), pp. 35-58.

32 Brebner, *Neutral Yankees,* p. 341 n. 137.

hospital ship in Halifax Harbour while awaiting the prisoner exchange cartel, brought him into contact with one Dr John Jeffries, a Boston Tory emigrant refugee who had arrived in Halifax in April 1776. Jeffries, whose patriot father was the long-time treasurer of the town of Boston, was surgeon to the General Hospital in Halifax from 1776 to 1779. In November 1776 Dr Jeffries had a casual conversation with Salter, with whom he was barely acquainted, in which the latter declared that "he was always of the Side of the Americans In their Conduct, untill they declared their Indypendence and then he quit or Left them".[33] Salter, who had carelessly assumed that Dr Jeffries, a scion of Boston gentry, was no less ardent a republican than his father — and Salter himself — was denounced to the authorities by his scandalized interlocutor.[34] Salter, who declared himself to be against American *independence,* was not opposed in principle to the American *rebellion,* which he saw as the continuation of political protest by other means. As a patriotic American, Salter could conceive of no lesser response to tyranny and oppression. It would be going too far to say that the old New England mercantile elite filled the role of a fifth column in Halifax during the war: "Merchants appear to have been equivocal, supporting resistance but taking a conservative stance about rebellion".[35] But Salter was atypical. He appears to have been unequivocal, supporting rebellion but taking a conservative stance about independence.

The government took a serious view of what they evidently construed as a deliberate attempt by a prominent local patriot to seduce a prominent Loyalist refugee from his allegiance. Salter was charged with speaking seditious words, indicted and tried for misdemeanour in the Supreme Court in February 1777. The only witness against him was the deponent, Dr Jeffries, who testified that the accused said, "he thought the Americans were Much in the Right of it to make the Stand they did". Though he was convicted, the verdict against Salter was qualified; the jury declined to return a general verdict of guilty as charged because the crown failed to prove seditious intention. As the court did not order a trial *de novo,* and the accused could not be granted an absolute discharge, Salter was bound over,

---

33 The Deposition of John Jeffries..., 16 November 1776, RG 1, vol. 342, doc. 77, PANS. The deposition was drafted by Attorney-General Nesbitt and sworn before Secretary Bulkeley. Concerning Dr Jeffries see Allan Everett Marble, *Surgeons, Smallpox and the Poor: A History of Medicine and Social Conditions in Nova Scotia, 1749-1799* (Montreal & Kingston, 1993), p. 343.

34 "He is the Tory refugee", wrote Thomas H. Raddall of Dr Jeffries, "who betrayed Malachi Salter to the courts": *His Majesty's Yankees* (New York, 1943), pp. 322, 324. The ordeal of Malachi Salter is a well-developed subtheme in Raddall's first historical novel, set in Nova Scotia during the revolutionary years, 1774-8. See generally Barry Moody, "The Novelist as Historian: The Nova Scotia Identity in the Novels of Thomas H. Raddall", in Alan R. Young, ed., *Time & Place: The Life and Works of Thomas H. Raddall* (Fredericton, 1991), pp. 140-53.

Elsewhere Raddall characterizes the 'Yankee merchants' (namely, Salter and Simeon Perkins) as typical of Nova Scotia's New Englanders: "cautious, measuring their American sympathies against the British strength by sea, and hoping that somehow the Nova Scotians could stay neutral in what seemed to them a ruinous brawl": Thomas H. Raddall, *The Path of Destiny: Canada from the British Conquest to Home Rule: 1763-1850* (Toronto, 1957), p. 79

35 Stuart, *United States Expansionism,* p. 18.

securities worth £1000 being ordered produced to ensure his good behaviour.[36] The case attracted attention in Boston, where John Gill's radical patriot *Continental Journal and Weekly Advertiser* described how Salter had been prosecuted "on account of some expressions in favour of America".[37] An immediate result of Salter's conviction was that when the next general commission of the peace was issued his name was omitted, though he had been a justice of the peace continuously for over 16 years.[38]

Despite Salter's notorious rebel sympathies, his 160-ton brigantine was at no less risk from American privateers than any other Nova Scotian merchantman. In July 1777 the inevitable happened: the *Rising Sun* was taken outside Liverpool *en route* to Halifax from Bermuda and was conveyed to Salem, Massachusetts.[39] From July to September Salter was in Boston, where he petitioned the council of state to be allowed to resettle, on the grounds that, "having Suffer'd severely, both in person & property on account of his political principles, and for the favor and assistance he afforded to the American Seamen & Others in Captivity there [Halifax], his residence in that Province must render him very unhappy".[40] Whether Salter was serious about returning to Halifax to collect his family and settle his affairs before removing permanently to his hometown of Boston, or the petition was merely a ruse calculated to procure his escape from Massachusetts, the council granted him safe conduct. By October Salter was back home in Halifax; he never set foot in Boston again. Before the end of the month the storm broke over his head. The government called in Solicitor-General Gibbons to advise "in the Case of Mr Salter lately from Boston Suspected of Treasonable & Criminal Practices &c."[41] Suspecting that he was at best a middleman, at worst a double agent who intended to convert Nova Scotian treasury bills and provincial warrants for the purpose of financing the rebel war effort, the government took decisive measures. Treasurer Benjamin Green (another former Bostonian) was ordered to stop payment on all warrants presumed to have originated in New England.[42]

Within days of his return, Salter was writing to his former business partner in Boston, the merchant Bartholomew Kneeland,

36 Crown Prosecutions, RG 1, vol. 342, docs. 77, 78; Pleas of the Crown, RG 39, series J (HX), vol. 1, p. 280 (Hilary Term 1777), PANS.

37 19 June 1777, cited in Clifford K. Shipton, comp., *Sibley's Harvard Graduates, Volume XV : 1761-1763* (Boston, 1970), pp. 421-2 n. 11.

38 Commission Book, 5 May 1777, RG 1, vol. 168, pp. 500-2, PANS.

39 Innis, *Simeon Perkins*, p. 157 (7 July 1777).

40 Edmund Duvar Poole, comp., *Annals of Yarmouth and Barrington (Nova Scotia) in the Revolutionary War* (Yarmouth, 1899), pp. 31-2, quoting Massachusetts Archives (manuscript documents series), vols. 159, p. 168; 183, p. 136.

41 The tortuous progress of *R*. v. *Salter* (2nd) can easily be followed through Solicitor-General Gibbons' cumulative statement of account, 1777-9 (2 April 1779): "Manuscript Documents of Nova Scotia", RG 1, vol. 248, doc. 13, PANS.

42 Brebner, *Neutral Yankees*, p. 341.

The times are Such I am almost afraid to put pen to paper...there is an order to the Treasurer to Stop paym.^{t} for my Treas.^{rs} notes. I am forbid to speak to the prisoners [of war], *and I apprehend my life to be in danger as I have been much threat'ned, for being suppos'd a friend to the Rebels*. ...I am forbid sending Money or any thing Else in the Cartel [prisoner exchange vessel]. I beg you will be cautious in what you write me, I stand on very ticklish ground, & must be very Circumspect...I could say many things but must forbear, you'll hear further from me soon. I am indeed very full of trouble.[43]

The letter, in which Salter indiscreetly mentioned that he hoped to sail for England "in about a month", was confiscated from the cartel before it sailed. A mere two days after the letter was written, the Council ordered Salter's arrest and detention on suspicion of "Crimes and Misdemeanours against Government"; Solicitor-General Gibbons was afterwards directed to draw up and transmit "an Opinion upon Mr Salters intercepted Letter".[44] Though he had not been charged, and so was not eligible for bail, Salter was ordered to post a £1000 bond to secure his release from custody and appearance at the next sitting of the Supreme Court, to answer any charges which might be found against him. Otherwise he would have remained one of "the Persons now confin'd in the Jail of Halifax for promoting Rebellion and such treasonable practices...".[45]

The moratorium on the redemption of treasury notes was repealed one week after its imposition, whether because the government already had the exhibit evidence they needed — the intercepted letter to Kneeland — in order to charge Salter with sedition; because Salter's creditors in Halifax, such as Councillor John Butler, wanted his debts repaid; or because the government thought the better of painting with the broad brush of sedition everyone holding redeemable treasury notes of possible New England provenance. To be sure, corresponding on any business matter, however innocuous, with anyone in New England (especially Boston) — the more so in that Salter's letter must have been smuggled on board the cartel, without the captain's knowledge — was *prima facie* evidence of sedition because it violated Governor Legge's proclamation of July 1775 prohibiting correspondence with the rebels. Crimes and misdemeanours against government were the only common law offences for which someone could be arrested on suspicion and held, thanks to the *Habeas Corpus Suspension Act*, which provided the legal pretext for detention without trial. Though appearances may have been deceptive in Salter's case, the government was legitimately concerned with both appearance and reality. Overburdened with 500 prisoners (both military and civilian) in custody, hopelessly inadequate penal facilities and an acting sheriff, Thomas Bridge, who just

---

43 M. Salter to B. Kneeland, 8 Nov 1777, Crown Prosecutions, RG 1, vol. 342, doc. 82, PANS (emphasis added).

44 For this and what follows see minutes of Council, 10, 15 and 22 November 1777, RG 1, vol. 189, pp. 433ff.; Solicitor-General's Statement of Account, RG 1, vol. 248, doc. 13, PANS.

45 Minutes of Council, 30 December 1777, RG 1, vol. 189, p. 436, PANS.

happened to be Salter's son-in-law as well as one of his sureties, the government had every reason to be deeply apprehensive of the continuing security risk posed by Salter.

It is probably no coincidence that Salter fled Nova Scotia for the relative safety of England the very month — January 1778 — when the *Habeas Corpus Suspension Act* was due to expire; he could not have learned of its renewal before his arrival overseas. Though Salter applied for and received from the lieutenant-governor a leave of absence to go to England on business, and was gone before any indictment could be preferred against him, he was in direct violation of his parole. Having broken a solemn undertaking that he would present himself to answer any charges which might be laid against him at the next sitting of the Supreme Court, Salter was rendering himself vulnerable to a process for outlawry.[46] In January 1778, after he had left the province, Salter was indicted for misdemeanour for secretly corresponding with the enemy; the only substantive evidence against him was his letter to the Boston merchant, Kneeland. Though a simple majority of the grand jury was prepared to accept Attorney-General Nesbitt's rather limited indictment, the panel was sharply divided over the merits of the crown's case. True bill was returned, but the indictment was null and void because an absolute majority (12) was required for the accused to be tried, and only 10 of the grand jurors were in favour. Nevertheless, the crown — now represented not by Nesbitt but by his deputy, Solicitor-General Gibbons — was granted a continuance; a *nolle prosequi* should have been entered or, more properly, a stay of proceedings ordered by the court.

In Easter Term 1778 *R.* v. *Salter* resumed. Solicitor-General Gibbons, taking no chances, drafted a new, longer and much more expansive indictment which charged constructive high treason. The grand jury voted 16 in favour of finding a true bill, whereupon counsel for the crown, in the absence of the accused, had no alternative but to move either for judgment of outlawry or that the recognizance be forfeited for non-appearance. Solicitor-General Gibbons chose the latter course, arguing that the recognizance was forfeitable because it had been made for personal, not legal, appearance. Counsel for the accused, former solicitor-general James Brenton, argued against the motion, which, if granted, would have led to forfeiture of the recognizance and made Salter, as well as his sureties, Thomas Bridge and John Fillis,[47] debtors to the crown for a substantial sum. Defence counsel then moved for leave to traverse (contradict) the indictment, which motion was denied by the court.[48] Unable to try the accused on the true bill found against him and unwilling

---

46 Clarke and Phillips, "Rebellion and Repression", pp. 192-5. For this and what follows, unless otherwise indicated, see Crown Prosecutions, RG 1, vol. 342, docs. 79-80, 82-5 [1777-9]; Pleas of the Crown, RG 39, series J (HX), vol. 1, pp. 311, 321, 340, 376 [1778-80], PANS.

47 John Fillis JP and MHA was Halifax's leading distiller and rum merchant; his daughter was married to Salter's son. See generally James F. Smith, "John Fillis, MLA", in *Nova Scotia Historical Quarterly*, 1, 4 (December 1971), pp. 307-23.

48 Justice Isaac Deschamps bench-book, under date 14 April 1778, Royal Nova Scotia Historical Society fonds, MG 20, vol. 221, file 91.5, PANS.

to order a stay of proceedings,[49] the court decided to continue both the recognizance and the indictment to the next term. This was but the first of 11 continuances, which were granted until Michaelmas Term 1780, eight months after Salter had returned to the province, having been absent for more than two years. Despite his return, he was neither tried nor granted a conditional discharge. Only his death, on 13 January 1781, a few weeks short of his 65th birthday, put an end to the interminable series of continuances and removed the oppressive indictment.

The crux of *R. v. Salter* is why proceedings continued after Trinity Term (July) 1778, when the lieutenant-governor — taking, as it were, the law into his own hands — ordered it stayed.[50] There are a number of possible explanations: a new lieutenant-governor had been appointed, and was to take office within the month; the new chief justice (Bryan Finucane) had only begun to preside; or, by far the likeliest explanation, Attorney-General Nesbitt took exception to a nonconsultative motion on the part of his junior by coming into court within days of the government's stay of proceedings order and moving successfully for another continuance. Given that the indictment was already subject to a continuance, the motion for a stay of proceedings had to be made in open court by senior crown counsel by right of preaudience. Precedence at the bar, therefore — no trifling matter among colonial British North American lawyers — may well have been the issue that ultimately frustrated Solicitor-General Gibbons' attempt to carry out the lieutenant-governor's executive order. In such a charged atmosphere, even the exercise of prosecutorial discretion would have been strictly circumscribed.

Ironically, it was this lawyers' imbroglio which enabled Malachy Salter to prolong his absence from Nova Scotia without suffering any adverse consequences to his property. He left Halifax under a recognizance and returned home two years later to find himself lying under indictment for constructive high treason. He might have met a far worse fate had the *Habeas Corpus Suspension Act,* which was subject to annual expiration, not been renewed regularly by special act of Parliament. Towards the end of the first year of the act's operation, the government of Nova Scotia was forced to consider the implications of non-renewal of the act for its strategy of legal repression. There was concern enough in official circles that the law officers were asked to develop a contingency plan which would provide for

---

49 The court was apparently also unwilling to issue process of outlawry against Salter; see generally Clarke and Phillips, "Rebellion and Repression", notes 122-6 and accompanying text. This would have permitted the immediate confiscation of his very considerable holdings of real estate. Salter owned all the property now occupied by Maritime Centre, St Matthew's Church and Government House, in the heart of the south suburbs of the old town of Halifax — not to mention large landholdings elsewhere on the peninsula and outside Halifax Township and County: Estate of Malachy Salter, Halifax County Court of Probate, file S 6 (mfm at PANS).

50 R. Bulkeley to R. Gibbons, 22 July 1778, Secretary's letter-book, RG 1, vol. 136, p. 266, PANS. The stay of proceedings ordered by the lieutenant-governor against the advice of Attorney-General Nesbitt was ignored by Solicitor-General Gibbons, who acted as chief crown prosecuting attorney until Salter's counsel, Brenton, replaced Nesbitt as attorney-general in October 1779. The solicitor-general's ability to act more or less independently of the attorney-general suggests that Salter may have been spared a trial on the second indictment because of a debilitating stasis between the law officers of the crown.

suspects to continue to be detained without trial, or prosecuted for some statutory or common law offence (e.g., sedition).[51] In England Salter was immune from a trial for high treason regardless of whether the *Habeas Corpus Suspension Act* was renewed or not. In Nova Scotia he was not, as the contents of the second indictment — constructive high treason disguised as sedition — showed clearly.

Salter's authorized and certainly well-publicized departure[52] for England in January 1778 coincided with the second proceeding against him. Once safely there, he remained for two years, perhaps not so much in order to attend to his tangled business affairs as to protect himself against the potentially fatal consequences of non-renewal of the disabling *Habeas Corpus Suspension Act*. After Attorney-General Nesbitt finally retired, in March 1779, and was duly succeeded by his protégé, Brenton (hitherto Salter's counsel), the prosecution was postponed for the duration of Salter's life.[53] Continued for more than two years, or eight terms, the indictment never came to trial. Despite Solicitor-General Gibbons' determination to charge Salter with high treason in April 1778, no useful purpose would have been served by indicting a suspected traitor for a crime for which he could not have been tried. Though Attorney-General Nesbitt certainly did not advise the lieutenant-governor to order a stay of proceedings, and interposed his authority in order to secure yet another continuance, it was Nesbitt's successor, Brenton, who saw to it that the ageing, worn-out and ill Salter was not subjected to the ignominy of a second sedition trial.

If, as Brebner argues, the affair of Governor Legge committed the oligarchy of Halifax officialdom to loyalism,[54] then the "dramatic increases in trade and shifts in its pattern"[55] on the eve of the American Revolution also committed the old New England mercantile elite of Halifax to a strategy of economic brinkmanship and politically untenable bipartisanship. Like the neutral Americans during the Napoleonic Wars, the "neutral Yankees of Nova Scotia" during the Revolutionary years wished to trade with both belligerents — in defiance of imperial and colonial government policy. In business as well as personal terms, therefore, Malachy Salter, the most prominent but least typical member of the elite, lost the war and did not survive long enough to contest the peace. The old, pre-planter New England mercantile elite died with him.

51   "As the Act of Parliament for Securing and detaining persons charg'd with or Suspected of the Crime of High Treason [*Habeas Corpus Suspension Act*] will expire at the end of this year; The Lieutenant Governor desires that you will consider the Consequence thereof in respect of such person[s] as may be now Confin'd in Jail in this Province under the Authority of said Act and how far such persons may be detained or prosecuted under any other Law": R. Bulkeley to W. Nesbitt, 16 December 1777 [copy], Secretary's letter-book, RG 1, vol. 136, p. 258, PANS. In response to the letter from the provincial secretary, Solicitor-General Gibbons submitted "a long Opinion respecting the State Prisoners in Gaol on the first of Jan.y 1778", Statement of Account, RG 1, vol. 248, doc. 13, PANS; the former document, regrettably, is not extant.

52   See, for example, Innis, *Simeon Perkins,* p. 175 (18 December 1777).

53   Buggey, "Salter", p. 696.

54   Brebner, *Neutral Yankees,* p. xiv.

55   Fischer, "Revolution without Independence", p. 101.

Nor was Salter the only Halifax merchant prosecuted in such a public and repressive manner: the New England Planter merchant, John Avery, was indicted in the summer of 1779 for carrying on trade, commerce and correspondence with the rebels. Having been arrested, imprisoned and then released after entering into a recognizance for £2,000, Avery was never subsequently tried on or discharged from the indictment which was found against him; his ordeal lasted for nearly five years. Despite the intervening passage of the omnibus amnesty act, the prosecution was continued from term to term, until April 1784, after Avery's premature death.[56] As a brother of one of the leading Cumberland insurrectionists, James Avery, John Avery was placed in a hopelessly compromising position.[57]

Yet John Avery did not form part of the New England quadrilateral on which Brebner based his "stifling of treasons" argument.[58] It will not do as an effective reinterpretation of the Nova Scotia government's strategy for suppressing sedition to place on an equal footing Judge Foster Hutchinson, the Boston Tory refugee lawyer and mandamus councillor;[59] the "seditious preacher", John Seccombe; the "ardent republican", Malachy Salter; and the oath-breaking conscientious objector, Timothy Houghton. The only thing these four New Englanders had in common was that they were all natives of Massachusetts and that they were suspected of disloyalty chiefly on account of their New England connections. Of the four, only Salter and Houghton were indicted and tried, and only against Houghton was an unconditional verdict of guilty of high misdemeanour recorded. That the government's overreaction to the crisis was reflected in the political use of the criminal law against New Englanders of *any* stripe, whether old settlers or recent refugee immigrants, suggests that, while the nature and degree of official repression could vary widely, its most characteristic form was legal. Moreover, by effectively banning treason trials, the *Habeas Corpus Suspension Act* narrowed the range of prosecutorial options available to colonial governments for suppressing rebellion and apprehending insurrection. A renewable war measures act designed to legalize

56 Pleas of the Crown, RG 39, series J (HX), vol. 1, pp. 348, 405; Crown Prosecutions, RG 1, vol. 342, docs. 51-7, PANS. See Norton, *New England Planters*, p. 33, §267.

57 A Connecticut Yankee whose family included prominent and active patriots such as his younger brother James, John Avery struggled unsuccessfully for the rest of his life to remove the stigma of the presumption of guilt by association which had attached itself to him. The literature on Avery is considerable: Ernest A. Clarke, "Cumberland Planters and the Aftermath of the Attack on Fort Cumberland", in Margaret Conrad, ed., *They Planted Well: New England Planters in Maritime Canada* (Fredericton, 1988), p. 44; Jean Stephenson, "The Connecticut Settlement of Nova Scotia Prior to the Revolution", *National Genealogical Society Quarterly*, 42, 2 (June 1954), p. 59; Julian Gwyn, "Capitalists, Merchants and Manufacturers in Early Nova Scotia, 1769-1791: The Tangled Affairs of John Avery, James Creighton, John Albro and Joseph Fairbanks", in Margaret Conrad, ed., *Intimate Relations: Family and Community in Planter Nova Scotia, 1759-1800* (Fredericton, 1995), pp. 190-212. See also *Nova Scotia Gazette & Weekly Chronicle* (Halifax), 25 November 1783, p. 1.

58 Brebner, *Neutral Yankees*, p. xiv.

59 Judge Hutchinson (younger brother of the last royal governor of Massachusetts Bay) arrived in Halifax in April 1776, and promptly arranged for inflammatory Congressional documents to be printed in the *Gazette: ibid.*, p. 340.

detention without trial on suspicion of high treason, it had the unanticipated side effect of limiting the scope of prosecutable crimes against the state to sedition. The latter was a utilitarian common-law misdemeanour comprehending a wide range of indictable offences from defamation to constructive high treason. Prosecutions for ancillary or collateral crimes against the state also served the limited monitory and exemplary purpose of legal repression better than statutory high treason, which posed serious political risks for the legitimacy, impartiality and credibility of the administration of criminal justice by colonial governments. Grand juries were less likely to find 'true bill' on high treason indictments, and petit juries less likely to convict for a crime for which the death penalty was mandatory and royal pardons unheard-of. Sedition, on the other hand, was a first-division misdemeanour, which might comprehend "treasonable and seditious words, libels or correspondence" — to quote the language of Nova Scotia's "Act of Grace", the omnibus *State Crimes Pardon Act* of 1783.[60] Unlike high treason, these crimes and misdemeanours against government were — in theory, at least — prosecutable by means of the *ex officio* criminal information as well as by regular indictment.

Even from indictments, however, if the prosecution was ordered by government during wartime, the only release was by death — as both Salter and John Avery discovered. It is therefore necessary to view the sedition proceedings — the most obvious method of dealing with rebel sympathizers — as but another of several aspects of the government's broad strategy of legal repression. A willingness to invoke the heavy hand of state security law also marked the Nova Scotia government's reaction to several other instances of real or imagined sedition during this period. Though none of these involved armed rebellion, the government's persecution of the expatriate New England merchants, Salter and Avery, shows that the official response to crimes against the state — less high treason, where the government's freedom of action was severely curtailed by imperial legislation, than sedition, where the limitless resources of the common law might be exploited fully — was heavy-handed legal repression. Parson Seccombe was not merely warned and asked to renounce republicanism; "he was ordered to find security in £500 for his good behaviour, and to be debarred from preaching until he had signed a recantation".[61] Timothy Houghton was tried and convicted of high misdemeanour for slandering the king and sentenced to fine and imprisonment. The charge against Malachy Salter was *not* dropped, despite the lieutenant-governor's stay-of-proceedings order, and he remained under indictment until finally discharged by death three years later.

The behaviour of the Nova Scotia government with regard to suppressing

---

60 *Statutes of Nova Scotia* (1783) 23 Geo. 3, c. 3: "An ACT for granting the King's Most Gracious Free Pardon, to all His Subjects in this Province, for all Treasons, Misprison of Treasons, or Treasonable Correspondence committed or done by them, or any of them, in adhering to, aiding or assisting, countenancing or abetting, His Majesty's late Subjects in the Thirteen Colonies, during their Rebellion". The second section enacted that all depending prosecutions, whether private or public, should cease. Such an act could not have been passed unless and until the overriding *Habeas Corpus Suspension Act* expired for good, which it did in January 1783.

61 Murdoch, *Nova-Scotia*, p. 584.

rebellion and sedition during the Revolutionary years was not consistent, thanks to the interposition of the imperial *Habeas Corpus Suspension Act.* Deprived of high treason as a triable crime against the state, the government focused maximum attention on sedition. In doing so, it consistently tended to exaggerate and to overreact to the apparent danger to state security posed by the New England 'underground'. The government, moreover, was prepared to use this temporary act as a cloak for subverting due process of law in the attempt to counter incitement to rebellion. Inevitably, political protest was criminalized. The authorities dealt vigorously with the Cumberland insurrection in late 1776, but though the siege of the fort had been lifted and the rebels dispersed or captured, the following and succeeding years were marked by an expanded strategy of legal repression, which from late 1776 onwards included prosecutions for sedition. The significance of *Salter* and the other sedition proceedings is precisely that dissent *was* "depicted as treason".[62] The policy of indiscriminate repression directed towards New Englanders, Planter and non-Planter alike, though perhaps a policy dictated to some extent by post-insurrection paranoia, was nonetheless one which treated true sedition — breach of allegiance — as constructive high treason. The aftermath of the Cumberland insurrection suggests that the government dealt leniently with treason and repressively with sedition in order not to have occasion to suppress rebellion again. The renewable, and five times renewed *Habeas Corpus Suspension Act* was flexible enough to permit the government either to inflict wholesale legal repression or to alternate repression and leniency.

If the ordeal of Malachy Salter provides a contribution to the historiography of political crime in 18th-century Nova Scotia, it also suggests the need for some modification of the Clarke-Phillips thesis, which extrapolates official restraint from a loyalty paradigm for the popular response to the American Revolution in Nova Scotia. Explanations of why Nova Scotia did not rebel, or was not invaded like Quebec — the *real* 'fourteenth colony'[63] — have stressed ideological over material factors and religious attitudes over practical economic, military and even epidemiological considerations (smallpox). Historians of the political economy of the American Revolution, such as Joseph Ernst, make the instructive point that Nova Scotia did not have the infrastructure to rebel even if it had wanted to: "What Nova Scotia missed...was not any dialogue over liberty, or the rise of nationalist sentiment, but a half-century or more of economic and political development, and of population growth, that created the pre-conditions for Revolution".[64] Economics and demographics aside, the New England Planter

---

62 Clarke and Phillips, "Rebellion and Repression", p. 201.

63 See, for example, S.D. Clark, *Movements of Political Protest in Canada, 1640-1840* ([1959] Toronto, 1978), pp. 75ff., 'The Struggle for the Fourteenth Colony', 1775; cf. "The fact that Nova Scotia was only one of fourteen colonies suggests that our line of approach ought to be by way of a comparison between conditions in Nova Scotia and those in the other colonies, especially in those which were more backward in accepting the revolutionary point of view [e.g., Georgia]": Kerr, "Merchants of Nova Scotia", p. 21.

64 Joseph A. Ernst, "English Canada and the American Revolution", *La Révolution américaine et l'Europe* (Paris, 1979), p. 518; see also Marc Egnal and Joseph A. Ernst, "An Economic

experience in "a marginal colony during the Revolutionary years" argues that historians should pay more attention to the varying degrees of *non*loyalty which the New England majority in general exhibited, not only in the "critical years", 1775 and 1776, but, indeed, throughout the war.[65] The planter majority — 75 per cent of Nova Scotia's approximately 20,000 population in 1775 was of New England origin[66] — was neither neutral nor loyal; neither was it disloyal. The New Englanders, like the nonjuring Acadians before them, simply wanted to be left alone in undisturbed possession of the status quo, anomalous and unsustainable though it was in the face of rebellion, civil war and revolution. The neutral Yankees' third way was not sincere or straightforward but time-serving and dissimulative — and the hard-pressed Nova Scotia government called their bluff. This article suggests that, in formulating its response to sedition, the oligarchy came to view the elite leadership of the New England church and community as constructive traitors.

Finally, if there is one main conclusion which may be drawn from this investigation of the ordeal of Malachy Salter, it is that historians who ignore or undervalue the role of the old New England mercantile elite in any study of Nova Scotia and the American Revolution do so at their peril. Halifax, as a minor metropolis, was by no means unique in its dependence upon trade.[67] The English or English-connected merchants who survived and even flourished during the war were the competitors-creditors of those New England merchants victimized as political criminals. The only way to understand the 'treason of the merchants' is to return once again to studying political dissent and protest and the impact of wartime conditions (e.g., privateering) on commercial competition. The fate of established American merchants as chosen victims of state crimes prosecution in Halifax during the Revolutionary years cannot be satisfactorily explained by the 'leniency' thesis. It is time to acknowledge the centrality of government repression, and of an official attitude of repressiveness, to an understanding of Nova Scotia in 1775-6 — when revolution was not so much "rejected" as prevented.

Interpretation of the American Revolution", *William and Mary Quarterly,* [3rd ser.], 29, 1 (January 1972), pp. 3-32; and Joseph Ernst, "'Ideology' and an Economic Interpretation of the Revolution", in Alfred F. Young, ed., *The American Revolution: Explorations in the History of American Radicalism* (DeKalb IL, 1976), pp. 159-85. (Ernst goes on to state, "In sum, the insistence by some historians of the Maritimes upon viewing the American Revolution as essentially an ideological and nationalist movement has tended to trivialize the study of Nova Scotia's history during the Revolutionary period": "English Canada", pp. 518-9.)

65 "Mr. Eaton declares positively that there was no reluctance on the part of the people 'to throw in their lot with their friends of the New England colonies' and ascribes their failure in so doing to their rural situation, paucity in numbers, dispersion in settlement, and lack of arms": Kerr, "Merchants of Nova Scotia", pp. 20-1, quoting Arthur Wentworth Hamilton Eaton, whose description (*History of King's County,* pp. 430-2), deriving from oral tradition, of the circumstances which resulted in provincial troops being dispatched to the New England Planter township of Cornwallis in the autumn of 1778 — to quench the "seditious spirit in King's" — gives one pause.

66 James E. Candow, "The New England Planters in Nova Scotia", *Planter Notes,* 6, 2 (April 1995), p. 5. Candow points out that the "American Revolution was perhaps the central phenomenon in the history of the New England Planters".

67 Fischer, "Halifax Merchants", p. 32.

NEIL MacKINNON

Reprinted from Vol. II, No. 2
(Spring 1973)

The Changing Attitudes
of the Nova Scotian Loyalists
towards the United States,
1783-1791

All great passions are difficult to sustain, and even more so when one is removed from the object of that passion. The Loyalists came to Nova Scotia at the very flood of their anger. Although they had sometimes been generous and conciliatory towards the American people during the revolution, the year of the peace and the expulsion traumatized them, and they lashed out, like a grievously hurt child, with an intensity more fierce than during the war. It was in this state that they came to Nova Scotia bringing with them what seemed to be a strong and enduring hatred of those who had expelled them, an emotion which permeated the settlements during their first years in Nova Scotia. But there are few constants. In Nova Scotia the refugees could not reserve for the Americans that obsessive concentration upon which hatred can thrive. With time, new circumstances, and new enemies, the memory of the revolution receded, the Loyalist attitude mellowed, and the American as enemy was relegated to a far corner of the Loyalist mind.

Although they had lost much in the revolution, the early Loyalist attitude was based on more than loss. They had not only been beaten; they had been dismissed. They had forced upon them the role of contemptuous foil for the virtue and progress of the triumphant revolution, and, unable to accept this, they were driven to make of their fate a positive thing. As revolution polarized America, the Loyalists, denied the centre, found themselves where they did not necessarily wish to be, on the right. In a world with no centre, they accepted the polarity into which they were thrust by enemy and events, adopting and exaggerating the postures of their position. Losers of a civil war, they became unbowed defenders of a noble cause. Unable to remain, they made of their leaving a virtue, being "Voluntary exiles to this place, Chusing [sic] rather than to live under the Tyrannic power of a republican Government to quit the lands of our Nativity."[1] Treated with contempt, they reacted with utter

1 Memorial of the inhabitants of Digby, 1 August 1785, Society for the Propagation of the Gospel, MG17, B1/1, vol. 1, Public Archives of Canada.

disdain for all that the new nation symbolized. It was this need to make a virtue of their situation which gave their anti-Americanism in the first years much of its aggressive quality.

There were brave epithets cast over their shoulders about quitting "this damned country with pleasure."[2] It was now a cursed place, "a land of banditti,"[3] and a special resentment was often reserved for those Loyalists who chose to remain in such a land, under the domination of petty tyrants.[4] To one Loyalist, the country had become Satan's Kingdom, the collapse of which he anticipated with certainty and pleasure.[5] "Was I once clear of them, I should not Care, how soon they went to the devil."[6] The humiliation of their expulsion was alleviated somewhat by these assertions that they had been about to leave anyway.

The impact of the lost war, however, is seen in the dreams and the expectations they held concerning their place of exile. Nova Scotia was not only a refuge, but a place in which the Loyalists would still triumph. "By heaven," said Edward Winslow, "we shall be the envy of the American States."[7] Brook Watson saw Nova Scotia as growing affluent and populous within the British Empire, while "Their neighbours, like vinegar fretting on their lees will soon curse the day which made them independent."[8] To many, Nova Scotia was to be an extension of the war, where Loyalists and their principles would triumph, while the independent states would slide inevitably into decline and anarchy. In an exile's verse the province was hailed as that happy land where peace, love and harmony would reign, where liberty would be extended.

> Under a Sov'reign whose mild sway
> We shall flourish and be free,
> While the land from which we fled,
> Shall be oppress'd with Tyranny.[9]

As early as 1779 Jacob Bailey was describing his escape from the regions of tyranny and rebellion to a land of freedom, tranquillity and affluence.[10] Within a few years he was hedging sharply on Nova Scotian affluence, but still

2 C. Clopper to Chas. Whitworth, 18 April 1783, Gideon White Collection, Public Archives of Nova Scotia.

3 J. Alptharp to John Wentworth, 20 February 1788, Wentworth Papers, vol. 2, P.A.N.S.

4 Jacob Bailey to Capt. Benjamin Palmer, 2 August 1784, Bailey Collection, vol. 15, P.A.N.S.

5 N. Ford to Gideon White, 23 August 1786, Gideon White Collection, P.A.N.S.

6 *Ibid.*, 8 June 1786.

7 Cited in W. H. Nelson, *The American Tory* (London, 1961), p. 169.

8 B. Watson to E. Winslow, 26 August 1785, in W. O. Raymond, ed., *The Winslow Papers* (St. John, 1901), p. 312.

9 Halifax *Nova Scotia Gazette and Weekly Chronicle,* 18 October 1785.

10 Jacob Bailey to Moses Badger, 1 July 1779, Bailey Collection, vol. 13, P.A.N.S.

preferred "the gloomy retreats of the wilderness" to the land of mobs and committees." This note was struck again by George Deblois who described the
new settlers as breathing "a much greater share of *Free Air* than those renown-
ed Sons of Freedom.":[12]
Despite their own difficulties, the Nova Scotian Loyalists clung tenaciously
to the belief that the troubles in the new states were worse, and their future
bleak. They still talked of the promise of their situation and the comparative
collapse of their enemy. One Nova Scotia refugee, in 1785, described the Americans — poor, tax-ridden and oppressed — as regretting their independence.
"They now look back with regret to those happy times, when, under the wings
of Great Britain, they enjoyed peace, plenty and real freedom."[13] Similarly, a
friend wrote to Gideon White describing the imminent collapse of the United
States. With exorbitant taxes, cramped trade, political and social uncertainty,
the country was on the brink of total dissolution and inevitable revolution.[14]
White, visiting New Hampshire in 1787, felt that, in comparison, Shelburne
was a veritable paradise, and an object of great envy by the unfortunate people
of that state.[15] Benjamin Marston in the same year was permitting himself the
luxury of sympathy for the revolted states. Although they richly deserved what
had already befallen them, Marston expressed some pity for them in the calamities yet to come.[16]
The extent of this early obsession with the United States is seen in a New
Year's verse found in the Shelburne *Packet*. The occasion appears to have
been a traditional attempt by the printer's man to sum up the year's events and
to wish the customers a happy new year, in light but laboured verse. This
particular example began with references to local places and events, but the
lightheartedness was abruptly dropped as the writer moved swiftly into a paean
to the King and his province of Nova Scotia. The bulk of the verse was then
concentrated upon the new nation, the many conflicts within it, and the ugly
fighting over the spoils of victory.

> Our trade protected shall each year increase
> And in its train bring freedom, plenty, peace;
> Whilst independence sons shall curse the hour
> That first gave birth to Independence pow'r.[17]

11 Jacob Bailey to Charles Inglis, 22 August 1783, Lawrence Collection, vol. 72, p. 110, P.A.C.

12 George Deblois to _____, May 1785, Lawrence Collection, vol. 20, p. 12, P.A.C.

13 *London Chronicle* (London, England), 25-27 August 1785.

14 N. Ford to Gideon White, 23 August 1786, White Collection, P.A.N.S.

15 Gideon White to Charles _____, 22 June 1787, *ibid.*

16 Benjamin Marston to Edward Winslow, 8 September 1787, in Raymond, *The Winslow Papers*, p. 347.

17 *Nova Scotia Packet*, 1 January 1787, in the White Collection, P.A.N.S.

Even in doggerel, intended for local amusement, this theme of Nova Scotia's rise and the States' failure was struck and was dominant. While the American experience faced imminent collapse, the Loyalists were "laying the foundations of a New Empire," and establishing "a *place* chosen by the Lords elect."[18]

The Loyalist newspapers played an important role in reflecting and extending this attitude, offering the refugees a steady flow of stories from and about the United States. In the summer and fall of 1786, the *Packet* was very busy with stories of discord and discontent within the United States, and particularly with the troubles in New Hampshire where, according to the *Packet,* a Cromwell had lately risen.[19] It also ran detailed stories on uprisings in Massachusetts, Rhode Island and Philadelphia, noting that with the continuing anarchy and confusion throughout the States, "many of the better thinking among them, are totally quitting them, and mean to seek an asylum from such distractions in this settlement."[20]

Where the American difficulties were reported with satisfaction, the American position in the commercial empire of Britain was debated with concern and fear, comments on the issue appearing repeatedly in the refugee newspapers. Its very prominence prodded the memories of revolution and provoked renewed comments on the past sins and possible future treachery of the independent states, on further rewarding rebellion, and on British credulity in the deceptions and designs of a desperate people.[21] *The Royal American Gazette* even reprinted fierce diatribes from American newspapers. One such letter from the *Boston Gazette,* having dredged up past British atrocities, described the Loyalists as pelf-hunting parasites and double faced tools of British intrigue.[22] Shortly after another Boston article was printed which, while commenting on the opposition of the Nova Scotian Loyalists to American involvement in British Trade, labelled the refugees as "nefarious outlaws" who were not only intent upon hurting American trade, but were also *"sucking the very vitals of our political existance* by means of their agents and emissaries."[23] The Shelburne newspapers were very sensitive to any American slighting of their communities, and answered in kind any derogatory comments they found. One column of a 1786 *Packet* contained a biting verse on affairs in the United States, and below it an attack on American distortion of Loyalist affairs in Nova Scotia. Commenting on the progress of shipbuilding in the province, the *Packet* stated that American newspapers deliberately exaggerated the difficulties of the refugees in order to stop the constant emigration of their citizens

18 Wm. Parker to Chas. Whitworth, 8 June 1784, White Collection, P.A.N.S.
19 *Nova Scotia Packet,* 13 July 1786.
20 *Ibid.,* 5 October 1786.
21 *Royal American Gazette,* 7 February 1785.
22 *Ibid.,* 1 August 1785.
23 *Ibid.,* 18 April 1785.

to Shelburne[24] The shipbuilding controversy was continued by the *Packet* with the launching of the brig *Governor Parr* at Shelburne. "Be hush'd ye inhabitants of Shelburne nor with your skyrending acclamations on these occasions, *disturb* the *quiet tranquility* of the *peaceable people of Massachusetts.*"[25]

By their constant attention to the United States, by their comparisons and contumely, the Shelburne newspapers helped to sustain the intensity of Loyalist hostility, for with three such newspapers in Shelburne, dragging the past in all its rancour before them, the Loyalists were given little respite from the war. The Shelburne papers, however, like their community, were short-lived, their demise coinciding with a shift in the Loyalist attitude towards the United States.[26] By the time of their passing, Loyalist antipathy was receding, the response to their former home less automatic and less harsh. Other comments on the United States can be found, but after 1787 the references, both in newspapers and private correspondence, were less frequent and less bitter.

The *Nova Scotian Magazine*, for example, produced in the last years of the decade to encourage both economic and cultural improvement within the province, contrasted sharply with the Shelburne newspapers in its attitude towards the United States. Originally published by William Cochrane, an Anglican minister who had come from New York after the Revolution, and later by John Howe, a Sandemanian Loyalist, it was dependent upon the support of Loyalist readers throughout the province, yet showed none of the blatant hostility of the Shelburne papers. It shamelessly borrowed many of its articles from American journals and sources, most of them on agricultural methods, but others on topics ranging from school systems to the fate of the free negro. There was one fierce Loyalist reaction in the magazine to a biased history of the Revolution[27] There was also a plan for education in Nova Scotia which made much of the weakness of the American system of education and the threat of American democratic institutions[28] But these seem isolated incidents in a journal otherwise void of derogatory comments on the Americans.

After 1786 there appeared an increase in, and easing of communication between Americans and Loyalists. Co-operation between the ethnic and fraternal societies on both sides of the border was more marked. The North British Society of Halifax, although studded with Loyalist members, thought it fitting to have representatives of the New York and Philadelphia societies in

---

24 *Nova Scotia Packet,* 9 November 1786.

25 *Ibid.,* 14 December 1786.

26 *The Royal American Gazette* and *The Port Roseway Gazeteer* had both ceased publication in Shelburne by September, 1787, while *The Nova Scotia Packet* existed as late as February, 1789. See Marie Tremaine, *A Bibliography of Canadian Imprints* (Toronto, 1952), pp. 612-617.

27 Halifax *Nova Scotia Magazine,* vol. 1, p. 204.

28 *Ibid.,* vol. 1, p. 105 ff., p. 199 ff., p. 364 ff.

attendance for its celebration of 1787.[29] Ties with relatives and friends, although frayed by division, emotion, and the wayward post, had not been sundered. With time, letters to and from the United States became more frequent and the circle of acquaintances broadened. As these ties were renewed and strengthened, visits to and from Americans increased.

One result of these visits, and perhaps also a cause, was the growing number of marriages between Americans and Loyalists. "I hear by accounts from Boston," wrote Mrs. Hutchinson, "that one of your youths has thought fit to detain one of our pretty girls by marrying her."[30] Andrew Belcher, another Loyalist, expressed delight at the engagement of his sister to a doctor from Cambridge.[31] The only derogatory comments were humorous ones by a friend who reminded Miss Belcher of her former opinion of doctors, and threatened to visit Boston to tease the prospective groom.[32] Those who had not long before severed their ties forever from Satan's Kingdom, now seemed happy to witness and encourage marriages with Americans. The scarcity of suitable matches in Nova Scotia would have overcome most obstacles, but what one notices is the lack of any comment on nationality as an obstacle.

Comments made by Loyalists visiting the United States after 1787 lacked the antagonism and bitterness found earlier. Although Gideon White painted a doleful picture of the state of New Hampshire upon his visit, he also stressed how impressed he had been by the kindness he had received, and by the many people he had call on him, all "very polite, friendly and social."[33] Frederick Geyer, writing of his visit to Boston in 1787, omitted any comment on public matters, "having long since determined to leave those matters to whom they are interested."[34] Gregory Townsend of Halifax had very much wanted to visit his friends in Boston.[35] Finally arriving in the spring of 1788, he had a delightful, if too brief, stay among "all our Boston Friends." Circumstances at home forcing him to cut short his visit, he "reluctantly left that best of Countries."[36] The family of Mather Byles, the Anglican clergyman, were also visiting the United States. An uncle had sailed in 1787, and in the following year Mather Byles III planned to visit relatives and childhood haunts.[37] In 1790 the elder Mather Byles journeyed to Boston to settle his father's estate. It was a sentimental journey, one of embracing sisters not seen for a decade, of prayers at

29 James S. Macdonald, *Annals of the North British Society of Halifax, N. S.* (Halifax, 1894), p. 55.

30 M. Hutchinson to M. Mascarene, 6 September 1783, Mascarene Papers, P.A.N.S.

31 Andrew Belcher to his sister, Betty, n.d. (c. 1790), Byles Papers, vol. 1, f. 3, P.A.N.S.

32 R. Altman to Miss Byles, 19 June 1790, *ibid.*

33 Gideon White to Chas.————, 22 June 1787, White Collection, P.A.N.S.

34 F. W. Geyer to Ward Chipman, 12 June 1786, Lawrence Collection, vol. 2, P.A.C.

35 G. Townsend to Ward Chipman, 19 November 1787, Chipman Papers, P.A.C.

36 *Ibid.,* 10 May 1788.

37 Mather Byles III to his aunts, 26 August 1788, Byles Papers, vol. 1, f. 2, P.A.N.S.

the family tomb, of visiting relatives, of entertaining and being entertained by a host of friends and acquaintances. He preached at Trinity Church, and was astonished to receive an invitation from a Mr. West to preach to his father's congregation at the new meeting house. It was a very happy trip, and the journal kept by this acerbic gentleman is noteworthy for the expressions of warmth, gratitude and generosity towards his American hosts. From the moment of his arrival, with his comments upon the politeness and courtesy of the customs official, until his return, there were no unkind comments on the Americans, no stirring of the Revolution's residue.[38]

Nor did it take a visit to express the altered views. One reads of the gradual softening in the letters of Margaret Hutchinson, from sharp hostility towards the new order to a casual acceptance. At the war's conclusion she would not entertain the idea of returning to the new Massachusetts. "The ideas I have of what it once was, and what it is now, has sufficiently wean'd me from it."[39] As the years passed she still did not return, but the altered America was no longer a factor. The reasons she later stressed were the difficulties of age and of leaving husband and family for any period of time.[40]

Even Jacob Bailey was softening. Few in Nova Scotia had written as much on the Loyalist fate in the Revolution, nor as violently against Britain and the rebels alike, as this Anglican minister in the Annapolis Valley. Towards the revolting states, the ambitious leaders, and their foolish supporters, he had been merciless in his ridicule.[41] With time, however, he turned more to Britain as the chief cause of Loyalist woes, and the Americans as villain receded somewhat into the background. In December of 1787 he wrote to the Rev. John Gardiner on his appointment to Bailey's former church at Pawnalborough, wishing the new minister well, and expressing his own continued affection for the parishioners. He had hoped to return after the war, he explained in most diplomatic terms, but the spirit of revolution had prevailed and gallic perfidy has led to a separation from Britain. "My long absence has not in the least diminished my tender regard for the happiness of those dear friends, which stubborn faction had compelled me to forsake."[42]

William Clark, an Anglican minister in Digby, by the end of the decade, also expressed new views on the revolted states, finding the Americans much changed from the earlier years. Having travelled to Boston in 1789, he commented on the immense difference he found in the people since the Revolution. "In times of Rebellion or public Commotion, the Body politic resembles a man under the Dilirium of a Fever, who when he gets well and returns to

38 Journal of Mather Byles, July-September 1790, Byles Papers, vol. 1, f. 2, pp. 29c-29i, P.A.N.S.

39 M. Hutchinson to M. Mascarene, 20 October 1783, Mascarene Papers, P.A.N.S.

40 *Ibid.*, 3 October 1786.

41 See, for example, Bailey's journal of the flight from New England, Bailey Papers, vol. 5, P.A.N.S.

42 Jacob Bailey to Rev. John Gardiner, 8 December 1787, Bailey Collection, vol. 15, P.A.N.S.

his natural Temper, is quite a different man."[43] Clark, far from condemning, now appeared to be rationalizing earlier American actions, and drawing a sharp distinction between revolutionary America and the moderation of the post-Revolution period.

The altered attitudes of such individuals as Clark and Bailey, White, Mrs. Hutchinson and the others, reflected the changing attitude of the Loyalists in general. The rank and file left few letters, but they did express themselves graphically by their actions, for they were now leaving Nova Scotia and returning to the United States. Although there had been an exodus of the uncommitted soon after the founding of the settlements, the majority had settled in and begun to build again. After the cessation of the King's allowance, however, another rush began to the United States. In the fall of 1787 an Anglican minister wrote of "the great Emigration from this Province to the States."[44] Governor Parr also described the great number leaving with the ending of provisions.[45]

A concurrent factor in encouraging many to return was the British decision which allowed half-pay officers to receive their pensions while residing outside the empire. The effect this had on emigration was so extensive that Jacob Bailey felt it would depopulate the province.[46] In 1790 William Clark wrote: "This Place is nearly desolated by emigrations, or more properly, re-emigrations."[47] The portable pensions had given many the opportunity of living where they wished and they apparently wished to live in the United States. Their return testified to the changing feelings of the refugees to their birthplace, a change in which the old rhetoric, the old cries of loyalty and treason, did not necessarily reflect the attitudes of the rank and file. It is difficult to return to a people you profess to hate. Since so many were returning with so little remorse, it might perhaps be assumed that the professions of hatred were no longer very extensive or very intense.

Hatred of the United States had been a dominant characteristic of the early Loyalist communities, for the first years had been too close to the Revolution to allow the abatement of harsh memories. The scars were still raw. Moreover, reality had not caught up with the Loyalists, and it was still imaginable to create

---

43 William Clark to Samuel Peters, 12 May 1790, Peters Papers, vol. 4, P.A.N.S.

44 Roger Viets to Samuel Peters, 12 October 1787, Peters Papers, vol. 3, P.A.N.S.

45 John Parr to Grenville, 25 May 1791, C.O. 217/63, P.A.C. Judith Fingard estimates that by 1790 Shelburne had lost 4/5 of its population, and Digby about one half. See Fingard, *The Anglican Design in Loyalist Nova Scotia* (London, 1972), pp. 43, 204.

46 Jacob Bailey to _____, 12 November 1787, Bailey Collection, vol. 15, P.A.N.S.

47 William Clark to Samuel Peters, 26 July 1790, Peters Papers, vol. 4, P.A.N.S. See also Jacob Bailey to _____, 12 November 1787, Bailey Collection, vol. 15, P.A.N.S., and Bailey to Morice, 12 November 1787, *ibid.* In a list of Shelburne residents who registered to leave the province in 1786-1787 approximately 74% stated they were returning to the United States. See White Collection, vol. 5, P.A.N.S.

in Nova Scotia what had been lost in the former colonies. The strength of this hope, spurring the many comparisons with the Americans, helped to keep alive the hostility. But the very intensity of their reaction was too much to sustain. The passage of time and the reality of Nova Scotia were bound to produce a mellowing patina for their views, and to elicit a more generous and friendly attitude to the United States. The revolutionary experience was, in effect, being supplanted by the Nova Scotian, the immediacy and the dominance of which overwhelmed the earlier trauma. If the hostility towards the United States was to be sustained, that country had to remain the principal focus of envy and hatred. In Nova Scotia, however, these hostile emotions were loosed upon Britain, local officials, Nova Scotians and one's fellow Loyalists.[48]

Twenty thousand Loyalists had descended upon Nova Scotia seeking retribution and opportunity from a province too poor to support them. The natural result was a fierce scramble among the Loyalists for the prizes. Moreover, the refugees were often placed in large, uncultivated areas, isolated somewhat from the rest of Nova Scotia. The discord and conflict inevitable in such a large task of transplanting was between and among Loyalists. The pent-up hostility and resentment of Loyalist grievances, instead of being channelled to the outside world, turned inward, Loyalist bickering with Loyalist over fundamental questions of property and place. Noting this on a tour of Shelburne, Andrew Brown wrote: ". . . all the bitterness seemed now to be shed between the different knots of Loyalists in Shelburne which they had lately directed undivided against the members of Congress and the independence of the United States."[49]

An even deeper resentment was soon expressed towards the officials of Nova Scotia. From the very beginning there had been harsh complaints of Governor Parr, of the treatment received and the obstacles placed in the way of settlement, and accusations of corruption, incompetence, and favouritism. To Charles Morris there were "unmeritted ungenerous complaints which have been made against all the officers of Government without exception."[50] These complaints and hostilities did not ease with time, for the Loyalists had come to a province ruled tightly by a small circle in Halifax, and their attempts to share in and to limit this power exacerbated feelings on both sides, deflecting much of the Loyalist venom onto the ruling body of Nova Scotia. Jacob Bailey declared that many of the respectable people returning to the United States had been in effect driven out by affairs in the province, where only the wicked prospered.[51] A returning Loyalist expressed his sympathy for the many remain-

48 Roger Viets to Samuel Peters, 12 October 1787, Peters Papers, vol. 3, P.A.N.S.

49 Prof. Andrew Brown, "History of North America" (unpublished MS), Andrew Brown Papers, p. 103, Edinburgh University.

50 Charles Morris to Maj. Studholm, 12 November 1784, Charles Morris Letterbook, P.A.N.S.

51 Jacob Bailey to_____, 12 November 1787, Bailey Collection, vol. 15, P.A.N.S.

ing Loyalists "who are obliged to live under the arbitrary, cruel & unjust Gov-
ernmt as at present administer'd in Nova Scotia."[52] The comments of the returning Loyalists represented a common attitude among the refugees towards
official Nova Scotia, for complaints had been both widespread and harsh.
"This is an ungrateful place, . . .", said one who had seen his son return in
1788.[53] They spoke as if they had fled a land under mob rule only to find themselves in Nova Scotia under a rule which seemed almost as arbitrary and exclusive. The bitterness once felt towards the revolted states was being shouldered aside by the growing anger and resentment felt towards the establishment
in Nova Scotia.

Britain also shared in the deflecting of Loyalist anger. Their early attitude
towards the mother country was somewhat disguised by the situation in which
they found themselves. Because of the circumstances of their defeat their
expressed enmity was focussed upon the revolting states. The corollary of this
attitude was the rite of loyalty in which they indulged so zealously. As antag-
onists of the rebel forces, they sought both to glorify and to symbolize the
antithesis of rebellion, the quality of loyalty.[54]

But what was of importance in their strenuous displays of devotion to the
crown was not the object of that loyalty but rather the virtue of loyalty itself.
They were to be distinguished from the rebels, and from other mortals, by the
possession of this selfless quality. Moreover, in the realm of Nova Scotia, since
they were uncomfortably dependent upon British largesse, and since their one
claim upon Britain was their loyalty, the ritualistic celebration of every imaginable royal event and birthday was as much a tactical as an affectionate re-
ponse, to keep alive in Britain a remembrance of the Loyalist sacrifices.

This combination of circumstances, however, obscured a festering resentment towards Britain. They had not accepted a peace which they felt betrayed
them to appease the rebels, and where ". . . such a number of the best of human
beings were deserted by the government they have sacrificed their all for?"[55]
To a degree judgment was withheld on Britain until it was seen how far she
would go to compensate the Loyalists for their losses. By 1788 they knew, for
by this date Britain had met her basic obligations. The land had been distributed, half-pay and pensions granted, provisions ended, and for many refugees,
too little given to too few. With their fate in Nova Scotia crystallizing, the
Loyalists tended to weigh less generously Britain's part in their fortunes, and
to place at her doorstep much of the blame once monopolized by the independent states. In 1790 William Clark wrote that "The People of New

52 Quoted by Clark in William Clark to Samuel Peters, 23 June 1789, Peters Papers, vol. 4, P.A.N.S.

53 J. Peters to Samuel Peters, 17 November 1788, Peters Papers, vol. 3, P.A.N.S.

54 See Neil MacKinnon, "Nova Scotia Loyalists, 1783-1785," *Histoire sociale/Social History* (November, 1969), pp. 23-24.

55 Sarah Winslow to Benjamin Marston, 10 April 1783, in Raymond, *The Winslow Fapers,* p. 87.

England never treated me with that Barbarity the Government of Old England has, all things considered."[56]

In contrast with the chill from Britain and Nova Scotia was the increasing warmth of the American response to the Loyalists. With time American anger subsided, and the returning Loyalists found a cordial welcome from the Americans. Settling in New York in 1790, a Dr. Huggeford wrote of how pleased he was with his reception, and only wished he had gone sooner.[57] Another found that the most friendly treatment was being paid to all the Loyalists returning to America.[58] Dr. Walter's return from Shelburne was well reported in an American newspaper of 1791:

> He has been invited to officiate in several of our Meeting-Houses, and met with universal approbation — the places of Worship have been crowded with the most respectable audiences on those occasions.[59]

Such examples of American generosity and cordiality would have done much by themselves to curb the Loyalist attitude, for the ebbing of American hostility weakened the foundations upon which Loyalist antipathy rested. No longer treated as an enemy, the Loyalist found it more difficult to act as one.

It would have been impossible in any case to sustain the intensity of the earlier attitude. Even hostility must have priorities, and the attention once focussed in splendid concentration upon the revolted states had been diverted in Nova Scotia to other, more immediate and more dominant objects of anger. With the Loyalist difficulties in the new land, the ugly conflicts with pre-Loyalists and fellow Loyalists, with the growing resentment of both the British and Nova Scotian governments, the American as enemy was relegated to a minor, somewhat distant role.

Republican institutions would remain alien to the Loyalists, for they had not shared that desperate American experience which had given birth to their political system. The influence of the French Revolution and its excesses would harden their attitude towards republicanism. Such events of the 1790's as Jay's Treaty and the American flirtation with the French, combined with the conservative regime of John Wentworth in Nova Scotia, with its emphasis upon the virtue of loyalty to the status quo, would rekindle some of the old rhetoric.[60] But it is easy to exaggerate the anti-Americanism of this later period in Nova Scotia,

56 William Clark to Samuel Peters, 12 May 1790, Peters Papers, vol. 4, P.A.N.S.

57 *Ibid.,* 4 September 1790.

58 Quoted in William Clark to Samuel Peters, 23 June 1789, *ibid.*

59 *Nova Scotia Gazette,* 20 December 1791.

60 Some Loyalists who entered the establishment in Nova Scotia retained a rhetoric of contempt and hostility. What is interesting in Nova Scotia is that the establishment, chiefly non-Loyalist under Parr, managed to usurp the image of loyalty and to brand some of the Loyalist reformers as suspect.

and misleading to see this later period, shaped by its own events, as a simple continuation of the 1780's. Between the bitterness of the exodus and the conservatism of the Wentworth years there was a marked pause in which the attitude of the Loyalists towards the American people, those detested rebels of the past, had mellowed remarkably.

SHANNON RYAN

Reprinted from Vol. XII, No. 2
(Spring 1983)

Fishery to Colony:
A Newfoundland Watershed, 1793-1815

ALMOST THREE CENTURIES after the discovery of the Newfoundland cod fish stocks, the British government still conceived of Newfoundland as a fishing station, the "Grand Cod Fishery of the Universe". As late as 1775 an act of parliament stipulated, among other things, ways to avoid the encouragement of a resident fishery in Newfoundland.[1] However, half a century later the condition of Newfoundland had changed. In 1824 the island at last received colonial status within the British Empire, and in 1832 Newfoundland acquired a system of representative government.[2] For Newfoundlanders the era of the French Revolutionary and Napoleonic Wars was a time of significant changes. In the years from the 1790s to the 1810s the island's permanent population increased substantially, and by 1815 the island's residents numbered 40,568 people. It was during these decades that the cod fishery was transformed from a migratory European business enterprise to a Newfoundland-based economic activity. As a result, Newfoundland's status as a fishing station could no longer be justified.

The beginning of war in 1793 had its usual immediate effects on the European migratory fisheries in Newfoundland waters. The French ceased all transatlantic fishing activity, not only because they did not have the naval strength to protect it, but also because it had always been French practice to fully mobilize her naval resources in her contests with England. As in earlier periods of war, once more the English West Country fishing fleets suffered from the impressment of large numbers of their fishermen into the Royal Navy and from the fears created by the threat of impressment, which scared many fishermen away from the English fishing ports. Although at first viewed as a temporary setback, such as had been experienced many times during the previous three centuries, this was, in fact, the beginning of the end of the migratory West Country-Newfoundland fishery.

The West Country migratory fishery had been in a remarkably healthy condition in the years since the American Revolution. From 236 ships, 2603 men and 22,535 tons in 1784, it had reached a peak of 389 ships, 4306 men and 28,846 tons in 1788.[3] Production rose steadily and dramatically from 131,650

---

1 Quoted in D.W. Prowse, *A History of Newfoundland* (London, 1895), p. 344.

2 For political developments in this period see A.H. McLintock, *The Establishment of Constitutional Government in Newfoundland, 1783-1832: A Study of Retarded Colonization* (London, 1941).

3 All statistics for this period, in the text and in the tables, unless otherwise stated are taken from the Annual Reports on the Trade and Inhabitants of Newfoundland in the CO 194 series, Public

cwts in 1784 to 412,590 cwts in 1789. This expansion was more than the market could cope with, and depressed prices caused a sharp decline in the size of the fleet, which numbered 304 vessels in 1789. During the following three years the fleet operated at a reduced but stable level, averaging 260 ships per year.[4] War in 1793 reduced the fleet to 148 ships. In the subsequent decades all three principal branches of the migratory fishery suffered difficulties and declined.

The bank fishery had been the major branch of this migratory fishery since the Seven Years war. In 1789-92[5] the bank fleet averaged 171 vessels annually and made up about two-thirds of all ships enumerated in the Annual Returns as British fishing ships. In 1793 the number dropped to 63 (out of 148) and in that year, for the first time, 19 bank ships were reported to be operating out of Newfoundland. Some of these were probably English bankers which decided to stay in Newfoundland during the winter rather than return to England, for the decline of the bye boat fishery and the business it had generated, combined with the hazards of war, made recrossing the Atlantic less attractive. Also, of course, the longer bank fishing season encouraged crews to remain on the island. In 1794, 201 fishing ships came from England, of which 100 were bankers; the figures for 1795 were 127 and 53 respectively. Meanwhile, the island-based banking fleet increased to 25 and then 62 vessels during these years. When the war was carried to the Grand Banks in 1796 by a French squadron of at least ten men-of-war under Admiral Richery, it appears that the bank fishery ceased altogether.[6] Although it recovered in 1797 and 34 British ships fished there, accompanied by 78 Newfoundland ships, indications are that the migratory fishery in Newfoundland was very weak during the next three years. By 1802 the bank fleet contained 71 Newfoundland ships and 58 British, and in 1803 there were 68 Newfoundland bank ships, while the British fleet numbered 64 ships. The size of the Newfoundland bank fleet remained the same in 1804, but in 1805 dropped to 30 ships and continued to decline until it had disappeared completely by the 1820s. The British bank fleet declined sharply in 1804 when war was resumed with France. In that year there were only 21 ships, and in 1805 only 12 ships, though after the Battle of Trafalgar there were about 20 ships annually. The fleet experienced another sharp decline during the 1812-14 war with the

Record Office [PRO], London. See Shannon Ryan, "Abstract of CO 194 Statistics", unpublished manuscript, Memorial University of Newfoundland, 1969. Also, see K. Matthews, "History of the West of England-Newfoundland Fishery", D.Phil. thesis, Oxford University, 1968, for a more complete discussion of the West of England-Newfoundland fishery prior to the 19th century.

4   Figures for the crews in 1790 are incomplete, as are the figures for tonnage in 1792.

5   No figures available for 1787 and 1788. All dates thus expressed are inclusive.

6   Governor James Wallace to Colonial Office, 29 September 1796, CO 194/39, fols. 25-46. English bank ships that stayed in Newfoundland and those that were built there were both referred to as island bank ships. Here they will be referred to as Newfoundland bank ships.

United States, but with the restoration of peace on all fronts in 1815, it again increased to 30 ships, and reached a total of almost 50 ships by 1818. After that year the fleet dwindled gradually but steadily until it had ceased to exist — certainly by the 1840s.

Another branch of the migratory fishery from Britain — the migratory ship fishery — was concerned with the inshore fishery, and the fate of this branch was much more swiftly sealed. This had been the original Newfoundland-England fishery but using a ship simply for transportation to and from Newfoundland proved to be uneconomical. Furthermore a shipload of experienced fishermen provided a bonanza for press gangs during war. In addition, good free fishing rooms had become increasingly scarce as settlement had slowly spread to the better harbours. Therefore, the fishing ships of the 1780s and 1790s carried small crews and few fishing boats. They came early, bringing supplies to the fishermen, and then produced what fish they could until a cargo could be acquired for Europe. The fishing ship fishery was a very limited one, and although three or four hundred fishing boats were involved and manpower per tonnage was stronger in the 1780s, by 1797 it had almost ceased to exist. By 1810 these ships were no longer enumerated and it is likely that, beginning in that year, they were included in the sack ship returns.

The third and only other branch of the British migratory fishery was known as the bye boat fishery.[7] This fishery involved individual small boat owners who left their boats in Newfoundland but who themselves migrated between the island and England annually. This too was an inshore fishery. The bye boat fishery reached its peak during the years 1771-1779, when the total number of keepers and servants averaged 525 and 5,691, respectively. The bye boat fishery had one major weakness — it easily became a resident fishery when it was convenient to do so. For example, it almost disappeared during the American Revolution when the bye boat men stayed in Newfoundland. This was necessary in order to retain their fishing rooms, which were increasingly under threat of encroachment by residents, whose numbers generally increased during periods of war. After the American Revolution, it was not able to recover and quickly declined. Bye boat keepers and/or servants were not enumerated after 1788, but there were reports up to 1801 of bye boats being employed in the fishery and reports up to 1803 of the quantities of fish caught by bye boat men. This decline had a significant effect on the viability of the other branches of the British migratory fishery, especially on that of the bank ships, for these ships lost a major source of their income — the annual transportation of the bye boat men and their equipment and supplies to and from Newfoundland. Nevertheless, the decline in the bye boat fishery as well as in the other migratory fisheries had a far greater impact on the economy of the West Country than it did on the fishermen them-

7   See Matthews, "West of England-Newfoundland Fishery", for a more complete discussion of this fishery.

selves, for the fishermen simply took up permanent residence in Newfoundland and the fishery continued.

The decline in the bank, fishing ship and bye boat fisheries was matched by a growth in the resident population and fishery. While it is probable that men were left behind during the last decades of the 16th century to care for equipment and buildings over the winters, the first known Europeans to establish a winter residence on the island since the Viking age were the small group of people brought to Cupids, Conception Bay, by John Guy in 1610. David Kirke's business venture in 1637 was the last in this brief series of organized colonization attempts. By 1660 the English government had become opposed to any colonization of the island and after a brief attempt to discourage settlement, generally ignored the residents' existence. Meanwhile, fishing captains, who had practised a crude "first come, first served" fishery in the 16th century, were granted their own charter in 1634, making their customs legal and giving the first captain to arrive in each harbour the authority to maintain law and order and to settle disputes. Gradually these fishing captains became more concerned with holding onto and improving the fishing premises they had taken the trouble to erect in the various harbours. This was especially so as independent ship owners evolved into companies with bigger investments in buildings, wharves, flakes and stages which, in turn, were getting increasingly expensive to erect as the forests became depleted. (The practice of using tree rinds as waterproof roofing material and for covering fish piles contributed to this depletion). Therefore, caretakers were left in the harbours over winter; they were expected to make certain preparations for the following summer and also to make sure that the fishing room was saved from falling into another's hands. The remnants of the colonization attempts and these caretakers laid the foundation for the growth of a Newfoundland resident population.

Although a steady stream of fishermen continued to settle in Newfoundland from the beginning of the 17th century and although certain family names in Newfoundland can be traced back to the very earliest residents, most fishermen treated Newfoundland as a temporary residence — either moving on to the Atlantic seaboard colonies or retiring to England. In 1650 there were about 1,500 European residents on the island; this figure had increased to about 3,000 by the end of the century, but then several decades of stagnation followed and it was almost mid-18th century before the number of people residing over the winter reached 5,000. The introduction of the potato at about this time provided a local substitute for imported flour and bread and also provided an important source of vitamin C. This assistance in the battle against starvation and malnutrition plus difficulties in the migratory fishery brought about a more rapid growth in population during the following decades. Furthermore, the success of the English colonies in establishing their independence curtailed migration there from Newfoundland after 1775. Moreover the establishment of a Newfoundland-West Indian fish, molasses and rum trade after the American Revolution gave further impetus to population growth and stability.

By the late 1780s the population had risen to nearly 20,000 but fluctuated until the latter stages of the French Revolutionary War. Furthermore, although the residents' share of the fish produced increased significantly after the American Revolution, well over one-half the dried cod fish was still being produced by the migratory fishermen. However, after the American Embargo Act of 1807 and the opening of the southern European ports by the British invasion of Spain in 1808, there was a stimulation in the Newfoundland dried fish trade which encouraged population growth. This growth intensified after the outbreak of the Anglo-American war in 1812. The number of people classified as residents grew to more than 30,000 by 1812 and to more than 40,000 by 1815. There was a comparative increase in the number of boats owned by inhabitants and in the quantity of fish produced by them. By 1815 residents owned almost all the fishing boats engaged in the fishery and were producing the entire yield of saltfish.

The disappearance of the migratory fishing fleets and the unprecedented growth in the population and their fishery were not simply opposite sides of the same coin. While it is true that the number of residents had always grown during wartime — certainly since Queen Anne's war — there had never been such an element of permanence involved. Although the wars initially caused severe difficulties for the fish export trade, the Newfoundland fishery was able to weather these market problems and to take successful advantage of available opportunities to market their produce.

The British-Newfoundland saltfish industry had entered a very healthy era after the American Revolution, and by 1788 nearly 950,000 cwts were produced, with southern Europe being the major market. In a report on the Newfoundland fishery written in 1781 but describing the period just prior to the American Revolution, John Cutter, a merchant in the fishery, summarized the trade and estimated the amount of fish produced in Newfoundland waters and its destinations.[8] Although his estimates of the quantity produced by British fishermen are probably too high, the report establishes the importance of Alicante as a market for British fish, followed by Leghorn, Lisbon, Naples/Oporto/Bilbao/the West Indies, and Barcelona. The size of the American fish trade in Bilbao and the extent to which it exceeded the British is also interesting because the British-Newfoundland saltfish trade experienced great difficulties in Bilbao after 1814 and was eventually displaced by Norway's. Cutter also pointed out that the French had a habit of sending saltfish that was surplus to home consumption to Genoa, Leghorn, and some Spanish ports; this was a practice which was also evident in the 19th century. The size of the American trade in the West Indies is certainly supported by other evidence and this presence also continued, with

8   "Remarks of a Merchant in the Newfoundland Fishery 1781 by John Cutter", CO 194/37, fols. 125-33.

Table I: Population of Newfoundland,
1796-1820

Year	Population
1796	-
1797	11,382
1798	-
1799	-
1800	-
1801[1]	14,902
1802	-
1803	19,029
1804	20,380
1805	21,975
1806	-
1807	25,234
1808	24,625
1809	25,157
1810[2]	12,553
1811	25,985
1812	30,772
1813	32,749
1814[3]	25,952
1815	40,568
1816	41,898
1817	43,409
1818	40,854
1819	40,937
1820	42,535

1 No figures for Bonavista, Trepassey and St. John's Island.
2 No figures for Bonavista, Conception Bay, Fortune Bay, Burin and Bay of Bulls.
3 Should no doubt read 35,952.

variations, during the 19th century. Certain ports were to be closed to foreign imports after 1814, but throughout the 19th century, the fate of the Newfoundland saltfish trade remained closely tied to developments in Spain, Portugal and the Italian ports.

High production up to 1789 caused a glut in the markets and a decline in prices. In 1790 and 1791 the fishery had retreated to a more reduced position with exports of 756,528 cwts and 772,121 cwts respectively; prices also recovered to 14s. per quintal. Part of the reason for the rapid growth in demand during the last part of the 1780s was the decline in the French fishery. In the six years ending in 1774, the French produced on an average 333,586 cwts of dried cod in Newfoundland waters, while in the three-year period ending in 1789, only 128,590 cwts, 241,262 cwts and 239,000 cwts were produced. Information is missing regarding 1790, but in 1791 and 1792 only 40,580 and 94,000 cwts, respectively, were produced. Meanwhile, the British fishery itself had declined to only 529,655 cwts in 1792; this triggered a stream of protests from the West Country merchants and a parliamentary committee was established early in 1793 to examine the situation.

Several of the witnesses called before the committee blamed Norway for taking over the market of Barcelona and also pointed out that the French and Americans were proving to be strong competitors in Spain. William Newman of Dartmouth complained as well about French and American competition. William Knox, also involved in the Newfoundland fish trade, claimed that American bank fish was competing too successfully with the British-Newfoundland product. When asked to name ports in Europe which had been markets for Newfoundland fish but which had recently been lost, he replied, "All the Spanish ports in the Bay of Biscay, particularly Bilbao, St. Sebastians and St. Andero which are now primarily supplied with American Fish". He also explained that the Danes, or Norwegians, were selling their stock fish — cod fish dried without salt —in both Italy and Spain. In addition, all the older firms joined in accusing those who had become established after 1763 or after 1783 as "adventurers and hucksters" who had, by their cut-throat competition, caused a trade crisis. For the most part, they joined in placing much of the blame on the British government, which was impeding their enterprise by collecting customs duties and entering and clearance charges in Newfoundland — a charge that was vigorously refuted by Richard Routh, the customs collector appointed to Newfoundland.[9] In retrospect, it seems that the limited success of the cod fishery in 1792 was mainly due to a catch failure, for the price in St. John's that autumn was a very healthy 15s. to 16s. per cwt.[10] In addition, of course, investment must have declined after the glut caused by overproduction in 1788.

9 Sheila Lambert, ed., *House of Commons Sessional Papers of the Eighteenth Century* (Delaware, 1976), Vol. 90, pp. 230, 139-40, 133, 289-96.

10 "Exports", BT 6/92, fol. 164, PRO.

The outbreak of war between France and Great Britain in 1793 was the beginning of a period of major disruptions in the Newfoundland fishery. British exports of saltfish from Newfoundland declined to 458,111 cwts in 1793 and the price for best quality fish went down to 13s. per cwt in St. John's.[11] Nevertheless, the southern European markets remained open and the following year there was a slight recovery, followed by another decline in 1795 which continued into 1796. It is impossible to explain satisfactorily the low productivity of these early years of the war, but no doubt there was a certain reluctance on the part of merchants to invest capital during these years, and the migratory fishery had been, as we have seen, substantially reduced. In 1796 a French squadron of ten men-of-war destroyed some fishing stations on the Labrador coast,[12] and this squadron also carried out raids against British-Newfoundland fishing ships south of St. John's, burning and sinking bankers and inshore shallops. Nevertheless, as Governor Sir Richard Wallace remarked, "The fishery this year [1796] has been interrupted but the injury done to it is by no means equal to what might have been expected when we consider the Force of the enemy that came to destroy it".[13] However, in 1796 Spain joined the French coalition, thus closing their markets to British fish, while at the same time cutting off a major source of salt. This latter factor, combined with unusually wet weather during the summer of 1797, resulted in the production of poor quality fish in 1797. Governor William Waldegrave wrote in August 1797: "Vast quantities of fish have been already brought into the different Ports of this Island, but the scarcity of salt and the unfavourable season for drying, has caused some part of it to be injured, and I fear some has entirely rotted".[14] The closure of the Spanish market and the lack of salt combined with wet weather to make the 1797 fishery the most disastrous since the American Revolution. Production declined to 374,940 cwts; it was also reported that 368,817 cwts were exported with a top price of 13s. 6d. per cwt.

In 1798 the situation improved somewhat, but not a great deal. In the absence of Spanish markets Portugal was being swamped with fish, and this kept the price low. In 1798 the top prices for fish in St. John's were only 10s. to 11s. per cwt,[15] while the price of provisions had risen considerably, with pork selling for nine to ten guineas per barrel.[16] The condition of the residents had worsened con-

---

11 *Ibid.* (In the CO 194 report it was stated that total exports amounted to 427,460 cwts.)

12 Report from Admiral Crofton, Commander of the HMS *Pluto*, to Admiral Waldegrave, CO 194/40, fols. 17-34. Information was collected in the summer of 1797 and the report is dated 10 January 1798.

13 Governor Sir James Wallace to the Duke of Portland, 24 November 1796, CO 194/39, fols. 27-45.

14 Governor Waldegrave to Colonial Office, 14 August 1797, *ibid.*, fols. 86-88.

15 BT 6/92, fol. 164; and Governor Waldegrave to the Duke of Portland, 30 October 1798, CO 194/40, fols. 135-37.

16 Frederick Warren, R.N., to Governor Waldegrave, 24 March 1798, CO 194/40, fol. 65.

siderably by the fall of 1789 and Governor Waldegrave reported that there was a serious threat of starvation.[17] To add to the misery, there was a partial potato failure in 1798. In one effort to relieve this distress, Waldegrave requested £1000 worth of copper coin from the British Treasury; this was provided and put into circulation. Almost immediately, loaves of bread went on the market at one and two pence each instead of at the minimum six pence (silver) which had been the former price.[18] This importation of copper coin from the British Treasury became a common practice during the following years. The British government had already given Waldegrave permission to allow imports of bread, flour and other food from the United States in order to keep prices down and prevent famine. (This permission was renewed annually until the Americans imposed an embargo in 1807, but by then the European scene had changed). In response to complaints from the merchants that crimes were being committed against their property during the winter by impoverished fishermen, the British government ordered in 1798 that the chief justice remain in Newfoundland on a fulltime basis.[19]

Conditions continued to be poor in the next four seasons. In 1799 exports exceeded 450,000 cwts but there was much poor quality fish. During this year, there were a large number of bankruptcies and a number of forced property sales by fairly well-established names in the fishery, including Harris and Roope, Thomas Stokes, and William Henley.[20] In 1800 and 1802 exports of salt-fish amounted to 517,348 and 461,144 cwts, respectively, and prices rose steadily from a high of 15s. to 27s. per cwt for the top quality product in St. John's.[21] For

17 Governor Waldegrave to the Colonial Office, 30 October 1798, *ibid.*, fols. 135-37. He computed the expenses of an average planter with four fishermen and two shoremen as follows:

four (4) fishermen's wages	@ £21 - £84
provisions for above	@ £10 - £40
two (2) shoremen's wages	@ £19 - £38
provisions for above	@ £10 - £20
bait for the boat	@ £11 - £11
boat, lines, hooks, and all her craft	@ £20 - £20
	£213

He went on to point out that in 1798 the average catch for this crew was about 280 cwts at an average price of 9s. per cwt. This would mean that the voyage was worth only £126, leaving the planter with a loss of £87. Salt was not included in the cost of the outfit for, as Waldegrave explained, the train oil produced generally covered the price of the salt. However, he added that the price of salt was rising while the price of oil remained the same.

18 Governor Waldegrave to the Colonial Office, 18 October 1798, *ibid.*, fol. 105.

19 Governor Waldegrave to the Colonial Office, 11 June 1798, *ibid.*, fol. 83. Another 20 years were to pass before the British government decided Newfoundland needed a fulltime governor. In the meantime, his annual tour in Newfoundland was confined to the fishing season and sometimes only a brief part of that.

20 Report of St. John's Magistrates to Waldegrave, 24 October 1799, CO 194/42, fol. 148.

21 BT 6/92. No information was available on 1801.

the most part, the fishery had suffered from the war but had made some adjustments, especially in becoming more sedentary. As Lieutenant Governor Robert Barton wrote in January 1802: "During the War the Fishery of the Island has been in a great degree sedentary, very few passengers have arrived from His Majesty's European Dominions during the period but it may be expected that great numbers will come out next year".[22]

Meanwhile, American fishing interests had not been idle. During the 1790s they employed 4,000 to 5,000 men annually, and during the ten-year period ending in 1800 they exported an annual average of 396,781 cwts of saltfish.[23] For the three-year period from 1798 to 1800, their exports to the West Indies averaged 175,897 cwts,[24] with the bulk of the remainder going to southern Europe. Much of this fish was produced on the Labrador coast, with as many as 1,500 American vessels being involved (as in 1805), each carrying 12 to 14 men.[25] One report in 1804 described the American fishery more fully. In that year about 1,360 American ships fished at Labrador and in the Gulf of St. Lawrence and employed about 10,600 men. The report went on to point out that the Americans sold their wet-salted cod to France and in the American home market, and their dry-salted product to the Mediterranean, with the worst of the latter being sent to the West Indies.[26] It was also reported that the United States was exporting 150,000 cwts of saltfish annually to the British West Indies by 1804, while Newfoundland sold only 50,000 cwts there.[27]

When war resumed in 1803, the Newfoundland fishery was much better able to deal with this interruption than it had been ten years earlier. Gibraltar began importing large quantities of saltfish for re-export; some of this was no doubt smuggled into southern Spain. Gibraltar took about 75,000 cwts in 1804 and about 100,000 in 1805.[28] Almost immediately after the outbreak of the war, the British government granted permission for Newfoundland to import provisions from the United States in an effort to depress food prices, wages, and fish prices.[29] However, the demand for servants increased as the number of passengers from the British Isles continued to decline: more than 6,000 came annually in 1787-88; 3,588 in 1800; 1,892 in 1802; a rise to 2,732 in 1803 because of the

22 Barton to Lord Hobart, 2 January 1802, CO 194/43, fols. 24-28.

23 Report laid before the House of Representatives by the Secretary of the Treasury respecting the fishermen of the United States on the 29th of January, BT 6/91, fol. 3.

24 Account of U.S. fish exports to the West Indies, *ibid.*, fol. 1.

25 Report from Captain James Murray, R.N., of H.M. Sloop *Curlew* on the Labrador coast, 23 July 1805, *ibid.*, fol. 116.

26 Lieutenant Morrison, R.N., Commander, HMS *Charlotte* to Governor Gower, September 1804, CO 194/44, fols. 24-25.

27 Gower to Lord Camden, 24 December 1804, *ibid.*, fols. 50-61.

28 BT 6/92, fol. 164. Computed by deducting 30,000 cwts for British and Irish consumption.

29 Order-in-Council, 2 March 1803, CO 194/43, fols. 284-89.

peace; down to 646 in 1804; 755 in 1805; and 600 in 1806.[30]

In 1804 Governor Sir Erasmus Gower reported that the fishery was carried out almost exclusively by the residents.[31] He also reported that fishermen were still in the habit of using Newfoundland as a stepping stone to the North American continent and, consequently, without a large annual influx of servants, wages would rise too high and profits would remain low. Of St. John's, Gower wrote in July 1805:

> ...this Harbour is no longer a mere fishing station, built round with temporary Flakes, Stages, and Huts of trifling value, but...it is a port of extensive Commerce...importing near two thirds of the supplies for the whole Island, and furnished with extensive Store-Houses and Wharfs for trade, containing a quantity of Provisions, Stores for the Fishery, British Manufacturers and West Indian Produce, as well as Fish and Oil ready for exportation, which together with the Buildings is computed to be worth more than a half a million Sterling.[32]

By 1806 Gower was explaining to the Colonial Office that the fishery was wholly sedentary and yet supplied all the available markets.[33] Similarly, local shipbuilding was becoming firmly established as well as a resident seal fishery. In this connection, Gower reported that 149 ships, all built in Newfoundland, prosecuted the seal fishery in 1804.[34]

The extensive exports of saltfish to Portugal glutted that country's markets repeatedly during this period so that much merchantable fish could not be sold in 1805 and had to remain in the island over the winter. To compensate to some degree, Great Britain prohibited Barbados, St. Vincent, and Grenada from purchasing fish from the United States, and Newfoundland's exports to the Caribbean rose from about 50,000 cwts annually before 1805 to 81,000 in that year and 101,000 in 1806. However, Jamaica and Demerara continued to purchase the American product. In addition, American traders had been buying some of Newfoundland's top quality fish for export to Spain and the amount thus purchased rose to 100,000 cwts in 1806.[35] In that year exports of saltfish totalled over 770,000 cwts, with top prices at 14s. per cwt. In 1807 about 675,000 cwts were exported and 13s. 6d. was the top price. Once again, there is a tone of comfort in the records and reports for 1807. The fishery was moderately successful and prices and wages were moderately high. Rapid changes were in the offing.

30 BT 6/92, fol. 164. These figures vary slightly from those reported in CO 194. See Ryan, "Abstract".

31 Gower to Colonial Office, 28 March 1804, CO 194/44, fols. 40-43.

32 Gower to Colonial Office, 18 July 1805, *ibid.*, fols. 115-17

33 Gower to Colonial Office, 29 April 1806, CO 194/45, fols. 61-69.

34 Gower to Colonial Office, n.d. 1805, *ibid.*, fols. 46-47.

35 Gower to Colonial Office, 9 November 1806, *ibid.*, fols. 155-59. See also Gower to Colonial Office, 9 November 1806, CO 195/14, fols. 50-54.

188 *The Acadiensis Reader: 1*

Table II: Codfish Caught By Inhabitants of Newfoundland, 1771-1791, 1796-1820 (quintals)

Year	Inhabitants	Total	Year	Inhabitants	Total
1771	261,240	639,919	1799	-	466,332
1772	298,605	759,843	1800	-	517,348
1773	366,446	780,328	1801[1]	195,400	255,740
1774	312,426	695,866	1802	-	461,144
1775	230,540	658,315	1803	410,188[2]	536,188
1776	205,448	549,903	1804	531,084	609,684
1777	-	-	1805	662,800	706,314
1778	205,840	501,140	1806	-	772,809
1779	262,500	409,670	1807	462,250	520,552
1780	-		1808	468,185	478,735
1781	168,150	255,150	1809	625,941	677,761
1782	-	-	1810[3]	299,515	317,415
1783	-	-	1811	601,894	618,494
1784	212,616	437,316	1812	674,611	709,163
1785	262,576	544,942	1813	819,250[4]	869,750
1786	257,547	569,142	1814	797,762[4]	865,132
1787	341,620	732,015	1815	802,668[5]	866,580
1788	457,105	948,970	1816	739,977	819,200
1789	339,260	771,569	1817	712,487	778,227
1790	302,974	649,092	1818	559,183	606,733
1791	229,770	536,287	1819	588,149[6]	717,909
1796	-	445,471	1820	736,524[7]	810,074
1797	261,570	374,940			
1798	-	485,764			

1 No figures for Bonavista, Trepassey and St. John's Island.

2 Also there were 25,720 quintals caught on North Shore by residents.

3 No figures for Bonavista, Conception Bay, Fortune Bay, Burin and Bay of Bulls.

4 In addition, caught on French Shore and Labrador by residents: 1813: 29,500 quintals, 1814: 44,050 quintals.

5 Includes amount caught by Labrador and French Shore residents.

6 In addition, caught on Labrador by residents: 76,000 quintals.

7 Includes amount caught by North Shore and Labrador residents.

The markets had finally been adjusted to compensate for the closure of the Spanish and Mediterranean ports. Gibraltar's imports had reached 130,000 cwts by 1807, while the British West Indies imported more than 100,000 cwts and the United States more than 155,000 cwts. The Americans exported their Newfoundland-purchased saltfish directly to southern Spain while the saltfish reexported from Gibraltar took clandestine routes. The American Embargo Act of 1807 reduced that country's imports of Newfoundland saltfish to about one-third its 1807 figure, and the French invasion temporarily closed the Portuguese ports to English commerce. These events and the beginning of the Peninsular War encouraged exporters to send more than 208,000 cwts to Gibraltar. However, there was a general hesitation in the industry during 1808 which was reflected in a lower catch and lower prices. Governor Holloway wrote that the number employed in the fisheries was down owing to the ports of Portugal being closed and the uncertainty of affairs with the United States.[36] The trade was discouraging, but at least Trafalgar (1805) had removed most of the maritime dangers and merchants were now sending their ships to market singly rather than in convoy so as not to create more gluts.[37] However, the closure of the American ports soon raised the price of provisions as the British West Indies were also forced to turn to British North America for supplies.[38]

In 1809 the ports of Spain and Portugal were being re-opened as a British army began to aid the Spanish and Portuguese in the Peninsular War. Portugal and Gibraltar bought almost 620,000 cwts of Newfoundland saltfish in all and the West Indies more than 133,000, but the Americans bought very little. Also, the price of the best fish did not rise above 13s. 6d per cwt, and the importation of supplies became a major problem. Governor Holloway wrote that a lack of supplies from the United States, Nova Scotia and Prince Edward Island had left the island "totally destitute of Beef for the Supply of His Majesty's Ships and the Inhabitants are deprived of it; I may therefore be under the necessity of allowing the Importation of Livestock, Grain and Fruit from the Azores or Western Islands, which I trust will meet your Lordship's approbation".[39] Similarly, in September Holloway complained about the lack of salt and stated that fish had to be thrown away for that reason. He also pointed out that 1808-09 had been a severe winter due to the great shortage of provisions because of the U.S. embargo. He also reported that the huge American fishery on the Labrador coast had ceased.[40] But, despite the unsettled market conditions and the scarcity of provisions, the saltfish exports exceeded 810,000 cwts.

By 1810, when the island produced 884,470 cwts for export, mainly to

36 Holloway to Colonial Office, 20 July 1808, CO 194/47, fol. 47.
37 *Ibid.*, fols. 52-53.
38 Holloway to Colonial Office, 18 November 1808, *ibid.*, fols. 61-68.
39 Holloway to Castlereagh, 19 July 1809, CO 194/48, fol. 23.
40 *Ibid.*

Table III: Markets for Newfoundland Codfish Exports, 1796-1820 (quintals)

Year	Spain, Portugal & Italy	British Europe	British West Indies	British America	United States	Brazil	Total
1796	-	-	-	-	-	-	445,471
1797	209,755	73,858	-	-	-	-	318,621
1798	-	-	35,008	-	-	-	485,764
1799	-	-	-	-	-	-	466,332
1800	-	-	-	-	-	-	517,348
1801[1]	107,037	45,002	162,878[2]	-	-	-	314,917
1802	-	-	-	-	-	-	461,144
1803	381,519	102,638	64,248	3,082	31,362	-	582,849
1804	425,446	41,480	41,590	15,757	35,169	-	559,442[2]
1805	377,293	65,979	81,488	22,776	77,983	-	625,519
1806	438,918	84,241	100,936	32,555	116,159	-	772,809
1807	262,366[3]	130,400	103,418	23,541	155,085	-	674,810
1808	154,669[3]	208,254	115,677	40,874	56,658	-	576,132
1809	326,781[4]	292,068	133,359	41,894	16,117	-	810,219
1810[5]	373,635	136,243	151,869	35,327	1,274	6,170	705,058
1811	611,960	139,561	152,184	18,621	1,214	-	923,540
1812	545,451	67,020	91,864	4,121	-	2,600	711,056
1813[6]	727,739	50,701	119,354	14,389	-	-	912,183
1814	768,010	55,791	97,249	24,712	-	2,049	947,811
1815	952,116	46,116	159,233	24,608	588	-	1,182,661
1816	770,693½	59,341½	176,603	37,443	2,545	-	1,046,626
1817	681,559	79,746	150,827	20,656	2,848	-	935,636
1818	560,632	57,258	116,716	-	-	-	751,818
1819	606,689	57,737	126,995	3,762	-	13,067	808,250
1820	626,644	81,014	139,484	19,741	-	7,723	874,606

1 No figures for Bonavista, Trepassey and St. John's Island.

2 Includes exports to the United States.

3 Amount exported to Portugal and Italy only.

4 Amount exported to Portugal only.

5 No figures for Bonavista, Conception Bay, Fortune Bay, Burin and Bay of Bulls.

6 Beginning in 1813, the name West Indies is used instead of British West Indies.

Portugal and Gibraltar, the island's exporters had adjusted to the new trade pattern. They had increased their exports to the British West Indies, displaced much of the American trade in southern Spain and continued to dominate the substantial trade to Portugal. Meanwhile, both wages and prices had risen since 1804.[41] In 1811 Spain and Portugal imported the enormous quantity of 611,960 cwts of Newfoundland saltfish,[42] while 140,000 cwts went to Gibraltar and more than 152,000 to the British West Indies, for a grand total of 923,540 cwts. By this time, moreover, the large British banking fleet had completely disappeared and the Newfoundland residents were producing the entire catch.

The year 1812 brought another war, and this time closer to home, as the Anglo-American war broke out. Security, not trade, became the top priority for both government and business. Of the fishery in 1812, Governor Sir John Thomas Duckworth wrote that it was "moderately successful and in some instances remarkably so". However, he also noted that merchants appeared unwilling to risk their vessels in the export trade: "There has been a want of shipping to export the produce of the season and a great proportion of it remains of necessity in the Stores of the Merchants. This circumstance has been the more regretted as the European Markets have been particularly advantageous, and the demand for fish unusually great".[43] In the meantime, a large cargo of bread and flour arrived from Quebec and, although prices were high, there was no scarcity of these items in the fall of 1812.[44] Total exports of saltfish amounted to 711,256 cwts in 1812, of which 545,451 went to Spain and Portugal (and possibly a little to Italy). Prices were abnormally high, reaching 22s. per cwt for top quality fish in 1811 and 22s. 6d. in 1812. Thus one can appreciate Governor Duckworth's lament in the fall of 1812 when he complained about the lack of sufficient ships. Nevertheless, while the war did discourage shipping to Newfoundland, the withdrawal of the Americans from the European saltfish trade helped create the unusual demand for the Newfoundland product. Indeed one traditional market, the British West Indies, was left short of supplies in 1812 as Newfoundland's exports there amounted to only 91,864 cwts. Similarly, exports to Gibraltar were reduced substantially as shipments there amounted to only 67,000 cwts. The growing importance of the resident fishery was becoming more obvious. Governor Duckworth, after consulting leading figures in the Newfoundland trade and in Newfoundland society, wrote in 1812 that "the Fisheries of Newfoundland are now decidedly sedentary, and that the war has been protracted so long as to make it very uncertain whether any change of system would be produced by the return of peace".[45]

41 Duckworth to Liverpool, 25 November 1810, CO 194/48, fol. 51-129.
42 This figure probably includes a little that was imported into Italy.
43 Duckworth to Earl Bathurst, 1 November 1812, CO 194/52, fols. 86-109.
44 *Ibid.*
45 Duckworth to Bathurst, 2 November 1812, CO 194/53, fols. 3-8.

In 1813 the fishery was again unusually productive, and 912,183 cwts of fish were exported. However, the weather for drying the fish was poor and, consequently, there was a lower proportion of merchantable fish.[46] This, no doubt, helps to explain why the best fish sold for 32s. to 42s. per cwt, which were unheard-of prices.[47] It was also reported that servants were being paid an average of £70 per season.[48] Again, supplies were plentiful in the fall of 1813 and were brought mostly from Great Britain.[49] Governor Sir Richmond Godwin Keats continued the practice begun by Governor James Gambier in 1803[50] of granting small plots of land to fishermen to enable them to better support themselves and their families.[51] Gower commented on the changes occurring in Newfoundland, especially in St. John's:

> St. John's became the Emporium of the Island in consequence of this extended war, with a population of nearly 10,000 inhabitants, seems to have grown out of its character from a Fishery to a large Commercial Town, and for a considerable time past has offered such advantages to the Farmer and Gardener as to surmount in a great degree all the restraints which Nature or the Policy of Government has laid on the Cultivation of a Soil, certainly less sterile than has generally been considered. But this character which it has latterly assumed, it is very doubtful if it will be able to support on the return of Peace.[52]

Like Duckworth, Keats recognized that the Newfoundland fishery had changed but, unlike Duckworth, he was not perceptive enough to conclude that the changes were becoming irreversible.

Peace was concluded in both Europe and North America in 1814 and, once again, exports of saltfish rose, this time to 947,811 cwts, of which 768,010 went to Spain, Portugal and into the Mediterranean. At the same time, the prices declined to 24s. 6d. per cwt for the merchantable quality. This was probably the most pleasant year of the whole period, with plenty of supplies from Great Britain and more about to arrive from the United States once peace was concluded. There was no danger from privateers and no signs yet of the violent loot-

46 Keats to Bathurst, 18 November 1813, CO 194/54, fols. 159-74.
47 See Edward Chapell, *Voyage of H.M.S. Rosamund to Newfoundland and the Southern Coast of Labrador* (London, 1818), pp. 245-247, and Ryan, "Abstract".
48 Society of Merchants, St. John's, to Keats, 23 June 1813, CO 194/54, fols. 55-56. According to Charles Pedley, *The History of Newfoundland* (London, 1863), p. 284, fish splitters received £90 - £140 in 1814.
49 Keats to Bathurst, 19 December 1813, *ibid.*, fols. 159-74.
50 Gambier to Hobart, 12 December 1803, CO 194/42, fols.175-78.
51 Keats to Bathurst, 18 December 1813, CO 194/54, fols. 159-74.
52 *Ibid.*

ings and other troubles which were to mar the immediate post-war, depressed years. The island enjoyed full employment, high wages, a large catch, and almost insatiable markets. Only Chief Justice Caesar Colclough saw, or imagined he saw, a very gloomy picture. Writing to Keats in March 1814, he pointed out that the high wages had encouraged greater dissipation among the inhabitants than usual. Then, foreseeing unemployment as a result of peace in Europe, he added rather gloomily that if low wages and unemployment ever returned, the ignorant people would find consolation or at least refuge in the bottle.[53] Indeed, by December the first cracks had begun to appear in the economic edifice as fish prices began to decline and information was received that the French fishery was recovering at St. Pierre and Miquelon and also on the Grand Banks, though not as yet on the "French Shore".[54]

Newfoundland had changed rapidly during the preceding decades. In 1795 Governor Wallace had complained that the merchants were staying and encouraging their men to do likewise.[55] This was a normal occurrence in wartime and had been observed and reported on numerous occasions during the 18th century. Just one year later, it was noted that "the population has so rapidly increased that in a few years an extensive fishery may be carried on there by the Inhabitants alone without receiving annual supply's [sic] of Men from England and Ireland as heretofore".[56] In 1804 Gower reported that the fishery in Newfoundland was carried out "almost wholly" by residents.[57] Again, this was not unusual because it had occurred during previous wars. In 1805 Gower reported that St. John's was "no longer a mere fishing station. . .but a port of extensive Commerce".[58] However, since St. John's had been the centre for the British bank fishery and since that had been disrupted because of the war, one can see why the port could not remain a fishing station and still prosper. Furthermore, St. John's was the most secure port on the island and had always been the naval governors' headquarters. In 1806 Gower reported again that the fishery was "almost wholly sedentary".[59] A few months later, he pointed out that the increase in the sedentary fishery and in the population was "likely to create a necessity for a resident Governor".[60] Governor Holloway's time was spent dealing with the American

53 Colclough to Keats, 21 March 1814, CO 194/55, fols. 233-41. Colclough also took a personal part in breaking up personal and fraction fights, which he seemed to think were seditious in nature. It is not surprising that he was forced to take early retirement back to England with nervous problems and stomach disorders.

54 Keats to Bathurst, 29 December 1814, *ibid.*, fols. 95-104.

55 Wallace to Portland, 25 November 1795, CO 194/41, fol. 105.

56 Captain Ambrose Crofton, R.N., to Waldegrave concerning his observations during the summer of 1796, 10 January 1798, CO 194/40, fols. 17-34.

57 Gower to Camden, 28 November 1804, CO 194/44, fols. 40-43.

58 Gower to Camden, 18 July 1805, *ibid.*, fols. 119-22.

59 Gower to Windham, 29 April 1806, CO 194/45, fols. 61-99.

60 Gower to Stephen Cottrel, 9 June 1806, *ibid.*, fols. 253-61.

embargo and with the prosperity which followed the opening of the Spanish markets after 1808, but in 1812 Governor Duckworth made it clear that "the Fisheries of Newfoundland are now decidedly sedentary"[61] and would remain so. In the meantime, Dr. William Carson, a Scotsman living in St. John's, attacked the system of naval government prevailing in Newfoundland, and advocated a system of representative government and the encouragement of agriculture.[62]

Since the migratory British fishery was bound to suffer in any major war, there was no real excitement generated by its decline immediately after 1793. Similarly, the usual growth in population at the same time elicited the usual perfunctory statements from the naval governors. During the course of the war period, however, this situation changed, and finally it became generally accepted, if not always appreciated, that Newfoundland's status as a fishing station had become inappropriate. The general evolution of the migratory cod fishery into a resident one was an important factor in this process. The length of the war, however, and the general prosperity that it created had encouraged the influx of large numbers of Irish.[63] Rapid population growth combined with the growth of a new industry — the spring seal fishery — were to make the migratory fishery redundant and ensure the survival of the colony with a broader economic base.

The settlement pattern of the Irish who arrived during the Napoleonic war period was different from those who came earlier because of the speed with which immigration took place. The Passenger Act of 1803 set stringent regulations on the transportation of British emigrants to North America. These regulations covered food, water, medical aid and sleeping accommodations, and stipulated the number of passengers per ton of burthen. Fishing ships proceeding to the Newfoundland fishery were excluded from the act, and this enabled Irish emigrants to travel to North America via Newfoundland at a lower price. Moreover, the demands for labour increased in Newfoundland as the market prospects improved and wages became attractive. Both these factors encouraged Irish emigrants to travel to the island under inhuman (but inexpensive) condi-

61 Duckworth to Bathurst, 2 November 1812, CO 194/53, fols. 3-8.

62 Dr. William Carson was one of the most influential promoters of representative government. See Prowse, *A History of Newfoundland,* and Frederick W. Rowe, *A History of Newfoundland and Labrador* (Toronto, 1980).

63 Irish Roman Catholics had had some connections with Newfoundland ever since Lord Falkland's settlement attempts in the early 17th century. They continued to come out to Newfoundland in limited numbers, on English fishing ships which called at Waterford and other Irish ports on their spring voyages for supplies of beef, pork, butter, cheese, and porter for the fishery. Immediately after the Treaty of Utrecht, relatively large numbers of Irish settled in Placentia Bay and St. Mary's Bay — areas which became vacant due to the expulsion of the French. Others settled in St. John's and its vicinity. For the most part, these Irish became integrated into the primitive resident fishing society that existed.

tions, sleeping on deck or on top of the bales of cargo.[64] With no fishing experience and very little, if any, capital, these Irish were fortunate to find that there was plenty of employment on the island. They consequently became servants for the established ship owners.

Ship owners, planter-fishermen, and new local entrepreneurs invested heavily in the fishery during these years of prosperity. They even began sending ships and crews to the northern part of the island where the French had fished, in relative peace, before the wars. Furthermore, they discovered that seals could be harvested by the thousands in early spring, and fishing vessels were sent to seek out cargoes of these sea mammals on the ice floes. This seal fishery, which involved activity during the months of February to May, provided a welcome supplement to the summer cod fishery. The seal fishery could be prosecuted only by residents and a comment by Lord Bathurst to the Newfoundland governor in 1812 neatly summed up the situation: "There can be no question that the present situation of that [Newfoundland cod] fishery from the long continuation of the War, and the great change which the recent introduction of the Seal Fishery must necessarily have occasioned, even if the War were now to terminate, will require a revision of the Laws and Instructions at present in existence".[65]

The movement towards a resident fishery was accelerated enormously during the war period by the extraordinary demand for Newfoundland's saltfish. The resulting near-monopoly situation encouraged local investment in the fishery and in the necessary infrastructure, especially shipbuilding. The expansion of the St. John's and Conception Bay fishing industry to the northern part of the island[66] resulted in the creation of a fishing fleet which was also able to participate in the harvest of the extensive seal herds. By the time the war had ended in 1815, Newfoundland's history as a British migratory fishery had come to a close and it was about to be recognized as another, albeit unique, British colony. Thus Newfoundland, which had always been a fishery based around an island, would finally become a colony based on a fishery.

---

64 Keats to Bathurst, 1 October 1815, CO 194/56, fols. 63-64.

65 Bathurst to Duckworth, 13 June 1812, CO 195/16, fols. 323-26.

66 This migratory vessel fishery to the island's north coast developed into a migratory fishery on the coast of Labrador after 1815. This was the origin of Newfoundland's "Labrador" cod fishery.

W. A. SPRAY

Reprinted from Vol. VI, No. 2
(Spring 1977)

The Settlement of the Black Refugees in New Brunswick 1815 - 1836

During the war of 1812, while the British navy blockaded the Atlantic coast of the United States and for a time occupied Chesapeake Bay, many black slaves seized the opportunity to escape from their owners in Virginia and Maryland and others were carried off by British sailors and marines. Most of these black fugitives were taken to the British base in Bermuda and even before the war ended about 1200 were dispatched to Nova Scotia. On the conclusion of the war the British authorities decided to send the remaining 1500 to 3000 there, despite considerable opposition from the House of Assembly, which felt that there were too many blacks in the province and that to bring in more would "tend to the discouragement of white labourers and servants, as well as to the establishment of a separate and marked class of people, unfitted by nature to this climate, or to an association with the rest of His Majesty's Colonists".[1] When Lieutenant Governor Sir William Sherbrooke was informed that an additional 1500 to 2000 black refugees were on their way to Halifax,[2] he was afraid of the reaction of the Assembly and attempted to alleviate the situation by sending some of the refugees to New Brunswick. On 13 April 1815, Major General Stracy Smyth, the Administrator of New Brunswick, asked his Executive Council to consider whether the province should receive 400-500 black refugees.

Although the Council agreed by a vote of 3 to 2 to accept the refugees,[3] the New Brunswick government was very reluctant to assume any responsibility for their welfare. Smyth and his Council were under the impression that a British Order-in-Council of 16 March 1808, which detailed the regulations for the execution of the Act for the Abolition of the Slave Trade, could be applied to the case of the black refugees, who could be treated as prizes of war and enlisted in the British armed forces or bound out as apprentices or indentured servants.[4] This was the basis for a public notice circulated throughout the province, asking those who were interested in settling the refugees on their land or in taking any of the men and women as servants to

---

1   Address of the House of Assembly to Sir John Sherbrooke, 1 April 1815, quoted in J. S. Martell, *Immigration to and Emigration from Nova Scotia, 1815 - 1838* (Halifax, 1942), p. 16.
2   Sherbrooke to Bathurst, 6 April 1815, quoted in *ibid.*
3   Executive Council Minutes, 13 April 1815, Rex/Px, vol. II, p. 111, Provincial Archives of New Brunswick [hereafter PANB].
4   Executive Council Papers, Rex/Px, Box 7, PANB.

apply to the Provincial Secretary's office in Fredericton or to the Collector of Customs at Saint John. A preference was to be given to those who could offer the best terms to families and who could settle them immediately.[5]

As the Collector of Customs at Saint John was ill, his assistant, William Scovil, reluctantly assumed responsibility for the reception of the refugees. Scovil, a servant of the British government, was cautious in incurring expenses since he did not know what reimbursement he could expect from the British authorities. Nevertheless, he prepared as best he could for the arrival of the refugees. He rented a storehouse in the Lower Cove for £5 per month to provide shelter and set about having new floors and partitions constructed. Under the impression that two groups of refugees would be arriving, Scovil considered the storehouse adequate "to accommodate the first importation", whom he hoped to dispose of before the second group arrived. He also suggested that some of the blacks be sent to Fredericton, Westmorland and other areas of the province.[6] His task was made more difficult when the President of the Executive Council informed him that he had no authority to purchase clothing or provisions for the refugees and that he should "adopt the same mode that has been pursued in Nova Scotia" for looking after the refugees,[7] which he could discover only by writing to the Collector of Customs at Halifax. The New Brunswick government's reluctance to take any financial responsibility was thus made clear and Scovil decided to consult a lawyer, Charles J. Peters, as to the limits of his own responsibilities. When Peters reported that the Collector of Customs had "nothing whatsoever to do with the *Black Refugees*" and that "any Indenture of apprenticeship made by him would have no validity whatsoever", Scovil informed Smyth that "as he had not the means for providing for their support, he must decline taking them in charge, unless His Honour will place funds at his disposal payable at one, two or three months, as he may think proper to direct".[8] Smyth was both alarmed and annoyed and wrote immediately to ask the Lieutenant Governor of Nova Scotia how the "unavoidable expense is to be defrayed until the people can be distributed".[9]

Before a reply was received, the *Regulus* arrived in Saint John harbour on 25 May 1815, carrying 371 black refugees, 111 women, 168 men and 92

5   Executive Council Minutes, 10 May 1815, Rex/Px, vol. II, p. 112, PANB.

6   Scovil to W. F. Odell, 14 May 1815, Provincial Secretary's Papers [hereafter RPS], Customs, PANB.

7   Odell to Scovil, 18 May 1815, *ibid.*

8   Scovil to Smyth, 20 May 1815, with an extract of a letter from Peters, dated 18 May 1815, *ibid.*

9   Smyth to Sherbrooke, 23 May 1815, Letter Book Military, no. 2, PANB.

children.[10] Both Scovil and the government were forced to take action. Smyth allowed Scovil to issue provisions from the military stores until the government was relieved of the charge of the refugees.[11] He also ordered a military medical officer to look after the sick refugees and informed the Lieutenant Governor of Nova Scotia of his willingness to accept more refugees.[12] By 29 June 1815 only 13 men, 5 women and 12 children remained under the care of the Acting Collector of Customs. Apparently some were taken by boat to Fredericton to find employment, but no records have been found of the number sent there or to other parts of the province, nor is there any mention of what happened to them in the newspapers. But it would appear from the letters of Smyth and Scovil that the majority found at least temporary employment in the Saint John area. Of the 30 refugees still under the care of Scovil in June 1815, 6 or 8 were considered by the medical officer to be unable to earn enough to survive and Smyth requested and later received permission to send these invalids to Halifax "in order to save the expense of any permanent Establishment for these people in this province".[13] Although Smyth had expected to receive some 500 refugees and had expressed a willingness to receive the remainder of those originally destined for New Brunswick, no other refugees were sent from Halifax.[14] Scovil later reported that the total expense he had incurred on behalf of the refugees was £536-16-1/4 and, after a lengthy wrangle, the British government agreed to repay this sum. The New Brunswick government, which had been put to almost no expense, had given little or no thought to the question of how the black refugees might be provided for in the future and was entirely

---

10   Scovil to Smyth, 25 May 1815, RPS, Customs, PANB. The nominal roll of the *Regulus* lists 381 black refugees, 169 men, 112 women and 100 children. "List of Black Refugees furnished by His Majesty's Ship *Regulus*", Colonial Office [hereafter CO] 188/22, pp. 41 - 3, on microfilm PANB. All CO references are to microfilm at PANB supplemented by photocopies at the UNB Library of enclosures not on PANB film. The nominal roll probably includes all those embarked at Bermuda and the discrepancy between the two figures would seem to indicate that some of the refugees died on the voyage. A number of others were sick when they arrived at Saint John.

11   Smyth to Sherbrooke, 16 June 1815, Letter Book Military, no. 2, PANB.

12   Smyth to Sherbrooke, 29 June 1815, *ibid.*

13   *Ibid.* and Sherbrooke to Smyth, 11 July 1815, CO 188/5, pp. 39 - 40.

14   Twenty-two blacks captured by the Americans on board British vessels during the war of 1812 - 4 and held in jail in Savannah were sent to New Brunswick in 1816 from the United States. The British Vice Consul at Savannah had intended sending them to Halifax but, when he was unable to find a vessel to accommodate them, they were sent to Saint Andrews. From there they were probably forwarded to Halifax since there are no records of their remaining in New Brunswick. Correspondence concerning these men can be seen in CO 188/5, pp. 137 - 52.

unwilling to assist them.[15]

The possibility of giving land to the refugees was first suggested by Lord Bathurst, the Colonial Secretary, who felt that in this way those black refugees who were "accustomed to agricultural labour" might in a short time be able to support themselves and thus cease to be an expense to the government.[16] On 29 July 1815 Smyth reported that, while he was prepared to act on this suggestion, it would be necessary to provide the black refugees with "some articles of husbandry and provisions until *at least* this period next year, before which time no industry would be able to procure a support from new land, at present an entire Wilderness".[17] In Nova Scotia the Lieutenant Governor received permission to issue provisions for the same period "as is allowed to discharged soldiers so settled, viz for two years".[18] Industrious settlers were also given seeds and farming implements and many of the blacks were settled on the land by 1816.[19] But in New Brunswick it was a year and a half before any attempt was made to implement a policy of land settlement and the initiative came not from the government, but from the black refugees themselves who were aware of what had been done in Nova Scotia. In 1816 they applied to the Executive Council for allotments of land in the Loch Lomond area, about 12 miles from Saint John, which was chosen because of its proximity to the city where the refugees might find temporary employment while clearing land for a settlement. The Executive Council referred the matter to Judge Ward Chipman of Saint John. The Council considered his report on 25 October 1816 and decided that 50 acre lots would be laid out for the black refugees at "their own expense". Although the blacks were to pay the cost of the survey they were not to be given title but to be issued licenses of occupation for a period of three years.[20] Land held under such licenses could not be sold and the refugees would have no security of possession since the government could refuse to reissue the licenses. No-one explained where the blacks were supposed to find the money to pay for the surveys.

It is quite clear that the black refugees were treated differently than white settlers. The policy in New Brunswick at this time was to give free grants of

15 A similar reluctance to assist the black refugees was evident in Nova Scotia. In 1816, Lord Dalhousie wrote: "the Legislature and Inhabitants of this Province generally consider them a Class of people that never will do well as Settlers and therefore will not give them any countenance or assistance". Dalhousie to Bathurst, 29 December 1816, RG I, vol. 112, pp. 8 - 9, Public Archives of Nova Scotia [hereafter PANS].

16 Sherbrooke to Smyth, 25 July 1815, CO 188/5, pp. 41 - 3.

17 Smyth to Sherbrooke, 29 July 1815, Letter Book Military, no. 2, PANB.

18 Sherbrooke to Smyth, 8 August 1815, CO 188/5, pp. 45 - 7.

19 Dalhousie to Bathurst, 16 May 1817, RG I, vol. 112, p. 25, PANS.

20 See Executive Council Minutes, 25 October 1816, Rex/Px, vol. II, p. 161, PANB.

at least 100 acres to white settlers. Disbanded soldiers, like those of the 104th Regiment, were also given free provisions for at least twelve months and "Tools and Implements of Husbandry".[21] In 1819 Welsh settlers in the Cardigan Settlement, near Fredericton, were given 200 acres if married and 100 acres if single and were personally assisted by the Surveyor General, Anthony Lockwood, and also by the Fredericton Emigration Society.[22] When licenses of occupation were issued to white settlers in 1818, they were issued "free of any expense" and large blocks of land were surveyed and laid out for immigrants before they arrived in order to facilitate settlement "by a class of men, born and nurtured in the British Empire".[23] These licenses of occupation were only temporary and once the immigrant settled on the land he could apply for a grant. In 1820 the New Brunswick legislature passed an act providing for an expenditure of £800 for surveying locations for immigrants. [24] Yet the black refugees were to get only 50 acres, they were to pay for the surveys, and they were to receive licenses of occupation for three years. There is no evidence to show that the New Brunswick government ever considered issuing provisions to the black refugees as was done in Nova Scotia.

Nonetheless, a site for a possible settlement was selected near Loch Lomond and Judge Chipman was asked to report on its suitability and to consult with the proprietors already in the area, "to whom the proximity of such neighbours may be a matter of importance."[25] In his report of 2 November 1816, Chipman supported the settlement, arguing that the black refugees would then "have a residence for their families where they can raise what may be necessary for their support in addition to the fish with which the neighbouring lakes abound, and within a convenient distance from the city for them to carry home the earnings of their labours at such seasons as they can find useful employment".[26] The proprietors near Loch Lomond, who were already in possession of the best lands, gave their support to the plan.[27]

---

21   Smyth to Col. Darling, 26 May 1818, Letter Book Military, no. 2, PANB.

22   Executive Council Minutes, 21 July 1819, Rex/Px, vol. II, pp. 333 - 4, PANB.

23   A. Lockwood to Smyth, 11 February 1820, Rex/Px, Surveyor General, 4, II, a, PANB, and enclosure in Smyth to Bathurst, 11 May 1819, CO 188/26, pp. 11 - 2.

24   "Observations on the Laws Passed, June 1820", CO 188/26, pp. 41 - 2.

25   W. F. Odell to Judge Chipman, 23 October 1816, Hazen Collection, New Brunswick Museum [hereafter NBM], Saint John.

26   Judge Chipman's Report, 2 November 1816, *ibid.*

27   Some of these men had received grants in 1817, while others had held land in the area for many years. George Matthews, who in later years acquired land in the black settlement, owned 716 acres near the settlement and was able to acquire another 385 acres in 1817. John Jordan owned 300 acres in 1817 and later acquired more. Francis Gilbert owned 500 acres and William G. Cody acquired 400 acres near the black settlement in 1817. There were many other grants issued for this area, most for 200 acres or more. Returns Entered in Auditors Office, nos. 787-1241, RNA 2/1/5, PANB.

Chipman suggested that licenses of occupation be issued until a "proper trial of their sincerity and exertion had taken place", and that land grants be made any time after three years of occupation and improvement.[28] However, he clearly did not expect the blacks to be able to support themselves solely by farming. This meant that they would always be in a precarious situation dependent on a demand for their labour in Saint John.

Several months passed before anything further was done. In February 1817 Charles Peters presented a petition from William Flood and 40 black refugees in the Saint John area to the House of Assembly.[29] Flood and the others had used up their money in buying food and clothing and they could not find employment during the winter when provisions and fuel were very expensive. They claimed that because of their destitute condition they could not settle and cultivate the land nor even pay to have the lots surveyed. Although they insisted that they wanted to support themselves, because of "their present forlorn and distressed situation in a country and climate to which they are strangers", they required government assistance in order to survive.[30] This petition was referred to the committee of supply, but there is no record of any assistance being given by the Assembly. The province's reluctance to aid the black refugees may have resulted from a belief that they would never make good settlers, for the unwillingness of the Assembly did not extend to the settlement of white British settlers. In 1816 it voted £1000 to encourage the introduction of settlers into the province, £896 of which was used to bring 125 people from Scotland and to supply them with food, clothing and supplies on their arrival.[31] In 1817 another £160 was given to assist a party of Scotch settlers in locating at Napan.[32]

Judge Chipman had been responsible for seeing that the 1817 petition of the black refugees had reached the House of Assembly and he continued to press their case.[33] During the winter of 1816-17, he had had copies of the petition presented to the Executive Council and to Lieutenant General Martin Hunter, Administrator of the province. This had produced no results;

28 Judge Chipman's Report, 2 November 1816, Hazen Collection, NBM.

29 New Brunswick, Assembly, *Journal* [hereafter JLA], 14 February 1817, p. 15.

30 Petition of William Flood, 1 February 1817, Records of the Legislative Assembly [hereafter RLE], 817/B/Pe/2, PANB.

31 "Account of a Settlement with James Taylor", 20 February 1817, and "Account of the Expenditures by the Commissioners for Introducing settlers into the Province", 23 January 1817, RLE/817/Re/H/1 and 2, PANB.

32 *JLA*, 27 February 1818, pp. 66 - 7.

33 Judge Chipman had assisted the blacks in New Brunswick earlier. As an opponent of slavery, in 1800 he had been one of two lawyers who as 'volunteers for the rights of humanity' had defended the slave Nancy in a case fought to test the legality of slavery in New Brunswick. See W. A. Spray, *The Blacks in New Brunswick* (Fredericton, 1972), p. 23.

nor had a letter from the mayor of Saint John, John Robinson. In April 1817 Chipman informed Hunter that the black refugees were "so bent upon making a settlement upon lands by themselves that they cannot be diverted from their purpose". Since some of the refugees had earned enough money in Saint John to pay for the surveying of their lots and others were willing to pledge their first earnings, Chipman felt that it was "a cruel thing that they should have been sent by Government to this, to them inhospitable climate, and left without any aid in making a settlement". Chipman urged the government to defray the costs of the survey out of provincial funds since "such a proportion of it cannot be applied more usefully".[34] Chipman's letter carried more weight with the Executive Council than Flood's petition and the Surveyor General instructed the Deputy Surveyor of Saint John, Bernard Kiernan, to lay out the lots for the refugees on vacant lands near Loch Lomond. When the government refused to pay the expenses of the survey and the blacks were unable to sustain the full costs, Ward Chipman Jr. and John Robinson stepped in to help. Believing that it was essential to settle the black refugees, who were "hovering about Saint John in a very distressed state, without any fixed habitation", on their lands early in the season so that they could plant their crops and grow food for the next winter, Chipman and Robinson agreed to make themselves responsible for the remaining expenses of the survey in the hope that the government would eventually compensate them.[35] Kiernan surveyed 112 fifty acre lots and received £14-18-6 from 62 of the black refugees, while £23-11-6 was advanced by Chipman and Robinson, who were later reimbursed by the government.[36]

There are no records of the number who attempted to occupy land in the settlement begun in 1817, which the whites referred to as "the Negro Settlement" or "Black Settlement" and later as Willow Grove. From later petitions it would appear that the majority of the blacks continued to live in Saint John while clearing the lots to raise crops,[37] but some did attempt to settle and the licenses of occupation were reissued in 1820. In 1823 the government ordered a new survey of the area, following frequent requests by whites for unoccupied lots in the settlement. Robert Foulis, Deputy Surveyor for the county of

34 Report of Judge Chipman, 22 April 1817, Land Petitions, St. John County, no. 478, PANB.
35 Petition of Ward Chipman and John Robinson, 19 February 1818, RLE/818/B/Pe/23, PANB.
36 *Ibid.,* and *JLA,* 27 February 1818, p. 64.
37 At least two black refugees turned down the opportunity to take possession of lots in the settlement near Loch Lomond. They found the land "very heavy timbered and difficult of improvement" and "sensible it was not in our power to go on it and make a living" decided to seek land in a "more feasible spot". They went to Springfield Parish in Kings County and in 1820 applied for land in that area. There request was refused since they were considered aliens. Petition of Benjamin Johnston and Henry Borum, 8 March 1820, Rex/Px, vol. 18, p. 955, PANB.

Saint John, was ordered to survey a block of 6160 acres between Loch Lomond and Black River and to divide the block into 112 lots of 55 acres each, five acres larger than those surveyed earlier since they included 10% for useless waste land. Foulis was instructed to report the names of both the original settlers and the present occupiers and to estimate the improvements made by each person.[38] In 1817 41 black refugees had been eager to settle on the land and 62 blacks had contributed to paying the costs of the survey. By 1827 the settlement had only 34 black residents, and at least 44 of those holding licenses of occupation were non-residents, most of them living and working in Saint John and using their lots only to raise food.[39] In 1828, although the blacks claimed that their settlement was growing, there were only 42 settlers on the land.[40] Perhaps part of the reason why conditions improved so slowly was the refusal of the government to give the refugees clear titles. The government's reluctance not only discouraged the blacks but also created tensions between black and white settlers in the area.

The practice of granting land in the settlement to whites began in 1822 when Charles Buck, a native of Cork, was recommended for six of the "unoccupied" lots in the "Black Refugee Tract".[41] The 112 lots in the settlement were numbered 1 to 56 on either side of a designated road and Buck was granted lots 37, 38 and 39 on each side of the road, while black settlers occupied land on either side of him. In 1823 the Surveyor General argued that since only about one quarter of the lots were actually occupied by the blacks, whites should receive grants of 100 and 200 acres in the settlement. Over 40 lots were offered to whites who had petitioned for them, although most failed to occupy the land.[42] One black, Peter Emerson, claimed that he had lived for three years on a plot given to a white settler and that he had cleared four acres and built a house.[43] This dispute was not settled immediately even though the Surveyor General reported to the Executive Council that Emerson's name had been recorded for one of the lots and that another that the white settler claimed was unoccupied had been surveyed for a black man

38   Petition of Robert Foulis, undated, RLE/826/G/Pe/44, PANB.

39   *New Brunswick Courier* (Saint John), 6 October 1827.

40   Petition of the Colored Population of the Settlement at Loch Lomond, 29 February 1828, RLE/828/E/Pe/63, PANB.

41   Petition of Charles Buck, 29 November 1829, Land Petitions, St. John County, no. 684, and Journal of Proceedings respecting allotments of Land, vol. 26, 12 January and 7 February 1822, PANB.

42   Petition of Patrick McKenna, 4 March 1823, with comments of Surveyor General, Land Petitions, St. John County, no. 731, PANB. Also see Journal of Proceedings respecting allotments of Land, vol. 26, pp. 12, 24, 26 - 9, 34, and 56, PANB.

43   Petition of Peter Emerson, [1823], Land Petitions, St. John County, no. 753, PANB.

named Reid, who was still living in the settlement.[44] When the whites attempted to occupy their grants, they were not welcomed. A Saint John newspaper of 5 June 1824 reported that:

> The Blacks of Loch Lomond have again been guilty of breaking the peace, and disturbing the quietness of that settlement. It appears that a number of females of that colour had collected together and mal-treated with the greatest severity a white man and his wife, threatening them even with the destruction of their lives and property. For this violent outrage they were taken into custody by order of a magistrate, but were soon after rescued by the lawless interposition of the 'Master Blacks'. An enquiry we think, ought to be instituted for the purpose of ascertaining the cause of the ill will which the Blacks in that settlement manifest against their white neighbours and if it is groundless let some effectual measure be adopted to prevent its recurrence.[45]

The grievances of the black settlers included the ease with which whites acquired large blocks of land in the area while they were unable to obtain titles to their small lots. There was also some question as to whether, in fact, some lots were really "unoccupied". When Charles Buck ran into strong opposition in trying to occupy and improve his grant, he requested aid in acquiring possession of the lots from which he had been driven by the blacks or a grant of land elsewhere and compensation for the improvements he had made.[46] The Executive Council refused to comply with his request for land in another area, but in an attempt to restore order, 10 blacks were convicted of assault in June 1824 and 13 were charged with rioting and 7 with arson in September 1824.[47] The arson charges were not proven but those convicted of assault and riot were given short sentences of from 7 to 12 days in the county jail.

This appears to have temporarily ended the disorders at Loch Lomond, but the grievances of the blacks were not resolved.[48] Agitation for clear

---

44 Petition of Daniel McIntosh, 18 August 1823, *ibid.,* no. 760, PANB. The petitions of McIntosh and Emerson were rejected at the time, but in 1836 Emerson's widow was granted one of the two lots in question. Description of Land Grants, vol. 18, no. 298, PANB.

45 *Saint John Globe,* 27 May 1905, extract from a newspaper of 5 June 1824.

46 Extracts from a petition of Charles Buck, Journal of Proceedings respecting allotments of Land, 4 January 1825, vol. 28, p. 39, PANB.

47 St. John County, Minutes of the Courts of the Quarter Sessions, 1 June and 7 September 1824, PANB.

48 *New Brunswick Courier,* 15 September 1827 has a report that 3 black women from Willow Grove were imprisoned for assembling with others and assaulting Thomas Buck.

titles continued throughout 1824 and 1825. In 1824 Lieutenant Governor Sir Howard Douglas apparently approved a recommendation from the Commissioner of Crown Lands that the blacks be given grants of 50 acres for what was considered the low price of 20s.[49] But the blacks were not informed of this decision and when they appealed to the Executive Council in 1825 for confirmation of their titles the Council decided not to give grants but to issue licenses of occupation for 99 years, perhaps because they feared that the possession of freehold titles might confer on the blacks the right to vote.[50] In 1834 Charles Simonds of Saint John, a member of the Assembly, was informed by the Crown Lands Office that the plan of 1824 had, in fact, been approved and that blacks were entitled to 50 acre grants if they could prove title to the land and pay 20s.[51] No reason was given for the long delay in informing the blacks of their rights.

In 1836 the House of Assembly established a committee to resolve the question of title.[52] The committee found that a report to the Crown Lands Office showed that the claims of 65 blacks were valid, while those of 10 others were doubtful. They also discovered that £75 had been received by the government on behalf of the blacks and that the delay in issuing grants had been caused "by the unsettled state of said ten claims".[53] Grants were finally issued on 16 September 1836 to 73 blacks.[54] When the list of those receiving land in 1836 is checked against the names of those who petitioned for land in 1817, it can be seen that for 18 blacks the struggle to obtain land titles had gone on for nearly twenty years. For most others it had lasted at least twelve years. A number of the original applicants were dead by 1836 and the grants were issued to their widows and children. Despite many complaints about the slow process of issuing land grants in New Brunswick, white settlers had never been treated this badly. Within the original 5600 acre "Black Refugee Tract", 1050 acres had been given to six white settlers, who thus held 21 lots of from 100 to 300 acres each, in marked contrast to the 50 acre farms of the blacks.[55]

The refusal of the government to grant land titles was, as William End suggested in the Assembly in 1836, one reason for the failure of the black

49   *JLA*, 27 February 1836, p. 132.

50   Executive Council Minutes, 17 May 1825, Rex/Px, vol. III, p. 230, PANB.

51   J. Beckwith to Charles Simonds, 15 November 1834, Letter Books (Baillie), vol. D, p. 178, PANB.

52   *JLA*, 25 February 1836, p. 127.

53   *Ibid.*, 27 February 1836, p. 132.

54   Grant to Hiram Taylor and 72 others, 16 September 1836, Description of Land Grants, vol. 18, no. 298, PANB.

55   J. Beckwith to Charles Simonds, 15 November 1834, Letter Books (Baillie), vol. D, p. 179, PANB.

settlement to prosper.[56] It was not the only factor. While other groups of settlers faced similar problems to those of the black refugees, they received more aid from Agricultural and Emigrant Societies, church organizations and other charitable groups. They were also assisted in settling near friends, relations or fellow countrymen. Indeed, as a committee for the settlement of immigrants in Charlotte County pointed out in 1820, newly arrived immigrants objected to being offered lands which were not "in the vicinity of their Countrymen or Connexions".[57] Sir Howard Douglas boasted in 1826 of having put into "active and successful operation", under the societies, "a system for receiving, locating and aiding Emigrants", which was in part financed by the government.[58]

The black refugees did not have friends to aid them and they received very little help from the Emigrant Society in Saint John. The Overseers of the Poor for the parish of Portland did grudgingly give aid to the blacks who were described as being "unaccustomed to the rigours of New Brunswick winters" and "incapable of providing subsistance for themselves and their families".[59] They were provided with seed potatoes in 1817 and in 1821 those who had been able to clear land were aided by a grant of £50 to purchase seeds and farming utensils, something Major General Smyth had considered necessary in 1815.[60] Free molasses, meal and material for making clothes were also supplied in 1823 and 1824.[61] But the Overseers of the Poor felt that it was unfair that the people of Portland had to bear these expenses, which "ought not to be chargeable upon any particular Town or Parish" but should be the responsibility of all the people of the province.[62] Since Saint John was a port city, many destitute refugees and immigrants arrived there yearly who required help and in all the years the Overseers of the Poor supplied aid to the black refugees much larger sums were spent on

56   *JLA,* 25 February 1836, p. 127.

57   Petition of Hugh McKay, John Campbell and Peter Stubs, 1 September 1820, Rex/Px/21/6, pp. 2370-2, PANB.

58   Petition of the Fredericton Emigrant Society, 27 January 1820, RLE/820/B/Pe/45, PANB, and Douglas to Horton, 16 November 1826, CO 188/133, p. 155. The expenditures of these societies in 1826 totalled £116.

59   Petition of the Justices of the General Sessions of the Peace for the City and County of St. John, 21 February 1826, RPS, Poor, PANB.

60   Accounts of the Overseers of the Poor for Portland Parish for 1820, *ibid.* See also *JLA,* 16 March 1821, p. 356 and 26 March 1823, p. 104.

61   Petition of the Justices of the General Sessions of the Peace for the City and County of St. John, undated, RPS, Poor, PANB.

62   Petition of the Justices of the General Sessions of the Peace for the City and County of St. John, undated, RLE/826/G/Pe/9, PANB.

"indigent" and "distressed" immigrants and paupers, particularly the Irish.[63]

Not all the black refugees were a burden to the parish. In 1825 only 10 were given assistance, but in the following years the numbers grew.[64] By 1827 the condition of the settlement had deteriorated and almost every person in the settlement was receiving aid, especially during the winter. Economic difficulties in the timber trade and the scarcity of jobs in Saint John meant that there was little opportunity for those who depended on employment outside the settlement to earn money, as they had to compete for the few jobs available with the rapidly increasing number of pauper Irish immigrants who were landing at Saint John. Even the most energetic settlers in the black settlement found it difficult to support their families and the Overseers of the Poor reported that "the condition of this wretched portion of the Inhabitants of the Parish, so far from being improved, is annually becoming more distressing, very little progress having been made by the most provident amongst them towards supporting themselves and families".[65] In 1827 the Saint John Agricultural and Emigrant Society attempted to assist the blacks and members of the Society visited the settlement to talk with various families.[66] Since one of the reasons for the destitute condition of many of the black refugees in the winter was apparently the result of their inability to procure seeds for planting in the spring so that they would have food for the following winter, the Society purchased seeds to the value of £20 for their use, in the hope that "having got a start they will be able to succeed better from year

---

63 Brereton Greenhous, "Paupers and Poorhouses. The Development of Poor Relief in Early New Brunswick", *Histoire Sociale/Social History*, no. 1 (April, 1968), p. 13, says that once an immigrant arrived in the province "neither government nor shipper nor speculator made any move to help him during those early years", but the government did help one particular group, the black refugees. This is incorrect. There was aid for immigrants from the Emigrant Societies and every year in the 1820s, 30s and 40s the magistrates of the city and county of St. John petitioned the legislature for large sums of money to reimburse them for aid to "indigent Emigrants" and "transient Paupers", just as they did for aid to indigent black refugees. The only difference was that most immigrants were only aided for a year or two, while some of the black refugees received meal and molasses — not the type of aid that would make them self-sufficient — for ten years or more. Moreover, paupers resident in any parish were also aided for years out of local funds. The reason for the steady stream of petitions to the legislature for aid to the black refugees was that the magistrates and parish officials felt that the blacks should not be the responsibility of the parish but of the government of the province since they had been settled in the area by the government.

64 The Petitions of the Overseers of the Poor for the Parish of Portland show 10 black refugees given aid in 1825, 15 in 1826, 31 in 1827 and 41 in 1828. RLE/826/G/Pe/15A and B, RPS, Poor (1826), RLE/828/E/Pe/23, RPS, Poor (1827), and RLE/829/E/Pe/2, PANB.

65 Petition of the Overseers of the Poor for the Parish of Portland, 1828, RLE/828/E/Pe/23, PANB.

66 *New Brunswick Courier*, 21 April 1827.

to year".[67] The Society was not happy with the results of their efforts. The treasurer reported in October 1827 that the people "continue to make the worst returns for the kindness extended towards them", although he added that "there are a few of the residents who are improving their lots in a very creditable manner".[68]

One of the greatest needs of the black settlers was a mill to grind their oats, buckwheat, barley and rye. Without such a mill they had to carry their grain 15 miles from the settlement. When the portable mill they had used for years broke down in 1828 due to continued use and the lack of "proper skill" to keep it in repair, they had virtually to abandon their attempt to grow grain and rely solely on Indian corn, "which they find best adopted for the miserable process of soaking and pounding in a mortar; the only method your Petitioners now possess for making it into bread". The construction of a grist mill would, they argued in a petition, "truly make it a land of pure delight and flowing with milk and honey" and also induce many of those who had leases of land in the settlement, but who spent their winters in Saint John and other places, to "set down to a diligent cultivation of their land and by the happy change that would be made thereby in their condition, serve as an example to point the way to others who are not so fortunate, to endeavour at procuring a similar bountiful privilege elsewhere".[69] This petition was supported by some of the whites living in the area. John Jordan, a local magistrate, and William G. Cody, a farmer and innkeeper, two of the largest landowners, claimed "a thorough knowledge of [the] peculiar disposition, habits, and condition" of the blacks and recommended that the legislature give serious consideration to the petition, as they conceived "it to be more happily adopted than any other kind of patronage or assistance whatever, to relieve the Blacks from the unstable habits too common to many in the settlement, and fix them in steady industry, and attention to their farms — a reform of which kind with them is now becoming essentially requisite for the safety, order and peace of the community".[70]   Eighteen other whites also argued that the mill would be "a means of rendering the Black settlers useful, and improve materially" their condition and enable them to provide for themselves and families "without the great difficulty which at present exists in their obtaining the means of support". The mill would discourage frequent trips to the city of Saint John, a temptation to the more unsteady members of the community, who "frequently acquire incitements to idle and dissipated

67   *Ibid.,* 28 July 1827.

68   *Ibid.,* 6 October 1827.

69   Petition of the Colored Population of the Settlement at Loch Lomond, 29 February 1828, RLE/828/E/Pe/63, PANB.

70   Statement of John Jordan and William G. Cody, 3 March 1828, *ibid.*

habits".[71] While the altruism of the whites may be questioned, there is no doubt that a mill would have been more beneficial to the settlement than steady rations of food and clothing. Nevertheless, there is no record of the blacks receiving the assistance they required to build one.[72]

In 1833 the local magistrates reported more optimistically that as many of the farms had been "improved to a very considerable extent", the owners no longer needed assistance, although other families, "who are utterly helpless, many of whom are aged and infirm", still needed aid.[73] After visiting the settlement, the magistrates petitioned for a grant of £50 from the Assembly to improve the road from William G. Cody's farm to the black settlement. This sum might be used to employ the blacks in clearing the road and it was expected that such employment would help "to introduce habits of industry" and reduce the amount of aid expended in the area. But while the House of Assembly agreed to reimburse the Overseers of the Poor for money already given in 1832, it decided that no further sums should be expended "unless to a very limited extent, under special circumstances".[74]

A severe winter in 1833-34 provided the special circumstances and the Overseers of the Poor were forced to spend over £59, although they informed the government that "the most rigorous measures" were adopted "to induce or compel such Black People as were capable of so doing to support themselves", and relief was given only to the sick, aged and infirm.[75] Provisions were supplied during periods of bad weather and the magistrates praised the efforts of the Overseers of the Poor and William G. Cody for his assistance in "conveying provisions to them through the snow drifts". In 1835 the Justices of the Peace reported that "poverty, sickness and distress" had prevailed at the settlement during the winter of 1833 and except for the efforts of Cody and the Overseers of the Poor many of the blacks would have starved since 10 or 12 of them were "so aged and infirm or so debilitated by the rigorous effects of the climate" that they were unable to maintain them-

---

71 Statement of the white settlers, 4 March 1828, *ibid.*

72 In 1828 a number of petitions were received by the House of Assembly for aid in constructing mills in various parts of the province. Very few received aid at that time unless the mill was already under construction. See *JLA*, 16 February 1828, p. 17. However, because of the number of petitions, the Assembly voted £1000 to the Lieutenant Governor to be used to encourage "the erection of Oat Mills and Kilns" but grants were only to be given if the mill "had been actually in operation previous to the claim for bounty". *Ibid.*, 31 March 1828, p. 135.

73 Petition of the Justices of the Peace for the City and County of St. John, presented 7 February 1833, RLE/833/Pe/41, PANB.

74 *JLA*, 19 February 1833, p. 52.

75 Petition of the Justices of the Peace for the City and County of St. John, presented 9 February 1835, RLE/835/Pe/98, PANB.

selves.[76] At least six visits had to be made to the settlement by Dr. Paddock of Saint John, who found that a state of near famine existed.[77] While conditions appear to have improved after 1836, some assistance was still necessary for several years, and in 1839 the Justices of the Peace for Saint John County complained that other parishes were sending black paupers to the Loch Lomond area so that they would not have to support them.[78] The annual requests for funds to reimburse the Overseers of the Poor for aid to black refugees ended in 1845, although occasional grants were made in later years.[79] But the black community did not grow substantially and did not prosper. In time, many lots passed into the hands of whites and the black settlement virtually disappeared.

The black refugees had come from the southern states to the harsh climate of New Brunswick. They had been settled on wilderness land which had to be cleared by methods with which they were totally unfamiliar. They did not know how to construct log huts; they had no money for seeds; and they were unaware of which crops they should plant. Born into slavery, they had never had any opportunity or encouragement to use their own initiative. In 1828 they pointed out that because of "their circumscribed ability" and their lack of knowledge, they found it almost impossible to adapt to a way of life which was foreign to them.[80] Without leaders who had experience of life in a backwoods settlement, they faced enormous difficulties which many were unable to overcome. Moreover, it was not just their "circumscribed ability" that accounted for the failure of their settlement. In 1851 Professor Johnson described the land the blacks had been given as "poor and stony".[81] In 1904 William Murdock claimed that the land in the vicinity of Willow Grove where Irish immigrants had settled in the 1820s "is wretched".[82] A modern soil survey report states that "in the main the Lomond soils" in the area of Willow Grove "are not suitable for agriculture", and that "experience had proved that even after much labour was expended on clearing the land

---

76   *Ibid.*, RLE/835/Pe/33, PANB.

77   *Ibid.*, and St. John County, Minutes of the Courts of the Quarter Sessions, 24 January 1835, PANB.

78   *Ibid.*, January 1836.

79   Aid requested in 1840 totalled £46-2-6; for 1841, £123-0-7; for 1842, £145-15-2; and for 1843, £55-8-16. Petitions of the Justices of the Peace for the City and County of St. John, RLE/841/Pe/119, RLE/842/Pe/177 and RLE/843/Pe/190, PANB.

80   Petition of the Colored Population of the Settlement of Loch Lomond, 29 February 1828, RLE/828/E/Pe/63, PANB.

81   James F. W. Johnson, *Notes on North America, Agricultural, Economical and Social* (Edinburgh, 1851), vol. 1, pp. 138 - 9.

82   William Murdock to W. F. Ganong, 4 April 1904, Ganong Papers, MS New Brunswick Settlements, vol. 1, p. 128, NBM.

and picking off the stones, the fertility of the soil, which is only mediocre, was not sufficient to offset the disadvantages of remoteness from markets".[83] The policy of giving small lots of marginal land to poor settlers was bound to fail, whether the settlers were white or black.[84]

White settlers could usually depend on some assistance from friends and fellow countrymen and if they still failed, like those Irish immigrants who also settled in the area of Willow Grove on land equally unsuitable for agriculture, they could move to other settlements in the province or to the United States. For the black refugees the alternative of moving to the United States was not appealing. Few attempted to settle in other parts of New Brunswick. Most preferred to remain among their own people, either on their tiny, unproductive lots in Willow Grove or to drift to the city of Saint John where they formed part of a "special class of permanent poor".[85] For this reason the settlement of the black refugees in New Brunswick can only be viewed as a failure.

83 H. Aulund and R. E. Wicklund, *Soil Survey Report of Southeastern New Brunswick* (Fredericton, undated), p. 70.

84 See John Richard's Report Respecting the Canada Waste Lands, 1831, Britain, *Parliamentary Papers*, 1831 - 2, vol. XXII, p. 37.

85 Judith Fingard, "The Relief of the Unemployed Poor in Saint John, Halifax, and St. John's, 1815 - 1860", *Acadiensis*, V (Autumn, 1975), p. 32.

T. W. ACHESON

Reprinted from Vol. VIII, No. 2
(Spring 1979)

The Great Merchant and Economic Development in St. John 1820-1850

One of the liveliest debates in recent Canadian business history has centred on the role of the nineteenth-century merchant in promoting or retarding the development of a locally controlled British North American industrial base. Supporters of the retardation theory usually argue that the colonial merchant was nurtured in a system based upon the export of raw and semi-finished produce and the import of fully manufactured materials. Dominating the ports and the transportation systems of British North America, he became the principal defender of the economic *status quo*, viewing any substantial re-arrangement of economic relations as a threat to his world. Thus he remained the harbinger of a form of economic colonialism which bound the destiny of British North America and of the forming Dominion of Canada in a subservient relationship to more advanced national economies, particularly those of the United Kingdom and the United States. Opponents of this theory have accepted the primacy of the merchant in the colonial economies but have argued that the gulf separating the merchant from other dynamic elements in the business community was less wide than the retardationists would have us believe. They maintain that the dramatic shift from commercial to industrial emphases and from external to internal markets in the last half of the nineteenth century occurred with the consent and participation of this dominant commercial element.[1]

There are several difficulties within this general argument. One of the most basic concerns the definition of "merchant". The meanest cordwainer in the mid-nineteenth century offered his shoes for sale to the general public; conversely, many important shippers and wholesalers owned, in whole or in part, the means to process the basic staple commodities of their region. Even a restricted use of the term leaves a group of businessmen involved in a variety of commercial, financial and transportation functions. In colonial Saint John, for example, "merchant" was a legal status conferred on certain men at the time of their admission to the freedom of the city. Within the hierarchy of occupations which were admissable as freemen, that of merchant was clearly the most important and this importance was reflected in the fees required of those admitted to the status. Although a merchant might also be a sawmill owner, a legal and social line was clearly drawn between merchants possessing a sawmill

---

1 The literature of this debate has been explored by L. R. MacDonald in "Merchants against Industry: An Idea and Its Origins", *Canadian Historical Review,* LVI (1975), pp. 263-81.

and sawmill owners by occupation whose status was lower. Moreover, there were a number of commercial functions characteristically performed by merchants, including the importing and wholesaling of produce, the export of fish and wood products, the transport of other people's goods, the purchase of staples produce on other people's accounts, the sale and auction of other people's goods, private banking, and acting as agents or directors for chartered banks, fire, marine and life insurance companies. In village business a single merchant might have exercised most of these functions; the most successful urban merchants were those who focussed their efforts on three or four. In time, the development of competing interests sharply limited the issues on which merchants were able to speak as a class or community. Indeed, on many issues, it is doubtful whether colonial boards of trade and chambers of commerce spoke for anything more than one of several elements within the business community.

Another important question raised by the retardation debate concerns the extent to which "normal" merchant behaviour was modified by the local environment. There can be little doubt but that all merchants in British North America responded to short term opportunities and that only rarely were they willing to sacrifice these opportunities on the alter of national, colonial or civic interest.[2] Yet, over time, a merchant became attached to the community in which he lived, his response to opportunity conditioned by the idiosyncracies of the local economy, the nature of the relationship between the local and metropolitan economies, and the impact of the economic cycle in reducing the short-term profitability of existing relationships. Any final assessment of the merchant's role in the economic development of British North America will therefore have to await the completion of a number of case studies of individual communities and firms.[3] The paper which follows is an attempt to explore the role of the merchant in the economic development of colonial Saint John. The city affords an interesting case study both because of its size — in 1840 it was the third largest urban centre in British North America — and because of the central role played by the trade in timber and deals in its economic life.

Traditionally the central problem in the study of the economy of Saint John has been to explain the failure of the city to make the necessary adjustments to compensate for the dislocations occasioned by the stagnation of the wood trade following Confederation. Recently, Peter McClelland has put the date of that stagnation back to mid-century, arguing that the shipbuilding industry, the most

2 A point most recently made by Professor Gerald Tulchinsky in *The River Barons* (Toronto, 1977), p. 234.

3 Nonetheless, a good beginning has been made with Tulchinsky's examination of the Montreal business community at mid-century, and in David Sutherland's study of the business strategies of Halifax merchants in the colonial period. Tulchinsky, *op. cit.;* David Sutherland, "Halifax Merchants and the Pursuit of Development 1783-1850", *CHR,* LIX (1978), pp. 1-17.

dynamic element in the provincial economy after 1850, added little to the well-being or growth of that economy.[4] McClelland has highlighted the role of New Brunswick businessmen in this problem by demonstrating the tenacity with which they stood behind the wooden shipbuilding industry, investing perhaps $8 million between 1870 and 1879 in a technology which was effectively obsolete.[5] These businessmen failed to make the transition to metal ships or to establish backward linkages from the shipbuilding industry — particularly those relating to the outfitting of ships and the manufacture of chains and anchors — which could develop in time into significant industries. McClelland has explained this failure in terms of "the absence of alternatives capable of giving to regional growth the sustaining force which timber was losing" after 1850.[6] But even if it is admitted that shipbuilding was unable to play this dynamic role — a thesis that is much more compelling in 1870 than in 1840 — McClelland offers scant evidence to prove that manufacturing and, to a lesser extent, fishing and agriculture, could not have contributed a dynamic element to the regional economy. To support his contention, he is forced to argue that they could not because they did not, an idea grounded in the assumption that by mid-century New Brunswick was backward relative to other colonial economies. To demonstrate this position McClelland offers an output analysis of New Brunswick and Ontario agriculture at the end of the nineteenth century, and points to the inability of some New Brunswick consumer goods producers to compete with central Canadian producers on the central Canadian market in the post-Confederation period. Much of this can be demonstrated for 1890, but it all presumes that what was true at that time must have been true a half-century earlier, and that the absence of a particular resource, say coal, must preclude the development of any industry which employed that resource.

The doubts raised by the ahistorical nature of this analysis are heightened by the persistence with which the provincial business community pursued and supported the wood trade and the wooden ship, even in the face of a technological obsolescence which by 1870 was obvious to all observers. This persistence suggests a commitment to a declining economic base understandable in the small resource-based village economies of much of the province, but more difficult to comprehend in the context of the complex, differentiated economy which existed in Saint John. Indeed, the continuance of these forms of activity and the failure of other kinds of development to occur may have been more the

---

4   Peter D. McClelland, "The New Brunswick Economy in the Nineteenth Century" (PhD thesis, Harvard University, 1966), pp. 3-4. McClelland argues that shipbuilding may have added no more than 2.6% to the gross regional product (p. 189) and that it had few significant backward or forward linkages.

5   *Ibid.*, pp. 229-30.

6   *Ibid.*, p. 4.

result of human factors than the absence of any particular material resource. Certainly Saint John in the colonial period possessed considerable potential. In 1840 the city was one of the largest urban centres in British North America, with a population of about 27,000. Its merchants possessed a monopoly of the commerce of the Saint John River Valley and its tributaries, a market of nearly 100,000 people. They also dominated the commercial life of the Bay of Fundy counties of New Brunswick and Nova Scotia, containing another 90,000 people.[7] The population of the Saint John River Valley exceeded that of the Home District of Upper Canada, while the city's whole market area compared favourably with the Quebec City District of Lower Canada.[8] Shipbuilding had been an important feature of the city's economy for two full generations by 1840 and the Saint John industry was clearly the most significant in British North America.[9] In addition, a substantial and diversified manufacturing sector designed to service both the timber trade and the growing consumer market of the area had emerged over the previous two decades, a development reflected in the strong labour movement which had become an important feature of city life in the years following the War of 1812.[10] By 1840 Saint John was marked as a growth centre with a distinct advantage over any other community in the Atlantic region. And this is of special significance because nineteenth-century manufacturing growth tended to be cumulative: early leaders generally improved their advantage over other communities as James Gilmour has demonstrated in his study of the spatial evolution of manufacturing in Ontario.[11]

In many ways the 1840s was the most critical decade of the colonial period. It witnessed the collapse of the preferences for colonial timber on the British market, a disaster which Saint John businessmen were able to overcome mainly by making the transition from the export of timber to the export of deals. Nonetheless, the trade in wood products reached its largest volume in that period and thereafter stagnated; the economy of the province grew increasingly dependent in the 1850s on the still further processing of wood into ships and their sale on the British market. The abrogation of the Old Colonial System was marked by several short term economic downturns which severely mauled

7   New Brunswick, *Journal of the House of Assembly*, 1841, pp. xvii-xxx; Canada, *Census of 1871*, IV, p. 125.

8   Canada, *Census of 1871*, IV, p. 128.

9   The early development of this industry is discussed by Lewis R. Fischer in "From Barques to Barges: Shipping Industry of Saint John, N.B. 1820-1914" (unpublished paper read to the Atlantic Canada Studies Conference, Fredericton, 1978).

10 Eugene A. Forsey, *The Canadian Labour Movement 1812-1902* (Ottawa, Canadian Historical Association, 1974), pp. 3-4; J. Richard Rice, "A History of Organized Labour in Saint John, New Brunswick 1813-1890" (MA thesis, U.N.B., 1968), ch. 1.

11 James M. Gilmour, *Spatial Evolution of Manufacturing: Southern Ontario 1851-1891* (Toronto, 1972).

the wood trades and raised serious doubts about the viability of an economy based upon them. At this point in time any group which persisted in subordinating all other interests to the needs of an already failing industry, it could be argued, can be perceived as contributing to the retardation of the provincial economy at a critical juncture in its history. If, by virtue of their influence within the political framework of the colony and their control of the principal sources of capital, merchants were able to promote or to inhibit certain kinds of development, then their role in determining the economic destiny of the city and its hinterland was as important as the presence or absence of any specific resource.

The study which follows will test this hypothesis in the context of merchant behaviour in the city of Saint John between 1820 and 1850. It will do so by examining the extent and nature of merchant wealth and the role of leading merchants in promoting or opposing development strategies in the first half of the nineteenth century. A major problem is the sheer size of the city's merchant community. During the colonial period about 800 men held the legal status of merchant and a number of others illegally participated in merchant functions. There were large numbers of transients whose residency in the city was confined to a few years, and even larger numbers of minor businessmen whose sole claim to the status of merchant seems to have been their role as small-scale importers. Their impact on the commercial life of the city was marginal and any attempt to include them in a study of this nature — even if sufficient information were available — could seriously distort its purpose. At the other extreme, the council of the Chamber of Commerce provides a definite group of the influential merchants but these might represent only one faction of important merchants. To overcome both of these difficulties an effort was made to determine which merchants played important roles in the commercial and public life of the city and province over a number of years. The criteria used in the selection included ownership of significant shipping, wharfing and waterfront facilities, directorships of important financial agencies, public esteem and influence as manifested in the press and in public documents, public service and personal wealth. Although the final decision of who to include is both arbitrary and subjective, for the purpose of this study forty leading commercial figures have been identified as "great" merchants. Members of this group comprehended a variety of commercial interests, but all participated in vital shipping and financial concerns of the port and all possessed substantial personal resources. Their influence stemmed not only from this control over most of the city's financial resources, but also from their ability to create a climate of public opinion which identified their interests with the welfare of the community at large,[12] and from

---

12 For the extent to which they succeeded in this goal see the testimonials to the merchants delivered by George Fenety and Henry Chubb, the city's most respected and influential newspaper editors in the 1840s. See *The Commercial News and General Advertiser* (St. John), 10 September 1839, and *The New Brunswick Courier* (St. John), 10 February 1843.

their access to the political institutions of the colony.[13] The group included 29 men who held the legal status of merchant, 4 mariners, 2 grocers, 1 fisherman, 1 clerk and 3 who were not freemen of the city.[14]

The great merchants were drawn from all elements within the broader community, but the most numerous were those of Loyalist or pre-Loyalist origins. Several, notably Ezekiel and Thomas Barlow, Noah Disbrow, Ralph Jarvis, John Ward, Stephen Wiggins and John M. and R.D. Wilmot, were scions of important Loyalist merchant families. Several others, such as Nehemiah Merritt, and Thomas and William Leavitt, were children of frugal Loyalist fishermen. Still a third group was the Simonds connection, the principal landed interest in the province, which included the pre-Loyalist, Charles Simonds, and the two fortunate young Loyalists who married his sisters, Thomas Millidge and Henry Gilbert. Equally as important as the natives were the British immigrants. By far the most significant were the Scots, Lauchlan Donaldson, John Duncan, James Kirk, Hugh Johnston, John Robertson and John Wishart, who greatly outnumbered the Protestant Irishmen, John Kinnear and William Parks.[15] All of these immigrants were the offspring of prosperous families and came to the colony as young men of substance, bringing with them at least some capital resources. From positions of comparative advantage in the early nineteenth century, these merchants rode the crest of the timber trade to wealth by the 1840s. Virtually all were involved, to some degree, in the timber trade itself. Frequently they shipped timber which their crews had harvested. More often they bought timber or deals from the producer or took them in trade. Sometimes they would ship them on consignment to the British market. Rarely was the timber merchandising a single activity. Usually it was part of a pattern of business endeavour which included the wholesaling and retailing of British and American imports, coastal shipping, and the purchase, use and sale of sailing vessels.[16]

13 This thesis is argued by Stewart MacNutt in his "Politics of the Timber Trade in Colonial New Brunswick 1825-40", *CHR*, XXX (1949), pp. 47-65.

14 This group includes L.H. Deveber, Thomas Barlow, Ezekiel Barlow, Jr., Issac Bedell, Robert W. Crookshank, Noah Disbrow, Jr., Lauchlan Donaldson, John Duncan, Henry Gilbert, James T. Hanford, John Hammond, David Hatfield, James Hendricks, Ralph M. Jarvis, Hugh Johnston, Sr., Hon. Hugh Johnston, Jr., John H. Kinnear, James Kirk, Thomas Leavitt, William H. Leavitt, Nehemiah Merritt, Thomas Millidge, D.L. McLaughlin, Thomas E. Millidge, William Parks, John Pollok, Robert Rankin, E.D.W. Ratchford, Hon. John Robertson, W.H. Scovil, Hon. Charles Simonds, Walker Tisdale, John V. Thurgar, John Walker, John Ward, Jr., Charles Ward, Stephen Wiggins, John M. Wilmot, R.D. Wilmot, John Wishart.

15 David Macmillan explores the early development of the St. John Scottish community in "The New Men in Action: Scottish Mercantile and Shipping Operations in the North American Colonies 1760-1825", *Canadian Business History: Selected Studies, 1497-1971* (Toronto, 1972), pp. 82-99.

16 A good description of these activities is found in Graeme Wynn, "Industry, Entrepreneurship

Central to the business activity of all leading merchants was involvement in or ownership of one or more of the three vital elements in city commerce: the banking system, the wharves of the port, and the ships. Most sat on the directorates of at least one of the three local public banks or the local advisory committee of the Bank of British North America.[17] Indeed, given the centrality of credit to the commercial system of the province, it was unthinkable that any substantial local firm would not have easy access to the financial stability which the banks offered, an access ultimately controlled by the bank directors whose committees met twice weekly to approve all loans. Access to the city wharves and water lots on the east side of Saint John harbour, the most valuable mercantile property in the colony, was also critical. The water lots had been leased in perpetuity by the city in return for the lessees' agreement to construct and maintain the wharves. In return for an annual rental of between £5 and £31, depending on location in the harbour, a merchant received the right to erect improvements on the wharf, to provide free wharfage for his ships and goods, and to charge the legal rates of wharfage to all ships choosing to load or unload at this landing.[18] Possession of this vital harbour resource provided the merchant with both the most geographically advantageous terminal for his sea and river commerce and a modest but continuous income.

The central feature of New Brunswick trade was its de-centralization. Most great merchants were not involved in the timber-harvest or the sawmilling industry. Similarly, although they bought, sold and contracted for the construction of vessels, they rarely participated directly in the shipbuilding industry. The role of most merchants was that of entrepreneur closing the links between the harbours of St. John and Liverpool. Their vehicle was the sailing vessel and by 1841 the port possessed nearly 90,000 tons of shipping, about equally divided between small coasting vessels and those designed for trans-Atlantic crossings.[19] There were great differences in patterns of ownership among the city's major mercantile firms. More than half of the port's tonnage was owned by its great merchants, several of whom possessed sizeable fleets. John Kirk owned 14 vessels totalling over 7,000 tons, Stephen Wiggins 10 vessels of nearly 7,000 tons and John Wishart 9 vessels of 4,500 tons. At the other extreme, a number of

and Opportunity in the New Brunswick Timber Trade" in Lewis R. Fischer and Eric W. Sager, eds., *The Enterprising Canadians: Entrepreneurs and Economic Development in Eastern Canada, 1820-1914* (St. John's, Memorial University of Newfoundland, 1979).

17 Reports revealing the directors and the financial state of affairs of each bank were published annually in *Journal of the House of Assembly.*

18 Schedule of Real Estate Belonging to St. John, Wharf Leases in Perpetuity, Records of the Executive Council, REX/PA, Miscellaneous, Provincial Archives of New Brunswick [hereafter PANB].

19 This description of the St. John fleet, containing information on the date of acquisition, size and ownership of each vessel, is found in "Customs House Account, Returns of Shipping, Port of Saint John, New Brunswick", *Journal of the House of Assembly,* 1842, cclvii-cclxvii.

merchants actually owned very little shipping, apparently preferring to ship through others. The large firm of Crookshank and Walker, for example, had only a single vessel in 1841. The different ownership patterns reflected the kinds of mercantile specialization that had developed by 1840. The large ship-owners were heavily committed to the timber trade, both as merchants and as carriers; Crookshank and Walker were West Indies merchants with strong ties to the coasting trade and played the role of commission merchant and auctioneer. But whatever the area of specialized activity an individual firm might tend to follow, the collective control by the great merchants of the financial structure, harbour facilities, and shipping industry of St. John placed them in the position both to accumulate personal wealth and to play a significant role in determining the kind of economy which might emerge in the city and the colony.

Most great merchants built up sizeable fortunes at some point in their careers. And while time and fortune were not always kind to them, the great majority managed to avoid calamitous failures.[20] Any attempt to establish the extent of personal wealth of an individual over time is an exceedingly treacherous enterprise, but it is possible to get a glimpse of the collective resources of the merchant community and to establish with some accuracy the holdings of most merchants at one point in their lives. Something of the size of St. John merchant capital can be glimpsed in the city's fleet. Assuming an average price of £5 a ton, a conservative estimate of the value of vessels registered in St. John in 1841 would be £450,000, and the capital investment of firms such as those of James Kirk or Stephen Wiggins would have been in the order of £30-40,000.[21] All firms had a basic business investment in offices, stores, warehouses, and the harbour-area land or wharves on which they were located. While the size of this investment varied with the scope of the facilities, even a single store in the harbour area was worth £3,000 by mid-century and the larger facilities of many merchants plus the value of stock on hand could multiply that figure five or six times. Yet few merchants committed most of their assets to their mercantile activities. In 1826 the firm of Crookshank and Walker, one of the largest in the city, owned assets valued at more than £50,000 ($200,000). Of this total only 20 per cent was represented by vessels (the firm owned four) and less than 10 per cent by goods on hand.[22] The remainder consisted of investments in property and notes. Johnston withdrew from the firm in 1826 and received the sum of £25,000 from his partner. He also retained ownership of his own firm, H. Johnston &

---

20 Two notable failures were the firms John M. Wilmot, in 1837 and James Hanford, Alex Yeats and J. & H. Kinnear, in 1843. *The New Brunswick Courier*, 4 March, 18, 25 November 1843; A.R.M. Lower, *Great Britain's Woodyard* (Toronto, 1973), p. 151.

21 Prices for New Brunswick-built vessels fluctuated between £5 and £12 a ton throughout the 1830s and 1840s.

22 Account Book I, pp. 5-10, Hugh Johnston Papers, New Brunswick Museum [hereafter NBM].

Co., and his total personal assets in that year amounted to over £40,000.[23]
Similar stories of substantial capital investment outside the major mercantile
operation can be constructed for other great merchants. Nehemiah Merritt died
in 1843 possessed of an estate worth about £60,000 ($240,000) exclusive of ships
and business stock.[24] In 1864 Stephen Wiggins left more than $700,000 to his
heirs, about half of it composed of assets not connected with the firm.[25] And still
later, in 1876, "The Lord of the North", John Robertson, passed on $454,000 for
the benefit of his children.[26] By 1840 there may have been a dozen merchants
each with assets exceeding a quarter of a million American dollars, and a large
part of this capital was available for investment beyond the primary enterprises
of their holders.

Not surprisingly the most important uses to which the great merchants of St.
John devoted their wealth were those designed to further the development
strategies which the merchant community deemed essential to its economic
well-being. While direction and emphasis of these strategies changed from time
to time in response to external circumstances, the broad outline is clearly visible
throughout the first half of the nineteenth century. Like their counterparts in
most North American ports, Saint John merchants emphasized a combination
of financial institutions, transportation links, resource exploitation and urban
development to enable them to facilitate trans-Atlantic trade and to dominate a
hinterland extending for 200 miles around the city. By 1840 their dominance in
shipping had turned the Bay of Fundy into a St. John lake and their location had
made the entire St. John Valley a satrapy of the city. Their greatest concerns
were the development of transportation facilities into the interior and to the
north shore of the province and the exploitation of the natural resources found
within this natural zone of control. To achieve the first, the merchants pressured
for a canal system to open the Grand Lake, some 60 miles from the city. After
1835 they sought to extend the city's control to the North Shore by means of a
combined ship-railroad system which would involve construction of short
railway lines between Grand Lake and Richibucto and between Shediac and
Moncton. To exploit the natural resources of the area, they proposed to develop
the sources of water power at the mouth of the St. John River and at the Grand
Lake, to mine the coal resources of the Grand Lake area, and to promote the
Bay of Fundy and southern whale fisheries.[27]

23 Schedule of Real and Personal Effects, May 1826, *ibid.*
24 Last will and testament of Nehemiah Merritt, Records of the Court of Probate, City and
County of St. John, Book G, pp. 131 ff., PANB. The totals include estimates of property values.
25 Stephen Wiggins, 1864, RG 7, RS 71, PANB.
26 John Robertson, 1876, *ibid.*
27 New Brunswick, Records of the Legislative Assembly [RLE], 1834, Petitions, vol. 2, no 41; 1836,
Petitions, vol. 5, nos. 70, 75, 81; 1834, Petitions, vol. 6, no. 130, PANB.

The most important institutions necessary to the maintenance of this commercial system were financial organizations, notably banks and insurance companies. Banks facilitated the transfer of funds in trans-Atlantic trade and control of the province's major credit agencies gave the leading merchants considerable leverage in their dealings with other parts of New Brunswick society. The Council of New Brunswick had co-operated with the merchant community to charter the first bank in British North America in 1820.[28] But the conservative policies and limited capital resources of the Bank of New Brunswick could not keep pace with the financial needs of merchants in a rapidly expanding colony and by 1836 they had secured royal charters for two more banking institutions, the Commercial and the City banks, over the opposition of the Executive Council of the province.[29] By 1845 the three banks possessed a paid up capital of £250,000 ($1,000,000), most of which was probably held within the city by the merchant community.[30] Through the period 1830-50 banking stock never yielded less than 8 per cent a year and was viewed not only as an excellent security but also a first class opportunity for speculation. Similar emphasis was placed on the city's two marine insurance companies, and on its fire insurance company. The £50,000 capital of the N.B. Marine Company, the largest of these firms, yielded an annual dividend of 10 to 60% in the 1840s,[31] and more than 80% of the stock of that company was held by city merchants in 1841.[32] The stock of these companies not only yielded an excellent dividend income, but provided the basis for a flourishing speculative trade in stocks.

Nonetheless, the most important single investment made by St. John merchants was in land. It is interesting to speculate on the reasons behind this phenomenon. Land was clearly acquired both incidentally, in payment for debts owed, and because of the high degree of security which it offered. As well, many merchants saw an opportunity to achieve a certain status in the possession of well-known farms and favoured city residences. The nature of the acquisitions reveals several motives on the part of the purchasers: a desire to emulate a landed gentry, to create the security of rental income, to speculate on rising land prices and, in the case of purchases outside New Brunswick, to escape the consequences of the provincial bankruptcy laws in the event of commercial

---

28 James Hannay, *History of New Brunswick* (St. John, 1909), II, pp. 428-9.

29 NB, RLE, 1836, Petitions, vol. 5, no. 64, PANB; Hannay, pp. 430-2.

30 These estimates are drawn from Bank of New Brunswick dividend payments, newspaper accounts of bank stock sales, and wills. There was no public statement disclosing the ownership of bank stock in colonial New Brunswick.

31 The annual reports of the N.B. Marine Insurance Company between 1830 and 1850 may be found in the appendices of the Journals of the New Brunswick House of Assembly.

32 New Brunswick, *Journal of the House of Assembly*, 1842, Appendix — Returns of Incorporated Companies, The N.B. Marine Insurance Company.

disaster. All merchants maintained one and sometimes two city residences. A large land-holder such as Noah Disbrow owned 12 city lots and 5 houses,[33] while John Robertson paid city taxes on real estate assessed at £25,000 ($100,000) — which almost certainly greatly underestimated its true market value — and held long term leases, through his brother, on more than 100 city lots.[34] At his death in 1876 Robertson owned city real estate valued at $250,000.[35] Virtually all merchants owned several city lots and most possessed long term leases on substantial tracts of city land in the harbour area.

Perhaps the most obvious case of land speculation on the part of leading merchants was the development of the suburban lands lying along the Marsh Road area directly north and west of the city. As early as 1819 most of this land had been acquired from the Hazen estate by several merchants — notably Nehemiah Merritt, Stephen Wiggins, Henry Gilbert, Hugh Johnston and Walker Tisdale — as building lots and farms.[36] By mid-century most of the land remained in the hands of the merchant-buyers, who were in the process of subdividing it into township building lots. The same assumptions concerning the development of the interior of the province marked the merchant's land acquisition in the St. John River Valley. Instead of buying up timber land, most merchants deliberately set about to acquire land bordering on the river. Their holdings were marked by a high proportion of intervale land, working farms and tenants, and comprised some of the most valuable agricultural resources in the province. The estate of Hugh Johnston alone contained nearly 12,000 acres of Valley land in 25 separate holdings scattered through Queens, Sunbury, York and Carleton counties in 1835.[37] A number of merchants also acquired extensive holdings in other areas, notably Nova Scotia, Maine, New York and Upper Canada. Nehemiah Merritt, for example, owned three houses at Greenwich & Amos Streets in New York City,[38] and he and Walker Tisdale each possessed more than 2,000 acres of land in Northumberland and Durham counties, Upper Canada.[39]

In addition to ownership of lands and financial institutions, the Saint John merchant sought security through the public sector of the economy. The debt of

33 Records of the Court of Probate, City and County of St. John, Book H, pp. 454 ff., PANB.

34 John Robertson to Common Council, 10 October 1849, Saint John Common Council Supporting Papers, vol. 20, Saint John Manuscripts, PANB; Saint John Schedule (etc.), 1842, REX/PA, Miscellaneous, PANB.

35 John Robertson, 1876, RG 7, RS 71, PANB.

36 Extract of Cash Received for Land Sold 1814-1821, Hon. William F. Hazen Papers, Daybook and Journal 1814-34, NBM.

37 Inventory of Estate of Hugh Johnston, 1 May 1835, Hugh Johnston Papers, Account Book I, NBM.

38 Probate Records, Book G, p. 131, PANB.

39 *Ibid.*, Book I, p. 267.

the city and the province and the financing of public utilities within the city offered ample opportunity for investment. The city, in particular, had no agency through which it could carry long term debt contracted for the construction of essential public works and from 1819 onward the merchant came to play an important role as city creditor.[40] By 1842 the municipal funded debt totalled £112,000 of which 40 per cent was held directly by merchants and their families and another 20 per cent by St. John banks and insurance companies.[41] The city's major public utilities were promoted and financed by its merchants. The water company was formed following the cholera epidemic of 1832 and by 1844 had expended £27,000 on the system.[42] The Gas Light Company and Reversing Falls Bridge Company were founded in the 1840s under the inspiration of the same group.[43]

Of all the potential investments in New Brunswick, the one that found least favour with the merchant community was secondary industry. Most merchant investment in this sector was related to the processing of natural resources produced in the province. In the wake of the growing English demand for deals in the mid-1830s several merchants acquired or constructed sawmills in conjunction with their shipping activities. Within the city John Robertson erected a large steam sawmill powered by sawdust and offal,[44] while less impressive operations were conducted by Robert Rankin & Co., Stephen Wiggins, R.D. Wilmot, Thomas and Ezekiel Barlow, and Nehemiah Merritt.[45] Outside the city the Kinnear brothers operated the Wales Stream mill.[46] Several others lent their support to the Portland Mills and Tunnel Company which proposed to cut tunnels through the Reversing Falls gorge to provide water power for a sawmill complex in Portland.[47] The most important industrial undertaking of any merchant before 1850 was the establishment of the Phoenix Foundry by the Barlow brothers in the 1820s. During the first two decades of its existence the firm introduced a number of technical innovations into the city, including construction of the first steamship manufactured entirely in the colony.[48]

40 The city debt rose from £4413 in 1822 to £115,366 in 1845. Minutes of the Common Council, vol. V, 5 April 1822; vol. XVII, 10 September 1845, Common Clerk's Office, Saint John City Hall.

41 Common Council Supporting Papers, vol. VI, 7/8-12/13 September 1842, Saint John Manuscripts, PANB.

42 NB, RLE, 1844, Petitions, vol. 7, no. 181, PANB.

43 *The New Brunswick Courier*, 27 March 1843.

44 *The New Brunswick Courier*, 11 September 1852.

45 *The Morning News* (St. John), 23 April 1841.

46 *The New Brunswick Courier*, 25 November 1843.

47 NB, RLE, 1834, Petitions, vol. 2, no. 41; 1836, Petitions, vol. 5, no. 75; 1839, Petitions, vol. 2, no. 43, PANB.

48 Common Council Minutes, vol. XV, 23 December 1840, 14 January 1841, Common Clerk's Office, Saint John City Hall.

However, these examples were the exceptions rather than the rule. Most leading merchants had no financial involvement with secondary industry before 1840; those who did, with exception of Robertson and the Barlows, had a very limited investment in the undertakings. There was little investment in the city's major secondary industry — shipbuilding — and most lumber, even in the St. John area, was made in 49 sawmills owned by a different group of men.[49] Quite clearly, comprehensive industrial development stood low on the list of merchant priorities in the period.

In view of the rapid pace of industrial growth in the city between 1820 and 1840, the low level of merchant participation is surprising. In 1820, apart from a few shipyards, sawmills, and flour mills, Saint John's secondary industry consisted of a wide variety of traditional crafts practiced in dozens of small workshops. Over the course of the next three decades, in response to the needs of a rapidly expanding provincial society, the city and its environs was transformed into an important manufacturing centre. This development occurred along a broad front. Most obvious and most significant was the growth of the shipbuilding and sawmilling industries. But there was also a host of industries producing for provincial consumers. Apart from the enterprises of the master tailors and shoemakers, these included 24 tanneries, 16 flour mills, 4 iron foundries, 2 brass foundries, 12 furniture and 4 soap manufacturers, 8 carriage makers, 2 breweries, a paper mill, and a number of minor industries.[50] The capacity and resources of these firms is perhaps best illustrated in the flour industry which by 1840 represented a capital investment of over £50,000 in mills capable of annually producing more than 150,000 barrels of flour, enough to feed the entire population of the province.[51] The tanners — 4 of whom were capable of generating more than 60 horsepower from their steam engines — made a similar claim for their industry.[52] The Harris Foundry comprised a block of buildings in 1846 with a replacement value of more than £10,000.[53] Most of these firms were developed by local entrepreneurs using their own skills and either their own capital or that of their family or friends.

Before 1840 most merchants either held this development at arm's length or viewed it with outright hostility. Wood and fish processing and shipbuilding were regarded as important elements in the commercial system and some

49 The most important of these was probably George Bond who held the lease for the tidal-powered Carleton mills, the most significant power source in the St. John area.

50 NB, RLE, 1840, Petitions, vol. 4, no. 122; 1843, Petitions, vol. 6, no. 149; 1850, Petitions, vol. 17, no. 357; 1850, Petitions, no. 414; 1836, Petitions, vol. 5, no. 112, PANB; *The New Brunswick Courier*, 12 October 1850, 5 July 1851.

51 NB, RLE, 1840, Petitions, vol. 4, no. 122, PANB.

52 *Ibid.*, 1845, Petitions, vol. 9, no. 298.

53 *The New Brunswick Courier*, 27 June 1846.

merchants were prepared to invest in these undertakings. When local grain and livestock production was expanding in the 1820s, several merchants indicated some support for the tanners in their efforts to exclude the cheap Canadian leather from the province, and even promoted the first steam flour mill to grind local wheat.[54] However, such support was rare. More common was a violent negative reaction. The special objects of the merchants' wrath were the millers and bakers. The latter had long protested because American flour entered the colony with a 5/-a barrel duty while bread entered free.[55] The merchants' reply was to demand the removal of provincial tariffs on both.[56] A clearer indication of the merchants' view of early industrial development is seen in the issues on which they took no position. These included virtually every request for assistance, support or tariff protection by every manufacturing industry and interest in the city between 1820 and 1840. Given the rapid growth of the manufacturing sector during this time, this lack of participation by the merchant community stood in sharp contrast to the support which the manufacturers were able to command in almost every other major segment of urban society.

The principal organization of the merchant community was the Chamber of Commerce and the world which the merchant sought to create and maintain before 1840 is clearly visible through its petitions to the municipal, provincial and imperial governments. The central doctrine in these petitions was the reciprocity of mercantilism and imperial economic preference in return for colonial deference and loyalty in matters economic and political. The merchant identified the prosperity of the colony with his right to buy cheaply and sell dear. To do this he must not only be able to sell colonial produce in a protected imperial market, but to purchase that produce in as free a market as possible. The latter doctrine carried a special significance for colonial producers for the merchant was prepared to use American timber and foodstuffs to keep costs as low as possible in the timber trade. Indeed, on any issue deemed vital to the prosecution of the timber trade the ranks of the great merchants never broke in nearly half a century. Thus woods resources held by the crown and after 1836 by the province must be leased at nominal fees[57]; severe penalties must be imposed on those stealing timber or making lumber, timber, fish and flour of inferior quality[58]; debtors must continue to be imprisoned lest British creditors lose

54 NB, RLE, 1834, Petitions, vol. 4, no. 91; 1828, Petitions, vol. 2, no. 43, PANB.

55 *Ibid.*, 1835, Petitions, vol. 4, no. 124; 1842, Petitions, vol. 3, no. 54.

56 *Ibid.*, 1833, Petitions, vol. 3, no. 102; 1840, Petitions, vol. 4, no. 121; 1842, Petitions, vol. 12, no. 237; 1851, Petitions, vol. 15, no. 457; *The New Brunswick Courier*, 4 February 1843.

57 W.S. MacNutt, "Politics of the Timber Trade in Colonial New Brunswick 1825-40", pp. 47-65; Graeme Wynn, "Administration in Adversity: The Deputy Surveyors and Control of the New Brunswick Crown Forests Before 1844", *Acadiensis*, VII (Autumn 1977), pp. 49-65.

58 NB, RLE, 1839, Petitions, vol. 3, no. 80; 1824, D, Petitions, no. 6, PANB.

confidence in the colony's will to protect them and cheap justice must be provided to permit the collection of debts[59]; no provincial duties could be imposed on timber, lumber, flour, bread, pork or manufactured tobacco; and provincial tariffs must stand at no more than 5 per cent so that the merchant might keep control of the commerce of the Annapolis Valley of Nova Scotia.[60] Until 1843 imperial regulations permitted the merchant to treat the entire eastern seaboard of the United States and New Brunswick as a single commercial entity for the purposes of the timber trade,[61] and New Brunswick timber makers found their prices set by American competition. Even more significant, in terms of its implications for the fortunes of farmers and millers, was the merchants' bitter and continued opposition to any attempts by either provincial or imperial parliaments to establish or maintain duties on flour or salted provisions, an opposition which finally led lieutenant-governor Sir John Harvey to express doubts as to what extent the St. John Chamber of Commerce "represents the real commercial interests of the province".[62]

By 1840 there is some evidence to suggest that a minority of merchants were prepared to dissent from the Chamber on economic issues not directly related to the timber trade. The flour trade was a case in point. While most fleet owners strongly supported free trade in wheat and flour in order to assure the cheapest provisions for their crews, a number of other great merchants came to see the commercial possibilities of a high tariff on foreign wheat and flour which would enable them to ship wheat from England for processing in St. John mills. And the rapidly expanding domestic market had persuaded a few that not only could greater returns be obtained by importing wheat, rather than flour, but that flour mills offered the best return of all.[63] Nonetheless, until the 1840s the vast majority of merchants still believed that low tariffs were essential.

After 1841 the assumptions upon which the merchants' system had been built were undermined by external factors. The first major jolt was the dramatic recession of 1841 occasioned by the collapse of the British timber market. As the ripples of this unusually severe crisis spread through the local economy, the layers of provincial society collapsed heirarchically, beginning with the ships labourers, passing into the minor shopkeepers and journeymen craftsmen, then

---

59 *Ibid.,* 1831, F. Petitions, vol. 2, no. 10.

60 *Ibid.,* 1850, Petitions, vol. 6, no. 138; *The New Brunswick Courier,* 24 February 1849.

61 *The New Brunswick Courier,* 20 January 1844.

62 Sir John Harvey to Lord Glenelg, 15 May 1838, CO 188/59, ff. 733-42, but also see Petition of St. John Merchants, 17 February 1834, CO 188/49, ff. 169-71; Sir John Harvey to Lord John Russell, 4 September 1840, CO 188/69, ff. 152-3; Sir William Colebrooke to Stanley, 29 March 1842, CO 188/75, ff. 341-5. Both Harvey and Colebrooke feared the economic and social consequences of an over-specialized staples economy.

63 NB, RLE, 1840, Petitions, vol. 4, no. 122, PANB. Among the dissenters were N. Merritt, R. Rankin, John Walker, D. Wilmot, I. Bedell, Wm. Parks.

into the ranks of the master craftsmen, shipbuilders, traders, contractors, small merchants, and lawyers,[64] finally claiming its victims among even the most stalwart with the bankruptcies of leading merchants such as James Hanford, Alex Yeats and J. & H. Kinnear in 1843.[65] Just as the economy was recovering from the recession in 1843, the British Government began its gradual dismantlement of the mercantilist structure with the regulations prohibiting the import of Maine-produced timber into the United Kingdom under the preferential tariff.[66] In the short run the regulations produced no significant impact on the timber trade other than to limit the merchants' choice of producers. The long run effect of the tariff declension between 1843 and 1849 was a sharp decline in the quantity and value of timber shipped from St. John, and a corresponding increase in the export of lumber and deals.[67]

The rapid change and threat of change in the early 1840s produced a crisis of confidence in the mercantile assumptions which had dominated the economy of New Brunswick since Napoleonic times. The producer, whether shoemaker, farmer, sawmill owner or founder, had existed in a gray area of semi-protection since the creation of the colony. Although the combination of imperial protective tariffs and provincial revenue duties had been sufficient to keep most local produce competitive with that from the United States, British produce entered the colony burdened only by the small revenue tariff. Provincial duties on British manufactures, for example, were fixed at 2½ per cent while those levied on American were 10 per cent.[68] The proposed elimination of the imperial tariff threatened to visit further disaster on an already badly demoralized artisan community. Hundreds of St. John artisans and mechanics had abandoned the city during the recession of 1841-2 and the exodus continued through 1842 and 1843 as economic prospects for the colony dimmed. By 1843 the city was divided by acrimonious debate between those prepared to follow the mother country into free trade, and those who argued that the wealth of colony was being dissipated on imported produce to the detriment of the producing classes. These protectionist views were strengthened by the emergence of a significant mechanics' revolt against what was perceived as the tyranny of the merchants. Out of the thriving mechanics community which had developed in the 1830s was formed, late in 1843, the Provincial Association, which brought together representatives of every major group of producers in the province.[69] The

64 *The New Brunswick Courier,* 4 March, 3 June, 15 July, 7 October 1843.

65 *Ibid.,* 4 March, 18, 25, November 1843.

66 NB, RLE, 1843, Petitions, vol. 9, no. 244, PANB.

67 Between 1840 and 1849 the value of timber exports from New Brunswick declined from £271,000 to £179,000; that of deals and boards increased from £180,000 to £266,000. New Brunswick, *Journal of the House of Assembly,* 1841, 1850, Customs House Returns.

68 *Ibid.,* 1842, Appendix, p. cclxxiv.

69 *The New Brunswick Courier,* 4 January 1844.

Association advocated protection and promotion of the interests of farmers, fishers, mechanics and manufacturers, through the use of duties, bounties, model farms and mechanics fairs. Among other things it urged the imposition of a substantial tariff on cordage and canvas, coupled with the payment of a bounty to farmers to grow hemp and flax.[70]

By 1844 the debate between free traders and protectionist had been transferred from the meeting hall to the Legislative Assembly, where the protectionists succeeded in imposing a compromise on the merchant interests after six close divisions in the House. Provincial duties were raised to 25 per cent on clocks, 20 per cent on wooden ware and chairs, 15 per cent on furniture and agricultural implements, 10 per cent on castings, cut nails and brick, and specific duties were imposed on cattle, oxen, horses and apples. At the same time any product required for the building of ships or the provisioning of crews, including flour, was placed on the free list. The debate over the most hotly contested duties, those on footwear and clothing, ended in a tie when a 10 per cent duty was imposed on footwear (a 5 per cent proposal was narrowly defeated) and clothing was admitted under a 4 per cent tariff.[71]

The compromise was only a temporary truce. Led by the St. John Chamber of Commerce, the free traders counterattacked at the 1845 sitting of the Assembly. Winning the support of several farmers who had voted with the protectionists the previous year, the free traders succeeded in reducing the tariff schedule to its 1843 levels, cutting some duties by as much as 60 per cent.[72] In response, one outraged protectionist leader vented his spleen in the columns of *The Morning News* on the "Free Trade Chamber of Commerce" of St. John, those "few selfish individuals" who were prepared to impose "this vicious system of one-sided free trade" on the "productive classes . . . the bone and sinew of the country".[73] However, this setback was temporary. Much to the chagrin of leading reformers like George Fenety, protection became a basic political issue during the 1840s and 50s, one that cut across the constitutional issues so dear to the hearts of reformers.[74] The Revenue Bill of the province was prepared each year by a select committee of the Assembly which acted on resolutions passed at each sitting of the Legislature. In 1847 the House, by a

70 *Ibid.,* 10 February 1844.
71 New Brunswick, *Journal of the House of Assembly,* 1844, pp. 152-7.
72 *The Morning News,* 24 March 1845. The defectors included Barbarie from Restigouche, Earle from Queens, Hanington and Palmer from Westmorland. See New Brunswick, *Journal of the House of Assembly,* 1845, pp. 219-21.
73 *The Morning News,* 19 March 1845.
74 Editor and publisher of *The Morning News* and later Queens Printer under the Liberals, Fenety was unsympathetic to the views of the protectionists. G.E. Fenety, *Political Notes and Observations* (Fredericton, 1867), I, chs. V, XXI. On the other hand both Lemual Allan Wilmot and Samuel Leonard Tilley supported the protectionist position.

21-10 majority, accepted the principle that "in enacting a Revenue Bill, the principle of protection to home industry, irrespective of revenue, should be recognized by levying duties on those productions and manufactures of foreign countries which the people of this province are capable of producing and manufacturing themselves".[75] The thrust of this resolution was directed against American produce and the Revenue Bill of that year introduced differential duties on British and foreign manufacturers. After 1850, however, the protectionists on the select committee were able to develop a policy of modest protection for a number of local industries. This included a 15% tariff on footwear, leather, furniture, machinery, iron castings (stoves, ranges, boilers, furnaces, grates), most agricultural implements, wagons and sleighs, veneers, cigars, hats and pianos.

The merchant community of St. John was ill-prepared to meet the threat posed by the rise of the Provincial Association. By 1843 it was still recovering from the blows dealt it by the collapse of 1841-2 and it perceived the major threat to its security among the British free traders rather than in a diverse group of local protectionists. While the Chamber of Commerce traditionally had been the principal vehicle of merchant views, by 1843 it had come to represent the great fleet owners in their struggle against the threats to the protected status of the colonial timber trade. The Chamber's initial reaction to the Provincial Association and its proposals to divert provincial resources from the timber trade into agriculture and manufacturing was negative. In strongly worded petitions to the provincial and imperial authorities it reiterated support for traditional mercantilist policies in the timber trade and for a maximum 5 per cent duty on all provincial imports.[76] Yet, while the majority apparently accepted the Chamber of Commerce position, a significant minority came out in support of the Provincial Association and its policies of economic diversification and protective tariffs.[77] Among the heretics were R.D. Wilmot, William Parks, the Jarvises, Henry Gilbert, John Walker, Noah Disbrow, Charles Ward and Walker Tisdale.[78] The principal spokesman for the movement in St. John in the mid-1840s was R.D. Wilmot. When the Provincial Association entered the political arena with its platform of the "new New Brunswick", Wilmot was returned to the House of Assembly where he replaced his cousin, Lemuel Allan Wilmot, as the province's leading protectionist. Meanwhile, in an effort to restore a semblance of unity to the divided merchant community, the Chamber of Commerce was re-organized in the spring of 1845 and the membership of its new directorate reflected the attempts made to provide representation from a

75 New Brunswick, *Journal of the House of Assembly*, 1847, pp. 190-1.

76 *The New Brunswick Courier*, 4 February 1844.

77 *Ibid.*, 10 February 1844.

78 NB, RLE, 1843, Petitions, vol. 6, no. 143, PANB.

wide range of merchant opinions and interests.[79] At the final crisis of mercantilism, in 1849, the Chamber played an important part in the organization of the New Brunswick Colonial Association which brought together the city's most distinguished citizens in an effort to define the province's role in the new economic order.[80] The early programme of the Association clearly represented an attempt to reconcile all viewpoints and included a proposal urging the encouragement of home industry.[81] These efforts muted but could not entirely conceal the tensions between merchant free traders and protectionists.

By 1850 the Colonial Association had dropped its proposal for the encouragement of home industry and offered reciprocity in trade and navigation with the United States as the sole panacea for the province's economic ills.[82] And in the House of Assembly the merchants and their supporters were able to impose a compromise on the protectionists the effect of which was to create two economic systems. The artisan and manufacturer were granted a moderate tariff on material not required in the prosecution of the wood trades, while virtually everything necessary to the lumber industry, the timber trade, the building of wooden ships, and the victualling of crews was admitted free to the New Brunswick market. The latter included mill engines, anchors, chain, canvas, cordage, tackle, felt, sails, spikes, cotton ways, and iron bolts, bars, plates and sheating, as well as rigging, tin and copper plate, sheathing paper, grain, flour, meal, bread, meats, fruit and vegetables.[83] In effect, every backward linkage that

79 *The Morning News,* 2 April, 16 April, 6 May, 7 May 1845; 25 February 1846.

80 *The New Brunswick Courier,* 28 June, 4 August 1849.

81 *Ibid.,* 15 September 1849.

82 *Ibid.,* 8 June 1850.

83 The evolution of New Brunswick policy between 1837 and 1860 is illustrated through the following commodities:

	1837		1842		1844	1845	1848		1855	1859
	Brit.	For.	Brit.	For.			Brit.	For.		
Wagons	2.5%	10%	2.5%	10%	10%	4%	4%	30%	15%	15%
Footwear	2.5%	5%	2.5%	10%	10%	7.5%	4%	30%	15%	15%
Agricultural Implements	Free	Free	Free	Free	10%	4%	4%	15%	15%	15%
Stoves	2.5%	10%	2.5%	10%	10%	7.5%	4%	15%	15%	15%
Chain	2.5%	10%	2.5%	10%	Free	Free	Free	Free	1%	1%
Canvas	Free	Free	Free	Free	Free	Free	Free	Free	1%	1%
Cordage	Free	Free	Free	Free	Free	Free	Free	Free	1%	1%
Mill Engines	Free	10%	Free	10%	Free	Free	Free	Free	10%	12.5%
Meat	Free	Free	Free	Free	Free	Free	Free	Free	Free	Free
Bread Flour	Free	Free	Free	Free	Free	4%	4%	10%	Free	Free

Source: Statutes of New Brunswick, 7 William IV, c.l.; 5 Victoria, c.l.; 7 Victoria, c.l.; 8 Victoria, c.2.; 11 Victoria, c.l.; 18 Victoria, c.1.

the rapidly growing shipbuilding and shipping industry might have provided to the provincial economy was discouraged by provincial policy. Ship builders were encouraged to import all materials required in the building process, other than wood. Merchants were rewarded both with the transportation costs of the building materials and with cheap vessels which they sold in the United Kingdom. It was a policy which permitted the application of a limited range of skills and the use of a small capital to produce a product which was competitive on the British market. Unfortunately such a policy conferred only limited benefits on the provincial economy and did not provide the flexibility or profit margins that gave the ship builder either the capital resources or the incentive to undertake any extensive technological innovation. More important it did not allow the development of substantial industries, dependent on these backward linkages, which might have promoted these changes.

Nonetheless, the activities of the Provincial Association remained an important theme in city politics into the 1850s. Of the 37 great merchants still living in St. John after 1842, 16 lent their support to at least some significant part of the protectionist programme and 12 of these consistently supported its general objective.[84] Not surprisingly, the merchants split on the issue of protection in terms of the emphasis which their business activities gave to the timber trade. Those with the most significant trading concerns — like John Ward, John Wishart and John Robertson — remained largely divorced from the concerns of other elements within the broader community. They were, as well, the major shipowners and their focus remained on the trans-Atlantic community. They did not, necessarily, oppose the protectionist impulse *per se*, but they did fear its emphasis on economic self-sufficiency, its inefficiencies, and, particularly, the stated goal of protectionists to transfer resources out of the timber industry and into manufacturing, agriculture and fishing.[85] Yet, while leading merchants opposed protectionist policies where they threatened to make the New Brunswick shipping industry uncompetitive on international runs by imposing substantial tariffs on flour, bread and pork, a number were prepared to accept the new order. Although it is difficult to generalize about them, they tended to include men whose principal activities had centred on the merchandising activities of the wholesaler and those whose interests were more concerned with New Brunswick than the trans-Atlantic community. While they were men of substance, none could match the personal fortunes amassed by the more substantial timber merchants, particularly those with heavy investments in ships. At his death in 1853, Noah Disbrow left over $80,000 (£20,800) to be divided among his 6 daughters and 2 sons,[86] and three years later Munson Jarvis'

84 NB. RLE. 1850. Petitions, vol. 6, no. 416, PANB.

85 *Ibid.*, 10 February 1843, 23 February 1850.

86 Noah Disbrow, 1853, RG 7, RS 71, PANB.

brother, William, a prominent dockside merchant left $50,000.[87] The next year William Parks placed a value of £17,484 (about $70,000) on the assets of his firm.[88] By comparison, Stephen Wiggins' share of the firm of Stephen Wiggins & Son was valued at $389,000 in 1863, most of which would have been in shipping.[89] Over the course of the 1850s, however, a minority of the great merchants did play an increasingly important role in the industrial development of the city through promotion of enterprises as diverse as woollen mills and coal oil refineries. As their industrial interests grew, their involvement in the staples' trade became less significant. Several had been or became agents for the transfer of resources from the staples to the manufacturing sector of the provincial economy in an attempt to create a more balanced economy. The Barlow brothers have been mentioned already in connection with the secondary iron industry. The hardware merchant, William Henry Scovil, established his cut nail factory in the early 1840s, while the wholesale grocer, William Parks, ended his career in the 1860s as proprietor of one of the first cotton mills in British North America.

Those who identified most closely with the community were generally most willing to commit capital to its internal development; those with strong British ties and alternatives were usually much less willing to make this commitment. The former characteristic is reflected in the relatively high proportion of merchants of Loyalist origins who supported the Provincial Association and its objectives. In essence, they viewed Saint John as the central element in a limited regional economy, in preference to its position in the larger metropolitan economy. It was merchants who had developed these more limited horizons and who saw their future in terms of local enterprise who came to the support of the manufacturers and artisans of the city, the group largely responsible for the not inconsiderable manufacturing development of the period from 1820 to 1850. The manufacturers and artisans were drawn from different origins, participated at different levels of civic society, and enjoyed a distinctly inferior status to their mercantile counterparts. Their special interests and ideas received serious consideration by the leaders of the community only during periods of economic crisis, such as the 1840s and 1870s. Even then the producers were able to achieve a position of influence only in alliance with a portion of the merchant community. When merchants closed ranks, they were able to establish the goals of the community at large and these goals were almost always designed to further the integration of the region into a larger trading complex in which the region was subordinated to the interests of a metropolitan community. So long

87 William Jarvis, 1856, *ibid.*

88 Partnership Agreements, William Parks Papers, F #3, NBM. This figure does not include Park's personal estate.

89 Stephen Wiggins, 1853, RG 7, RS 71, PANB.

as the imperial economic system was possible, the merchants used their capital and their great influence to maintain and further that system, largely ignoring the interests of farmers, manufacturers and other producers in the province. Nowhere was this more evident than in the crucial area of credit. Not only did they use the financial institutions in the city to direct the available credit to their own commercial purposes, but they successfully thwarted every effort by producers to obtain their own banking facilities.

The great merchants certainly organized and financed the commercial and financial super-structure needed for the conduct of the timber trade in a major sea port and they played important roles in providing capital for the exploitation of the natural resources of the region and for the construction of public works and utilities within the city. A minority, distinguished by their wholesaling concerns and native origins, began to participate in some fashion in the development of a more diversified urban economy. But the majority of great merchants retained a commitment to an unmodified staples economy. In the early nineteenth century it was this group which produced the dominant economic class, the institutions and myths — particularly that of commerce as the great creator of prosperity — which formed the community of St. John. Throughout the period they were able to mould the economy to their essentially interregional export-oriented needs. In so doing, they exploited the province's natural resources of timber and stimulated the development of major sawmilling and shipbuilding industries both of which produced significant short-term benefits for the economy. Ancillary benefits were derived from the provision of shipping, credit facilities and insurance services.

The manufacturing sector of the New Brunswick economy did grow rapidly in the 1850s and 60s. Gordon Bertram has demonstrated that in 1871 the *per capita* output of the province's manufacturing industries rivalled that of Ontario and Quebec and was nearly twice that of Nova Scotia.[90] Nearly half of the industrial output of New Brunswick was produced in and around the city of St. John.[91] McClelland suggests that there was an average annual growth of one per cent in New Brunswick's deal and lumber exports during the period.[92] Not surprisingly, the largest components of the province's industrial output were sawmill products and wooden ships (44% for the province and 38% for the city).[93] Apart from these traditional staples, however, virtually every industry which had received

90 Gordon W. Bertram, "Historical Statistics on Growth and Structure in Manufacturing in Canada 1870-1957", in J. Henripen and A. Asimakopulas, eds., *Canadian Political Science Association Conference on Statistics 1962 & 1963* (Toronto, 1964), p. 122. The figures for Ontario, Quebec, New Brunswick and Nova Scotia were $69.60, $62.60, $59.80, $30.70.

91 St. John County output totalled $8,312,627; that of the province was $17,367,687. Canada, *Census of 1871*, vol. III, Table LIV.

92 McClelland, p. 124.

93 *Ibid.*, Tables XXII, XXXIX.

even a modest degree of protection in the previous generation flourished. Foundry products, footwear and clothing all exceeded shipbuilding in value, while furniture and carriage making, boiler making, saw and file manufacture, and tin and sheet iron output and leather making all played significant roles in the local economy.[94] Some backward linkages from shipbuilding, which earlier tariff policies had done so little to encourage, were also able to develop by the late 1860s. The most obvious example was the small rope making industry functioning in the city and there can be little doubt that at least some of the foundry activity was stimulated by the market created by the ship builders.[95]

Yet the outlines of the earlier emphases were still visible in the city's industrial structure. There was, apparently, no industry capable of producing the chain, anchors, and canvas used in the shipbuilding industry, nor to provide the machinery employed in the province's 565 sawmills.[96] Although steam engines had been constructed in St. John in the 1840s, there was no engine building firm in the province by 1870.[97] A similar situation existed in the basic food industries. The ancient flour industry had been virtually eliminated and only a miniscule meat curing industry survived.[98] There were no distilleries and only four small breweries.[99] The debate over the virtues of the ordered pastoral life as opposed to the disordered and transient nature of the timber industry was a recurring theme in nineteenth-century New Brunswick. The debate came to be couched in such explicit moral terms that it is difficult to make any assessment from it of the economic viability of provincial agriculture in the period, or to determine the extent to which the agricultural development of the province was effected by the timber trade.[100] The rapidity of agricultural development between 1840 and 1870 would seem to indicate that there was some truth to the charges of the timber critics; at the very least, the combination of rewards which the trade could offer to the rural inhabitants coupled with the refusal of the provincial legislature to provide any protection for the nascent colonial agriculture, severely retarded the

94 The shipbuilding industry produced vessels to a value of $538,042 and employed 647 men. Foundry output, including fittings, nails, and tacks, was $786,000 (507 employees); clothing $826,660 (1033 employees); footwear $539,230 (565 employees). Canada, *Census of 1871*, vol. III, Tables, XXI, XXXII, XXIII, XXIV, XXXVI, XXXVI, XXXIX, XLV, LI, LII, LIII.

95 *Ibid.*, Table L.

96 The number of sawmills in the province had declined in the 1860s. There were 609 Water-powered and 80 steam-powered sawmills in 1861. Canada, *Census of 1871*, vol. IV, pp. 336-43.

97 Canada, *Census of 1871*, vol. III, Table XLVI.

98 *Ibid.*, Tables XXI, XXXVII.

99 *Ibid.*, Table XXXV.

100 Soil maps would seem to indicate that the agricultural potential of the province is limited. However, since the arable area comprises several million acres of land, this source is only useful as an indicator of the upper limits of agricultural growth. In the short run the province possessed a considerable potential as the rapid growth of mid-century reveals.

development of a substantial agriculture in the early nineteenth century.[101]

This retardation was of vital importance to the health of the colonial economy. New Brunswick ran a perennial deficit in its current account and in most years the entire trade imbalance resulted from the substantial imports of foodstuffs for use within the province. The most prominent example of this phenomenon was American wheat and flour, but it was reflected, as well, in large imports of rye flour, Indian meal, pork, beef, lamb, butter, potatoes, vegetables, fruit and even oats. The proportion of agricultural products ranged from just over 20% of the province's total imports in 1840 to just under 40% in 1855.[102] Wheat and flour imports alone exceeded the value of timber exports by 1852 and by 1855 the 170,000 barrels of flour and 110,000 bushels of wheat, worth £334,000 in all, rivalled the £380,000 in deals shipped from the province.[103] New Brunswick agricultural conditions were not particularly suited to the production of wheat, although the doubling of output following the National Policy of 1879 indicates that a much larger production than occurred up to Confederation was possible.[104] But it is more difficult to explain the import of most other foodstuffs which could be produced domestically. Given the fact that substantial quantities of these products were grown in the province in the 1840s, that the land for producing more was readily available, and that there was a substantial local demand for these foodstuffs which could not be met by local producers, it seems probable that the incentives offered by the timber trade, and the refusal of the province to afford even nominal protection to local producers were the major factors in inhibiting the growth of a more substantial agricultural sector before 1850.

In the final analysis there is no simple answer to the question of merchant responsibility for economic growth or retardation in St. John and New Brunswick. While they agreed on the validity of the concept of economic growth, merchants rarely spoke with a single voice when the subject of a specific development strategy was raised. Most were prepared to permit, and some to

101 Acreage of cultivated land increased from 435,861 in 1840 to 1,171,157 in 1870 at a rate much more rapid than that of population growth. Consequently the number of cultivated acres *per capita* rose from 2.7 to 4.6. In the single decade of the 1860s the number of farmers in the province rose by nearly 30%; the population by 13%. Canada, *Census of 1871*, vol. III, pp. 90-1; vol. IV, pp. 129, 336-43.

102 New Brunswick, *Journal of the House of Assembly*, 1841, pp. cclxxvi-cclxxvii; 1856,pp. clxiii-clxvi.

103 Flour and wheat to the value of £169,000 was imported in 1854. This compared with exports of 134,000 tons of timber valued at £165,000. Two years later the respective values of the two commodities was £286,000 and £160,000, and in 1855 imported flour and wheat totalled £377,000, a value rivalling that of the provinces lumber output (£437,000). See New Brunswick, *Journal of the House of Assembly*, 1853, 1855, 1856, Customs House Returns.

104 Canada, *Census of 1881*, vol. III, pp. 42-3, 120-1, 158-9. New Brunswick wheat output rose from 204,911 bushels in 1871 to 521,956 in 1881.

support a strategy which included the development of certain kinds of secondary industry. These efforts were generally successful although this success was due more to the efforts of the city's artisans than to its merchants. Merchant endeavours were particularly aimed at supporting and preserving the traditional timber staple and its milling, shipping, and shipbuilding ancilliaries. The manufacture of producers goods used in any of these activities, including mill engines and machinery, shipbuilding materials, and domestic foodstuffs needed for ship crews, woods workers and mill labourers, were afforded no encouragement. In effect two economic systems based upon mutually exclusive values were the result of the synthesis which emerged from the conflicts of the 1840s. The most obvious victim of that synthesis was the shipbuilding industry, potentially the most dynamic element in the provincial economy, which was locked into the more conservative timber trade economy. Thus a city containing a number of secondary iron and steel firms, which for decades had possessed the capability of manufacturing complete steamships and engines, and a labour force skilled at working in both wood and iron was unable to manufacture metal ships or even to make any substantial adjustment in the face of technologial changes which were gradually eroding this vital industry. In the course of 1860s and 70s the ship builders built and the timber merchants bought and sold ships in the traditional way simply because they could not perceive the industry apart from the timber trade or from the lumber which was basic to both building and trade. While the timber merchants were not alone able to shape the provincial economy to their perceptions, they provided an effective and powerful leadership to substantial interests in the province which identified with the traditional timber trade. By 1871 the economy was becoming increasingly diversified and self-sufficient and the dynamic elements in this development were to be found in secondary industry and in agriculture, but the influence of the great merchants delayed this development by two critical decades. In this sense they contributed to the retardation of a viable industrial base in the city.

JUDITH FINGARD

Reprinted from Vol. V, No. 1
(Autumn 1975)

The Relief of the Unemployed Poor in Saint John, Halifax, and St. John's, 1815 - 1860*

As the leading commercial centres in eastern British America, Saint John, Halifax, and St. John's sheltered within their environs a significant proportion of the region's meagre population. This included not only the most comfortable and affluent colonists, but also three categories of poor inhabitants whose problems were never far from the minds of public-spirited citizens. Prominent among the disadvantaged were the permanent or disabled poor — a motley collection that embraced the helpless aged, the physically and mentally infirm, as well as destitute widows and orphans, those unproductive elements in the community without kith or kin to act as providers. The plight of these unfortunates aroused the greatest outward display of local sympathy, though their inescapable presence was largely taken for granted and their welfare sadly neglected. A second group consisted of immigrants who annually swelled the ranks of the poor that infested these major Atlantic ports. These included refugee blacks from the United States, settled near Halifax and Saint John after the War of 1812, who became a special class of permanent poor in town and suburb, as well as the meanest of the urban labourers. Most significant in point of numbers was the incessant flow of poverty-stricken Irish who, on arrival, crowded into the poorhouses of Saint John and Halifax and augmented the paupers of St. John's.[1] Subsequently, as resident

---

1 Minutes, 10 November 1847, Saint John Common Clerk, MSJ, Provincial Archives of New Brunswick [hereafer PANB]; Letter from A, *Public Ledger* (St. John's), 6 March 1838.

Residence Indicated for Inmates of Halifax Poorhouse, 1833-7

	Halifax*	N.S.	England	Scotland	Ireland	NFLD.	N.B.	U.S.	Other
1833	300	99	94	27	299	17	17	12	32
1834	339	79	80	27	330	27	20	22	41
1835	298	64	77	27	248	10	10	10	47
1836	280	98	71	23	243	9	12	8	62
1837	350	74	53	25	270	10	20	8	45

* With no orphanage or lying-in-hospital in Halifax more than half of the town inmates were children.
Source: *Journals of the Legislative Assembly*, Nova Scotia [hereafter JLA], 1834-8.

* This essay is a product of a programme of research supported by the Canada Council whose assistance I gratefully acknowledge.

labourers, the Irish frequently re-emerged as members of the third category — the casual poor.[2] Found amongst these casual poor were individuals or families dependent on a hand-to-mouth existence, who became temporarily incapacitated through sickness or misfortune, and the seasonally unemployed, those perennial casualties who formed the most intractable problem for the commercial towns. While the majority of this latter group consisted of common labourers, they were often joined in penury by skilled journeymen thrown out of work or underpaid in wintertime. In St. John's the whole operative class of resident fishermen habitually found themselves idle and destitute for seven months out of twelve, a situation which gave the colony "a larger proportion of poor than in other British settlements."[3] Each of these categories — permanent, immigrant, and casual poor — posed its special difficulties for the community, but as constituent elements of society, each was thought by benevolent and judicious townsmen to be entitled to some form of assistance during the period of privation. In the fluid, uncertain conditions of colonial society, prosperous inhabitants were chastened by the possibility "that the calamities which have befallen others may soon overtake ourselves, and that their distressing lot may soon become our own."[4]

When a conjunction of diverse circumstances, including overseas immigration and economic recession, forced urban poverty to the forefront of public attention in the period after the Napoleonic Wars, the towns of the Atlantic colonies, in contrast to those of the Canadas, could draw on a tradition of state poor relief. This government involvement took the forms of locally enacted poor laws providing for municipal assessments in Nova Scotia and New Brunswick and of executive initiative for appropriating colonial revenue in Newfoundland. The methods of dispensing these funds in Saint John, and eventually in St. John's, involved a mixture of both indoor and outdoor relief, whereas in Halifax public assistance was confined to the poorhouse.[5] But the existence of facilities for public relief did not preclude individual involvement in civic welfare measures. Citizens continued to feel that they had a direct role to play both in aiding the poor and in determining the guises that public and voluntary assistance assumed. For one thing, they were well aware that the scale of public relief was inadequate to meet emergencies, a

2 Petition of JPs, Saint John, 1839, RLE/839/pe/3, No. 61, PANB.

3 *Free Press* (Halifax), 23 December 1827.

4 17th Annual Report of Saint Andrew's Church Female Benevolent Society, *Guardian* (Halifax), 22 January 1847.

5 In St. John's the piecemeal organization of indoor relief began in 1846 with the erection of the relief sheds or 'Camps', notorious hovels designed to house the fire victims of that year. These were not replaced until a poorhouse was opened in 1861, followed by the discontinuance of relief for the able-bodied for the first time in 1868.

deficiency starkly demonstrated every time fires, crop failures, business re-
cessions, heavy immigration, or ineluctable winter exacted their toll. Haligonians experienced these harsh circumstances in the decade after 1815,
when large numbers of poor immigrants and unemployed labourers were
thrown on the mercy of a town that had abandoned outdoor relief under public auspices and that had, therefore, to rely on voluntary efforts to ward off
the threat of starvation and social disorder.[6]

Moreover, goaded by tender consciences and insistent churches, some
colonists regarded benevolence as a christian duty. Within a society that
prided itself on its christian ethos, the laws of God and humanity dictated
that the poor could not be permitted to starve; the sick and aged poor must
be cared for. But starvation did occur, and the numerous sick and aged poor
in the towns necessitated the erection of institutions to minister to their
afflictions. In the absence of this kind of large-scale capital expenditure
which city councils or provincial legislatures were reluctant to undertake,
privately organized dispensaries and societies for the relief of the indigent
sick played a vital role in treating accidents and common illnesses.[7] For
the chronically ill, however, circumstances were different. Halifax, for example, possessed no specialized institution for dealing with any category of
sick poor until the opening of the lunatic asylum in 1859.[8] The failure "to
ameliorate the condition of suffering humanity" offended christians who witnessed ample investment in facilities for transportation and commerce; the
neglect of social amelioration seemed to be at odds with mid-Victorian
notions of progress.[9]

In these circumstances townspeople responded sympathetically to acute
destitution because they considered the existing forms of poor relief outdated
and unprogressive. The purely custodial care of destitute lunatics in the temporary asylum established in St. John's in 1846, for example, was said to be

6 *Free Press*, 4, 11, 25 February, 4 March 1817; G. E. Hart, 'The Halifax Poor Man's Friend
Society, 1820-27: An Early Social Experiment, *Canadian Historical Review*, XXXIV (1953),
109-23. The Poor Man's Friend Society (admittedly helped by the legislature) aided as many
as one-tenth of Halifax's inhabitants during the winters of the early 1820s. *Annual Reports*
of the Halifax Poor Man's Friend Society. Similarly in St. John's the Poor Relief Association of
1867, a voluntary organization, aided one-fifth of the inhabitants during a winter of great distress
when government relief was insufficient. *Newfoundlander* (St. John's), 10 May 1867.

7 *Public Ledger*, 5 March 1847; Editorial, *Times* (St. John's), 7 July 1849; 'Death from Starvation!', *Patriot* (St. John's), 5 February 1853; Letter from J. Slayter, M.D., *Acadian Recorder*
(Halifax), 20 January 1855; 'The Poor,' *Morning Journal* (Halifax), 28 December 1855; Editorial,
Newfoundlander, 11 February 1856; Speech by Dr. Grigor, Legislative Council Debate, 3 March
1857, *Acadian Recorder*, 7 March 1857.

8 G. Andrews, 'The Establishment of Institutional Care in Halifax in the Mid-Nineteenth
Century," (honours essay, Dalhousie University, 1974).

9 Editorial, *Christian Messenger* (Halifax), 10 January 1851; 'Lunatic Asylum and General
Hospital,' *Acadian Recorder*, 21 May 1853.

inconsistent with the age of improvement.[10] Citizens were particularly out-spoken when their local pride was offended. To lag behind other towns in the provision of specialized facilities for the poor seemed unpatriotic as well as undesirable. The example of Saint John, where a lunatic asylum was opened in 1836 and firmly established in a permanent edifice in 1848, was constantly paraded by social critics before the lethargic citizenry of Halifax and St. John's.[11] This call for imitation grew out of a search for self-esteem, since colonial towns aspired to social responsibility and an acknowledgment of their benevolence and modernity.[12]

In an age that witnessed both the heyday of the philanthropic society and in North America the 'discovery of the asylum', the custom of fostering benevolence by means of association also encouraged citizen involvement in directing local poor relief. The bewildering variety of associations, both ephemeral and permanent, that emerged for the social, physical, and moral improvement of the poor fulfilled a basic middle-class instinct for collective efforts as well as for emulating the fashionable course. While few of the large-scale societies and the asylums they sometimes sponsored could exist without some government aid to augment charitable donations, voluntary management provided communities with excellent experience in organization, fund-raising, and social investigation. At the same time, however, voluntary associative benevolence underwent a fragmentation which meant that by mid-century every church and every ethnic and interest group had its own charitable society or charitable function. This occurred despite attempts throughout the period by the most public-spirited citizens to promote the comprehensive, non-partisan relief of the urban poor, on the ground that "we are but a part of one great human family".[13]

Particularly significant was the bifurcation of urban society between Catholics and Protestants, which emerged most graphically in the 1840's, when Irish immigration, the introduction of unfamiliar religious orders, the ravages of

10 Letter from Aqua, *Public Ledger*, 15 December 1846.

11 J. M. Whalen, 'Social Welfare in New Brunswick, 1784-1900,' *Acadiensis*, Vol. II, No. 1, (Autumn 1972), p. 61; *Sun* (Halifax), 8 January 1851; New Brunswick Lunatic Asylum,' *ibid.,* 15 October 1851.

12 'Benevolent Enterprise', *Morning Post* (Halifax), 10 March 1845; 'Fancy Balls versus Hospitals and Asylums,' *Presbyterian Witness* (Halifax), 16 March 1850; Speech by Dr. Grigor, Legislative Council Debate, 12 March 1851, *Sun*, 17 March 1851; 'Public Hospital,' *Morning News* (Saint John), 17 October 1856.

13 Editorial, *Public Ledger*, 7 March 1837; The Poor — God Help Them! Let Man think of them too! Great Suffering in consequence of Scarcity of Fuel," *Morning Post*, 10 March 1846; *Morning News*, 31 July 1846; Address to the Public by the Halifax Poor Man's Friend Society, *Acadian Recorder*, 19 February 1820; Report of Indigent Sick Society, St. John's, *Public Ledger*, 5 May 1840; Appeal of Committee of Ladies' Benevolent Society, Halifax, *Morning Post*, 7 October 1844.

epidemics, and the cry of 'papal aggression' led colonial Protestants to resent the indisputable fact that the larger proportion of poor rates and voluntary contributions went towards the relief of poor Catholics. Piqued Protestants did not tire of reminding their Roman Catholic neighbours that nine-tenths of the inmates of the poorhouse in Halifax were Catholics, or that it was the Protestant citizenry in St. John's who supported the Catholic poor.[14] To such an extent did the Catholics constitute the labouring and disabled poor in the towns that the more bigoted Protestants began to pronounce publicly that the Roman Catholics were improverished because they were Catholics.[15] Not surprisingly, a host of 'separate' charitable societies and institutions resulted. Consequently, vertical divisions in the population of the towns, not only between Catholics and Protestants, but also between Methodists and Anglicans, Irish and native-born, loyalists and non-loyalists, took precedence over the fledgling regard for the corporate well-being.

Finally, the colonist became concerned about poor relief in his capacity as a citizen of a town in which he had a vested interest, and protection of that stake demanded that the community should reflect his own particular values. When he talked therefore about subordinating the relief of the poor to the good of the community, he meant subordinating it to his own purposes. It is these underlying values, shared by contemporaries in three pre-industrial towns of Atlantic Canada, and the various schemes they spawned, that provide the focus of the ensuing discussion. Amongst the townsman's preconceptions, it was his reverence for the family, his regard for the dignity of labour, his preoccupation with good order, and his search for economy which led him to the fundamental conclusion "That the truest charity is to find employment that will give food; and not food without employment."[16]

Those citizens who viewed the relief of the poor within the wider context of the welfare of urban society at large undoubtedly represented the most respectable, dependable, moderately reformist, and middle-class elements in the towns. Whether they paraded as newspaper proprietors, clergymen, assemblymen, or aldermen, they were motivated by a concept of responsibility to the public, the congregation, or the electorate. They expected other men in positions of leadership and authority to take their civic duty as conscientiously as they did themselves. At the base of urban society the leadership they discerned was that of the male head of the organic unit, the family. Since the interests of the family in society received priority over those of the individual, the claims of the poor were likely to elicit a more sympathetic response if they could be fitted into the familial framework. In this respect a

14 Letter from P. Power's Friend, *Guardian*, 19 March 1847; Editorials, *Public Ledger*, 18 April 1834, 8 December 1835, 6 May 1842.

15 'Popery in Newfoundland', *Public Ledger*, 25 September 1855.

16 *Free Press*, 21 October 1817.

special sanctity was accorded the interdependent relationship between the provider and his spouse and offspring. Only sickness and unexpected unemployment were thought to constitute legitimate excuses for the failure of bread-winners to take seriously their duty as providers.[17] Drunkenness, improvidence, low wages, laziness, and fecundity were problems with which the wretched family had to contend alone, though the editor of the *Morning News* wondered whether, in cases of drunkenness as the cause of family poverty, the state should not be vested with the right to intervene and regulate employment and expenditure of wages.[18]

When it came to the vital circumstance of sickness, public health officers recognized that unless the labourer was retained in health, "the family of the victim becomes a charge upon the town for a much longer time" than the duration of his illness.[19] Where sickness of a poor or struggling head of the family led to his death, the citizenry displayed an appropriate concern for the widow and children, as it did for the orphan in the case of double bereavement.[20] Nevertheless, talk about society's responsibilities towards widows and orphans was considerably more energetic than the framing of humane measures to provide for their sustenance. Admittedly, concerted efforts for temporary assistance to widows and orphans sometimes followed severe epidemics or summers of excessive immigration, but attention to the welfare of the fatherless remnant of the family was haphazard and ephemeral.[21] In a society based on commerce, hard physical labour, and male political power, women were utterly expendable. Children, on the other hand, were exploitable as cheap labour. Orphans and foundlings were greatly in demand in the pre-industrial period as apprentices by farmers, householders, and craftsmen, apprenticeships secured by indentures that again tended to emphasize the family ambience.[22]

17   Editorial, *Public Ledger*, 9 December 1828.

18   Editorial, *Times* (St. John's), 29 July 1848; Investigator, No. III, *ibid.*, 4 November 1854; 'Drunkenness, Poverty and Suffering.' *Morning News*, 11 January 1860.

19   Board of Health, Saint John. Report for 1858, p. iv, New Brunswick. *JLA* (1857-58), Appendix.

20   Letter from RP, 'Queen's National Fund,' *New Brunswick Courier* (Saint John) 13 June 1840; 'Bazaar,' *Morning News*, 12 November 1855.

21   An example is provided by the Emigrant Orphan Asylum established in Saint John in 1847. J. M. Whalen, 'New Brunswick Poor Law Policy in the Nineteenth Century,' (M.A. thesis, University of New Brunswick, 1968), pp. 32, 35-36; also the Church of England Asylum for Widows and Orphans founded in St. John's after a cholera epidemic. *Times* (St. John's) 27 December 1854, 20 January 1855; *Newfoundland Express* (St. John's), 20 February 1858, 19 February 1859.

22   Abstract of R. J. Uniacke's Evidence before the Select Committee of the House of Commons on Emigration, 22 March 1826, *Novascotian* (Halifax), 19 October 1826. Arranging such places for orphans was the principal aim of the Orphan Benevolent Society of Saint John which dissolved only after the city's orphanages were well established. *New Brunswick Courier*, 8 August 1840, 23 January 1858.

Society showed its greatest concerted anxiety about family welfare when large numbers of heads of families were thrown out of work. While this concern might sometimes extend to female bread-winners, it was the men as labourers and mechanics who commanded the most attention. In those instances where public measures were taken to meet the temporary emergency of seasonal unemployment, preference was given to family men. In fact the work itself, never sufficient to satisfy the demand, was usually confined to heads of families.[23] About 600 of these employed on civic works in Saint John in 1842 received from 1s. to 3s. a day according to the number of their dependents.[24] Coincident with family considerations, this preoccupation with the labouring poor stemmed from the emphasis placed by the well-to-do on the material progress of the town. As the basis of the socio-economic pyramid, the very fabric of urban society was thought to depend on the labourers' contributions, not only as hewers of wood and drawers of water, but as "the bone and marrow of the country."[25] When 'honest' working men faced starvation, self-interested leaders of society invariably urged the expeditious relief of "that most indispensably useful part of the community," preferably through employment, but if necessary through relief without labour.[26]

Citizens' attitudes towards poor relief were also influenced by the need to distinguish between the honest, deserving, labouring poor and those who were undeserving, profligate, or even criminal. For the public remained anxious that the poor should not endanger the social order of the towns and that relief should preserve a properly balanced relationship between the 'haves' and the 'have-nots.' This determination to ensure that the 'haves' maintained the upper hand goes far to explain the universal abhorrence of mendicancy; begging transferred the initiative to the poor when it ought to remain with their economic betters. Mendicancy was a form of free enterprise, an activity not to be encouraged in the poor who were certain to misuse it. A successful beggar might see in crime his road to further advancement. Beggars were,

23 'Stonebreaking,' *Novascotian*, 20 December 1832; Matthew to Mayor, 3 January 1842 and Communication from Chamberlain upon the subject of distress of labouring poor, 3 January 1842, RLE/842/22/2, PANB. The use of the very cheap labour of British soldiers and incarcerated criminals on public works sometimes reduced the opportunities for the unemployed poor. W. Moorsom, *Letters from Nova Scotia; comprising Sketches of a Young Country* (London, 1830), p. 34; Letter from Clerk of the Peace to Commissioners of Streets for Halifax, Special Sessions, September 1837, RG 34, Vol. 10, Public Archives of Nova Scotia (hereafter PANS).

24 'Employment of the Poor,' *New Brunswick Courier*, 4 December 1841; 'Frightful Extent of Pauperism in the City,' *ibid.*, 5 March 1842.

25 Editorial, *Patriot*, 9 November 1839.

26 Letter from An Inhabitant of Halifax, *Acadian Recorder*, 14 December 1816; Letter from Beneficus, *ibid.*, 1 February 1817.

therefore, not only an expensive nuisance,[27] but a threat to society, whose guardians through their beneficence in furnishing food and clothing might unwittingly admit to their houses imposters or thieves. Such unbecoming and potentially subversive behaviour in the poor might be avoided if the rich took it upon themselves to seek out poor families in their dwellings and investigate their degree of penury and deservedness. The efficacy of social investigation was reiterated as often as hordes of beggars descended on the towns and it became the standard practice of voluntary associations and government agencies.[28]

Despite the need for precautionary measures to safeguard the interests of the town and the welfare of the honest poor, it was often that same apprehension for the good order of society that stimulated citizens to urge generous public relief in times of severest want. In the winter of 1816-17 the first voluntary relief committee in Halifax feared that if the sufferers were "abandoned to the horrors of starvation . . . they may be induced by despair to commit depredations."[29] Thereafter the preference given to civic employment schemes as the most propitious form of assistance pinpointed unemployed labourers as the element in the population most likely to threaten the good order of the city. The spectre of hungry mobs of workers conjured up in the mind of the authorities frightening thoughts of uncontrollable outrage and seething insubordination. Poverty was regarded as a 'evil' which could not be allowed to reach "that stage where it is not stopped by stone walls, or locks, bolts, or bars."[30]

27 Letter from A Friend to the Deserving Poor, 'Beggars,' *Acadian Recorder*, 29 March 1834; 'Charity,' *Novascotian*, 25 December 1844; 'Pauperism in Saint John,' *Morning News*, 17 November 1847.

28 (Halifax Poor Man's Friend Society) Address to the Public, *Acadian Recorder*, 19 February 1820·, (St. John's Dorcas Society) Letter from Clericus, *Public Ledger*, 5 February 1833; (St. John's Indigent Sick Society) *ibid.*, 27 February 1835; *Times* (Halifax), 20 December 1836; (Government relief, St. John's) Resolution of the commissioners for the distribution of 300 for relief of the destitute poor, *Newfoundlander*, 27 February 1840; (St. George's District Visiting Society, Halifax) *Morning Post*, 27 January 1842; (Samaritan Society, Saint John) *New Brunswick Courier*, 2 January 1847, *Morning News*, 8 March 1847; (St. John's Fire Relief Committee) *Public Ledger*, 30 March 1847; (Outdoor relief, St. John's) Speeches by Little and the Speaker, Assembly Debate, 22 March 1853, *Newfoundland Express*, 2 April 1853; (St. Vincent de Paul Society, St. John's) Editorial, *Newfoundlander*, 9 February 1854, Letter from A Clergyman, 'How the Poor may be Relieved,' *ibid.*, 28 January 1858; (St. Vincent de Paul Society, Saint John) *Morning Freeman* (Saint John), 22 November 1859.

29 Memorial of the Committee for distributing relief to the labouring poor in Halifax, 14 March 1817, RG 5, Series P, Vol. 80, PANS.

30 Letter from Civis, 'Feed the Hungary and the Poor — Clothe the Naked,' *Morning News*, 30 November 1857·, 'Employment of the Poor,' *Novascotian*, 5 January 1832; Gilbert and Develier to Odell, 30 March 1842, RLE/842/22/2, PANB.

Self-interest also demanded economical relief. The search for economy encouraged attempts to eliminate some forms of poverty amongst labourers by the prevention and treatment of diseases and accidents. On its establishment in 1857 the Saint John Public Dispensary for outpatients undertook to diminish the number of inmates accommodated in the tax-supported almshouse. Its managers therefore appealed to the public not solely as a benevolent institution "but a *money saving one to our citizens.*"[31] Similarly, the need for welfare might be reduced by the more rigorous enforcement of the board of health regulations in the city. Otherwise, the health officer argued, "Sickness, debility, death, widowhood and orphanage, connected with pauperism, are expensive contingencies" which the town must sustain.[32] Financial considerations were also pa. amount in the discussion of the relative merits of indoor and outdoor relief. It was popularly but by no means universally maintained that institutional care was cheaper than outdoor measures. This assumption led to the repeated advocacy of various types of asylums which would offer both centralized and more economical relief. Enthusiasts for the erection of a poorhouse in St. John's claimed that such an institution in Halifax housed more paupers than were then supported in St. John's and did so at less expense.[33] Where outdoor relief was essential, the economy-minded suggested that food, fuel, and clothing should be provided at reduced rates or at cost rather than given away gratuitously to the poor. Not only would the available charitable funds then be less liable to misuse and made to go further, but those suffering from a state of temporary destitution would be retained in their constructive role as colonial consumers.[34] Interest in the poor man as a consumer also afforded a major reason why citizens preferred employment relief to charitable relief in the form of cheap food and old clothes. If he earned subsistence wages, the poor man would still continue to participate in the retail trade of the town at full market prices.[35]

A mindfulness of both economy and order led the benevolent to expect a return on their investment in alms-giving, charitable subscriptions, and poor rates. Gratuitous charity represented the worst sort of investment for an enterprising community. It precluded a productive return on welfare expenditure and did nothing to foster the virtues of thrift and self-reliance amongst the labouring poor, whereas labour extracted from the recipient of relief constituted the ideal recompense, the favoured *quid pro quo.*[36] As a correspon-

---

31   'St. John Public Dispensary.' *New Brunswick Courier*, 4 April 1857. Similarly *Report* of the Governors of Halifax Visiting Dispensary for 1860 (Halifax, 1861), p. 6.

32   Board of Health, Saint John, Report for 1858, p. iv, New Brunswick, *JLA*, (1857-8), Appendix.

33   Speech by Barnes, Assembly Debate, 8 April 1845, *Times* (St. John's), 12 April 1845.

34   'The Season,' *Morning Post*, 19 February 1845.

35   'Relief of the Poor,' *Patriot*, 30 March 1839.

36   Editorial, *Times*, (St. John's), 29 September 1847.

dent to the *Acadian Recorder* explained, "every penny given in charity to a healthy person, able to work, is a serious injury to society at large, unless that penny produces its own value by some mode of industry."[37] The guarantee that a poor person or family relieved through charity or employment was in fact deserving formed another precautionary, money-saving consideration. Most public relief schemes or welfare services — voluntary or government sponsored — required a means test in the form of a certificate of genuine destitution from a respectable citizen or designated official.[38] Poor youths supplied their *quid pro quo* in another form. All towns and many churches within them organized clothing societies which aimed primarily at sheltering poor children against the inclemency of winter weather. But in return for free clothing, the children were expected to attend Sunday school of catechism classes where proper ideas of christian citizenship were carefully inculcated.[39]

With their interest in economy, good order, and the wider welfare of the town, social commentators of every description urged consistently from the 1810's until the 1860's and beyond that the able-bodied poor should be relieved only in return for an equivalent in labour. Work was seen as the great panacea for the prevailing urban malaise produced by seasonal unemployment, dangerous mendicancy, and exorbitant, gratuitous aid. Effective employment relief would benefit both the poor and the town. For individual recipients, employment would supply what the majority professedly preferred — the means of obtaining the necessaries of life without sacrificing completely their independence by becoming degraded objects of charity.[40] Provision of work would eliminate reliance on charity which was both demoralizing and induced wasteful habits of idleness, intemperance, improvidence, and even worse forms of anti-social behaviour.[41] As far as the town itself was concerned, or more specifically its leading citizens, employment

---

37   Letter from Agenoria, *Acadian Recorder*, 29 November 1823.

38   *Morning News*, 11 September 1846; Notice of Commissioners for the Relief of the Poor, *Newfoundland Express*, 23 January 1861.

39   Catechistical Society, *Cross* (Halifax), 7 August 1847. The Saint John and Portland Ladies' Benevolent Society loaned clothing to the sick poor and if it was returned in good order, the party received a gift of some of the articles. *New Brunswick Courier*, 22 June 1844.

40   Editorial, *Acadian Recorder*, 6 February 1836; 'Relief of the Poor', *Patriot*, 30 March 1839; Letter from Observer, *Newfoundland*, 9 March 1848·, Petition of Irish labourers (Halifax) to Sir John Harvey, 25 April 1848, RG 5, Series GP, Vol. 7, PANS; Speech by Shea, Assembly Debate, 14 December 1848; *Newfoundlander*, 21 December 1848; Speech by Hayward, Assembly Debate, 10 February 1854, *Newfoundland Express*, 18 February 1854; Speech by Surveyor General Hanrahan, Assembly Debate, 12 March 1856, *ibid.,* 31 May 1856.

41   Letter from Humanus, *New Brunswick Courier*, 2 February 1833; Editorial, *Newfoundlander*, 30 September 1847·, Report of Committee of HM Council upon the expenditure on account of paupers in the district of St. John's, *Public Ledger*, 3 July 1849.

relief was designed to "subserve the Public interest."[42] In the first place, work was favoured as a security measure, the object being to avoid public mischief by keeping the labouring poor busily occupied.[43] Secondly, from the 1840s onwards, when middle-class faith in progress and improvement clearly emerged in debates on social welfare, as it did in the matter of education, relief in the shape of employment was valued as a means by which the poor could contribute significantly to the economy and development of the town and colony. The editor of the *New Brunswick Courier* aptly referred to it as a way "in which the necessities of the labouring poor could be made to dovetail with the general interest of the whole community, so that they might be benefited by receiving work, while those who pay for it might be equally benefited by having it done."[44] As one Halifax paper put it, "the poor might earn a loaf, and at the same time benefit the city."[45] Such a mutually beneficial situation obtained in Saint John in 1842 when the city council spent a grant of 2500 from the executive on the employment of the poor in winter. With the consequent removal of rock from the town squares, "the City was improved and the poor people were relieved at the same time."[46] Similarly in St. John's, the editor of the *Times* applauded the insistence of the governor in 1847 that the able-bodied must work for their relief and favoured the ubiquitous resort in Newfoundland to road works as the method by which the poor could secure their subsistence while "the country at large is benefited."[47]

The public interest would equally be served if such employment reduced the number of those supported by government and voluntary charity. Stephen March, an assemblyman in Newfoundland, was typical of those colonists who believed that poverty was synonymous with unemployment, and therefore that the availability of sufficient work would materially diminish the legislature's staggering appropriation for relief of the poor.[48] In 1829 the editor of the *New Brunswick Courier* claimed that the programme of street building undoubtedly relieved Saint John of potential parish burdens.[49] This interest in economy also motivated those who were less sympathetic towards the poor, and who argued that relief for the able-bodied in the form of com-

---

42 'Employment for the Poor,' *Morning News*, 29 January 1858; also *New Brunswick Courier*, 30 January 1858.

43 'Employment of the Poor,' and editorial comment, *Novascotian*, 12 January 1831.

44 'Winter Employment for Outdoor Labourers,' *New Brunswick Courier*, 30 January 1858.

45 *Novascotian*, 11 January 1858.

46 'Employment for the Poor,' *Morning News*, 29 January 1858; 500 not used in 1842 was used in 1858, Common Council, *ibid.*, 19 February, 5 March 1858; 'Employment of the Poor,' *New Brunswick Courier*, 4 December 1841.

47 Editorial, *Times* (St. John's), 9 October 1847.

48 Speech by March, Assembly Debate, 3 February 1853, *Patriot*, 12 February 1853.

49 *New Brunswick Courier*, 19 September 1829.

pulsory labour would soon send idlers and imposters scurrying to their own resources, or better still, as far as commentators in St. John's were concerned, encourage them to emigrate.[50] A similarly rigorous attitude can be discerned in the workhouse ethic that emerged in the management of the almshouse in Saint John, an institution which, unlike the Halifax poorhouse, catered to the able-bodied as well as to the disabled poor.[51] Anxious to reduce the burden of the poor rate on its citizens, the grand jury of Saint John suggested in its review of the almshouse in 1842 that "even nursing mothers should be required when in health to earn their living."[52] Faced with overwhelming numbers of applicants, the administrators of the almshouse advocated the enforcement of labour to render the institution unattractive to the able-bodied poor. In 1849, the lieutenant-governor of New Brunswick pointed out that "the immediate profit of the work, is not the object of main importance. The able-bodied men, as a class, may earn much less than their maintenance costs the public, but if the knowledge that hard work is required acts so as to deter others from entering the Alms House, a saving to the ratepayers will be effected, and the industry of individuals will be promoted out of its precincts."[53]

Finally, employment relief was singularly attractive to colonial capitalists and ratepayers who relished the existence of a cheap, exploitable labour force. A report of a committee of the Newfoundland legislative council in 1849 clearly delineated how the interests of employers could be served by replacing gratuitous assistance with employment relief. It proposed that the St. John's poor commissioner's office should act as a labour bureau where "artisans and labourers might at the time be had at rates a degree lower than their ordinary rate of wages."[54] In Saint John, a city which in contrast to St. John's was keen to retain its highly mobile labourers, the inhabitants felt a particular urgency to afford employment relief for the seasonally destitute and portrayed with complacent satisfaction those "starving for want of work" as a potentially cheap labour force.[55] For this reason, G. E. Fenety, the civic-conscious editor of the *Morning News*, proposed that the prosecution of

50 *Newfoundlander*, 7 June 1855.
51 Letter from an Inhabitant of Halifax, *Acadian Recorder*, 14 December 1816; Letter from An Old Tax Payer, 'Poor House,' *Morning News*, 16 March 1842.
52 Grand Jury Presentment, March 1842, RMU, Csj, 1/10, PANB; see also 'The Almshouse &c, &c', *Morning News*, 27 September 1850.
53 J. R. Partelow, Provincial Secretary, to the Commissioners of the Alms House and Work House, Saint John, *New Brunswick Courier*, 29 September 1849. Work was not consistently provided, see Charges against the Alms House Commissioners, October 1860, RMU, Csj, 1/15, PANB.
54 Report of Committee of HM Council upon the expenditure on account of paupers in the district of St. John's, *Public Ledger*, 3 July 1849.
55 Letter from The Poor Man's Friend, 'How to Employ the Poor,' *Morning News*, 19 February 1858; 'Employment for the Poor,' *ibid.*, 29 January 1858; Letter from Citizen, *Morning Freeman*, 26 March 1859.

public works should be reserved for seasons of scarcity and depression when they would not only benefit the poor by supplying work but the urban authorities would obtain the best return on the expenditure of the citizen's money in the form of useful labour, cheaply done.[56]

The range of proposals for furnishing socially-useful employment for the poor was far greater than the number of schemes actually undertaken. Initially, contemporaries viewed work as a palliative for distress in a very pessimistic light. One sceptical correspondent in Saint John in 1832 urged the citizens to consider whether they had in fact any responsibility in the matter, and if so, whether such a programme of work was feasible. They should determine, the correspondent suggested without expectation of a favourable response, "Either that it is not our duty as members of a Christian community to endeavour to provide for the employment of the poor as well as their relief. Or, that it is an object which we cannot reasonably expect to attain by any united efforts in this place."[57] Part of the trouble was that the people who took it upon themselves to advise the community on this issue tended to be men given to idle talk or theorizing, not practical men of business — newspaper editors, politicians, and bureaucrats rather than merchants, contractors, builders, and entrepreneurs. Moreover, with very few exceptions, the schemes implemented were not placed on a systematic footing, despite the necessity for regularizing employment relief advocated by the amateur political economists of the day. The projects themselves, both in conception and in practice, were of two varieties: heavy outdoor labour and indoor factory work. Public efforts were concentrated chiefly on the former because society was male-oriented and reflected the outlook of a pre-industrial age.

The most widely discussed forms of employment and the jobs most frequently organized can both be subsumed under the general heading of public works. These differed more in time, location, and sponsorship than in form or variety. In Halifax the urgent need for outdoor relief in the years following the Napoleonic Wars forced citizens' committees, in the absence of government measures, to address themselves to the question of providing employment. Much to the disappointment of its energetic proponents and the satisfaction of its critics, the Poor Man's Friend Society in the 1820s failed in its persevering endeavours to find work for the poor, being unable to do more than serve as a labour bureau.[58] Its successors, however, were determined to base their schemes for relieving the labouring poor on employment. Accordingly, a long tradition of outdoor relief for able-bodied men through stone breaking for the metalling or macadamizing of the roads began in the winter of 1830-1 and was revived for the benefit of at least 200 family men according

56 'A Word in Season — or, a Practical Lesson for the Times,'*Morning News*, 3 January 1855; 'Work for Labourers,' *ibid.*, 21 September 1857.

57 Letter from Homo, 'Employment of the Poor,' *New Brunswick Courier*, 14 January 1832.

58 Editorial, *Free Press*, 5 March 1822; *Acadian Recorder*, 7 February 1824.

to need over the next three decades.[59] While the sponsorship of this menial, degrading enterprise passed from the voluntary citizens' committees to the city corporation in the 1840s, it continued to be funded largely by private charity with the mayor still appealing to the inhabitants for subscriptions or contributions in stone.

Meanwhile in Saint John and St. John's stone breaking was also promoted, and requests for financing it, as well as more sophisticated activities like pipe laying and rubbish removal, were often directed to the respective executive governments by hard-pressed civic-leaders.[60] But road works remained the ideal form of public works in St. John's and the outports. Initiated principally through the efforts of Sir Thomas Cochrane in the 1820s, road making and repairing became a perennial resort as relief for the able-bodied and for seasonally unemployed fishermen. To such an extent was this enterprise popularly believed to mitigate distress, that until reforms of the late 1860s the road bill came to be associated with other appropriations for eleemosynary aid and therefore considered as little more than a euphemism for a poor relief bill.[61] Indeed, despite approval for the 'dovetailing' nature of this work — that it secured "real value to the country while relieving the necessities of the industrious poor" — the amount of labour provided on the roads was apparently determined by the degree of distress rather than by a comprehensive transportation policy.[62] That some contemporaries were prone to criticize this tendency can be attributed to their preference for a systematic approach to employment relief which would supplant the 'make work' nature of the existing enterprise.

59 'Employment of the Poor,' *Novascotian*, 12 January 1831; 'Employment of the Poor,' *Acadian Recorder*, 15 January, 31 December 1831; *Weekly Observer* (Saint John), 3 January 1832; 'Employment of the Poor,' *Novascotian*, 12 January 1832; 'Stone Breaking,' *ibid.*, 20 December 1832; 'The Employment of the Industrious Poor,' *ibid.*, 3 January 1833; 'Stonebreaking,' *ibid.*, 21 February 1833; *Guardian*, 4 January 1843; *Sun*, 4 February 1848.

60 Letter from Homo, 'Employment of the Poor,' *New Brunswick Courier*, 14 January 1832; *ibid.*, 10 February 1838; Editorial, *Public Ledger*, 23 March 1838; Common Council resolutions, *New Brunswick Courier*, 27 November 1841·, Letter from Civis, 'Feed the Hungry and the Poor — Clothe the Naked,' *Morning News*, 27 November 1857; 'Winter Employment for Outdoor Labourers,' *New Brunswick Courier*, 30 January 1858.

61 Speech by Hogsett, Assembly Debate, 22 March 1853, *Newfoundland Express*, 2 April 1853· Speech by Hayward, Assembly Debate, 10 February 1854, *ibid.*, 18 February 1854; Speech by Hanrahan, Assembly Debate, 11 April 1854, *ibid.*, 29 April 1854; Editorial, *Public Ledger*, 24 August 1855; Speech by Prendergast, Assembly Debate, 21 January 1856, *Newfoundland Express*, 30 January 1856; Speech by Surveyor General Hanrahan, Assembly Debate, 12 March 1856, *ibid.*, 31 May 1856·, Editorial, *Newfoundlander*, 12 October 1857.

62 'State of the Poor — Its Causes,' *Newfoundlander*, 10 October 1853. Moreover by the sixties road money was occasionally granted without a strict adherence to the exaction of labour on the ground that poor men "could not, on their spare diet, be sent four or five miles out of town to work on the roads." Assembly Debate, 22 February 1866, *ibid.*, 19 March 1866.

At the opposite extreme to such 'make work' arrangements stood the entirely fortuitous opportunities for employment of the able-bodied poor created by the march of progress in the Atlantic colonies. By the middle of the century skilled and semi-skilled labourers in substantial numbers, sometimes large enough to siphon off the burdensome surplus of the towns, were engaged on railway works in the environs of Saint John and Halifax, on road building for the overseas telegraphic cable in Newfoundland, and on the construction of a variety of impressive civic buildings, such as the city hospital, provincial lunatic asylum, and city prison in the Halifax area.[63] For the private contractors a pool of unemployed poor supplied cheap labour at the termination of the shipping season; for the public authorities the works saved them the trouble of devising, and more important, financing an alternative employment scheme; for the community, large-scale productive labour meant a positive boon as a result of the exchange of wages for local services. As Fenety pointed out in 1858, railway construction during the depression involved "something like a thousand pounds *distributed*, as it were, among the labouring classes every week, which in turn finds its way into the stores, and thus keeps business moving."[64] But by its nature the work was short term and often interrupted by undercapitalization. Moreover, the climatic limitation imposed on the work when it was most needed meant that rail lines laid on frozen mud near Saint John sank in the spring thaw; that autumnal road building in Newfoundland was inefficient and could not be pursued at all in winter; and that ambitious building operations had to be halted in Halifax when frost attacked new masonry.[65] Unfortunately, such enterprises did not lay the basis of a sustained and systematic employment policy. The jobs tended to terminate with the completion of the railway, the telegraphic communications, or the public buildings concerned.

Those colonists with sufficient foresight to suggest projects. that were neither wholly 'make work', nor fortuitous, nor seasonal in character, appear from the perspective of the 1970s to have had common sense to their credit.

---

63 Speeches by Parsons and Hanrahan, Assembly Debate, 11 April 1854, *Newfoundland Express*, 29 April 1854; 'Winter Work for the Industrious,' *Morning Chronicle* (Halifax), 27 January 1855; 'Remember the Poor,' *Morning News*, 27 November 1857; *Morning Journal*, 28 April 1858; *Evening Express* (Halifax), 26 May May 1858; 'Business and Prospects,' *Morning News*, 29 September 1858.

64 'Ship Building and Saw Mills about St. John — Hard Times — The Way to Relieve Distress,' *Morning News*, 10 December 1858.

65 'Employment for the Poor,' *Morning News*, 29 January 1858; Evidence of James Douglas before the Select Committee appointed to inquire into the Appropriation of Monies voted by the Legislature for the Relief of the Poor, *JLA*, Newfoundland, 1848-9, Appendix, p. 691; *Patriot*, 27 December 1852; Editorial, *Newfoundlander*, 12 October 1857; Speech by Surveyor General Hanrahan, Assembly Debate, 10 March 1858, *ibid.*, 18 March 1858·, 'The Weather vs House Building,' *Morning Journal*, 12 December 1859.

Shrewd commentators flourished most noticeably in Saint John's, the town amongst the three which suffered most relentlessly from chronic poverty. While the distress of the inhabitants was undoubtedly complicated by the supply system practised by the merchants, contemporaries ascribed it more generally to the predominance of a single economic activity that was seasonal in nature and underdeveloped in scope. In such circumstances alternative forms of employment could be fruitfully designed to meet the demands of the local consumer market or to act as ancillary pursuits to the primary business of the fishery. Several newspaper editors and government reports recommended that both unemployment in winter and one persistent deficiency of supply in the local market might be overcome by setting the able-bodied poor to work in the woods producing lumber on a systematic basis. While many of the seasonally unemployed resorted to the woods on their own initiative, they functioned as independent, small-scale producers without the stimulus of attractive marketing facilities in town. The press suggested several times that the government ought to open a wood yard or depot in St. John's on a cash basis where the poor could be sure of an equitable return for their labour and the sale of all manner of wood and primary wood products on terms advantageous both to themselves and to the public treasury.[66] A perceptive government inquiry in 1856 went a step further by advocating that the poor should be organized in supervised gangs for a more comprehensive and profitable system of employment relief in the woods.[67] Other proposals regarded employment schemes as a means of augmenting the fishery. The government report of 1856 strongly favoured the promotion of shipbuilding through tonnage bounties paid to those shipbuilders who employed a required proportion of government paupers. Not only was this a labour-intensive industry and directly related to the staple export business of the colony, but it would create many additional jobs in auxiliary areas.[68]

Alternative projects for supplementing the fishery depended on the facilities for indoor work, the other variety of employment advocated in the towns as a means of relief. The forward-looking government report of 1856, for example, claimed that publicly-sponsored factories might offer employment, in lines of work suited to the country — principally the manufacture of nets and

66 Editorial, *Public Ledger,* 29 March 1839; 'Relief of the Poor,' *Patriot,* 30 March 1839; Editorial, *Public Ledger,* 30 September 1853.

67 Report of Committee of Enquiry into the State of the Poor, 26 March 1856, *Newfoundland Express,* 23 April 1856. Another winter activity which was urged in Saint John and Halifax was the ice trade. *Saint John Herald,* 10 December 1845; *Morning Journal,* 26 January 1857.

68 Report of Committee of Enquiry into the State of the Poor, 26 March 1856, *Newfoundland Express,* 23 April 1856; also Speech by March, Assembly Debate, 10 December 1860, *ibid.,* 25 December 1860.

seines (imported from Britain at a cost of over 30,000 in 1860,[69] as well as small-scale wooden products such as staves and shingles, the picking of oakum (25 tons of which was imported every year, according to the *Public Ledger* in 1839),[70] and the production of domestic clothing. That report, however, was published almost twenty-five years after a factory for the relief of the able-bodied had been established in St. John's, an institution which had served as an inspiration for the government report and a point of departure for many other suggestions that emanated from St. John's. It was a quite unique institution which in terms of longevity, popularity, non-partisanship, and 'dovetailing' was the most successful of the few sustained ventures in the Atlantic towns for employing the labouring poor in this period.

The St. John's factory, a non-resident and therefore non-correctional institutional, was begun in December 1832 by a group of community-conscious women who aimed primarily to teach "carding, spinning, net making" to the children of the poor and to afford useful employment to the indigent of St. John's.[71] Like any new institution, however, the managers of the factory initially encountered difficulties in obtaining appropriate raw materials to be worked into consumer goods and in raising sufficient funds to subsidize its activities.[72] Subscriptions and charity balls raised enough money to finance the construction of a permanent building in 1834 and subsequently financial assistance came from a variety of sources: bazaars, balls, benefit performances by the local theatrical group, public subscription campaigns, and fairly regular aid from the legislature.[73]

Since the factory suffered its share of vicissitudes and never achieved self-sufficiency, its community-conscious efforts were more noteworthy than its long-term accomplishments. In the first place, the factory undertook to promote industry in place of charity as a means of poor relief. This emphasis, it was popularly believed, would foster all the appropriate virtues and habits in the poor. In a community where dire poverty was endemic and the expense of

69 Speech by March, Assembly Debate, 10 December 1860, *Newfoundland Express*, 25 December 1860.

70 Editorial, *Public Ledger*, 29 March 1839.

71 Editorial and Report of the Meeting of Committee of Ladies for establishing a Factory for the purpose of giving useful Employment to the Poor of the Town, *Newfoundlander*, 13 December 1832.

72 *Public Ledger*, 26 February 1833; *Newfoundlander*, 18 April 1833; Letter from A Friend, *Public Ledger*, 28 March 1834; Report of St. John's Factory, *ibid.*, 27 November 1835.

73 St. John's Factory, *Newfoundlander*, 4 September 1834; *ibid.*, 18 September 1834; St. John's Factory, *Public Ledger*, 16 January 1835·, *ibid.*, 27 February 1835; Report of St. John's Factory, *ibid.*, 16 August 1836; *Newfoundlander*, 23 March 1837; *ibid.*, 15 June 1837; Assembly Debate, 1 October 1838, *Patriot*, 6 October 1838·, *Public Ledger*, 28 February 1840, 28 February 1851; *Newfoundland Express*, 22 October 1853; R. H. Bonnycastle, *Newfoundland in 1842* (London, 1842), Vol. 2, p. 232.

poor relief crippling, the encouragement of self-reliance, independence, and self-respect amongst the poor was enthusiastically endorsed by the articulate.[74] By supplying work and useful industrial training as well as wages, the managers of the factory hoped "to improve and elevate the mind and feeling of the poor and needy, above relying on eleemosynary aid" from other sources.[75] This was a vital consideration in St. John's where the accustomed rhythm of summer fishing followed by winter distress discernibly undermined the morale and spirit of the working class and disposed them "to lean altogether on public charity for support."[76] The factory also undertook to supply much of its work in the slack commercial season when unemployment was at its height.[77] To those who contributed to its operations, the system pursued by the factory assured the desirable *quid pro quo* in labour. Not only did this ease the qualms of the benevolent about fostering idleness, but it stressed employment as "the panacea for the amelioration" of the condition of the St. John's poor.[78] It was also no mean consideration that the factory might reduce the burden of poor relief on the community since "every shilling earned here is so much withdrawn from the demands on the public which pauperism engenders."[79]

In the second place, the factory endeavoured both to employ those elements in the town population most in need of work and to extend its operations to meet emergencies that arose. Initially the institution catered to the most destitute poor of St. John's, employing some 30 work people.[80] Its normal complement of workers had risen to about 60 by the severe winter of 1837-8.[81] With financial aid from the executive during the famine year of 1847-8, the factory was able to employ between 100 and 150 a day.[82] Within a few years of its foundation experience had shown that indoor employment relief was most eagerly sought by women and children, who constituted two segments of society usually neglected in the pre-industrial period but most in

74 Speech by Carson, Assembly Debate, 21 March 1835, *Public Ledger*, 24 March 1835; Editorial, *Newfoundlander*, 28 March 1839.

75 Letter from R. Prowse, *Public Ledger*, 26 February 1847·, Report of St. John's Factory, *ibid.*, 16 August 1836.

76 Annual Report of Committee of Factory, *Public Ledger*, 3 August 1849.

77 Report of Factory Committee, *Newfoundlander*, 3 August 1837; Report of St. John's Factory, *Times* (St. John's), 3 August 1842.

78 Editorial, *Newfoundlander*, 28 March 1839.

79 Report of Committee of St. John's Factory, *Newfoundlander*, 14 September 1843; Annual Report of Committee of Factory, *Public Ledger*, 3 August 1849.

80 Report of St. John's Factory, *Public Ledger*, 27 November 1835.

81 Editorial, *Newfoundlander*, 5 July 1838; Report of St. John's Factory Committee, *Public Ledger*, 27 July 1838.

82 Report of St. John's Factory, *Newfoundlander*, 10 August 1848; *Times* (St. John's) 23 March 1849.

need of work since they comprised the majority of the year-round, as opposed to the seasonally, unemployed.[83] Its essential service as an employer of women and children was noted by the attorney general in 1856 when he asserted that "from the effects of disease and shipwreck" St. John's had more widows and orphans "than in any other city or town of the same size."[84] Priority of employment was given to females of every creed between the ages of 12 and 60. They laboured daily from 10 a.m. to 4 p.m. and were paid on a piece-work rate. Although the actual rate is unknown, contemporaries claimed that workers usually earned between 1s. and 1s.6d. a day, a typical relief wage. One hard-working female was reputed in 1849 to be earning as much as 12s. a week making nets. But on the basis of detailed figures for two months in 1838, the averages of the women and children fell between 3s.6d. per week, starvation wages at best. On the assumption that the adolescents were less productive and paid at a lower rate than the mature women, it is not surprising that commentators declared that it was the "industrious" female who could earn her support at the factory. Advocates of the establishment also proudly boasted that the factory was the agency through which whole families of widows and their children could work together and earn a complete livelihood.[85] One wage packet was clearly inadequate to maintain a family.

Finally, the factory offered specialized training and concentrated on manufactures that were most needed in the community and therefore presumably guaranteed a ready, local market. Two types of manufactures were undertaken: fishing nets for the primary industry of the colony and domestic textiles required by local merchants for sale in their stores. The factory committee was proud of the quality of the nets and publicized them as being superior or at least comparable to the imported commodity.[86] Moreover, the preoccupation with net-making as an activity beneficial to the family and the community at large was frequently celebrated.

> The advantages to the colony by this branch of industry are incalculable —
> the women and children are taught to make nets for their husbands and

83 Letter from Malthus, Poor Man's Friend Society, No. 5, 'Answer to My Opponents.' *Nova-Scotian*, 16 February 1825.

84 Speech by Attorney General Little, Assembly Debate, 8 April 1856, *Newfoundlander*, 10 April 1856.

85 Account of persons employed at Factory, *Newfoundlander*, 5 July 1838; Letter from R. Prowse, *Public Ledger*, 26 February 1847; Editorial, *Newfoundlander* 11 March 1847; 'The Factory,' *Times* (St. John's), 8 September 1847·, *ibid.*, 23 March 1849; Speech by Warren, Assembly Debate, 8 April 1853, *Newfoundland Express*, 28 April 1853; Speech by Prowse, Assembly Debate, 8 April 1856, *Newfoundlander*, 10 April 1856.

86 Report of St. John's Factory, *Public Ledger*, 16 August 1836; Annual Report of Committee of Factory, *ibid.*, 3 August 1849.

fathers, and thus to employ the hitherto unprofitable season of winter — while the fisherman has only to provide the twine instead of the more expensive article, the net or seine, which latter is often beyond his means, and the want of it is not unfrequently a serious hindrance to his getting on in the world.[87]

Money otherwise sent outside the colony could thereby be kept in circulation, generating employment which would result in "an immense saving" to the colony.[88] At the same time, the training in net-making was thought to promote "an exceedingly useful art" in the economic circumstances of Newfoundland.[89] The needlework, always a supplementary activity, was aimed at producing necessary items of wearing apparel for local consumption. This textile branch, originally of a finishing nature, blossomed into the manufacture of textiles in 1850 when Lieutenant Governor LeMarchant provided several looms for the weaving of homespun, a fabric well suited to ordinary domestic wear and hitherto not produced in the colony. This had the advantage of adding another type of industrial training to the factory's regimen, though the institution's inability to find a qualified weaver in St. John's by 1868 casts doubt on the success of the undertaking.[90]

Despite support from the legislature, endorsement by select committees, and the intermittent interest of governors, official attempts to exploit factory production as an extensive system of poor relief amounted to little more than brief enthusiasm.[91] Whatever their reasons, many prominent citizens were critical both of the management of the factory and of the quality and cost of the nets it produced. Moreover, the retail merchants of St. John's did not absorb all the ready-to-wear clothing made at the factory. If the institution had been designed to employ men in winter rather than women the year round, it might have excited a more lively public concern. It is also possible that prospective workers did not always take advantage of the factory's facilities for voluntary employment. Ultimately, by the 1860's, the management of the institution came to devolve, not on a general committee of citizens as formerly, but on the Catholic St. Vincent de Paul Society, a change that was accompanied by a concentration on purely hibernal operations.[92] Nonetheless, the St. John's factory was the one genuine house of industry in

87 Report of Factory Committee, *Newfoundlander*, 3 August 1837.

88 Report of St. John's Factory, *Newfoundlander*, 10 August 1848.

89 *Times* (St. John's), 23 March 1849.

90 Editorial, *Public Ledger*, 22 January 1850; *Times* (St. John's), 23 January 1850; Speech by Emerson, Assembly Debate, 22 March 1850, *Public Ledger*, 26 March 1850. See criticism voiced by Prendergast, Assembly Debate, 31 May 1852, *Newfoundland Express*, 4 June 1852·, Report of Proceedings of St. Vincent de Paul Society, *Newfoundlander*, 22 December 1868.

91 Report of Committee of HM Council upon the expenditure on account of paupers in the district of St. John's, *Public Ledger*, 3 July 1849·, Editorial, *Newfoundland Express*, 3 May 1856.

92 Report of Society of St. Vincent de Paul, *Newfoundlander*, 20 December 1867.

the Atlantic region. In spite of musings about a house of industry as a palliative for poverty, Haligonians did no more than toy with the idea of providing indoor employment relief and seemed unable to devise forms of work that would fit in with the wider interests of the city and thereby appeal to the philanthropy of the townspeople.[93] After public agitation a residential house of industry for women and children was opened briefly through voluntary assistance in Saint John in 1834, but it was intended mainly as a self-supporting school of domestic industry which also trained household servants for the city.[94]

Indoor employment, therefore, did not prosper more noticeably than outdoor measures of relief. It is not difficult to discern why employment schemes foundered. For one thing, colonists believed that the conditions which caused unemployment were beyond their control and could neither be anticipated nor rectified in towns whose economies were subject to fluctuating external and international trends.[95] The sudden influxes of immigrants and erratic business depressions made the colonists feel singularly helpless. If leading townsmen felt helpless in the face of such circumstances, they would hardly be capable of helping others to help themselves. Moreover, the launching of extensive schemes for employment required capital, and no agency in the towns appeared willing to sustain a socially useful experiment in the early stages before it could become a self-supporting or even profitable operation. Despite, or perhaps because of, the amazing array of enterprises partially subsidized by government, the provincial legislatures refused to risk their revenues on long-term employment schemes or to favour leading towns at the expense of the other inhabitants in the colony.[96] For their part, the corporations of Saint John and Halifax were not wealthy enough to embark on ambitious projects and were reluctant to resort to unpopular taxation. Nor were colonists agreed how far the various levels of government should involve

93 "Proposal for the Establishment of a House of Industry in connexion with an Orphan Asylum," *Nova Scotian*, 10 February 1836; "An Appeal to the Public on behalf of the Establishment of a House of Industry in connexion with Orphan Asylum," *ibid.*, 28 March 1839; Letter from One of the Society, 'House of Industry, Hints to the Benevolent,' *Morning Chronicle*, 11 March 1845; 'House of Industry,' *Guardian*, 14 March 1845; 'House of Industry,' *Morning Post*, 26 March 1845; Letter from a Friend to the Poor, 'Help for the Poor,' *Sun*, 19 January 1846·, 'The Reclamation of Vagrants, *Morning Journal*, 22 February 1856.

94 Letter from Homo, 'Employment of the Poor,' *New Brunswick Courier*, 14 January 1832; Letter from Humanus, 'Employment of the Poor,' *ibid.*, 2 February 1833; 1st Report of the House of Industry, *ibid.*, 26 July 1834; Petition of Managing Committee of Female House of Industry in City of Saint John, 2 February 1835, RLE/835/pe/4, No. 82, PANB. It also provided home employment relief for women on a piece-work basis. Report of St. John Female House of Industry, *New Brunswick Courier*, 17 January 1835.

95 Letter from a Sympathizer, 'The Present and Former Government', *Morning News*, 1 February 1856.

96 'Who are the Suffering Poor?', *Morning News*, 22 February 1858.

themselves in manipulation of the labour market. The editor of the *New-foundland Express*, for example, pointed out that the government report of 1856 on employment for the poor "proceeds upon an assumption which has proved a failure wherever it has been attempted to give practical effect to it — the assumption that the *organization of labour* can be effected by the state."[97]

Left to private capitalists, however, the pauperizing patterns of unemployment were reinforced and exploited because merchants were content to employ town labourers in summer and abandon them to the mercy of government, charity, occasional public works, or sharply reduced wages in the private sector during winter.[98] With the notable exception of shipbuilders in Saint John, entrepreneurs were as yet unwilling to invest in industry and thereby ease some of the seasonal fluctuations, and this despite a general conviction by mid-century that sufficient wealth and tradition of prudence existed to sustain "promising and well-considered commercial speculation" in local manufactures.[99] In these circumstances, voluntary, non-profit-making agencies did what they could. Such denominational societies as the St. Vincent de Paul in St. John's and the visiting societies attached to St. Matthew's and St. George's churches in Halifax went unpretentiously about the business of providing essential, if token, indoor work for women and children.[100] But more generally, associations found it easier to dispense discriminating charity without labour and thereby salve their consciences rather than campaign for effective employment relief. In fact society's inability to attack pre-industrial poverty at its source, which was unemployment, led by the 1850s to a marked preoccupation with the symptoms of poverty, especially intemperance, and a corresponding interest in social amelioration as moral rather than economic reform.[101]

97   Editorial, *Newfoundland Express,* 23 April 1856; Speech by Attorney General, Assembly Debate, 21 February 1866, *Newfoundlander,* 15 March 1866; Speech by Receiver General, Assembly Debate, 6 March 1868, *ibid.,* 11 March 1868.

98   Speech by Hogsett, Assembly Debate, 3 April 1854, *Newfoundland Express,* 11 April 1854; 'Our Trade System,' *Newfoundlander,* 1 February 1855; J. Fingard, 'The Winter's Tale: The Seasonal Contours of Pre-Industrial Poverty in British North America,' Canadian Historical Association, *Historical Papers* (1974), pp. 65-94.

99   Editorial, *Sun,* 24 December 1853.

100   St. Vincent de Paul Society, *Newfoundlander,* 2 April 1857; *Newfoundland Express,* 10 December 1861; St. Matthew's Church District Society, *Guardian,* 15 November 1850; St. George's Ladies' Benevolent Society, *Colonial Churchman* (Lunenburg), 15 June 1837; *Morning Post,* 15 January 1842; St. George's District Visiting Society, *Church Times* (Halifax), 3 December 1853.

101   For example, 'Providing for the Poor,' *Morning News,* 18 January 1860.

RUSTY BITTERMANN

Reprinted from Vol. XVIII, No. 1
(Autumn 1988)

The Hierarchy of the Soil:
Land and Labour in a 19th Century
Cape Breton Community*

THE IMPRESSIVE RENAISSANCE OF MARITIME HISTORIOGRAPHY over the past
two decades has concentrated on issues located outside of the countryside, while
the rural spaces in which most of the region's population lived and the bulk of
the region's economic activity occurred have received relatively little study.
Despite this lack of attention, some common perceptions permeate the
literature. It is assumed that farming was basically "subsistence" in nature for
much of the 19th century and that rural residents enjoyed a rough equality of
condition. The immigrant encounter with the rural environment of the region is
perceived as generating, at least initially, a society characterized by rough
equality and the supposed absence of markets for farm goods coupled with
relatively open access to land resources is thought to have sustained egalitarian
social structures.[1] Significant markets for Maritime agricultural goods are
typically construed as a relatively late development.[2] The literature concerning
rural Cape Breton in the 19th century is certainly no exception to these
statements. Indeed, those districts settled by Highland Scots have commonly
been portrayed as enclaves of self-sufficiency, since Highlanders, it is claimed,

*I would like to thank David Frank, Brian Tennyson, and Graeme Wynn for their comments on an
earlier version of this paper and the participants in the 15th Conference on the Use of Quantitative
Methods in Canadian Economic History for their responses to some of the methodology informing
it. As well I wish gratefully to acknowledge the support for this research provided by Queen's and
doctoral fellowships from the Social Sciences and Humanities Council of Canada.

1   See for instance John Warkentin, "The Atlantic Region", in R. Cole Harris and John Warkentin,
    eds., *Canada Before Confederation: A Study of Historical Geography* (Toronto, 1977), pp.
    169-231; Graeme Wynn, "The Maritimes: The Geography of Fragmentation and Underdevelop-
    ment", in L.D. McCann, ed., *A Geography of Canada: Heartland and Hinterland* (Scarborough,
    1982), pp. 156-213. For exceptions to this statement see Debra McNabb, "Land and Families in
    Horton Township, N.S., 1760-1830", M.A. thesis, University of British Columbia, 1986 and
    James W. St. G. Walker, *The Black Loyalists: The Search for a Promised Land in Nova Scotia
    and Sierra Leone, 1783-1870* (New York, 1976).

2   Melville Cumming, "Agriculture in the Maritime Provinces", in Adam Shortt and Arthur
    Doughty, eds., *Canada and its Provinces* (Toronto, 1913), XIV, p. 648; W.T. Easterbrook and
    H.G.J. Aitken, *Canadian Economic History* (Toronto, 1956), pp. 240-1; Peter Sinclair, "From
    Peasants to Corporations: The Development of Capitalist Agriculture in the Maritime
    Provinces", in John A. Fry, ed., *Contradictions in Canadian Society: Readings in Introductory
    Sociology* (Toronto, 1984), pp. 276-93; Stephen Hornsby, "Scottish Emigration and Settlement
    in Early Nineteenth Century Cape Breton", in Kenneth Donovan, ed., *Cape Breton Historical
    Essays* (forthcoming) and "An Historical Geography of Cape Breton Island in the Nineteenth
    Century", Ph.D. thesis, University of British Columbia, 1986.

knew little of agriculture, were uninterested in material progress, and farmed primarily for subsistence.[3] Gaelic cultural traits supposedly combined with the absence of markets for farm goods to generate rural communities characterized by the most rudimentary forms of subsistence farming. Egalitarian social structures were thus rooted in a shared material poverty.

A close examination of the history of one fragment of the 19th century Maritime countryside, the Cape Breton community of Middle River, suggests the need to reconsider these assumptions. Settlement in this district was not a leveling but rather a differentiating process, as inequalities in the initial distribution of land resources laid the basis for enduring socioeconomic divisions. Because there were markets for agricultural products, land, and labour, and because some Highlanders were not uninterested in material progress, these inequalities deepened as they were reproduced over time. Nineteenth century Middle River was not a collectivity of essentially self-sufficient farm units, although census figures might cause it to appear so in aggregate. From the earliest decades of European settlement, there was a substantial export trade in farm products from the district, but not all households were involved to the same extent. Unequal access to resources, particularly land, meant that some households were in a position to produce substantial amounts of goods for export, while others were unable to meet household needs from their farm holdings. Middle River's 19th century history is grounded in the tensions induced by these differing relations to local resources. To relinquish rural visions rooted in the myth of self-sufficiency is to discern a social dynamic within the countryside.

Middle River, like other European communities in the Maritimes, was moulded by the pre-existent economies of the northern fisheries and southern plantation production. Agricultural goods, drawn by the demand for provisions to supply both fishermen and slaves, were produced and shipped from rural regions all about the eastern and western shores of the Atlantic basin. Perched on the busy western rim of seaborne communications between these two zones of demand, and with no area of land more than 30 miles from salt water, rural Nova Scotia was inexorably shaped by these patterns of trade. The economies of plantation and fishery which created demand for Maritime agricultural goods

---

3   Charles Dunn, *Highland Settler: A Portrait of the Scottish Gael in Nova Scotia* (1953, reprinted Toronto, 1980); Louis Gentilcore, "The Agricultural Background of Settlement in Eastern Nova Scotia", *Annals, Association of American Geographers*, 46 (1956), pp. 378-404; D. Campbell and R.A. MacLean, *Beyond the Atlantic Roar: A Study of the Nova Scotia Scots* (Toronto, 1974); R.A. MacLean, "The Scots Hector's Cargo", in Douglas F. Campbell, ed., *Banked Fires: The Ethnics of Nova Scotia* (Port Credit, Ontario, 1978), pp. 106-30; John Warkentin, "The Atlantic Region", pp. 186, 196. This characterization of Highland farming skills has been ably challenged in Alan MacNeil's study of farming in Pictou and Antigonish counties, "A Reconsideration of the State of Agriculture in Eastern Nova Scotia, 1791-1861", M.A. thesis, Queen's University, 1985.

also served to bring American agricultural production into competition with that of the Maritimes. Vessels transporting fish to the West Indies brought back not just Caribbean goods but foodstuffs — particularly flour — purchased at American ports on the route home. American vessels moving north to fish also played a significant, albeit immeasurable, role in transporting those agricultural goods that could be produced more cheaply in the United States than in Nova Scotia. Agriculture in the region assumed its unique shape not in the absence of market forces but in the presence both of strong sources of demand *and* of alternative sources of supply for foodstuffs.[4]

Like many other agricultural regions in Cape Breton, Middle River was particularly well-situated to take advantage of the Newfoundland market. The agricultural core of the district, the pear-shaped Wagamatcook River Valley, was located roughly six miles from the protected salt waters of the Bras d'Or Lakes. The distance from Indian Bay, the mouth of both the Baddeck and the Wagamatcook rivers, to St. John's was less than 500 miles, a voyage that could be hazarded by relatively small vessels. The farmers of the adjacent Baddeck Valley had established direct trading links with the Newfoundland market before the arrival of the first European settlers to Middle River.[5] Though in time Middle River too would have direct trade with St. John's, the ports of Arichat and Sydney acted as intermediaries in the first exchanges originating from the Wagamatcook Valley.[6] While Arichat had a considerable involvement with the Caribbean market, Sydney primarily served as a conduit for foodstuffs moving to Newfoundland.[7] After being transported to the lakeshore, Middle River's farm goods were conveyed by open boat to these centres. Sydney soon supplanted Arichat and by the 1840s the Newfoundland market would

4   Harold Innis, *The Cod Fisheries: The History of an International Economy* (1940; reprinted Toronto, 1978), pp. 231, 267; Testimony of Mr. Morrison, general produce merchant of Halifax, "Report of the Select Committee on the State of the Coal Trade and for the Promoting of Inter-Provincial Trade", Canada, House of Commons, *Journal*, 1877, vol. XI, p. 38, App. 4; Graeme Wynn, "Late Eighteenth Century Agriculture on the Bay of Fundy Marshlands", *Acadiensis*, VIII, 2 (Spring 1979), p. 89. For reports indicating the trading activities of American fishing vessels along the coasts of Cape Breton at the time of early settlement in Middle River see Ainslie to Bathurst, 18 May 1817, CO 217, vol. 135, pp. 66-8 and Ainslie to Bathurst, 8 October 1818, CO 217, vol. 136, pp. 110-1.

5   W. James MacDonald, ed., *Patterson's History of Victoria County* (1885, reprinted, Sydney, 1978), p. 52.

6   Letter of John McLennan cited in Mrs. Charles Archibald, "Early Scottish Settlers in Cape Breton", *Nova Scotia Historical Society Collections*, 18 (1914), p. 90.

7   Thomas C. Haliburton, *History of Nova Scotia* (1829; reprinted Belleville, Ontario, 1973), II, p. 221; R. Montgomery Martin, *History of Nova Scotia, Cape Breton, the Sable Islands, New Brunswick, Prince Edward Island, the Bermudas, Newfoundland, etc. etc.* (London, 1837), pp. 102-4; C. Bruce Fergusson, ed., *Uniacke's Sketches of Cape Breton and Other Papers Relating to Cape Breton Island* (Halifax, 1958), pp. 48-9.

overwhelmingly be the destination for Middle River's farm production.[8] It is difficult to gain a clear sense of the chronology of the early growth of agricultural exports from the Middle River district. Even before road improvements and haulage with horses, there is evidence that during the shipping season 20 or more teams of oxen might be engaged in transporting farm produce to the lakeshore on sledges drawn across bare ground.[9] As cattle and sheep might make their own way, such figures indicate that the early agricultural trade of the valley was conducted on a considerable scale. The first specific data on farm exports is from mid-century. According to the reports of Middle River's Agricultural Society, in 1847 300 cattle, 500 sheep, 400 firkins of butter, and a "considerable quantity of pork" were shipped out of the district, a not inconsiderable trade for a population of probably less than 800 people.[10] Production of the two most significant agricultural exports, beef and butter, increased by 200 and 500 per cent respectively over the period 1847-1851 to 1858-1860.[11] The rich agricultural potential and locational advantages of Middle River were drawn into the mercantile nexus of sugar and fish long before industrialization and urbanization generated nearer markets.

Markets permitted and encouraged agricultural specialization in Middle River. Because these forces did not lead to extreme — single crop or single animal — forms of agriculture, the considerable degree of specialization that did exist is often overlooked. Though a mixture of crops and livestock were raised in Middle River, this variety did not entail a concomitant "mixed" economic strategy, for the agricultural economy, as elsewhere in northeastern Nova Scotia, overwhelmingly centred on the cow.[12] By mid-century, the importance of cattle to Middle River's agricultural economy was as great, or greater, than that of wheat to the economy of the agricultural districts of Ontario during the booming

8   Annual Reports of the Middle River Agricultural Society, RG 8, vol. 16, nos. 173-195, Public Archives of Nova Scotia [PANS].

9   Letter of John McLennan cited in Archibald, "Early Scottish Settlers in Cape Breton", p. 90.

10 Annual Report of the Middle River Agricultural Society, 29 December 1847, RG 8, vol. 16, no. 185, PANS. Population estimates are based on the 1838 and 1860/61 Nova Scotia Census figures. "1838 Census of Nova Scotia", RG 1, vol. 449, nos. 55-57, PANS; Nova Scotia, Census, 1860/61, PANS.

11 Annual Reports of the Middle River Agricultural Society, RG 8, vol. 16, nos. 173-234, PANS.

12 The output of agricultural goods was calculated using the aggregate census figures. Field crop production figures were utilized as given and intermediary products deducted from the estimates. The returns to animal husbandry were calculated not on the basis of recorded slaughters and sales, but on the basis of the more reliable inventory figures through the use of production coefficients. Valuation of the farm products was based on both Halifax and local prices. Full details of the procedures used can be found in Rusty Bittermann, "Middle River: The Social Structure of Agriculture in a Nineteenth Century Cape Breton Community", M.A. thesis, University of New Brunswick, 1987, App. III and IV.

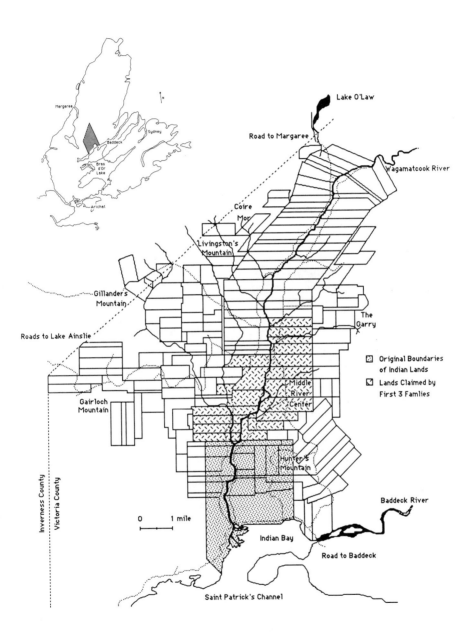

years of the wheat trade.[13] Beef and milk products accounted for roughly two-thirds of the value of all agrarian end-products in Middle River in 1860/61 (see Figure 1). As agricultural exports, beef and milk played an even more prominent role. More than 80 per cent of the agricultural exports shipped from the nearby port of Baddeck over the years 1858 to 1865 originated with the string of dairy animals.[14] Sheep and swine were important secondary agricultural products. Though roots and grain were raised, the people of Middle River specialized in livestock production and most households, to varying degrees, obtained breadstuffs by purchase. While it is possible, indeed likely, that the concentration on animal husbandry had increased over time because of failures with potato and grain crops and in response to surer and cheaper supplies of flour, the orientation toward animal husbandry is clearly discernable from the earliest reports of the Agricultural Society in the 1840s. As a consequence, hay was the pre-eminent field crop. Small grains and roots — most particularly oats and potatoes — were grown, but hay was by far the most important crop, accounting for roughly three-quarters of the value of all Middle River's field crop production.[15] The quantities of livestock that could be carried on Middle River's farms was determined by the success of this single crop, harvested in a few short weeks.

13 The relative status of wheat within the farm economy of the region which would become Ontario has been a matter of some dispute. In *Unequal Beginnings: Agricultural and Economic Development in Quebec and Ontario Until 1870* (Toronto, 1980), John McCallum claims that it accounted for roughly 75 per cent of farm receipts and contends that in terms of "cash income" it was "more important to the Ontario farmer of the 1850s than to the Saskatchewan farmer of today" (p. 24). Marvin McInnis' analysis of a sample (1100 farms) of the 1860/61 census returns for Canada West in "Marketable Surpluses in Ontario Farming, 1860", *Social Science History*, 8, 4 (Fall 1984), pp. 395-424, tends to support McCallum's figures. On these farms, wheat accounted for just under 70 per cent of total surpluses (p. 413). While not denying the "strategic" (p. 415) significance of wheat to Ontario's agrarian economy, Douglas McCalla, on the basis of a close analysis of the records from a dozen Ontario farms and roughly the same number of retail firms, has argued in "The Internal Economy of Upper Canada: New Evidence on Agricultural Marketing Before 1850", *Agricultural History*, 59 (1985), pp. 397-416 that McCallum exaggerates the relative significance of wheat. If one accepts McCallum's and McInnis' figures, the relative importance of wheat to Ontario's agriculture and cattle to that of the Middle River region are roughly the same. If, on the other hand, McCalla is correct, then cows are relatively more important to Middle River's agriculture than wheat was to that of Ontario.

14 Baddeck exports were recorded beginning in 1858. During the period from 1858 to 1865 agricultural goods averaged 88 per cent of total exports. Animal products comprised, on average, 85 per cent of these agricultural goods. Nova Scotia, House of Assembly, *Journals*, 1859-1866, "Trade Returns". The reports of the Agricultural Society, including marketing information, are found both in the *Journal of Nova Scotia Agriculture* and RG 8, vol. 16, nos. 173-234, PANS.

15 The value of field crop production was estimated from data obtained from the Nova Scotia Census, 1860/61. The prices used are available in Bittermann, "Middle River: The Social Structure of Agriculture in a Nineteenth Century Cape Breton Community", App. III.

Figure I: **Middle River Endproduct Production 1861**

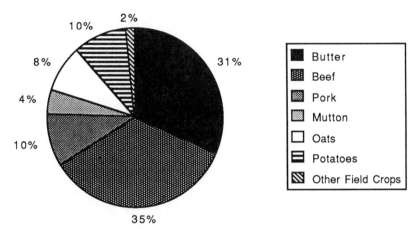

Source: Nova Scotia, Census, 1861

The landbase of the Middle River district of Cape Breton, like that of much of the Maritimes, is sharply variegated. Rich meadowland is seldom far removed from difficult upland. Varieties of soil, drainage, steepness, stoniness, and micro-climate sharply delimit the agricultural potential of different portions of the region's soils. The returns to capital and labour on the fertile intervale land along the central portions of the valley were considerably greater than those to be gained by applying similar investments to the soils found in the glens and on the hills around the periphery of the valley. With settlement, as the lines of private property encircled land assets of sharply varying potential value, this geography would come to articulate a social structure as variegated as the landscape. Each successive wave of settlers encountered the diminished crown assets left by the choices of those who had proceeded them. The costs of acquiring land did not, however, reflect its relative quality. Prior to changes in crown land policy in 1827, these differing opportunities were obtained at constant cost, one of the many mechanisms which operated to generate inequality during the course of the settlement process. Subsequently the differentiating affects of the mechanism were intentionally enlarged when a new lands policy, introduced after the best locations had been alienated, increased the cost of obtaining crown land. The new regulations, officially announced for British North America in 1827, replaced a "free land" policy with purchase by sale at auction combined with a reserve price fixed by the government.[16]

16 R.G. Riddell, "A Study of the Land Policy of the Colonial Office, 1763-1855", *Canadian Historical Review*, 18 (1937), p. 390. In Cape Breton, implementation of this policy was delayed

The first Europeans who settled in Middle River in 1811 enjoyed the strong markets engendered by the War of 1812 and by British restrictions on American trade with the British Caribbean.[17] The first three families had eight years of New World agricultural experience behind them.[18] At least two, perhaps all three, had been recruited from what one historian has described as "the more prosperous possessor class" of the tenantry of the Scottish Highlands selected for Lord Selkirk's settlements on Prince Edward Island.[19] One of these families had possessed sufficient resources to construct a vessel, purchase stock, and depart Selkirk's lands, first for more favorable areas of settlement on the Island and subsequently for Middle River.[20] All three of the first families had children reaching maturity.[21] Reportedly drawn by Middle River's rich interval lands, and possessing capital, Maritime agricultural experience, and considerable supplies of familial labour, these households were in a strong position to exploit the considerable natural resources and locational advantages of the Wagamatcook Valley.[22] Exclusive of 4500 acres of land reserved for Micmac use at the mouth of the Wagamatcook, the first three families had the pick of the lands of the district. Being veteran settlers they chose wisely. As well, they chose repeatedly. Despite their modest numbers, they were able, both through grants

for five years. "Free" land grants never were, in fact, without cost and the *actual* changes in the costs to the settler of acquiring land have yet to be closely calculated. In terms of officially sanctioned fees, Stephen Hornsby has estimated that the new land policy resulted in a fivefold increase in costs. Stephen Hornsby, "Scottish Emigration and Settlement in Early Nineteenth Century Cape Breton". Consideration of the impact these changes in land policy had on the social structure of Upper Canada is provided in Leo Johnson, "Land Policy, Population Growth and Social Structure in the Home District, 1793-1851" in J.K. Johnson, ed., *Historical Essays on Upper Canada* (Toronto, 1975), pp. 32-57, and Joy Parr, "Hired Men: Ontario Agricultural Wage Labour in Historical Perspective", *Labour/Le Travail*, 15 (Spring 1985), pp. 91-103.

17 John Young, *The Letters of Agricola on the Principles of Vegetation and Tillage* (Halifax, 1822), p. xiii; W.T. Easterbrook and Hugh G.J. Aitken, *Canadian Economic History* (Toronto, 1965), pp. 142-50, 228-38. A fuller treatment of the settlement process can be found in Bittermann, "Economic Stratification and Agrarian Settlement: Middle River in the Early Nineteenth Century", in Donovan, ed., *Cape Breton Historical Essays*.

18 John A. Nicholson *et al.*, *Middle River: Past and Present History of a Cape Breton Community 1806-1985* (Sydney, 1985), pp. 288-91; John Murray, *History of the Presbyterian Church in Cape Breton* (Truro, 1921), p. 91; Archibald, "Early Scottish Settlers in Cape Breton", p. 90.

19 J.M. Bumsted, ed., *The Collected Writings of Lord Selkirk, 1799-1809*, vol. II (Winnipeg, 1984), p. 34. See too Patrick C.T. White, *Lord Selkirk's Diary, 1803-1804: A Journal of His Travels in British North America and the Northeastern United States* (Toronto, 1958), pp. 33-5.

20 Nicholson *et al.*, *Middle River*, pp. 288-91.

21 Cape Breton Census, 1818, in D.C. Harvey, ed., *Holland's Description of Cape Breton Island and Other Documents* (Halifax, 1935), pp. 163-4.

22 A traveller's report from 1827 remarking with favour upon the "very independent circumstances" of some of the Valley's households was undoubtedly referring to some of the first families. Glasgow Colonial Society Correspondence, M-1352, p. 129, Public Archives of Canada [PAC].

and occupation, to acquire roughly 4000 acres of the best of the district's land and their acquisitions, in conjunction with the lands reserved for the Micmacs, engrossed the first seven miles of land along the lower course of the Wagamatcook River.[23] Subsequent settlers would either have to contest the claims of these families, or the Indians, or settle further upstream or on lots not bordering the river.

The next influx of settlers, like the first, did not come directly to Middle River from the Old World. Rather they came from various Atlantic locales — Newfoundland, Prince Edward Island, Nova Scotia, and elsewhere on Cape Breton. Between 1812 and 1817 at least 13 claims were made for new grants in Middle River.[24] While most of these were filed by Highlanders, two of the petitioners were from Ireland and one from England. Unlike the first families, these settlers did not persist. By 1820 when a new wave of immigrants arrived in the valley, all of those who had migrated between 1812 and 1817 had either previously vacated their grants or were willing to sell their claims to the newcomers. The reasons for their departure are not clear, but it is possible that they lacked sufficient capital to develop their claims in an environment that was initially relatively remote from work opportunities.

The third wave of immigrants, who began arriving in 1820, was the first to come directly from the Old World. Between 1820 and 1823, roughly 100 emigrants, arrayed in 23 households, joined the population established by the first three families.[25] The limited evidence available suggests both that these immigrants were not impecunious and that they applied their resources toward the development of livestock production in the district.[26] While some complained of the costs of filing land claims, virtually all appear to have acquired legal claim to their lands soon after arrival. Like the first settlers established in the valley, the newcomers were Protestant Highlanders and they took up the holdings of the immigrants of the 1812 to 1817 period and acquired all the remaining agricultural land fronting on the river. Some even encroached upon

23 It is impossible to determine precisely the amount of land they attempted to alienate. Legal claims were supplemented by occupation and/or improvement of additional lands. See for instance the petition of Donald MacRae, Series "A", Land Papers, reel no. 78, PANS. The sources for my estimates are Series "A", Land Papers, PANS; Cape Breton Land Papers, 1787-1848, PANS; Nicholson *et al.*, *Middle River*, pp. 157-266. The boundaries of the Indians' lands are indicated in "Petition of the Cape Breton Indians", RG 5, Series "GP", Miscellaneous "A", 1855-58, vol. 3, no. 163, PANS.

24 Cape Breton Land Papers, 1787-1848, PANS.

25 Series "A", Land Papers, PANS.

26 One petition reports the misfortune of a widow on a 100 acre lot, who was forced to sell her land because she lost "all her cattle" to disease. Widowhood, the possession of only 100 acres, and the specific location of her farm all suggest that she would be among the poorer of this group of immigrants. Yet her petition indicates that she possessed a number of livestock a few years after arrival in Middle River. Cape Breton Land Papers, 1787-1848, p. 243, PANS.

the claims of the first three families and a few infringed on Indian lands. As well as initiating a period of significant growth in the settlement, the influx seems to have stimulated a concern on the part of the original families to define more sharply the boundaries of their lands.

There were significant differences in the quality and quantities of land obtained by the settlers of the early 1820s and those held by the first three families and their offspring. As well as having obtained the most favorable locations, the first settlers controlled greater quantities of crown land than the subsequent immigrants. Although some of the new households with mature sons applied for multiple grants, none was able to acquire more than 500 acres. The mature male to land ratio of the first settlers was in excess of 300 acres in the mid-1820s; that of the latter group was approximately 175. Although the distinctions between households just beginning the pioneer phase and those with a decade of improvement behind them was an important factor shaping access to new opportunities and capital accumulation, their differing circumstances were shaped as well by considerable variation in the landbase they controlled. Yet, despite these distinctions, the immigrants of the early 1820s shared a number of important characteristics with the first group of settlers. With few exceptions they too had acquired lands of sufficient quantity and quality to permit rapid farm-making and to justify hopes of meeting household needs from farm resources. Although one-third of these families had left the valley by 1838, most, like the first group of settlers, would persist in their residence.[27] By and large both groups appear to have prospered in the 1820s and 1830s. The teams of oxen bearing produce to the lake shore originated with both sets of households.[28]

The final phase of settlement extended from the late 1820s to mid-century. Those arriving in the valley in this period were confronted with a sharply reduced supply of crown land. The best agricultural lands fronting on the Wagamatcook River had been claimed and these earlier claims were increasingly protected by clear title. Adding to the new settlers' difficulties were the changes in government land policy which had sharply increased the costs of acquiring crown land. Those with the last pick of public lands encountered the steepest costs. The immigrants of this period were probably the least able to bear this financial burden, since contemporary reports leave little doubt of the initial poverty of those who settled the backlands in Middle River and elsewhere in Cape Breton.[29] Many had lacked the resources even to provide for their own

27 1838 Census of Nova Scotia, RG 1, vol. 449, nos. 55-7, PANS.

28 Letter of John MacLennan, quoted in Mrs. Charles Archibald, "Early Scottish Settlers in Cape Breton", p. 90.

29 RG 5, Series "P", vol. 81, PANS; Glasgow Colonial Society Correspondence, M 1354, no. 98, no. 125, PAC; J.S. Martell, *Immigration to and Emigration from Nova Scotia, 1815-1838* (Halifax, 1942), pp. 57, 65-6, 77, 84. The pattern of increasing poverty has been noted at source too. See James Hunter, *The Making of the Crofting Community* (Edinburgh, 1976), pp. 39-49; Eric

passage across the Atlantic. Without the capital to participate in the active market in privately-held river front lands or to travel on to colonies where more valuable crown lands remained available, the last group of immigrants to enter the valley settled on crown lands located to the rear of the riverfront lands and on the Micmac lands. It is not accidental that the last group of settlers to acquire lands were also the poorest. Nor is it simply a result of the pattern of Highland out-migration. As the community grew, new socioeconomic niches were created at the bottom at the same time that the opportunities for those with modest means, capable of going elsewhere, narrowed. The geographical epithet adhering to this group of settlers, "Backlander", came to indicate not just the location of their holdings, or chronology of arrival, but, more importantly, their status and position in rural society. With few exceptions the quality of the lands they acquired made farm-making arduous and costly. Many of them, either because they had settled on Indian lands or because they lacked the means to pay for the crown lands, held their lands as squatters rather than as owner occupiers. Their legal status mirrored their precarious financial circumstances.

Because the Backlanders were confined to marginal agricultural lands, they also lost control over much of their labour power. The more marginal the land, the greater the capital and labour inputs necessary to wrest a living from the soil. Lacking the means of subsistence, the labour of Backlanders had, of necessity, to be directed off the farm in order to make ends meet. For many this proved an inescapable conundrum. Labour needed for farm-making had to be committed to off-farm employments, while the returns gained, which were needed for farm capitalization, were diminished by the demands of basic sustenance. Dreams of future independence on the land had to be weighed year by year against the advantages of applying one's labour elsewhere. Backlanders perpetually operated under the necessity of dual commitments: at issue was the relative mix of self-employment and wage work.

The fate of the Indian lands during this period is a reminder of the important role the state played in protecting the acquisitions of the first settlers from the land pressure engendered by subsequent waves of immigration. Despite the legal claim of the region's Micmacs to the lands lying along the lower three miles of the Wagamatcook River and their legal and physical resistance to its loss, squatters overran Indian lands, and subsequently persuaded the government to sanction these new property rights.[30] The intruders contended that the Micmacs

Richards, *A History of the Highland Clearances: Emigration, Protest, Reasons* (London, 1985), II, pp. 245-6.

30 Nova Scotia House of Assembly, *Journals*, 1844-5, App. 16; *ibid.*, 1847, App. 19; *ibid.*, 1849, App. 45; *ibid.*, 1851, App. 64; *ibid.*, 1860, "Indian Reserves", pp. 392-98; *ibid.*, 1860, "Report of the Committee on Indian Affairs", pp. 214-5; *ibid.*, 1862, "Indian Reserves", and "Indian Affairs", App. 29-30; *ibid.*, 1863, App. 16, "Indian Affairs", Petition of John Richard on behalf of the Indians of Wagamatcook, 1849, RG 5, Series "P", Misc. "B", vol. 49, no. 39; Petition of Paul Christmas and Andrew Christmas, 9 March 1864, RG 5, Series "P", vol. 18, no. 167.

were not utilizing their lands and that the squatters' needs, coupled with their cultivation of the soil, gave them greater claim to the property. Because they possessed quantities of land well in excess of current levels of use, many of the families located along the river frontage faced similar potential threats from the immigrants of the 1830s and 1840s. A shared Scottish heritage had not prevented these pressures from forcing a rearrangement of the property lines of well-situated Highlanders in the 1820s. In this case newcomers had pleaded the right to bring into production, and possess, lands which, though claimed, were not being utilized.[31] In subsequent decades, however, the pressure of population on resources forced a rearrangement of the property lines only of Indian holdings. Behind this pattern lay the differing degrees of protection afforded by the state to private property in land.[32]

Because the process of settlement in Middle River was differentiating, the early European residents of Middle River did not encounter one another as equals. While some of the more prosperous residents of Middle River were expanding their economic activities and constructing substantial houses during the 1830s and 1840s, many of the backlanders were fighting for their very existence. Stripped of personal resources by the capitalist transformation of the Scottish Highlands, they faced the difficulties of farm-making on marginal New World lands during unusually severe weather and the spread of diseases that ruined successive potato and grain crops.[33] Like the rural poor elsewhere in the western world during these decades, they suffered from the combined misery inflicted by agricultural failures coupled with more general economic downturns. Both their returns from the soil and their opportunities for wage work, were sharply reduced. The disparities in the personal circumstances of rich and poor were considerable. In May 1835 Kenneth MacLeod Jr., one of Middle River's wealthier farmers, expanded his holdings with the purchase of an

31 See petition of Roderick MacKenzie, 11 October 1821, reel no. 66; petition of Alexander Finalyson, 10 November 1824, reel no. 82; petition of Kenneth MacLeod Sr., 27 July 1825, reel no. 66; RG 20, Series "A", Land Papers, PANS.

32 It should be noted that the state was responding to grass roots political pressure. Some Crown officials were very sympathetic to the Indians' position and attempted to stem the erosion of their lands. Support for the squatters, however, seems to have been one of the few issues on which there was broad consensus among the Highlanders of Middle River. In part this support appears to have originated from a desire to have the roads passing across Reserve Lands improved, something which, given the statutory labour approach to road construction, would not occur without European settlement. Petition of Kenneth MacLeod *et al.*, 1 January 1839, RG 5, Series "P", vol. 106, no. 12; Petition of the Middle River Agricultural Society, 1 Feb. 1859, RG 5, Series "P", vol. 55, no. 6; Nova Scotia House of Assembly, *Journals*, 1844-5, App. 16; *ibid.*, 1847, App. 19; *ibid.*, 1849, App. 45; *ibid.*, 1851, App. 64.

33 Accounts of some of these disasters are found in Robert Morgan, " 'Poverty, wretchedness, and misery': The Great Famine in Cape Breton, 1845-1851", *Nova Scotia Historical Review*, 6, 1 (1986), pp. 88-104 and Hornsby, "Scottish Emigration and Settlement in Early Nineteenth Century Cape Breton" and "Historical Geography of Cape Breton Island", pp. 175-90.

adjacent farm for £155; the following month Peter Morrison, a backlander, mortgaged his entire farm to the Baddeck merchant C.J. Campbell for £5-13s-4d. worth of provisions.[34] One of the valley's finest stone houses was constructed in 1848, the same year that starvation was reported to be "stareing many in the face".[35] The account, probably from Middle River, of the death from exposure and weakness of "a poor woman at the head of a large and weak family in a rear settlement [who], while her husband was away was constrained in midwinter to leave her home and collect what meal she could in the settlement for her famishing children" is a story of backland circumstances.[36] Poverty, remote locale — her body was found on a footpath, not a road — and the sort of male occupational pluralism that left women and children alone for prolonged periods to fend for themselves, were regular features of life in the hill lands. During these years, when famine stalked the backlands, the reports of the Middle River Agricultural Society indicate the regular shipment of vast quantities of foodstuffs out of the district. The Secretary of the Society, while reporting in 1847 that once again the potato crop had been utterly destroyed by disease and that by spring the district would be "destitute of potatoes", continued his letter with news concerning the other crops and the happy arrival of a shipment of farm implements from the United States that would be a "great saving of time and labour".[37] Extreme poverty lived cheek by jowl with comfort and modest affluence; crises of sustenance coexisted with considerations of agricultural efficiency.

While we know that the inequalities grounded in the early years of settlement persisted, indeed deepened, during the second quarter of the 19th century, we know little about how the tensions induced by these divisions were socially handled. In times of scarcity the poor sought, and received, charity. The Reverend Norman MacLeod of the nearby community of St. Ann's has described how the human disaster induced by the potato blight of 1848 "made it impossible for the most saving to shut their ears and eyes from the alarming claims and craving of those around them, running continually from door to door, with the ghastly features of death on their very faces".[38] There are suggestions from elsewhere in rural Cape Breton that theft may have served on occasion to convey that which charity did not obtain. In the spring of 1848, H.D.

---

34 Deed Book "K", pp. 348-9, "M", p. 98.

35 W. Kidston to A. Scott, 18 April 1848, RG 8, vol. 16, no. 245, PANS.

36 Letter quoted in Archibald, "Early Scottish Settlers in Cape Breton", p. 80.

37 Annual report of the Middle River Agricultural Society, 29 December 1847, RG 8, vol. 16, no. 185, PANS. That foodstuffs were being exported from districts suffering from famine was noted in the local press. Letter to the editor, "R", *Cape Breton Spectator* (North Sydney), 3 June 1848.

38 "Letters of the Reverend Norman MacLeod, 1835-1851", in D.C. Harvey, ed., *Bulletin of the Public Archives of Nova Scotia*, 2, 1 (1939), p. 22.

Sellon travelled through the rural districts about Baddeck and St. Ann's and reported that "many that have provisions and property talk of removing to the States in the Fall, so that the little they have may not be plundered and devoured by the famishing population".[39] As well as acting as protector of private property from forcible requisitions, the state was summoned to alleviate these tensions through the provision of relief.[40] The crises were created by nature, as magistrates' reports and editorials alike agreed, but nature had exposed a social structure where some lived on the margin and others did not.

The linkage between the varied contours of the religious history of Cape Breton and the different rural class experiences of these decades deserves closer attention. Reverend Norman MacLeod, adhering to the Calvinist pole of Presbyterianism, appears to have had no difficulties justifying the very considerable wealth which he maintained in a sea of rural poverty.[41] In his view wealth was indicative of moral worth and the potato famine of the 1840s was God's response to "unthriftiness and offensive indolence".[42] But what of the evangelists whom he so roundly castigated, men like the Reverend Peter MacLean of Whycocomagh who drew crowds of thousands to his emotional religious services and who was himself from a crofter's background?[43] While some theologies provided a defense of accumulation, others may have posed a challenge to this order and/or provided succour to its victims. James Hunter has suggested that in the Highland context, evangelical religion responded to the

39 H.D. Sellon to the editor, *Cape Breton Spectator*, 12 May 1848. See too Petition of John C., 12 May 1847, RG 5, Series "P", vol. 83, no. 144, PANS; *Spirit of the Times* (Sydney), February 1848. Margaret MacPhail's novel, *Loch Bras d'Or* (Windsor, N.S., 1970), which is rooted in rural Cape Breton's rich oral traditions, portrays the prosperous mid-19th century farmer, John MacNab, as needing to secure and lock his goods from potential thieves. Her treatment of the tensions between rich and poor embraces two traditions. From the perspective of the more prosperous, the poor were "lazy fellows, who did not provide for long winter months" and who would "prowl at night to steal food and fodder". For the poor, though, MacNab was a likely target for their raids because he "seemed to have more than he needed and was considered a bit stingy and too ambitious", and he paid poorly those who worked in his fields (pp. 15-6).

40 Petition of the Magistrates of the County of Cape Breton, 12 February 1847, RG 5, Series "P", vol. 106, no. 83; H.D. Sellon to the editor, *Cape Breton Spectator*, 12 May 1848; "R" to the editor, *Cape Breton Spectator*, 3 June 1848.

41 Reverend Norman MacLeod's farm encompassed 1200 acres. In the midst of the mid-century economic and agricultural crisis it sold for the very tidy sum of $3000. Flora McPherson, *Watchman Against the World* (Toronto, 1962), pp. 147-8. The wealth of this minister was not unique. Laurie Stanley has noted the fruitful merger of ministerial duties and capital accumulation by other Presbyterian clerics. Her attempt to discern "typical" behaviour obscures the important fact that there were significant differences in outlook both among ministers and believers. *The Well-Watered Garden: The Presbyterian Church in Cape Breton, 1798-1860* (Sydney, Nova Scotia, 1983), p. 126.

42 Petition of Reverend Norman MacLeod, 18 March 1848, RG 5, Series "P", vol. 84, no. 68. See too the potato famine prayer in *Presbyterian Witness* (Halifax), 9 December 1848.

43 Stanley, *The Well-Watered Garden*, p. 133.

needs of the dispossessed.[44] In that setting, evangelicals used Biblical injunctions concerning the rights of all men to access to the fruits of the earth to challenge the property rights of great proprietors. How might such notions have been translated in a Cape Breton context that lacked such great accumulations of landed wealth and yet in which the lines of property segregated desperation from modest comfort and affluence? Those who shouldered the burden of developing the backlands in the 1830s and 1840s did not do so because these were the only lands available, but because they could not afford to compete in the market for better agricultural lands. While some backlanders struggled to develop marginal land, considerable acreages of good agricultural land acquired well in advance of the potential for use remained under forest. As late as 1871 roughly half the best (class II and III) agricultural lands in the Middle River district still had not been brought into production.[45] Although class lines were less starkly drawn in the New World, as in the Highlands the social distribution of resources underlay the economic plight of much of the population. More consideration needs to be given to the possible class dimensions of the differing religious affiliations within Cape Breton's Presbyterian community and to the social aspect of the religious disputes which agitated settlements like Middle River for much of the 19th century.[46]

How the social divisions in communities like Middle River affected the regional political experience deserves more attention as well. The cleavages and tensions between rich and poor appear to have been particularly strong in the 1840s. Letters to the editor and petitions speak of the resistance of those inhabiting "humble cottages" to the concentration of power in the hands of the wealthy. Road commissioners who were also prosperous farmers were accused of placing the poor in their debt for provisions when they ran short over the winter and then pocketing their less fortunate neighbors' share of the road monies the following spring. Magistrates were denounced for imposing fines on

---

44 Hunter, *The Making of the Crofting Community*, pp. 94-106, 159-60. See too Iain Fraser Grigor, *Mightier Than a Lord: The Highland Crofters' Struggle For the Land* (Stornoway, 1979), pp. 83, 125.

45 Estimates were established by correlating census data on land utilization with land records and modern soil maps. Canada, *Census*, 1870/71; D.B. Cann, J.I. MacDougall, and J.D. Hilchey, *Soil Survey of Cape Breton Island*, Nova Scotia Soil Survey, Report no. 12 (Truro, 1963). See Bittermann, "Middle River", App. VI.

46 Religious disputes and factional struggle for control of church property animated Middle River's Presbyterians for much of the 19th century. The clashes could at times be violent. Attempts to block the ascension of a new minister in 1864 saw rival groups armed with clubs and stones, and in at least one case a gun, battle it out at the church entrance on Sunday morning. Queen v. Simon MacRae, *et al.*, Victoria County Supreme Court Records, 1868, RG 39 "C", PANS; Petition of Alexander MacRae *et al.*, 1 February 1845, RG 5, Series GP, vol. 1, no. 122; John Murray, *History of the Presbyterian Church in Cape Breton* (Truro, 1921). Debra McNabb has raised similar questions concerning the social basis of the "New Light" movement in western Nova Scotia in "Land and Families in Horton Township", pp. 86-7.

the poor in order to requisition a labour force to work in their fields and censured for their indifference to the plight of the poor during periods of crop failure. In Middle River, those accused of the abuse of civic power reported "factions" forming and warned how "rebellion plans her accursed plots and prepares to blow settlements to ruin".[47] The scattered evidence suggests recurring conflict between front settler and backlander, rich and poor.

The implications of rural inequality can be most easily traced in the economic sphere. Differential access to resources, and the related circumstances of differences in the stages of farm-making, shaped local exchanges and patterned local relationships. Countryfolk met one another as buyers and sellers of foodstuffs and buyers and sellers of labour. They competed with one another for limited local resources. Depending upon their economic circumstances, rural residents interacted in different fashions with the broader environment in which they lived. While some households were integrated into the regional economic fabric primarily as commodity producers, others, despite having access to land, participated in markets primarily through the sale of labour.

During the 1830s and 1840s, when Backlanders repeatedly faced crises of life on the margin, the more prosperous early settlers extended their control over local resources. Because there were markets for agricultural production, and for the factors of production — such as land — used to generate these goods, the early settlers, who possessed farms of considerable productivity, were able to utilize the capital accumulated from the sale of agricultural goods, and from the increasing potential value of their farm assets, to enlarge their economic activities through purchases and investments. Some of these initiatives were directed toward acquiring more agricultural lands and making other investments to expand agricultural production. Because others did not share this affluence, the wealthier households were able to proceed beyond the limits on the extent of their agricultural production imposed by the capacities of household labour supplies. By 1860 roughly one-quarter of Middle River's farms were operating on a scale that necessitated the procurement of labour from beyond the household at harvest time.[48] These were the farms which

---

47 "Aonghus Liath" to the editor, *Spirit of the Times*, 19 July 1842; Angus MacLeod to the editor, *ibid.*; petition of Kenneth MacKenzie *et al.*, 19 May 1848, RG 5, Series "P", vol. 49, no. 168; "R" to the editor, *Cape Breton Spectator*, 3 June 1848. The conversion of road monies into farm income for the wealthier farmers through a form of debt peonage appears to have been widespread. See Captain W. Moorsom, *Letters From Nova Scotia: Comprising Sketches of a Young Country* (London, 1830), p. 288.

48 Estimates of the relationship of household labour supply to farm needs focused on the critical demands at harvest time. In the case of Middle River the key crop underpinning the agricultural regime was hay. The requirements for its harvest were calculated by combining figures concerning the length of the haying season and the labour requirements per acre with the manuscript census figures concerning the number of acres mown and the household labour force. Figures for the amount of time available for hay-making were calculated from contemporary

constituted the commercial core of agricultural production. In 1860 the most prosperous quartile of the district's farms accounted for half of the surpluses in livestock production. By contrast the least affluent half of all farm households produced only 15 per cent of the surplus production.[49] Fully 85 per cent of all livestock surpluses were the product of the wealthier two quartiles of Middle River's households. Overwhelmingly these were the farms of the first three families and the immigrants of the early 1820s and their descendents.[50]

While a significant portion of the population invested in the growing export-oriented agricultural economy of the district, a more limited group purchased hydraulic sites and established processing facilities. In the 1830s the son of one of the original three families expanded an earlier modest milling establishment by acquiring one of the best sites for hydraulic power in the district and by procuring new milling equipment. Some of the capital necessary for the expansion was raised by mortgages secured against his agricultural holdings.[51] Yet another son of one of the first three families began construction of another grist mill in 1848.[52] Two years later the grandson of one of the first families attempted to found a fulling, dying, and dressing establishment. Once again the loans for this enterprise were secured with mortgages against his valuable agricultural holdings. The capital was supplied by the Reverend Hugh MacLeod, a wealthy Presbyterian minister residing in Sydney.[53] Other substantial farmers from the district became involved in the expanding shipbuilding industry along the rim of the Bras d'Or basin. Data from the first years of settlement are lacking, but in the period 1854-1869 a cluster of prosperous Middle River farmers financed the construction of at least three vessels ranging

Maritime reports. The labour requirements of hay-making were computed on the basis of a 19th century United States government study of agricultural hand labour. A full explanation of my estimating procedure and sources is contained in Bittermann, "Middle River", App. V.

49 Surplus production was calculated on a household basis from the manuscript census returns (see note no. 12). Household consumption needs, estimated on the basis of contemporary sources concerning diet and calculated to include the differentials in adult and child caloric requirements, were deducted from gross farm livestock output calculations to generate figures for livestock production surpluses. Full details of the procedures used can be found in Bittermann, "Middle River", App. IV.

50 This was determined by linking household level analysis of the census data with the district's land records. It should be noted that because of the concentration on animal husbandry many households which did not have positive net farm incomes did have livestock surpluses.

51 Some of these were held by family members at 6 per cent interest and others by outside interests. A sum of £107 was raised from John Tempest of Dartmouth, repayable with interest over 4 years. Deed Books "N", p. 495; "T", p. 258; "N", p. 532, PANS.

52 Petition of Finlay MacRae, 14 December 1847, RG 5, Series "P", vol. 53, no. 120, PANS. It is not clear how he financed this enterprise.

53 The mortgage, dated 1850, was for £125 payable with lawful interest in 3 years — penal sum £250. Deed Books, "R", p. 394, PANS.

from 75 to 94 tons.[54] It would appear that these vessels were constructed both to serve the produce trade to Newfoundland and as speculations for resale.[55] Like their shipbuilding counterparts elsewhere in Cape Breton, these farmer-entrepreneurs relied upon the availability of cheap labour supplies for their initiatives. Because the capital requirements for all these enterprises were considerable, they tended to be the ventures of offspring of the first three families, men able to exploit the advantages gained from considerable aggregations of agricultural wealth.[56]

Even in years without severe weather conditions and crop failures, the economic strategies pursued by those occupying the other end of the agrarian spectrum were quite different. Many of Middle River's residents, from the earliest days of settlement through to the contemporary period, have found it necessary to live with one foot on the land and with the other in near and distant work environments. As Victoria County's Crown Surveyor, D.B. MacNab, observed in 1857, there was a distinct rural "class" which survived by constructing distended household economies: "by means of farming, conducted by their wives and children, and going themselves during the summer season to distant parts of the province or to the United States, they eke out the means of a scanty subsistence".[57] In the third quarter of the 19th century roughly one-half of the households in Middle River were dependent on the returns of off-farm work for their survival.[58] More than 80 per cent of these households were those of Backlanders.[59] Patterns of life which for many had begun in the Highlands were continued in Nova Scotia. Rural residents whose heritage embraced seasonal labour on Thomas Telford's canals and roads, with the Dutch herring fleet, on the Lowland "hairst", or in Scottish industrial centres, found themselves

54 John P. Parker, *Cape Breton Ships and Men* (Toronto, 1967), pp. 67, 70.

55 See the advertisement for the *Roderick MacRae* in *The Times and General Commercial Gazette* (St. John's), 26 October 1870, the year following the vessel's construction.

56 The patterns of capital accumulation in Middle River suggest that the ability of local merchants to control the terms of trade, and thus extract rural surpluses, has often been exaggerated. See, for instance, Sinclair, "From Peasants to Corporations: The Development of Capitalist Agriculture in the Maritime Provinces", p. 278. Once again the difficulty lies with the assumption of a shared rural condition. While dependence on the local merchant and the barter economy are often identified with the countryside as a whole, the evidence suggests that not all rural residents were equally powerless in the face of local terms of exchange. Some farmers were able to buy with cash and to sell directly in more distant markets; they were in a position to effectively bargain for competitive prices.

57 D.B. MacNab to Uniacke, 3 January 1857, Nova Scotia House of Assembly, *Journals*, 1857, App. 71, p. 421. See too W.J. Ousley to Uniacke, 19 February 1857, *ibid.*, App. 71, p. 413.

58 Based on a household level analysis of production and consumption using the 1860/61 and 1870/71 manuscript census returns. Full details of the procedures used can be found in Bittermann,, "Middle River", App. II-IV.

59 Household level analysis of net farm income was linked with the district's land records.

working on North American roads, canals and rail lines, with the American fishing fleet, on their neighbor's harvest, and in New World cities.[60] Improvements in North American transportation systems permitted these distended family economies to be stretched across greater distances over time. By the mid-19th century some residents of Middle River were working seasonally in the United States. By the end of the century they were involved with labour markets in the western sectors of the continent, both in the United States and in Canada. For the poorer strata, rural life was not, and had seldom been, insular.

Middle River's 19th century experience does not conform to the idea that the social organization of the countryside was an obstacle to capitalist growth and the creation of a capitalist labour market.[61] Nor does it fit well with the idea that the generation of a labour force from rural regions was primarily the result of demographic processes and population densities.[62] It was Middle River's social structure — rooted in the relative wealth of the immigrant population and in the unequal distribution of local resources — which created a peripatetic labour force constantly on the move between potential zones of wage labour. From the early years of settlement, long before there was actual pressure on the district's arable lands, many found it necessary to labour for others in order to survive. The existence of these peripatetic labourers generated opportunities for those with capital and propelled capitalist growth. The explanation for the massive growth of Cape Breton's shipbuilding industry in the mid-19th century is to be found not just in the demand created by local staples and the growth of trans-Atlantic and international trade but also in the ready supplies of cheap labour originating in the countryside.[63] So too the cyclonic development of Cape

60 A.J. Youngson, *After the Forty-Five: The Economic Impact on the Scottish Highlands* (Edinburgh, 1973), pp. 182-4; T.M. Devine, "Temporary Migration and the Scottish Highlands in the Nineteenth Century", *Economic History Review*, 32 (1979), pp. 344-59; William Howatson, "The Scottish Hairst and Seasonal Labour 1600-1870", *Scottish Studies*, 26 (1982), pp. 13-36; E.J.T. Collins, "Migrant Labour in British Agriculture in the Nineteenth Century", *Economic History Review*, 29 (1976), pp. 38-59.

61 Michael Merrill, " 'Cash is Good to Eat': Self-Sufficiency and Exchange in the Rural Economy of the United States", *Radical History Review*, 3 (1977), pp. 42-71; James Henretta, "Families and Farms Mentalité in Pre-Industrial America", *William and Mary Quarterly*, 3rd ser., 40 (1978), pp. 3-32; Allan Greer, "Wage Labour and the Transition to Capitalism: A Critique of Pentland", *Labour/Le Travail*, 15 (1985), pp. 7-24.

62 MacLean, "The Scots: Hector's Cargo", pp. 118-9, Del Muise "The Making of An Industrial Community: Cape Breton Coal Towns, 1867-1900", in Don Macgillivray and Brian Tennyson, eds., *Cape Breton Historical Essays* (Sydney, 1980), p. 81; Dunn, *Highland Settler*, pp. 124-6.

63 John P. Parker, *Cape Breton Ships and Men*; Keith Matthews, "The Shipping Industry of Atlantic Canada: Themes and Problems", in Keith Matthews and Gerald Panting, eds., *Ships and Shipbuilding in the North Atlantic Region* (St. John's, 1978), pp. 1-18. Ian McKay has noted the challenge that the abundant and cheap supply of peripatetic rural craftsmen — the "botchers" as the unionized termed them — posed to the wage rates of Haligonian carpenters, *The Craft Transformed* (Halifax, 1985), pp. 13-6.

Breton's coal industry in the late 1850s and 1860s was the product not just of the termination of the GMA monopoly, the Reciprocity Treaty, and enormous American demand, but also of the ready availability of an inexpensive rural labour force.[64] The expansion of coal mining in this period was dependent upon the labour of perhaps as many as 1500 new workers.[65] Further afield, and at other moments in the 19th century, Cape Breton's mobile, rural-based, labour force played a part in, among other things, manning the American fishing fleet, constructing Boston's streetcar suburbs, and bringing in the harvest on the Canadian prairies.[66] The social structure of rural communities like Middle River induced labour-injected patterns of economic change.

While the mobility of this labour ensured its usefulness for capitalists operating outside of the Middle River region, indeed even outside of the country, it posed difficulties for local entrepreneurs. By their movements, rural labourers brought the wage rates offered by local employers into competition with those

64 Richard Brown, *The Coal Fields and Coal Trade of the Island of Cape Breton* (London, 1871); S.A. Saunders, "The Maritime Provinces and the Reciprocity Treaty", *Dalhousie Review*, 14 October 1934), pp. 355-71.

65 An estimate of the size of the work force in and about Cape Breton's mines in 1855 was made by using Richard Brown's figures of manpower and production from 1838 to calculate roughly manpower from the production figures of 1855. Assuming a steady man/ton ratio, roughly 900 men were working at the mines in 1855. The provincial mines report from 1864 provides a partial list of the workforce employed by Cape Breton's coal mines at this time. The figures, available for 11 of the 19 mines listed in the report, indicate an "average" workforce of 1,809 for 1864. The 1864 investments for four of the other mines are given as $63,059. If we divide this by the man to investment ratio indicated with the other data — $270 per man — it would indicate that these mines perhaps employed an additional 233 men. This still leaves the workforce at four of the other enumerated mines unaccounted for. As well there were other smaller operations that are not listed in these returns. A workforce figure of 2500 for all of Cape Breton's coal mines during this period of the coal boom would probably not be far off. The number of men who had worked at the coal operations at some point over the course of the year would be yet a higher figure as there appears to have been significant turnover. Inventory by Richard Brown, RG 1, vol. 463, no. 32, PANS; Brown, *The Coal Fields and Coal Trade of the Island of Cape Breton*, pp. 98, 111-39; Nova Scotia House of Assembly, *Journals*, 1865, "Mines Report", App. 6.

66 It was estimated at mid-century that roughly 4000 Nova Scotians were working with the American fishing fleet. Many of these men were recruited from the Strait of Canso region by vessels destined for the Gulf of St. Lawrence. Paul Crowell to James Uniacke, 10 February 1852, Nova Scotia House of Assembly, *Journals*, 1852, App. 25; John MacDougall, *History of Inverness County* (Truro, 1922), p. 17. On the Boston linkage see Alan Brookes, "The Exodus: Migration From the Maritime Provinces to Boston During the Second Half of the Nineteenth Century", Ph.D. thesis, University of New Brunswick, 1978. On the involvement of Maritime labour in the Prairie harvest see A.A. MacKenzie, "Cape Breton and the Western Harvest Excursions, 1890-1928", in Ken Donovan, ed., *Cape Breton at 200: Historical Essays in Honour of the Island's Bicentennial, 1785-1985* (Sydney, 1985), pp. 71-84; W.J.C. Cherwinski, "The Incredible Harvest Excursion of 1908", *Labour/Le Travailleur*, 5 (Spring 1980), pp. 57-80; John Herd Thompson, "Bringing in the Sheaves: The Harvest Excursions, 1890-1929", *Canadian Historical Review*, 59 (1978), pp. 467-89.

available elsewhere. They pitted demand in Middle River against that in other regions and they pitted the labour rates available within the agricultural sector against those available from other sectors of the economy. The social distribution of resources in Middle River, coupled with the seasonal nature of demand for agricultural labourers, ensured that many would be involved in continuous comparison and choice-making between the returns of labour on the home-holding, the neighbor's holding, and the wages to be obtained elsewhere. Reciprocally, the uncertainties of off-farm work, no doubt, contributed to the decisions of many to maintain dual commitments, rather than cast their lot entirely to the whims of the labour market. Such comparisons could create difficulties for local farmers and others reliant upon hired labour. They placed limits on the rates of capital growth and concentration within Middle River.

During the third quarter of the 19th century, the rapid growth of the industrial economy pitted commercially-oriented farmers against very strong regional competitors for labour. The complaint of shortages of harvest labour in the countryside in the 1860s and 1870s was widespread.[67] Rural wages were not keeping abreast of industrial ones. When they laboured off their own holdings, the small farmers who had traditionally provided the supplementary labour for the harvest activities of the larger farms were altering their pluralistic strategies to operate in the more rewarding industrial sector. Larger farmers felt the pinch of this choice. As one Sydney area farmer lamented in 1871: "farmers and their sons by hundreds, nay, thousands, [are] leaving their farms to the women, and seeking employment at the collieries and railways springing up in every direction, and the cry-out here is for more hands. Can nothing be done? If it go on, we must have Chinese or Coolies".[68] Despite this particular suggestion, the response of prosperous farmers during this period focused on the demand end of their dilemma — reduction of the need for agricultural labour through mechanization — rather than on strategies designed to increase the supply of labour in the countryside. In Middle River mechanization began with the introduction of horse rakes and mowers in the 1860s. Linkage of census data concerning implement ownership with an analysis of household labour supplies indicates that the first steps in this transformation were undertaken primarily by those households lacking sufficient family labour resources to get in their hay without recourse to supplementary labour.[69] Arguably it was peripatetic labour that forced these new capital investments and the greater reliance of the more prosperous farmers on industrial sources of supply. The timing of the transformation and the hand wringing of the elite of the agrarian community

---

67 *Journal of Agriculture for Nova Scotia*, April 1865, p. 19; *Acadian Recorder* (Halifax), 3 March 1866; *Journal of Agriculture for Nova Scotia*, May 1867, p. 237; *ibid.*, July 1871, p. 652.

68 *Journal of Agriculture for Nova Scotia*, July 1871, p. 652.

69 Hay harvest labour estimates were correlated with census data on implement ownership. Canada, *Census*, 1870/71.

strongly suggest that mechanization was a response to agricultural labour moving into other areas. The machines were, perhaps, drawn into the vacuum left behind more than they acted as a force of propulsion. Once in place, however, they irreversibly transformed the patterns of work in the countryside, changing the relations between the commercial and sub-subsistence farms, and changing the relations within families.

Middle River's history does not fit well with prevailing characterizations of the rural Maritimes in the early 19th century: economic independence arising from simple access to land resources, an agriculture of self-sufficiency, social organization characterized by an equality grounded in household independence, localized life experiences. None of these prevailing myths concerning the countryside holds up well under close inspection. Is Middle River's history likely to be representative of the patterns of other agrarian Maritime communities? Certainly there are grounds for doubting the representativeness of this community study. Cape Breton's sharply varied topography and the extreme poverty of many of the Highland immigrants who peopled the region while not unique to the Maritimes — poor immigrants did settle on difficult terrain elsewhere — still might suggest that the patterns of rural social structure and development in Middle River would be limited to other similar situations. Perhaps too the particular timing of the European settlement of this district might have played an important role in shaping its social configuration. Yet Middle River's history suggests that the land form simply articulated — rather than caused — the social structure. While the initial poverty of many of the original immigrants was a factor shaping the social organization of Middle River, the presence of impecunious settlers within the district was not fortuitous. The type of economic development which occurred was fostered by general factors in no way unique to Middle River — state policy, markets for farm products, and accumulative behaviour. These created the socioeconomic niches which attracted and initially sustained (and constrained) the rural poor. Middle River was probably not an anomaly.

Debra McNabb's fine study of Horton Township during the period 1760-1830 provides a particularly useful comparison since the land base of the settlement, the nature of the immigrant population, and the chronology of the peopling of the district were quite different from those of Middle River. Horton was settled by relatively prosperous pre-Loyalist immigrants who arrived in the wake of the Acadian deportations. The lands they acquired were among the best in Nova Scotia. Yet the social structure which developed was very similar to that of Middle River in the early 19th century. McNabb argues that in Horton access to abundant land resources never produced an egalitarian society characterized by household self-sufficiency. There too economic stratification emerged in the early years of settlement and many residents lacked the agricultural resources necessary for economic independence.[70] While only further studies of other rural locations will provide truly persuasive evidence concerning the broad contours of the social landscape of the rural Maritimes in the early and mid-19th century, the evidence suggests that the patterns revealed in Middle River's case may well have been more general.

If Middle River was not an anomaly, this study indicates the need to ask new questions about the Maritime countryside and to reconsider the role of the rural population in regional history. Virtually every aspect of the rural experience, from agricultural commodity production through to family life and religious orientation, might usefully be examined and considered (or reexamined and reconsidered) in stratification-conscious terms. Studies which explain agricultural change in terms of "average" farm statistics, political behaviour in terms of a singular rural response, or provide a generalized portrait of rural ways of life need to be treated skeptically. Conceptualizing rural life in terms of household self-sufficiency and rough equality has provided a justification of sorts for the urban focus of contemporary historiography. With the exception of the supposedly inexorable pressures of demography, such a countryside is primarily static. Change originates elsewhere. To discern the currents inducing transformation one looks to the economic, social and intellectual forces arising in urban and industrial centres. Change in all its guises — markets included — originates here and "penetrates" the countryside. Middle River's history suggests the need to reconsider urban-focused explanations of regional transformation and to modify them with an appreciation of the critical role rural regions played in shaping and propelling change.

70 McNabb, "Land and Families in Horton Township", p. 72.

GAIL G. CAMPBELL

Reprinted from Vol. XVIII, No. 2
(Spring 1989)

Disfranchised but not Quiescent: Women Petitioners in New Brunswick in the Mid-19th Century*

CANADIAN WOMEN'S PARTICIPATION IN THE POLITICAL life of their society is usually dated from their struggle for and achievement of the vote.[1] Yet denial of the franchise had not prevented women from being actively involved in the political life of their communities. Indeed, from the earliest times, women had found ways to influence their government.[2] In the period prior to the introduction of manhood suffrage — a period characterized by deferential

*This paper builds on a data base that was created while I was a post-doctoral fellow at the University of New Brunswick. This particular study is part of a much broader project dealing with political culture in mid-19th century New Brunswick.

1 Although New Brunswick women were not disfranchised by statute until 1843, historians have found no record of even propertied women in the colony voting before that time. John Garner, *The Franchise and Politics in British North America, 1755-1867* (Toronto, 1969), pp. 155-6. While it is true that in debates on franchise extension in later years politicians claimed that women of the province had voted before their specific exclusion in 1843, the only evidence that has been found to support their claims is a single letter to the editor that appeared in the *Gleaner and Northumberland Shediasma* in 1830, cited in Elspeth Tulloch, *We, the undersigned: A Historical Overview of New Brunswick Women's Political and Legal Status, 1784-1984* (Moncton, 1985), pp. 3-4. Garner argues that exclusion by statute did not represent a new restraint on the franchise. For centuries, women in Great Britain had not exercised the franchise despite the lack of a formal legal restraint, having, as one judge argued, "always been considered legally incapable of voting for members of Parliament". This exclusion by convention had been accepted by the colonies as part of their legal heritage. Garner, *The Franchise and Politics*, p. 156. Indeed, evidence from extant newspapers suggests that the purpose of the 1843 statute was mainly to clarify the law in order to "promote the public peace at elections". By giving convention the weight of law, the revised statute provided county sheriffs with clear guidance in deciding whether a demanded scrutiny should be carried out. The disfranchisment of women was quite incidental to the amendments and went unnoticed by the newspapers of the day and, apparently, by their readers as well. See "The Election Law — The Loan Bill — And the Legislative Council in a Ferment", *The Standard or Frontier Gazette* (St. Andrews), 6 April 1843; "Prorogation of the Legislature", *ibid.*, 20 April 1843; *Weekly Chronicle* (Saint John), 31 March 1843 and "House of Assembly", *ibid.*, 14 April 1843; "Provincial Legislature", *The Gleaner and Northumberland, Kent, Gloucester and Restigouche Commercial and Agricultural Journal* (Miramichi), 14 February 1843, and "Editor's Department", *ibid.*, 13 March 1843; "The New Election Law", *The Loyalist* (Saint John), 23 March 1843; and "Parliamentary", *St. John Morning News and General Advertising Newspaper*, 31 March 1843.

2 For example, following a long-established European tradition, the women of New France took to the streets during the late 1750s to protest food shortages. Terence Crowley, "Thunder Gusts: Popular Disturbances in Early French Canada", Canadian Historical Association, *Historical*

politics — distinctions between men's and women's political behaviour were often blurred. Women, as well as men, regularly participated in politics by petitioning legislatures to achieve specific political goals.[3] Women, like men, were involved in creating the political culture of their society.

Political culture, which involves much more than participation in the formal political system, is shaped by those values and attitudes that are so widely accepted they are taken for granted. Such values provide the underpinnings for the development of formal political institutions and structures.[4] The role of women both in maintaining and in shaping societal values requires further investigation. While women undoubtedly had a significant indirect impact on government and politics through their influence within their own families and as members of voluntary groups and organizations within their communities, this paper will focus on women's direct political participation by analysing the nature and extent of political lobbying by women from three New Brunswick counties, as measured by the number and content of their petitions to the Legislative Assembly during the mid-19th century. In political terms, the decade selected for analysis — 1846 through 1857 — was a highly significant one. Political parties emerged during this period. Those great moral questions, temperance, and then prohibition, became, for a time at least, the major political issue. And it was on the moral issue that women began to petition the Legislature in numbers during the decade.

While petitions do not represent a new source for the historian, researchers have not normally attempted to identify petition signatories unless they happen to be active members of a specific organization. Often researchers have been satisfied to count the number of petitions, identify the specific sponsoring group

Papers (1979), pp. 19-20. And evidence from the pre-history period strongly suggests that Iroquois women, at least, had enormous political influence in their society. See especially Judith K. Brown, "Economic Organization and the Position of Women Among the Iroquois", *Ethnohistory*, 17 (1970), pp. 153-6.

3   In an article discussing the role of women in American political society, Paula Baker has made this argument very effectively. Of course, the political transition which separated male and female politics occurred much earlier in the United States where the introduction of manhood suffrage (demonstrating definitively to women that their disfranchisement was based solely on sex) and the rise of mass political parties dated from the early 19th century. Paula Baker, "The Domestication of Politics: Women and American Political Society, 1780-1920", *American Historical Review*, 89 (1984), pp. 620-47. For a review of the literature concerning the role of deference in male political behaviour during the antebellum period, see Ronald P. Formisano, "Deferential-Participant Politics: The Early Republic's Political Culture", *American Political Science Review*, 68 (1974), pp. 473-87.

4   For similar definitions of political culture, see Robert R. Alford, *Party and Society: The Anglo-American Democracies* (Chicago, 1963), pp. 2-6; Gabriel A. Almond and G. Bingham Powell Jr., *Comparative Politics: System, Process, and Policy* (2nd ed., Boston, 1978), ch. II, pp. 25-30; Ronald P. Formisano, *The Transformation of Political Culture: Massachusetts Parties, 1790s-1840s* (New York, 1983), p. 4.

and note the number of signatories.[5] In the past, then, petitions have been used only as supplementary evidence. Yet for those who wish to analyse the nature and significance of women's political role in the 19th century, petitions provide the key. Only through the medium of petition could a woman gain official access to her government or express her views about policy to the legislators. Thus, the petition provides a useful measure of the signatory's knowledge of the way government worked, her degree of interest in the issues of the day, and her attitudes concerning those issues.

Petitions and petitioners can be divided into two discrete categories. The first category includes petitioners seeking to use the law in some way: to apply for a government subsidy to which they were legally entitled, to redress a grievance, to appeal for aid at a time of personal distress, or to request a grant from public monies to carry out a worthy public project. Individual petitioners normally fall into this first category, and while such petitions do not reveal the petitioner's opinions on the issues of the day, they do suggest the extent to which she both understood the system and was able to use it to her advantage. The second category includes petitioners seeking to change the law in some way. Through the medium of the petition, they sought to influence their government, to persuade the legislators to accept their view. Occasionally such people petitioned as individuals, but usually they petitioned in concert with others. Legislators would, after all, be more inclined to take a petition seriously if they could be persuaded that a majority of their constituents supported it. Regardless of the success or failure of the petition, such documents can provide important insights concerning societal attitudes. Whether the signatories were members of an organized group with a specific platform and goals, or a group of unorganized individuals who coalesced around a specific issue, an analysis of the demographic characteristics of the supporters of the issue can enhance our understanding of political attitudes and political culture.

The petition process was a popular political strategy used by men as well as women. During the ten-year period from 1846 through 1857, between 400 and 500 petitions to the New Brunswick Legislature were received annually. On average, between 25 per cent and 30 per cent of these were rejected and approximately 50 per cent were granted, while the remainder were tabled or sent to Committee. However, if they persisted in their petitions, even those who had initially been rejected could eventually achieve their goals. Moreover, legislators

---

5 See, for example, Carol Lee Bacchi, *Liberation Deferred? The Ideas of the English-Canadian Suffragists, 1877-1918* (Toronto, 1982), pp. 34, 38, 75, 82, 143; Catherine Cleverdon, *The Woman Suffrage Movement in Canada* (Toronto, 1970), pp. 23-110, 160-220; Wendy Mitchinson, "The WCTU: 'For God, Home and Native Land': A Study in Nineteenth Century Feminism", in Linda Kealey, ed., *A Not Unreasonable Claim: Women and Reform in Canada, 1880-1920s* (Toronto, 1979), pp. 155-6.

did not prove more responsive to petitions from men whose votes they might risk losing at the next election.[6] Although a minority among petitioners, women demonstrated their ability to use the strategy effectively.

This study is concerned with the women petitioners of the counties of Charlotte, Sunbury and Albert in the mid-19th century. All three counties are in the southern half of the province. Charlotte is a large, economically diverse county in the south-west corner. Sunbury is an agricultural county in the central region, just east of Fredericton; and Albert is in the south-east region between Saint John and Moncton, on the Bay of Fundy. Although originally selected because of the richness of their sources for the study of political history, Albert, Charlotte and Sunbury proved typical in many ways. Thus, while these three counties cannot be considered a microcosm of the province as a whole, they did encompass a broad spectrum of 19th century anglophone New Brunswick society, including areas of pre-Loyalist, Loyalist and post-Loyalist settlement and encompassing rural communities, villages and even large towns. Moreover, one-fifth of New Brunswick's petitioners came from one of these three counties.[7]

Together the three counties included over 30,000 people at mid-century, nearly half of them female. A large majority of those people (over 80 per cent) lived in nuclear families, although a small minority of such families (perhaps as many as 10 per cent) included one or more single or widowed relations, apprentices, boarders or servants. Over 80 per cent of the inhabitants had been born in New Brunswick of American or British stock. Of the immigrant population, nearly 70 per cent had been born in Ireland. Although the three counties included substantial numbers of Episcopalians, Baptists, Presbyterians, Roman Catholics and Methodists as well as a few Universalists and Congregationalists, among others, in both Albert and Sunbury the Baptists were stronger by far than any

6 Although these figures represent the average yearly percentages, the success rate varied significantly from year to year, with legislators proving decidedly more sympathetic some years than others. But in no case did male petitioners prove more successful than their female counterparts. Even election years did not necessarily bring a greater likelihood of success than other years. Petitions to the New Brunswick Legislature are located in Record Group 4, Record Series 24, 1846-57/Petitions [RG4, RS24, 1846-57/Pe], Provincial Archives of New Brunswick [PANB]. It is also possible that the success rate of certain types of petitions varied over time. In her analysis of the WCTU and its impact, for example, Wendy Mitchinson has suggested that the petition campaign was not a particularly effective strategy and that women were naïve in their belief that they could achieve legislative change through the medium of petition. Mitchinson, "The WCTU", p. 156. If women were naïve in this belief, however, they were certainly not alone, for the majority of petitioners were men.

7 Of the 5,081 petitions considered, 1,029 originated in one of the three counties. This suggests that the people of Albert, Charlotte and Sunbury were slightly over-represented among the colony's petitioners, comprising 20.25 per cent of petitioners as compared to 16.3 per cent of the total population of the province. (The discrepancy is not statistically significant, however, as differences of plus or minus five per cent could occur entirely by chance.)

other denomination, comprising almost 62 per cent of Albert's population and one half of Sunbury's population in 1861.[8]

In both Albert and Sunbury counties, the farm sector accounted for more than half the workers. Even in Charlotte County, which contained very little good agricultural land, over one-third of the population were engaged in agriculture, providing for the needs of the fishery and the lumbering industry. Fifteen per cent of Charlotte's families were employed in the fishery while one-quarter of that county's population depended on the lumbering industry for their livelihood. In each of the three counties 17 per cent of those whose occupation was listed were skilled artisans; a further 15 per cent listed their occupation merely as labourer; and approximately four per cent of all families were headed by merchants and professional men.[9] While the men were occupied in the farming, fishing, and lumbering industries, or as skilled artisans or professionals, the women were scarcely idle. Approximately one in every four women of child-bearing age actually bore a child in 1851 and, aside from running their households and caring for the needs of their 14,600 children, the 6,289 women of the three counties churned 689,363 pounds of butter and wove 94,019 yards of cloth on their hand looms.[10] Yet, despite the demands of their busy and productive lives, hundreds of women in the three counties found the time to petition their government.

A wide variety of motives persuaded these women to put their names to petitions. Many of the women in the first category of petitioners — those who sought to use the law in some way — were widows seeking financial compensation or support which they knew was their due. A cursory examination of their petitions would seem to give credence to the common notion that women were "forever dependent" on men, and that women who lost their husbands were left destitute, dependent on their sons, family or the charity of the

8   Information on denominational affiliation is not available for 1851 and therefore the 1861 census was used in this case. See *The Census of the Province of New Brunswick, 1861* (St. John, 1862).

9   Unless otherwise noted, all information contained in the demographic profiles provided for the three counties under study is drawn from *The Census of the Province of New Brunswick, 1851* (St. John, 1852).

10 The 6,289 figure refers only to women over the age of 20. For a discussion of women's role in the dairying industry in British North America during this period, see Marjorie Griffin Cohen, "The Decline of Women in Canadian Dairying", in Alison Prentice and Susan Mann Trofimenkoff, eds., *The Neglected Majority: Essays in Canadian Women's History, Volume 2* (Toronto, 1985), pp. 61-70, and *Women's Work, Markets, and Economic Development in Nineteenth-Century Ontario* (Toronto, 1988), pp. 59-117. While the 1851 census does not specify who the weavers are, the manuscript census of manufacturing for 1861 indicates that virtually all of the hand loom weavers engaged in this cottage industry were women. The manuscript census of manufacturing for 1871 also supports this assumption. See Manuscript Census for Charlotte County, 1861 and 1871, PANB.

public for support.[11] A more careful reading of the individual petitions leads to quite a different interpretation. Unless their husbands had been soldiers, widows did not generally petition the Legislature for support and those rare women who did appeal to their government for aid at a time of personal distress were not begging for charity or long-term support. In fact, most such petitioners were following an accepted and established formula used by men as well as women, to request compensation for the sacrifices they had made for their country and their community.

In 1848, for example, Margaret Baldwin, widow of the late Thomas Baldwin, of St. Andrews Parish in Charlotte County, petitioned the Legislative Assembly for help. Her husband had been employed in the early part of the previous summer by the medical attendant at Hospital Island to help with the care of sick and destitute 'emigrants'. He proved so satisfactory in the discharge of his duties that when a second group of 'emigrants' arrived later in the year he was employed a second time. This time, however, he contracted typhus fever and died, leaving his wife destitute with no means of support for either herself or their two children.[12] Margaret Tufts faced a similar situation. Her husband, Benjamin, had also been employed on Hospital Island. He had been contracted to erect the pest house and repair the public buildings. While he was so employed, a large number of sick 'emigrants' were landed on the island and Benjamin "devoted all his spare time in administering to the wants of the sick". While so engaged, he was himself taken ill with typhus fever of which, in a few days, he died, leaving his wife destitute, with "a large and helpless family" to support. In petitioning her government for help, Mrs. Tufts pointed out that she had, since her husband's death, subsisted on the meagre sum of £10, the balance owing to him at that time. At the time when she filed her petition, she had no visible way of making a living and feared that she must, for the coming winter at least, be dependent on the sympathy of the public.[13]

Both Margaret Baldwin and Margaret Tufts received grants from a sympathetic Legislature. On the surface, these two petitions, which were the only petitions of this general nature to be submitted during the entire decade, appear

11 This view of women as forever dependent on men is argued by Rosemary Ball, " 'A Perfect Farmer's Wife': Women in 19th Century Rural Ontario", *Canada: An Historical Magazine* (December 1975), pp. 2-21. And even historians like David Gagan, who recognize that "the fact of subordination was partially, if not wholly, mitigated by environment which cast women in a central role in the farm family's struggle to improve, and endure" often conclude that "for those women who outlived their partners, widowhood...was a calamity the consequence of which clearly troubled even the stoutest hearts". David Gagan, *Hopeful Travellers: Families, Land, and Social Change in Mid-Victorian Peel County, Canada West* (Toronto, 1981), pp. 89-90.

12 RG4, RS24, 1848/Pe 4, PANB.

13 RG4, RS24, 1848/Pe 5, PANB.

to be the kind one might expect from women. However, although these petitions do point out these women's potentially destitute condition, that is not the focal point of their arguments. Margaret Baldwin and Margaret Tufts were not asking their government for charity: they were demanding, in very proper and formulaic terms, money they believed to be their just due in consideration of the services their husbands had rendered to their community. Having received their grants, neither woman saw fit to petition for money a second time. Margaret Baldwin and her family soon left the parish, while Margaret Tufts managed by sharing a house with another family and taking in a lodger. [14]

A more unusual widow's petition came from Mary Ann Storr. Mrs. Storr and her family had made their entry into the province in April 1854, by way of Partridge Island. Her husband had died there, a victim of the cholera epidemic. In 1855, Mary Ann and her children were living in St. Andrews Parish in Charlotte County. In that year Mrs. Storr petitioned for, and was granted, compensation for the clothing and bedding of herself and her children which had been destroyed by direction of the authorities at the Quarantine Station in an effort to prevent the spread of cholera. Mrs. Storr was not asking for charity, only for just compensation. [15]

The majority of widows who petitioned the Legislature were the widows of 'old soldiers', men who had fought in the American Revolution. The "Act for the Relief of Old Soldiers of the Revolutionary War and their Widows", passed on 28 March 1839, entitled widows of veterans to an annual pension of £10. Despite the formulaic nature of their petitions, it would seem that the women themselves initiated their petitions, and continued to press their claims against apparently deaf officials until they were satisfied. Many such petitions referred to the women as indigent, if not destitute, and assured the Legislature that the petitioner had insufficient property to support herself and had not divested herself of any property in order to be eligible for a pension under the terms of the Act. Most of the women who applied for the widow's pension reported that their husbands had, in the past, been recipients of the pension. [16] An analysis of the

14 New Brunswick Manuscript Census, 1851, PANB. Not only were women less likely to petition their government for charity than were men, the Overseers of the Poor in each parish, in requesting reimbursement for monies expended on poor relief, more often listed men than women as recipients of that relief. On the rare occasions when individual men and women did petition their government for help in times of distress, they pressed their claims in very similar ways.

15 RG4, RS24, 1855/Pe 162, PANB.

16 See *Acts of the General Assembly of Her Majesty's Province of New Brunswick* (Fredericton, 1839-45), 2 Victoria, Chapter 27; amended 4 Victoria, Chapter 16 and 6 Victoria, Chapter 36. Under the terms of the Act widows were eligible for the same annual pensions their husbands had received. Moreover, the eligibility clauses in the oath drew no distinction between veterans and their widows: the formulaic wording for initial applications, as set out in the 1839 Act, was the same for both.

content of their petitions indicates that these were not desperate and destitute women begging for charity, but, rather, capable and competent women claiming and, if necessary, persisting in claiming pensions as their right. And they needed to be persistent. Although widows' pensions were routinely granted by the Legislature, some such petitions were rejected. Seven of the women who applied for the pension received at least one rejection by the Legislature. Jerusha Black, who was living in Pennfield Parish, Charlotte County at the time of her husband's death in 1846, left that parish after his death and her first petition was filed from St. George Parish in 1848. She was granted her pension that year, but the following year, when she applied from St. David Parish, she was denied support. Back in St. George in 1850, she received her pension once more. The following year, at age 79, she returned to her childhood home, Campobello Island, where she and John Black had married in 1793. There is no record of her application in that year, but in the following year, 1852, she was receiving her pension in Campobello.[17]

Of the 23 women who petitioned the Legislature for pensions as the widows of 'old soldiers', only six were able to sign their own names. But, illiterate or not, these women were apparently responsible for initiating their own petitions. Thus, in 1852, Nancy Leonard, of West Isles in Charlotte County, requested that she be granted her pension for the previous year as well. She noted that "on account of ill health and great infirmity your petitioner neglected to furnish the usual petition as she had previously done for these nine years".[18] Ruth McFarlane, of St. Patrick Parish in the same county, had been receiving the allowance of £10 by annual application since her husband's death in 1841. However, as she explained in her petition of 1849, in 1848 she had been told by county officials that there was no need to petition each year. As a result of this misinformation, she had not petitioned and she had not received her pension for 1848. Mrs. McFarlane, at 82, may have been "infirm and poor", but she knew her rights; she requested, and was granted, £20.[19] Martha Pendleton, of West Isles, was equally annoyed with the apparent incompetency of local officials. Her husband, who had regularly received a pension as an 'old soldier', died in 1845, leaving her with no property or other means of support. According to her petition of 1849, she had filed petitions each year following his death but had received no pension. Upon inquiry, she was informed that her petitions had been mislaid.[20] By the winter of 1849-50, she had reason to believe that her persistence

---

17 RG4, RS24, 1848/Pe 152; 1849/Pe 13; 1850/Pe 56; 1852/Pe 67, PANB.

18 RG4, RS24, 1852/Pe 68, PANB.

19 RG4, RS24, 1849/Pe 39, PANB.

20 Nor has any earlier petition from Martha Pendleton been found among the petitions to the Legislature.

had finally been rewarded, for the Legislature awarded her £30 for the three years she had been without support. She was informed that her application had been granted and that payment would be made through the Clerk of the Peace. Mrs. Pendleton's triumph proved short lived, for, as she reported in her petition of 1850, the Clerk had only agreed to certify her petition for £10, thereby depriving her of the retroactive award.[21] Petitioners, even elderly and infirm ones, could not count on local officials to look after their interests, since the officials were not always cooperative or even very well informed.

That women were aware of their rights, and counted on their government to uphold and protect those rights is nowhere more evident than in the case of the large group of young single women who fall within the first category of petititioners. Teachers, regardless of their sex, were required to petition the Legislature in order to receive the provincial school allowance. The licensing procedure was the same for both men and women, and only licensed teachers were eligible to receive the provincial subsidy. Although the criteria changed somewhat during the decade, as the Normal School was established and became generally accepted, the change was gradual and the basic requirements remained consistent until 1853, when the requirement that teachers petition the Legislature directly was dropped. Women remained at a disadvantage throughout the period. The School Act of 1837, which eliminated the previous distinction between a grant issued to a female teacher and one issued to a male, also stipulated that not more than three women teachers per parish were eligible for certification by the trustees in their semi-annual reports. Moreover, the School Act of 1852 restored the distinction between grants issued to male and female teachers. Women teachers holding a third class certificate were to receive £4 less than their male counterparts while grants to women who had attained a first class certificate were a full £10 lower than those received by men who held first class certificates. The community also had a significant responsibility in the process, for the school proprietors were required to provide a building and to match the amount paid by the province and teachers' petitions had to be certified by the local trustees.[22]

For Alice Thomson of Charlotte County, the fact that only three female teachers per parish could apply for the provincial allowance meant that although she had taught in St. Andrews for 18 months, she received the provincial allowance for only the first six. In her petition of 1847, she informed the legislators that the trustees had refused to report her for the last 12 months "by reason of the too great number of female schools in the parish at that

21 RG4, RS24, 1850/Pe 42, PANB.

22 Katherine F.C. MacNaughton, *The Development of the Theory and Practice of Education in New Brunswick, 1784-1900* (Fredericton, 1946), pp. 89, 149.

time".[23] This was a not infrequent occurrence in St. Andrews, which was a large parish. In 1849, both Lydia Thomson and Mary O'Neill reported that, although they had been certified by the trustees, their petitions of the previous year could not be returned to the Legislature "as the number of female schools allowed by law had already passed".[24] Nor was the problem confined to large and populous parishes. Susannah Rogers of Coverdale, the smallest parish in Albert County, reported in 1850 that she could not be certified in the usual way for 1849 because the parish had exceeded its allotment of female school teachers.[25] These four young women, faced with an obstacle their male counterparts did not have to deal with, persisted in pressing their claims and all four eventually received their allowances, delayed by a full year in each case.

Nonetheless, the legal restriction did have the desired effect: significantly fewer women than men applied for the provincial subsidy each year. In Sunbury County only two of the 15 petitions from teachers were from women, and one of those was requesting remuneration not for her services, but rather for the services of her late husband. In Albert four of the 28 petitioning teachers were women. But in Charlotte County 45 of the 96 teachers who petitioned the Legislature for remuneration were women, and, although one of the female petitions was from a woman requesting the school allowance due her late husband, one of the male petitioners was requesting payment for the services of his late wife, while another was claiming the school allowance of his late daughter.

In some cases teachers counted on the good will of their employers when accepting teaching positions. When they responded to 'emergency' situations, teachers recognized that they were taking a risk which would make them vulnerable to rejection. This is clearly evidenced by the cogent arguments such teachers developed in their efforts to convince legislators to grant them an allowance to which they were not legally entitled. Women were more likely than men to respond to 'emergency' situations, and occasionally they suffered as a result. Isabella Fogg, of St. Patrick, a licensed teacher of the third class, agreed to step into the breach while the man who had been teaching in her district went off to attend the Training School in Fredericton. When he returned she was obliged to close her school. Six months of continuous teaching were required in order to be eligible for the provincial subsidy and Isabella's school had been open for only three months. She argued her case so effectively, however, that the legislators granted her petition to be paid for those three months.[26] Other

23 RG4, RS24, 1847/Pe 471, PANB.
24 RG4, RS24, 1849/Pe 91; 1849/Pe 209, PANB.
25 RG4, RS24, 1850/Pe 21, PANB.
26 RG4, RS24, 1851/Pe 35, PANB.

women were not so lucky. Sophia Flagg of Campobello lived in a district which had been unable to attract a licensed teacher. When approached by the local trustees, she agreed to help out in the hope that, allowing for the circumstances, she might be granted the usual subsidy. She taught for six months but her petition for the provincial school allowance met with rejection.[27] Mary Hitchings of St. Stephen taught in a remote district of that parish for nine months in 1845. She did not apply for a licence because she "did not contemplate pursuing the business of teaching but was induced to teach as long as she did from the solicitation of a number of inhabitants in the district and from its destitute condition as to the means of education". Her application for the provincial allowance was rejected because she did not have a licence.[28] Rebecca Pratt of St. George agreed to teach on Pleasant Ridge in St. Patrick Parish despite the fact that the few poor inhabitants could not afford to remunerate a teacher. She taught for six months in the hope of receiving the provincial allowance, but her petition was denied.[29] Male teachers rarely put themselves in such vulnerable situations.[30]

In some cases the trustees themselves proved peculiarly lax, often at the expense of female teachers. In St. David Parish in Charlotte County, women teachers frequently found themselves at the mercy of seemingly incompetent trustees. In 1845, Mary Jane Perkins, a native of the parish, completed her education and applied for her teaching licence. She filled out all the necessary papers and paid the 30s fee. Then she accepted a job teaching school in the parish. However, when it came time to certify her for the provincial allowance, she was told her papers had been lost.[31] Susan Rogers was also teaching in the parish in 1846. She had passed her licensing examination in 1839 and had been duly certified as qualified to teach spelling, reading, writing, arithmetic and English grammar. When her licence was cancelled, she had immediately applied for a new one but had been told that renewal was unnecessary. Since then the trustees had apparently changed their minds, for they refused to certify her petition in the usual manner because her licence had not been renewed.[32] Just two years later Rachel Hawes faced a similar problem. An 18 year old native of the parish, Rachel had been employed to teach for a six month period. Yet she was discouraged from applying for her teacher's licence. She was told not to go to the expense because "licences would soon be cancelled and issued only from

27 RG4, RS24, 1849/Pe 95, PANB.

28 RG4, RS24, 1848/Pe 158, PANB.

29 RG4, RS24, 1848/Pe 131, PANB.

30 Two per cent of male teachers as compared to 10 per cent of female teachers fall into this category

31 RG4, RS24, 1846/Pe 60, PANB.

32 RG4, RS24, 1846/Pe 261, PANB.

the Training School".[33] In order to grant the petitions of these three young women, the legislators were required to exhibit extraordinary flexibility in their interpretation of the law. The women had understood the provisions of the law and had attempted to comply with them, yet had been prevented from doing so by the trustees, the men who should have understood the School Act better than anyone else, since they were responsible for its enforcement. In the end, not one of the women involved was denied her allowance. Yet it is perhaps significant that no male teacher in any parish reported having been told by the trustees not to bother applying for a licence.

Some of the reasons for rejection were, of course, common to both men and women. Young single teachers of both sexes proved very mobile. One of the most common problems encountered by both men and women involved their failure to transfer their licences when moving from parish to parish. Fortunately the legislators proved flexible concerning this rule, often allowing teachers to renew their licences 'after the fact'. Yet whether the problems they faced were shared by both sexes or clearly gender related, women teachers demonstrated their superior skill in the petitioning process. Three of Sunbury's 15 teachers received rejections from the legislators: all three were male. Rejection was rare for Albert County petitioners with only two of the 28 petitions being turned down by the Legislature, both of them from men. In Charlotte County, 18 male petitioners and seven female petitioners were rejected. In general, it appears that women were not more likely to be rejected than were their male counterparts.[34] Moreover, as in the case of soldiers' widows, it was the women themselves who pressed their claims and ultimately, sometimes through sheer doggedness, gained their allowance.

Married women did not typically petition the Legislature as individuals.[35] Nor did they sign petitions calling for the building of roads, wharfs, bridges and other public works. They did not petition for the incorporation of either the Roman Catholic bishop or the Loyal Orange Order. Nor did they join in requests for the division of parishes or the creation of free ports. Their husbands, in contrast, did all these things. The failure of women to become involved in such lobbying campaigns can cause historians to draw misleading conclusions about women and their role within the broader society. Because 19th century women were denied the vote and because they did not lobby their

---

33 RG4, RS24, 1848/Pe 162, PANB.

34 RG4, RS24, 1846/Pe; 1847/Pe; 1848/Pe; 1849/Pe; 1850/Pe; 1851/Pe; 1852/Pe, PANB.

35 There were four exceptions to this general rule in the three counties during the twelve year period under study. They include a woman who had been named executrix of her father's estate and three married teachers. One of the latter had continued to teach after her marriage while the remaining two were applying for allowances earned prior to marriage. See RG4, RS24, 1851/Pe 239; 1852/Pe 25; 1849/Pe 84; 1850/Pe 49.

Legislature as part of an organized group, it has been assumed that women were not knowledgable about political issues and that they were not active politically. Politics has been regarded as an activity outside the 19th century woman's 'proper sphere', as defined for her by a patriarchal society and women's political involvement is usually dated from the rise of provincial and national women's organizations in the late 19th century. The political awareness evinced by the women who joined such organizations is viewed as a new departure which saw women becoming active outside the domestic sphere for the first time.[36] Yet there was a far greater degree of continuity than such interpretations would lead one to expect. At least some married women in mid-19th century New Brunswick understood the system and quickly learned to use it effectively. These women had stepped beyond the domestic sphere long before the advent of national, or even provincial women's organizations.

Take the case of John and Alice Wilson of St. Andrews Parish in Charlotte County. John was a highly successful merchant. In 1851 he was 64 years old. Alice, his American-born wife, was 58. According to the census of that year, their household also included a hired man, two female servants, and an errand boy. John and Alice had sundry relatives living in the parish including their married son Thomas, a lawyer, and John's two younger brothers who were also merchants. Between 1846 and his death in 1855, John Wilson petitioned the Legislature no less than 21 times. Some of the petitions he initiated involved lobbying for parish improvements, while others were more personal in nature. In 1847, for example, he petitioned for and received a grant of money to improve Dark Harbour, Grand Manan. In 1849 he asked to be reimbursed for the money he had expended in the care and maintenance of 'emigrants' from Ireland brought over to work for the St. Andrews and Quebec Railroad Company, of which he was president. His petition was rejected. In 1851 he requested a further

---

36 For a discussion of women's lack of power within the family, see Margaret Conrad, "'Sundays Always Make Me Think of Home': Time and Place in Canadian Women's History", in Veronica Strong-Boag and Anita Clair Fellman, eds., *Rethinking Canada: The Promise of Women's History* (Toronto, 1986), pp. 69, 75-7. For examples of the view that the rise of provincial and national women's organizations signalled a 'new day' for women in terms of political activity, see Deborah Gorham, "Flora MacDonald Denison: Canadian Feminist", in Kealey, ed., *A Not Unreasonable Claim*, pp. 48, 58-64; Wendy Mitchinson, "The WCTU", pp. 152-4, 166-7; and Veronica Strong-Boag, "'Setting the Stage': National Organization and the Women's Movement in the Late 19th Century", in Susan Mann Trofimenkoff and Alison Prentice, eds., *The Neglected Majority: Essays in Canadian Women's History* (Toronto, 1977), pp. 87-103. Historians have not altogether ignored women's political activity during this period, but in general women's participation in the petitioning process has been characterized as exceptional rather than normal. For the best discussion of women's political activity during this period, see Alison Prentice, Paula Borne, Gail Cuthbert Brandt, Beth Light, Wendy Mitchinson and Naomi Black, *Canadian Women: A History* (Toronto, 1988), pp. 105, 174-5 (for references to petitions and petitioners, pp. 70, 81, 102, 105).

grant to deepen the channel at Dark Harbour, which was, he argued, the only safe harbour in the area in the event of a storm. Once more the Legislature granted his request. In 1855 he requested yet another grant for the purpose of further improvements at Dark Harbour.[37]

During that entire decade, Alice Wilson did not sign a single petition to the Legislature. But there is every reason to assume that she understood precisely what her husband had been doing. In his will, John named his "dear wife Alice" his sole executrix, leaving her all his "real estate viz. land, buildings, mills, wharfs, stores" as well as all his "personal estate of every description consisting of household furniture, all my books, debts, notes of hand, bonds, bank stock, bridge and steamboat stock, money, vessels and of all description property termed personal estate".[38] John's obvious faith in the abilities of his 'dear wife Alice' proved fully justified. Less than a year after his death, Alice petitioned the Legislature for the first time. She asked to be reimbursed the amount expended by her late husband in opening and improving Dark Harbour, Grand Manan. The following year she petitioned for the appointment of a person to look into the expenses incurred by her late husband in constructing a breakwater at Dark Harbour. That same year she requested that the government suspend the issue of debentures to the New Brunswick and Canada Railroad and Land Company until reparation had been made her for the claims of her late husband. When that request was tabled, she followed it up with a second petition.[39] Clearly Alice Wilson was a force to be reckoned with. Indeed, her immediate facility with the petition process makes one wonder if perhaps Alice had not always been the 'petitioner' in the family. Whatever her role may have been in the process while her husband was alive, after his death she quickly proved herself fully capable of handling his affairs. While Alice Wilson is undoubtedly the best example of a widow who used petitions to promote her business interests after the death of her husband, she was by no means the only example.[40]

Custom — and perhaps some husbands — prevented married women from signing more petitions dealing with individual and family affairs, but one should not assume either a lack of knowledge about or a lack of interest in the political system and the way it worked, on the part of such women. Moreover, starting in 1853, married women began to sign petitions in numbers. The petitions they signed were qualitatively different from the petitions women had signed up to

37 RG4, RS24, 1846/Pe 285; 1847/Pe 67, 116, 154, 313, 402; 1848/Pe 365, 389; 1849/Pe 7, 89, 355; 1851/Pe 333, 334; 1852/Pe 320, 321; 1853/Pe 260; 1854/Pe 37, 105, 354; 1855/Pe 291, 292, PANB.

38 Charlotte County Probate Court Records, RG7, RS63B3, 1852, PANB.

39 RG4, RS24, 1856/Pe 5; 1857-58/Pe 7, 9, 164, PANB.

40 For examples of other widows who were involved in the economic life of their communities, see RG4, RS24, 1846/Pe 216; 1849/Pe 195; 1852/Pe 17, 202; 1854/Pe 215, 225, PANB.

that time. Such women fell into the second category of petitioners: those who sought to change the law. The issue that finally mobilized them to take up their pens was, not surprisingly, a reform issue. By the final decades of the century it would be an issue closely associated with the organized women's movement. The issue was temperance.

The temperance movement was well entrenched in New Brunswick by 1853, the first formal temperance organization having been established in 1830. Drawing inspiration and encouragement from both Great Britain and the United States, the New Brunswick movement had gained ground steadily throughout the 1830s and 1840s.[41] Temperance societies were established in Fredericton, Saint John, Dorchester, Chatham, St. Stephen and St. Andrews and temperance *soirées* and teas were very popular.[42] During the early years, the goal had been to encourage moderation and sobriety but by the mid-1840s many temperance activists were advocating total abstinence.[43] As the depression of the late 1840s began, temperance advocates, in their search for explanations, increasingly associated drinking with the broad social problems of crime and poverty.[44] In 1847, the Sons of Temperance, the most successful of the American total-abstinence organizations, established its first division in British North America at St. Stephen, New Brunswick. The Sons of Temperance and its affiliates, the Daughters of Temperance and the Cadets of Temperance, had

41 For evidence of British and American influences, see J. K. Chapman, "The Mid-Nineteenth Century Temperance Movement in New Brunswick and Maine", *Canadian Historical Review*, 35 (1954), pp. 43, 48-50 and T. W. Acheson, *Saint John: The Making of a Colonial Urban Community* (Toronto, 1985), pp. 140-50. Analysts of the 19th century temperance movements in Great Britain and the United States tend to characterize the movement as an Anglo-American crusade. The American and British campaigns began at the same time and nourished each other. See, for example, Brian Harrison, *Drink and the Victorians: The Temperance Question in England, 1815-1872* (Pittsburgh, 1971), pp. 99-103; W. R. Lambert, *Drink and Sobriety in Victorian Wales, c. 1820-c. 1895* (Cardiff, 1983), pp. 59-61; and Ian R. Tyrell, *Sobering Up: From Temperance to Prohibition in Antebellum America, 1800-1860* (Westport CT, 1979), pp. 135, 299.

42 Chapman, "The Mid-Nineteenth Century Temperance Movement", p. 48.

43 Acheson, *Saint John*, p. 138. The British and American movements had made this shift somewhat earlier. Teetotalism had gained popularity in Britain by the late 1830s while the "Washingtonians" popularized teetotalism in the United States after their inception in 1840. Lambert, *Drink and Sobriety*, p. 59; Tyrrell, *Sobering Up*, pp. 135-90.

44 While the prohibition advocates of a later period would focus on the effects of drinking on individual families, the women petitioners of this early period, like their male counterparts, regarded drinking as a community rather than a family problem. The petitions that went beyond a formulaic request for the enactment of "a Law to prevent the importation, manufacture and sale of all intoxicating Liquors within this Province", generally decried intemperance as "a great public evil". As the authors of one 1851 petition succinctly put it, "your petitioners are convinced that crime, pauperism and lunacy in nine cases out of ten are the direct result of drinking habits". See RG4, RS24, 1846/Pe 45; 1848/Pe 270; 1849/Pe 87; 1849/Pe 151; 1849/Pe 363; 1851/Pe 228; 1854/Pe 220; 1854/Pe 394; 1854/Pe 395; 1854/Pe 404; 1854/Pe 465.

widespread appeal. Teas, picnics, and steamer excursions provided family diversions and attracted many to the great crusade.[45] By 1850 there were branches all over the southern part of the province.[46]

For many years temperance advocates sought to achieve their goals by moral suasion, but by the late 1840s some had become convinced that moral suasion alone was not enough. For a time, they focussed their efforts on gaining control of liquor consumption within their own communities through attempts to secure limitations on the number of tavern licences issued by county and city councils.[47] But such efforts proved unsuccessful. In Maine, temperance crusaders facing a similar failure had appealed to a higher authority. By 1851 they had gained enough support in the Legislature there to achieve an effective prohibition law. The 'Maine Law', which was the first prohibitory liquor law in North America, had a significant effect on the New Brunswick temperance movement. In 1852, a so-called 'monster petition' calling for the prohibition of the importation of alcoholic beverages was presented to the House of Assembly.[48] The 9000 signatures on the petition so impressed the province's legislators that they were persuaded to pass "An Act to Prevent the Traffic in Intoxicating Liquors". This act "forbade the manufacture within New Brunswick of any alcoholic or intoxicating liquors except for religious, medicinal or chemical purposes. Beer, ale, porter and cider were excepted".[49]

Women had, of course, been involved in the temperance cause from the time of its first appearance in New Brunswick in 1830. But men had always outnumbered women in temperance organizations and until 1853 the vast majority of temperance petitions were submitted by and signed by men.[50] Urban women were the first to take up their pens in the temperance cause: the "Ladies' Total Abstinence Society for the City and County of Saint John" submitted the first recorded petition from women on the issue to the Legislature in 1847. Three years later

45 Acheson, *Saint John*, p. 149; Chapman, "The Mid-Nineteenth Century Temperance Movement", p. 50.

46 W. S. MacNutt, *New Brunswick, A History: 1784-1867* (Toronto, 1963, 1984), p. 350.

47 Acheson, *Saint John*, p. 141. Similar attempts were made in New England to control licensing at the local level. Tyrrell, *Sobering Up*, pp. 91, 242-3.

48 RG4, RS24, 1852/Pe 406, PANB. The Maine Law also had a significant impact in England and within the United States. See Harrison, *Drink and the Victorians*, p. 196; Tyrrell, *Sobering Up*, p. 260.

49 Chapman, "The Mid-Nineteenth Century Temperance Movement", p. 53.

50 New Brunswick women were by no means atypical in this regard. Barbara Epstein argues, for example, that during this period American women in the temperance movement were generally relegated to subsidiary roles — influencing sons and husbands. Barbara Leslie Epstein, *The Politics of Domesticity: Women, Evangelism, and Temperance in Nineteenth-Century America* (Middletown CT, 1981), p. 91.

Woodstock's Victoria Union No. 4 of the Daughters of Temperance submitted a petition opposing the granting of tavern licences. The following year the "Ladies of Woodstock" went even further, calling for "an act to prevent the sale of spiritous liquors". In 1852, the Daughters of Temperance from Woodstock were joined in the campaign by women from Fredericton and the surrounding area.[51] Rural women, including the subjects of this article, in contrast, did not sign temperance petitions to the Legislature before 1853. Yet this cannot be taken as an indication of either a lack of knowledge or a lack of interest. Some, like the women of Albert County, had, for several years, regularly signed petitions addressed to their local county councils opposing the issuance of tavern licences.[52] Such women signed petitions not as members of any organized temperance group, but rather as members of their local community; and this pattern was to continue when they turned their attention to the Legislative Assembly in 1853. Rural women had not participated in the legislative lobbying campaign that had culminated in the drafting of the Liquor Bill. Yet they were very much in the mainstream of the temperance movement as it gathered force, attempting first to achieve sobriety through moral suasion, then seeking local solutions through no licensing campaigns. And they would soon have the opportunity to demonstrate their support for the new legislation.

The new law was to come into force on 1 June 1853. In fact, it never came into effect. No sooner had it passed into law than the lobby against it began. Petitions calling for the repeal of the new law flooded in from nearly every county in the province. And the legislators were disposed to listen. Perhaps they had, after all, been just a little too hasty. The Legislative Assembly depended mainly on customs duties for its disposable revenue and duties on rum alone represented over one third of that revenue.[53] It was at this stage that the women of New Brunswick mobilized for action. Women who had never before signed a petition took up their pens. They begged their legislators not to repeal the new law. Men had achieved the law; the women were determined to keep it.[54]

51 See RG4, RS24, 1847/Pe 465; 1850/Pe 445; 1851/Pe 431; 1852/Pe 348; 1852/Pe 402; 1852/Pe 407, PANB. The early involvement of urban women is not surprising. Harrison argues that the temperance movement in England owed much to industrialization. Led by pioneers among whom doctors, coffee traders, evangelicals and industrialists figured prominently, the movement spread out from the towns (Harrison, *Drink and the Victorians*, pp. 92-8). Similarly, Tyrrell argues that temperance "flourished in a society in transition from a rural to an urban industrial order", receiving its strongest support from the promoters of that change (Tyrrell, *Sobering Up*, pp. 7, 209, 241, 252). A comprehensive study of the New Brunswick temperance movement during this period remains to be done, but the pattern of petitioning is suggestive of the need for a careful comparative analysis.

52 RG18, RS146, B9 (1851), PANB.

53 Chapman, "The Mid-Nineteenth Century Temperance Movement", p. 44.

54 Women from both Charlotte and Sunbury participated in the 1853 campaign against the repeal

After the election of 1854, temperance advocates, many of them women, redoubled their efforts. Through the medium of petitions, they urged their newly elected Assembly to enact yet another law "to prevent the importation, manufacture and sale of all intoxicating liquors within this province". Sunbury prohibitionists, for example, addressed three separate petitions to their legislators in 1854. Those petitions contained no less than 915 signatures and 488 of those names were female.[55] Three hundred and seventy-five (77 per cent) of these women were living in the county when the census was taken in 1851.[56] They represented well over 30 per cent of the county's 846 families. One hundred and fifty-five of these women (just over 40 per cent) were married and the majority of them (95) petitioned with their husbands and children. Thus, fathers and sons signed the petition from "the male inhabitants of Sunbury County" while mothers and daughters were signing the petition from "the female inhabitants of Sunbury County". Often fathers signed on behalf of their sons, and mothers on behalf of their daughters. Occasionally parents included the names of very young children on the petition: 16 of the daughters listed were under ten years of age in 1854 (see Table 1). In very rare cases, one parent signed both petitions on behalf of the entire family, but these amounted to less than five per cent of the total signatures.

Typical of those who signed as families were the Carrs of Burton Parish. Free Will Baptists, they were prepared to take a stand on the prohibition issue. Mary Ann Carr who was 44 in 1854, signed the petition on behalf of herself and her daughter Louisa, who was 17; Huldah, at 24, signed on her own behalf. Mary Ann's husband, William, 11 years her senior, a farm owner and operator, also signed the petition, as did their 21 year old son, Alexander. Sarah and Andrew Smith also supported the call for a new prohibitory liquor law. Sarah was 42 in 1854, while Andrew was 49. Like the Carrs, they were Free Will Baptists and farm owners. Their three oldest children, Frances, 23, George, 19, and Abigail, 17, joined their parents in supporting the petition. Similarly, Margaret Nason, a 34 year old weaver, her farmer husband, and her two sons, aged 14 and 15, all signed. Residents of Lincoln, they were, like the Carrs and the Smiths, Free Will Baptists. Augusta Perley's family was less typical. Her husband, George, a 47 year old Maugerville farmer, had signed a petition urging temperance legislation

of the Act. See the index of the *Journal of the New Brunswick House of Assembly*, 1853, which refers to: Petition 366, Lucinda Garcelon, Clara A. McAllister, Margaret Robinson and 300 others, female inhabitants of Charlotte, and Petition 386, Israel Smith, Thomas H. Smith, Esq. and 996 others of Sunbury and York. Other petitions for Charlotte which might well have numbered women among their signatories include: Petition 318 from Charlotte County, Petition 354 from St. Andrews and Petition 355 from St. George. None of the above has survived in the PANB.

55 RG4, RS24, 1854/Pe 394, 1854/Pe 395, 1854/Pe 404, PANB.
56 Manuscript Census for Sunbury County, N.B., 1851, PANB.

TABLE 1

Sunbury County: Women Temperance Petitioners by Signing Category and Age Group

Age	Wives whose husbands signed	Wives whose husbands did not sign	Widows	Daughters signing with one or both parents	Daughters whose parents did not sign	Other women signatories	Totals	% of women petitioners
0-9				16			16	4
10-14				37	11		48	13
15-19				45	13	2	60	16
20-29	14	12		38	20	11	95	25
30-39	28	20	1	8	4	5	66	18
40-49	21	14	1	1			37	10
50-59	20	10	1				31	8
60-69	9	3	3				15	4
70-89	3	1	2			1	7	2
Totals	95	60	8	145	48	19	375*	100
% of women petitioners	25	16	2	39	13	5		100

*Women identified in the 1851 census (77 per cent of all women signatories).

in 1852. In 1854, Augusta, then 38, joined him in his fight for the cause, as did their daughters, Mary Frances, 19, and Charlotte, 17, and their eldest son, Walter, 15. The Perleys, however, were one of only 23 Episcopalian families to sign the petition.

Although 60 married women signed the petition even though their husbands had not, the majority of these women did not sign alone. For example, Gertrude Harris, the wife of a Blissville farmer, signed the petition without her husband, but her three eldest children, Thomas, 17, Mary, 14, and Hannah, 12, signed with her. Like the majority of Sunbury signatories, the Harrises were Free Will Baptists. Mary Glasier, the Irish-born wife of a Lincoln lumberman, signed the petition on behalf of her 13 year old daughter, Melissa, as well as herself; her mother, Catherine O'Brien, also signed. The Glasiers were Methodists, a group that provided close to 20 per cent of Sunbury's petitioners. Some married women signed alone, independent of their families as well as of their husbands. Among them was Ann Tosh, the 26 year old wife of an Irish labourer in Sheffield. Such women were, however, usually strengthened by religious as well as moral conviction. Ann Tosh, for example, like so many other signatories, was a Free Will Baptist.

Almost 60 per cent of the female signatories were not married. Eight were widows, while the remaining 212 were single. Of the single women, 68 per cent signed with one or both of their parents. While the majority of married women who signed were between 30 and 39 years of age, the single women signatories were somewhat younger on average. Typical of the young single women who signed were Alice and Mary Ann Patterson, aged 31 and 27 respectively. Both were dressmakers, living with their parents, a dressmaker and a tenant farmer, and their three younger brothers. All the members of this family signed. Margaret Barker, 24, and her sister Mary, a 21 year old schoolmistress in Sheffield Parish, signed the petition along with their widowed mother and elder brother. A farm family, they were Congregationalists. The five daughters of William Smith, Phebe, aged 30, Mary, 27, Hepzedah, 23, Adeline, 21, and Sarah, 20, all signed, as did their brother Steven, aged 26. Not surprisingly, they were Free Will Baptists. Yet their older brother and their father did not sign.

Denominational affiliation could be determined for only 71 per cent of the 303 Sunbury families.[57] Baptists, Methodists and Congregationalists were slightly over-represented among signatories, while Roman Catholics were significantly under-represented (see Table 2). Thus, women who belonged to Protestant

---

57 These included 61.7 per cent of Sunbury's 488 women petitioners. Information concerning religious denomination was drawn from the Manuscript Census for 1861, PANB. Thus, almost 40 per cent of all female signatories had removed from their parish of residence by 1861, suggesting that women petitioners were not likely to be more geographically stable than were their contemporaries.

TABLE 2

Sunbury County: Religion of Women Temperance Petitioners

Religion	Blissville	Burton	Lincoln	Maugerville	Sheffield	Totals	% of Identified Petitioners	% of Total in County
Baptist	70	24	37	13	25	169	56.1	51.0
Methodist	2	9	3	8	30	52	17.3	14.1
Episcopalian		10		18	4	32	10.6	11.5
Congregational				4	14	18	6.0	2.3
Presbyterian		2	1	1	4	8	2.7	5.4
Roman Catholic	7	3	4	2	2	18	6.0	15.5
Disciples		3				3	1.0	.1
Covenanter	1					1	.3	.1
TOTALS	80	51	45	46	79	301*	100.0	100.0

*Women present when the 1861 census, which includes religious affiliation, was taken (61.7 per cent of all women signatories).

evangelical sects were more likely to sign temperance petitions than were women of other denominations. However, in Sunbury County, where over 50 per cent of the families were Baptist and the numbers of other denominations were small, patterns among the other denominational groups prove difficult to discern with any degree of precision.

The wives and daughters of labourers were under-represented among petition signatories from Sunbury, but so, too, were the wives and daughters of artisans. In contrast, farm families were significantly over-represented. Thus, while 56 per cent of the workforce classified themselves as farmers in 1851, 71 per cent of the female petitioners were the wives or daughters of farmers (see Table 3). The occupations of some of the women signatories were also listed in the census. These included five weavers, three dressmakers, four schoolmistresses, a trader and four servants.

On the whole, then, the women who signed the Sunbury petitions of 1854 were very ordinary women, unremarkable within their community. The average signatory was relatively young, between 20 and 29 years of age, and was likely to sign with some other member of her family. Like the majority of her contemporaries, she was probably part of a farm family and attended either a Baptist or Methodist Church. Although she had never before signed a petition, she was prepared to stand up and be counted in support of her beliefs or those of her parents or friends. She may not have been either sophisticated or worldly, yet her interests and knowledge extended beyond the domestic sphere. The action she took was a decidedly political one and it would be difficult to argue, at least in the case of any of the 109 women over the age of 20 who signed the petition independent of any husband or parent, that she did not understand the principle behind that action. And, for one brief moment, her action had the desired effect, for in 1855, the Legislature did pass yet another prohibitory liquor act.

Of course, the women of Sunbury did not achieve their goal single handed. In 1854, at about the same time as the people of Sunbury were presenting their petitions, a second 'monster petition' was presented to the House of Assembly. It was far longer than the petition that had so impressed the legislators back in 1852; this petition included over 20,000 signatures. Moreover, it suggested more broadly based support. Whereas the signatories of the earlier 'monster petition' had been drawn largely from Saint John City and County, this time they came from at least half of the 14 counties of New Brunswick, although not from Sunbury. Well over half of the 20,000 signatories were women, including 143 women from Hillsborough in Albert County, and 198 women from Charlotte County, 93 from St. Stephen Parish and 105 from the parish of St. Andrews.[58]

58 RG4, RS24, 1854/Pe 465, PANB.

Table 3

Sunbury County: Occupations of Heads of Households of Petitioning Families

Occupational Categories	Blissville	Burton	Lincoln	Maugerville	Sheffield	Totals	% of Families	% of Total in County
Professions	2	1	2		2	7	2.6	1.4
Trade & Commerce		1		1		2	.7	1.7
Agriculture	44	28	40	27	52	191	71.0	55.7
Artisans	6	7	3	5	17	38	14.1	17.9
Fishermen					1	1	.4	.7
Labourers	3	2	7		18	30	11.2	19.2
Miscellaneous								3.4
TOTALS	55	39	52	33	90	269	100.0	100.0

The patterns that emerged in Sunbury were repeated in Hillsborough. Eighty per cent of Hillsborough's women signatories were living in the parish when the census was taken in 1851.[59] They included representatives of more than one-quarter of the parish's families. Forty-eight were married women, while a further six were widows (see Table 4). The husbands of 28 of these women could be identified as having signed temperance petitions in the past. Elizabeth Steeves was typical of the married women who signed. Her husband George, a Baptist farmer descended from the Pennsylvania Germans who had settled the parish in the previous century, had signed temperance petitions to both his local County Council and the Provincial Legislature in the past. Now his wife, joined by her two daughters and her daughter-in-law (aged 28, 26 and 26 respectively), signed the 'monster petition' of 1854. Margaret Duffy was the wife of the Baptist minister. Although her husband was an Irish immigrant, she was of German descent and had been born and raised in the parish. She and her daughters, Jane, 22, Theora, 12, and Margaret, 10, added their names to the petition. Mary Gross also traced her roots to the original German settlers. She, too, was a Baptist. In the past, her husband Robert had signed temperance petitions and now she and her daughters, Ruth, 18, Hannah, 14, and Anne, 12, took up their pens. Dillah Steeves and her husband shared a common background, but he was not, apparently, as interested in the temperance cause as his wife. While her farmer husband never signed a temperance petition, Dillah, at age 48, signed her first. Her daughters, Elizabeth, 23, and Jane, 17, signed with her.

Of the 61 single women who signed, 48 were the daughters of temperance advocates. Isaac Milton, a Baptist farmer, had signed a petition calling for prohibition in 1851. In 1854, his daughters, Ruth, 21, and Mary, 20, joined the campaign. Elizabeth Steeves, 25, and her sister Permelia, 22, the daughters of a widowed farmer who had, in the past, been a temperance advocate, also added their names. They, too, were Baptists. Occasionally women signed independent of parents or siblings. Twenty-one year old Jane Boyd signed the petition despite the fact that no one else in her large family signed with her, but Jane was exceptional. Only 13 of the 61 single women signatories identified could claim to have taken a stance independent of their parents. As was the case in Sunbury, the wives and daughters of the farmers of Hillsborough were over-represented among the signatories: although only 59 per cent of the parish's families were headed by farmers, 72 per cent of the women signatories came from farm families. The Baptists were again significantly over-represented.[60] While Bapt-

---

59 Manuscript Census for Albert County, N.B., 1851, PANB.

60 Religious affiliation was drawn from the 1861 Manuscript Census for Albert County, PANB. Fully 72 per cent of Hillsborough's female signatories were located in the 1861 census. In this case, marriage records were used to trace those women who may have removed to another parish within the county. This, coupled with the tendency to greater geographical stability within Albert County as a whole, accounts for the high rate of record linkage for Hillsborough.

TABLE 4

Albert County: Women Temperance Petitioners by Signing Category and Age Group

Age Groups	Wives whose husbands had been temperance advocates	Wives whose husbands had not been temperance advocates	Widows	Daughters whose parents were temperance advocates	Daughters whose parents had not been temperance advocates	Other women signatories	Totals	% of women petitioners
0-9				5	3		8	7
10-14				12	1		13	11
15-19				15	3		18	16
20-29	8	6		16	3	2	35	30
30-39	7	3			1		11	10
40-49	8	7	1				16	14
50-59	3	3					6	5
60-69	1	1	2				4	3.5
70-89	1		3				4	3.5
TOTALS	28	20	6	48	11	2	115*	
% of women petitioners	24.5	17.5	5	41.5	10	1.5		100

*Women identified in the 1851 census (80 per cent of all women signatories).

ists comprised 76 per cent of the parish population, fully 92 per cent of the Hillsborough women who signed the 'monster petition' of 1854 were Baptists (see Table 5). Many were descendants of the original German settlers who had begun immigrating to the parish from Pennsylvania as early as 1765. On the whole, then, the Hillsborough women were a more cohesive group than the Sunbury women, although their demographic profile is very similar.[61]

The Charlotte County signatories, drawn mainly from the two major towns in the county, were a more diverse group of women. They were also more mobile. Of the 260 women who signed either the 'monster petition' or another petition calling for prohibition in 1854, only 63 per cent had been living in the county when the census taker called in 1851.[62] The women were older on average than the women in either Hillsborough or Sunbury. Forty-eight percent of the signatories were married, while a further six percent were widows. The majority of the married women ranged in age between 30 and 50, while the majority of single women who signed were in their twenties (see Table 6). In Charlotte County, the temperance movement was clearly a middle class movement, attracting supporters from the families of professional men, merchants and skilled artisans as well as from the most prosperous farm families.

In St. Stephen, many of the most prosperous members of society belonged to the Congregational Church and a high proportion of these were temperance advocates. Mary and Frances Porter, daughters of George M. Porter, one of the wealthiest lumber merchants in the county, signed the 'monster petition'. Mary Ann Murchie also signed: her husband, James, listed himself merely as a farmer in the census, but he was much more than that, controlling nearly 20,000 acres of land. Charlotte Hitchings, another signatory, was the wife of a lawyer. Her daughter Frances, then 17, also signed, as did Mary and Louisa Todd, the daughters of a local merchant. All these women were Congregationalists.

In St. Andrews, the picture proved somewhat more varied. Ann Berry, a Scottish-born Presbyterian, was the wife of a house carpenter. Her husband, Thomas, had signed a temperance petition as early as 1848. In 1854, she and her daughters, Helen, 23, and Isabella, 13, followed his example. Jane McCracken was an Irish-born Presbyterian. A 43 year old widow, she made her living as a dressmaker. Her sister Susan, also a widow, and her niece lived with her: they, too, were dressmakers. Elizabeth Clark, 35, and her daughter Jane, 17, were Methodists, a denomination often associated with the temperance cause; yet

---

61 It should be noted, however, that the Hillsborough Baptists were quite different from the Sunbury Baptists. While the Hillsborough Baptists traced their roots back to the religious traditions carried as part of their cultural baggage by the original Pennsylvania German immigrants, Sunbury Baptists had been strongly influenced by the New Light movement of the late 18th century.

62 RS 24, 1854/Pe 220 and 1854/Pe 465, PANB; Manuscript Census for Charlotte County, N.B., 1851, PANB.

TABLE 5

Hillsborough Parish, Albert County: Religion of Women Temperance Petitioners

Religion	No. of Identified Petitioners	% of Identified Petitioners	Denomination as % of Parish Population
Baptist	95	92.2	75.6
Methodist	8	7.8	9.8
TOTALS	103*		

*Women present when the 1861 census, which includes religious affiliation, was taken (61.7 per cent of all women signatories).

TABLE 6

Charlotte County: Women Temperance Petitioners by Signing Category and Age Group

Age Group	Wives whose husbands had been temperance advocates	Wives whose husbands had not been temperance advocates	Widows	Daughters whose parents were temperance advocates	Daughters whose parents had not been temperance advocates	Other women signatories	Totals	% of women petitioners
10-14				5	1		6	4
15-19				16	11	2	29	18
20-29	3	5		19	12	3	42	26
30-39	10	15	2	2	3		32	19
40-49	16	15	3				34	21
50-59	6	4	4				14	8
60-69	2	3	2				7	4
TOTALS	37	42	11	42	27	5	164*	
% of women petitioners	22	26	7	26	16	3		100

*Women identified in the 1851 census (63 per cent of all women signatories).

there is no record of Obadiah, the 40 year-old mariner who was husband to Elizabeth and father to Jane, ever having signed a temperance petition. Perhaps he was too much away at sea to find time for such things. Like the Clarks, Christiana Stevenson, an American-born immigrant, was a Methodist. But her husband, Robert, a tanner and currier, and his brother, Hugh, had both signed temperance petitions to the Legislature in 1848. Elizabeth Harvey, the wife of a ship's carpenter, was an Episcopalian who supported the great crusade; she was 33 in 1854. Just 22 in 1854, Mary Stickney, the young wife of a watchmaker, was, like Elizabeth Harvey, an Episcopalian who rallied to the temperance cause. None of these women was unusual among St. Andrews' petitioners, who were drawn largely from among Presbyterians, Methodists and Episcopalians, and represented many of the families of the skilled craftsmen of the parish. Women like Ann Chesty, the 26 year old daughter of an Irish-born Roman Catholic labourer, were rare indeed among the signatories.

The Charlotte County experience raises questions about the role of religion in determining which women would prove most likely to support the movement. The representation of a particular religious denomination among the Charlotte County petitioners seems to have depended on organization (see Table 7). In St. Stephen, Congregational Church women proved the most likely to sign although Congregationalists comprised only five per cent of the total population of the parish. In St. Andrews, Presbyterian and Methodist and, surprisingly, Episcopalian women predominated. The tiny contingent of signatories from St. Patrick were almost exclusively Baptist (nine of 12 families). Were petitions passed around at church meetings? If so, the denominational affiliation of the majority of signatories in any single parish may well be accidental. Nonetheless, in comparing the denominational affiliation of the women who signed petitions calling for prohibitory liquor legislation with the denominational affiliation of the men who signed petitions calling for the repeal of such legislation, clear trends do emerge. Roman Catholics and Episcopalians were over-represented among the repeal petitioners. And while Episcopalians were only slightly under-represented among the women petitioners, Roman Catholic signatories were rare indeed.[63]

The typical Charlotte County woman signatory was married or widowed and was between 30 and 50 years of age. She lived in one of the two major towns in the county and was solidly middle class, the wife of a relatively prosperous merchant or artisan. Her daughters were likely to sign with her. She might be a

63 Information concerning the religious affiliation of petitioners was drawn from the Manuscript Census for Charlotte County, 1861, PANB. Denominational affiliation was determined for 81 of the 115 families identified. These included 113 women in all, just 43.5 per cent of the county's 260 female petitioners. Charlotte County was characterized by a high degree of geographic mobility during this period and female temperance petitioners were not atypical in this regard.

TABLE 7

Charlotte County: Religion of Women Temperance Petitioners

Religion	St. Andrews	St. Patrick	St. Stephen	Totals	% of Identified Petitioners	% of Total in County
Baptist	1	14	2	17	15.0	22.3
Methodist	18		11	29	25.7	11.9
Episcopalian	14		5	19	16.8	24.1
Congregational			17	17	15.0	1.1
Presbyterian	23	2		25	22.1	19.0
Roman Catholic	5			5	4.4	15.2
Universalist			1	1	1.0	1.8
Totals	61	16	36	113*	100.0	100.0

*Women present when the 1861 census, which includes religious affiliation, was taken (43.5 per cent of all women signatories).

312 The Acadiensis Reader: 1

Congregationalist, a Presbyterian, a Methodist or possibly an Episcopalian, but whatever her religious faith, she would be joined in the temperance crusade by other members of her local congregation.

As significant and impressive as the petition campaign was, the petitioners did not comprise a majority of the adult population of the province. And the 1853 act had not proved popular. Thus, it is scarcely surprising that the newly elected government proved reluctant to act. Early in November, however, a vote in the House of Assembly went against the government and the government of the day resigned. The Lieutenant-Governor called upon the Liberal opposition to form a government; and among the leaders of this new government was Samuel Leonard Tilley, a man who had recently been chosen Most Worthy Patriarch of the Sons of Temperance in North America.[64] Shortly thereafter, in the parliamentary session of 1855, Tilley put forward, as a private member, a new prohibitory liquor bill, which passed narrowly in the House of Assembly and in the Legislative Council. Despite personal reservations, the Lieutenant-Governor, John Manners-Sutton, gave his assent on the advice of his Executive Council and the act was scheduled to become law on 1 January 1856.

For a brief moment it seemed as if the fight had been won. But, as was the case in 1853, agitation for repeal began almost immediately. Petitions opposing the new law poured in. No women were among the signatories of these petitions.[65] After a brief, ineffectual attempt to enforce the act, the legislators gave up. Yet they did not repeal the act. The Lieutenant-Governor demanded that they either repeal it or enforce it and the entire issue became so controversial that the Lieutenant-Governor forced a dissolution of the House and yet another election was called. Shortly after that election, which was held in 1856, the act was repealed. The temperance fight, for the moment at least, was over.

Even though the fight was ultimately lost, the role women played in it is highly significant. The very fact that two prohibitory liquor acts were passed demonstrates the power of the petition as a political tool in mid-19th century New Brunswick. Petitions and petitioners were taken seriously. Nor was it suggested that women had less right than men to petition their Legislature. There is no evidence to suggest that women's signatures carried any less weight than men's.[66]

---

64 Chapman, "The Mid-Nineteenth Century Temperance Movement", p. 53.

65 This is not so surprising as it might appear. Women were not involved in repeal campaigns in the United States, either. In general, 19th century women saw drinking as a male vice and sought to reform men. Epstein, *The Politics of Domesticity*, pp. 1, 110; Tyrrell, *Sobering Up*, p. 181.

66 In discussing women signatories of the 'monster petition' of 1852, Mr. Hatheway, the Representative for York County, argued that women's signatures on petitions were "a sufficient reason" for passing the Liquor Bill then before the House. He believed a politician needed "the good opinion of the fair portion of the community" and declared that he "would always rather have one lady canvasser than a dozen men". *Reports of the Debates and Proceedings of the House of Assembly of the Province of New Brunswick* (Fredericton, 1852), p. 101. In the 1854

By analyzing the women signatories, we can gain new insights concerning 19th century politics and political culture. It is true that wives and daughters of men who signed repeal petitions are rarely to be found among the signatories calling for prohibition. At the same time, almost half of the married women who signed petitions were not joined by their husbands in their fight for the cause. Moreover, there is some indication that mothers were more influential than fathers, for sons proved twice as likely to follow their mothers in signing temperance petitions as they were to follow their fathers in signing repeal petitions. But daughters were even more likely to follow their mothers' lead than were sons. More important than any of these considerations, the women's decisions to take up their pens in the cause of temperance when they did, demonstrates that women had followed the political progress of the temperance legislation and were prepared to take a public political stand on an issue they believed to be important. And in many cases their stand was quite independent from that of their husbands.

Of those inhabitants who petitioned the Legislative Assembly during the 12 years covered by this study, women represented only a very small minority. Thus, while female petitioners from each of the three counties numbered in the hundreds, male petitioners numbered in the thousands. Nonetheless, in Sunbury, the county for which the most complete records are available, women from over 30 per cent of the families listed in the 1851 census signed at least one petition to their Legislature during the period. Petition signatories included women of all ages, all classes, all ethnic and religious groups. But no matter what their age, ethnicity, religious denomination or economic status, the very fact that significant numbers of women signed petitions is historically important. Women did not have the right to vote in the mid-19th century. Yet, in New Brunswick, at least, women were not passive and they were not silent. Many understood the law and were determined to make it work for them. They petitioned for pensions and subsidies to which they were legally entitled and, from time to time, they petitioned for redress of personal grievances. Most were successful in achieving their ends. Many more women became politically active during the decade, seeking, through the medium of petitions, to influence their government to change the law. Working in concert with others of like mind, they effectively

debates, while some members questioned the signatures of "children in schools", the right of women to sign was generally accepted. Indeed, the majority of those who rose in the House to comment on the 1854 Bill argued that 30,000 signatures in favour of the Bill, as opposed to 4,000 against, was strong evidence of the public feeling. *Reports of the Debates and Proceedings* (1854), pp. 70-3. Similarly, American and British legislators attacked the validity of children's signatures on temperance petitions but did not question the signatures of non-voting women for, as the women themselves argued, "although they did not themselves vote, their husbands did, and their husbands would be heeding the advice of their spouses". Harrison, *Drink and the Victorians*, p. 229; Tyrrell, *Sobering Up*, pp. 279-80.

demonstrated their power to persuade, although ultimately they failed to achieve their goal. Whether they petitioned as individuals or in association with others, whether they were seeking to change the law or merely to use it, whether they succeeded or failed, these 19th century New Brunswick women had stepped outside the domestic sphere and into the world of politics. Their lives had a political dimension and, by exercising their rights as subjects under the crown, they helped to shape the political culture of their province.

JANET GUILDFORD

Reprinted from Vol. XXII, No. 1
(Autumn 1992)

"Separate Spheres": The Feminization of Public School Teaching in Nova Scotia, 1838-1880

IN 1838 THE NOVA SCOTIA ASSEMBLY decided that local school boards could hire women.[1] The Assembly was responding to a shortage of public school teachers and the decision was popular with both school boards and women teachers. Within 40 years women made up two-thirds of the public school work force in the province.[2] Both the recruitment of large numbers of women teachers and its consequences illustrate the ambiguities and contradictions inherent in the 19th-century, middle-class gender expectations usually referred to as the ideology of "separate spheres".[3] The feminization of public school teaching, and the gender ideology that encouraged it, had important implications for the struggle of Nova Scotia teachers to achieve professional wages and decent working conditions. Women were recruited as teachers because school administrators and politicians, persuaded that men and women belonged to separate spheres of activity, believed that women were inherently suited to the care and teaching of young children. But this widely shared gender ideology was inimical to teachers' claims to professional status, claims based on the possession of a set of acquired and scientifically based skills and knowledge. This contradiction inhibited successful collaboration between men and women within the public school work force and prolonged the struggle for higher wages and professional autonomy.

Women did not begin teaching school in Nova Scotia in 1838; rather, it was from that date that women teachers began to move from private schools to state-subsidized public schools.[4] Moreover, despite the periodic expression of fears and reservations about the feminization of public school teaching, Nova Scotians appeared to regard the development as a natural one. The feminization of public school teaching accompanied the creation of the reformed, state-supported elementary school

---

1 *Statutes of Nova Scotia*, 1838, ch. 23, s. VI.

2 *Annual Report of the Common, Academic and Normal and Model Schools of Nova Scotia* [*Annual Report*] (1880), Table B.

3 For a discussion of the contemporary debate about separate spheres as a conceptual framework see Mary P. Ryan, *Women in Public: Between Banners and Ballots, 1825-1880* (Baltimore and London, 1989), pp. 5-8.

4 Alison Prentice, "The Feminization of Teaching in British North America and Canada, 1845-75", in Susan Mann Trofimenkoff and Alison Prentice, eds., *The Neglected Majority: Essays in Canadian Women's History, Vol. 1* (Toronto, 1977), pp. 49-69.

systems in North America and Britain, a phenomenon that has attracted considerable attention from historians in the past few decades.[5] As David Allison, the superintendent of schools for the province, reported in 1877: "It may be desirable that we should have more male teachers, yet we are not to expect that Nova Scotia will be an exception to...almost every country where common school instruction [is] freely brought to the people".[6]

Contemporary observers believed that women teachers were recruited because they were willing to work for low wages and because, according to the prevailing ideology of gender roles, women had a natural aptitude for working with young children. Women became teachers because they had few opportunities for other paid employment and because they, too, believed that they had a natural aptitude for the job.[7]

Between 1838 and the passage of the Nova Scotia Free School Act in 1864, which eliminated tuition and introduced greater centralized supervision of public schooling

5   In the United States 60 per cent of teachers were women by 1870. David B. Tyack and Myra H. Strober, "Jobs and Gender: A History of the Structuring of Education Employment by Sex", in Patricia A. Schmuck, W.W. Charters, Jr. and Richard O. Carlson, *Educational Policy and Management: Sex Differentials* (New York, 1981), pp. 131-52. Women formed the majority of the public school teaching force in Quebec and Ontario by 1871. Marta Danylewycz, Beth Light and Alison Prentice, "The Evolution of the Sexual Division of Labour in Teaching: Nineteenth Century Ontario and Quebec Case Study", *Histoire sociale/Social History*, XVI, 31 (mai-May 1983), pp. 81-110. In England women formed 75 per cent of the work force by 1914. Frances Widdowson, *Going Up Into the Next Class: Women and Elementary Teacher Training 1840-1914* (London, 1983), Foreword. In Scotland 70 per cent of teachers were women by 1911. T.C. Smout, *A Century of the Scottish People, 1830-1850* (New Haven and London, 1986), p. 220. See also Helen Corr, "The Sexual Division of Labour in the Scottish Teaching Profession, 1872-1914", in Walter M. Humes and Hamish M. Patterson, eds., *Scottish Culture and Scottish Education, 1800-1980* (Edinburgh, 1983).

For a thorough recent overview of the literature on women teachers see Alison Prentice and Marjorie R. Theobald, "The Historiography of Women Teachers: A Retrospect", in Alison Prentice and Marjorie R. Theobald, eds., *Women who Taught: Perspectives on the History of Women and Teaching* (Toronto, 1991), pp. 3-36. The editors have also included an extensive bibliography. See also Wendy E. Bryans, "'Virtuous Women and Half the Price': The Feminization of the Teaching Force and Early Women Teacher Organizations in Ontario", M.A. thesis, University of Toronto, 1974. For the British experience see Barry Bergen, "Only a Schoolmaster: Gender, Class and the Effort to Professionalize Elementary Teaching England, 1870-1910", *History of Education Quarterly*, 21, 1 (1982), pp. 1-21; Dina M. Copelman, "'A New Comradeship between Men and Women': Family, Marriage and London's Women Teachers, 1870-1914", in Jane Lewis, ed., *Labour and Love: Women's Experience of Home and Family, 1850-1940* (Oxford, 1986), pp. 175-94; Widdowson, *Going Up*. The American experience is addressed in Tyack and Strober, "Jobs and Gender"; Redding S. Sugg, Jr., *Motherteacher: The Feminization of American Education* (Charlottesville, Virginia, 1978); Madeleine R. Grumet, *Bitter Milk: Women and Teaching* (Amherst, 1988).

6   *Journals of the House of Assembly of Nova Scotia [JHA]* (1877), App. 5, Annual Report, xviii.

7   See, for example, Prentice, "The Feminization of Teaching"; Tyack and Strober, "Jobs and Gender", Widdowson, *Going Up*. For a somewhat expanded discussion of the recruitment of women into public school teaching in the last half of the 19th and early 20th-centuries in the United States see Geraldine Joncich Clifford, "'Daughters into Teachers': Educational and Demographic Influences on the Transformation of Teaching into 'Women's Work' in America", in Prentice and Theobald, *Women who Taught*, pp. 115-35.

in the province, the change proceeded slowly. In 1851 just under 20 per cent of Nova Scotia public school teachers were women; in 1861 women formed a third of the public school work force.[8] Feminization was much more rapid in the decade following the 1864 Free School Act. In less than five years women constituted nearly half of all teachers both winter and summer.[9] In 1870 the provincial superintendent of schools reported that:

> The rapid increase of female teachers, as compared with those of the other sex, is worthy of note. While the former increased 81% in 5 years, the number of male teachers increased only 51%. The proportion of female teachers is greater in summer, 53% of those employed in the summer, 41% employed in winter being female teachers.[10]

By the end of the 1870s two-thirds of the province's teachers were women (see Table One).

The relationship between school reform and feminization is obviously an important one. To understand it we must consider both the function of the reformed public school systems and the mid-19th-century ideological concept of separate spheres for men and women. Nineteenth-century advocates of public school reform promised many benefits, but time and again they returned to a single theme: universal free public schooling would provide moral training for the young and produce a generation of hard-working, law-abiding citizens.[11] The inculcation of these social and political values was generally more important to the aims of school reformers than the provision of either religious or intellectual education.[12] Reformed public school systems, therefore, required a large work force capable of teaching the values and attitudes deemed appropriate by the school reformers, as well as a smaller number of administrators and teachers with strong academic background for the senior (and especially the male) students. The recruitment of women as public school teachers seemed natural to 19th-century legislators, school administrators and parents who were imbued with the separate spheres ideology.[13]

Reformed public school systems occupied an ambiguous place in the mid-19th-century social landscape. They created institutions in which some of the work of the private sphere — the training of children — was performed in a public arena under the jurisdiction of the state. They attest to the difficulty of applying the middle-class

---

8   Prentice, "The Feminization of Teaching".
9   Prentice, "The Feminization of Teaching".
10 *Annual Report*, (1870), p. xxi.
11 See, for example, Alison Prentice, *The School Promoters* (Toronto, 1977); and Sugg, *Motherteacher*.
12 Sugg, *Motherteacher*; Grumet, *Bitter Milk*.
13 For a discussion of this idea see Nancy F. Cott, *The Bonds of Womanhood: "Woman's Sphere" in New England, 1780-1835* (London, 1977). More recently a debate has arisen about the usefulness of the idea of separate spheres as an analytical approach. See for example, Linda Kerber, "Separate Spheres, Female Worlds, Women's Place: The Rhetoric of Women's History", *Journal of American History*, 75 (June, 1988), pp. 9-39; Alice Kessler-Harris, "Gender Ideology in Historical Reconstruction: A Case Study from the 1930s", *Gender and History*, 1, 1 (Spring, 1989), pp. 31-49; and Ryan, *Women in Public*.

ideal of a division of labour along sexual lines, an ideal that confined male activity to the public world of economics and politics and female activity to the private world of the family and reproduction. While it seemed natural that women, suited by nature to the moral training of children, should be hired as public school teachers, public schools were more than extensions of the domestic sphere. They were also arenas for both collaboration and competition between men and women. The boundaries between the private and the public spheres were not always clearly defined, and were under constant revision. This overlapping of the private and public spheres had important ramifications in the teachers' struggle to gain recognition for their work.

Historians have continued to debate the relative importance of ideology and economics in the recruitment of women to public school teaching.[14] It can be argued, however, that the two were in fact intimately related and mutually reinforcing. Women were paid low wages because they were performing the work of the private sphere, work usually performed outside the formal economy. Women were recruited as teachers because they were believed to have a special aptitude for the job. Concepts of gender were thus central to the 19th-century division of labour. When we remember that the mid-19th century was also the period when professional police forces were first recruited in many parts of British North America it becomes clear that sex and notions of gender played an enormous role in decision making. It was never suggested that women, because they were willing to work for low wages, would make an ideal police force. Reverend Robert Sedgewick, speaking to the Halifax Young Men's Christian Association in 1856, expressed his derision of such an idea when he asked the rhetorical question "What can be more unfeminine than a woman thief-catcher?"[15] While women were certainly attractive employees because of their willingness to work for low wages, ideology played a very large part in their recruitment to public school teaching. The conjunction of public school reform and the idea of separate spheres for men and women was central to the change. As Geraldine Joncich Clifford has argued, the movement of elements of the work of social reproduction from the household to the public school played an important role in turning "daughters into teachers".[16]

The ideology of separate spheres had wide acceptance in mid-19th-century Nova Scotia. Reform politician George Young, for example, writing in 1842, described women as "queens of the household" and urged the education of women for motherhood.[17] In 1846 the anonymous author of an essay on the "Improvement of Female Education" argued that women were "admirably adapted to the sacred charge

---

14   See, for example, Bryans, "Virtuous Women".

15   Robert Sedgewick, "The Proper Sphere and Influence of Woman in Christian Society", in Ramsay Cook and Wendy Mitchinson, eds., *The Proper Sphere: Woman's Place in Canadian Society* (Toronto, 1976), p.15.

16   Clifford, "Daughters into Teachers".

17   George R. Young, *On Colonial Literature, Science and Education; written with a view of improving the Literary Educational and Public Institutions of British North America*, v. 1 (Halifax, 1842), p. 126.

of watching the young".[18] Nova Scotians were also well aware of international debates on the role of women. In the early 1850s two Halifax newspapers, both of them published by women, regularly carried items about separate spheres and the mid-19th-century debates about women's proper sphere and women's rights.[19] Reverend Robert Sedgewick tackled these debates directly in his 1856 address to the Halifax Young Men's Christian Association in which he claimed unequivocal support for rigidly distinctive roles and natures for men and women.[20]

The attitudes of Nova Scotia politicians, school administrators and teachers were imbued with the ideology of separate spheres for men and women. Nova Scotians accepted the idea that women were the queens and moral rulers of the home, but very few advocated the full equality of the sexes. The question of women's equality did, however, emerge several times within the Sons of Temperance. In 1856 the "full and unequivocal membership of the female sex" was proposed at the provincial annual meeting, but it was rejected.[21] The issue resurfaced in a letter to the order's journal in 1868, when "A friend of the order" asked "Has not God made man and woman equal?" The editor disagreed. He recommended that women should retain their status as "visitors".[22] The public participation of women, even in worthy causes, remained troublesome. In 1862, when Mrs. Nina Smith appeared alone on the platform of the Temperance Hall to solicit aid for the poor, she addressed a slim and critical audience. One listener did admit that while he was "utterly opposed to the theory of female oratory", Mrs. Smith had performed so well that it "made his heart bleed" and he moved a vote of thanks to "the lady who had so unselfishly braved the prejudices of society to relieve the destitute".[23]

Public school reform and the acceptance of the separate spheres ideology in Nova Scotia help us to understand the general trend toward the feminization of the public school work force, but when we average relative numbers of men and women teaching in the province as a whole we miss some important local differences. There were significant variations in the timing and extent of feminization. The city of Halifax was among the first school districts in which the majority of teachers were women. The predominance of women in urban teaching forces has been widely noted by other historians. Urban areas were the first to develop bureaucratic school systems with large numbers of female teachers in the younger classes of graded schools and a smaller number of men in supervisory positions.[24] As Table One demonstrates, Halifax followed the pattern of other urban areas. Very soon after the

18 Anon. "Improvement of Female Education", *Essays on the Future Destiny of Nova Scotia* (Halifax, 1846).
19 See, for example, *Mayflower*, 1, 1 (May 1851), pp. 6-7; *Provincial Magazine*, March 1852, p. 86.
20 Sedgewick, "Women's Sphere".
21 *Abstainer*, 15 November 1856.
22 *Abstainer*, 25 November 1868.
23 *Acadian Recorder*, 22 February 1862.
24 Danylewycz, Light and Prentice, "Evolution", pp. 82-3.

implementation of the Free School acts of 1864-7, Halifax had a predominantly female work force supervised by a corps of male principals and administrators.[25]

Table One
Female Teachers as a Percentage of All Teachers (average winter-summer)

School District	1851	1859	1861	1869	1871	1877	1879
Annapolis				38			48
Antigonish				25			40
Cape Breton				24			27
Colchester				60			77
Cumberland				63			80
Digby				50			59
Guysborough				49			70
Halifax Co.				62			81
Halifax City	36	55	52	58	65		81
Hants				59			65
Inverness				13			26
Kings				41			60
Lunenburg				52			76
Pictou		27		45			59
Queens				52			73
Richmond				42			47
Shelburne		64		51			75
Victoria				19			40
Yarmouth				48			69
Nova Scotia	20	39	30	45	47	61	66

Sources: Prentice, "The Feminization of Teaching", p. 57; Annual Report (1859), p. 157; Annual Report (1877); Annual Report (1879). Until 1864 School Districts and Counties did not conform. Halifax City remained one school district for statistical purposes throughout the period.

The situation in rural areas must be examined more closely, and with careful attention to local conditions. The retention of male teachers in the eastern counties is particularly significant. All four Cape Breton counties still had more men than women teaching in public schools in 1879. In Antigonish County 60 per cent of the teachers were male. The only exception to this pattern was Pictou County, where women constituted 59 per cent of the teachers, still below the provincial average of

25   *Annual Report*, (1870), Report of the Board of School Commissioners for the City of Halifax for 1870, pp. 9ff.

66 per cent women. Although other factors may have played a part in this trend, the influence of Scottish educational traditions, including that of the male teacher, is a useful point of departure. Traditional sexual divisions of labour played an important role in the timing of the feminization of public school teaching. Danylewycz, Prentice and Light have argued that the tradition of female teaching orders in Quebec hastened the acceptance of women teachers in the province.[26] While John Reid, in his study of Scottish influences on higher education in the Maritimes, reminds us of the need for careful attention to the transmutation of Scottish traditions, it can safely be argued that the Scottish parish school system did not foster the acceptance of women teachers.[27]

The Scottish immigrants to northeastern Nova Scotia brought with them the tradition of the parish school system, established in the 17th century. This system had two characteristics that would preclude women teachers. One was the religious duties performed by many parish schoolteachers. The parish teacher usually doubled as the session clerk and often led the reading of the psalms at Sunday services, public tasks that could not be performed by a female teacher.[28] The second was the role of the parish school in preparing its students for further intellectual training at the burgh schools, or county academies, and at university. Unlike the situation in either North America or England and Wales, provision was made for some students to progress from the parish elementary schools through to the burgh secondary schools and then to university. It is significant that the feminization of the Scottish public school teaching force did not really begin until after the passage of the British 1872 School Act. This act, by providing funding only for primary schools and not for secondary schooling, changed the orientation of the Scottish school system and eliminated the link between primary education and the universities.[29] The persistence of male teachers in counties with high proportions of Scottish immigrants and their descendants owes some debt to the legacy of the parish school system.

Further research is needed to reach firm conclusions on the matter of recruiting women teachers, and other factors must be weighed. Prentice and Theobald, in their recent review of the historiography of women teachers, emphasize the complexity and local variation in the recruitment of women teachers to public school teaching.[30] At this point any conclusions about the reasons for the regional variations within Nova Scotia in the rate of feminization are premature, but the rich literature in the

26   Danylewycz, Light and Prentice, "Evolution", p. 94.

27   John G. Reid, "Beyond the Democratic Intellect: The Scottish Example and University Reform in Canada's Maritime Provinces, 1870-1933", in Paul Axelrod and John G. Reid, eds., *Youth, University and Canadian Society: Essays in the Social History of Higher Education* (Montreal, 1989), pp. 275-300. See also R.D. Anderson, *Education and Opportunity in Victorian Scotland: Schools and Universities* (Oxford, 1983).

28   Bruce Lenman, *Integration, Enlightenment and Industrialization: Scotland 1746-1832* (Toronto, 1981), p. 12.

29   Helen Corr, "The Sexual Division of Labour in the Scottish Teaching Profession, 1872-1914", in Walter M. Humes and Hamish M. Paterson, eds., *Scottish Culture and Scottish Education, 1800-1980*, (Edinburgh, 1983); Smout, *Scottish People*, pp. 221-2; Anand C. Chitnis, *The Scottish Enlightenment: A Social History*, (London, 1976), p. 127.

30   Prentice and Theobald, "The Historiography of Women Teachers".

field suggests a number of interpretative approaches. Strober and Tyack, in their study of American teachers, argue that it was only in the areas that rejected other educational reforms that large numbers of male teachers remained in the public school system.[31] This interpretation flies in the face of the conventional Scottish reputation for a love of learning, and further research on the public schools of Cape Breton would be needed to test it. However, the willingness of Pictou County school boards to hire women in the 1870s is interesting, as that county maintained a reputation for the quality of its schools.

A further line of inquiry presented by Danylewycz, Light and Prentice must also be explored. They argue that the presence of other more lucrative opportunities for paid work for men was an important variable in their participation in public school teaching.[32] This factor may have been of considerable importance in mid-19th century Cape Breton. It is interesting to note, however, that counties on the south shore of the province, especially Queens and Shelburne counties, which also experienced poor economic conditions in the 19th century, were much more likely to hire women. By 1879 three-quarters of the teachers in both counties were women (see Table One). Variations in attitudes toward female teachers among Protestant denominations may have played a role in these counties. Baptists and Methodists, in contrast to Presbyterians, sometimes had less rigid views of women's role in education.[33] A number of questions about the local contours of feminization in Nova Scotia remain unanswered.

Attitudes to the general process of feminization in the province varied considerably throughout the period. Politicians appeared to have very little difficulty accepting the idea of women teachers in the public schools of Nova Scotia. The idea of free schools supported by local property assessment was a controversial issue from the late 1830s to the mid-1860s, and denominational education remained contentious throughout the period.[34] The subject of women teachers paled in comparison to these thornier subjects. In 1837 the Education Committee of the Nova Scotia Assembly prepared a package of school reforms. Among the recommendations was a somewhat grudging acceptance of women teachers. The committee recommended that "Female Teachers, who are often the most valuable that can be obtained" should be entitled to a share of the provincial education grants.[35] Both the Assembly and the Legislative Council accepted the recommendation without debate. It was agreed "that where a female Teacher can be more advantageously employed than a male teacher", the local school board could hire a woman.[36]

The change was totally ignored in the local press. The *Novascotian* published three letters in early March supporting the Assembly's other school reforms. A letter

31   Tyack and Strober, "Jobs and Gender", p. 137.
32   Danylewycz, Light and Prentice, "Evolution".
33   I would like to thank one of the anonymous *Acadiensis* readers for raising this important point.
34   For a discussion of education debates in Nova Scotia see Janet Guildford, "Public School Reform and the Halifax Middle Class, 1850-1870", Ph.D. thesis, Dalhousie University, 1990. The Nova Scotia government passed free school legislation in 1864. *Statutes of Nova Scotia*, 1864, ch. 58.
35   *JHA* (1837-8), App. 72, p. 161.
36   *Statutes of Nova Scotia*, 1838, ch. 23, s. VI.

writer from Musquodoboit apparently did not expect to see large numbers of women enter the occupation. The writer hoped for other reforms that would "raise the character of this class of men, by increasing their means; and making their profession an object of ambition to men of talents and acquirement".[37] The lack of interest in the question of women teachers was strikingly apparent in the one statistical survey of the Nova Scotia school system in the 1840s. In 1842 the report of the short-lived Nova Scotia Central Board of Education presented a multitude of tables, but it did not provide an analysis of male and female teachers. While the language of the report assumed that teachers were male, it is impossible to determine whether or not the members of the board strongly preferred male teachers in the common schools.[38]

Considerably more light was thrown on attitudes to women teachers during the 1850 session of the Legislature. In the course of the general debate on public schooling, female teachers and the education of women were discussed a number of times. Practical approval of female teachers was expressed in the form of a grant to the Amherst Female Seminary, which trained female teachers.[39] While members on both sides of the House expressed general approval for educating girls and hiring women as teachers, apprehension and ambivalence also emerged, and the discussion of women teachers was always couched in the language of separate spheres.[40] Reform leader Joseph Howe hoped that local school boards would be unrestricted in hiring women teachers, but he believed that any Nova Scotia woman would rather be married to a yeoman than "head the best school in the country".[41] The member for Hants County "highly eulogized the character and acquirements of the female teachers" in his riding, claiming that there was a "kindliness in female teachers which was of utmost value to children". His attitude, however, revealed inconsistencies. Despite his apparent approval for women as teachers he argued, without explaining why, that school boards should not hire only female teachers if men applied.[42] The politicians' attitudes toward women were perhaps best revealed by their humour. During one debate a member earned "roars of laughter" when he commented about women, "I love them, sir, as I would love my mother, and I could stand here and plead all night for them".[43] On another day Conservative leader J.W. Johnston evoked a good response when he reminded his fellow members that it was dangerous to introduce the subject of ladies into the debate because "they have already thrown us off our track".[44] Talking about women in the Assembly elicited laughter because women were not part of the public sphere of politics, but belonged in the private sphere of the household.

37   *Novascotian*, 1 March 1838.
38   *First Annual Report of the Nova Scotia Central Board of Education* (Nova Scotia, 1842).
39   *JHA* (1851), App. 51, Report of the Education Committee, p. 185.
40   *Novascotian*, 6 May 1850.
41   *Novascotian*, 6 May 1850.
42   *Novascotian*, 6 May 1850.
43   *Novascotian*, 6 May 1850.
44   *Novascotian*, 2 February 1850.

Education administrators, on the other hand, never made jokes. They were an earnest breed, dedicated to fighting ignorance and vice wherever they found it. Unlike the situation in Upper Canada where one man dominated the educational affairs of the province for 40 years, Nova Scotia had six different senior education administrators in the 30 years between 1850 and 1880.[45] To varying degrees all the Nova Scotia superintendents of education expressed qualified support for hiring women teachers, and all did so in terms of the special abilities of women in caring for young children. Certainly the superintendents of education in Nova Scotia discussed the situation in ideological terms. All, with the possible exception of J.W. Dawson, had some misgivings about the feminization of public school teaching, and all endorsed a strict division of male and female labour within the school system.

Nova Scotia's first school superintendent, J.W. Dawson (1850-3), a young Pictou County geologist and bookseller, actively promoted the recruitment of female teachers.[46] His own formal education had begun in a "Dame School", a small private school for young children run by a woman.[47] In 1850, after a trip to Massachusetts, he reported very favourably on the number and ability of women teachers in the state.[48] As a patriotic Nova Scotian Dawson saw a further advantage in training his countrywomen as teachers. He believed that it would stem the out-migration of Nova Scotia women.[49]

About 20 per cent of Nova Scotia teachers were women during Dawson's brief regime as superintendent, but he noted that they were usually hired only for the summer term, and replaced by men, who during the summer may have been drawn into agricultural or other work. He felt this practice was "injurious" to the state of education, and advocated the retention of good teachers, whether male or female, during the whole year.[50] Dawson was impressed with the quality of some of the women teachers he found at work in Nova Scotia. He singled out the women teachers of Barrington, in Shelburne County on the province's south shore, for special praise. They were "especially deserving of credit for their knowledge of the branches required in their schools and of improved methods of teaching".[51] Dawson's superintendency was a brief one; he resigned from the position after just two years. For the next two years educational affairs in the province were overseen by two regional inspectors. Hugh Munro, the inspector for eastern Nova Scotia, made no comment at all on women teachers; no doubt he encountered very few.

45   Alison Prentice, *The School Promoters* (Toronto, 1977).

46   J. William Dawson, *Fifty Years of Work in Canada: Scientific and Educational* (London, 1901).

47   Dawson, *Fifty Years*. For a discussion of dame schools see E. Jennifer Monaghan, "Noted and Unnoted School Dames: Women as Reading Teachers in Colonial New England", Conference paper for the 11th Session of the International Standing Conference for the History of Education, Oslo, Norway, 1989.

48   *JHA* (1851), Annual Report.

49   Out-migration from the province was female led. See Patricia Thornton, "The Problem of Out-Migration from Atlantic Canada, 1871-1921: A New Look" *Acadiensis*, XV, 1 (Autumn 1985), pp. 3-34.

50   *JHA* (1851), App. 53, Annual Report; *JHA* (1852), App. 11, Annual Report, pp. 72-3.

51   *JHA* (1852), App. 11, Annual Report, p. 67.

Charles D. Randall, responsible for western Nova Scotia, was a strong supporter of female teachers and argued that it was not sex that mattered in a teacher, but qualifications. This kind of comment must always be regarded with suspicion. The sex of the teacher obviously did matter to Randall because he noted that women were "natural guardians of the young".[52]

Alexander Forrester (1854-64), a Scottish-trained minister and zealous educational reformer, was Nova Scotia's second superintendent of public schools.[53] His attitude toward female teachers was considerably more ambivalent than either Dawson's or Randall's, and his support was dependent on the conventions of a rigid delineation of separate spheres for men and women. He spelled out his approach in the teachers' textbook he published in 1867. He noted that "both by the law of nature and revelation" there was a "position of subordination and of dependence assigned to women", and thus there ought to be "situations in educational establishments better adapted to the one sex than the other".[54] In other words, women were acceptable as teachers of young children, but men should retain their jobs as the teachers of older children and as supervisors.

In 1864 Forrester, a long-time Liberal partisan, was demoted by the Conservative government and replaced by Theodore Harding Rand (1864-70), an Annapolis Valley Baptist who had been a teacher at the Normal School in Truro.[55] Rand, too, endorsed the idea of separate roles for male and female teachers. Addressing the Provincial Education Association in 1870 he tried to reassure the male teachers who wanted to "throw a shield around male teachers, lest their lady associates drive them all out of the province".[56] Rand did not believe that male and female teachers were in competition for the same jobs. While men lacked "maternal sympathies so requisite for the conduct of the lower grades...[w]e must retain a certain proportion of the masculine element" for more advanced students.[57]

Rand was fired as superintendent of schools in February 1870 because he bucked the Council of Public Instruction (CPI) during a separate school dispute in Cape Breton.[58] He was replaced by Rev. A.S. Hunt (1870-7), a successful Baptist minister who lacked any experience with the public school system of the province. Forrester and Rand had demonstrated that professional educators were independent and obstructive, and the CPI chose Hunt because its members felt he would support their political policies and smooth over the separate school question, which he did until

52   *JHA* (1854), App. 73, Report of the Education Committee, p. 374.
53   Judith Fingard, "Alexander Forrester", *Dictionary of Canadian Biography*, Vol. IX (Toronto, 1976), pp. 270-2.
54   *The Teachers' Text Book*, (Halifax, 1867), pp. 565-6 cited in Prentice, "The Feminization of Teaching", p. 61.
55   Margaret Conrad, "Theodore Harding Rand", *Dictionary of Canadian Biography*, Vol. XII (Toronto, 1990), pp. 879-84.
56   *Journal of Education*, 29 (February 1870), p. 450.
57   *Journal of Education*, 29 (February 1870), p. 450.
58   Conrad, "Theodore Harding Rand".

his death in 1877.[59] But Hunt's lack of experience with the public school system left him unprepared for the extent of feminization in the early 1870s. He also had to contend with the fact that some people complained about the increasing numbers of women teachers, while others "had a very decided preference" for them.[60]

Hunt's own attitude to women teachers was complex. While initially he deplored the feminization of the public school work force, he gradually changed his opinion. Although there were echoes of the separate spheres ideology in his thinking, he was not entirely confident of the natural ability of women to exercise a good influence on children, and his approval for women teachers was closely tied to their educational attainments. Hunt's thinking on the question is most interesting because it contains elements of both older ideas about the depravity of women and newer ideas about the need for specialized training in the making of an effective school system.

In his first report Hunt commented that the "evil" of large numbers of female teachers was "operating unfavourably upon the public welfare".[61] And he may have been one of the few Canadians to take satisfaction in the depression of the 1870s, because it dried up new work opportunities for male teachers and kept them in the school system.[62] These denunciations reflect only one facet of Hunt's complex attitudes toward women. Although he was imbued with the separate spheres ideology, Hunt was not persuaded of the value of women's natural aptitude for mothering or teaching, and he was apprehensive about the effect of "ignorant" women on the development of children. He advocated the introduction of more rigorous training for girls in the public school system and hoped that women teachers would also receive better training.[63] He explained his thinking to the provincial Education Association in 1872:

> Our common schools are open alike to the sexes, and I am of the opinion that our colleges and academies also ought to be, and in a few years, I think will be, open to females...[T]he most highly cultivated intellect is requisite to train a child in his early years. It is most unsafe for the moral and intellectual, as well as for the physiological welfare of a young child, to trust it to the keeping of ignorant and uncultivated persons. Here is at once a reason why mothers should have the best education that the country can afford, for mothers must have charge, some of them exclusive charge, of

---

59   For obituaries of Hunt see *Christian Messenger*, 31 October 1877; *Acadian Recorder*, 24 October 1877. It is probably a comment on Hunt's lack of professional credentials that no biographical work has been published on his career. For a brief discussion of his appointment see Conrad, "Theodore Harding Rand".

60   *Annual Report* (1876), pp. ix-x.

61   "Our Public Schools", *Journal of Education*, 37 (June 1871), p. 573.

62   *Annual Report* (1876), pp. ix-x.

63   "Our Public Schools", *Journal of Education*, 37 (June 1871), p. 573; Superintendent's Address to the Education Association of Nova Scotia, *Journal of Education*, 44 (August 1872), p. 50.

the earlier years of their children — an ignorant woman in such a position is a sad object to contemplate.[64]

With longer experience in the public school system of Nova Scotia Hunt did moderate his position on women teachers. He felt that the complaints about feminization would dissipate as the level of training among women teachers improved.[65] By the time David Allison, a classical scholar and the president of Mount Allison College, assumed the superintendency 1877 feminization was a fait accompli and no longer the source of much discussion.[66]

Feminization and the separate spheres ideology that promoted it had important ramifications for teachers' efforts to improve their wages, working conditions and political power. By 1870 Nova Scotia school administrators were speaking confidently and optimistically about the "dignity of the teacher's profession". An editorial in the provincial *Journal of Education* claimed that

Teaching is no longer an ignoble pursuit, nor a field for scholastic ambition, but a profession engaging the public confidence, demanding great talents and industry, and securing great and satisfactory rewards.[67]

These claims must have read like wishful thinking to the teachers of Nova Scotia. The struggle to achieve professional status was long and difficult, and teachers had made little progress by 1870. There has been debate among historians about whether "professionalization" is the most accurate description of teachers' efforts to improve their situation, but the term has been adopted for this study because it was used by contemporary education administrators and teachers in their struggle for improved wages, working conditions and status.[68] References to teaching as a profession began to appear in the Nova Scotia press as early as the 1830s and continued to be used throughout the period.[69] Alexander Forrester, for example, asked in a pamphlet promoting the Normal School, "Would it...not prove of incalculable service to the cause of education to have the business of teaching exalted to the rank and dignity of one of the learned professions?"[70] In 1870 the *Journal of Education* used the

---

64 Superintendent's Address to the Education Association of Nova Scotia, *Journal of Education*, 44 (August 1872), p. 50.

65 *Annual Report* (1876), pp. ix-x.

66 "David Allison", in Henry James Morgan, ed. *The Canadian Men and Women of the Time: A Handbook of Canadian Biography* (Toronto, 1898), p. 18. For Allison's initial impressions of feminization see *JHA* (1877), App. 5, Annual Report, p. xviii.

67 *Journal of Education*, 32 (August 1870), p. 498.

68 For a discussion of recent approaches to the history of teachers efforts to improve their situation see Wayne J. Urban, "New Directions in the Historical Study of Teacher Unionism", *Historical Studies in Education/Revue d'histoire de l'education*, 2, 1 (Spring/printemps 1990), pp. 1-15. Also useful is Jennifer Ozga and Martin Lawn, *Teachers, Professionalization and Class* (London, 1981).

69 See, for example, *Novascotian*, 1 March 1838; *Provincial Magazine*, 2, 2 (February 1853), p. 52.

70 *Register and Circular with Brief History and Condition of the Normal School of Nova Scotia 1862* (Halifax, 1862), p. 12.

teachers' claims to professional status as the basis for higher wages for teachers.[71] The professionalization model is helpful in understanding the position of teachers if we adopt Barry Bergen's approach to the question. He argues that professional-ization must be examined as "the process of constituting and controlling a market for special services, expertise or knowledge".[72]

A second useful point can also be drawn from the literature on the professional-ization of teaching. Ozga and Lawn point out that claims for professionalization played an ambiguous role in the teachers' efforts to improve their conditions. The state could and did use professionalism to control teachers, by encouraging them to tie their aspirations very closely to the level of service they provided to the community, thereby discouraging unseemly demands for personal gain. However, teachers also used their claim to professional status in order to assert their right to higher wages and greater control of the conditions of their work, to which they felt entitled by virtue of their specialized knowledge and skills.[73]

There can be little doubt that Nova Scotia teachers, like their counterparts in other places, failed in their early bids for professional status. While wages did improve for a few men in senior positions, most male teachers continued to earn a wage comparable to that of labourers, and women were paid on a scale very similar to the wage rates of domestic servants.[74] Even the most senior male education officers in the province were powerless to assert their claims to professional control against the interference of elected political officials. The demotion or firing of three well-qualified senior officials in the decade following the passage of the Free School Act in 1864 made this point very clear. Alexander Forrester was demoted to principal of the Normal School in 1864 by the Conservative Nova Scotia government because of his long-time support for the opposition Liberals.[75] At the same time the provincial government stripped the Normal School of its right to confer teaching licences on its graduates and instituted a new licensing examination system. In 1867 F.W. George, an experienced educator, was fired as inspector of schools for Cumberland and replaced with a political appointee.[76] And in 1870 superintendent T.H. Rand was fired for opposing the government's separate school policy.[77] By 1880 Nova Scotia teachers did not control access to the profession, wages or the conditions of their work.

The teachers did try a variety of strategies to improve their lot, and their efforts illustrate both the strengths and weaknesses of professionalization as a political tool.

71   *Journal of Education*, 30 (April 1870).
72   Barry H. Bergen, "Only a Schoolmaster: Gender, Class, and the Effort to Professionalize Elementary Teaching in England, 1870-1910", *History of Education Quarterly*, 22, 1 (1982), p. 8.
73   Ozga and Lawn, *Teachers, Professionalization and Class*.
74   *Halifax Daily Reporter and Times*, 12 January 1874; Ian McKay, "The Working Class of Metropolitan Halifax, 1850-1889", Honours Essay, Dalhousie University, 1975.
75   Fingard, "Alexander Forrester".
76   F.W. George to Lt.-Gov. Sir Hastings Doyle, 7 September 1869 Provincial Secretary's Correspondence, RG 7, vol. 69, Public Archives of Nova Scotia [PANS].
77   T.H. Rand to the Provincial Secretary, 5 February 1870, Provincial Secretary's Correspondence, RG 7, vol. 69, PANS; *JHA* (1870) App. 22, Arichat Schools.

Sometimes the actions were short-lived, as was the case when 22 teachers petitioned the Halifax School Board for higher wages in 1855.[78] Others attempted to improve their skills by attending government-sponsored Teachers' Institutes.[79] A teacher who attended an institute at Truro in 1852 reported:

> I have returned with a feeling of delight...one source of regret alone I feel regarding it, and that is that we continued together for so short a time...I feel happier in my work, because many of the plans I have tried in doubt have been tried by others, and that with success.[80]

Teachers' Institutes could also be adapted to serve more autonomous professional goals. In 1870 nine teachers from the town of Pictou conducted their own Teachers' Institute, holding semi-monthly meetings and operating a library "of the best works on Education and practical teaching".[81]

Teachers began to create sustained autonomous organizations in the early 1860s. The Halifax and Dartmouth Teachers' Association was formed in 1862 by 17 men and five women to elevate the status of teachers.[82] A few months later 14 teachers, ten men and four women, established a province-wide organization. At first the group called itself the United Teachers' Association of Nova Scotia, but six months later the name was changed to the Provincial Education Association (PEA). The change in name suggests a shift in the political orientation of the organization from the elevation of the status of the teacher to the improvement of educational services within Nova Scotia.[83] While these two goals were always associated by the teachers' organizations they were not identical, and the contradictions expose the ambiguity of professionalism.

Between 1862 and 1880 the PEA functioned as a combination lobby group and scientific society for the teachers of Nova Scotia. Its membership, open to teachers of both sexes, was dominated by senior male teachers, many of them teachers and principals of academies rather than elementary schools, and county inspectors. With the one exception of Amelia Archibald, a Halifax teacher who served as a member of the Management Committee of the association in 1873, the executive was entirely male.[84] The PEA was moribund between 1876 and 1879, and in 1880 it was superseded by the Educational Association of Nova Scotia. The change represented a loss of autonomy by the teachers. The new Educational Association was established under the auspices of the Council of Public Instruction, and the membership included all provincial education officials and everyone associated with provincial colleges as

78 *Presbyterian Witness*, 22 December 1855.
79 *JHA* (1851), Annual Report.
80 *JHA* (1852) Annual Report, App. 11, p. 60.
81 *Annual Report* (1870), Inspector's Report, Pictou County, p. 54.
82 *Constitution of Halifax Dartmouth Teachers Association* (Halifax, 1862)
83 Minutes of the Provincial Education Association [PEA], 16 May 1862, 25 September 1862, PEA Minute Book, RG 14, vol. 69, PANS.
84 See PEA Minutes, 1862-80 and Petitions, RG 5, Series P, vol. 77, no. 86, 20 February 1864 and vol. 77, no. 165, 11 February 1868, PANS.

well as teachers. The format of the first convention resembled a teachers' institute rather than the scientific society form used by the PEA.[85]

The records of the PEA are, unfortunately, sparse, but there is no evidence that the association regarded the feminization of public school teaching as a professional or political issue. Although it was open to all teachers in the province, the PEA attracted only a handful of women, and it can be assumed that these women were dedicated professionals. For the most part they were treated by their male colleagues with a protective paternalism appropriate to the conventions of the separate spheres ideology. The association recognized the salary differentials between men and women by collecting lower membership dues from women teachers, and in 1869 it voted to sell Alexander Forrester's *Teacher's Text Book* to "Lady Members" for one dollar instead of two.[86]

Male members also protected women from having to expose themselves to censure by speaking on a public platform. On the few occasions when women teachers prepared papers for meetings the papers were read by men and the writer remained anonymous. In July 1871, for example, Halifax school principal C.W. Major read a "paper by a lady teacher entitled 'Miscellaneous Observations of the Studies of Girls'", and in 1873 F.W. George, principal of the New Glasgow Academy, also read a paper from an anonymous "lady teacher".[87] The pattern was interrupted in 1874 when Dartmouth teacher Maria Angwin stood on the public platform to read her own paper, ironically entitled "The Old is Better".[88] Angwin, later the first women licensed to practise medicine in Nova Scotia, was obviously out of step with her colleagues, and the next year another male teacher read a paper "handed in by a lady".[89]

Although women were clustered at the low end of the occupation and paid considerably less than men at each licence level, the participation of even a few in the PEA demonstrates that some women were ambitious to improve their standing.[90] In the early 1850s women teachers attended Teachers' Institutes sponsored by the

---

85   *Report of the First Annual Convention of the Education Association of Nova Scotia* (1880), PEA Minute Book.

86   *Journal of Education*, 25 (June 1869), p. 396; PEA Minutes, December 1873.

87   PEA Minutes, 20 July 1871 and December 1873.

88   PEA Minutes, December 1874.

89   PEA Minutes, December 1875; Lois Kernaghan, "'Someone Wants the Doctor': Maria Angwin, MD, (1849-1898)", Nova Scotia Historical Society *Collections*, Vol. 43, (1991), pp. 33-48.

90   *JHA* (1869), Annual Report, App. 7, Table 1.

Winter Term.	Acad.	1st class	2nd class	3rd class	Total
Male	13	231	260	290	794
Female	0	232	182	90	504

The salary differentials for 1869 were: Male 1st class: $397; Female 1st class: $256; Male 2nd class $253; Female 2nd class: $181; Male 3rd class: $186; Female 3rd class: $150. RG 14, vol.30, #471, 1869, PANS.

Nova Scotia superintendent of schools, J.W. Dawson.[91] In 1858 Forrester published an essay by a young woman pupil at the Normal School in the *Journal of Education and Agriculture* on teachers' need for special knowledge about the nature of child development.[92] From the time it opened in 1854 the provincial Normal School at Truro always had a large proportion of female students. It was not until 1869 that female teachers were eligible to take the examination for first-class licences. In October 1869 a 16-year-old Normal School student was the first woman to gain a first-class licence.[93] However, the highest licence granted in the province was the academic licence, not the first class. Therefore women were still ineligible for teaching in provincial secondary schools. The two medal winners at the Normal School in 1877 were both women, and the four students with highest marks in the licensing examinations in 1881 were women.[94]

A few women were active in professional activities beyond the PEA and the Normal School, and some won recognition for their efforts. In 1870 Miss H.M. Norris of Cape Canso won a ten-dollar prize from the Provincial Education Association for the best educational tract, "Five Days a Week, or the Importance of Regular Attendance at School".[95] Letitia Wilson, who taught the school in Doctors Cove, Shelburne County, attained both respect and financial reward. In 1870 the trustees of her school found her services so profitable "both educationally and financially" that they increased her salary sufficient to make her the highest paid teacher in her class in the county.[96]

Such success was unusual, and the PEA did not provide a forum for women's professional ambitions. In the early 1870s two women took their grievances to a wider audience. Both these women were unhappy about the lack of financial remuneration they received as well as their lack of status. The language they employ is as significant as their arguments. They argued their cases explicitly in terms of women's special aptitude for teaching the young, and called on the chivalry of their colleagues and employers rather than demanding recognition of their professional skills. Both women wrote anonymously. Apparently even complaints couched in socially acceptable terms were likely to be met with resistance and criticism.

The first was written to the provincial *Journal of Education* in 1871. The author developed her argument systematically:

> Have the friends of right, and the keen discrimination of providential arrangements, considered these conclusions? What place does the woman occupy in the family? Who does not know that in the most important

---

91   Of 68 teachers attending a Teachers Institute at Truro in November 1851, 24 were female. *Journal of Education*, 3 (January 1852); Five female teachers (Susan Best, Annie Kidson, Esther Gould, Mary E. Troop, C.A. Troop) also attended an Institute at Truro in April 1851. Forty men also attended. *Novascotian*, 28 April 1851.

92   *Journal of Education and Agriculture*, 1, 3 (September 1858), pp. 36-8.

93   *Journal of Education*, 27 (October 1869), p. 413.

94   *JHA* (1877), App. 5, Annual Report, p. xviii; *Annual Report* (1881), App. A.

95   *Journal of Education*, 29 (February 1870), pp. 446-7.

96   *Annual Report* (1870), p. 41.

institution in the world, *Home*, woman's mind is the governing power? Who does not know that all minds receive the first training, the first direction, the first noble, generous pulsation of future ambition, under the moulding and elevating authority of the female? Take from our homes this female training; take from society, generally, this element, and what are our homes or what our country? There is a part of the great system of instruction in which woman towers immensely above man. The teacher's office is specially suited to women — who are natural educators.[97]

She went on:

When it is stated that, for the same labour, females receive less pay, though that labour may be as well, if not better, performed, we are compelled to feel that an aspersion is cast upon our sex, from which our past history and present influence ought to save us, and if it has any meaning at all, is a sad commentary upon the chivalry and gallantry of our countrymen.[98]

The second anonymous woman teacher brought her complaints to a Halifax newspaper in 1874. Her tone was more urgent than that of the letter writer three years earlier, but her argument, that male gallantry ought not to permit the underpayment of women teachers, was similar:

Now, Mr. Editor, when we take into account the time, trouble and expense given in order to obtain a first-class license, and the loss of dignity entailed in interviewing the Commissioners, one by one, and in appealing to every feeling known to humanity (save that of qualification for the office), it will be granted that the salary given is not glaringly liberal....The only remedy for this evil is increase in salary....It is pitiable to reflect that the only city officials so treated are *women*, whom one would suppose the chivalrous instinct of a *gentleman* would lead him to protect, not oppress.[99]

The deeply held gender attitudes of both male and female teachers crippled their ability to address their situation directly and to negotiate collectively with the state. Reformed public schools provided moral training for children, work associated with the unpaid reproductive labour of the private sphere. But that work was performed in the public sphere for wages. The separate spheres ideology could not fully accommodate the novel institutional setting of the public school which did not fit neatly into it. This uneasy fit made it very difficult for male and female teachers to negotiate collectively to improve their working conditions. The gender ideology had special meaning for teachers of both sexes. And it is important to remember that, whatever reassurances were attempted by school administrators such as T.H. Rand,

97   "Female Teaching", *Journal of Education*, 36 (April 1871), p. 559.
98   "Female Teaching", *Journal of Education*, 36 (April 1871), p. 559.
99   *Halifax Daily Reporter and Times,* 12 January 1874.

men and women were in competition for jobs. Rand himself pointed to this competition indirectly in the *Journal of Education* in 1870 in an item on selecting teachers. He complained that when it came to hiring, many local school boards made inappropriate choices, and nearly all those poor choices were women teachers. He said that very few "real Teachers" applied for teaching jobs. Most were "estimable young ladies without money" who were hired because the local school trustees believed that money raised in town should help the poor, or they were untrained school girls hired because they were local or because their fathers were influential in the locality.[100]

Superintendent Hunt also tried to reassure male teachers that they need not compete with women for jobs. In 1871 he argued that women teachers simply could not compete with men "in inculcating what we may call the severer studies so necessary to fit young men for the hard, practical duties of life".[101] He believed that it was a false economy for school trustees to take advantage of the supply of cheap female teachers.[102] The report of the inspector for Pictou County in 1870 refers very explicitly to the competition:

> Though painful to acknowledge, it is a humiliating fact that too many sections are influenced in their selection of teachers more by dollars and cents than by the merits of candidates. Many young men, holding first-class licenses, experienced difficulty in obtaining situations, because they objected to labour for the paltry salaries offered. Trustees also complain of the scarcity of teachers. The fault and the remedy rest with themselves.[103]

J.B. Calkin, the principal of the Normal School, offered the most modern solution to the competition. In 1874 he argued that teaching salaries should be based on qualifications, not sex.[104] It is eloquent testimony to the durability of the separate spheres ideology that his was virtually a lone voice. The editor of a Halifax newspaper expressed a much commoner attitude in a tirade against equal rights for women when he stated that "a sensible and practical woman can always get her rights".[105]

In reality the separate spheres ideology prescribed the expectations and attitudes of Nova Scotia women teachers in ways that made it difficult for them to bargain effectively in the public sphere. Women teachers, as the two writers quoted above attest, believed that they had a natural aptitude for teaching. A natural aptitude does not constitute a learned skill, or in Bergen's words, "special service, expertise or knowledge".[106] Expertise and skill are political constructs; that is, the recognition of

100 *Journal of Education*, 30 (April 1870).

101 *Journal of Education*, 37 (June 1871), p. 573.

102 *Journal of Education*, 37 (June 1871), p. 574.

103 *Annual Report* (1870), Inspector's Report, Pictou County.

104 *Annual Report* (1875), Report of the Provincial Normal School, App. B, p. 95.

105 *Presbyterian Witness*, 21 August 1869.

106 Bergen, "Only a Schoolmaster", p. 8.

skill depends on the success of its possessor in persuading society of its value, not on the degree of difficulty or length of time involved in acquiring it. Women have historically been less successful than men in that process because the skills of women have been defined as belonging to the private sphere, outside the economic values that permeate the public sphere. One measure of this difficulty is found in the descriptions of male and female teachers in mid-19th-century Nova Scotia. Male teachers were recognized for their "careful training and ability".[107] Female teachers, on the other hand, were admired for their "affectionate solicitude" and "unimpeachable fidelity".[108] Women were praised for their innate characteristics, while men were valued for their acquired or learned skill.

Because women were performing work that they were divinely called to, and rested their claims for status on God and nature, they lacked a language in which to advance their claims in the public sphere. This is evident in the women teachers' appeals for chivalry, language that carried more weight in the private sphere than in the public. It is very significant that both of these women used the language of chivalry and natural ability rather than that of human rights and acquired skill.

The full extent of these disadvantages can be understood when we take a longer view of the impact of the separate spheres ideology on the life cycle of women. This ideology proposed that marriage and motherhood were the routes to economic security and social influence. More research is needed to determine just how long women remained in the public school work force, but we do know that women teachers in Nova Scotia were not encouraged to remain in their positions after marriage.[109] The inspector for Cumberland County was the only provincial education official to broach the subject of married teachers directly. He wrote:

> Married ladies are necessarily unable to give steady attendance to school duties, the higher law of maternity compelling them often to be at home. The law of nature seems to be that ladies should, on entering the married state, devote themselves to domestic and social cares, and not to public duties. The family is the school in which the married lady should teach.[110]

The inspector from Pictou County simply assumed that women moved out of the work force at marriage, and coyly reported that "Cupid's intrigues have carried off

---

107 Minutes of the Commissioners, 12 June 1850, Records of the Board of Commissioners of Schools for the City of Halifax, RG 14, no. 29, PANS.

108 Minutes of the Commissioners, 12 June 1850, Records of the Board of Commissioners of Schools for the City of Halifax, RG 14, no. 29, PANS.

109 The experience of Nova Scotia teachers differed from that of their counterparts in London and in France where married teachers were encouraged to remain in the work force. See Copelman, "A New Comradeship", and Leslie Page Moch, "Government Policy and Women's Experience: The Case of Teachers in France", *Feminist Studies*, 13, 2 (Summer 1988), pp. 301-24. Jean Barman has argued that in British Columbia women teachers often had careers at least as long as their male counterparts: Jean Barman, "Birds of Passage or Early Professionals? Teachers in Late Nineteenth-century British Columbia," *Historical Studies in Education*, 2, 1 (Spring 1990), pp. 17-36.

110 *Annual Report* (1876), Inspector's Report, Cumberland County, p. 30.

seven of our female teachers".[111]

The forced retirement of women teachers at marriage again reminds us that public school teaching was conducted in the public sphere. It is oversimplifying a complex process to argue that public school rooms became an extension of the private sphere. The public school system was created by male politicians, administered and supervised by male education officers, and its senior teaching positions were retained for male teachers. The men within the public school system were insistent in their claim to specialized knowledge and their position as professionals. Bureaucratization created career ladders for male teachers, with a few lucrative and socially prestigious positions within their sight, if not their grasp. Yet, unlike medical doctors, who were successful in masculinizing their occupation as part of the process of professionalization, male teachers had to wage their struggle in a field that by 1880 was dominated by women. Pictou County school inspector Daniel McDonald, an active member of the Provincial Education Association, identified professionalization quite explicitly with men. In his report for 1870 he lamented that the number of "professional men is small" and stressed the importance of educating the public "to provide salaries adequate to the comfortable maintenance of a family, and to render the schools permanent institutions before young men can be expected to devote their lives to teaching".[112]

While the competition of women in the field may have generated bitter resentment among many men, the separate spheres ideology to which they were committed demanded that they treat their female colleagues with paternalism and chivalry. The strong representation of Scottish-trained academy teachers in the Provincial Education Association in the 1860s and 1870s intensified the dichotomy between elements of the public and private spheres in public education, making it more difficult to negotiate the boundaries within the profession and to present common cause. These men had to press their claims to professional control of a feminized and degraded institution with politicians for whom feminization and the associated low costs were acceptable and even desirable. For male teachers, as for female teachers, the acceptance of a rigid distinction between the public and private spheres inhibited successful collaboration and thus professionalization.

Gender analysis must be applied broadly to the question of public education in mid-19th-century Nova Scotia. Public school reform in the mid-1860s created a demand for a large work force that was capable of providing moral training for young children. The separate spheres ideology accorded women a special role in the nurture of young children, and women quickly became numerically predominant in that work force. They were not hired because of their special training or skills but because they had what were believed to be natural characteristics that they shared with all women. The separate spheres ideology that promoted the recruitment of women teachers thus proved highly problematic to both men and women working within the reformed public schools. Nineteenth-century Nova Scotia teachers were unable to persuade politicians and taxpayers that they controlled the market on a special skill.

111 *Annual Report* (1877), Inspector's Report, Pictou County, p. 34.
112 *Annual Report* (1870), p. 53.

IAN ROSS ROBERTSON

Reprinted from Vol. XV, No. 1
(Autumn 1985)

Political Realignment in Pre-Confederation Prince Edward Island, 1863-1870

IMPORTANT POLITICAL CHANGES OCCURRED in Prince Edward Island between 1863 and 1870. Historians have usually been attracted to Island history in these years by the theme of colonial union, and perhaps as a consequence have tended to underestimate the significance of issues predominantly local in character. But to understand the period and what followed, it is necessary to redirect the focus of analysis away from the question of Confederation. The details of the story are not tidy, but Island politics were not a tidy affair in these years.[1]

The political realignment of this period took place in two stages, and the Confederation question was decisive at neither. Following the split in the Conservative leadership over Confederation in 1864-65, the most potent factors causing political change were the land question and sectarianism. The land question separated the Conservatives from their grassroots supporters in rural Queens County and determined the Liberal election victory of 1867. Sectarianism, embodied in the issue of denominational grants, separated virtually all Roman Catholic legislators from the Protestant leadership of the Liberal party following the election of 1870, thus providing the opportunity for a coalition government to be formed under the leadership of Conservative James Colledge Pope. The alliance of convenience between Conservatives and Roman Catholics developed into a political juggernaut which ruled for 17 of the next 21 years and brought the Island into Confederation in 1873. Thus close examination of the political impact of the land question, which scattered Conservative forces in 1867, and sectarianism, which scattered Liberal forces three years later, is essential for understanding the configuration of political factions after 1870 and for a realistic comprehension of the genesis of Confederation on the Island. It was in these years, and in a local context conditioned by strife over the land question and sectarianism, that the political vehicle for Confederation was assembled.

Over the decades of the 1840s and 1850s, in response to the issues of responsible government and land reform, partisan divisions on the Island had developed largely on the basis of ideology and class interest. The Liberals, under George

The author wishes to thank M. Brook Taylor for his advice in revising this paper. Research was facilitated by the support of the Social Sciences and Humanities Research Council of Canada, through its Leave Fellowship and Research Grant programmes.

1 See F.W.P. Bolger, *Prince Edward Island and Confederation 1863-1873* (Charlottetown, 1964), F.W.P. Bolger, ed., *Canada's Smallest Province: A History of P.E.I.* (Charlottetown, 1973), Chs. 6-9, Harry Baglole and David Weale, *The Island and Confederation: The End of an Era* (Summerside, 1973).

Coles, were the party of progressive reform and made a point of appealing to the tenantry. After the achievement of responsible government in 1851 they placed particular emphasis upon widening the franchise, ensuring universal access to non-denominational education, and enabling as many tenants as possible to become freeholders, while bettering the lot of those whose landlords refused to sell. The Liberals encountered considerable frustration over the land question: only one major landlord could be persuaded to sell during their years in office, and ameliorative legislation they passed, such as that designed to indemnify evicted tenants, was diluted or disallowed by the Colonial Office.[2] The inescapable conclusion was that the Liberal programme of moderate reform had failed, and indeed the census of 1861 revealed that only 40.4 per cent of the occupiers of land were freeholders.[3] Yet the land question was not an issue which could bring the Conservative party back to office, for many of its leaders were landlords or land agents or both, and the party was intimately linked in the public mind with the proprietary system. Instead, the Conservatives won the elections of 1859 and 1863 by mobilizing the Protestant majority against perceived threats to their interests from the Roman Catholics, who constituted approximately 45 per cent of the population. After both elections the Conservatives formed all-Protestant governments, and by 1863 Protestant constituencies were returning only Conservatives and Roman Catholic constituencies only Liberals.[4]

Confederation generated little public support on the Island, but provoked a major split in the Conservative leadership. Premier John Hamilton Gray and the powerful colonial secretary, William Henry Pope, supported the Confederation movement. The attorney general, Edward Palmer, a former premier who had led the Conservatives to victory in 1859 and 1863, opposed it vehemently, taking a central role in rallying public opinion against it. As a consequence first Gray, in December 1864, and then Palmer, in January 1865, resigned from the cabinet.[5] Despite Palmer's departure, he had the satisfaction of knowing that a divided Conservative party could not lead the colony into Confederation. The new premier, James Pope (William's younger brother), remained discreetly ambiguous about his views on the issue, but in 1866, under pressure of public opinion, he presented to the House of Assembly the "no terms" resolution, which denied the possibility of *ever* achieving satisfactory terms of union.[6] In

2 See Ian Ross Robertson, "George Coles", *Dictionary of Canadian Biography*, X (Toronto, 1972), p. 185.

3 Calculation based on Andrew Hill Clark, *Three Centuries and the Island: A Historical Geography of Settlement and Agriculture in Prince Edward Island, Canada* (Toronto, 1959), p. 95, Table III.

4 See Ian Ross Robertson, "The Bible Question in Prince Edward Island from 1856 to 1860", *Acadiensis*, V, 2 (Spring 1976), pp. 3-25, and "Party Politics and Religious Controversialism in Prince Edward Island from 1860 to 1863", *Acadiensis*, VII, 2 (Spring 1978), pp. 29-59.

5 Prince Edward Island, Executive Council Minutes, 20, 22 December 1864, 6, 7 January 1865, microfilm, Public Archives of Prince Edward Island [PAPEI].

6 See Prince Edward Island, House of Assembly, *Debates and Proceedings, 1866*, pp. 52, 54.

effect, there was such a strong anti-Confederate consensus that the question became more or less dormant, with opposition to Confederation being a virtual test of political orthodoxy. To campaign for public office as an advocate of Confederation in these years was to invite defeat, as Edward Whelan, the only prominent pro-Confederate Liberal, discovered in 1867. William Pope, who remained strongly in favour of union of the colonies, resigned from the cabinet in 1866 and contested no more elections. Confederation became a non-issue, and the dynamics of political change on the Island were elsewhere.

Shaken at the top by the Confederation issue, the Conservative party was shaken at the base by the events surrounding the history of the Tenant League. For a generation Island tenants and squatters had heard various solutions to their problems proposed by radical Escheators, more moderate Liberals, and Conservatives. The Escheators, who flourished in the 1830s and early 1840s, had advocated dispossession of proprietors for failure to fulfill the granting terms of 1767. Given the elapse of time and the Escheators' disregard for property rights, the British government considered their proposals utterly beyond the pale of serious discussion. Their leader, William Cooper, although representing a majority in the assembly, was refused an audience when he went to London in 1839.[7] As the party in power in the 1850s the Liberals had relied heavily on their Land Purchase Act of 1853, which authorized government purchase of proprietary estates, with the consent of their owners, for resale to the occupiers of land. But many proprietors, including some of the largest, refused to sell, and the British government would not contemplate compulsory legislation. As a consequence, in the early 1860s the majority of Island farmers were still tenants or squatters. After extensive public hearings in 1860, a report by a land commission, and a delegation to England, the only measure the Conservatives were able to implement by 1864 was the so-called 15 Years Purchase Bill. This legislation gave certain tenants the right to buy the land they occupied at a rate most Island tenants considered exorbitant. Over the next four years only 45 tenants availed themselves of the act, and hence only 2,911 — or 0.82 per cent — of the 353,537 acres to which it applied were converted from leasehold to freehold under its provisions.[8] In the wake of these disappointing experiences with political parties a new tenants' movement took shape.

A brief account of the origins, strategy, tactics, and repression of the Tenant League is necessary in order to explain its political impact in 1867. Founded formally at a convention in Charlottetown on 19 May 1864, the League put its faith in direct action, with no government serving as intermediary between landlord and tenant. Each township was to have a local committee, which would decide upon "a fair and reasonable price" to be offered to the proprietors for their lands. Any difficulties in this process were to be referred to the ten-man

7   See Harry Baglole, "William Cooper", *Dictionary of Canadian Biography*, IX (Toronto, 1976), pp. 156-8.

8   *Statutes of Prince Edward Island*, 27 Vic., c. 2; "Statistics respecting Land Tenure", in Colonial Office [CO] 226/104, p. 311, microfilm, Public Archives of Canada [PAC].

Central Committee of the League. The programme of the Tenant League differed in principle from that of the earlier Escheat movement in that the new organization did not advocate expropriation without compensation. The convention even resolved that "any tenant who shall refuse to make a fair offer ...shall forfeit the sympathy and all the advantages of this Union". But the convention also left no doubt about its determination to bring the leasehold system to an end, by publishing a "Tenant's Pledge", to be taken by its members. Those subscribing to the pledge were "to withhold the further liquidation of rent and arrears of rent; and...to resist the distraint, coercion, ejection, seizure, and sale for rent and arrears of rent".[9] In other words, no further rent was to be paid, and, if necessary, members were to resist the processes of law in order to exert pressure on landlords to sell.

George F. Adams, a tavernkeeper from eastern Queens County who had also, according to his own account, purchased leasehold rights from proprietors more than once, emerged from the founding convention as the most visible single member of the Tenant League. He explicitly rejected the view that the movement should wait for the next election (which would normally be held in 1867) and make its weight felt at the polls; rather, he argued that the issue could be settled before then through united direct action. The exclusion of assemblymen and legislative councillors from the convention emphasized the leaguers' lack of faith in parliamentary means of land reform. Indeed Adams, an Englishman who would soon be described privately by Lieutenant Governor George Dundas as "a wild Chartist",[10] cited examples from British history in which reforms were won "by the *people themselves* demanding them, and in many instances, shedding their *blood* for *them*, and that *too without a murmur*". Stating that the League had no desire for political power, but aimed solely to resolve the land question, he appealed to all sympathizers to lay aside political and religious differences "until this all important grievance is redressed".[11] The Tenant League was clearly a movement beyond the control of the established political élite of Prince Edward Island.

By the early months of 1865 the movement began to present a direct challenge to authorities. On 10 March 1865 James Curtis, under-sheriff for Queens County, made a trip to Fort Augustus and the Monaghan Settlement, ten or 12 miles east of Charlottetown. His purpose was to serve writs on several tenants, including James Callaghan, an early militant in the movement for a tenant league, at the suit of the landlord, Father John McDonald. Curtis encountered various obstructions, and one of Callaghan's sons, whom he met on the road, even made a threat upon his life. Callaghan's son was carrying a tin trumpet,

9 *Ross's Weekly* (Charlottetown), 26 May 1864. The name actually adopted at the convention was "The Tenant Union of Prince Edward Island", but the organization was commonly referred to as the "Tenant League".

10 Dundas to Arthur Blackwood, 6 June 1864, private, in CO 226/100, p. 230. Also see *Ross's Weekly*, 26 May 1864, *Examiner* (Charlottetown), 23 May 1864, 19 June 1865.

11 *Ross's Weekly*, 26 May 1864.

which was the trademark of the League and which had a dual function: it was the means by which supporters passed on the warning that a suspicious person or group was approaching, and the clamour created by dozens of horns could intimidate such persons and make their horses difficult to control. Eventually Curtis turned back, for the community was arming itself with sticks and other weapons against him, and "the trumpets were blowing in every direction". He concluded, and his superior agreed, that it would be "useless" to undertake such missions in that area in future, "without being backed up with a strong force".[12] One week later the Tenant League held a public procession in Charlottetown, headed by a band and displaying flags, some with such inscriptions as "Vox Populi", "Tenant Rights", and "Free Land for All". Even critics of the League conceded that the demonstration was orderly. But a breach of the peace occurred when Curtis attempted to arrest Samuel Fletcher, a rank and file Tenant Leaguer against whom he had a writ for refusing to pay rent. With the assistance of others, Fletcher escaped, tin trumpet in hand, and instantly became an enduring symbol of successful popular resistance to authority.[13]

In the late spring and the summer of 1865 matters assumed a more menacing aspect. On the night of 27 May a fire broke out on the estate of John Archibald McDonald (a nephew of Father John), an unpopular landlord in eastern Queens known for short leases, high rents, and ruthlessness in the use of distraint and eviction. A barn and stable, valued at £150, were destroyed. Although no direct connection with the Tenant League was ever proved, the fire was apparently the work of incendiaries angered by a series of writs for rent served on known Tenant Leaguers by the sheriff's bailiff and McDonald earlier in the day.[14] On 18 July Curtis was assaulted and injured some six miles west of the capital while returning from an expedition with writs issued for non-payment of rent. In the course of the affray a group of Tenant Leaguers rescued a horse and wagon which had been seized, but Curtis and his three assistants managed nonetheless to capture "the ring-leader", Charles Dickieson, a farmer for whose arrest a warrant had already been issued.[15] When Dickieson, who was charged in connection with the incident, was to be brought before a justice of the peace in Charlottetown, the authorities feared that sympathetic demonstrators might set him free. Hence about 25 special constables were armed to escort him between the jail and City Hall. They succeeded, although they were pelted with stones by a crowd numbering in the hundreds in from the countryside.[16] These events raised

12 Curtis to John Morris, 14 March 1865, in Accession 2514/10, PAPEI; also see Morris to J.C. Pope, 15 March 1865, in *ibid.*

13 See Theophilus DesBrisay to Morris, 18 March 1865, and Morris to J.C. Pope, 18 March 1865, in *ibid.*; *Islander* (Charlottetown), 24 March 1865; *Examiner*, 10 April 1865; Robert Hodgson to Edward Cardwell, 2 August 1865, in Prince Edward Island, *Assembly Journal, 1866*, appendix G.

14 See *Examiner*, 5 June 1865; *Royal Gazette* (Charlottetown), 7 June 1865.

15 See affidavits of Curtis and Jonathan Collings, 19 July 1865, in *Assembly Journal, 1866*, app. G; *Islander*, 21 July 1865.

16 See Thomas W. Dodd to W.H. Pope, 26 July 1865, and W.H. Pope to Dodd, 26 July 1865 in

the question of possible means of aid to the civil power, for it was evident that in Queens County the sheriff was finding it increasingly difficult to discharge his duties without the assistance of an armed force. On 1 August the administrator of the colony, Robert Hodgson, with the full support of the government led by James Pope, took the fateful step of requesting that soldiers be sent to the Island from Halifax. Five days later two companies, totalling 134 men, arrived in Charlottetown.[17]

The idea of rent being collected "at the point of a bayonet" — a local metaphor referring to any active involvement of soldiers in the enforcement of leasehold obligations — was anathema in the political universe of Prince Edward Island. Hodgson and Pope were gambling that the mere presence of regular troops in Charlottetown would have a stabilizing effect on the Island as a whole. The all-Protestant Conservative government faced an awkward political dilemma, for the League had displayed particular strength in areas which had voted Conservative in recent elections. The first signs of formation of a new tenant organization had appeared in Protestant districts. Around the beginning of 1864, tenants at a meeting in southern Kings County had passed resolutions pledging resistance to distraint proceedings and expressing determination to prevent occupation of farms seized for rent, and had appended a declaration that "we are, or the majority of us, supporters of the present Government".[18] Whelan had greeted this with undisguised amusement, if not glee, and had republished the report of the meeting under the heading "Government Supporters in Arms Against the Government".[19]

The Conservatives doubtless felt acutely uncomfortable at the prospect of having to use the military in districts which had voted Conservative, but by October of 1865, with resistance to the officers of the Queens County sheriff continuing, they had little alternative. On 3 October James H. Peters, assistant judge of the Supreme Court, complained to Hodgson that on the previous day when travelling west to hold court in Prince County he had had to pass through a "tumultuous assembly" of some 200 persons, equipped with tin trumpets, near Hunter River, in Queens County, apparently gathered "to prevent the Sheriff serving writs from the Supreme Court". A former land agent who had established a formidable Island-wide reputation in the ten years before his appointment to the bench in 1848, Peters urged the administrator to take prompt action, lest "the lawless spirit which appears at present confined to certain districts, will soon extend through the whole country, then only to be suppressed by a loss of life which one shudders to contemplate".[20] Within days Hodgson and the Pope government sent 27 soldiers with the Queens County sheriff on the first

Accession 2514/10, PAPEI; Hodgson to Cardwell, 2 August 1865, in *Assembly Journal, 1866*, app. G.

17 See Hodgson to Sir R.G. McDonnell, 1 August 1865, in *ibid.*; *Examiner*, 7, 14 August 1865.

18 *Ross's Weekly*, 28 January 1864.

19 *Examiner*, 1 February 1864.

20 Peters to Hodgson, 3 October 1865, in CO 226/101, p. 482.

of two expeditions to four townships in the western half of the county.[21]

Although capable of intimidating or repelling small bodies of civilian law enforcement officers, the Tenant Leaguers had no intention of challenging regular soldiers. The sheriff's party encountered no resistance in western Queens, and in November the sheriff, accompanied by 43 soldiers, made a ten-day visit to the five adjacent townships of eastern Queens where the League appeared to be strongest and where its leadership was concentrated. In serving writs they met some passive hostility, including the destruction of three small wooden bridges. But Hodgson felt able to report to London that "I am inclined to believe that this and the previous demonstration [in October] have had a good effect; and that although the animosity of the tenantry on the rent question has not subsided, the dread of incurring heavy costs has induced many to come forward and endeavor to effect a settlement of their arrears".[22] Rent had been collected "at the point of a bayonet".

Furthermore, the Tory government launched several prosecutions, including one against the publisher of the pro-Tenant League *Ross's Weekly* newspaper for libel because of references to the Supreme Court judges, the sheriff, and the bailiff in an article entitled "The Tenant Union and the Courts of Law".[23] The government also undertook to purge the ranks of magistrates, other minor officials, and district school teachers of League supporters.[24] Under these pressures the Tenant League organization and leadership appear to have disintegrated. The local government felt sufficiently in command of the situation to release its Tenant League prisoners, including Dickieson, in August of 1866, and the imperial government withdrew its troops on 27 June 1867.[25]

Thus repression had effectively destroyed the Tenant League as an organization capable of defying the law. Indeed its existence as an organization of any sort was problematic by the autumn of 1866.[26] Yet no one claimed that pro-League sentiment was dead, and close examination of the electoral results of 26 February 1867 suggests that events surrounding the history of the League played

21 See Hodgson to Cardwell, 11, 25 October 1865, *Assembly Journal, 1866*, app. G.

22 Hodgson to Cardwell, 22 November 1865, *ibid.*

23 See Executive Council Minutes, 7 October, 13 November, 12, 19 December 1865; Prince Edward Island Supreme Court Minutes, 12, 13, 16, 17, 18, 19, 20, 22, 24 January 1866, PAPEI; "The Queen v John Ross", Indictment for Libel, Prince Edward Island, Supreme Court Case Papers, PAPEI; *Herald* (Charlottetown), 24 January 1866, reprinted from *Patriot* (Charlottetown), 20 January 1866; *Royal Gazette*, 20 September 1865; *Islander*, 3 November 1865. The article, which appeared in *Ross's Weekly*, 16 March 1865, does not appear to survive.

24 See Hodgson to Cardwell, 25 September 1865 (with enclosure), in CO 226/101, pp. 430-7; Extract from Minutes of the Board of Education, 27 July 1865, in Accession 2514/9, PAPEI; John McNeill to Clerk of Executive Council, 5 October 1865, in *ibid.*; Executive Council Minutes, 1, 14 August, 19 September, 7 October 1865.

25 See *Herald*, 8 August 1866; *Islander*, 28 June 1867.

26 Reports of meetings of the League's Central Committee in August and September of 1866 appeared in *Herald*, 22 August, 19 September 1866, but no hard evidence of subsequent activity as an organization survives.

a decisive role in the outcome. Six newly-elected assemblymen, five of them from rural Queens County, the focal point of League support during its heyday, were believed to be sympathetic to the movement. Each of the six replaced a Conservative, and these reversals were sufficient to determine which party won the election. Without them, the Liberals would have lost, 17 to 13, instead of winning, 19 to 11.

A more detailed analysis, focusing on the available results for individual polls, supports the hypothesis that suppression of the League engendered hard feelings which caused a decisive shift in the assembly election of 1867. For example, in the western half of Queens, comprising the 1st and 2nd Districts, all four successful Liberal candidates were considered to be pro-Tenant League, and they all won by wide margins. In the 1st District, Peter Sinclair and Donald Cameron, the pro-Tenant League candidates, took more than 90 per cent of the votes at the Lot 22 poll. Lot 22 was the first township to which troops had been despatched in October of 1865, following two major incidents of Tenant League defiance of the sheriff's officers in the area, one of which resulted in the indictment of 16 persons. In the 2nd District, the New Glasgow and Wheatley River polls, located in the home districts of the most prominent Tenant League prisoners, provided the margin of victory for Henry J. Callbeck and William S. McNeill. Finally, Benjamin Davies, the pro-Tenant League candidate elected in eastern Queens, gained his margin of victory through overwhelming support at the polls on Lots 49 and 50, the home townships of several Tenant League leaders, including Adams; troops had been sent to both in November of 1865.[27] The returns from these polls in 1st, 2nd, and 4th Queens confirm Palmer's analysis of the election in a letter to his anti-Confederate ally in Nova Scotia, Joseph Howe. The government's loss, he stated, "proceeded more from the effects of the Tenant League, than from the confederation differences within our Conservative party".[28] Rural Queens County had delivered six of eight seats to the Tories in 1863, but four years later only one Tory survived in rural Queens.

Further scrutiny of voting trends on the Island in the aftermath of the Tenant League disturbances reinforces the conclusion that Queens County, the most prosperous, the most populous, the most Protestant, and at recent elections the

27 Calculations based on *Examiner*, 11 March 1867.

28 Palmer to Howe, 8 March 1867 (draft), Item 256, Palmer Family Papers, PAPEI. It may be worth noting that all five townships in 4th Prince, where Alexander Laird Jr., who was believed to be a League sympathizer, replaced James Pope, bordered on western Queens. It is also possible that this reversal was related to Pope's behaviour as a landlord. The constituency included Lot 27, approximately 7,500 acres of which belonged to Pope. In 1868 Dundas reported to London that during the preceding five years Pope's average *actual* rental had been exceeding his *nominal* rental. This meant that he had been collecting arrears during the mid-1860s, when it was very controversial to do so. His political support on Lot 27 appears to have been weak from the beginning of his political career, for in 1857, when first elected at a byelection, 606 to 507, he lost the Lot 27 poll, 134 to 87; thus he won only 39.4 percent of the votes cast at that poll, while winning 58.2 percent of the votes in the remainder of the electoral district. See Dundas to the Duke of Buckingham and Chandos, 3 June 1868, CO 226/104, pp. 333-4; percentage calculations based on electoral data in *Examiner*, 8 June 1857.

most Tory of the three Island counties, had suddenly become hostile territory for the Conservatives, and that their repressive measures against the League explained the change. Evidence in the papers of John McEachern, a self-described "moderate Conservative"[29] residing in a disturbed township of western Queens, provides additional corroboration. Although there is no reason to believe that McEachern, a tenant farmer, was ever actively involved with the Tenant League, he appears to have been in arrears to his landlord on Lot 65, Colonel B.H. Cumberland. In a diary entry for Thursday, 19 October 1865, he wrote that the sheriff had passed through his district that day, accompanied by soldiers. There was a gale on the following day, but on Saturday, when the weather had cleared to some extent, he went to Charlottetown "to settle with Chas. Wright",[30] the agent of Cumberland. McEachern was thus apparently conforming to the pattern subsequently noted by Hodgson, whereby tenants in arrears, anticipating visits from the sheriff supported by soldiers, acted before this happened to them. In a retrospective entry dated 1 January 1866, McEachern stated that in the autumn of 1865 landlords had "distrained upon tennants [*sic*] that never attended Union meetings, which causes much dissatisfaction among many of the former supporters of the present Government".[31] At the Legislative Council election of 19 December 1866 the Conservatives lost both Queens County seats at stake, though they had won both at the first election for the upper house, in 1863. One Charlottetown newspaper attributed the results to "the stop-at-home disease"[32] among Conservative voters, and McEachern, in recording the tally at his local poll, Nine Mile Creek, reported that "many remained home". Indeed the decline in the number of voters at Nine Mile Creek between 1863 and 1866 — from 91 to 51 — was so dramatic as to require a special explanation.[33]

Even more significant were the identities of the two victors in Queens, and the majorities by which they won. John Balderston, a delegate to the founding convention of the Tenant League, who had been dismissed as a commissioner of small debts in September 1865 for his connection with the movement, won 62.7 per cent of the votes in the western half of the county. Robert P. Haythorne, a former estate owner who had disposed of his lands according to the League's prescription, won 58.9 per cent of the votes in defeating the incumbent Conservative member for eastern Queens.[34] Many years later, Haythorne would

29 Fragments of Family History of John McEachern, Diary, undated entry at the commencement of 1870, microfilm, PAPEI. Concerning McEachern, see David Weale, "The Emigrant", *The Island Magazine*, 16 (Fall-Winter 1984) and 17 (Summer 1985).

30 McEachern Diary, 19, 20, 21 October 1865. Although the part of the collection entitled "Sundry Accounts" gives no figures for the 1860s, between 1844 and 1851 McEachern, who had arrived in 1830, had been as much as 11.8 *years* in arrears.

31 McEachern Diary, 1 January 1866.

32 *Herald*, 9 January 1867.

33 McEachern Diary, 19 December 1866; also see 11 February 1863.

34 Calculations based on data in *Islander*, 4 January 1867. Concerning Balderston's dismissal, see

state publicly that "I was returned...[in 1866] in great measure through the influence of that body [the Tenant League]".[35] Thus there can be no doubt that rural Queens County was in the process of shifting its political allegiance in a fundamental way, and that this shift was intimately related to the brief but spectacular career of the Tenant League.

This was the last time the land question played a major divisive role in local politics. In 1866 the largest estate on the Island, comprising more than 15 per cent of its land mass, was sold to the local government by the Cunard family.[36] The sale was a decisive turning-point in the struggle against leasehold tenure, for afterwards the terms of the debate within Prince Edward Island were never quite the same. It was as though many supporters and beneficiaries of the old order knew that its days were numbered. There was at least one significant land purchase by the government in every succeeding year through 1871, as several proprietors, particularly resident ones with political connections, sold out; the sellers included James Pope, T. Heath Haviland Jr., and the Palmer family.[37] In 1871 Haviland declared in the Legislative Council that "it is altogether contrary to the spirit of the people to remain any longer under the proprietary system. I do not think any party would have the boldness, at the present time, to rise up in the Legislature, or in any public place and say that it should be perpetuated. The hand writing is on the wall and it must go down".[38] Die-hard proprietors remained, but they had little or no political support on the Island. There were virtually no defenders of leasehold tenure left in the legislature, and when unpopular landlords were criticized, no one rose to explain away their actions. The necessity of resolving the land question had become part of the political consensus, and at least some of the credit belonged to the Tenant Leaguers, for their agitation and resistance had helped to persuade the Tories that the cost of maintaining and defending the system was too great — both politically and in terms of the divisive impact of disorders and repression in the countryside. Issues other than the land question would be the prime determinants of Island political groupings after 1867.

One of the first major tasks the new Liberal government undertook was educational reform. Coles acted rapidly to restore "free education", the system his party had established in 1852, by which the colonial treasury paid the entire salaries of school teachers.[39] In 1863 the Tories had reduced the salary paid to

Executive Council Minutes, 1 August, 19 September 1865, and Balderston to Charles DesBrisay, 17 August 1865, in Accession 2514/10, PAPEI.

35 Prince Edward Island, Legislative Council, *Debates and Proceedings, 1874*, p. 166. Given that the Tenant League appears to have ceased functioning as an organization prior to the Legislative Council election of December 1866, it is probable that what Haythorne really meant was that he had been returned in large part through the influence of individuals whom he knew *had been* active in the League.

36 Calculation based on Clark, *Three Centuries and the Island*, pp. 46, 52.

37 See *Assembly Journal, 1875*, app. E.

38 *Legislative Council Debates, 1871*, p. 21.

39 See Resolution number one in *Assembly Journal, 1867*, p. 48.

each teacher by £15, expecting that each district would provide the final £15 of the teacher's salary through local assessment. The change had not been a success, as the provisions for ensuring the desired result were inadequate, and simply led to litigation and ill will. In fact, by 1867 the Tories realized that the experiment had failed, for they did not oppose the restoration of "free education". Now led in the assembly by Haviland, they asked that it not be treated as a partisan matter. One even stated that "I believe it was the intention of the majority of the Conservative party, had the government remained in their hands, to amend the law in this particular".[40]

In 1868 the Liberal government carried out a major consolidation and amendment of the existing laws relating to education. The primary objectives were to clarify the principles and to increase the efficiency of the Island's educational system, and in these respects the statute of 1868 was successful.[41] But it was not so effective in matters upon which religious denominations differed. It was a compromise, and the Liberals gave all they thought politically feasible to the strong-willed and increasingly ultramontane Roman Catholic bishop of Charlottetown, Peter McIntyre. The public and non-denominational Normal School would no longer be compulsory for the candidates for teaching licences. The statute enlarged the Board of Education to 11 members, and when appointed, they included five Roman Catholics. Furthermore, Father Angus McDonald, rector of the Catholic St. Dunstan's College, was one of the members who were named "examiners" of teaching candidates. For the Acadian areas the Liberals re-enacted certain concessions made in 1864, and attempted to address a chronic problem, namely, the shortage of French-speaking teachers, which had been worsened by the abolition of the special category of "French Acadian" schools in 1863. As many as 20 extra salary grants of £5 each would be paid to teachers instructing ten or more children in the French language, on condition that local trustees raised a like sum by voluntary subscription.[42] The new act also increased the number of school visitors from two to three, and the Liberals appointed a Roman Catholic to one of the visitorships.

But this was not enough for the bishop. On 3 March McIntyre had sent a memorial to the government, in which he recalled the public support given to St. Andrew's College during its brief existence, between 1831 and the mid-1840s. He pointed out that through St. Dunstan's and three female schools his church was educating close to 500 pupils at no cost to the treasury. Hence, it was "a grievance that he [the bishop] gets no aid from the Public School Fund of the Colony, not even as much for the number of children taught free, as should be paid for them if they attended District Schools".[43] On 18 March the executive

40 See Colin MacLennan in *Assembly Debates, 1867*, p. 32.

41 *Statutes*, 31 Vic., c. 6.

42 See Georges Arsenault, *L'Education chez les Acadiens de l'Ile-du-Prince-Edouard 1720-1980 ou La survivance acadienne à l'Ile-du-Prince-Edouard* (Summerside, 1982), pp. 34, 55, 58-9.

43 *Assembly Journal, 1868*, app. FF. For a modern history of St. Dunstan's, see G. Edward MacDonald, "'And Christ Dwelt in the Heart of His House': A History of St. Dunstan's Univer-

council resolved not to submit the proposed grant to the legislature, and this refusal of the bishop's request was consistent with the principles of the new Education Act, which had cut off all aid to schools in which sectarian religion was taught.[44] But the government's decision did not close the issue. The Conservative Opposition saw the opportunity to embarrass the religiously composite Liberal administration, and had the memorial tabled for discussion.[45] Their leader, Haviland, questioned "whether...an education that is not founded upon the principles of religion...is a healthy system...for a mere secular education, unless founded upon religious instruction, is utterly futile".[46] Frederick Brecken asked Coles, who in 1860 had supported a motion favouring equal endowments for St. Dunstan's and the publicly-established and secular Prince of Wales College, why he now refused the bishop's memorial. Brecken also asserted that McIntyre held the power to overthrow the government, and went on to say that George Howlan, the leading Roman Catholic assemblyman, disagreed with the premier on educational policy.[47]

The Conservatives succeeded in provoking quite diverse statements of position from the government side of the house. Coles replied that although he had voted for a grant of £75 to St. Dunstan's in 1858, and for equal endowments in 1860, "the Government do not at present feel themselves in a position to give a grant to the College. Yet in my own individual opinion, the Bishop is entitled to a grant. But...individual opinion is entirely a different thing from political duty".[48] The attorney general, Joseph Hensley, stated, however, that "you cannot depart from...secular education unless you break up the whole system of the present common school education altogether".[49] Howlan advocated a system of separate schools for the colony. "But", he asked, "where can I go for redress?"[50] Two other Roman Catholic Liberal members expressed their agreement with Howlan as to the necessity of mixing religious and secular training.[51] Hensley replied that

sity 1855-1955", Ph.D. thesis, Queen's University, 1984; pp. 124-33 concern the controversies between 1868 and 1870 surrounding a proposed grant of public money to St. Dunstan's and follow the account in Ian Ross Robertson, "Religion, Politics, and Education in Prince Edward Island from 1856 to 1877", M.A. thesis, McGill Univerity, 1968, ch. 7. *Assembly Journal, 1845*, p. 43 records a grant of £75 to St. Andrew's College, but MacDonald, p. 52 gives the year of closure as 1844, without citing a source.

44 Two such schools which had formerly been aided were given a year of grace to meet the requirements of the Education Act. See *Assembly Journal, 1868*, p. 76, Joseph Hensley and Coles in *Assembly Debates, 1868*, pp. 152, 153, *Executive Council Minutes*, 18 March 1868.

45 *Assembly Debates, 1868*, p. 130.

46 *Ibid.*, p. 155.

47 *Ibid.*, pp. 160-1. Concerning the motion in 1860, see Robertson, "Party Politics and Religious Controversialism in Prince Edward Island from 1860 to 1863", pp. 30-2.

48 *Assembly Debates, 1868*, p. 176. Concerning the grant to St. Dunstan's in 1858, see Robertson, "The Bible Question in Prince Edward Island from 1856 to 1860", pp. 16-7.

49 *Assembly Debates, 1868*, p. 45.

50 *Ibid.*, pp. 162, 164.

51 See *ibid.*, pp. 169. 171.

if such a programme were practicable, he would favour it, and said that the Tories were merely trying to divide the Liberal Catholics and Protestants, for the Opposition had committed themselves to nothing.[52] Another executive councillor, Davies, claimed that, given the provisions of the Free School Act, the bishop's schools were unnecessary, adding that "a sectarian system of education is a wrong one".[53]

In part this range of viewpoints could be attributed to the very co-existence of Protestants and Roman Catholics in the same government at a time when the local bishop was becoming more assertive in his requests for public support. But another factor accounted for the way in which these contradictory opinions were allowed to run riot in public: the weakened state of the Liberal leadership. James Warburton, a veteran Prince County Protestant Liberal possessing a long history of good relations with Island Catholics (including the Acadians, whose language he probably spoke, given that he had spent two years at a Jesuit college in France), had more or less retired from active politics. Whelan, who had had political responsibility for Kings, the most Catholic of the three counties, had died in December 1867, and his death had deprived the Liberals of a tremendously influential Catholic layman strongly committed to the non-denominational system of education.[54] Perhaps most important of all, Coles' mind had begun to deteriorate. In August 1868 Coles requested and received six months' leave of absence; in the session of 1869 he rarely spoke; and by 1870 he was unable to take his seat in the assembly.[55] His political career had come to an end. Thus, in a year and one-half — between December of 1866 and the summer of 1868 — the Liberals had lost their three most prominent leaders of the post-responsible government period, all of whom had worked successfully across sectarian lines in the past.

Moreover, these losses had come at a time when the government was facing increasing pressure from several directions. In February 1868 the Free-Secession Presbytery had expressed "their strong condemnation of state grants in aid of any sectarian institution...[and pledged to] use all their lawful endeavours to prevent such endowments".[56] The Protestant Liberals were clearly in a delicate situation. Under conflicting external pressures, two solid blocs were forming among the executive councillors: Howlan and Andrew A. McDonald, the only Roman Catholics, against Davies, Callbeck, Alexander Laird Jr., and W.W. Lord. It is likely that Coles and Hensley sided with the Davies group, and Hay-

52 See *ibid.*, p. 172.

53 *Ibid.*, p. 180. Davies had been an MHA in 1852, when the Free Education Act was passed.

54 On this point, see Ian Ross Robertson, "Edward Whelan", *Dictionary of Canadian Biography*, IX, p. 833; also see Warburton in *Assembly Debates, 1857*, p. 54.

55 See Executive Council Minutes, 20 August 1868, and resolution of sympathy to Mrs. Coles and family, in *Assembly Journal, 1870*, p. 96.

56 Minutes of the United Presbytery of Prince Edward Island, 26 February 1868, Archives of Pine Hill Divinity Hall, Halifax [APH]. Access to the collections at Pine Hill was granted by the archivist, the Rev. E. Arthur Betts.

thorne with Howlan. The position of the Protestant bloc worsened as Coles slipped into mental impotence. In the Education Act and the subsequent appointments, they had made all the concessions they could afford to give to McIntyre. Hensley had emerged as the *de facto* leader of the government, but whether he could keep the Liberal party together was an open question. Although he lacked the charisma of a Coles or Whelan, Hensley nonetheless combined qualities of moderation, good sense, and firmness, all of which were important in the circumstances.

The Protestant Liberals could derive no comfort from the course which the *Islander* and the *Examiner*, traditionally the leaders of public opinion in the colony, were taking. In the early months of 1868 William Pope, editor of the Conservative *Islander*, outlined his new position regarding Roman Catholics and education. It was a policy of limited concessions to the Roman Catholic Church. Pope had perceived the vulnerability of the Coles-Hensley government, and in February he came out in favour of a grant to St. Dunstan's College, without mentioning any conditions to be met. He went on to say that "we believe that all who profess and call themselves Christians should be anxious that *religious* education should be imparted to children, in fact that it should underlie all other education". In so doing, the former colonial secretary, reputedly a freethinker, warned of the tendency of the age to infidelity, and in an apparent change of heart since the early 1860s, when he had abused Roman Catholic beliefs mercilessly, recommended that Catholics "force" the school question upon the government.[57] Throughout early 1868 he kept continual pressure on the Liberals, eventually publishing a draft bill embodying his desired amendments to the Education Act.[58]

If the about-face on the part of the *Islander* surprised the Liberal leaders, that of the *Examiner*, which had been Whelan's paper, shocked them. Soon after Whelan died it came out in support of the St. Dunstan's endowment,[59] and then began to move to an increasingly pro-clerical position. In April the *Examiner* asserted that "the first duty of a State is to make due provision for the religious and moral training and the necessary or useful secular instruction of its youth". Anyone who disagreed with this truism was guilty of "open and unabashed bigotry and audacious uncharitableness".[60] Walter C. Grant became editor in the middle of April, and under his guidance the *Examiner* grew less friendly to the party which had given it birth; it seemed only a matter of time before a complete break would be made.

57 *Islander*, 21 February 1868. The endowment was to bear the same proportion to the Prince of Wales College grant as did the Roman Catholic population of the Island to the Protestant population.

58 See *Islander*, 29 May 1868. A Roman Catholic and Liberal editor wrote that "we [Roman Catholics] hardly know how to express our gratitude....What a generous, tolerant, large-minded soul W.H. Pope is in adversity!"; *Herald*, 5 February 1868. Nonetheless, he endorsed Pope's draft bill: see *Herald*, 3 June 1868.

59 See *Examiner*, 17 February 1868.

60 *Examiner*, 6 April 1868.

On 8 July 1868 Gray, the pro-Confederate former premier, who had lost his nomination in 1867, followed the example of William Pope. At the public examination of St. Dunstan's College he expressed the hope that "the day was not far distant, when the Institution would be acknowledged, both publicly and privately". If he had a son, "he would, without hesitation, send him to St. Dunstan's".[61] When an assembly seat for Summerside fell vacant in late 1868, James Pope, who had not contested the general election of the previous year, announced his candidacy and published an electoral card promising aid to all "efficient schools" open to government inspection, regardless of who controlled them; in the same card he claimed to be "opposed to the endowment of any Sectarian institution".[62] This "Summerside card" did not restrict the number of schools which would be eligible for grants from the treasury, perhaps because deciding upon such a limitation involved practical political difficulties. If Pope were to limit support to schools already in existence in October 1868, he would be liable to the charge of giving exclusive privileges to Roman Catholics, for no other denomination at that time supported private schools of significance. On the other hand his open-ended plan left the way clear for McIntyre to establish an unlimited number of Catholic schools, and receive public money for each. The Pope brothers evaded these questions by having William maintain that the new provisions would apply only to institutions established in towns and villages,[63] while James was never explicit on the point.

It was a hard-fought campaign. On the one side were the *Islander*, the Popes, Haviland,[64] and McIntyre.[65] They relentlessly claimed "common justice". On the other side were a Protestant-oriented and anti-Confederate Conservative Charlottetown newspaper, the *Patriot*, the two Summerside newspapers, the Presbyteries,[66] the Liberal party, and the Liberal candidate, Angus McMillan.[67]

61 Reported in *Examiner*, 13 July 1868. Gray had also attended the public examination of St. Dunstan's in 1867, and had stated then that he "felt proud" of the college: *Examiner*, 15 July 1867. In the late 1850s Gray had been founding president of an ultra-Protestant group, the "Protestant Combination", which had been formed to defend against "the encroachments of the Romanists"; see Robertson, "The Bible Question in Prince Edward Island from 1856 to 1860", pp. 11, 15.

62 *Islander*, 16 October 1868.

63 See his draft bill in *Islander*, 29 May 1868. William held to this position throughout the campaign.

64 See editorial in *Islander*, 27 November 1868; and letter of Haviland to the editor of the *Islander*, dated 24 November 1868.

65 See *Patriot*, 21 November 1868; *Islander*, 29 January 1869, 17 June 1870; *Progress* (Summerside), 23 November 1868, 8 March 1869.

66 See Minutes of the Kirk Presbytery of Prince Edward Island, 5 November 1868, APH; Minutes of the United Presbytery of Prince Edward Island, 9 November 1868, APH. Both Presbytery resolutions were published in *Patriot*, 12 November 1868.

67 McMillan avoided comment on the school question, on the ground that a general election was the only time when such discussion would be meaningful. This was consistent with Premier Hensley's view that "the whole house were returned at the last Election on the tacit understanding as I thought that for this House at least the question of separate Grants was to slumber". See

The *Examiner* and another Roman Catholic newspaper, the *Herald*, stood aside, the former because of its long-time allegiance to the Liberal party, and the latter because its publisher was queen's printer. On 19 November McMillan scored a decisive victory for the Liberals, as he took 58 per cent of the Roman Catholic votes and 59 per cent of the Protestant votes.[68] Why did so capable and so influential a man as James Pope lose so badly in his home town to a political novice? Among Roman Catholics there appear to have been two poles of opinion: some believed that he did not go far enough, and others that he went too far.[69] But aside from the merits of the position taken by Pope, there is the fact that he was attempting, in the course of one byelection campaign, to effect a major change in Island political alignments.

The traditional loyalty of Roman Catholics to the Liberal party was probably at least as important as their devotion to the non-sectarian Free Education Act. The Liberal party, especially in the recent past, had been the political home of the Catholics' friends among the Protestant majority on the Island; conversely, residual antipathy towards William Pope for his polemics against Catholic beliefs earlier in the decade was damaging to his brother James, although the latter had never associated himself with these attacks. Finally, the role of the bishop seems to have been controversial among Island Catholics. In a private letter to one of McMillan's campaign organizers on 28 October, Premier Hensley wrote that, in the Charlottetown area at least, "a large number" of Catholics were "very indignant at the pressure brought to bear upon them so suddenly".[70] Among the Protestants, David Laird, editor of the *Patriot*, pointed out that McIntyre, despite the failure of his memorial, was founding new educational institutions. Since March he had established convents in Summerside and Tignish, and he was planning a boys' school in Charlottetown. Sooner or later he would presumably request public support for them, as well as the ones existing in March. Now was clearly the time to draw the line.[71] Laird also caught the logical dilemma in William Pope's "towns and villages" plan:

> Poor sinners, say we, those people in the country, who will have to pay for and retain 'mixed schools' — schools which are hurrying their children headlong into infidelity — and yet have to assist the 'rich and wealthy and wealthy and rich' people of Charlottetown, Summerside, and Georgetown to support *additional* schools to those now in operation.[72]

The Summerside byelection pried the *Examiner* loose, once and for all, from

Examiner, 26 October 1868; electoral card of McMillan, dated 29 October 1868, in *Progress*, 2 November 1868; Hensley to Richard Hunt, 28 October 1868, Item 306, Hunt Papers, PAPEI.

68 Calculations based on data in *Islander*, 27 November 1868.

69 See George W. DeBlois in *Assembly Debates, 1877*, pp. 25, 53-4.

70 Hensley to Hunt, 28 October 1868, Item 306, Hunt Papers, PAPEI.

71 See *Patriot*, 31 October 1868.

72 *Patriot*, 7 November 1868; "rich and wealthy and wealthy and rich" was a description which

the Liberal camp. Four days after Pope's defeat, Whelan's old paper declared that the Liberal party "has deceived its supporters" and "is no longer worthy of their confidence".[73] On 30 November the *Examiner* specifically naméd Coles, Hensley, Davies, and Alexander Laird Jr., and accused them of "concealed enmity" to Roman Catholicism, citing in particular grievances with regard to the distribution of public offices. Concerning education, Grant took the same position as James and William Pope, with the "towns and villages" rider.[74] In succeeding weeks the editor lost all restraint, and embarked upon a virulent campaign of bombast against the Protestant Liberals: their "ruling idea seems to be hatred and injustice to Catholics...one [government] more intensely stupid and bigoted than the present never swayed the destinies of this Colony".[75]

Notwithstanding the *Examiner's* conversion, the defeat of James Pope caused the school question to recede rapidly from view. The loss undermined the arguing position of the Popes, Haviland, and the Roman Catholic leaders. Whatever explanations were advanced, it was indisputable that 58 per cent of the Roman Catholic electors polled on 19 November had not felt strongly enough about the question of denominational grants to vote against the Liberal party. The Popes realized this, and decided to let the matter stand for the present. Their attempt to inaugurate a new party system on the basis of an alliance between the pro-Confederate Conservatives[76] and the Roman Catholic Liberals had been premature. Hence the school question caused little public stir in 1869; only one or two assemblymen mentioned it at all during the session.[77] But the Liberal party was still racked by internal differences of opinion. Apparently Hensley attempted in March to effect a compromise by supporting in caucus a grant of £300 to St. Dunstan's. This failed to gain acceptance, and Howlan was rumoured to have tendered his resignation. If he did, he also withdrew it when he realized that it would not force any concession.[78]

Hensley's decision in June to retire from politics and become a member of the Supreme Court was more serious. His resignation created a genuine leadership crisis for the Liberals. On the day after Hensley was appointed to the bench, David Laird, whose brother Alexander Jr. was a member of the Executive Council, wrote that "what is left of a government may as well begin to dig their political graves".[79] The Liberal party had been decapitated: Coles, Whelan,

James Pope had applied recently to the people of Summerside.

73 *Examiner*, 23 November 1868.

74 *Examiner*, 30 November 1868.

75 *Examiner*, 7 December 1868.

76 Haviland and William Pope were openly-declared pro-Confederates; concerning James Pope's position on the Island's entry into Confederation, see Ian Ross Robertson, "James Colledge Pope", *Dictionary of Canadian Biography*, XI (Toronto, 1982), pp. 700, 704.

77 See Samuel Prowse and Kenneth Henderson in *Assembly Debates, 1869*, p. 66.

78 See *Patriot*, 6, 27 March, 24 June 1869; *Examiner*, 29 March, 5 April 1869; *Journal and Western Pioneer* (Summerside), 1 April 1869.

79 *Patriot*, 19 June 1869.

Warburton, and Hensley were all gone from active politics. To choose the aggressive Davies or the blustering Howlan would be an invitation to a quick rupture. The only alternative seemed to be Haythorne, the Government Leader in the upper house. Although timid and a most inexperienced and unskilful politician, he was the only remaining prestigious Liberal who was not identified with one of the two hostile camps within the party. A man of considerable education and intelligence, Haythorne recognized the weakness of his government and attempted to persuade two Conservative legislative councillors, including Palmer, to join his cabinet.[80] He failed, but nevertheless the government survived the session of 1870 intact. Howlan seemed appeased by being named Government Leader in the assembly,[81] and the Roman Catholic members generally ignored the jibes of Haviland and Brecken.[82]

The Liberal government soon had to face an election, as the assembly had sat for four years. Fearing the silence of the Roman Catholic Liberal members, the Presbyteries held a joint conference on 19 May.[83] They then appointed an eight-man committee, chaired by Gray, to take what action they deemed necessary concerning the school question. Gray's committee responded by issuing on 1 June an open letter "To the Presbyterians of Prince Edward Island", reminding them that it was their duty to "give their suffrages only to men, whose established principles will be a sure pledge that, by no partial or unjust measures, any denomination of Christians shall receive educational advantages or support at the expense of their fellow-subjects".[84] In other words, there must be no change in the non-denominational character of the educational system. The Wesleyans were equally vigilant, and at their annual District Meeting they warned against giving public money to denominational institutions under any circumstances.[85] The effect of these vigorous actions on the part of the Presbyterians and Wesleyans was to choke off serious discussion of the school question during the campaign.

Haythorne won the election on 18 July 1870 by a margin of 17 to 13, largely on the strength of his own and his party's anti-Confederate record. The Tory leadership was badly divided. Palmer and James Pope were again candidates for the assembly, and Haviland lost his nomination in Georgetown, owing to his unpopular stands on Confederation and the school question. The Liberals won at least as much on the Tories' weakness as on their own strength. But the election decided who would control the Conservative party: Palmer and David Laird lost and James Pope won. On 22 July the *Islander* was jubilant at the defeat of the

---

80 At the time, the overtures were an open secret. See *Islander*, 25 June, 2 July 1869; *Patriot*, 29 June 1869; *Examiner*, 28 June 1869. In 1870 Haythorne confirmed their existence; see his letter to the editor of the *Islander*, dated 5 October 1870, *Islander*, 7 October 1870.

81 See *Assembly Debates, 1870*, p. 70.

82 See *Assembly Debates, 1870*, pp. 10, 52-3.

83 See Minutes of the Kirk Presbytery of Prince Edward Island, 19 May 1870, APH.

84 See *Islander*, 10 June 1870.

85 See the report of the meeting on 10 June in *Islander*, 17 June 1870.

anti-Confederate leaders within the party, and did not even mention the triumph of the government. The former colonial secretary devoted his columns to gloating: "Mr. Palmer was, in the language of the turf, *nowhere*".[86]

For the Liberals, victory soon proved a sobering experience. Haythorne precipitated a crisis by speaking out on the school question on Declaration Day, 29 July. The *Islander* reported:

> That the Premier designated the Prince of Wales College a Protestant institution which had been established for the benefit of Protestants and asserted 'That he was prepared to propose a grant from the public funds in aid of St. Dunstan's College. That should he find himself unable to carry a grant for St. Dunstan's College he would propose the disendowment of the Prince of Wales College. That should he be unable to carry a grant for St. Dunstan's College, or to procure the disendowment of the Prince of Wales College, he would resign'.[87]

This of course brought on a confrontation between the Howlan and Davies factions. It was an unauthorized policy statement, and came with virtually no warning, for Haythorne, a legislative councillor, had not had to publish a card embodying his political platform during the campaign for the assembly.[88] Decapitated by Hensley's resignation in the previous year, the government now disintegrated. Feelings were already high in the Liberal party, for at the late election Howlan's group had eliminated two of Davies' allies. Protestants representing Roman Catholic constituencies, they had expressed opposition in the assembly to denominational grants; two Catholics replaced them.[89]

The storm broke on 18 and 19 August when the Liberal caucus met in Charlottetown. Seventeen assemblymen and seven legislative councillors attended, of whom 14 were Protestants and ten were Catholics. Led by Howlan, the Catholics were adamant: the St. Dunstan's grant was a *sine qua non* of continued support for the government. Haythorne and three other Protestants agreed; the rest were immovable.[90] On the second day, Davies and Sinclair pre-

86 *Islander*, 22 July 1870.

87 *Islander*, 5 August 1870.

88 Haythorne later claimed that on at least four public occasions prior to the election he had expressed his support for a grant to St. Dunstan's. He also said that he had made it clear he was opposed to denominational grants in general: "I considered St. Dunstan's a special case". Yet he voted for McDonald's caucus resolution of 19 August 1870, which certainly was not confined to St. Dunstan's. See letters of Haythorne to the editor of the *Patriot*, dated 1, 15 December 1870, in *Patriot*, 3, 17 December 1870. From these letters, he does not appear to have thought out his position very carefully. In any event, the Liberal Protestants of the Davies group did not consider Haythorne's views on the school question to be agreed-upon Liberal party policy.

89 See *Patriot*, 21 July 1870; letter of Haythorne to the editor of the *Patriot*, dated 1 December 1870, in *Patriot*, 3 December 1870; letter of W.W. Sullivan "To George Howlan", dated 29 November 1871, in *Examiner*, 4 December 1871.

90 See *Patriot*, 20 August 1870; Howlan, Sinclair, McMillan in *Assembly Debates, 1871*, pp. 45, 45-6, 57.

sented a resolution expressing general satisfaction with the existing Education Act.[91] This met no opposition;[92] but McDonald submitted an amendment, to the effect that

> When any school shall have been opened by any sect or denomination it shall be placed under the Board of Education and be subject to the rules and regulations thereof. Save and except that nothing herein contained shall prevent the parents and guardians from selecting their own textbooks, and choosing their own teachers.[93]

The amendment was carried, with the support of Haythorne's Protestants.[94] The Roman Catholics then attempted to lessen the deleterious effects of their victory by adding a slightly ambiguous "conscience clause", which would supposedly limit religious instruction to before or after the regular hours.[95] But this provision meant little, for citizens were already permitted to use the local schoolhouse for whatever purpose they desired, following the hours of secular instruction[96] The point to the Catholic programme lay in McDonald's first amendment. On the executive council matters were equally grim; Davies and Sinclair prevailed by a margin of four to three.[97] As David Laird remarked, "it was plainly seen that the breach was irreparable and that to carry out their policy, each of the parties must seek new political associates".[98]

The Roman Catholics succeeded in finding new allies, but not in enforcing their views on the school question. The Conservative pro-Confederates had been looking on with interest, and waiting for the split to occur. When this happened, James Pope joined with Howlan and his followers to form a coalition government. In the meantime William Pope had prepared the way for his brother to refuse to meet the demands of Howlan and McDonald. No Protestant Conservative had submitted the question of denominational grants to his con-

---

91 See *Patriot*, 20 August 1870.

92 See letter of Howlan to the editor of the *Patriot*, dated 22 August 1870, in *Patriot*, 25 August 1870.

93 See Howlan in *Assembly Debates, 1872* (2nd Session), p. 237; editorial in *Patriot*, 20 August 1870.

94 See letter of Haythorne to the editor of the *Patriot*, dated 15 December 1870, in *Patriot*, 17 December 1870. The *Patriot* editorial, 20 August 1870 appears to be mistaken on this point, as it asserts that Haythorne opposed McDonald's amendment.

95 For the text of the second proposed amendment to the Davies-Sinclair resolution, see Howlan in *Assembly Debates, 1872* (2nd Session), p. 237.

96 See *Statutes*, 24 Vic., c. 36, s. 23. This was pointed out by Sinclair in *Assembly Debates, 1871*, p. 46.

97 See Hodgson to the Earl of Kimberley, 6 September 1870, CO 226/106, pp. 225-7. The division was as follows: Davies, Sinclair, Callbeck, and Lord against Haythorne, Howlan, and McDonald. Coles was incapacitated and Alexander Laird Jr. was absent, as he had been defeated by James Pope.

98 *Patriot*, 20 August 1870.

stituents at the last election, and nothing, William said, could be done without a mandate from the people.[99] In maintaining this, he also undermined Haythorne's position with the Protestant population. Furthermore, the premier's plan to disendow Prince of Wales College was "the most objectionable". William reasoned that "If the denying Catholics a grant for their schools constitutes injustice, the injustice is in no degree lessened by spoiling the Public College, and thereby doing injustice to the public generally".[100]

On 10 September James Pope formed a new government, with the Roman Catholics receiving three seats on the executive council.[101] The leading Tories in the government were Pope, Haviland (who was elected to the Legislative Council for Charlottetown in October), and Brecken. The basis of the alliance, in terms of public policy, was a mutual self-denying pledge: nothing would be done on the Confederation or school questions until they were submitted to the people at the polls.[102] Thus, without repudiating the "Summerside card" in principle, the Tories had avoided wading in the troubled waters of the school question. They had also won over the Roman Catholic members and returned to power. Manipulation of the "religion and education" issue had brought the Popes and Haviland effective control of the government, and they responded by burying the issue. As for the Catholics who were party to the coalition, editor and assemblyman Edward Reilly stated their point of view succinctly: "If it be said that the school question is to be kept in abeyance for a period, it should be remembered that Mr. Pope's four years are greatly preferable to Mr. Sinclair's eternity".[103] They could see no advantage in sitting by while Davies and Pope formed a new all-Protestant government, after the pattern of the Conservative administrations from 1859 to 1867.

In analyzing the realignment in Prince Edward Island politics between 1863

99 He first used this argument in the *Islander*, 5 August 1870. Also see report of speech by James Pope on 11 October 1870 in *Islander*, 21 October 1870. The only Roman Catholic Conservative elected in 1870 was Emanuel McEachen.

100 *Islander*, 5 August 1870. The Baptist Association of Prince Edward Island made Haythorne's position even more uncomfortable by announcing its unequivocal opposition to all denominational grants; see letter of the Rev. John Davis to "*Mr. Islander*", dated 19 August 1870, in *Islander*, 19 August 1870.

101 Executive Council Minutes, 10 September 1870. Haythorne remained with the other Protestant Liberals, while all Liberal Roman Catholics but James R. McLean followed Howlan. McLean had supported Howlan and McDonald in August, but apparently saw no point in joining the Conservative Confederates when no concessions were being offered. He also objected to committing himself in writing to the coalition: *Assembly Debates, 1875*, p. 359.

102 See *Islander*, 9 September 1870; electoral cards of Brecken (who faced a byelection because of his acceptance of the office of attorney general), dated 13 September 1870, and Haviland, dated 16 September 1870, in *Islander*, 23 September 1870; Brecken in *Assembly Debates, 1872* (1st Session), pp. 45-6; James Pope in *ibid.* (2nd session), p. 230, and *ibid.*, 1875, p. 349; McEachen in *ibid.*, p. 358. At the request of Dr. James Robertson, the agreement between the two factions was embodied in a written pledge, the text of which does not appear to have survived.

103 From the *Herald*, cited without a precise date, in *Patriot*, 29 September 1870. This number of the *Herald* does not survive.

and 1870, which had major long-term implications for the Island, it is necessary to recognize the leading roles of the land question and sectarianism, both of which had been important sources of internal conflict for many years. No account which fails to examine these two issues can explain adequately contemporary political changes or what happened after 1870.[104] The bad feelings generated by repression of the Tenant League alienated from the Conservative party the Protestant voters of rural Queens County. This important segment of the party's electoral base shifted to the Liberals.[105] Sectarianism, which had been dormant as a force in Island politics, resurfaced in the issue of denominational grants. The ambitious policies of the Roman Catholic bishop, who in the course of the 1860s broadened the scope of his request for public aid from a single institution to an expanding system of denominational education, presented the Liberal leadership, which had been weakened by attrition, with a challenge they proved ultimately unable to contain. Defining a space somewhere between the polarizing camps of the Catholic politicians apparently directed by the bishop, and the Protestant Liberals adhering to the policies Coles and Whelan had defended in the 1850s, the Pope brothers and Haviland found a means of regaining power. That was no small accomplishment, for William Pope, still widely regarded as the political mastermind of the faction to which he belonged, was strongly identified wih the Confederation project, which remained intensely unpopular on the Island.

The coalition formed in 1870 was essentially one of opportunism. The land question, for generations the staple of Island politics, was receding in importance. The sense that the demise of the leasehold system was inevitable left little room for partisan advantage, and, among other things, this consensus had the effect of removing the land question as the possible source of a decisive lure for entry into Confederation. Those uncommitted to union of the colonies seemed to believe that they could resolve the problem on their own, without the Dominion of Canada, sooner or later. With the land question now a source of political consensus rather than conflict, and with the issues of denominational grants and Confederation too dangerous to raise, the initial unifying principle of the Pope-Howlan alliance appeared to be the simple maxim that it was better to be

104 J.M. Bumsted has recently drawn attention to the general lack of study by Island historians of "racial, religious, and social tensions" in the colonial period, and, more specifically, to the failure to examine seriously the possible relationship of "popular conflict such as that resulting from the Tenant League agitation" to the Confederation question on the Island. See "'The Only Island There Is': The Writing of Prince Edward Island History", in Verner Smitheram *et al.*, eds., *The Garden Transformed: Prince Edward Island, 1945-1980* (Charlottetown, 1982), pp. 19, 29.

105 The five pro-Tenant League assemblymen from Queens County were re-elected in 1870. As an example of the bitterness remaining after the events of 1865, relations between James Pope and McNeill, the most vocally pro-Tenant League assemblyman, were strained for many years. In 1872 McNeill would refer to Pope's "attempt to rule the Island by the bayonet, the handcuffs, and the jail"; later in the same session Pope called McNeill "the Communist General" and "a man whom he believed might be guilty of committing crimes similar to those perpetrated by the communists of France": *Assembly Debates, 1872* (2nd Session), pp. 117, 167, 169.

in office than in opposition. Yet the coalition arrangement represented a great strategic coup for the pro-Confederate minority centering on William Pope, whose objective of splitting the Liberals and gaining Roman Catholic support had become evident in 1868, with the Summerside byelection. William was not in public office, but he remained closely linked to his brother, who was premier; and as of 21 October the colonial treasurer was their father, Joseph, a forceful man who was known to be a strong Confederate.

Within months of assuming office, the coalition found a programme: construction of a railway, which fitted in well with contemporary notions of "progress" and "development". Although James Pope could not claim to have an electoral mandate for the project, it was nonetheless entirely consistent with his personal record as a vigorous and progressive entrepreneur. He was a businessman with interests in virtually all sectors of the Island economy, and had long been involved in promoting improvements in transportation and communications. His brother William had been advocating a railway for several years, and perhaps by coincidence, perhaps not, building the Prince Edward Island Railway would prove to be an indirect means towards William's goal of Confederation. A mere eight days after his brother returned to the premier's office, William had written a "private and confidential" letter to the prime minister of Canada, Sir John A. Macdonald. In William's view, it was time for the Colonial Office to "put on the screws". Islanders must be told that if they did not re-open negotiations with Ottawa, "Her Majesty's ministers will be compelled to take matters in hand and settle the terms for them". But all this must be done "without any communication being had upon the subject with our Executive *or any member of it*", for "it is important that our friends in the Executive could have it in their power to say that they have not had any intercourse with Canada on the subject".[106] It is impossible to state definitively whether James Pope had any knowledge of his brother's letter to Macdonald, for William was not explicit on this point. If James was not aware of it, then William's caution to Macdonald would serve to keep both his own brother and the Canadian prime minister in the dark as to the actual role he was playing.[107]

Whatever the motives of the Popes in 1870, it is clear that the influence of the Tenant League and the issue of denominational grants both weakened traditional party allegiances during the course of the 1860s. These changes in political alignment prepared the way for the Tory pro-Confederates to return to power. In the process of capitalizing upon the tensions within the Liberal party, the Popes created a political machine which would dominate local government for two decades and bring the Island into Confederation. The Island's road to Confederation was not a direct one. Islanders believed they had put Confedera-

106 Pope to Macdonald, private and confidential, 18 September 1870, vol. 119, pp. 48221-6, Sir John A. Macdonald Papers, Public Archives of Canada.

107 It is by no means certain that the Pope brothers were in precise agreement on the Confederation question in 1870, for they had had public differences over the issue in the past; see Ian Ross Robertson, "William Henry Pope", *Dictionary of Canadian Biography*, X, p. 596.

tion behind them after the commotion in 1864-65 among the Conservative leaders. In order to follow the real road to Confederation, more prosaic matters of immediate concern to the people of the time must be examined, for they explain how the Popes and Haviland, who would lead Islanders into the Dominion of Canada, gained the power to do so. No longer isolated after 1870, the pro-Confederate minority was in a position to determine the political agenda of Prince Edward Island.

PHILLIP A. BUCKNER

Reprinted from *The Causes of Confederation*
(Acadiensis Press, 1990)

The Maritimes and Confederation:
A Reassessment*

A number of years ago E.R. Forbes in an important article challenged the stereotype of Maritime conservatism and attempted to show how it had distorted the way in which the history of the Maritimes has been portrayed in the post-Confederation period.[1] Yet it can be argued that this stereotype has also influenced our interpretation of the pre-Confederation era in a variety of ways. Nowhere is this more true than in studies of the role of the region in the making of Confederation. The failure of the Maritime colonies to respond enthusiastically to the Canadian initiative for Confederation in the 1860s has come to be seen as yet another example of their inherent conservatism. The impression that emerges from the literature is of a series of parochial communities content with the status quo and trapped in intellectual lethargy who were dragged kicking and screaming into Confederation. This stereotype leads to several misleading conclusions. First, it encourages historians to underestimate the degree of support which existed within the Maritimes for the ideal of a larger British North American union and to exaggerate the gulf that divided the anti-Confederates from the pro-Confederates. Second, it oversimplifies and trivializes the very real and substantive objections which many Maritimers had to the kind of union that they were eventually forced to accept. Recent American historiography has led to a substantial re-thinking of the debate that took place in the United States over the ratification of the American constitution in the 1780s and a similar re-assessment of the debate over the Quebec Resolutions in the Maritimes in the 1860s is long overdue.

The first studies of Confederation, in fact, devoted little time to this issue. Reginald George Trotter in *Canadian Federation: Its Origins and Achievement* (Toronto, 1924) barely mentions the debate over Confederation in the Maritimes and M.O. Hammond in *Confederation and Its Leaders* (Toronto, 1917) simply ascribed the views of anti-Confederates like Albert J. Smith to their "opposition to change of any kind" (p. 237). In the first scholarly article on "New Brunswick's

---

* This paper is also published in the "Dialogue" section of the *Canadian Historical Review* in March 1990, along with two critiques, and I am grateful to the editors of the *CHR* for allowing me to reproduce the paper here. I am also grateful to a number of colleagues and friends for agreeing to comment on an earlier draft, including Ernie Forbes, Bill Acheson, David Frank, Ken Pryke, Jack Bumsted and Brook Taylor. I hasten to add that none of them agreed with everything that I said, although no two of them disagreed with the same thing.

1   E. R. Forbes, "In Search of a Post-Confederation Maritime Historiography, 1900-1967", *Acadiensis*, VIII, 2 (Autumn 1978), pp. 3-21.

Entrance into Confederation", George Wilson assumed as a given New Brunswick's hesitancy and focused on the factors — the loyalty cry, Canadian campaign funds and the "educational work of Tilley" (p. 24) — which he saw as critical in persuading New Brunswickers to vote for union.[2] D.C. Harvey also concentrated on the idealism of the expansionists in his paper on "The Maritime Provinces and Confederation" in 1927.[3] Writing at a time when there was a feeling in the Maritimes that Confederation had not delivered what had been promised,[4] Harvey stressed that union could have been accomplished relatively easily if the "factious" opponents of Confederation had not been "able to whip up an opposition that caused no end of trouble to the unionist statesmen and left behind a legacy of suspicion and ill-will which has been like an ulcer in the side of the Dominion" (p. 44). Harvey called for Maritimers to "recapture" the initial enthusiasm of the pro-Confederates and to abandon the tendency to blame Confederation for their problems. By implication, then, the critics of Confederation both in the 1860s and the 1920s lacked vision and statesmanship.

This perspective was also implicit in William Menzies Whitelaw's *The Maritimes and Canada before Confederation.*[5] In his preface Whitelaw declared that he had focused the book around "the struggle between an incipient nationalism and a rugged particularism" (p. xix). The book was published in 1934 after the collapse of the Maritime Rights Movement and the onset of the Great Depression, at a time when most Canadian historians were beginning to see the advantages of a strong central government and Maritimers were again discussing the chimera of Maritime Union. Not surprisingly, Whitelaw approached the topic with a strong bias in favour of Confederation and preferably a highly centralized federal system. From the beginning the emphasis of the book was on the relative backwardness of the Maritimes and the persistence there of "early particularism", the title of one of the first chapters. Whitelaw ended his study in 1864 with an insightful chapter on "Maritime Interests at Quebec", which showed how the Canadians manipulated the Quebec Conference and outmanoeuvred the divided Maritimers.[6] Interestingly, he did not discuss the actual debate over the Quebec Resolutions but concluded with a brief lament over the decision to abandon Maritime Union. In his review of the book in the *Canadian Historical Review*, Chester Martin with some justification declared that Whitelaw "leaves an impression not only of 'particularism' but of parochialism: of particularism run to seed, too inert to defend or even to discern

---

2   *Canadian Historical Review*, IX (1928), pp. 4-24.

3   Canadian Historical Association, *Annual Report* (1927), pp. 39-45.

4   The roots of this sentiment are discussed in E. R. Forbes, *Maritime Rights: The Maritime Rights Movement, 1919-1927* (Montreal, 1979).

5   I have used the reprint edition which contains a valuable introduction by Peter Waite (Toronto, 1966).

6   Whitelaw pointed out that there was only one recorded vote at Quebec on which Canada was outvoted by the four Atlantic Provinces uniting together. See *The Maritimes and Canada before Confederation*, p. 240.

their own interests in the presence of the expansive forces then abroad in Canada and the United States".[7]

In the 1940s A.G. Bailey contributed two important articles to the small corpus of serious scholarly literature on the Maritimes and Confederation.[8] In "Railways and the Confederation Issue in New Brunswick, 1863-1865" he focused rather narrowly on the debate over the western extension, which he argued was the "most potent" factor behind the opposition to Confederation in the colony (p. 91).[9] The problem with explaining the debate in New Brunswick in these terms is that many pro-Confederates wanted the western extension, not a few anti-Confederates wanted the Intercolonial and a large number of New Brunswickers wanted both, although they could afford neither.[10] In his next article on "The Basis and Persistence of Opposition to Confederation in New Brunswick", Bailey adopted a broader approach. Although starting from the assumption that "in the early stages of the union movement there was a misapprehension of its significance, together with some degree of apathy, rather than a reasoned opposition" (p. 93), Bailey went on to explore with some subtlety the roots of anti-Confederation sentiment. The rapid collapse of the anti-Confederate government he again ascribed primarily to its failure to complete the western extension but he also emphasized mounting pressure from the imperial government, as well as "the exaggerated menace of Fenian invasion" (p. 117) and Canadian campaign funds. He also recognised that many of those who opposed union "directed their attacks not so much against the principle of Confederation as against the specific terms of union which had been embodied in the Quebec Resolutions" (p. 115). Indeed, the failure of the pro-Confederates to make substantial alterations in those resolutions in London accounted, he suggested, for "the remarkable persistence of opposition" to Confederation after 1866 (p. 116). But he did not emphasize this point which is made as a kind of aside in the conclusion of the article.

7   *CHR*, XVI (March 1935), p. 72. Cited in Waite's Introduction to *The Maritimes and Canada before Confederation*, p. xv. Waite includes this excerpt as "an illustration of the best and the worst of Chester Martin — that is, of the comprehensiveness of Martin's thinking and his inability to change it". Yet it seems to me a fair interpretation of Whitelaw's perspective.

8   One might include James A. Roy, *Joseph Howe — A Study in Achievement and Frustration* (Toronto, 1935) as a serious study but it is a perverse work that simply reiterates the myths about Howe perpetuated in earlier studies. For a critique of the book, see J. Murray Beck, "Joseph Howe and Confederation: Myth and Fact", *Transactions of the Royal Society of Canada* (1964), pp. 143-44. Perhaps because the issue of Confederation was not put to the electorate in Nova Scotia as it was in New Brunswick, the early writing on Nova Scotia focused almost exclusively on the perversity of Howe in opposing Confederation.

9   "Railways and the Confederation Issue in New Brunswick, 1863-1865" and "The Basis and Persistence of Opposition to Confederation in New Brunswick" first appeared in the *Canadian Historical Review*, XXI (1940), pp. 367-83 and XXIII (1942), pp. 374-97, but both are reprinted in Bailey's *Culture and Nationality* (Toronto, 1972), from where the quotations in the text are drawn.

10   For example, Timothy Warren Anglin was not opposed to the Intercolonial although he thought the western extension should be the priority. See William M. Baker, *Timothy Warren Anglin 1822-96: Irish Catholic Canadian* (Toronto, 1977), p. 54. Baker also notes that many pro-Confederates supported the western extension although frequently as a second choice (p. 55).

The next major study of Confederation came from Chester Martin. In the *Foundations of Canadian Nationhood* (Toronto, 1955), Martin dismissed the opposition to Confederation in the Maritimes as "too general to be the result of personalities or sheer parochialism" (p. 347). This insight might have provided the basis for a fundamental re-assessment of the debate in the Maritimes, but Martin quickly reverted to the stereotype of Maritime conservatism. Indeed, one of the major sub-themes in the book is that the original decision to partition Nova Scotia into a series of smaller units had inevitably promoted parochialism: "Where local division had been deliberately planted and thriven for three-quarters of a century, provincialism was only too apt to degenerate into sheer parochialism" (p. 290). Because he saw Confederation as forced upon the British North American colonies by (in what was the *leitmotif* of this section of the book) "events stronger than advocacy, events stronger than men" (p. 291) and the opposition to it as a natural instinct (see p. 297), Martin also accepted that "there were solid reasons for resistance based upon conflicting interests and a long train of policy" (p. 355). Nonetheless, the clear implication of his approach was that the fundamental motivation behind the widespread Maritime opposition to the Quebec Resolutions was the deep-seated conservatism of the region.

During the early 1960s writing on Confederation became a growth industry as Canada approached its bicentennial. Since most Canadian historians were still influenced by the consensus approach, which minimized the significance of internal conflicts by focusing on the things which united Canadians and distinguished them from other people, they tended to downplay regional concerns and to interpret the making of Confederation as a success story of which all Canadians should be proud.[11] The best of these studies was Peter B. Waite's *The Life and Times of Confederation 1864-67* and it is a tragedy that it has been allowed to go out of print.[12] Although Waite does not indicate that he was directly influenced by Chester Martin, there are a number of parallels in their interpretations. Like Martin, Waite saw Confederation as forced upon the British North Americans by external pressures. Although he was less deterministic and did not see Confederation as an inevitable response to these pressures, he concluded that Confederation was "imposed on British North America by ingenuity, luck, courage, and sheer force" (p. 323). Like Martin, he argued that the opposition to Confederation was rooted in the "innate conservatism" of the smaller communities across British North America (p. 14) and that this conservatism was particularly strong in the Maritimes. But reflecting the spirit of the 1960s, Waite also saw the tentative stirrings of a sense of

11 The concept of a consensus approach is, of course, taken from American historiography but, as I have tried to argue elsewhere, it seems to me applicable to Canadian historiography. See my "'Limited Identities' and Canadian Historical Scholarship: An Atlantic Provinces Perspective", *Journal of Canadian Studies*, XXIII, 1&2 (Spring-Summer 1988), esp. pp. 177-78.

12 I have used the second printing (Toronto, 1962), which contains "a few minor corrections" (Preface, p. vi). As will become apparent I have drawn heavily upon Waite's sources in the discussion which follows.

Canadian nationalism in the 1860s. By 1864, he concluded, "Whether for good or ill, there was a national spirit stirring in the Maritime provinces" (p. 72); in fact, the Maritime pro-Confederates were even more eager than the Canadians to escape from "the littleness of provincial pastures" (p. 89). Since Waite clearly accepted that Confederation was necessary and desirable and that the Quebec Resolutions were an imaginative and ingenious recipe for union, he had limited patience with the anti-Confederates who are seen as "men of little faith".[13] His impatience with their unwillingness to accept the Quebec terms is revealed in his treatment of the "Poor, tired, rather embittered" Joseph Howe who might "have supported Confederation had he had an opportunity similar to Tupper's" (p. 210). And it is even more clearly revealed in his assessment of L.A. Wilmot: "It may have been that Wilmot was perfectly genuine in his conversion to Confederation. But if so, it was not his main motive. With Wilmot perquisites usually triumphed over policies" (p. 256). Waite accepted that Nova Scotians had some reason for resentment since the Quebec Resolutions were imposed upon them against their will but he did not extend the same sympathy to New Brunswick and Prince Edward Island, which he described as totally mired in an all-pervasive parochialism: "Of both Fredericton and Charlottetown Goldwin's Smith's unrepentant aphorism is not altogether inappropriate: 'The smaller the pit, the fiercer the rats'" (p. 233).[14] It was the "ferocity of politics" which accounted for the "primeval character" of the discussion of Confederation in New Brunswick (pp. 233-34). As for Prince Edward Island their opposition is more simply explained. Most Islanders had never been away from the Island in their lives (at least according to George Brown) and they had "had little opportunity to cultivate larger loyalties". "Like the Acadians a century before, they simply wanted to be left alone" (pp. 180-81).

Waite's emphasis on the parochialism and conservatism of New Brunswick and Prince Edward Island was reinforced by two more specialized studies which appeared in the early 1960s. There was always a curiously ambivalent attitude in the work of W.S. MacNutt toward his adopted province. Because he was disappointed with the province's performance in the post-World War Two era, he took up the cause of Maritime unity in the 1950s and railed against those local politicians who were obsessed with the distribution of local patronage and lacked a vision of grandeur.[15] In *New Brunswick: A History: 1784-1867* (Toronto, 1963), he projected this anger backwards and his impatience with the provincial politicians

---

13　I do not know if Waite had read Cecelia M. Kenyon, "Men of Little Faith: The Antifederalists on the Nature of Representative Government", *William and Mary Quarterly*, 3d ser., XII (1955), pp. 3-43 but his approach was certainly in line with the American historiography of the period.

14　I attempted to trace the context of Goldwin Smith's remark but Waite's source was G. M. Wrong, "Creation of the Federal System in Canada" in Wrong *et al., The Federation of Canada, 1867-1917* (Toronto, 1917), p. 17 and Wrong does not indicate his source. It seems likely, however, that the quote referred to Canadian politics in the post-Confederation era and reflected Smith's somewhat biased view of his adopted home.

15　Forbes makes the same point about J. Murray Beck in his "In Search of a Post-Confederation Maritime Historiography", p. 55.

shines through. Although MacNutt felt it was "difficult to allow very much praise for the politicians" of the province (p. 460), at least "A few leaders of imagination and daring had made themselves the instruments of the grand idea that was British North America's response to the problems of the time, the urge for mergers and the manufacturing of great states" (p. 454). Francis W.P. Bolger adopted a not dissimilar approach in *Prince Edward Island and Confederation 1863-1873* (Charlottetown, 1964). During the years that Confederation was discussed Island politics, he noted, "remained personal, parochial, and violent" (p. 14) and it was inevitable that the Island would resist with all its might the pressures for union.[16]

It is difficult not to come away from these works with the impression that there was virtually no support for Confederation in the Maritimes, except for a handful of prescient individuals who had the imagination to accept the leadership of the more far-sighted and progressive Canadians. Yet all three studies revealed very clearly that anti-Confederation sentiment in the region was generated as much by the unpalatability of the Quebec Resolutions as by opposition to the idea of Confederation itself. All three historians also accepted that the terms adopted at Quebec city reflected Canadian needs and Canadian priorities and, like Whitelaw, they clearly assumed that the Maritime delegates to Quebec had failed to secure better terms because of the superior acumen and organization of the Canadian delegation. It is, of course, true that the exigencies of Canadian politics forced the members of the Great Coalition to adopt a relatively united front on the constitutional issues under discussion while the Maritime delegations were divided both internally and amongst themselves at Quebec. But one could as easily attribute the failure of the Maritime delegates to their realism and to the extent of their desire for some kind of union. Their basic problem was that the two regions were of such unequal size. At Philadelphia in 1787 the Americans were forced to resort to equal representation in the Senate, not solely to appease the small states, but also for reasons of *"regional* security", in order "to safeguard the most conspicuous interests of North and South".[17] In the end it was the comparative equality of the two regions which compelled the delegates at Philadelphia to agree to the "Great Compromise". No such pressure existed at Quebec in 1864. Because of the uneven size and power of the two regions, the Maritime delegates were compelled to agree to union on Canadian terms, if they wanted union at all.

The leading Maritime politicians at Quebec had no illusions about the limited room they had for manoeuvre. Even at Charlottetown Samuel Leonard Tilley and W.H. Pope opposed the suggestion that Maritime Union should precede Confederation on the grounds that the Maritime Provinces would be able to arrive

---

16   Bolger also contributed the chapters on Confederation to *Canada's Smallest Province: A History of Prince Edward Island* (Charlottetown, 1973), where his larger work is synthesized.

17   See Jack N. Rakove, "The Great Compromise: Ideas, Interests, and the Politics of Constitution Making", *William and Mary Quarterly*, 3d ser., XIV, 3 (July 1987), esp. p. 451.

at better terms with Canada by negotiating separately rather than united.[18] Indeed, Charles Tupper believed that the gradual withdrawal of Britain had made the subordination of the Maritimes to Canada inevitable and that the goal of the Maritime delegates at Quebec must be to gain the best terms of union that they could.[19] The Maritimers did try to offset their weakness in the House of Commons by insisting on sectional equality in the Senate and the majority of them also sought to ensure that the provinces would be left with control over those local matters of most immediate concern to their constituents. Although Jonathan McCully failed to have agriculture removed from the list of federal responsibilities, Tilley persuaded the delegates to transfer control over roads and bridges to the provinces.[20] Upon returning to New Brunswick Tilley worked out that only five of the fifty-nine acts passed by the New Brunswick legislature in the previous session would be found *ultra vires* of the provincial government under the proposed division of powers.[21] And both Tilley and Tupper pointed out forcefully at the London Conference that their intention had not been to create a "Legislative Union".[22] Yet, even after it became clear to them how unpopular the Quebec Resolutions were, the pro-Confederate leadership recognized that there were limits to the concessions the Canadians could make without destroying the fragile unity of the Great Coalition. Reluctantly, therefore, they accepted that, if Confederation was to take place in the 1860s, "it is the Quebec scheme & little else we can hope to have secured".[23]

Although the pro-Confederate leadership was probably right in this assumption, the Quebec Resolutions weakened the potential support for union in the region. Even many of those sympathetic to the ideal of Confederation felt that a second conference should be called to re-negotiate the terms of union.[24] Both Bailey and MacNutt attributed much of the lingering resentment to Confederation in New Brunswick after 1866 to the failure of the efforts of the New Brunswick delegates at the London Conference to make substantial alterations in the unpopular Quebec plan.[25] Bolger also accepted that the Island rejected the initial proposals because they were not "sufficiently attractive".[26] Much of the debate in the Maritimes revolved not over the issue of whether union was desirable but whether the Quebec Resolutions adequately met Maritime needs and concerns. Indeed, the strength of the anti-Confederate movement throughout the region was that it could appeal both

18   See G. P. Browne, ed., *Documents on the Confederation of British North America* (Toronto, 1969), pp. 38-39.

19   See K.G. Pryke, *Nova Scotia and Confederation* (Toronto, 1979), p. 190.

20   See Browne, ed., *Documents*, pp. 77-78.

21   *Ibid.*, p. 171.

22   *Ibid.*, p. 211. Tupper personally supported the idea of a legislative union, but he was undoubtedly influenced by the knowledge that this position was not shared by most Nova Scotians.

23   McCully to Tilley, 8 June 1866, quoted in Pryke, *Nova Scotia and Confederation*, p. 28.

24   See Pryke, *Nova Scotia and Confederation*, pp. 22-23, 26.

25   Bailey, "The Basis and Persistence", p. 116; MacNutt, *New Brunswick*, pp. 456-57.

26   Bolger, *Prince Edward Island and Confederation*, pp. v, 293.

to those whom Waite describes in Canada West as the "ultras", who opposed Confederation on any terms, and the "critics", who had specific objections to the Quebec scheme, although not opposed to Confederation on principle.[27] In Canada West most of the critics were easily convinced to put aside their objections; in the Maritimes, the proponents of the Quebec resolutions had an uphill battle to bring the critics on side. Unfortunately Waite does not present the struggle in the Maritimes in quite these terms, but lumps the critics together with the ultras, thus creating the impression that die-hard opposition to union was stronger than it was. He therefore concludes that "New Brunswick was pushed into Union, Nova Scotia was dragooned into it, and Newfoundland and Prince Edward Island were subjected to all the pressure that could be brought to bear — short of force — and still refused".[28] In a literal sense these comments are true but they gloss over the fact that what the Maritimes were pushed, dragooned and (in the case of P.E.I.) "railroaded" into was a union on *Canadian* terms.[29] MacNutt and Bolger also admitted that there were severe imperfections in the Quebec Resolutions from the perspective of the Maritimes but they too ignored the implications of this argument and bunched together all anti-Confederates as conservatives who lacked foresight.

This was also the conclusion of Donald Creighton in *The Road to Confederation: The Emergence of Canada 1863-1867* (Toronto, 1964). As in all his works, Creighton's writing was infused with a strong moral tone and a rigid teleological framework which emphasized that Confederation was the logical destination at the end of the road. Those who stood in the way of his vision of what was both right and inevitable were dismissed as narrow-minded obstructionists and he began his book by approvingly paraphrasing Arthur Hamilton Gordon's description of the Maritimes as "half a dozen miserable fragments of provinces" where the "inevitable pettiness and the lack of talented and devoted men in public life could not but make for parochialism, maladministration, and low political morality in every department of provincial life" (p. 8). Throughout the book Creighton contrasted "the lofty nationalist aims of the Canadians" (p. 154) with the parochialism of the Maritimers. "If the Charlottetown Conference was likely to end up as an open competition between confederation and Maritime union", he wrote scornfully, "the Maritimers seemed placidly unaware of the prospect, or disinclined to get excited about it. They appeared to be simply waiting without much concern, and even without a great deal of interest, to see what would turn up" (p. 91). To Creighton the opposition of the Maritimers to Confederation was almost incomprehensible. Since "Maritimers showed, again and again, that they could not but feel their ultimate destiny lay in North American union" (p. 75), their opposition could only be based upon a natural lethargy. A much more sophisticated

27 See *Life and Times of Confederation*, p. 122.

28 *Ibid.*, p. 5.

29 "Railroaded" is the clever aphorism used by Peter Waite in his chapter in Craig Brown, ed., *The Illustrated History of Canada* (Toronto, 1987), p. 289.

study of the Confederation era was W.L. Morton's *The Critical Years: The Union of British North America, 1857-1873* (Toronto, 1964). But Morton too had limited sympathy with the Maritimers' failure to see what he described as the "moral purpose of Confederation" (p. 277). New Brunswick's opposition he ascribed to the lack of moral integrity of its politicians and the lack of principle of its electorate, which "was largely composed of individuals who were politically indifferent, or took no interest in politics except to sell their votes" (p. 172).

The later 1960s and the 1970s also saw a considerable number of more specialized studies, mainly by academics coming from or living in the Maritimes, and they usually took one of two forms. On the one hand, some of these historians attempted to show that Maritime pro-Confederates had played a more significant role in the Confederation movement than had previously been assumed, although they did not question the view that the pro-Confederates possessed a larger vision than the vast majority of the inhabitants of the region.[30] Del Muise in his study of the debate over Confederation in Nova Scotia took a different and much more significant tack. Moving beyond the rather narrow political boundaries in which the whole debate had come to be cast, he argued that the battle over Confederation was between the proponents of the old maritime economy of "wood, wind and sail" and the younger, more progressive members of the regional elites who were prepared to make the transition to a continental economy based upon railroads and coal and committed to industrialization.[31] Muise's interpretative framework was particularly convincing in explaining — really for the first time — why pro-Confederates like Tupper, who were from areas with the potential for industrialization, were prepared to support union even on the basis of the somewhat unpalatable Quebec Resolutions and he successfully established that "certain regions and interests in the Province wanted and carried Confederation".[32] Muise's thesis also helped to explain why those most committed to an international economy based on shipping and shipbuilding were so vehemently opposed to Confederation on almost any terms. By rescuing the debate from a narrowly political framework and focusing on the economic interests of the participants, Muise challenged the stereotype that most Maritimers were motivated by a rather simple-minded conservatism. Yet he also

30   See Alan W. MacIntosh, "The Career of Sir Charles Tupper in Canada, 1864-1900", Ph.D. thesis, University of Toronto, 1960 and Carl Wallace, "Sir Leonard Tilley, A Political Biography", Ph.D. thesis, University of Alberta, 1972. MacIntosh presents a very traditional portait of Tupper, who is seen as accepting and following the overweening vision of Macdonald. Wallace makes a more successful effort to place Tilley in a regional context, but he too believes that "a good argument can be put forward to prove that Confederation was little more than a smokescreen for a diversity of local issues" (p. 209).

31   This argument is presented in "The Federal Election of 1867 in Nova Scotia: An Economic Interpretation", *Collections of the Nova Scotia Historical Society* (1968), pp. 327-51 and developed at greater length in "Elections and Constituencies: Federal Politics in Nova Scotia, 1867-1878", Ph.D. thesis, University of Western Ontario, 1971.

32   Muise, "Elections and Constituencies", p. iv. For an application of the Muise thesis, see Brian Tennyson, "Economic Nationalism and Confederation: A Case Study in Cape Breton", *Acadiensis*, II, 1 (Autumn 1972), pp. 38-53.

fell into the classic trap by identifying the pro-Confederates as younger men while their opponents come across as conservatives resisting the forces of change. The work of the Maritime History Group has undermined this fallacious dichotomy, for they have shown that those who remained committed to the traditional economy — or at least to the shipping and shipbuilding industries — were among the most dynamic economic entrepreneurs in the region and that they were motivated not by a misplaced conservatism but a sensible analysis of the economic benefits still to be derived from investing in the traditional sectors of the economy.[33] Although it was not his intention, by portraying the division of economic interests in the province in terms of the old versus the young (and by implication those representing the future against those wedded to the past), Muise's thesis inadvertently reinforced the stereotype that the anti-Confederate forces were motivated by parochialism and unprogressive attitudes.

Moreover, the attempt to divide the whole province into pro-Confederates and anti-Confederates on the basis of their commitment to the economy of wood, wind and sail was too deterministic. By the 1860s there was a growing desire to participate in the evolving industrial economy but, as Ben Forster has pointed out in his recent study of the rise of protectionist sentiment in British North America, the Saint John manufacturing interests "had divided opinions as to the value of Confederation" and Pryke makes the same point about Nova Scotian manufacturers.[34] Public opinion in those communities tied to "wood, wind and sail" was also more deeply split than Muise's thesis allowed. As he admitted, when Stewart Campbell introduced his resolution against Confederation in March 1867, only nine of the sixteen members of the Nova Scotia legislature who supported it were from areas committed to the traditional economy, and while twenty-five of the thirty-two members who opposed it represented areas "with at least some commitment to the emerging economy of coal and railroads", the degree of that commitment varied considerably.[35]

Although Muise's approach was extremely valuable in helping to explain the extremes of opinion — the views of the ultras on both sides — it could not adequately explain the motives of the large body of men who were prepared to consider union with Canada but who disliked the Quebec Resolutions. We do not know precisely how many Maritimers fell into this category and we may never know, since the issue of accepting or rejecting the Quebec Resolutions temporarily

33 This argument is developed in a variety of works published by members of the group but most recently and most fully in Eric W. Sager and Gerry Panting, "Staple Economies and the Rise and Decline of the Shipping Industry in Atlantic Canada" in Lewis R. Fischer and Gerald E. Panting, eds, *Change and Adaptation in Maritime History: The North Atlantic Fleets in the Nineteenth Century* (St. John's, 1985). For an interpretation which incorporates this approach, but one that builds upon Muise's insights, see John G. Reid, *Six Crucial Decades: Times of Change in the History of the Maritimes* (Halifax, 1987), esp. pp. 113-16.

34 Ben Forster, *A Conjunction of Interests: Business, Politics, and Tariffs 1825-1879* (Toronto, 1986), p. 62. On Nova Scotia, see Pryke, *Nova Scotia and Confederation.*

35 Muise, "The Federal Election of 1867 in Nova Scotia", pp. 337-38.

forced most Maritimers to identify themselves as pro- or anti-Confederates on that basis. What is certain is that a variety of interests and ideological and cultural perspectives were represented in both camps. Years ago Bailey pointed out that in New Brunswick "The cleavage of opinion seems not to have followed either occupational or class lines" and suggested that there were strong ethnic and religious overtones to the struggle.[36] Subsequent studies of New Brunswick have re-affirmed Bailey's insight and have emphasized cultural over economic factors. Similar patterns can be found in the other Maritime provinces. Traditionally Canadian historians have emphasized the growing independence of the British North American colonies after the grant of responsible government. Yet these were also decades when in a variety of ways the colonies were becoming increasingly anglicized.[37] The Quebec Resolutions, which so clearly sought to follow imperial and British institutional models, appear to have been most strongly supported by those who welcomed movement in this direction and particularly by the British-born, less enthusiastically endorsed by the native-born (of whom there was a much larger number in the Maritimes than in Canada West), and viewed with greatest suspicion by cultural minorities such as Irish Catholics and Acadians. Nonetheless, as W.M. Baker has shown, "the whole idea of a monolithic response by Irish Catholics to Confederation is highly questionable".[38] Desirable as it may be to come up with matching sets of dichotomous interests or ethno-religious categories, one can do so only at the risk of obscuring the diversity that existed on both sides in the struggle.

The second major emphasis of the more recent scholarship has been on analyzing the position of those Maritimers who opposed union. J. Murray Beck spent most of a life-time trying to correct the negative image of Howe embodied in the literature, although he did not deny that Howe "set store by the wrong vision".[39] Similarly, Carl Wallace dissected the motives of Albert J. Smith, who, he claimed, "exemplified the true mentality of New Brunswick in this era" and who, like New Brunswick, "turned to the past, unable to adjust to the changing present".[40] Other

36   Bailey, "The Basis and Persistence of Opposition to Confederation", p. 99. Peter Toner emphasises "the Irish threat, real and imagined" in his discussion of the politics of Confederation in "New Brunswick Schools and the Rise of Provincial Rights" in Bruce W. Hodgins, Don Wright and W. H. Heick, eds, *Federalism in Canada and Australia: The Early Years* (Waterloo, 1978), esp. pp. 126-27.

37   The increased anglicization of the Thirteen Colonies in the decades prior to the American Revolution is a major theme in Jack P. Greene, "Political Mimesis: A Consideration of the Political Roots of Legislative Behaviour in the British Colonies in the Eighteenth Century", *American Historical Review*, 75 (1969-70), pp. 337-67. It is a theme which has yet to be adequately explored in the evolution of *British* North America in the mid-decades of the nineteenth century.

38   Baker, *Anglin*, p. 79.

39   "Joseph Howe and Confederation: Myth and Fact", p. 146 and *Joseph Howe: Volume II The Briton Becomes Canadian 1848-1873* (Kingston and Montreal, 1983), p. 211.

40   Carl Wallace, "Albert Smith, Confederation and Reaction in New Brunswick: 1852-1882", *Canadian Historical Review*, XLIV (1963), pp. 311-12. An extended version of this argument is

historians, strongly influenced by the debate over the continuing underdevelopment of the region and a feeling that Maritimers may have made a bad deal when they entered Confederation, produced a series of studies that were more sympathetic to the anti-Confederate position. W.M. Baker wrote a finely crafted book on Timothy Warren Anglin, pointing out that "in his original criticism of Confederation Anglin had been correct on many counts".[41] Robert Aitken supplied a sympathetic portrait of Yarmouth, that hotbed of anti-Confederation sentiment.[42] David Weale resurrected Cornelius Howat as the symbol of the desire of Prince Edward Island to retain control of its own destiny and in *The Island and Confederation: The End of an Era* he produced with Harry Baglole a lament for the decision of the Island to enter Confederation.[43] K.G. Pryke contributed an extremely balanced and very sophisticated study of *Nova Scotia and Confederation* (Toronto, 1979). Although he argued that Nova Scotians "had little alternative but to acquiesce" in a plan of union designed to meet Canadian needs, he explained the willingness of Nova Scotians to accept their "unwelcome subordination" to Canada by factionalism among the anti-Confederates and imperial pressure. His conclusion was that "By default, then, Nova Scotia entered into and remained in Confederation" (p.xi). Whereas earlier historians had consigned the Maritime anti-Confederates to the dust-basket of history, the revisionists rescued them from obscurity and emphasized that they were the true standard-bearers of the wishes of the majority of the population. Unfortunately revisionism carries its own risks, for this approach often portrays the most vehement of the die-hard anti-Confederates as the legitimate voice of the Maritimes. Moreover, once again inadvertently, the revisionists also tended to reinforce the image that Maritimers were motivated by an all-pervasive parochialism and stubborn conservatism which explained the depth of anti-Confederation sentiment in the region.

It is time to challenge this stereotype. If one turns the traditional question on its head and asks not why were so many Maritimers opposed to Confederation but why so many of them agreed so easily to a scheme of union that was clearly designed by Canadians to meet Canadian needs and to ensure Canadian dominance — which virtually everybody who has written on the subject agrees was implicit in the Quebec scheme — then the Maritime response to the Canadian initiative looks rather different. It may be true that there had been little discussion of the idea of an immediate union before the formation of the Great Coalition made Confederation an issue of practical politics but the idea of British North American union, as Leslie

contained in "The Life and Times of Sir Albert James Smith", M.A. thesis, U.N.B., 1960, which concludes with the statement that "He lacked the depth and vision to be a great statesman" (p. 210).

41   Baker, *Anglin*, p. 116.

42   Robert M. Aitken, "Localism and National Identity in Yarmouth, N. S., 1830-1870", M.A. thesis, Trent University, n.d.

43   David Weale, *Cornelius Howat: Farmer and Island Patriot* (Summerside, 1973) and David Weale and Harry Baglole, *The Island and Confederation: The End of an Era* (n.p., 1973).

Upton pointed out years ago, had been in the air since the arrival of the Loyalists.[44] In an unfortunately much neglected article written in 1950, John Heisler concluded from a survey of "The Halifax Press and British North American Union 1856-1864" that "It seems unlikely that a sense of British North American Unity had ever been wholly obscured".[45] Many Maritimers appear to have thought like the anonymous correspondent to the *Provincial Wesleyan* who in 1861 referred to "our home" as "Eastern British America", thus implying some sense of a common destiny with Canada.[46] As Peter Waite pointed out, the initial response of the Maritimers at Charlottetown and in the regional press was certainly not unfavourable to the idea of union. Even Anglin, perhaps the most committed anti-Confederate elected to the New Brunswick legislature, admitted that he did "not know of any one opposed to union in the abstract".[47] Indeed, Anglin himself believed union was desirable as a future goal, though on terms so favourable to New Brunswick that they were undoubtedly impracticable.[48]

It was the terms agreed upon at Quebec which hardened Maritime attitudes as the ranks of the ultras swelled with support from the critics of the Quebec scheme, to use Peter Waite's terminology. Even then what is surprising is how much support the pro-Confederates had. In New Brunswick, the only province in which the issue was put to the electorate, the supporters of the Quebec plan were initially defeated at the polls but for their opponents it proved to be a pyrrhic victory.[49] From the beginning the new government included a large number of men who were sympathetic to the idea of Confederation, if not the Quebec Resolutions, and who were converted fairly easily into pro-Confederates, once it became clear that union was not possible except on the basis of those resolutions. The attitude of the premier, A.J. Smith, toward Confederation was somewhat ambiguous and he was surrounded by others like R.D. Wilmot who were even more clearly critics of the Quebec scheme rather than die-hard opponents of union.[50] Ultra sentiment may have been more widespread in Nova Scotia than in New Brunswick but the victory

44   L.F.S. Upton, "The Idea of Confederation, 1754-1858" in W. L. Morton, ed., *The Shield of Achilles: Aspects of Canada in the Victorian Age* (Toronto, 1968), pp. 184-204.

45   *Dalhousie Review*, 30 (1950), p. 188.

46   *Provincial Wesleyan*, 16 January 1861. I am grateful to John Reid for supplying me with this reference.

47   Baker, *Anglin*, p. 103. I am grateful to a student in one of my seminars, Mary McIntosh, for supplying me with this reference.

48   *Ibid.*, pp. 58, 64-65.

49   Historians remained divided over the scale of the victory. Waite suggests in *The Life and Times of Confederation*, p. 246 that the election results were comparatively close but Baker in *Anglin*, p. 75 argues that the anti-Confederates won at least 60 percent of the popular vote.

50   Once again historians are not agreed on whether Smith did convert to Confederation prior to the defeat of his government. Baker in *Anglin*, p. 102 argues that he did not but Wallace feels that Smith was willing to lead the province into union. See "Albert Smith, Confederation and Reaction in New Brunswick", pp. 291-92. In his "Life and Times of Smith" Carl Wallace points out that as early as 1858 Wilmot had indicated his belief in the inevitability of British North American union (see p. 23).

of the anti-Confederate forces at the polls in 1867 was roughly of the same dimensions as in New Brunswick two years earlier and may have been distorted by the legitimate feeling of outrage that many Nova Scotians felt against the undemocratic way they had been forced into the union and by the fact that the Nova Scotia election took place after it had become certain that there would be no substantial alterations in the Quebec plan.[51] In any event any anti-Confederate government in Nova Scotia would have suffered from the same internal divisions as did the Smith government in New Brunswick and would probably have met much the same fate in much the same way. At least that is a viable reading of Ken Pryke's study of what happened to the deeply divided anti-Confederation movement after Confederation. Indeed, Pryke suggests that those who advocated "an extreme stand towards union during the election represented a small minority of the anti-confederates".[52]

Even Prince Edward Island's opposition is easily exaggerated. There is in Island historiography a powerful tradition of Island "exceptionalism" and there is undeniably some justification for this approach. Prince Edward Island was small, its future on the edge of a large continental nation was bound to be precarious, and opposition to the idea of union was stronger than on the mainland. Yet it is doubtful whether the Islanders' commitment to the protection of local interests differed more than marginally from a similar commitment by other British North Americans.[53] After the Charlottetown Conference the majority of the Island's newspapers came out in favour of a federal union "upon terms that the Island may reasonably stipulate for" and at Quebec the Prince Edward Island delegates never opposed the principle of union.[54] Of course, the support of the Island elite for union was not unconditional and the forces favouring Confederation would have faced a difficult battle in persuading the majority of Islanders that Confederation was necessary in 1867. But what appears to have decisively swayed Island opinion was the failure of

---

51   Del Muise points out that about 60 percent of the Nova Scotia electorate voted for anti-Confederates in 1865 which is roughly comparable to Baker's figure for New Brunswick.

52   See *Nova Scotia and Confederation 1864-1874*, p. 49.

53   For a different point of view see Weale and Baglole, *The Island and Confederation*. I have two major disagreements with the authors. First, they create an image of harmony and unity on the Island that ignores the very real ethnic, religious and class divisions which existed on the Island and thus postulate a unified response to Confederation. Second, they imply that Islanders had developed a strong desire to be separate that almost amounted to a sense of Island nationalism. But the Island had never been an independent and autonomous state and there is no evidence that any sizeable number of Islanders ever wanted it to become one. Indeed, the tendency to equate resistance to Confederation in the Maritimes to a kind of "provincial nationalism" is, I believe, utterly wrongheaded. What most Maritimers wanted (and Prince Edward Islanders were no exception) was to protect the corporate identities of their long-established Assemblies. For a development of this theme in American historiography, see Jack P. Greene, *Peripheries and Center: Constitutional Development in the Extended Politics of the British Empire and the United States, 1607-1788* (Athens Ga, 1987).

54   Bolger, *Prince Edward Island and Confederation*, pp. 59, 61, 86.

the Quebec Conference to respond sympathetically to any of the Island's needs.[55] Thanks to the resistance of the French Canadians and the Maritimers, the preference of some of the delegates for a legislative union was abandoned. But to their requests for changes in the composition of the Senate and an additional member of the House of Commons (or even for larger House in which the Island would have six representatives), for a recognition of the peculiar financial position of the Island with its very low debt and limited sources of potential revenue, and for financial assistance to resolve permanently the land question, the delegates from the other colonies turned a deaf ear. It is easy to dismiss the Island's demands, particularly the desire for adequate representation in the new federal Parliament, as unrealistic. But, during the discussions at Quebec, Alexander Tilloch Galt offered an alternative system of representation in the House of Commons that would have given the Island the six federal representatives they wanted and an additional senator for the Island was surely not a radical demand.[56] Indeed, after Confederation the principle of rep of pop was abandoned to meet the needs of the West.[57] It was the obduracy of the Canadians and the refusal of the other Maritime delegations to support Prince Edward Island's demands, not the latter's unwillingness to compromise, that isolated the Islanders and delayed the Island's decision to enter Confederation.

Not surprisingly the Islanders refused to consider the degrading terms which were offered to them and defiantly declared in the famous "no terms" resolution that they would never enter Confederation. Although in 1869 they again rejected a set of marginally better terms offered by the Macdonald administration they found themselves inexorably drawn within the orbit of Canada. They adopted the Canadian decimal system of coinage and were forced to follow Canadian policy in regulating the Atlantic fisheries.[58] Unable to negotiate reciprocity on their own and eager for an infusion of money to resolve the land question, the Island leadership did not abandon negotiations with Canada. Undoubtedly the financial crisis generated by the building of an Island railway explains the timing of Confederation but as the debate in 1870 when the legislature rejected Canada's 1869 offer shows, the number of MLAs prepared to accept Confederation if the terms were fair was growing steadily even before the Island approached insolvency. When the Canadian government offered "advantageous and just" terms in 1873, giving the Island much of what it had demanded at Quebec in 1864, the opposition to Confederation

---

55   Unfortunately most of the literature on Confederation simply dismisses the Island's needs as irrelevant, including even Bolger. See *ibid.*, pp. 68ff.

56   For Galt's plan and the discussion of the extra Senator, see Browne, *Documents*, p. 106. Today we accept a much wider departure from the principle of rep by pop than P.E.I. requested in 1864.

57   David E. Smith, "Party Government, Representation and National Integration in Canada" in Peter Aucoin, ed., *Party Government and Regional Representation in Canada* (Toronto, 1985), p. 14.

58   See Frank MacKinnon, *The Government of Prince Edward Island* (Toronto, 1951), p. 132.

evaporated.[59] If Cornelius Howat was the authentic voice of the ultras on the Island, his was very much a voice in the wilderness by 1873.

From a longer perspective what is remarkable is not that there was opposition to Confederation in the Maritimes but how ineffectual it was. In Ireland the union with Britain was never accepted and ultimately resulted in separation and partition and even today there are secessionist movements in Scotland and in Wales. The imperial government was so impressed with the success of the Canadian experiment that it would try to reproduce it elsewhere, but except for Australia and South Africa — and in the latter it was imposed by force — few of the federations it created survived for long. In fact, unlike other areas of the world forced into federation on terms considered unjust, the Maritime opposition to Confederation was remarkably weak and evaporated remarkably quickly. Although there remained pockets of secessionist sentiment, Maritime separatism has never been a potent force.[60] The simple explanation for this phenomenon is to attribute it to the willingness of the Maritime leadership to sell their birthright for a mess of Canadian potage. But the assumption that Maritime politicians and the Maritime electorate were more venal and more corrupt than politicians elsewhere is an assumption which cannot be sustained. Historians have for too long quoted enthusiastically the comments of Arthur Hamilton Gordon and other imperial visitors to the colonies. Inevitably, they were critical of what they saw, since they came from a more patrician political culture controlled by an elite who feared any movement in the direction of democracy. But much of what they disapproved of — the scrambling of different interest groups, the narrow self-promoting nature of much of the legislation, the continual catering to popular demands — is what popular politics is all about. The ideal of the disinterested gentleman-politician made little sense in colonies where there were virtually no great landed estates and limited inherited wealth and no hereditary ruling caste. Much of the opposition to the Quebec scheme seems to have come from those who feared, legitimately, that it was designed to create just such a caste and to place power in the hands of an elite which professed the ideal of disinterestedness while lining their own rather larger pockets.[61]

The belief that politics in the Maritimes were individualistic and anarchic is also mythical. During the transition to responsible government the Maritime provinces had begun to evolve parties in the legislatures at pretty close to the same pace as

59 Bolger, *The Island and Confederation*, pp. 210, 262.

60 The only serious expression of separatist sentiment was the repeal movement of the 1880s and it was in part, indeed perhaps in large part, simply a strategy for better terms. See Colin Howell, "W. S. Fielding and the Repeal Elections of 1886 and 1887 in Nova Scotia", *Acadiensis*, VIII, 2 (Spring 1979), pp. 28-46.

61 I have drawn for inspiration in these comments on Gordon S. Wood, "Interests and Disinterestedness in the Making of the Constitution" in Richard Beeman, Stephen Botein, and Edward C. Carter II, eds, *Beyond Confederation: Origins of the Constitution and American National Identity* (Chapel Hill & London, 1987), pp. 69-109.

they evolved in Canada and in the decades before Confederation all of them were in the process of developing party systems with roots deep in the constituencies, even New Brunswick.[62] If Confederation disrupted this development and brought about a major political realignment and considerable political confusion, it was because of the far-reaching implications of the measure, not because of the inherent pliability or lack of principle of Maritime politicians, and it had the same effect in Ontario and Quebec, which also had their share of loose fish. Similarly the belief that Maritimers were either by nature or because of the scale of their political structures more susceptible to patronage and corruption should be challenged. Gordon Stewart has advanced the claim that the Canadian political system before Confederation was more corrupt and more patronage-ridden than in the Maritimes, since Canadians had adopted the spoils system with greater enthusiasm and consistency during the transition to responsible government.[63] In fact, there may be a reverse correlation between size and patronage in pre-industrial societies. In a larger political unit politicians are more remote from the people they serve and less likely to be drawn from a clearly defined local elite. They can not command the same degree of deference and therefore require access to a larger fund of patronage to cement the more impersonal bonds of party loyalty. Certainly those Maritime politicians who held posts in the new federal administration, like Tilley and Tupper, claimed to be appalled by the ruthlessness of the Canadians in distributing patronage along party lines, although they soon began to pursue similar policies to ensure a fair distribution for their own constituents and their own re-election.[64] By proving that the new political system was not totally biased in favour of the Canadians the Maritime political leadership did something to dissipate the lingering fears that it would be dominated by Canadians and Canadian needs. But this evidence cannot be used to explain the success of the pro-Confederates in the first place nor does it adequately explain the rapidity with which integration took place.

The degree of support for Confederation in the region can only be explained by abandoning the notion that all but a handful of Maritimers were inherently parochial and conservative. Maritimers did not live in a dream world. They had experienced a period of rapid economic and demographic growth and they were aware of the changes taking place around them. They were acutely aware that external events had made some form of larger union desirable in the 1860s. British pressure, the American Civil War and the cancellation of reciprocity, and the Fenian raids helped to drive home this message, as they did in the Canadas. But no

62   See Gail Campbell, "'Smashers' and 'Rummies': Voters and the Rise of Parties in Charlotte County, New Brunswick, 1846-1857", *Historical Papers* (1986), pp. 86-116.

63   Gordon Stewart, *The Origins of Canadian Politics: A Comparative Approach* (Vancouver, 1986), pp. 88-89.

64   The latter statement is based upon an examination of the patronage files in the Tilley and Tupper papers during the 1870s in the National Archives of Canada. I discuss the question of patronage at more length in "The 1870s: The Integration of the Maritimes" in E. R. Forbes and D. A. Muise, eds, *The Atlantic Provinces in Confederation* (in press).

external pressures could have compelled the Maritimes to join Confederation if ultimately they had not been convinced that it was in their own interests to do so. That is the lesson which can be drawn from the failure of the earlier initiatives on Confederation in the 1830s and 1840s.[65] In all these cases, despite the strong advocacy of the Colonial Office and enthusiastic support from British officials in the colonies, the union movement collapsed because of lack of colonial support. Similarly the Maritime Union movement, despite strong imperial pressure, collapsed because of lack of colonial enthusiasm. Undoubtedly imperial support helped to sway the more conservative groups in the colonies, like the hierarchy of the Catholic Church.[66] But imperial interference could also unleash a colonial reaction. As allies, men like Gordon were a mixed blessing and it is quite possible that the pro-Confederates won their victory in New Brunswick in 1865 despite, not because of, Gordon's interference in the politics of the province.[67] The combined pressures generated by the American Civil War and the British response to it were critical factors in the timing of Confederation. Without those immediate pressures union might not have come about in the 1860s and it would certainly not have come about on the basis of the Quebec Resolutions, since it was those pressures which persuaded so many Maritimers to accept union on those terms. But since the idea of Confederation does seem to have had widespread and growing support, at least from the elites in the region, it does not follow that in the 1870s negotiations between the Canadians (now presumably united in their own federal union) and the Maritimers could not have been successful, albeit on a somewhat different basis.

By the 1860s, a variety of indigenous forces were, in fact, leading an increasing number of Maritimers to the conclusion that some form of wider association was desirable. The restlessness of provincial elites may have been, as Peter Waite suggested, part of the reason for the enthusiasm for a larger union but this restlessness cannot be related solely to their political ambitions and their immediate economic self-interest. Support for the idea of union was, indeed, too widespread

---

65 On the earlier attempts to achieve Confederation see Ged Martin, "Confederation Rejected: The British Debate on Canada, 1837-1840", *Journal of Imperial and Commonwealth History*, XI (1982-3), pp. 33-57 and B. A. Knox, "The Rise of Colonial Federation as an Object of British Policy 1850-1870", *Journal of British Studies*, XI (1971), pp. 92-112. My interpretation of Ged Martin's "An Imperial Idea and Its Friends: Canadian Confederation and the British" in Gordon Martel, ed., *Studies in British Imperial History: Essays in Honour of A. P. Thornton* (New York, 1985), pp. 49-94 is that while British support was essential for Confederation, it was the circumstances within British North America which gave the British something to support.

66 For example, Bishop MacKinnon wrote to Tupper that "Although no admirer of Confederation on the basis of the Quebec Scheme; yet owing to the present great emergency and the necessities of the times, the union of the Colonies upon a new basis, we receive with pleasure" (Pryke, *Nova Scotia and Confederation*, p. 27). MacKinnon's reservations are not spelled out but they were likely similar to those of Archbishop Connolly who wrote that "The more power that Central Legislature has the better for the Confederacy itself and for the Mother Country and for all concerned" (Connolly to Carnarvon, 30 January 1867, in Browne, *Documents*, p. 262). See also K. Fay Trombley, *Thomas Louis Connolly (1815-1876)* (Leuven, 1983), esp. pp. 302-44.

67 Wallace, "Life and Times of Smith", p. 47.

for it to be simply the result of individual ambition. Clearly there must have been some co-relation between an individual's socioeconomic position and his response to the Confederation issue, but it would be foolish to revert to the kind of Beardian analysis which American historians have come to find less and less useful.[68] In any event without the support of a wide cross-section of the articulate public any effort at union would have been pointless.

It can hardly be denied that much of the support for a larger union came from those who equated consolidation with material progress and modernization, as most historians have recognized. What they have been less willing to accept is that these intellectual pressures were growing stronger in the Maritimes as in the Canadas and affected many of the opponents of the Quebec scheme as well as its advocates. Even prior to Confederation governments in the Maritimes took on new responsibilities as the nineteenth century revolution in government filtered across the Atlantic.[69] Maritimers shared with other British North Americans an enthusiasm for railways, for expanded and more highly centralized schools systems,[70] for improved social services, and for governments with enhanced access to credit. In a recent book on *Inventing Canada: Early Victorian Science and the Idea of a Transcontinental Nation* (Toronto, 1987), Suzanne Zeller has argued that the diffusion of early science was another of the pressures encouraging the establishment of larger units of government and that the inventory methods of Victorian science "laid a conceptual and practical foundation for the reorganization of British North America" (p. 9). Unfortunately, Zeller focuses almost exclusively on developments in the United Province of Canada. But the Maritimes had their share of scientists influenced by similar notions and a wider political community similarly affected by the diffusion of scientific knowledge and it seems likely that the same developments were occurring there.[71] Nonetheless, Zeller's book points to the direction which studies of the movement for Confederation must now take. What is required now are detailed analyses of the intellectual milieu in which literary figures and the growing number of professionals functioned, of clerical

---

68   The reference here is, of course, to Charles Beard's economic interpretation of the making of the American constitution. As Richard Beeman notes in his "Introduction" to *Beyond Confederation*, the prolonged historiographical debate over Beard's interpretation has come to be seen as important by "ever-decreasing numbers" of American historians (p. 14).

69   See Rosemary Langhout, "Developing Nova Scotia: Railways and Public Accounts, 1849-1867", *Acadiensis*, XIV, 2 (Spring 1985), pp. 3-28.

70   As Ian Robertson points out, Prince Edward Island claimed to be the first place in the British Empire to introduce "a complete system of free education" with the adoption of the Free Education Act of 1852 and Nova Scotia was the next British North American colony to follow suit, in 1864. See his "Historical Origins of Public Education in Prince Edward Island, 1852-1877", unpublished paper given at the Atlantic Canada Studies Conference, University of Edinburgh, May 1988, pp. 3, 5.

71   A. G. Bailey points out that the Maritime universities, like the central Canadian universities, "tempered their concern for the classics with a lively concern for the sciences" during the Confederation period. See "Literature and Nationalism in the Aftermath of Confederation" in *Culture and Nationality*, p. 66.

thought, and indeed of changing views of the role and function of the state held by entrepreneurs and by other groups in society. One suspects that such studies will reveal support, in the Maritimes as elsewhere in Canada, for the emergence of larger and more powerful institutional units of government.

Yet it does not follow that all of the supporters of Confederation were on the side of an expanded role for government and material progress, while all of those who opposed the Quebec scheme were not. The most vehement opposition to Confederation in the Maritimes came, as D.A. Muise correctly pointed out, from those whose economic interests seemed most directly threatened by union with Canada. It is, however, far from self-evident that they were opposed to the other changes that were taking place in their colonial societies. Some of the opposition to Confederation in the Maritimes, as in the Canadas, did come from those whose social ideal was reactionary and anti-modern in several respects, but not all anti-Confederates, perhaps not even a majority, opposed commercial development or technological change. There does appear to have been an overlap between those who resisted government intervention, feared increased taxation and resented outside interference with community institutions and those who opposed Confederation. Yet many pro-Confederates shared these concerns. In summarizing the vast literature dealing with the politics of the early American republic, Lance Banning points out the futility of trying to describe the Federalists as liberal and progressive and their opponents as conservative and reactionary: "If revisionary work has taught us anything, it has surely taught us that both parties were a bit of each".[72]

It has long been known that the Fathers of Confederation were not democrats and that they were determined to secure the protection of property and to create barriers against the democratic excesses which in their minds had led to the collapse of the American constitution and to the American Civil War.[73] For this reason they limited the size of the House of Commons so that it would remain manageable, chose to have an appointed rather than an elected second chamber, and sought to ensure that both houses of the proposed federal legislature were composed of men who possessed a substantial stake in society. Most of the Maritime delegates at the Quebec conference shared these anti-democratic and anti-majoritarian objectives. So, of course, did many of the most prominent anti-Confederate leaders — even that tribune of the people, Joseph Howe. Ironically, a considerable part of the initial opposition to the Quebec Resolutions came from those — like Howe and Wilmot — who, like the leading pro-Confederates, were wedded to British constitutional models but who rejected the Quebec plan for not

72 Lance Banning, "Jeffersonian Ideology Revisited: Liberal and Classical Ideas in the New American Republic", *William and Mary Quarterly*, XLIII, 1 (January 1986), p. 14.

73 See Bruce Hodgins, "Democracy and the Ontario Fathers of Confederation" in Edith G. Firth, ed., *Profiles of a Province: Studies in the History of Ontario* (Toronto, 1967) and "The Canadian Political Elite's Attitude Toward the Nature of the Plan of Union" in Hodgins *et al.*, eds, *Federalism in Canada and Australia*, pp. 43-59.

establishing a legislative union or because they feared it might lead to the disruption of the empire. But once convinced that legislative union was impracticable, primarily because of the determined opposition of the French Canadians, and that Britain was solidly behind the Quebec scheme, many of these critics were converted fairly easily into supporters of union, although they continued to ask for marginally better terms for their provinces.

The more serious and determined opposition came from those who believed that the Quebec plan would create a monster, an extraordinarily powerful and distant national government, a highly centralized federal union in which Maritimers would have limited influence. It is easy to dismiss these arguments as based on paranoia, irrational fears or perhaps some kind of psychological disorder, particularly since the worst fears of the anti-Confederates were not realized. But the opposition to centralizing power in a distant and remote government was deeply rooted in Anglo-American political thought. Elwood Jones has described this attitude as "localism", as a world view that was held by many articulate conservatives and reformers on both sides of the Atlantic and was "an integral part of the British North American experience".[74] This approach has the merit of indicating the considerable overlap between those who supported and those who opposed the Quebec Resolutions. Those Resolutions were capable of more than one interpretation and many of the Canadian pro-Confederates supported Confederation because it promised more, not less, autonomy for their provinces.[75] Nonetheless, the term "localism", with its implication of parochialism, to some extent distorts the nature of the opposition to the Quebec Resolutions. It reinforces the notion that the pro-Confederates were drawn from the men of larger vision, usually described in American historiography as the cosmopolitans, while their opponents were men of more limited experience and a more local, and thus more limited, frame of reference.[76] In American historiography, however, the "men of little faith" are now taken more seriously than they used to be and it is time to re-assess the criticisms made by those who fought hardest against the Quebec scheme.[77]

74   Elwood H. Jones, "Localism and Federalism in Upper Canada to 1865" in Hodgins *et al.*, *Federalism in Canada and Australia*, p. 20.

75   See A.I. Silver, *The French-Canadian Idea of Confederation 1864-1900* (Toronto, 1982), pp. 33-50 and Robert Charles Vipond, "Federalism and the Problem of Sovereignty: Constitutional Politics and the Rise of the Provincial Rights Movement in Canada", Ph.D., Harvard University, 1973, pp. 82-87.

76   In American historiography the notion of the Federalists as cosmopolitans and the Anti-federalists as provincials, found for example in Jackson Turner Main's *The Antifederalists: Critics of the Constitution, 1781-1788* (Chapel Hill NC, 1961) and *Political Parties before the Constitution* (Chapel Hill, 1973), has been challenged by Wood in "Interests and Disinterestedness in the Making of the Constitution".

77   See, for example, James H. Hutson, "Country, Court and Constitution: Antifederalism and the Historians", *William and Mary Quarterly*, 3d ser., XXXVIII, 3 (July 1981), pp. 337-68; Isaac Kramnick, "The 'Great National Discussion': The Discourse of Politics in 1787", *ibid.*, XLV, 1 (January 1988), pp. 3-32 and Richard E. Ellis, "The Persistence of Antifederalism after 1789" in Beeman *et al.*, eds, *Beyond Confederation*, pp. 295-314.

Only a minority of the Maritime anti-Confederates appear to have denied the need for some kind of a union, but since the Maritimers were not, like the Canadians, trying simultaneously to get out of one union while creating another, they were less easily convinced of the merits of the Quebec Resolutions. Following the Charlottetown Conference, the *Acadian Recorder* expressed the belief that when "the delegates . . . have to let the cat out of the bag" it would be found that the cat was "a real sleek, constitutional, monarchical, unrepublican, aristocratic cat" and that "we shall ask our friends the people to drown it at once — yes to drown it".[78] It will not do to create yet another oversimplified dichotomy, pitting democratic anti-Confederates against aristocratic pro-Confederates. Yet clearly the anti-Confederates did attract to their cause those who were suspicious of the aristocratic pretensions of the designers of the new constitution. Whether such critics were true democrats or simply adherents of an older classical republican tradition, whether they drew upon English opposition thought, classical liberalism or Scottish common sense philosophy, or whether they simply drew eclectically upon the host of Anglo-American intellectual currents available to them, can not be established until more detailed studies have been completed of their rhetoric.[79] But it does seem likely that it is on the anti-Confederate side that one will find many of those who were most sympathetic to wider popular participation in government and to the movement toward democracy already underway in the Maritimes.[80] And such men surely had good reason to be suspicious of the ideological goals of those who had drafted the Quebec Resolutions.

The critics of the Quebec Resolutions were also surely correct to believe that the proposed constitution went further in the direction of centralization than was necessary or desirable in the 1860s. The real weakness in the analysis of most of what was written in the 1960s, and it is particularly apparent in the work of Morton and Creighton, is that it focuses too much on the twentieth-century *consequences* of

---

78   *Acadian Recorder*, 12 September 1864, quoted in R. H. Campbell, "Confederation in Nova Scotia to 1870", M.A. thesis, Dalhousie University, 1939, p. 80.

79   I am, of course, calling for the kind of intellectual history associated with American scholars such as Bernard Bailyn and Gordon S. Wood and British scholars like J. G. A. Pocock. The only serious attempts to apply this approach to the Confederation era have been by Jones, "Localism and Federalism" and by Peter J. Smith, "The Ideological Origins of Canadian Confederation", *Canadian Journal of Political Science*, XX, 1 (March 1987), pp. 3-29. Unfortunately both efforts seem to me flawed by the effort to deal with too wide a time frame and to apply to the mid-nineteenth century categories developed for the eighteenth century.

80   It is worth noting that the Maritimes were at least as far, if not further, advanced in this direction than the Canadas. According to John Garner, *The Franchise and Politics in British North America, 1755-1867* (Toronto, 1969), Nova Scotia had been "the first colony in North America to introduce manhood suffrage" (p. 33). Although Nova Scotia subsequently drew back from the experiment, all of the Maritimes had wide franchises and Prince Edward Island had virtually universal male suffrage by the 1860s. After Confederation, when the federal government decided against vote by ballot, there was an outcry from New Brunswick, which had adopted the ballot in 1855. Indeed, it was this increasingly democratic climate that annoyed men like Gordon and that perhaps accounts, at least in part, for the desire of some members of the colonial elites for a wider, and preferably a legislative, union.

what was done rather than on the more immediate *context* of the late nineteenth century.[81] The Quebec plan, after all, never worked out as the far-sighted Macdonald and his associates hoped. Despite Macdonald's expectations, the provincial governments did not dwindle into insignificance after Confederation. Because of pressure from the provinces and the decisions of the Judicial Committee of the Privy Council, as well as Macdonald's own retreat from an extreme position on such issues as the use of the power of disallowance, the ability of the federal government to interfere with the activities of the provinces was constrained in the late nineteenth century and the constitution was effectively decentralized. This decentralization made considerable sense at a time when, by our standards, the people and politicians had a remarkably limited concept of the role of government in society, particularly of the role of a remote federal government.[82] Twentieth-century historians like Creighton and Morton may, for very different and to some extent contradictory reasons, lament the fact that those who lived in the late nineteenth century were not prepared to accept a twentieth-century role for the federal government but it does not alter the reality. In fact, Macdonald shared with his contemporaries this limited conception of the role of the federal government and he did not wish a highly centralized federal system either to introduce the degree of control over the economy that Creighton longed for in the 1930s or because of any commitment to the nation-wide bilingualism and biculturalism policy that Morton espoused in the 1960s when he was converted to a Creightonian conception of Confederation. It is time to abandon the Creightonian myth that Macdonald and the other advocates of a federal union that was a legislative union in disguise were simply practical politicians engaged in the necessary work of building the Canadian nation.[83] Confederation certainly did not require that the federal government should attempt to "treat the provinces more 'colonially' than the imperial authorities had latterly treated the provinces" through its control over the lieutenant-governors and the resurrection of the anachronistic power of reservation.[84] The Fathers of Confederation were not philosopher-kings but neither did they live in the intellectual vacuum that much of the traditional literature seems to assume existed throughout British North America, but particularly in the Maritimes. In fact, the roots of the thought of the exponents of centralization

81   I have been influenced here by Beeman, "Introduction", *Beyond Confederation*, pp. 5-8.

82   There has been a heated debate over the role of the Judicial Committee of the Privy Council, but much of the controversy centres around the consequences in the 1930s of the decisions taken under very different circumstances in the 1880s and 1890s. For a summary of the recent literature, see Frederick Vaughan, "Critics of the Judicial Committee of the Privy Council: The New Orthodoxy and an Alternative Explanation", *Canadian Journal of Political Science*, XIX, 3 (September 1986), pp. 495-519. Unfortunately Vaughan is also primarily concerned with the implications of the decisions, this time in the 1980s, and expresses fear that the JCPC "left us with a federal system that is seriously lacking an institutional body which to bind the several provinces at the centre so as to ensure the continued existence of Canada as a one nation" (p. 505).

83   This point is also made in Smith, "The Ideological Origins of Canadian Confederation", pp. 3-4.

84   Vipond, "Federalism and the Problem of Sovereignty", pp. 128-29.

emerged not out of a vacuum but out of a body of conservative thought that was deeply suspicious of democracy and their opponents were surely correct to place little faith in the motives of such men and the scheme they proposed. Many of the anti-Confederates were clearly marching to a different drummer.[85]

Ideological and sectional considerations did not take place in isolation from each other and what initially united the Maritime anti-Confederates, regardless of their ideological differences, was their feeling that the Quebec Resolutions did not adequately protect their sectional interests. As the anti-Confederate newspaper, the *Woodstock Times*, noted, "union is one thing and the Quebec scheme is quite another".[86] The scheme that emerged out of the Quebec Conference was designed to mollify its potential critics in two ways: by ensuring that sectional interests would be protected through federal institutions such as the Cabinet and the Senate and through the creation of a series of provincial legislatures with control over local matters. Yet those critics who argued that the Senate would be too weak and ineffectual to defend regional interests would be very quickly proved correct after Confederation. Indeed, by making the Senate an appointed body the Fathers of Confederation had intentionally ensured that the decision-making body in the new federal system would be the House of Commons. This was no accident, for, as Robert MacKay pointed out, Macdonald's intention was to grant "the forms demanded by sectional sentiments and fears", while ensuring "that these forms did not endanger the political structure".[87] Traditionally, Canadian historians and political scientists have laid great stress on the principle of sectional representation in the Cabinet as one of the primary lines of defence for the protection of regional interests. Yet this argument ignores the fact that, however important individual ministers may be, the policies that emerge from the collective decisions of the Cabinet must inevitably reflect the balance of power in the House of Commons. The fears of the Maritime critics of the proposed constitution were undoubtedly exaggerated but they were surely correct to believe that in the long run there was no effective guarantee that their vital interests were adequately protected at the federal level.[88]

---

85   James H. Hutson in "Country, Court and Constitution" has suggested that the division between federalists and the antifederalists in the 1780s was between those committed to a Country and a Court ideology. The Court party supported commercial expansion and were profoundly statist in orientation, while their Country opponents defended agrarian interests and feared any substantial increase in state power. These categories have some value, but British North America in the 1860s was not the United States in the 1780s. There were very few self-sufficient agricultural communities, even in the Maritimes in the 1860s, and it is doubtful whether the majority of the anti-Confederates were any less market-orientated than their opponents. Ideological determinism is as distorting as any other kind and there is the danger of turning all the pro-Confederates into Hamiltonians and all the critics of the Quebec Resolutions into Jeffersonians.

86   Quoted in Waite, *Life and Times*, p. 252.

87   See Robert A. MacKay, *The Unreformed Senate of Canada* (rev. ed., Toronto, 1963), p. 43.

88   This is one of the major themes in Forbes, *The Maritime Rights Movement* and is implicit in T. W. Acheson, "The Maritimes and Empire Canada" in David Bercuson, ed., *Canada and the Burden of Unity* (Toronto, 1977).

Similarly, they were surely correct to be suspicious of federalism as it was presented to them in the 1860s. The question of whether the anti-Confederates leaned toward a different and less centralized model of federalism than the supporters of the Quebec scheme is a controversial and ultimately unanswerable one, since it depends upon which group of anti-Confederates one takes as most representative. In Halifax, as Peter Waite showed, there was considerable support for a legislative union, at least as reflected in the city's newspapers.[89] But in Nova Scotia outside of Halifax and in New Brunswick and Prince Edward Island there seems to have been considerably more sympathy for the federal principle.[90] Federalism was viewed suspiciously by conservatives who believed that it would leave the government without the power to govern and such fears were expressed by both sides in the Confederation debate. They were, however, most forcefully expressed, in Halifax and elsewhere, by the pro-Confederates and the Quebec Resolutions went a long way to pacifying most of those who wanted a purely legislative union. But the Quebec Resolutions did little to mollify those who feared that the proposed provincial legislatures would be nothing more than glorified municipal institutions and that all real power would be concentrated in the federal Parliament. As Richard Ellis points out, during the debate over the American constitution, the supporters of ratification "preempted the term 'Federalist' for themselves, even though, in many ways, it more accurately described their opponents".[91] Until detailed studies of the Confederation debate in the three Maritime Provinces have been completed, it would be premature to assume that the Maritime anti-Confederates anticipated the provincial rights movement of the 1880s and argued for a form of co-ordinate sovereignty. But many of the critics of the Quebec Resolutions in the region clearly believed that their provincial governments would be left with inadequate powers and resources. In this regard they were also more prescient than the pro-Confederates. The Maritime governments required special grants to cover their deficits in the later 1860s and 1870s and were forced to turn time and again to the federal government for financial assistance. We know little about how Maritimers responded to the provincial rights movement of the 1880s since the literature assumes that Ontario and Quebec were the key players while the Maritimers were motivated solely by the desire for larger subsidies, but it is plausible to assume that the movement was

89   See "Halifax Newspapers and the Federal Principle, 1864-1865", *Dalhousie Review*, 37 (1957), pp. 72-84.

90   See Waite, *Life and Times*, pp. 238-39 on New Brunswick. Vaughan in "Critics of the Judicial Committee of the Privy Council" argues that the main anti-Confederate alternative to Confederation in the Maritimes was an imperial union (p. 510), but then admits a few pages later that an examination of the Confederation debates in the Maritimes shows clearly that much of the resistance there was based upon a very clear perception of the centralist philosophy which lay behind the Quebec Resolutions (p. 512).

91   Ellis, "Persistence of Antifederalism", p. 302.

supported in the region by many of those who had resisted the Quebec scheme of union.

If the enthusiasm of Maritimers for Confederation upon the basis of the Quebec Resolutions was less pronounced than in Canada (or at least in Canada West), it was, then, not because they lagged behind intellectually but because they obviously had more to lose in a federation which was not designed to meet their needs. It was not an obtuse conservatism which led so many Maritimers to oppose the terms that were initially offered to them in 1864 but a feeling that those terms were patently unfair. They were motivated not by an intense parochialism which manifested itself in separatist tendencies but by a desire to find a place for themselves in a union which protected their interests. Under the pressure of events the majority (at least in New Brunswick and eventually in Prince Edward Island) did agree to union on terms which they did not like. But what most Maritimers sought in the Confederation era was not a future for themselves outside of Confederation but a more equitable union than seemed to be promised by the Quebec Resolutions.